While Men Slept...

Jane -

I pray for God's blessings
on you through our
Lord Jesus Christ.

Kirby F. Fa

12 - 12 - 04

While Men Slept...

A Biblical and Historical Account of the New Universal Christianity

Second Edition

Kerby F. Fannin, Ph.D.

Life's Resources Inc.
Addison, Michigan

The cover is adapted from a public domain photograph of the earth and the moon taken by the Galileo spacecraft on December 16, 1992. The Jet Propulsion Laboratory, California Institute of Technology, Pasadena, California managed the Galileo Project for the United States National Aeronautics and Space Administration. Edwin V. Bell, II, author/curator, National Space Science Data Center, NASA Goddard Space Flight Center, Greenbelt, MD 20771, USA.

International Standard Book Number: 0-944835-02-3

Library of Congress Control Number: 2002090975

But while men slept, his enemy came and sowed tares among the wheat, and went his way.

—Matthew 13:25

Beloved, when I gave all diligence to write unto you of the common salvation, it was needful for me to write unto you, and exhort *you* that ye should earnestly contend for the faith which was once delivered unto the saints. For there are certain men crept in unawares, who were before of old ordained to this condemnation, ungodly men, turning the grace of our God into lasciviousness, and denying the only Lord God, and our Lord Jesus Christ.

— Jude 1:3-4

For such *are* false apostles, deceitful workers, transforming themselves into the apostles of Christ.

—2 Corinthians 11:13

We are of God: he that knoweth God heareth us; he that is not of God heareth not us. Hereby know we the spirit of truth, and the spirit of error.

—1 John 4:6

And in that day shall the deaf hear the words of the book, and the eyes of the blind shall see out of obscurity, and out of darkness.

—Isaiah 29:18

But blessed *are* your eyes, for they see: and your ears, for they hear.

—Matthew 13:16

Contents

Contents

Summary

The goal of the change in thinking marked by the French Revolution, which began on July 14, 1789, was to overthrow the old order of the world's system and replace the authority of God with that of man and his reason. Plato, the Greek philosopher, had taught that reason could be relied upon to bring one to an enlightened understanding of reality. After the life of Jesus on earth, early Christians in Alexandria, Egypt blended Christian beliefs with the teachings of Plato into a philosophy known as Neo-Platonism. Additionally, the Unitarian belief known as Arianism, soon emerged to challenge the divinity of Jesus Christ. This view was hotly debated among Roman Christians and repressed at the Council of Nicea in A.D. 325. Arianism was, however, revived within a few years and was becoming dominant while influential fourth-century Greek manuscripts of the Bible were being produced.

After the Romans took firm control of Christianity, making a form of it the universal religion, they also made the Latin Vulgate the official Bible. Although the Roman Catholic Church underwent a major split in A.D. 1054, it still maintained strong control over its constituents, who had little access to the Scriptures. Englishman John Wycliff challenged the lack of access to the Scriptures by the common people. His influence on Bohemian John Hus brought challenges against church authority to mainland Europe. In Germany Martin Luther used the Scriptures to mount a doctrinal challenge against church practices, leading to the Reformation. Within a few years, King Henry VIII separated England from the authority of the Roman Catholic Church over the issue of his personal divorce. With this separation, the Church of England, known as the Anglican Church, was formed.

In an effort to counter the Reformation and the split of the Anglican Church from the Roman Catholic Church, Ignatius Loyola formed the Society of Jesus, also known as the Jesuits. This organization operated in much of Europe, developing significant influence in secular governments. Their power soon led European kings to demand that the pope abolish the Jesuits, which he did in 1773. The leaders of Prussia and Russia, however, refused to recognize the papal ban and allowed the Jesuits to continue operations in their countries. Meanwhile, Prussian and German influences, working through such eminent thinkers as Emanuel Swedenborg, Immanuel Kant, Georg Hegel, and Samuel Taylor Coleridge, laid the groundwork of enlightened reason on which others could build a new universal Christianity.

The pope restored the Jesuits in 1814, enabling them to operate more openly. Soon, strong efforts were made to unify the Christian churches. However, when the king of Prussia required union of the Reformed and Lutheran Churches in 1817, resistant Lutherans fled the country. After religious freedom was granted to Roman Catholics in England in 1829, more subtle plans were initiated toward unifying the churches. The Oxford Movement, which began at Oxford University in England on July 14, 1833, provided the means by which key future leaders of the British Government, the Anglican Church, and the Roman Catholic Church established strong bonds with a goal of unification.

One member of the Movement, Frederick Denison Maurice, was a nineteenth-century Anglican priest with strong Universalist Unitarian views. Maurice described a Utopian-like society, which he called the "Kingdom of Christ." He said man would establish the Kingdom on earth through a movement called "Christian Socialism" and bring the state and church into global union. Through Maurice's influence, Daniel and Alexander Macmillan arranged for the development and publication of a new Greek New Testament. This new text relied heavily upon the fourth-century Greek manuscript in the possession of the Vatican. It was used to replace the text based on the work of Desiderius Erasmus, which had been the basis for Protestant Bibles for nearly three hundred years. During the writing of the new Greek New Testament, the authors were heavily influenced by Maurice and privately made clear their agreement with his theological positions.

In 1870, through the work of close Oxford Movement friends, especially Henry Edward Manning and Samuel Wilberforce, the pope was declared to be infallible and the Protestant Bible was said to be in error. Consequently, a major revision of the Bible was planned and the first meeting of the Revision Committee was held on July 14, 1870. Although it was billed as a revision of the Authorized Version of the Bible, the new version relied heavily upon the unfinished critical Greek New Testament authored by Westcott and Hort, rather than on the Received Text of Erasmus, on which the existing Protestant Bible was based. The authors of the unfinished new Greek New Testament were placed on the English Bible Revision Committee, where they, while working secretly together, exerted a strong influence on its operation, demanding direct Unitarian participation in the work.

Also in 1870, Asa Mahan, while president of Adrian College in Adrian, Michigan, wrote a book called *The Baptism of the Holy Ghost*, which served as the basis for the modern Pentecostal and Charismatic Movements. Mahan soon traveled to Oxford, England, where he helped lay the foundations for seeking the baptism of the Holy Spirit in the Keswick Conventions, which began in 1875. Under the influence of Keswick theology, major spiritual revivals, including those of 1901 in Topeka, Kansas, 1904 in Wales, and 1906 in Los Angeles, California, occurred. Controversy followed amidst reports of both true and false spiritual manifestations.

In 1893 the World's Parliament of Religions in Chicago introduced the concept of a global "Christianity" that included all of the existing world religions. The Hindu Swami Vivekananda, through his prayers to the goddess Kali, brought a message of unity in diversity by which all religions would be united under the banner of Christianity. The Roman Catholic Church stressed that unity among religions would be achieved by providing social good for humanity. A new universal "Christianity" was to be attained through social justice and by ordered government. By the early 1900's, significant progress had been made toward the goal of unifying the church and state to build the earthly Kingdom of God, much as Maurice had proposed.

Those who promoted this goal became known as postmillennialists because they believed that mankind would first establish the Kingdom of God on earth, prior to Christ's returning to assume power. That is, they believed He would return *after* the millennial Kingdom is established on earth through ordered global laws, and their enforcement. Premillennialists, on the other hand, believed that the world would continue to degrade until Jesus Christ returns to establish His millennial Kingdom.

While Men Slept...

By the 1940's the church organizations promoting the postmillennial view of the earthly Kingdom of God had made significant progress. Revisions were made in the Revised Bible, giving it a broader ecumenical appeal. Through the coordinated efforts of the World Council of Churches and the Roman Catholic Church, the Second Vatican Council embraced the new Bibles as being more suitable for a new universal Christianity. More revisions followed.

Also out of the Second Vatican Council, a further unifying force was brought to the world. A new outpouring of the "Holy Spirit" was globally introduced into Protestant churches through the efforts of the Roman Catholic, Anglican, and Episcopal Churches. This Charismatic Movement, while resembling the Pentecostal Movement of the early 1900's, was characterized by de-emphasizing the importance of biblical doctrines, such as that of salvation by faith in the atoning sacrifice of Jesus Christ. Many participants in the Movement also embraced extra-biblical manifestations of spiritual power. Because signs and wonders were presented with the new spiritual movements, they were accepted by many as being of God. Even though the Bible is clear that the great deception in the last days will come by means of lying signs and wonders, many throughout the world have refused to try the spirits to see whether they really are from God.

Many who cannot see the biblical and historical basis for the new universal Christianity are likely to be deceived into accepting a social gospel, instead of believing in salvation through faith in the shed blood of Jesus Christ alone. Some, who stand for the witness of Jesus Christ and for the Word of God, may feel that they are alone. However, when the prophet Elijah stood against hundreds of prophets of Baal, the LORD assured him that he was not alone:

> Yet I have left *me* seven thousand in Israel, all the knees which have not bowed unto Baal, and every mouth which hath not kissed him.
>
> —1 Kings 19:18

The Apostle Paul, in his letter to the Romans, also reminded us that there remains a remnant of true believers, according to the election of grace.

Preface

When the Apostle Paul addressed the learned people of Corinth, he did so with great humility. He knew that his knowledge of Greek philosophy was no match for that possessed by the Corinthians. So, rather than trying to compete with them in the wisdom of the world, Paul said:

> And I, brethren, when I came to you, came not with excellency of speech or of wisdom, declaring unto you the testimony of God. For I determined not to know any thing among you, save Jesus Christ, and him crucified. And I was with you in weakness, and in fear, and in much trembling. And my speech and my preaching *was* not with enticing words of man's wisdom, but in demonstration of the Spirit and of power: That your faith should not stand in the wisdom of men, but in the power of God.
>
> —1 Corinthians 2:1-5

I, too, bring this book to you with great humility, and in weakness, and in fear, and in much trembling. Knowing that it will be counted as foolishness by the wisdom of this world, I submit this book believing the words that Paul continued to write to the Corinthians:

> Now we have received, not the spirit of the world, but the spirit which is of God; that we might know the things that are freely given to us of God. Which things also we speak, not in the words which man's wisdom teacheth, but which the Holy Ghost teacheth; comparing spiritual things with spiritual. But the natural man receiveth not the things of the Spirit of God: for they are foolishness unto him: neither can he know them, because they are spiritually discerned.
>
> —1 Corinthians 2:12-14

Many of the people written about in this book progressed from a desire to learn more about God to a desire to learn more about nature. My progression, on the other hand, was from wanting to learn more about nature to wanting to learn more about God. My formal education and training is in natural science, rather than in theology.

I recall making my decision to study the natural sciences in college. I reasoned with myself that, since both truth and life were important, the most logical path by which to learn those things that were important was through the study of the natural science of biology. Therefore, it seemed that, through the study of biology, I would learn the truth about life. Still looking at the natural realm, it seemed that, if we were to preserve life on this planet, the most important specialty to study would be that of environmental science. I was convinced that, by the application of reason through science, the keys of objective truth could be found for solving the most pressing global problems. Therefore, the tools with which I was equipped were those used to discover truth through the observation of nature.

As I observed spawning salmon, struggling to swim upstream and even leaping over obstacles that were in their way, it became clear to me that they were trying to fulfill the purpose for their lives. Some salmon even swam more than a thousand miles in the ocean before beginning their treacherous struggle to reach the place of their origin, so they could lay and fertilize their eggs. Once they succeeded, however, only a small percentage of those eggs survived to hatch and an even smaller percentage of the young fish actually succeeded in their journey to the ocean.

Why do salmon struggle so hard to swim upstream? Why do they spend so much energy for such a relatively small return? They do it because they must. God has put the desire in them to accomplish the purpose He has for their lives. They are not doing their own will but they are doing the will of Him that created them.

We can learn much about God by observing nature. We see the evidence of the instructions that God has given to His creation. The Apostle Paul explained that God reveals Himself to us through His creation, which we call nature:

> For the invisible things of him from the creation of the world
> are clearly seen, being understood by the things that are made,
> *even* his eternal power and Godhead; so that they are without
> excuse:
>
> —Romans 1:20

While learning that God reveals Himself to us through nature, it took
me many years, however, to discover that the truth I had been searching for in nature is but a shadow of the real truth, that being the spiritual things of God. Having given me the gift of reason, it was God,
through His Holy Spirit, who brought me to search for truth. I soon
found that truth did not lie in my reason, which was the filter through
which I interpreted the things that I observed in nature. Instead, I
found that the truth I was searching for could only be found in God
who, through His Word, created all of nature, including my reason.

In my search, it soon became evident to me that God is Truth. Through
the work of my reason and my faith, I accepted that there is one true
God. I eventually came to my present understanding that the Word of
God is the revelation of God to man. It then became clear to me that
the one true God revealed Himself through His Word by His will
through the inspiration of His prophets and apostles as recorded in
the Scriptures, which were supernaturally preserved. The Word of
God was also revealed by the manifestation of God Himself, known
as Jesus.

Because the Word of God *is* God revealed, it is Truth. Therefore, it is
objective and not relative. As Truth, it cannot change or be changed
by the will or reason of man. Because it is Truth, the Word of God can
be used as the standard by which all other things may be measured.
Understanding that Jesus was God manifest in the flesh, the Holy
Ghost is the Spirit of God, who is the Spirit of Jesus Christ, and who
is also known as the Spirit of Truth. As the Spirit of Truth, He draws
us to and guides us in the Word of God, as revealed in the written
Word and in Jesus Christ. Once this was realized, my search for a
greater understanding of Truth moved beyond the study of the natural sciences to the study of God and His Word, Theos (Θεος) and
Logos (Λογος), which many call theology.

While Men Slept...

This book is intended to provide a biblically and historically documented account of the progression of Christian theology as it moved away from a belief in objective truth and toward a belief in subjective truth. As such, it is moving the world toward a belief in Universalism. I believe that this book will help the discerning Christian see how Satan is trying to accomplish his centuries-old plan to deceive the whole world into denying the saving sacrifice of Jesus Christ on the cross. To accomplish the plan, Satan is using the Spirit of Error to subtly counterfeit the Word and Spirit of God to lead the world into a new universal Christianity.

Kerby F. Fannin
Addison, Michigan
March 25, 2002

Acknowledgments

I am truly grateful for the patient and helpful support that was given to me by my wife, Annette, during the research and preparation of this book. I am also very grateful to my sister, Anna Sue Irving, who gave me prayerful encouragement and strength during my work.

Elizabeth Greenwood, Mary Lou Kersh, Jeffrey Kersh, Marty McGinn, and William Oestrike provided careful readings of the manuscript and posed challenging questions on detailed editorial issues. I thank Paul E. Paino, Kelley Fannin, David Genee, and Michael Shirkey for offering encouraging insight and comments concerning the manuscript. I appreciate the prayerful support of Rex, Barb, and Jody Bernstein. The questions and comments offered by skeptical critics were especially beneficial because they encouraged closer examination and more thorough documentation of the issues which they doubted.

I thank God for waking me up from my slumber and giving me eyes and ears to receive His Word. I also thank Him for blessing me with supportive children, Kelley, Kent, and Austin Fannin, and with a praying father and mother, Epp and Hazel Fannin.

While Men Slept...

Chapter 1. Introduction

Therefore speak I to them in parables: because they seeing see not; and hearing they hear not, neither do they understand.

—Matthew 13:13

Without Controversy

Ironically, one of the greatest controversies during the nineteenth century revision of the English Bible was caused by a verse written by the Apostle Paul that proclaimed itself to be without controversy:

And without controversy great is the mystery of godliness: God was manifest in the flesh, justified in the Spirit, seen of angels, preached unto the Gentiles, believed on in the world, received up into glory.

—1 Timothy 3:16

The controversy, as will be discussed later in this book, was over whether the Scripture should read that Jesus was "God" or whether Jesus was "He." Despite the factual evidence to the contrary, the revisors insisted that the text should read "He" rather than "God."

As Paul knew, facts should be without controversy. As we have learned, however, even clear factual evidence is often disputed and discarded when it is in conflict with the agenda of our reason. This book is intended to be without controversy by relying upon clearly documented factual evidence to inform the reader of the underlying theologies, philosophies, and histories of the people directly and indirectly involved in rewriting the Bible and developing a new universal Christianity. The reader may agree with these theologies, philosophies, and histories and welcome the changes that are underway. Alternatively, the reader may choose to prayerfully explore the issue further. Some, however, may choose to ignore the factual evidence.

1

While Men Slept...

Ignoring Factual Evidence

There are many reasons why we might choose to ignore factual evidence on an issue. One reason is that accepting evidence as true may require us to make a change in our system of beliefs or our method of behavior that we are not willing to make. Another reason may be that we are caught up in pride and are unwilling to entertain the notion that we should reconsider a position that we have long held.

A very enduring example of someone who refused to accept the clear evidence of truth was illustrated by a nineteenth century Danish storyteller named Hans Christian Andersen (1805-1875). In *The Emperor's New Clothes*, Andersen told of two clever robbers who developed a scheme to take advantage of the Emperor's vanity.[1] They pretended to weave cloth that they claimed to be of the most beautiful colors and magnificent patterns. They said this cloth was special, because it was invisible to anyone who was either unfit for his office or who was very stupid. Those who were fit for their offices or who were very clever were the only ones who could see the magic cloth.

The Emperor had a suit of clothes made for himself out of the nonexistent cloth. He reasoned that, "If I had a suit made of this magic cloth, I could find out at once what men in my kingdom are not good enough for the positions they hold, and I should be able to tell who are wise and who are foolish."[2] Not wanting to be exposed as being unfit for their positions or as being foolish, almost everyone, including the Emperor, pretended to see the clothes.

As the Emperor paraded through the streets in the nonexistent clothes, that he and almost everyone else pretended to see, a child cried out that the Emperor was wearing no clothes! It took the eyes of a child who was not concerned about the opinions of others to admit the truth. Even though all could see that what the child said was true, they were afraid to admit the truth for fear of what others would say or think about them.

---

[1] Hans Christian Andersen, *The Emperor's New Clothes*, Virginia Lee Burton, design and illustration (Boston: Houghton Mifflin Co., 1949).

[2] Ibid., p. 8.

But finally, they all knew the truth. When they came to the knowledge of the truth they all cried out together, "But he has nothing on at all!"[3] The Emperor felt very silly because he knew the people were right. But he thought, "The procession has started and it must go on now."[4] Those who had been pretending to hold up the imaginary train of the Emperor's nonexistent clothes then took greater trouble to pretend to hold up what they knew wasn't there at all.

Some of us, when faced with plain evidence that others do not appear to see, tend to question our own wisdom. In doing so, we may find ourselves agreeing with others who may also be unwilling to take a position based on the evidence rather than on what they perceive as the "conventional wisdom." Many times we discover that it takes "fresh eyes," such as those of a child, to put aside our vanity and see the truth as it really is rather than continuing to see things as we would like to see them.

Underlying Influences on Christianity

Few people are aware of the profound underlying influence that Unitarians, Universalists, and Socialists have had on redefining Christianity. Neither are they aware that those influences have also led to a belief in Universalism that has led them down a path toward a new universal Christianity, which is based on works rather than on the sacrifice offered by Jesus Christ. The debate between the Unitarian and Trinitarian beliefs on the nature of God extends back into the first century A.D. It continues to the present. Today, however, the messages of Unitarianism, Universalism, and Socialism are successfully and subtly entering churches all over the world. In fact, some of the most educated and highly respected theologians in the world today unknowingly embrace and rely on Bibles that have had principles of Unitarianism and Universalism injected into their very core.

"How can this be?" you may ask. Surely, there must be some mistake. We now have the most advanced schools of theology and the "oldest

---

[3] Ibid., p. 43.

[4] Ibid., p. 44.

and best" manuscripts of the Bible that have ever been available to humans. In some cases, we may even know personal friends or acquaintances who have been directly involved in some phase of producing one of the modern day versions of the Bible or espousing the new universal Christianity. Most of these people are probably sincere Christians. Without further considering the issue, you may simply brush off the assertion of Socialist, Unitarian, and Universalist influence on modern Christianity because you know that "this simply cannot be true."

However, you probably do agree that, for the past several decades, there has been a general growing apostasy, or falling away from a belief in the saving grace of Jesus Christ. Many present day believers who still attend church find themselves sitting in "spiritually dead" pews. Many of the churches that are flourishing today are basing their growth on emotional excitement and innovative marketing programs rather than on a true love for God, devotion to His Word, and the power of the true Spirit of God. What is behind the apparent loss of direction by many modern-day professing Christians?

Seeing Through a Glass Darkly

It would be wise for you to pause for a moment before you continue reading. You may wish to ask yourself if you are ready to hear truth, especially when it may seem to be contrary to what you have been taught or told. Do most people generally believe the truth? You might recall Noah, Elijah, Jeremiah, Amos, Stephen, Paul, and Jesus. Popular wisdom rejected them.

Not everyone wants to know the truth and not everyone is able to understand the truth. This has always been a very great challenge for many of us. Why can't all understand? Jesus spoke in parables so that not all could understand what He was saying. Recall the words of Jesus and the exchange he had with his disciples. As Jesus was speaking in parables about sowing seeds, he said that some would bring forth fruit and some would not. He said:

Who hath ears to hear, let him hear. And the disciples came, and said unto him, Why speakest thou unto them in parables? He answered and said unto them, Because it is given unto you to know the mysteries of the kingdom of heaven, but to them it is not given. For whosoever hath, to him shall be given, and he shall have more abundance: but whosoever hath not, from him shall be taken away even that he hath. Therefore speak I to them in parables: because they seeing see not; and hearing they hear not, neither do they understand.

—Matthew 13:9-13

If you really do not have a love for the truth of God's Word and are not willing to look at plainly documented historical evidence with fresh eyes, then there is no need for you to read any further. None of us should pretend to see when we do not see. It may not be the time for you to see these things yet. I urge you to put this book down and pray that the Holy Spirit will show you His will and purpose for you at this time.

If, however, you have a genuine love for the truth of God's Word, then I urge you to pause from reading right now and pray to the LORD God (YHWH Elohiym) in the name of Jesus that, through His True Holy Spirit, He will enable you to understand. Ask Him to give you the wisdom to discern Truth from error, knowing that "...the wise shall understand." (Daniel 12:10b) Recall Jesus' words as He says:

But blessed *are* your eyes, for they see: and your ears, for they hear. For verily I say unto you, That many prophets and righteous *men* have desired to see *those things* which ye see, and have not seen *them*; and to hear *those things* which ye hear, and have not heard *them*.

—Matthew 13:16-17

Many who read this book may strongly disagree with the basic premises I hold concerning God as Truth. However, a discerning reader will understand that we all see the world through the filter of our own eyes and that we, therefore, are often at different levels of our understanding of Truth. The Apostle Paul explains that we now neither see all nor know all:

> For now we see through a glass, darkly; but then face to face: now I know in part; but then shall I know even as also I am known.
>
> —1 Corinthians 13:12

Those who see truth as within their own reason, shining through their own eyes, which may be viewed as a darkened glass, will certainly have a much different view of the world than one who sees truth as being objective and independent of his own reason. It is the difference in where we believe truth lies that has led to disputes over determining what God really said ever since Eve's interaction with the serpent in the Garden of Eden.

Do You Know With Whom You Speak?

It appears from the account of Eve's interaction with the serpent in Genesis 3 that she allowed herself to be deceived by her reason. In her encounter with the serpent, she also demonstrated the truth of the expression that I have heard throughout my life, "It's not what you know, but who you know that makes the difference." When the serpent came to Eve, she would have been much less likely to have been deceived had she focused on who was talking to her and not just on what he was saying. If she had learned more about who this serpent was before she entered into a dialogue with him, she might have realized that he had an agenda to deceive her. Had she understood his agenda, she would have immediately become suspicious when he challenged the truth of God's Word by asking in Genesis 3:1, "Yea, hath God said, Ye shall not eat of every tree of the garden?" She never even called the serpent by his name. Had she really known him, she might have said his name. She might have questioned him, rather than engaging in a dialogue with him.

When we compare Eve's interaction with the serpent to Jesus' interaction with the devil in Luke 4, we can see some very major differences. Jesus accepted the Word of God as true, without doubting, and used that Word to challenge the devil. Then, in His final rebuke of the devil, Jesus called him by name when he said in Luke 4:8, "...Get thee behind me, Satan...." In other words, Jesus knew exactly with whom He was dealing. Because He knew Satan, He knew his agenda. Satan's agenda was exposed.

With an understanding of the difference between Eve's and Jesus' encounters with the tempter, it is clear that one of the major tools Satan has to use against God's people is anonymity. If we do not know who he is, we would be much less likely to challenge his agenda than if we know with whom we are dealing. God makes it clear through the prophet Isaiah that His people are taken into captivity because they lack knowledge:

> Therefore my people are gone into captivity, because *they have* no knowledge: and their honourable men *are* famished, and their multitude dried up with thirst.
> —Isaiah 5:13

Moses knew the importance of a name. When God was sending him to Egypt to bring the Israelites out of captivity, Moses had a question for God:

> And Moses said unto God, Behold, *when* I come unto the children of Israel, and shall say unto them, The God of your fathers hath sent me unto you; and they shall say to me, What *is* his name? what shall I say unto them?
> —Exodus 3:13

The essence of the question that Moses asked of God was, "What is your name? Who are you?" God answered him plainly:

> And God said unto Moses, I AM THAT I AM: and he said, Thus shalt thou say unto the children of Israel, I AM hath sent me unto you. And God said moreover unto Moses, Thus shalt thou say unto the children of Israel, The LORD God of your

> fathers, the God of Abraham, the God of Isaac, and the God of Jacob, hath sent me unto you: this *is* my name for ever, and this *is* my memorial unto all generations.
>
> —Exodus 3:14-15

God told Moses, "I AM THAT I AM." Then He said I AM the LORD God, YHWH Elohiym (יהוה אלהים). God makes it clear that this is His name forever. Moses knew with whom he was speaking. God reveals Himself openly.

Satan often operates anonymously, doing much of his work in secret so that the light of truth cannot shine upon it. The prophet Daniel, however, explains that the LORD God *reveals* secret things:

> He revealeth the deep and secret things: he knoweth what *is* in the darkness, and the light dwelleth with him.
>
> —Daniel 2:22

This book was written to help shed light on many things that have been performed in secret, under the cover of darkness, which has been behind the developing new universal Christianity. The work is presented believing that if one can see the unfolding of historically documented events in the light of the Word of God, he will, perhaps, be able to discern truth from error.

The purpose of this book, therefore, is not to dispute about the shades of meanings of words, to argue about Bible versions or manuscripts, or to debate about various spiritual or theological movements. Neither is this book intended to criticize those who have differing theological views or social perspectives. Instead, it is the goal of this book to humbly present the factual evidence to *help the reader to get to know some of the people and the underlying agenda* that led up to the modern process of redefining Christianity. The focus of this book is toward *understanding* more about the *"who and why"* of those that have been working for centuries to lay the foundations of a *new* universal Christianity.

Section 1. The Background

While Men Slept...

Chapter 2. The Path to the Enlightenment and the French Revolution

And no marvel; for Satan himself is transformed into an angel of light. Therefore *it is* no great thing if his ministers also be transformed as the ministers of righteousness; whose end shall be according to their works.
—2 Corinthians 11:14-15

The Winds of Change

The French Revolution began on July 14, 1789, which became known as Bastille Day. The event marked a major change in the course of modern history. It left an indelible mark on the history of civilization and provided a reference point for the major change in thinking that was to reshape the world. It was the symbol that man had assumed a position to challenge the sources of all of the authorities to which he had been required to submit. The challenge was against the previously held beliefs in the authority of God, the Scriptures, the church, and the king. The old order of authority was replaced by a new order.

Reason, the power of the intellect of the rational mind, was pronounced to be the new source of all authority. This belief in the authority of reason was responsible for the great changes that occurred in the church, as well as in the state. This change toward a belief in the authority of reason has also occurred in the thinking of many that call themselves Christians. For many, this belief has also caused a falling away from believing in the saving grace of Jesus Christ. To understand what happened, it is useful to begin by focusing on the events in the eighteenth century that led up to the French Revolution. The new wave of thinking was sweeping across much of the western world. It was a time of great contrasts, and a time when great thinkers, writers, and theologians proliferated.

Writers like Charles Dickens (1812-1870), himself a childhood victim of the social impact of economic hardships among the masses, chronicled the conditions in eighteenth century England. He especially described the difficulties faced by many children who were unfortunate enough to have been born without privilege. It was those conditions and difficulties, which Dickens wrote of in *Oliver Twist,* that provided a backdrop for winning popular support for the French Revolution. In his novel, *A Tale of Two Cities,* Dickens described this time as one of great contrasts:

> It was the best of times, it was the worst of times, it was the age of wisdom, it was the age of foolishness, it was the epoch of belief, it was the epoch of incredulity, it was the season of Light, it was the season of Darkness, it was the spring of hope, it was the winter of despair, we had everything before us, we had nothing before us, we were all going direct to Heaven, we were all going direct the other way—in short, the period was so far like the present period, that some of its noisiest authorities insisted on its being received, for good or for evil, in the superlative degree of comparison only.

> There were a king with a large jaw and a queen with a plain face, on the throne of England; there were a king with a large jaw and a queen with a fair face, on the throne of France. In both countries it was clearer than crystal to the lords of the State preserves of loaves and fishes, that things in general were settled forever.[1]

Amidst these great contrasts, however, there was also a swelling storm of discontent. Change was in the air. Thinkers were emerging who challenged the very foundations of the status quo. The seeming disparity between the great wealth of the few and the severe poverty of the many was being intensely brought into question. The masses were being stirred. The very source of authority and power was being challenged. But what was this authority that was being challenged? Where did it come from?

---

[1] Charles Dickens, *A Tale of Two Cities,* In *Charles Dickens: Four Complete Novels* (Avenel, New Jersey: Gramercy Books/Random House Value Publishing, Inc., 1982), p. 589.

The Path to the Enlightenment and the French Revolution

Authority from God

Most civilizations throughout time, including the Egyptians, the Greeks, and the Romans, for example, have accepted the existence of a god, or gods, having power and authority over the earth and the things that are in it. The early Hebrews understood that God, who was known to them by the name יהוה (YHWH), which has been commonly translated as LORD, had authority over everything:

> Thine, O LORD, *is* the greatness, and the power, and the glory, and the victory, and the majesty: for all *that is* in the heaven and in the earth *is thine*; thine *is* the kingdom, O LORD, and thou art exalted as head above all.
> —1 Chronicles 29:11

Throughout history, however, the Hebrews rejected and disobeyed God, refusing to submit to His authority. During the pre-king days of Israel, the people relied upon their own reason to decide what was right and what was wrong. That which was right was determined by each man's individual perspective, as he saw it through his own eyes:

> In those days there was no king in Israel: every man did that which was right in his own eyes.
> —Judges 21:25

When God saw that the people both wanted and needed a king, He gave them one. It was God, and not the people, who chose the king to rule over the Hebrews:

> And Samuel said to all the people, See ye him whom the LORD hath chosen, that *there is* none like him among all the people? And all the people shouted, and said, God save the king .
> —1 Samuel 10:24

The kings had authority only because God gave it to them. First He chose Saul and then He chose David to be the kings over Israel. After that, there were many kings, some who were righteous and some that were unrighteous, which followed in succession.

While Men Slept...

Prior to the changes in thinking that led to the French Revolution, most Europeans commonly accepted that all authority, whether of the Scriptures, the church, or the king, existed because God ordained it to be so. This was what Paul confirmed to the New Testament church when he told the Romans that every soul should be subject to higher powers. He wrote that there is no power except that it comes from God:

> Let every soul be subject unto the higher powers. For there is no power but of God: the powers that be are ordained of God.
> —Romans 13:1

Authority of Rome

During the centuries before Christ, the world surrounding the Mediterranean Sea underwent major changes in the powers that ruled it. The Egyptians gave way to the Assyrians, who gave way to the Babylonians, who gave way to the Persians and the Medes, who gave way to the Greeks, who gave way to the Romans. It was the Romans who ruled a great empire that encompassed much of the western world during the time of the birth of Jesus Christ.

The power and authority of Rome was great. The Roman emperors believed that their authority to rule came from the Roman gods. It was the Roman emperor, Caesar Augustus, who, by the great authority of Rome and of the Roman gods, made the decree that caused the birth of Jesus to be in Bethlehem:

> And it came to pass in those days, that there went out a decree from Caesar Augustus that all the world should be taxed.
> —Luke 2:1

Because of the decree, Joseph was required to travel, with his espoused wife, Mary, to the City of David, which was named Bethlehem, where Jesus Christ was born. The power and authority of the Roman Emperor was enormous. When he spoke, the world was required to obey.

14

The Path to the Enlightenment and the French Revolution

The Romans continued to rule the great empire throughout the life of Jesus. It was they who, based on the condemning accusations of Jewish leaders, crucified Jesus Christ. Following the Crucifixion, the Romans continued to persecute those who followed and believed in Jesus. Many of His disciples, who became known as "Christians," were martyred during the first century. Among those were Stephen, Paul, Peter, and many others.

During the latter part of the third and the early part of the fourth centuries, Emperor Diocletian (A.D. 245-313) established a four-person rulership, known as a tetrarchy, over the Roman Empire. He tried to bring stability to the Empire by establishing a unified pagan religion to appease the Roman gods. As part of the process, he required everyone to sacrifice to pagan idols or be subject to severe punishment or even execution. This policy resulted in a great persecution of Christians when they refused to offer the sacrifice.[2]

The Roman Emperors who ruled prior to Diocletian were unsuccessful in suppressing Christianity by removing the rulers and teachers. Diocletian better understood that the Christian faith was being preserved not only by its rulers and teachers, but also in the Scriptures. Therefore, he reasoned that if he could destroy the Scriptures, which were the very foundation of the church, he could extinguish Christianity.[3] Diocletian and his subordinates set out to accomplish his objectives.

In A.D. 303, Diocletian, unleashed terror against the Christians. By one account it was just before dawn on A.D. February 23, 303 when he came to the Church of Nicomedia with his chief military and civil officers. There he found and burned the copies of the Scriptures and also burned the church.[4] The next day, he published an edict against all Christians, stripping them of any rights they may have previously

---

[2] Walker et al., *A History of the Christian Church*, 4th ed. (New York: Charles Scribner's Sons, 1985), pp. 122-123.

[3] Edward Backhouse, *Early Church History to the Death of Constantine*, 2nd ed., Charles Tylor, ed. (London: Hamilton, Adams & Co., 1885), p. 351.

[4] Ibid., p. 349.

had. All accessible copies of the Scriptures were publicly burned and the churches were destroyed. On A.D. April 30, 304, Maximian (d. A.D. 310), one of the tetrarch rulers, issued an edict that required, among other things, that all copies of Bibles be burned. The edict also required, without exception, that all Christians sacrifice to the gods under the threat of death.[5] According to one account, during the nineteenth year of the reign of Diocletian:

> ...the imperial edicts were every where published, to tear down the churches to the foundation, and to destroy the sacred Scriptures by fire, and which commanded, also, that those who were in honourable stations, should be degraded, but those who were freedmen should be deprived of their liberty, if they persevered in their adherence to Christianity....it was not long before other edicts were also issued, in which it was ordered that all the prelates in every place, should first be committed to prison, and then, by every artifice constrained to offer sacrifice to the gods.[6]

Intense Christian persecution continued until Constantine (A.D. c.272-337), who had reportedly converted to Christianity, seized power in A.D. 312 to become the new Roman Emperor.[7] The legendary history of the way in which Constantine seized power over the Empire has been thoroughly reported elsewhere and will not be elaborated upon here. However, it is critical to understand that Constantine reportedly saw a vision in the sky of a cross that convinced him that Christ would protect him in the battle for the Empire. When he won the battle, he legalized Christianity and sought to unify the divisions between the pagans and the Christians. Using his great power and

---

[5] Philip Schaff, *History of the Christian Church,* vol. 2, *Ante-Nicene Christianity, A.D. 100-325* (New York: Charles Scribner's Sons, 1883), p. 66.

[6] Valesius, *Annotations on the Life and Writings of Eusebius Pamphilus*, S. E. Parker, trans., In *The Ecclesiastical History of Eusebius Pamphilus, Bishop of Caesarea, In Palestine*, Christian Frederick Cruse and Isaac Boyle, trans. and eds. (Grand Rapids, Michigan: Baker Book House, 1990), p. 320.

[7] *Helvidius, Post-Nicene Fathers,* vol. 6, Philip Schaff and Henry Wace eds. (Grand Rapids, Michigan: Eerdmans Pub. Co., 1892; rep. 1983), p. 338.

wealth as persuasive tools, Constantine sought to bring the religions of the pagans and the Christians into a state of unity. He believed such unity would help stabilize the destabilized Roman Empire.[8]

In other words, Constantine sought to unify the pagans and the Christians by bringing them into one religion. To accomplish his goal, he ended the era of Christian persecution that had recently preceded his rise to power. The Christians who were cooperative with his plans received money and power. Many who could not agree with his plan to unify the pagans with the Christians were exiled or worse.

Being a practicing pagan, Constantine exerted great pressure to include certain pagan traditions into the Christian church. Constantine gave himself the title held by the chief priest of the Roman pagan religion, "Pontifex Maximus."[9] The modern word, pontiff, which the pope is also called, was derived from the office of Pontifex Maximus.[10] Thus, under Constantine, the Christian church became part of the state.

Once Constantine was able to get agreement among key figures in the religious world, he declared that he had established the "universal" or "catholic" church. Since there could be only one universal church, as declared by the great authority of the Roman Empire, it became known as the Catholic Church. As the authority of the Roman Empire declined, the authority of the Catholic Church rose.

Leo I (A.D. c.400-461), called "The Great," was the bishop of Rome from A.D. 440 to 461. He established the primacy of the bishop of Rome over the other bishops. At the Council of Chalcedon in A.D. 451 Leo I, asserting his authority by virtue of apostolic succession,

---

[8] Walker et al., *A History of the Christian Church,* pp. 125-130.

[9] Kenneth Scott Latourette, *A History of Christianity to A.D. 1500,* vol. 1 (New York: Harper San Francisco, 1975), p. 184.

[10] G. H. Joyce, *The Pope,* In *The Catholic Encyclopedia*, Charles G. Herbermann et al., eds., vol. 12 (New York: The Encyclopedia Press, 1913), p. 270.

declared that "Peter has spoken through Leo."[11]   By asserting that Jesus had given Peter all authority, Leo concluded that, by apostolic succession, all authority was then his. Leo saw himself as the supreme ruler and teacher.[12]

Thus, through the union of the Roman Empire, which had all secular power, and the Catholic Church, which Leo claimed had all religious power, there was no other power on earth. Leo I even got Emperor Valentinian III to issue an edict that commanded all to obey the bishop of Rome.[13] By A.D. 494, Leo's successor, Gelasius, declared that the Roman Church ruled the whole world, including the Emperor.[14]   The bishop of Rome acquired the distinctive title, *the* pope, near the beginning of the sixth century. Before then, other metropolitan bishops had each been called "papa" or "pope."[15]

After the first millennium, things began to change. Challenges were being made against the authority of the Roman Church. First, there was a major division in 1054 when the Eastern Church split from the Roman Church.[16] Then, during the Crusades, the Crusaders severely destabilized and weakened the Eastern Church by their conquest of Constantinople in 1204. Using their growing wealth and power, the Crusaders also challenged the authority of the Roman Church.[17] They were at odds with King Philip IV (1285-1314) and with the pope over the great wealth they had amassed during the Crusades. Consequently, some of the former Crusaders were brutally suppressed. Notable among the suppressed Crusaders was a group known as the Knights of the Temple, or the Templars.[18, 19]

---

[11] Walker et al., *A History of the Christian Church,* p. 152.

[12] Ibid., p. 152.

[13] Latourette, *A History of Christianity*, vol. 1, p. 187.

[14] Ibid.

[15] R. W. Thompson, *The Footprints of the Jesuits* (Cincinnati: Cranston & Curts and New York: Hunt & Eaton, 1894), p. 22.

[16] Latourette, *A History of Christianity*, vol. 1, p. 410.

[17] Walker et al., *A History of the Christian Church,* p. 288.

[18] Ibid., p. 286.

[19] Latourette, *A History of Christianity*, vol. 1, p. 413.

The Path to the Enlightenment and the French Revolution

Despite the many challenges that were made against the authority of the Roman Catholic Church, it continued to maintain its position as the center of power and authority in the western world through the close of the fifteenth century. As the fifteenth century closed, the Roman Catholic Church was under the firm control of the powerful Medici family of Florence, Italy. Having received brilliant political instruction from Niccolo Machiavelli (1469-1527) in his writing, *The Prince*, "Magnificent" Lorenzo de Medici (1449-1492) had a strong grip on the wealth and power possessed by the Roman Catholic Church. Machiavelli instructed Lorenzo de Medici on how to acquire and maintain power. One of Machiavelli's key points of instruction was that what one appears to be is more important to a position of power than what one actually is. He taught that it was more important to "appear" to have good qualities than to actually "have" good qualities.

The most important quality that a "prince" needed, according to Machiavelli, was that he should *appear* to be religious. He explained that a prince should take great care to say things so that:

> ...he should appear all mercy, all faith, all honesty, all humanity, all religion. And nothing is more necessary to appear to have than this last quality. Men in general judge more by their eyes than by their hands, because seeing is given to everyone, touching to a few. Everyone sees how you appear, few touch what you are....[20]

Heeding the advice of Machiavelli, Lorenzo de Medici set out to establish his son as having the appearance of "all religion." The Medici family used their great wealth and power to have Lorenzo's son, Giovanni de Medici (1475-1521), appointed as a cardinal at the age of thirteen and then elected as Pope Leo X in 1513.[21] Pope Leo X

---

[20] Niccolo Machiavelli, *The Prince, A New Translation with an Introduction by Harvey C. Mansfield, Jr.* (Chicago: The University of Chicago Press, 1985), pp. 70-71.

[21] Richard P. McBrien, *Lives of the Popes: The Pontiffs from St. Peter to John Paul II* (New York: HarperCollins Publishers, Inc., 1977), p. 272.

enjoyed the power and authority of being the head of the Roman Catholic Church, through which he exerted his authority over kings.

Authority of Kings

The King's Church

Ironically, while the Roman Catholic Church claimed its authority to rule came from Peter by apostolic succession, it was Peter who had also urged believers to submit to the authority of the kings and to honor the king:

> Submit yourselves to every ordinance of man for the Lord's sake: whether it be to the king, as supreme; Or unto governors, as unto them that are sent by him for the punishment of evildoers, and for the praise of them that do well.
>
> —1 Peter 2:13-14

> Honour all men. Love the brotherhood. Fear God. Honour the king.
>
> —1 Peter 2:17

But to whom did God give the authority to rule in sixteenth century England? Until 1534, England was under papal authority. However, King Henry VIII (1491-1547) and Pope Clement VII (1478-1534) had a major conflict concerning the issue of divorce. The king wanted the pope to allow him to divorce his wife, Queen Catherine, so that he could marry Anne Boleyn. The pope refused. Therefore, Henry established himself as the head of the Church of England and severed his ties with Rome.[22] In 1534, the Parliament forbade payment of a tax levied by the pope, known as Peter's Pence, to Rome and declared the king, instead of the pope, to be the supreme head of the Church of England.[23] By July 1536, it was illegal for a person in England to submit to the "feigned and pretended authority" of the pope.[24]

---

[22] Will Durant, *The Reformation: A History of European Civilization from Wyclif to Calvin: 1300-1564* (New York: MJF Books, 1957 and 1985), pp. 536-550.

[23] Latourette, *A History of Christianity*, vol. 2, p. 802.

[24] *English Historical Documents: 1485-1558*, C. H. Williams, ed. (New York: Oxford University Press, 1971), pp. 743-760.

The Path to the Enlightenment and the French Revolution

The King of the British: James I

Ironically, the death of King Henry VIII in 1547 left England in religious confusion. Henry's son by Jane Seymour, Edward VI, briefly reigned through a Protestant "Protector" until his death at the age of sixteen. After Queen Mary I, who was Henry VIII's daughter by Catherine, assumed the throne in 1553, her efforts to return England to Roman Catholicism were marked by common scenes of public executions. Many who opposed her religious views were burned at the stake. She died in 1558 and was succeeded to the throne by the daughter of Henry VIII and Anne Boleyn, Queen Elizabeth I (1533-1603). Born outside the sanction of the Roman Catholic Church, Elizabeth had little sympathy for returning England to the authority of Rome.[25]

Elizabeth's cousin, Mary Stuart (1542-1587), was the queen of Scotland and granddaughter of Margaret, who was the sister of Henry VIII. The Roman Catholic Mary Stuart considered herself to be the legitimate heir to the throne of England because Elizabeth was born in a marriage that was not recognized by the Roman Catholic Church. As the queen of Scotland by birth and having spent much of her life living in France, where she became the queen of France by marriage, Mary declared herself to be the "Queen of England, Scotland, and France." Mary was forced to abdicate her Scottish throne in 1567 and she fled to England. While Mary was in England, numerous attempts were made by Roman Catholics against the life of Queen Elizabeth in an effort to give the throne to the Catholic Mary. Based on testimony that Mary had known about and encouraged the plots to assassinate the queen, Mary was executed in 1587.[26]

Mary Stuart had a son, James Stuart (1566-1625), who as an infant was crowned James VI, king of Scotland, when his mother was forced from the throne. Despite the dispute between Queen Elizabeth and Mary Stuart, the queen selected James VI to succeed her to the throne of England in 1603. As the King of England, he was known as King James I and strongly supported the doctrine of the Divine Right of

---

[25] Edward P. Cheyney, *A Short History of England* (Boston and others: Ginn and Company, 1904), pp. 309-334.

[26] Ibid., pp. 340-362.

While Men Slept...

Kings.[27] This doctrine was that the king had received his authority to rule from God and that he, therefore, ruled by "divine right." Consequently, his right to rule could not be questioned or challenged, except by God. The ascension of a Scottish King to the throne of England and Ireland had the effect of uniting the previously divided Britain. The union of Scotland, Ireland, and England under King James I brought a high level of political stability to the British Isles.[28]

Authority of Scripture

Looking Toward the Scriptures

Only one thing could successfully challenge the assertion by the pope of the absolute authority of the Roman Catholic Church. That was the belief that God had given to man through His divine inspiration an even higher authority, the Scriptures. Following the Crusades, there was a renewed interest in looking to the Scriptures, rather than to the Roman Catholic Church, for the revelation of God's will to man. There was an increased level of interest in making the Scriptures available directly to the people, without the filter of the Roman Catholic Church.

The Roman Catholic Church and the kings of Europe, however, resisted efforts to make the Scriptures directly available to the people. Consequently, intense efforts arose to translate the Scriptures outside the governance of the Roman Catholic Church and the kings. Such actions were met with strong and often hostile opposition from the existing authorities. Nevertheless, by the fourteenth century John Wycliff (c.1320-1384) had caused the Bible to be translated into English.[29] Asserting that the Scriptures were the authority of the church, Wycliff maintained that popes might err and that they were not essential for the administration of the church.[30] Wycliff insisted that the

---

[27] Ibid., pp. 383-388.

[28] J. C. Becket, *A Short History of Ireland* (London: Hutchinson University Library, 1958), p. 69.

[29] Alfred W. Pollard, *Records of the English Bible: The Documents Relating to the Translation and Publication of the Bible in English, 1525-1611* (London & New York: H. Frowde, Oxford University Press, 1911), p. 1.

[30] Latourette, *A History of Christianity*, vol. 1, p. 663.

relationship of man to God was direct and that no intermediary, such as the church or a priest, was required.[31] The followers of Wycliff, known as "Lollards" or "mumblers," were ruthlessly suppressed and many of them were burned. Consequently, many of Wycliff's followers went underground.[32] In 1387 King Richard II prohibited, under penalty of imprisonment and confiscation of property, the work of Wycliff.[33]

Significantly, King Richard II (1367-1400) of England married the Bohemian princess Anne in 1382.[34] This provided a connection between Bohemia and England that enabled John Wycliff's teachings to spread to mainland Europe by way of Bohemia and Moravia. Notably, John Hus (c.1372-1415) of Bohemia became an avid student of Wycliff's work. He believed that it was Christ and not the pope who was the head of the true Christian church. Like Wycliff, Hus believed that the only law of the true church was found in the Bible.[35, 36] Sometime between 1450 and 1456, Johann Gutenberg (1398-1468), a German, printed the first Bibles. The established Roman Catholic Church responded to the surge of interest in reading the Bible by passing laws banning the reading of Scripture.[37]

Despite the bans on Bible reading by the authorities, the interest in bringing Bibles to the people continued to increase. The work on producing readable Scriptures continued even within the Roman Catholic Church. By the sixteenth century, Desiderius Erasmus (c.1466-1536) found himself in a very unique and strategic position. He was a loyal Catholic who had close personal relationships with Pope Leo X, with King Henry VIII, and with Martin Luther (1483-

---

[31] Durant, *The Reformation*, p. 31.

[32] Walker et al., *A History of the Christian Church,* pp. 380-381.

[33] George Haven Putnam, *The Censorship of the Church of Rome and Its Influence Upon the Production and Distribution of Literature*, vol. 1 (New York: Benjamin Blom, 1967), pp. 69-70.

[34] Walker et al., *A History of the Christian Church,* pp. 380-381.

[35] Ibid., pp. 381-382.

[36] The Count Lutzow, *The Life & Times of Master John Hus* (London: J. M. Dent & Co. and New York: E. P. Dutton & Co., 1909), p. 27.

[37] Putnam, *The Censorship of the Church of Rome*, vol. 1, pp. 69-70.

1546). Although Erasmus spent considerable time in both England and in Rome, he rejected lucrative offers by King Henry VIII to live in England and also declined the offer by Pope Leo X to be made a cardinal in the Roman Catholic Church. Erasmus insisted on maintaining his freedom. He used that freedom to produce the first printed edition of the Greek New Testament.[38] This text, which Erasmus compiled in 1516, served as the foundation for later editions of the Greek New Testament, which by 1633 became known as the *Textus Receptus*, or the Received Text.[39]

The Scriptures: The Foundation of the Reformation

With the availability of a printed Greek New Testament, a dedicated Roman Catholic monk and teacher named Martin Luther was able to translate the Bible into German.[40] Other translations soon followed. William Tyndale (c.1484-1536) relied heavily upon the work of Erasmus, Luther, and others to produce a printed Bible that could be read by English speaking people.[41]

While Pope Leo X spent his time in leisure, in cultivating the arts, and in amassing great wealth through the sale of indulgences, Martin Luther was studying the Scriptures. Although Luther is historically credited with being the leader of the Reformation, he considered the Bohemian reformer, John Hus, to be his forerunner.[42] Thus, like John Wycliff and John Hus, Luther found the teachings of the Scriptures to be in conflict with the teachings of the Roman Catholic Church. Luther also agreed with Wycliff and Hus that God revealed Himself to man through the Scriptures, rather than through the pope.

---

[38] Durant, *The Reformation*, pp. 271-292.

[39] Edward Miller, *Introduction* to John William Burgon, *The Traditional Text of the New Testament,* In *Unholy Hands on the Bible*, Edward Miller, ed., vol. 1, Jay P. Green, ed. (Lafayette, Indiana: Sovereign Grace Trust Fund, 1990), p. 2.

[40] Kenneth Scott Latourette, *A History of Christianity: A.D. 1500-A.D. 1975,* vol. 2 (New York: HarperSanFrancisco, 1975), pp. 704-706.

[41] Brooke Foss Westcott, *A General View of the History of the English Bible*, 1st ed. (London and Cambridge: Macmillan and Co., 1868), pp. 31-42.

[42] Lutzow, *The Life & Times of Master John Hus*, p. 312.

Using the Scriptures, Luther then challenged the authority of the pope on such basic issues as the means to salvation and the requirements for paying indulgences.[43] In his studies, Luther found that the church and Scriptures did not agree on the fundamental doctrinal issue concerning the means for salvation. He said that the Scriptures maintained that salvation was obtained by faith alone and could not be achieved, as was taught by the Roman Catholic Church, by performing works. Instead of believing that salvation was through the authority of the pope, Luther declared that salvation was by faith alone, by trusting in the "Word of God."[44]

Using the Scriptures, Luther challenged the absolute authority of the pope. It was noon on October 31, 1517, the day before All Saints Day, when Luther posted his theses on the door of the All Saints Castle Church in Wittenberg, Germany.[45] With his "Ninety-Five Theses," Luther emphasized the importance of believers following Scripture, rather than the teaching of the Roman Catholic Church where they differed from each other. Stressing the need for repentance and God's grace, he disputed the great emphasis that the pope had placed upon the payment of money for the remission of sins.[46]

Although Luther was extremely loyal to the pope and to the Roman Catholic Church, he stood by his convictions. He maintained that the pope was wrong in asserting his authority beyond what the Scriptures could support.[47] As he studied canon law, Luther reached the conclusion that, as late as the fourth century, the bishop of Rome was not recognized as the head of the universal church. He even argued that before the twelfth century the whole jurisdictional authority of the papacy did not exist.[48]

---

[43] Walker et al., *A History of the Christian Church,* p. 426.

[44] Ibid., pp. 424-425.

[45] Durant, *The Reformation*, pp. 340-341.

[46] Walker et al., *A History of the Christian Church,* pp. 424-426.

[47] Philip Schaff, *The History of the Christian Church*, vol. 7, *History Of Modern Christianity, The German Reformation*, 2nd ed. (Grand Rapids: Wm. B. Eerdmans Publishing Co., 1980; Revised, Charles Scribner's Sons, 1910), pp. 160-166.

[48] Hajo Holborn, *A History of Modern Germany: The Reformation* (New York: Alfred A. Knopf, 1976), p. 136.

While Men Slept...

Despite intense pressure from the Church of Rome, Luther refused to compromise on his convictions of what he believed to be the truth.[49] Those Christians who accepted the authority of Scripture became Protestants whereas those who remained in the Roman Catholic Church maintained that the pope, and tradition, had authority over the Scriptures. Thus, Luther effectively challenged every professing Christian to address the question of whether the authority of God belonged with the Scriptures or with the pope.

Luther's challenge to the authority of the pope manifested itself amidst growing doubts that the Roman Catholic Church was a faithful witness of the Word of God. Luther held that the error of the Roman Catholic Church was that it had compromised with human reason.[50] With the growing skepticism toward the church, there had been an increased interest in turning to the Scriptures as a means of determining what God had actually said. If the church were not the faithful witness that preserved God's revelation to man, then the Scriptures had to be looked to as the preserved Word of God to man.

The events Luther initiated brought about the Protestant Reformation, which declared the authority of Scripture. He asserted that from Scripture came forth the simplicity of the doctrine of Jesus Christ. In 1522, Luther preached in Wittenberg that the Gospel consists of the knowledge of sin, forgiveness through Christ, and love for one's neighbor. The alterations by the church that had caused so much turmoil had to do with externals.[51]

Inspiration of the Scriptures

Once it is believed that God gives all authority and that all of creation is subject to Him, then it is critical that man understands what it is that God has willed for him. What is God's purpose for man? What is God's plan? If the Scriptures are God's Word to man, then it follows that the Scriptures are to be looked to as the revelation of the author-

---

[49] Robert Herndon Fife, *The Revolt of Martin Luther* (New York and London: Columbia University Press, 1957), pp. 670-691.

[50] Fulop-Miller, *The Power and Secret of the Jesuits*, p. 443.

[51] Walker et al., *A History of the Christian Church,* p. 434.

ity of God to man. Therefore, it is then necessary to study Scripture to determine what it is that God is saying to man.

Paul wrote these words to Timothy concerning the inspiration of Scripture by God:

> All scripture *is* given by inspiration of God, and *is* profitable for doctrine, for reproof, for correction, for instruction in righteousness: That the man of God may be perfect, throughly furnished unto all good works.
>
> —2 Timothy 3:16-17

If all Scripture is divinely inspired, it follows that the authority of Scripture proceeds from its inspiration.[52] Some might argue that one could not prove the authority of Scripture by using Scripture because such a proof represents a circular argument. On the other hand, as one writer put it:

> For anyone who by faith accepts the authority of the Scriptures as the Word of God, the matter is settled: the authority of the Bible is not to be defended, but affirmed (as in the case of the existence of God and of the excellence of Jesus Christ).[53]

The Protestant view of the authority of Scripture was clarified, for example, in the Westminster Confession of Faith, which was originally published in 1646 and agreed to by the churches in the kingdoms of Scotland, England, and Ireland in 1647. It made the following confession concerning the authority of Scripture:

> The authority of the holy scripture, for which it ought to be believed and obeyed, dependeth not upon the testimony of any man or church, but wholly upon God (who is truth itself), the author thereof; and therefore it is to be received, because it is the word of God.[54]

---

[52] Rene' Pache, *The Inspiration and Authority of Scripture*, Helen I. Needham, Translator (Salem, Wisconsin: Sheffield Publishing Company, Moody Bible Institute of Chicago, 1969), p. 305.

[53] Ibid., p. 306.

[54] *Westminster Confession Of Faith* (Glasgow: Free Presbyterian Publications, 1990; first published in 1646), pp. 17-21.

While Men Slept...

The Counter Reformation

The Jesuits

The challenges of Martin Luther, in favor of Scripture, and King Henry VIII, in favor of himself, against the authority of the pope was rejected by a group of Roman Catholics who formed an organization on August 15, 1534[55] known as the "Company of Jesus." The group, formed during the same year in which England separated itself from Roman Catholic authority, later organized itself into the "Society of Jesus" on September 27, 1540 under the authority of Pope Paul III and became known as the Jesuits.[56] As a Jesuit, one was required to submit his will completely to the authority of his superiors in absolute "holy obedience," learning to feel that obeying his superiors was the same as obeying God.[57] The Society was organized in a military style, with its head called the "General," which was known as the "Black Pope" because of his black cassock.[58]

Ignatius Loyola (c. 1491-1556), who was the founder of the Jesuits, had the avowed purpose of using the organization as the tool by which to suppress the Reformation and to declare the beliefs of the resultant Protestant Movement as unpardonable heresies.[59] As such, the Jesuits were the key movers in the Counter Reformation of the Roman Catholic Church.[60, 61] Five years after the formation of the Jesuits, the Roman Catholic Church took a significant step against the Protestant Reformation. On December 13, 1545, Pope Paul III opened the Council of Trent. A key function of the Council was to condemn the writings of Martin Luther. Specifically, the Council condemned Luther's

---

[55] Note: August 15 had been known as the Feast Day of the Goddess Diana. It was known to Roman Catholics as the Feast Day of the Dormition of Mary and, after 1950, it was known as the Feast Day of the Assumption of Mary.

[56] F. A. Ridley, *The Jesuits: A Study in Counter-Revolution* (London: Secker and Warburg, 1938), pp. 150-151.

[57] Durant, *The Reformation*, p. 912.

[58] Ibid., p. 913.

[59] Thompson, *The Footprints of the Jesuits*, pp. 31-33.

[60] Walker et al., *A History of the Christian Church,* pp. 508-509.

[61] Holborn, *A History of Modern Germany: The Reformation*, p. 274.

assertion of the authority of Scripture as the sole source of doctrine. Instead, the Council concluded that doctrine was derived from Roman Catholic Church tradition as well as from Scripture.[62] To further discredit Martin Luther, the Council stated that individuals had no right to interpret Scripture. That right, it said, belonged only to the Roman Catholic Church because it alone had the power of the Holy Ghost.[63]

Even though Pope Leo X had approved of the work of Erasmus on the Greek New Testament and Pope Adrian VI had asked Erasmus to do a similar work on the Old Testament, the Council of Trent rejected his work. In its effort to discredit the Scripture that Luther had used as a basis for his claim on its authority, the Council condemned the Greek New Testament that Erasmus had prepared. While rejecting Erasmus' Greek Text, the Council asserted that Jerome's Vulgate was the only authentic Latin Version of the Bible.[64]

The Roman Catholic English Bible

The Jesuits dominated the Council of Trent.[65] As we have learned, the Council condemned Erasmus' work, which was the very basis of the Reformation and for the English Bible of William Tyndale. No alternative Bible was available to the English-speaking people that was acceptable to the Roman Catholic Church. Nevertheless, Bible reading in England became more widespread and, without an official presence of the Roman Catholic Church in that country, the people were being weaned from "pomp and ceremony" of religion and the cause for the Reformation was steadily advancing.[66]

---

[62] Brooke Foss Westcott, *The Bible In The Church; A Popular Account of the Collection and Reception of the Holy Scriptures in the Christian Churches* (London & Cambridge: Macmillan and Co., 1866), pp. 255-256.

[63] Edward McNall Burns, *The Counter Reformation* (Princeton, New Jersey: D. Van Nostrand Company, 1964), p. 50.

[64] Durant, *The Reformation*, p. 285.

[65] Benjamin G. Wilkinson, "Our Authorized Bible Vindicated, In *Which Bible?*, David Otis Fuller, ed. (Grand Rapids, Michigan: Institute for Biblical Textual Studies, 1990), p. 235.

[66] Ibid., pp. 237-238.

While Men Slept...

To try to influence the English people back toward Roman Catholicism, the Jesuits worked in Continental Europe to prepare a Roman Catholic Bible for English speaking people. Working in Rheims, France, the Jesuits prepared an English New Testament in 1582 based on Jerome's Latin Vulgate, instead of on Erasmus' Greek New Testament, to displace the then popular Tyndale Bible. A Roman Catholic Old Testament in English, published in Douay, France, followed in 1609-1610.[67] This Bible became known as the Douay-Rheims Bible.

The Protestant English Bible

Not withstanding the presence of a pre-Reformation English Bible and a post-Reformation and post-Council of Trent English Roman Catholic New Testament, the Puritans requested that King James I of England authorize the translation of a post-Reformation Protestant English Bible. Although King James I was the official head of the Church of England, he had been raised under the influence of Calvinism as a Scottish Presbyterian. Consequently, he did not share with the Anglicans their interest in church ritual.[68] In April 1603, the Puritans presented a petition to the king with requests for reform. The outcome of the petition was that King James I held a conference at Hampton Court in January 1604 to resolve matters between the Puritans and the English bishops. It was out of this conference that the king authorized a new translation of the English Bible that became known as the "Authorized" or "King James" version that was eventually produced in 1611.[69]

After King James I had authorized the translation of the Bible into English at the 1604 Hampton Court Conference, the Jesuits accelerated their efforts to prevent its production. A group of Jesuits dug underneath the Houses of Parliament during 1604 and 1605. They then undertook a treasonous plot whereby they placed barrels of gunpowder under the Houses of Parliament in an attempt to assassinate

---

[67] Ibid., pp. 238-241.

[68] George Macaulay Trevelyan, *England Under the Stuarts* (London: Methuen & Co. Ltd. and New York: G. P. Putnam's Sons, 1924), pp. 73-79.

[69] Walker et al., *A History of the Christian Church,* pp. 548-549.

King James I and Members of Parliament. The "Gunpowder Plot," as it was called, was discovered before harm was done. However, the failed plot had the effect of solidifying the unpopularity of Roman Catholics among the people of England.[70] The consequence of the failed plot was that rigorous laws were enacted and enforced that prevented toleration of the Roman Catholic Church in England. The priests, especially the Jesuits, were banished and persecuted.[71] Thereby, England was maintained as an Anglican, rather than a Roman Catholic, nation.

The King James Bible was distinctly Protestant. It contained stern warnings in the Dedication and in the message from the Translators to the Reader about the "Popish" persons who would desire to keep the people in ignorance and darkness:

> So that, if on the one side we shall be traduced by Popish persons at home or abroad, who therefore will maligne vs, because we are poore Instruments to make GODS holy Trueth to be yet more and more knowen vnto the people, whom they desire still to keepe in ignorance and darknesse: or if on the other side, we shall be maligned by selfe-conceited brethren, who runne their owne wayes, and giue liking vnto nothing but what is framed by themselues, and hammered on their Anuile; we may rest secure, supported within by the trueth and innocencie of a good conscience, hauing walked the wayes of simplicitie and integritie, as before the Lord; and sustained without, by the powerfull Protection of your Majesties grace and fauour, which will euer giue countenanace to honest and Christian endeuours, against bitter censures and vncharitable imputations.[72] [Letters are untranslated from the original.]

---

[70] Trevelyan, *England Under the Stuarts*, pp. 92-99.

[71] Leopold Von Ranke, *The History of the Popes During the Last Four Centuries*, vol. 2 (London: G. Bell and Sons, Ltd., 1913), p. 244.

[72] Dedication Letter, In *The Holy Bible, 1611 Edition, King James Version: A Word-for-Word Reprint of the First Edition of the Authorized Version Presented in Roman Letters for Easy Reading and Comparison with Subsequent Editions* (Nashville: Thomas Nelson Publishers, Undated).

While Men Slept...

Toleration: Moving England Back to Rome

To escape persecution, the Jesuits operated secretly and, despite their repression, they were key to keeping Roman Catholicism alive in England.[73] After the reign of King James I, there were resurgences of Roman Catholicism in the country. In 1670, for example, the treaty of Dover created an alliance between Anglican England and Roman Catholic France against their common enemy, the Dutch Republic. That treaty was actually used as a cover for another secret treaty whereby King Charles II (1630-1685) attempted to re-establish Roman Catholicism in his country of England. Some believed that he used this treaty as a basis for declaring himself to be a Roman Catholic and that he saw the prearranged quarrel with the Dutch as a means for re-establishing Romanism in England.[74] After the death of Charles II in 1685, King James II (1633-1701) continued the efforts to bring England back to the Roman Catholic Church. Using the disguise of complete toleration for all parties, James II issued the Declaration of Indulgence in 1687 that gave full rights for public worship to Roman Catholics.[75]

Toleration was seen by some as the mark of the true church. John Locke (1632-1704), for example, while attacking the doctrine of the Divine Right of Kings, argued in favor of natural law and in favor of religious toleration. In his *A Letter Concerning Toleration* written in 1689, Locke stressed tolerance as the key characteristic of the "true church." Locke opened his writing by saying:

> Since you are pleased to inquire what are my thoughts about the mutual Toleration of Christians in their different professed religion, I must needs answer you freely, that I esteem that toleration to be the chief characteristic mark of the true church.[76]

[73] Edmund Sheridan Purcell, *Life of Cardinal Manning: Archbishop of Westminster*, vol. 1 (New York: Macmillan and Co., 1896), pp. 655-656.

[74] M. W. Patterson, *A History of the Church of England* (London: Longmans, Green and Co, 1909), p. 363.

[75] Ibid., p. 369.

[76] John Locke, *The Works of John Locke, Four Letters on Toleration* (London: Ward, Lock and Co., Undated), p. 2.

The Path to the Enlightenment and the French Revolution

A careful look at Locke's theology, however, revealed that his beliefs were largely Unitarian [we will see that he had a major influence on the new universal Christianity]. Believing that religion exercised a strong moral force, he believed it to be true and saving only when it acted as the inward persuasion of the mind. In his view, the concept of punishment was inappropriate because it could have no effect.[77] Committed to the "humanization of Jesus," Locke reduced Him to the "status of an exalted and inspired prophet" and also reduced the status of the Holy Ghost.[78] David Hume (1711-1776) took the unconventional beliefs of Locke even further by saying that the existence of God as the primal cause was invalid, that polytheism preceded monotheism, and that miracles were not valid.[79]

The seventeenth century Puritans believed that accepting the doctrine of tolerance for the Roman Catholic Church in particular would be self-destructive. According to one writer, the Puritans were probably correct. He said:

> It was clear to them that the first use that the Roman Catholics would make of toleration would be to employ it as a fulcrum for the destruction of Protestantism.[80]

Papal Suppression of the Jesuits

Amidst increased calls for toleration of Roman Catholicism in England during the seventeenth and eighteenth centuries, the power of the Jesuits continued to increase. The strong influences they developed over the temporal powers of sovereign nations, including France, Spain, Portugal, and Naples (a kingdom at that time), caused their kings to mount challenges to the powers of the pope. In a conciliatory gesture toward those and other kings who found themselves threat-

---

[77] B. W. Young, *Religion and Enlightenment in Eighteenth-Century England: Theological Debate from Locke to Burke* (Oxford: Clarendon Press, 1998), pp. 24-25.

[78] Ibid., p. 26.

[79] Latourette, *A History of Christianity*, vol. 2, p. 1004.

[80] Patterson, *A History of the Church of England*, p. 316.

ened by the increasing power of the Jesuits, Pope Clement XIII (1693-1769) promised them that he would abolish the Society of Jesus. In 1769, on the night before the day appointed for him to publicly sign the decree abolishing the Jesuits, Pope Clement XIII "was suddenly seized with convulsions, and died, leaving the act unperformed, and the Jesuits victorious." Some were convinced that the pope had been poisoned.[81]

Clement XIV (1705-1774) was elected as the new pope in 1769 by cardinals who were divided over their support for the Jesuits.[82] Monarchs of sovereign nations, however, continued to resist the influence of the Jesuits. Charles III of Spain finally presented the pope with an ultimatum. He said that unless the Jesuits were utterly and completely dissolved, he would break away from the Roman Catholic Church and set up an independent Spanish Church, similar to the Church of England.[83]

On July 21, 1773, Pope Clement XIV officially banned the Jesuits.[84] He issued a decree concerning the Jesuits that said:

> We deprive it [the Society of Jesus, known as the Jesuits] of all activity whatever, of its houses, schools, colleges, hospitals, lands, and, in short, every other place whatsoever, in whatever kingdom or province they may be situated. We abrogate and annul its statutes, rules, customs, decrees, and constitutions, even though confirmed by oath, and approved by the Holy See or otherwise...We declare all, and all kind of authority, the general, the provincials, the visitors, and other superiors of said society, to be *forever annulled and extinguished*, of what nature soever the said society may be, as well in things spiritual as temporal... Our will and pleasure is, that these our letters should forever and to all eternity be valid,

---

[81] Thompson, *The Footprints of the Jesuits*, pp. 224-227.

[82] Ibid., p. 225.

[83] Manfred Barthel, *The Jesuits: History & Legend of the Society of Jesus*, Translated & adapted by Mark Howson (New York: William Morrow and Company, Inc., 1984), p. 229.

[84] Thompson, *The Footprints of the Jesuits*, pp. 222-224

permanent, and efficacious, have and obtain their full force and effect, and be inviolably observed by all and every whom they do or may concern, now or hereafter, in any manner whatsoever.[85]

After suppressing the Jesuits, the pope died in the following year on September 22, 1774. There was considerable controversy over the cause of his death. Some reported that a post-mortem examination of the body showed the presence of poison and implicated the Jesuits. The Jesuits disputed those findings and treated such an account as an act of libel.[86]

Despite the unequivocal order of the pope, many Jesuits did not consider themselves abolished. Within a month of their dissolution, Frederick the Great of Prussia offered to accept the Jesuits in his territories. He was especially hopeful that this move would help enhance the loyalty toward him by the Catholics in the province of Silesia. In addition, Catherine the Great of Russia refused to acknowledge that the pope had dissolved the Jesuits. Therefore, the Jesuits flourished in Prussia and in Russia during the time of their suppression.[87]

Re-Emergence of the Jesuits

Even though Pope Clement XIV had abolished the Jesuits, "forever and to all eternity" in 1773, they were restored in 1814 by Pope Pius VII.[88, 89] The universal head of the Jesuits then became General Brzozowski, who was in Russia.[90] Soon there came out of Prussia, where the Jesuits had been working even though they had been offi-

---

[85] Quoted from Nicolini, *History of the Jesuits*, pp. 387-406, In Thompson, *The Footprints of the Jesuits*, pp. 231-232.

[86] Thompson, *The Footprints of the Jesuits*, pp. 227-233.

[87] Barthel, *The Jesuits*, pp. 231-233.

[88] Joseph de Guibert, *The Jesuits: Their Spiritual Doctrine and Practice*, William J. Young, Translator, George E. Ganss, ed. (St. Louis: The Institute of Jesuit Sources, 1964), p. 462.

[89] Barthel, *The Jesuits*, p. 237.

[90] Francis Edwards, *The Jesuits in England: From 1580 to the Present Day* (Tunbridge Wells, Kent: Burns & Oates, 1985), p. 162.

cially banned by the Roman Catholic Church, the Prussian Plan for Union, requiring the unification of the churches. Specifically, the king of Prussia, Frederick William III (1797-1840), proclaimed a plan to requiring the unification of the Lutheran and Reformed Churches. It was encouraged and endorsed by theologian and Bible critic, Friedrich Ernst Daniel Schleiermacher (1768-1834). The king required that the churches treat the differences between themselves as nonexistent. Thousands of orthodox Lutherans responded by refusing to submit to the proclamation and emigrated to America.[91] The edict was brought forth in 1817, 300 years after Martin Luther had sparked the separation of faith-based Christians from the Roman Catholic Church. The effect of this requirement was that it caused a strong reaction among conservative Lutherans. Those Lutherans eventually organized themselves into the German Evangelical Synod and later became known as the Lutheran Church (Missouri Synod). As such, they resisted ecumenical efforts to establish a union with other churches.[92, 93]

Having been officially absent from Rome for over forty years, the Jesuits sought to restore their work in educational systems. As such, the Jesuit teachers in Rome requested volunteer catechists to help in their schools. A young man named Giovanni Maria Mastai-Ferretti (1792-1878) accepted their call.[94] Young Mastai-Ferretti, who was destined to become Pope Pius IX, assisted in teaching young boys in religious and elementary education. Pope Pius VII became interested in Mastai and consented in 1817 for him to become a deacon and then

---

[91] Henry Renaud Turner Brandreth, "Approaches of the Churches Towards Each Other in the Nineteenth Century," In *A History of the Ecumenical Movement, 1517-1948*, ch. 6, Ruth Rouse and Stephen Charles Neill, eds. (Philadelphia: The Westminster Press, 1954), p. 287.

[92] Ruth Rose, "Voluntary Movements and the Changing Ecumenical Climate," In *A History of the Ecumenical Movement, 1517-1948*, ch. 7, Ruth Rouse and Stephen Charles Neill, eds. (Philadelphia: The Westminster Press, 1954), p. 325.

[93] Philip Schaff, "The Reformation In Prussia. Duke Albrecht And Bishop Georg Von Polenz, § 99, Propagation And Persecution Of Protestantism In Germany Till 1530, ch. 6, The Reformation from A.D. 1517 to 1648," vol. 7, In *The History of the Christian Church*, http://www.ccel.org/s/schaff/history/7_ch06.htm.

[94] Frank J. Coppa, *Pope Pius IX: Crusader in a Secular Age* (Boston: Twayne Publishers, A Division of G. K. Hall & Co., 1979), p. 25.

a priest at the age of twenty-seven. For the next three years, Priest Mastai received Jesuit instruction. After the death of Pope Pius VII in 1823, his successor, who was Pope Leo XII, appointed Mastai as an archbishop in 1827. Mastai, who was under strong Jesuit influence, then went on a religious retreat under the direction of the Jesuit fathers in order to prepare himself for his new office.[95, 96] As we shall see, Mastei, as Pope Pius IX, would lead the Roman Catholic Church during a period of great change, which included reopening England to the Church of Rome. He was to play a key role in establishing the foundation for building the new universal Christianity.

The Enlightenment

Challenges to Authority

After the challenge to the authority of the Roman Catholic Church in the sixteenth century that brought about the Reformation, other traditionally held ideas were subject to question. All did not agree that an independent sovereign God was the source of all authority, whether it was imparted to the church, the king, or the Scriptures. The world's fundamental view of the universe was challenged when Galileo (1564-1642) used scientific inquiry to confirm the Copernican system that the earth revolved around the sun. His success helped to build the foundation for the "Enlightenment."[97] Seventeenth century philosophers, such as René Descartes (1596-1650), continued to build a case for enlightened thinking. He made a bold declaration that might seem to many to be an assertion of his own divinity when he wrote, "I think, therefore I am." Thus, Descartes defined his own existence by his own mind.[98] This kind of language had been previously reserved for God (Yahweh), who identified Himself to Moses as "I AM:"

---

[95] Ibid., pp. 26-31.

[96] Edwards, *The Jesuits in England: From 1580 to the Present Day*, 170. [88] Joseph de Guibert, *The Jesuits: Their Spiritual Doctrine and Practice*, William J. Young, Translator, George E. Ganss, ed. (St. Louis: The Institute of Jesuit Sources, 1964), p. 462.

[97] Walker et al., *A History of the Christian Church*, p. 569.

[98] Ibid.

> And God said unto Moses, I AM THAT I AM: and he said,
> Thus shalt thou say unto the children of Israel, I AM hath sent
> me unto you.
>
> —Exodus 3:14

Eighteenth century philosophers were emboldened by the success of philosophy during the preceding centuries. As chinks in the armor of the traditional order continued to be made, a significant number of eighteenth century thinkers began to challenge it. During the "Enlightenment," philosophers and writers argued in favor of man's intuitive thinking capacity as the basis for his authority.

The Prussian philosopher Immanuel Kant (1724-1804) defined "Enlightenment" as being able to know without being told. In his words, enlightened thinking was:

> ...man's release from his self-incurred tutelage. Tutelage is
> man's inability to make use of his understanding without di-
> rection from another. Self-incurred is this tutelage when its
> cause lies not in lack of reason but in lack of resolution and
> courage to use it without direction from another.[99]

Restoration of "Divine Truth"

The German Enlightenment, in which Kant was a key participant, laid the foundation that changed modern Christian theology. In contrast to traditional Christianity that believed in an active God with a will and personality, the new view was that God was remote. It was believed that He set in motion the laws of the universe, but reason was to be the means by which the intentions of God were to be understood. Thus, religion was made subordinate to rationalism.[100, 101] In other words, it was believed that God was no longer participating in

---

[99] Immanuel Kant, *Foundations of the Metaphysics of Morals and What is Enlightenment?*, 2nd ed., rev., Lewis White Beck, trans. (Upper Saddle River, New Jersey: Prentice-Hall, Inc., 1997), p. 83.

[100] Holborn, *A History of Modern Germany, 1648-1840*, pp. 311-312.

[101] Ibid., p. 485.

the activities of the universe, but that He had left man and his reason in charge. Kant was influenced by the writings of Emanuel Swedenborg (1688-1772). In his criticism of Swedenborg's works, Kant introduced principles of metaphysics that resulted in the publication of his *Critique of Pure Reason.*[102]

Swedenborg said that in 1743 "the Lord himself" called him to a "holy office." He said the Lord opened his eyes to see the spiritual world and revealed to him things that had "never before come to the knowledge of any man." These included matters concerning the true worship of God, the spiritual sense of the Word, and many other concerns "conducive to salvation and true wisdom."[103] Swedenborg taught that God had uniquely showed him the "last judgement," which took place in the spiritual world in 1757.[104] According to Swedenborg, the Lord cannot manifest Himself in person to the world. However, He would as He foretold, "...come and establish a New Church, which is the New Jerusalem."[105] Therefore, Swedenborg taught, the Lord would use a man to receive the doctrines of the New Church and communicate them through the press. According to Swedenborg, he was that man:

> That the Lord manifested himself before me his servant, that he sent me on this office, and afterwards opened the sight of my spirit, and so let me into the spiritual world, permitting me to see the heavens and the hells, and also to converse with angels and spirits, and this now continually for many years, I attest in truth; and further, that from the first day of my call to this office, I have never received any thing relating to the *doc-*

---

[102] Robin Larsen, et al., eds. *Emanuel Swedenborg: A Continuing Vision* (New York: Swedenborg Foundation, Inc., 1988), p. 418.

[103] William White, *Life of Emanuel Swedenborg, Together with A Brief Synopsis of His Writings, Both Philosophical and Theological* (Philadelphia: J. B. Lippincott & Co., 1884), p. 62.

[104] Emanuel Swedenborg, *The True Christian Religion; Containing the Universal Theology of the New Church, Foretold by the Lord in Daniel, VII. 13, 14, and in the Apocalypse, XXI. 1, 2.*, trans. of the Latin (New York: American Swedenborg Printing and Publishing Society, 1873), p. 761.

[105] Ibid., p. 766.

trines of that church from any angel, but from the Lord alone, while I was reading the Word.[106]

He believed that he was the human recipient of the "Divine Truth" that came into the world.[107] Swedenborg taught that there was not a trinity of persons in the Godhead. Instead, he said, there was a trinity of essentials. They were the Father as the Divine Love, the Son as the Divine Truth, and the Holy Spirit as the Divine Proceeding, which was operating in the preservation and regeneration of man. Swedenborg claimed that he restored the original teachings of Christianity and set them up on a new and advanced rational basis.[108] According to Swedenborg, "everyone receives truth, in such proportion as he is in good."[109]

The Authority of Reason

Thus, based on Swedenborg's teachings, Divine Truth was restored to the world to be interpreted on the basis of man's rational thinking, or reason. Under such an influence, Kant was able to confer a divine status to reason. A belief in a transfer of Divine Truth from the authority of God to the reason of man could then be expressed in freedom of human thought and action. The Jesuits agreed and by emphasizing this freedom helped fuel the Enlightenment. They promoted human reason and ethical freedom, rather than yielding to the authority of God.[110]

---

[106] Ibid.

[107] Charles W. Ferguson, *The New Books of Revelations: The Inside Store of America's Astounding Religious Cults* (Garden City, New York: Doubleday, Doran & Company Inc., 1928; printed for Chicago: The Private Editions Company, 1930), p. 355.

[108] Ferguson, *The New Books of Revelations*, p. 361.

[109] Emanuel Swedenborg, *On the New Jerusalem and Its Heavenly Doctrine, As Revealed from Heaven, to Which are Prefixed Some Observations Concerning the New Heaven & the New Earth*, trans. from Latin, 5th ed. (London: Society for Printing and Publishing the Writings of the Hon. Emanuel Swedenborg, 1812; Originally published in 1758), p. 12.

[110] Hajo Holborn, *A History of Modern Germany, 1648-1840* (New York: Alfred A. Knopf, 1964), pp. 126-127.

Reason became the unifying and central point of eighteenth century philosophy. As one writer put it, that century was "...imbued with a belief in the unity and immutability of reason."[111] Reason was seen as the one thing of permanence, from which all other things could be defined. Once this belief was established, then the definition of God became relative to the mind and could, therefore, be defined by one's own reason. Reason could then be used as the basis for defining the universe. Therefore, all authority would be subject to reason, which could grant it to whomever it willed. Thus, rule by the authority of God could then be replaced by rule by the authority of the reason of the people.

By accepting this authority of reason, the Scripture became without any authority, except for that which was given to it by reason. Therefore, the tendency of those who served reason was to deny the inspiration of the Scriptures. For example, a nineteenth century Oxford scholar on Hinduism and natural religion, Max Muller, described his skepticism of the New Testament this way:

> We are never told in the Gospels that they were written by the Founder of the Christian religion Himself. They only profess to give us what the four Apostles had to tell of the life and doctrine of Christ...[112]

Once Swedenborg taught that Divine Truth was given to his reason and after Kant transmitted this new thinking throughout Germany, other German theologians went even further. Friedrich Ernst Daniel Schleiermacher (1768-1834), a leader in German textual criticism, explained that: "Everything human is holy, for everything is divine."[113] Therefore, if the reason of man were holy, he could actually use it to

---

[111] Ernst Cassier, *The Philosophy of the Enlightenment*, Fritz C. A. Koelln and James P. Pettegrove, Translators (Princeton, New Jersey: Princeton University Press, 1979), p. 6.

[112] F. Max Muller, *Natural Religion: The Gifford Lectures Delivered before the University of Glasgow in 1888* (London: Longmans, Green, and Co., 1889), p. 561.

[113] Friedrich Schleiermacher, *On Religion: Speeches to Its Cultured Despisers*, Introduction, Translation, and Notes by Richard Crouter (Cambridge: Cambridge University Press, 1988), p. 188.

41

define that which is holy. Once one believes that everything is divine, it then follows that everything should be worshipped. Schleiermacher said the universe should be "intuited" and worshipped with innumerable possible forms of religion:

> Let the universe be intuited and worshipped in all ways. Innumerable forms of religion are possible, and if it is necessary that each become real at some time, then it would at least be desirable that one could have an intimation of many at all times...A new creation always arises out of nothing, and religion is virtually nothing in all members of the present age when their intellectual life opens up for them in power and fullness.... In each, the holy remains secret and hidden from the profane. Let them gnaw at the shell as they may, but do not prevent us from worshipping the God that is within you.[114]

Once reason was established as the sovereign authority, it became the standard for all things and the basis for criticism was established.[115] No longer did mankind have to be subjected to the authority of Scripture. Where Scripture and reason were not in agreement, it was Scripture that had to yield to reason. Where God, the church, the pope, or the king did not agree with reason, they, too, had to be redefined.

Illuminated Reason: The Secret Knowledge

As reason replaced faith as the guide to all things, it became evident that not everyone possessed the same capacities for reasoning. As such, it was believed that some had a more "enlightened" reason than others. Such thinking was consistent with the belief that there is a body of secret knowledge (gnosis) that, when it is acquired, leads one to become a god, as was believed by the Gnostics. Understanding this reality, much of the Gnostic teaching had a deliberate riddle-like dimension so that only those "in the know" could comprehend it.[116]

---

[114] Ibid., pp. 222-223.

[115] Cassier, *The Philosophy of the Enlightenment*, p. 141.

[116] Walker et al., *A History of the Christian Church*, p. 63.

Many of those who believed they were capable of understanding the secret knowledge also accepted the concept of "natural religion, " believing that they possessed inborn knowledge and rational thought. As reliance upon enlightened reason increased, the new abilities were applied to nature and to religion. The "Deists" spoke of a "universal" religion that could be comprehended by enlightened reason. Believing that God is the "Great Architect" of the universe, Deists believed that He created the world and put reason into man. Through this reason, they believed, God gave man the moral law by which He governs the universe with laws that are in harmony with reason.[117, 118] Deists believed that all phenomena could be explained by the interaction between man and his environment, excluding a directing role by God. The leading tenets of Deists could be regarded as acknowledging the existence of a reasonable, all-wise, all-powerful, all-good God who created the world, set it going, and then left it alone to work out its own destiny.[119]

Members of the Freemasons were among those who adopted Deist views.[120] Andrew Michael Ramsay (1686-1743), the founder of French Freemasonry, was among those who edited and published eighteenth-century writings on Deism. Although he was raised as a Protestant, Ramsay converted to Catholicism, reportedly because of his "universal religious aspirations."[121] While there has been a significant public rivalry between the Freemasons and the Jesuits, some Masonic historians were convinced that Jesuits had infiltrated their organizations, tampered with their rituals, and introduced higher degrees. Whether it was with or without the influence of the Jesuits, the Freemasons entered into a relationship with the Enlightenment through members such as Francois Marie Arouet de Voltaire (1694-1778) and by the

---

[117] Kerry S. Walters, *Rational Infidels: The American Deists* (Durango, Colorado: Longwood Academic, 1992), pp. ix-x.

[118] Latourette, *A History of Christianity*, vol. 2, p. 984.

[119] Patterson, *A History of the Church of England*, p. 388-389.

[120] Latourette, *A History of Christianity*, vol. 2, p. 1003.

[121] C. J. Betts, *Early Deism in France: From the So-Called "Deistes" of Lyon (1564) to Voltaire's "Lettres Philosophiques" (1734)* (The Hague, Boston, and Lancaster: Martinus Nijhoff Publishers, 1984), pp. 235-236.

writings of Jean Jacques Rousseau (1712-1778), and Thomas Paine (1737-1809).[122, 123, 124, 125]

Among the "enlightened" thinkers in Germany, an association known as the "Order of the Illuminati" (which means "Enlightened Ones") was formed on May 1, 1776. The Order was related to the Freemasons and was formed by Adam Weishaupt, a professor at Ingolstadt University who had been a member of the then banned Jesuits. He designed the Order to employ some of the techniques that had been used by the Jesuits since their formation. These techniques included the requirement of unconditional obedience, far-reaching mutual surveillance, and confession of inferior members to superior members.[126,127]

"Enlightened" reason sought to put all things under its authority by removing the concept of "God-ordained rule" and replacing it with its own rule. Encouraged by philosophers and practitioners of reason, the masses were placed in direct opposition to the established order. Soon after, the belief in reason ignited the spark that lead to the American Revolution. On July 4, 1776, the people overthrew the authority of the king with the United States Declaration of Independence.

Encouraged by the success of the American Revolution, English-born Thomas Paine used writings such as *Common Sense*, *The Rights of Man*, and *The Age of Reason* to challenge the prevailing Christian belief in God. As Paine wrote of the challenge of the masses to the privileges and titles of the pre-Revolutionary era, he applied "god" status to reason when he wrote:

> The patriots of France have discovered in good time that rank and dignity in society must take a new ground. The old one has fallen through. It must now take the substantial ground of character, instead of the chimerical ground of titles; and they

[122] Fulop-Miller, *The Power and Secret of the Jesuits*, pp. 436-437.

[123] Walker et al., *A History of the Christian Church,* p. 584.

[124] Ibid., p. 627-628.

[125] Betts, *Early Deism in France*, pp. 95-96.

[126] Pat Robertson, *The New World Order* (Dallas, London, Vancouver, and Melbourne: Word Publishing, 1991), p. 67.

[127] Walker et al., *A History of the Christian Church,* p. 435.

have brought their titles to the altar, and made of them a burnt-offering to Reason.[128]

Within six years after he formed the Order of the Illuminati, Adam Weishaupt infiltrated the Continental Order of Freemasons in 1782 and created the "Illuminated Freemasonry." Frederick the Great of Prussia became the sovereign grand commander and Philippe of France, Duc 'Orleans, became the grand master of the grand orient of the Continental Order of Freemasons.[129] Soon, the spark of reason ignited the masses in France.[130] On July 14, 1789, the people overthrew the final symbols of God-ordained authority: the king and the church! With a cry for redistributing power and wealth, the new order was established. The new rule was directed by human reason and not by the authority of God.

In her 1907 play, *The Goddess of Reason*, Mary Johnston described the effects of the Revolution in a scene set in 1794 France:

> ...Old things are past. To-day we welcome new.
> Gone are the priests, gone is the crucifix;
> Chalice and paten whelmed beneath the Loire!
> Kings, princes, nobles, priests, all crumbled down!
> Death on a pale horse hath ridden o'er them,
> The ravens and the sea mews pick their bones.
> Theirs are yesterdays, the ci-devants! —
> Liberty, Equality, Fraternity!
> We worship Thee, Triune and Indivisible! —
> O Mother Nature, pure, beneficent,
> Redeemed from darkness of the centuries,
> Smile on thy children, come to worship thee!
> And thou, supernal Reason, Crown of Man ...
> We worship thee![131]

---

[128] Thomas Paine, *Rights of Man* (Lunenburg, Vermont: The George Macy Companies, Inc., 1961), p. 54.

[129] Robertson, *The New World Order*, pp. 67-68.

[130] William Gibson, *Church, State, and Society, 1760-1850 (New York: St. Martin's Press, 1994), p. 51.*

[131] Mary Johnston, *The Goddess of Reason* (London: Archibold Constable & Co., 1907), p. 129.

While Men Slept...

Chapter 3. Foundations of Universal Christianity

**That your faith should not stand in the wisdom of men,
but in the power of God.**

—1 Corinthians 2:5

Greek Philosophy: Platonism

Knowledge vs. Belief

Greek philosophy provided a framework on which to construct the Unitarian and Universalist theology that provided the basis for the new universal Christianity. Plato (427-347 B.C.) laid the foundations of Greek philosophy on which others have been building for nearly twenty-four hundred years.[1] In *The Republic*, for example, Plato described the concept of enlightenment to truth. Reason, he argued, could be relied upon to bring one to an enlightened understanding of reality. Using very simple but logical discussions in a dialogue technique, Plato clearly distinguished between those who have opinions and those who have knowledge.[2]

Presenting a theory that knowledge and belief are two different and opposite states of mind, Plato argued that knowledge could not be defined by belief. Because he saw the relationship between man and nature as one in a constant flux, he believed that everything is relative and nothing is permanent. Knowledge, he reasoned, is relative to changing facts. Everything is relative unless one's mind is enlightened to the degree that it ascends from specific objects or ideas that are grasped by the senses to universal truths that do not change. Thus, only through enlightenment can one grasp the universal truth.

---

[1] John M. Cooper, *Introduction*, In *Plato: Complete Works*, John M. Cooper and D. S. Hutchinson, eds. (Indianapolis, Indiana: Hackett Publishing Company, 1997), pp. vii-viii.

[2] Plato, *The Republic*, In *Plato: Complete Works*, John M. Cooper and D. S. Hutchinson, eds. (Indianapolis, Indiana: Hackett Publishing Company, 1997), p. 1132.

While Men Slept...

Allegory of the Cave

Plato illustrated, for example, the difference between knowing something to be true and only believing something to be true by using an allegory of a cave with people trapped in it. He reasoned that if people in a cave were restrained so that they could not see from side to side, then their view of reality would be limited. If they were able to only see shadows of people walking about, rather than the people themselves, they might actually believe that the shadows were reality. Thus, they would have limited knowledge because they could only see the shadows and not the people themselves.

Now suppose, as Plato explained, that one of those trapped in the cave was able to get loose from his bonds. Once he was loose, suppose he were able to go out and discover that the shadows were not real people at all. Suppose he found, instead, that the shadows were only formed in places where light was unable to pass through the bodies of real people who were walking about in the light. Plato explained that the one who was now able to see the people in the light knew something that those who were still trapped in the cave did not yet know. To the one who could see the people in the light, the shadows that he once believed to be reality were not real at all. Instead, they were only the shadows of real people. Thus, this one who saw the people illuminated by the light would have reached a level of enlightenment. Being enlightened, he was able to see the truth that those who were still trapped in the cave could not comprehend.[3]

Control by the Enlightened

The allegory of the cave simply demonstrates the concept that those who possess knowledge, which others do not yet have, are enlightened to the truth. Those who do not yet know the truth still see only shadows which they think are real. While believing certain things to be true, they do not yet comprehend reality. Plato believed that there are some that will:

---

[3] Ibid., pp. 1132-1135.

...be compelled to lift up the radiant light of their souls to what itself provides light for everything. And once they've seen the good itself, they must each in turn put the city, its citizens, and themselves in order, using it as their model.[4]

Plato's position was that the City (or the State) should be controlled by those who could "lift up the radiant light of their souls," those who were enlightened, those who see the truth, and not by those who are still trapped in the cave. In other words, those who "know" or possess "gnosis" should, for the benefit of the entire society, rule over those who do not yet know. It was his view that education was a process of putting sight into blind eyes.[5] Education was seen as an "enlightening" process of bringing light to the darkness. Plato taught that reason could be used to see the very truth and essence of things.[6] Believing that reason is divine, he wrote that the virtue of reason :

...seems to belong above all to something more divine, which never loses its power but is either useful and beneficial or useless and harmful, depending on the way it is turned.[7]

Neo-Platonism: The Blended Christianity of Alexandria

Alexandria, Egypt

Early Christians in Alexandria, Egypt sought to fuse the teachings of Plato into Christianity in a philosophy known as "Neo-Platonism." The Neo-Platonic teachers took Plato's basic philosophy on the essence of reason even further than he did. They taught that thought and being, each in their simple essence of truth, are one and the same.[8] Therefore, they taught that one could attain union with God by contemplation.[9]

---

[4] Ibid., p. 1154.

[5] Ibid., p. 1136.

[6] James H. Rigg, *Modern Anglican Theology with a Prefix of the Memoir of Canon Kingsley,* 3rd ed. rev. (London: Wesleyan Conference Office, 1880), p. 128.

[7] Plato, *The Republic*, p. 1136.

[8] Rigg, *Modern Anglican Theology,* p. 128.

[9] Latourette, *A History of Christianity*, vol. 1, pp. 26-27.

While Men Slept...

Philo (c.20 B.C.-A.D. 50), who was born into a leading Jewish family in Alexandria, sought to reconcile Greek philosophy, especially Platonism, with Judaism.[10] While he sought to achieve this reconciliation, he became known as the father of Neo-Platonism, especially among Christians.[11] As a mystic himself, Philo believed that the object of the soul's striving was an immediate vision of God.[12] Max Muller, the nineteenth century authority in Indian culture of whom we shall learn more later, explained that this vision of God was believed to be "...the knowledge of the divine element in the soul, and of the consubstantiality of the divine and human natures."[13]

Plotinus (A.D. 205-270) brought the Neo-Platonic philosophy of Philo into the third century. Reason, he stressed, is not a faculty of the individual. Instead, it is a ray or a flash of the universal reason, which is diffused throughout the universe.[14, 15] The Neo-Platonic philosophy was pantheistic, with the essence of God consisting of "The One, Reason or Intelligence, and the Soul of the World."[16] As a Neo-Platonist, Plotinus taught of a Primal Being to which the soul yearns for a union. Having paid close attention to Eastern religion and superstition in search for divine wisdom, Plotinus considered the Neo-Platonic doctrines to be mysteries, which should not be brought before the uninitiated.[17]

Plotinus further taught that "the One" in a transcendent Unity is the First Principle of all reality and the prolific source of all being. From

---

[10] Kenneth Scott Latourette, *A History of the Expansion of Christianity, vol. 1, The First Five Centuries* (Grand Rapids, Michigan: Zondervan Publishing House, 1970), p. 42.

[11] Rigg, *Modern Anglican Theology*, p. 131.

[12] Latourette, *A History of the Expansion of Christianity*, vol. 1, p. 42.

[13] F. Max Muller, *Theosophy or Psychological Religion; The Gifford Lectures Delivered before the University of Glasgow in 1892* (London, New York, and Bombay: Longmans, Green, and Co., 1903; First edition published in 1893), p. 424.

[14] Latourette, *A History of the Expansion of Christianity*, vol. 1, p. 20.

[15] Rigg, *Modern Anglican Theology*, p. 130.

[16] Ibid., p. 132.

[17] Muller, *Theosophy or Psychological Religion*, pp. 427-428.

this source, he taught, everything moves down graded levels of being, of awareness, and of value. The highest level is the Intellect in which being and awareness of being are as close as possible to one thing. On the next level is the Soul, where time appears and awareness takes the form of serial apprehension and reasoning. On the final level, Nature, being and awareness become external to each other and the body appears. Plotinus taught that each of these levels shows the reality of its Source and each strives to Unity. Therefore, the Neo-Platonists believed that the human person is called to follow a self-disciplined path toward unity of being and awareness of "the One."[18]

Alexandria: The Seat of Unitarianism

For the Greeks, Christianity was simply Neo-Platonism. As the Neo-Platonic Christianity matured in Alexandria, the city became the seat of intellectual Christianity. As such, it became the natural location for founding a school for teaching Christianity. As one of the early heads of the school at the close of the second century, Clement of Alexandria had a tremendous influence of the direction of Christian thought. Consistent with Neo-Platonism, Clement looked toward the divinity of man. He was able to boldly reconcile human divinity with Christianity as he wrote:

> It is time, then, for us to say that the pious Christian alone is rich and wise, and of noble birth, and thus call and believe him to be God's image, and also His likeness, having become righteous and holy and wise by Jesus Christ, and so far already be like God.[19]

As the school developed, it became the major center of Greek scholarship and was where the foundations of Unitarian beliefs were forged.

---

[18] Walker et al., *A History of the Christian Church,* pp. 120-121.

[19] Clement of Alexandria, "Exhortation to the Heathen," In *The Ante-Nicene Fathers: Translations of The Writings of the Fathers down to A.D. 325*, vol. 2, *Fathers of the Second Century*, Alexander Roberts and James Donaldson, eds. (Grand Rapids: Wm. B. Eeerdmans Publishing Company, Reprinted 1979), p. 206.

While Men Slept...

The third century theologian Origen (c.186-254 A.D) was a pillar of Unitarianism at the Alexandrian School. Born in Alexandria, Origen was a student of Greek philosophers, including Plato, and was also a well-known Bible scholar and prolific writer.[20] Origen, along with many of his admirers and followers, apparently believed that it would be an honor for Christianity if it were to be brought into harmony with Platonism, as modified into Neo-Platonism.[21]

Those who blended their Christian beliefs with the great emphasis on knowledge taught by the Greek philosophers were, as has been discussed, called Gnostics. Gnosticism blended Christianity with ideas from eastern and western heathenism, such as Greek philosophy and Oriental mysticism.[22] Origen believed that certain people are on a higher intellectual plane than others and that they can be raised to the level of God through the contemplation of God. Thus, through the possession of a secret "gnosis," or knowledge, one can be freed from the physical world and be released into the spiritual world.[23]

Believing that they were capable of knowing and understanding all things, Gnostics tended to reject the divinity of Jesus Christ and His role as the redeemer of mankind. Instead, as explained by Philip Schaff, they believed that "redemption" is the "...liberation of the light-spirit from the chains of dark Matter." This release, they believed, is "...affected by *Christ*, the most perfect aeon, who is the mediator of return from the sensible phenomenal world to the supersensuous ideal world...."[24] The divinity of Jesus Christ did not fit within the set of logical principles they were applied to all other realms of life. Therefore, Gnostics denied the Triune nature of God by making Jesus a created being, rather than the Creator of all things.

---

[20] W. H. Lord, *The Modern English Pulpit*, In *The Presbyterian Quarterly and Princeton Review*, New Series, No. 8, October, 1873, p. 576.

[21] Review of *The Works of Plato*, In *The Princeton Review*, vol. 36, no. 2, April, 1864, pp. 244-245.

[22] Schaff, *History of the Christian Church*, vol. 2, p. 448.

[23] Latourette, *A History of Christianity,* vol. 1, p. 26.

[24] Ibid., p. 455.

The Gnostics believed that only "enlightened" ones, who possess the secret knowledge, will be able to rise to the level of God. This concept was also the foundation for the "Age of Enlightenment."[25] Many of what are viewed as significant finds of biblical history, including the finding in 1945 of thirteen codices at Nag Hammadi in Egypt near a fourth century monastery, contained largely Gnostic works.[26] To understand the "gnosis," or knowledge believed by the Gnostics, it is prudent to study Greek philosophy, especially the writings of Plato who frequently used allegories to illustrate key concepts. By such study, early Gnostics such as Origen came to believe that the Bible should be interpreted allegorically and not literally.[27]

Both Origen and his predecessor at the Alexandrian School, Clement of Alexandria, attempted to synthesize Christianity and Greek philosophy.[28] While Origen's teachings were significant and far-reaching, many of them became condemned as heresy and have been the source of great controversy among Christians throughout the centuries. Among the many heresies that Origen taught in the Alexandrian School was that Jesus Christ was a created being and was not eternal. As the nineteenth century theologian, Philip Schaff, explained:

> ...he [Origen] taught with equal clearness a separateness of essence between the Father and the Son and the subordination of the Son, as a second or secondary God beneath the Father, and thus furnished a starting point for the Arian heresy. The eternal generation of the Son from the will of the

---

[25] J. W. Hanson, *Universalism: The Prevailing Doctrine Of The Christian Church During Its First Five Hundred Years* (Boston and Chicago: Universalist Publishing House, 1899), pp. 93-94.

[26] R. M. Grant, *Gnosticism and Early Christianity*, 2nd ed. (New York & London: Columbia University Press, 1966), p. 5.

[27] Ronald Heine, *Reading the Bible with Origen*, In *The Bible in Greek Christian Antiquity*, Paul M. Blowers, ed. and trans., Based on *Bible De Tous Les Temps*, vol. 1, *Le monde grec ancien et la Bible*, C. Mondesert, ed. (Notre Dame, Indiana: University of Notre Dame Press, 1997), p. 135.

[28] Walter Nigg, *The Heretics*, Richard and Clara Winston, trans. and eds. (New York: Alfred A, Knopf, Inc., 1962), p. 99.

Father was, with Origen, the communication of a divine but secondary substance, and this idea, in the hands of the less devout and profound Arius, who with his more rigid logic could admit no intermediate being between God and the creature, deteriorated to the notion of the primal creature.[29]

Eusebius of Caesarea (A.D. 260-340), who will be discussed later, wrote a history of the early church in which, among other things, he described the life and teachings of Origen. Even though Eusebius greatly admired the life and work of Origen, he wrote:

...Origen, a Greek educated in Greek learning, drove headlong towards barbarian recklessness; and making straight for this he hawked himself and his literary skill about; and while his manner of life was Christian and contrary to the law, in his opinions about material things and the Deity he played the Greek, and introduced Greek ideas into foreign fables. For he was always consorting with Plato...[and other Greeks]...from whom he learnt the figurative interpretation, as employed in the Greek mysteries, and applied it to the Jewish writings.[30]

Augustine (A.D. 354-430) also expressed his astonishment at some of Origen's heretical views. One of these was that the world was created in order that sinful souls might be accommodated with bodies, in which they would be shut up as in a prison. Therefore, the more sinful soul would have a more earthly body in which to be bound.[31] If this argument were to be followed further, it might be concluded that

---

[29] Philip Schaff, *History of the Christian Church,* vol. 3, *Nicene and Post-Nicene Christianity from Constantine the Great to Gregory the Great, A.D. 311-600,* 5th ed., rev. (Grand Rapids: Wm. B. Eerdmans Publishing Company, 1981; Charles Scribner's Sons, 1910), pp. 619-620.

[30] Eusebius, *The Ecclesiastical History,* vol. 2, ed. published with H. J. Lawlor, J. E. L. Oulton, trans. (London: William Heinemann Ltd., 1932), p. 59.

[31] *St. Augustin's City of God,* Marcus Dods, trans., 1871, In *A Select Library of the Nicene and Post-Nicene Fathers of the Christian Church,* Vol. 2, *St. Augustin's City of God and Christian Doctrine,* Philip Schaff, ed. (Grand Rapids, Michigan: Wm. B. Eerdmans Publishing Co., 1979; reprint of the 1886 ed.), p. 218.

Jesus came in a body because He was less good than was God the Father or God the Holy Ghost.

Philip Schaff described the Neo-Platonic philosophy, which was taught at the school of Alexandria, as the enemy of Christianity. As he explained, it blended Christianity with paganism and elements of various other religions:

> The last enemy [of Christianity] was the Neo-Platonic philosophy, as taught particularly in the schools of Alexandria and Athens even down to the fifth century. This philosophy, however, as we have before remarked, was no longer the product of pure, fresh heathenism, but an artificial syncretism of elements heathen and Christian, Oriental and Hellenic, speculative and theurgic, evincing only the growing weakness of the old religion and the irresistible power of the new.[32]

Merging Christians into the Roman Empire

Unity of Religion

As Paul and others spread the Gospel of Jesus Christ throughout the Greek world, those whom they encountered had been accustomed to worshipping Greek gods. As they were converted to Christianity, many still could not totally reject the Greek teachings with which they had been raised. Receiving mixed messages, the people found themselves confused about what to believe. An example of this occurred as Paul was preaching to the worshippers of the goddess Diana of Ephesus. After the silversmiths incited a riot by crying, "Great is Diana," among the people, the whole city was "…filled with confusion…." (Acts 19:29) As the crowd entered the theater:

> Some therefore cried one thing, and some another: for the assembly was confused: and the more part knew not wherefore they were come together.
>
> —Acts 19:32

---

[32] Schaff, *History of the Christian Church,* vol. 3, p. 73.

While Men Slept...

As we have learned, many Christians suffered severe persecution by the Roman government prior to Constantine's rise to power. As he took control of the Roman Empire, the persecutions of A.D. 249 to 251 under the rule of Decius, of A.D. 303 to 305 under the rule of Diocletian, and of A.D. 305 to 311 under the rule of Galerius in the East were a recent memory.[33] Suddenly, however, the Christians gained favor with the Roman Emperor. Although he had been a practicing pagan, Constantine reportedly converted to Christianity. The pagans, which had been the favored group in the Roman Empire, were losing some of their prestige. However, they had the prospect of retaining many of their practices if they could compromise with the Christians. Now the Christians had the opportunity to legalize their worship under the name of "Christianity," if they would compromise with the pagans.

Using his power and authority, Constantine was determined to bring unity among pagan and Christian religions and the Roman government. He brought Christians and Romans into one religion, adopting a symbol of the Greek letters X-P (Chi-Rho), which are frequently overlaid upon each other. These letters are thought to be the designation of the first two letters in the word "Christ."[34] The letters also represent the first letter of each of the words, Χριστιανος Ρωμαιος, or "Christian Romans." In bringing Christians and Romans together, Constantine blended some aspects of each religion into the new State religion. For example, in A.D. 314, he put the Christian cross on coins, which also retained the figures of *Sol Invictus* (the sun god) and *Mars Conservator* (the god of war, Mars). As noted previously, Constantine assumed the title of "pontifex maximus," as the chief priest of the pagan state cult.[35] The title means "supreme bridge builder." Indeed, Constantine was seeking to build the bridge between pagans and Christians.

One compromise concerned the day of worship. Constantine legislated that the Day of the Sun (Sunday), also known as the Christian

---

[33] F. G. Kenyon, *The Text of the Greek Bible* (London: Gerald & Co., Ltd., 1975), p. 9.

[34] Latourette, *A History of Christianity,* vol. 1, p. 92.

[35] Ibid., pp. 92-93.

"first day," would be a weekly holiday.[36] Proclaiming "sun's day," which was the name of a pagan Roman holiday, to be the day of worship and the day of rest for Christians, Constantine sought to distinguish it from the Jewish "Sabbath," which was on the last day of the week. Thus, Constantine adopted the inclusive views of the Neo-Platonists as he attempted to create unity through the synthesis of a universal Christianity.

"Christ" by Whatever Name

Eusebius of Caesarea was careful to explain that the word "Christ" was not unique to Jesus. He clarified that the term "Christian" could be applied to anyone who had a "testimony of righteousness." Indeed, he emphasized that there were many anointed men, who were therefore called "Christs," who had lived since ancient times. He also said:

> Whence it is evident that the religion delivered to us in the doctrine of Christ is not new nor a strange doctrine; but if truth must be spoken, it is the first and only true religion.[37]

Clearly, the Christianity that Eusebius of Caesarea spoke of was not the same as that of which the Apostle Paul preached. According to Paul, the doctrine that he preached was unique. The doctrine of the gospel of Jesus Christ that Paul preached had been kept secret since that world began and only became clear after Jesus Christ was crucified. Paul wrote:

> Now to him that is of power to stablish you according to my gospel, and the preaching of Jesus Christ, according to the revelation of the mystery, which was kept secret since the world began, But now is made manifest, and by the scriptures of the prophets, according to the commandment of the everlasting God, made known to all nations for the obedience of faith:
>
> —Romans 16:25-26

---

[36] Walker et al., *A History of the Christian Church,* p. 129.

[37] Valesius, *Annotations on the Life and Writings of Eusebius Pamphilus*, pp. 26-28.

What was the "mystery" that Paul wrote about? It was that we have redemption through the blood of Jesus Christ:

> In whom we have redemption through his blood, the forgiveness of sins, according to the riches of his grace; Wherein he hath abounded toward us in all wisdom and prudence; Having made known unto us the mystery of his will, according to his good pleasure which he hath purposed in himself:
>
> —Ephesians 1:7-9

Therefore, Paul determined not to dispute with the wisdom of man but to preach the simple gospel of Jesus Christ and Him crucified:

> And I, brethren, when I came to you, came not with excellency of speech or of wisdom, declaring unto you the testimony of God. For I determined not to know any thing among you, save Jesus Christ, and him crucified. And I was with you in weakness, and in fear, and in much trembling. And my speech and my preaching *was* not with enticing words of man's wisdom, but in demonstration of the Spirit and of power: That your faith should not stand in the wisdom of men, but in the power of God.
>
> —1 Corinthians 2:1-5

Jesus: Creator or Creature? The Great Debate

But Whom Say Ye That I Am?

Despite Paul's clear teaching of the revelation of the mystery of the unique sacrifice of Jesus Christ for sin, Jesus remains the subject of great controversy. Was He really the promised Messiah that the Jews had been awaiting? Was He the Christ? Was He the Son of God? Was He God who came in the flesh to save the world? His very name testified of His purpose. Jesus is the English name for יהושע (YAHushua), meaning YAHWEH is salvation.

Some of Jesus' contemporaries, such as Peter, declare that He was the Christ, the Son of the living God, as recorded in Matthew 16:16 and in John 6:68-69. Others, such as John, confess that, not only was

He the Logos (Λογος), or the Word, but that He was in the beginning and was, Himself, God. As John wrote:

> In the beginning was the Word, and the Word was with God, and the Word was God.
>
> —John 1:1

In other words, John explains, the Word was not created. Instead, He already was in the beginning. Furthermore, John goes on, it was by Him that all things were made. Speaking of the Word, John explains:

> All things were made by him; and without him was not any thing made that was made.
>
> —John 1:3

These are strong statements from Peter and John who were among Jesus' closest associates on earth, His disciples. They declare that He was indeed the Son of God and was also, himself, God. John further clarifies the three Person nature of God, in the now very controversial Scripture, as he describes that there are three heavenly witnesses who are One:

> For there are three that bear record in heaven, the Father, the Word, and the Holy Ghost: and these three are one.
>
> —1 John 5:7

This concept that God is one but that He is expressed as three co-equal Persons was, and still is, very difficult for many people to understand. The concept is spiritual and not physical. Therefore, it was especially difficult to comprehend for those who were accustomed to the worship of tangible physical idols. Those who were accustomed to idol worship saw their gods as distinct objects, rather than as spiritual beings.

The Arians: the Fourth Century "Unitarians"

During the fourth century, the debate about the nature of Jesus intensified. Those who rejected His divinity accepted many of Origen's views. This great debate became very public in the church of Alexandria and spread rapidly. By one account, the circumstances that brought the debate to the public arena were as follows:

> It happened that Alexander, bishop of Alexandria, in Egypt, disputing one day, in the presence of his presbyters and other clergy, on the subject of the three divine persons, and being desirous of making a display of his knowledge, remarked, that in the Trinity there was a unity. Arius, one of his presbyters, who was well versed in the art of reasoning and in metaphysical distinctions...inclined to an error directly opposed to it, and replied, with great asperity, that if the Father begat the Son, the latter must have had a beginning; from which, he continued, it clearly followed that there was a time when he was not, and that his substance was made from nothing.[38]

Thus, putting his trust in reason, Arius (A.D. c.250-c.336) entered into the debate on the basis of logic. By using the logic that the Son came from that which was not, Arius placed the Son into the same category as all other beings—that of being created. Thus Arianism could be described as a set of the following ideas:

> God was not always the Father. God was once alone and was not yet Father. He became Father subsequently. The Son was not always. As everything came to be from what is not, as they are things created and things made, so God's Logos himself came to be from what is not. He was not. He also had as a beginning the fact of being created.[39]

The implications of this argument are enormous. If the position of Arius were taken to be true, then the Son would be a different kind of

---

[38] *Council of Nice*, In Valesius, *Annotations on the Life and Writings of Eusebius Pamphilus*, Translated by S. E. Parker, In *The Ecclesiastical History of Eusebius Pamphilus, Bishop of Caesarea, In Palestine*, Translated from the Original with an Introduction by Christian Frederick Cruse and an Historical View of the Council of Nice by Isaac Boyle (Grand Rapids, Michigan: Baker Book House, 1990), pp. 6-7.

[39] Colm Luibheid, *Eusebius of Caesarea and the Arian Crisis* (Dublin: Irish Academic Press, 1981), pp. 8-9.

God. Therefore, those who believed Jesus to also be God would have then conceded to the principle of pagan polytheism.[40] If, on the other hand, the Son were also God, who offered Himself as the perfect sacrifice for sin, then the need for further sacrifices would be eliminated.

Due to the controversy, Arius was exiled from Alexandria and went to Palestine where he found a sympathetic supporter for his views in Eusebius of Nicomedia (d. about 342). Arius' supporters argued that Alexander was advocating that there were two coequal gods- two "unbegottens."[41] Thus, they were accusing those who did not support their position as being polytheists.

Did God, as argued by Arius, create Jesus or was the Son begotten of the very essence of God? The key to this issue was the interpretation of the Greek word "γεννετος" (gennetos) as it applied to the Son. Although it is traditionally translated as "begotten:gennetos," in Greek philosophy it was a broader and more vague concept. The latter translation meant anything which in any way "came to be."[42] Arius had adopted the view of Origen, which was that Jesus was lower than God, who created Him. Thus the Logos was subordinate to God and was generated in the same manner that all other creatures were generated. When pressed on his views, Arius' position was that Jesus was a creature and was, therefore, not God who had come in the flesh. Arius' position was known as "Arian" and those who held that view were known as "Arians."

Athanasius (A.D. c.297-373), on the other hand, took an opposite position from that of Arius. He maintained that it was impossible to say that God was ever without the Logos. In other words, God the Father was never without God the Son. He argued that God could not be viewed as a monolithic and static abstraction, but that He is dynamic. The Logos is, therefore, not subject to time's limitations

---

[40] F. J. Foakes-Jackson, *Eusebius of Pamphili* (Cambridge: W. Heffer & Sons Ltd., 1933), p. 45.

[41] Walker et al., *A History of the Christian Church,* p. 132.

[42] Ibid., p. 132.

and is eternal with the Father. He rejected Origen's belief that the Logos is a "second god" to the very God. He maintained that the Son does not become God, but is God.[43]

This argument over whether Jesus was a created being severely divided the Christian Church. It threatened to destroy the harmony that Constantine was promoting as he was establishing the ecumenical "One World Religion," or "Universal Church," in which both pagans and Christians would agree and worship together.

The Council of Nicea: Settling the Confusion

Bringing the worshippers of Roman gods and the Christians together on the day of worship, however, was not enough. There were still disputes among Christians over key doctrinal issues that kept them out of unity with each other. The disputed matters concerned establishing the date of the Christian Passover, as it was called, and changing its date to distinguish it from the Jewish Passover. The Christian Passover controversy became known as the "Quartodeciman" or the "Fourteenth-day" controversy. It was so named because of being celebrated on the same day as the Jewish Passover, which was the fourteenth day of the month of Nisan.[44] The other key dispute was over the deity of Jesus Christ. Was Jesus a created being or was He, indeed, God manifested in the flesh?

To resolve these differences, the Roman Emperor Constantine brought disputing Christians together in A.D. 325 for the First Council of Nicea in Asia Minor. According to one account of the Council of Nicea, Eusebius of Caesarea had the first seat on the right hand of Constantine and "in the name of the whole synod addressed the emperor Constantine, who sat on a golden chair between two rows of the opposite parties."[45] Christians were given the opportunity to unify

---

[43] Alvyn Pettersen, *Athanasius* (London: Geoffrey Chapman, 1995), pp. 164-174.

[44] Arthur Penrhyn Stanley, *Lectures on the History of the Eastern Church* (New York: Charles Scribner's Sons, 1900), pp. 145-146.

[45] Valesius, *Annotations on the Life and Writings of Eusebius Pamphilus*, p. xii.

their faith under the watchful eye of the Roman Emperor. As is done in most conflict resolution negotiations, compromise was sought. That meant that no one really got what he wanted but most got enough of what they wanted that they were, for whatever purpose, willing to agree.

The day for celebrating the Christian Passover was agreed upon. The Christians who believed in the deity of Jesus Christ were willing to make a compromise. They named the day of the Resurrection, "Easter," after the pagan goddess of spring and fertility, Ishtar or Eastre. They were, however, unwilling to compromise concerning their central belief about Jesus Christ. The debate centered on the question:

> Was Jesus really God manifest in the flesh, as believed by Athanasius and his supporters, or was He a creature created by God, as promoted by Arius and his followers?

Resolving this key question required great skill. With Constantine exerting pressure to have the controversy resolved, attempts were made to reach an acceptable and "face-saving" agreement. During the debate, the non-Scriptural terms, "homoousion" (ομοος) and "homoiousion" (ομοιος) were introduced. Introducing the term homoousion (from "homos," meaning the same, and "ousia," meaning essence) was supposed to clarify the discussion. Those theologians taking the "homoiousion" position believed that the three persons in the Trinity were similar, but not the same. The word "homoousion," on the other hand, was taken to mean that the three persons in the Trinity were of the "same substance."[46] The terms were confusing and had vague meanings to many of the participants in the discussion. The debate centered on the difference of one "I" or "iota." The supporters of Athanasius, who are frequently called Trinitarians, favored the term "homoousion." The Arians and those who took a middle position in the argument, who were called semi-Arians, preferred the term "homoiousion."

---

[46] Philip Schaff and Henry Wace, eds., *A Select Library of Nicene and Post-Nicene Fathers of the Christian Church: St. Athanasius: Selected Works and Letters, Prolegomena*, ch. 2, pt. 3, 2nd series, vol. 4 (Grand Rapids, Michigan: Wm. B. Eerdmans Publishing Company, 1971), pp. xxx-xxxiii.

While Men Slept...

Because Eusebius of Caesarea appeared to be in a very favorable position with Emperor Constantine, his position on this matter was critical to the course of the debate. Unfortunately, his position on this subject seemed to depend upon the particular theological or political setting in which he found himself at any given time. At first, he refused to support the "homoousion" position.[47] Instead, he took a semi-Arian, or middle, position on the argument. That position taught that Christ is not a creature, but co-eternal with the Father. However, it also taught that He was not of the same essence as the Father, but that He was of like essence. Therefore, He was subordinate to the Father.[48] Eusebius of Caesarea proposed his doctrine to the Council of Nicea, but it was rejected.

The followers of Athanasius were unwilling to bend to the desires of Eusebius of Caesarea and others who wanted to agree that Jesus was a created being. This time the compromise at the Council of Nicea would have to come from those who rejected the deity of Jesus Christ. Therefore, after very careful wording and descriptions of the wording, both Eusebius of Caesarea and Eusebius of Nicomedia, wanting to please Constantine, signed the creed. It was signed by all but two of the bishops at the Council. In the end, the official position of the Council of Nicea, adopted under pressure from Constantine, was that Jesus was of the same substance as God and, therefore, was part of the three-person nature of God. The creed was intended to exclude Arianism.[49] Because Constantine treated religious questions solely from a political point of view, he assured unity by banishing the bishops who would not sign the new profession of faith.[50]

Eusebius of Caesarea finally agreed with the position which he had previously rejected, that Jesus was "consubstantial" [homoousion]

---

[47] Ibid. p. xiii.

[48] Philip Schaff, *History of the Christian Church Chapter IX: Theological Controversies, and Development of the Ecumenical Orthodoxy* (Oak Harbor, WA: Logos Research Systems, Inc., 1997, according to the 1910 ed. of Charles Scribner's Sons; Dallas, TX: The Electronic Bible Society, 1998), http://www.ccel.org/s/schaff/history/3_ch09.htm#_edn1

[49] Walker et al., *A History of the Christian Church*, p. 135.

[50] Nigg, *The Heretics*, p. 127.

with God. Some were convinced, however, that his new position was not his own but that he was actually coerced into the agreement by the entire circumstances of the Council of Nicea. They believed that his fear of the emperor, rather than his own conviction, was a critical factor that caused him to accept the "consubstantial" position.[51]

Second Thoughts on the Trinity

The Arian Resurgence

To the casual observer it would appear that the Arian debate was settled at the Council of Nicea, as it was presented in the Nicene Creed. The Creed had clarified the view of Athanasius and other Trinitarians. Jesus was indeed part of the Triune God, namely God the Father, God the Son, and God the Holy Ghost. Constantine, the most powerful man in the world, and Eusebius of Caesarea, a very learned man and confidant of Constantine, had even finally agreed on the deity of Jesus Christ. Arius had been cast out of fellowship and Athanasius was put in communion. With the acceptance of the Nicene Creed, all appeared to be in agreement.

However, shortly after the Council of Nicea, there was a definitive move back toward the Arianism that had just recently been rejected. Constantine, who was under significant theological influence from Eusebius of Caesarea, was having second thoughts about Arianism. It was shortly after the Council of Nicea that Eusebius of Nicomedia, a strong supporter of Arius, was established as bishop of Nicomedia where he served from A.D. 329 to 339. He was then established as the bishop of Constantinople in A.D. 339.[52] Eusebius of Nicomedia found himself, and the cause of Arianism, being significantly enhanced by the increasing favor he found with Constantine.

Much of the widely read history concerning the life of Constantine, the role of Eusebius of Caesarea during and following the Council of Nicea, and the post-Nicean Arianism was written by Eusebius of

---

[51] Valesius, *Annotations on the Life and Writings of Eusebius Pamphilus*, p. xii.

[52] B. J. Kidd, *A History of the Church to A.D. 461*, vol. 2, A.D. 313-408 (Oxford: The Clarendon Press, 1922), p. 53.

While Men Slept...

Caesarea himself. However, Socrates Scholasticus, another church historian, gives a more objective history of the circumstances surrounding the post-Nicean Arian controversy. According to Socrates, his intent was to state the particulars of the history that Eusebius of Caesarea had left out. In introducing his work on church history, he criticized Eusebius of Caesarea for his inaccurate statement of the facts. Socrates accused Eusebius of:

> ...being more intent on the rhetorical finish of his composition and the praises of the emperor, than on an accurate statement of facts.[53]

After the Council of Nicea and during the last years of his rule, Constantine was under the domination of the Arians.[54] Although many believe that the Creed of the church was settled at Nicea, there remained significant factions and divisions within the church. Arius was still alive and his friend Eusebius of Nicomedia rapidly regained influence over Emperor Constantine. Because of this influence, Constantine reconsidered his position regarding the exile of Arius and in A.D. 335 he was readmitted into communion.[55] Athanasius, however, held to his position concerning the deity of Jesus Christ, without compromise, by refusing to have communion with those who were "fighting against Christ." Soon, however, a conspiracy rose up against Athanasius, who was the archbishop of Alexandria.

In an effort to unseat Athanasius as the archbishop of Alexandria, those who favored Arianism accused him of cruelty, sorcery, and murder for unlawfully putting a bishop to death. Although Athanasius easily cleared himself of those charges, during the summer of A.D.

---

[53] Socrates Scholasticus, *The Ecclesiastical History*, bk. 1, ch. 1, A. C. Zenos, rev. and notes, In *A Select Library of Nicene and Post-Nicene Fathers of the Christian Church,* vol. 2*, Socrates, Sozomenus: Church Histories*, Philip Schaff and Henry Wace, eds. (Grand Rapids, Michigan: Reprinted by Wm. B. Eerdmans Publishing Co., 1979), p. 1.

[54] John William Burgon, *The Traditional Text of the New Testament,* In *Unholy Hands on the Bible*, Edward Miller, ed., vol. 1, Jay P. Green, ed. (Lafayette, Indiana: Sovereign Grace Trust Fund, 1990), p. 85.

[55] Duane Wade-Hampton Arnold, *The Early Episcopal Career of Athanasius of Alexandria* (Notre Dame, Indiana: Notre Dame University Press, 1991), p. 161.

335 his enemies arranged to have him ordered to appear before a council in Tyre that was to sit in judgement of his conduct. Realizing that there was a predetermined plan to condemn him, Athanasius fled from Tyre to Constantinople to make a direct appeal to the emperor. He had determined to make what was called a "...bold and dangerous experiment, whether the throne was inaccessible to the voice of truth."[56] Thus, Anthanasius presented himself before the emperor, requesting that his accusers be brought face to face with him in the presence of the emperor. As one writer explained:

> The leaders of the Tyrian council, amongst the most conspicuous of whom were the two Eusebii, were accordingly summoned to Constantinople just after they had celebrated, at a great dedication festival at Jerusalem, the condemnation of Athanasius and the restoration of Arius to church communion.[57]

The result of the conspiracy against Athanasius was that he was exiled to Gaul, where he remained until the death of Constantine in May A.D. 337. Constantine II later returned Athanasius to Alexandria.[58, 59] Alexandria, however, was under the jurisdiction of another of Constantine's sons, Constantius (A.D. 317-361) who assumed the throne in the East. Eusebius of Nicomedia, along with Theognis of Nicea, continued his work to reintroduce Arianism into the church. Based on the historical account of Socrates Scholasticus:

> After the death of the Emperor Constantine, Eusebius, bishop of Nicomedia, and Theognis of Nicaea [sic], imagining that a favorable opportunity had arisen, used their utmost efforts to expunge the doctrine of *homoousion*, and to introduce Arianism in its place.[60]

---

[56] Ibid.

[57] Ibid.

[58] Scholasticus, *The Ecclesiastical History*, bk. 2, ch. 3, p. 37.

[59] Walker et al., *A History of the Christian Church*, p. 137.

[60] Scholasticus, *The Ecclesiastical History*, bk. 2, ch. 2., p. 36.

They were able, through the use of eunuchs, to convert the empress who was then able to convert Constantius back to Arianism. After Athanasius returned to Alexandria, there arose a conspiracy among the Arians who again succeeded in having him banished. It was about A.D. 340, when Eusebius of Caesarea, who also called himself Pamphilus, died. Also, the younger Constantine was killed in a battle by the soldiers of his brother, Constantius.[61] Constantius later appointed Eusebius of Nicomedia, the strong advocate of Arianism, to be the bishop of Constantinople.

An account of the events that followed were that:

> He [Constantius] in his turn fell, as his father had done, more and more under the influence of the Nicomedian Eusebius, now transferred to the see of Constantinople. A second expulsion of Athanasius was accordingly resolved upon. The old charges against him were revived, with the addition of his having set at naught the decision of a council. It was further resolved on this occasion to put another bishop in his place. Accordingly, in the beginning of the year 340, a Cappadocian named Gregory, said to be an Arian, was installed by military force on the throne of the great defender of the faith, who, to save his followers from outrage, withdrew to a place of concealment.[62]

The Council of Antioch: Confusing the Creed

Within five years of the death of Constantine, Eusebius of Nicomedia organized another council, held at Antioch, for the purpose of overturning the Trinitarian actions that had been taken at the Council of Nicea. There, the Arians again brought charges against Athanasius accusing him for, among other things, resuming his episcopal authority in Alexandria following his return from exile without the license of a general council of bishops.[63]

---

[61] Ibid., book 2, chs. 4 and 5, p. 37.

[62] *Athanasius, St, Bishop of Alexandria*, http://ccel.wheaton.edu/a/athanasius/athanasius-EB.html.

[63] Scholasticus, *The Ecclesiastical History*, bk. 2, ch. 8, p. 38.

After again exiling Athanasius, Eusebius of Nicomedia proposed a replacement for him as the bishop of the Alexandrian Church. Eusebius surnamed Emisenus was ordained as bishop of Alexandria by Eusebius, who was then bishop of Constantinople. However, Eusebius surnamed Emisenus was afraid to go to Alexandria because its people strongly supported Athanasius. Consequently, the Council of Antioch then designated Gregory as bishop of Alexandria.[64]

In addition to replacing Athanasius as the bishop of Alexandria, those attending the Council of Antioch intensified their efforts to overthrow the Trinitarian doctrine that came out of the Council of Nicea. Specifically, they subtly altered the Nicene Creed using discrete techniques. Their approach was to not directly condemn anything in the Creed. Instead, they changed it. According to Socrates Scholasticus, their strategy was to:

> ... subvert and nullify the doctrine of consubstantiality by means of frequent councils, and the publication of various expositions of the faith, so as gradually to establish the Arian views.[65]

In other words, the plan was to make subtle and frequent changes in a manner that would go unnoticed by all but the most discerning readers. In doing so, they would gradually insert their Arian views into the Creed. They avoided confrontation by not attacking the Creed. Instead, they undermined it by inserting changes that gradually moved it toward Arianism. Eusebius of Nicomedia has been called a "master of intrigue" because he used such subtle and non-confrontational techniques to accomplish his goals.[66] For example, while remaining at the Council of Antioch, those of the Arian persuasion appeared to confirm the decisions made at the Council of Nicea in a new edition of the Creed. In it, they said that they believed in one God who was the Creator of the Universe and in one "only-begotten Son of God." They wrote a letter, which they distributed to the bishops in every city, saying:

---

[64] Ibid., bk. 2, ch. 9, p. 39.

[65] Ibid., bk. 2, ch. 10, pp. 39-40.

[66] B. J. Kidd, *A History of the Church to A.D. 461*, vol. 2, *A.D. 313-408* (Oxford: The Clarendon Press, 1922), p. 53.

> ...We have learned from the beginning to believe in one God of the Universe, the Creator and Preserver of all things both those thought of and those perceived by the senses: and in one only-begotten Son of God, subsisting before all ages, and co-existing with the Father who begat him, through whom also all things visible and invisible were made....[67]

While that letter was still circulating, the Council remained at Antioch where they continued to make changes in the Nicene Creed. They then published another letter containing a slightly altered Creed. This one appeared to negate portions of the one they had earlier issued. Those changes tended to further blur the role of the Father and the Son in the Creation. This time, they said it was the Father and not the Word who was the Creator. They continued to say, however, that all things were made through the Son, who they called "God the only begotten." Then they went on to embellish the Creed with hyperbole concerning the Son so that those who believed in the deity of Jesus Christ could not argue against the revised Creed. It then read:

> In conformity with evangelic and apostolic tradition, we believe in one God the Father Almighty, the Creator and Framer of the universe. And in one Lord Jesus Christ, his Son, God the only-begotten, through whom all things were made: begotten of the Father before all ages, God of God, Whole of Whole, Only of Only, Perfect of Perfect, King of King, Lord of Lord; the living Word, the Wisdom, the Life, the True Light, the Way of Truth, the Resurrection, the Shepherd, the Gate; immutable and inconvertible; the unaltering image of the Divinity, Substance and Power, and Counsel and Glory of the Father; born 'before all creation'; who was in the beginning with God, God the Word, according as it is declared in the Gospel, and the Word was God, by whom all things were made, and in whom all things subsist: who in the last days came down from above, and was born of the virgin according to the Scriptures....[68]

---

[67] Scholasticus, *The Ecclesiastical History*, bk. 2, ch. 10, pp. 39-40.

[68] Ibid., bk. 2, ch. 10, pp. 39-40.

The essence of this change was that, instead of reading that we "...believe in one God of the Universe, the Creator and Preserver of all things both those thought of and those perceived by the senses: and in one *only-begotten Son of God* " it had now become we "...believe in one God *the Father Almighty, the Creator and Framer of the universe. And in one Lord Jesus Christ, his Son, God the only-begotten* through whom all things were made...." [Italics were added for emphasis.] Thus, the effect of the *new* Creed was that the *Father* was the Creator and Framer of everything, *making him also the Creator of God the Son*, through whom everything else was made.

Gregory, the new bishop of Alexandria who had not yet entered the city, subscribed to the newly published Antiochian Nicene Creed, which was an Arian revision of the original Nicene Creed. Equipped with the new Creed, he then entered Alexandria with a military escort and forced Athanasius to flee. Although Gregory reportedly had an escort of about five thousand soldiers, along with a number of Arian supporters, Athanasius was able to escape being captured. After Gregory, with his Arian views, had taken over the church, the people of Alexandria, set the church on fire.[69]

Resurgence of Christian Persecution

As Gregory became less popular, he was not considered by the Arians to be sufficiently zealous in promoting Arianism. Therefore, he was removed as bishop of Alexandria and was replaced by George, who acquired a reputation for being an able advocate of Arianism.[70] Following the death of Constantius, his cousin, Julian Caesar (A.D. 331-363), became the Roman Emperor. Although Julian was reared as a Christian under the guidance of Constantius, he was taught the Arian position (denying the deity of Jesus Christ), which was held by Constantius. As a youth, Julian was strongly attracted to paganism, as represented by Neo-Platonism, and became an enthusiastic adherent of that philosophy.[71]

---

[69] Ibid., bk. 2, ch. 11, p. 40.

[70] Ibid., bk. 2, ch. 14, p. 41.

[71] Latourette, *A History of the Expansion of Christianity*, vol. 1, pp. 176-177.

While Men Slept...

As his belief toward Neo-Platonistic paganism developed, Julian's hatred toward Christians intensified. He initiated a persecution against Christians and commanded that all the pagan temples in the East be reopened. Practicing his beliefs in the pagan religion, Julian actively participated in pagan worship and openly offered sacrifices to the pagan gods.[72] During his great persecution of Christians, Julian banned Christians from attending public schools and from learning the Greek language.[73] This effectively prevented Christians from developing what he considered "argumentative and persuasive power" and also prevented them from studying the Greek Scriptures. As a consequence, Christians were prevented from knowing whether those who wished to deceive them had, indeed, corrupted any surviving Scriptures.

Arian View of Eusebius of Caesarea

What Eusebius of Caesarea believed and what he publicly said often seemed to disagree with each other. To understand his true views on the nature of Jesus Christ, it is most useful to examine his relationship with others who had clearly established positions on the Arian controversy. Origen, for example, who had a clearer position in his view that Jesus was lower than God, exerted a strong influence on the theology of Eusebius of Caesarea. Pamphilus was a pupil of Origen and Eusebius of Caesarea was a pupil of Pamphilus.[74] Pamphilus, a presbyter of Caesarea and close personal friend of Origen, played such a role in the life of Eusebius of Caesarea that, after his death, Eusebius took on the name, "Eusebius of Pamphilus."[75] It was

---

[72] Salaminius Hermias Sozomen, *The Ecclesiastical History of Sozomen, Comprising a History of the Church from A.D. 323 to A.D. 425*, bk. 5, chs. 1-3, Nicephorus Callistus, arranger, Chester D. Hartranft, rev., In *A Select Library of Nicene and Post-Nicene Fathers of the Christian Church*, vol. 2, *Socrates, Sozomenus: Church Histories*, Philip Schaff and Henry Wace, eds. (Grand Rapids, Michigan: Wm. B. Eerdmans Publishing Co., reprinter, 1979), pp. 325-328.

[73] Sozomen, *The Ecclesiastical History of Sozomen,* p. 340.

[74] Heinrich Greeven, *The Gospel Synopsis From 1776 to the Present Day*, Robert Althann, translator, In *J. J. Griesbach: Synoptic and Text-critical Studies, 1776-1976*, Bernard Orchard and Thomas R. W. Longstaff, eds. (Cambridge: Cambridge University Press, 1978), p. 23.

[75] Foakes-Jackson, *Eusebius of Pamphili,* p. 36.

Pamphilus who, along with Eusebius of Caesarea, devoted significant time and energy, even while in prison, defending the work of Origen. One account of the evidence of the great admiration that both had for Origen is shown below:

> To the influence of Pamphilus, the devoted admirer and en-
> thusiastic champion of Origen, was doubtless due also in large
> measure the deep respect which Eusebius showed for that il-
> lustrious Father, a respect to which we owe one of the most
> delightful sections of his Church History, his long account of
> Origen in the sixth book, and to which in part antiquity was
> indebted for the elaborate *Defense of Origen*, composed by
> Pamphilus and himself, but unfortunately no longer extant....
> During the two years of Pamphilus' imprisonment Eusebius
> spent a great deal of time with him, and the two together com-
> posed five books of an *Apology for Origen*, to which Eusebius
> afterward added a sixth.[76]

As a result of this strong influence by Origen, Eusebius of Caesarea held his views concerning the nature of Jesus Christ. Even though Eusebius of Caesarea finally agreed to the other position at the Council of Nicea, he was suspected of favoring the "Arian" or "Semi-Arian" position because he shared the views of Origen concerning the divinity of Jesus Christ.[77]

Eusebius of Caesarea was also a strong supporter of Eusebius of Nicomedia, who was a staunch defender of the position of Arius. In addition, Arius claimed to have the support for his doctrine concerning the deity of Jesus Christ by a number of bishops, including Eusebius of Caesarea, who wrote a letter to Alexander in defense of Arius for

---

[76] Arthur Cushman McGiffert, "Prolegomena. The Life and Writings of Eusebius of Caesarea, The Life of Eusebius," ch. 1, Arthur Cushman McGiffert, trans. with Prolegomena and notes, In *Nicene and Post-Nicene Fathers of the Christian Church*, series 2, vol. 1, Philip Schaff and Henry Wace, eds. (Grand Rapids, Michigan: Reprinted by Wm. B. Eerdmans Publishing Co., 1979), pp. 8-9.

[77] Philip Schaff, *History of the Apostolic Church with a General Introductin to Church History*, Edward D. Yeomans, trans. (New York: Charles Scribner, 1859), p. 52.

his position.[78, 79] There are various other references that link Eusebius of Caesarea, Eusebius of Nicomedia, and Arius in which they appear to agree with each other on the Arian theology. However, some believed those references to be "…too exiguous, too imprecise to yield any ultimately decisive information."[80] Whether or not one agrees that the available information proves that Eusebius of Caesarea was Arian, in the traditional sense of the word, it is clear that he did have a Father-centered theology. This was demonstrated by his use of expressions implying the subordination of the Son to the Father.[81]

While Eusebius' position on the central Arian issue concerning the deity of Jesus Christ was not clear because he oscillated on his public views, it is clear that he took a position close enough to Arianism to give Arius encouragement.[82] Further evidence of Eusebius' views concerning the nature of God is provided by his position on the Holy Ghost. One author described Eusebius' views this way:

> The Holy Ghost belongs to the Holy Trinity but is only the greatest of the creatures made by the Son to whom He is inferior. The Holy Ghost was produced…is a creation of the Son, because "all things were made by Him."[83]

Eusebius of Caesarea and the Pagan Sacrifice Implication

Having close association with and the respect of Constantine, Eusebius of Caesarea was in a strategic position to have a major influence on the newly legalized Christianity. He was, however, the source of many rumors concerning his true beliefs. For example, some claimed that he sacrificed to idols in order to exempt himself from the persecution

---

[78] Luibheid, *Eusebius of Caesarea and the Arian Crisis*, p. 25.

[79] J. Stevenson, *Studies in Eusebius* (Cambridge: Cambridge University Press, 1929), p. 75.

[80] Luibheid, *Eusebius of Caesarea and the Arian Crisis*, p. 121.

[81] Ibid., p. 124.

[82] Stevenson, *Studies in Eusebius*, p. 89.

[83] Ibid., pp. 89-90.

that many other Christians were experiencing.[84]   In a specific accusa-
tion, Potamo, bishop of Heracleopolis, questioned whether Eusebius
of Caesarea was fit to sit in judgement of Athanasius because of the
implication that he had sacrificed to idols. Potamo said:

> …Were you not in custody with me, during the time of the
> persecution? And I truly, in defence of the truth, lost an eye;
> but you are injured in no part of your body, neither did you
> undergo martyrdom, but are alive and whole. In what manner
> did you escape out of prison, unless you promised to our per-
> secutors that you would commit the detestable thing [sacri-
> fice to idols]? And perhaps you have done it.[85]

Eusebius of Caesarea did not deny the charge. Rather than continue
the discussion, however, he dismissed the council, which he had headed
for the purpose of sitting in judgement of Athanasius.

The implication by Potamo that Eusebius had sacrificed to the Roman gods during the time of the Roman persecution of Christians was
very significant. If Eusebius did indeed sacrifice to the Roman gods in
exchange for his freedom, then his sincerity in his subsequent work
on behalf of Christianity might be suspect. Those who would want to
rely on Eusebius' work, whether it would be on his church history, his
actions at the Council of Nicea, or his work on biblical revision, would
certainly hope that he would be free from the tainting that would be
associated with submitting to a sacrifice to the Roman gods.

Joseph Lightfoot (1828-1889), one of the three who used the fourth
century Greek Bibles believed to have been written under Eusebius'
direction as the primary basis for rescinding the *Textus Receptus*, came
to his defense. Lightfoot's defense of Eusebius of Caesarea against
the implication that he actually did sacrifice to the pagan gods was

---

[84] Valesius, *Annotations on the Life and Writings of Eusebius Pamphilus*, S. E.
Parker, trans., In *The Ecclesiastical History of Eusebius Pamphilus, Bishop of
Caesarea, In Palestine, Translated from the Original with an Introduction by
Christian Frederick Cruse and an Historical View of the Council of Nice by Isaac
Boyle* (Grand Rapids, Michigan: Baker Book House, 1990), p. ix.
[85] Ibid., p. xv.

made on the basis that Potamo never actually called Eusebius "the sacrificer." In Lightfoot's view, this indicated that there was no direct evidence to prove that Eusebius did indeed sacrifice.[86] Many accept Lightfoot's defense at face value, perhaps without considering his level of objectivity on this matter. Accepting his defense is crucial to accepting the biblical revisions based on the work of Eusebius. Lightfoot may have been correct in asserting that Potamo did not have direct proof of a pagan sacrifice by Eusebius of Caesarea. One should, however, also consider the other implicating evidence.

During the Christian persecutions before A.D. 303, those who were suspected of being Christians were required to make a sacrifice. If they did, they normally received a certificate of sacrifice. An original certificate of an A.D. 250 sacrifice, for example, located at the University of Michigan in Ann Arbor was issued to a woman and her daughter in Egypt. According to the editors of the collection, the certificate:

> ...testified that they had obeyed the imperial edict to participate in pagan sacrifices as proof of their loyalty to the government. Since faithful Christians would not sacrifice to pagan gods, the edict served as a means for identifying Christians and making them liable for punishment or imprisonment.[87]

Whether or not Eusebius of Caesarea possessed such a certificate is not known.

In A.D. 303 the Christian persecution intensified. During its height, Emperor Diocletian issued an edict saying that those Christians which were in prison who were willing to sacrifice to idols could be set free. Those who refused would then be subject to torture to require them to offer incense to the gods.[88]

---

[86] McGiffert, "Prolegomena. The Life and Writings of Eusebius of Caesarea, The Life of Eusebius," ch. 1, p. 10.

[87] In *The Evolution of the English Bible: From Papyri to King James*, Kathryn L. Beam and Traianos Gagos, eds. (Ann Arbor: University of Michigan Press, 1997).

[88] Edward Backhouse, *Early Church History to the Death of Constantine*, p. 354.

Although Eusebius of Caesarea and Pamphilus were in prison together, Pamphilus was martyred in A.D. 310 by beheading for refusing to sacrifice to idols.[89] Eusebius of Caesarea was set free. It is clear that he survived imprisonment while those around him were either severely injured or executed. Eusebius of Caesarea witnessed the martyrdom of Christians, but he was released unharmed. By at least one account, he:

> …was the eye-witness of martyrdoms; at Tyre he witnessed the contest of the martyrs with wild beasts, and the miraculous reluctance of the animals to touch them; in the Thebaid he saw many Christians put to death in a single day, some by fire, others by the sword; so many were there that the sword was blunted and the executioners were worn out.[90]

Whether Eusebius of Caesarea sacrificed to idols or not may never be conclusively established on this earth and may be the subject of further discussion. It does, however, remain unclear how he escaped the great persecution of those who would not sacrifice to idols while those around him were maimed and martyred. How he was able to witness the great physical hardships that other Christians endured without himself being subjected to similar hardships, unless he had renounced his faith by sacrificing to the Roman gods, is difficult to understand.

---

[89] Stevenson, *Studies in Eusebius*, p. 54.
[90] Ibid., p. 51.

While Men Slept...

Chapter 4. The Eusebius-Origen Bibles

I have thought it expedient to instruct your Prudence to order fifty copies of the sacred Scriptures...[1]
—Emperor Constantine to Eusebius of Caesarea

Bibles for the Fourth Century Roman Church

Ordered by the Roman Emperor

Desiring to bring peace to the Roman Empire, Emperor Constantine looked for a Bible that would facilitate the amalgamation of the pagan Roman religion and Christianity into one universal religion. It was during the controversial fourth century Arian resurgence that Eusebius of Caesarea, in obedience to the command of the Roman Emperor Constantine, prepared fifty copies of the Bible. This well-known church historian, Eusebius of Caesarea, wrote of Constantine's request:

> EVER careful for the welfare of the churches of God, the emperor addressed me personally in a letter on the means of providing copies of the inspired oracles, and also on the subject of the most holy feast of Easter.[2]

Showing his great admiration for Eusebius of Caesarea, Constantine wrote:

> I am, notwithstanding, filled with admiration of your learning and zeal, and have not only myself read your work with pleasure, but have given directions, according to your own desire,

---

[1] Eusebius Pamphilus, "The Life of the Blessed Emperor Constantine," bk. 4, ch. 34, Ernest Cushing Richardson, rev. trans. with Prolegomena and notes, ed., In *A Select Library of Nicene and Post-Nicene Fathers of the Christian Church*, vol. 1, 2nd Series, Philip Schaff and Henry Wace, eds. (Grand Rapids, Michigan: Wm. B. Eerdmans Publishing Company, 1979), p. 549.

[2] Ibid., p. 548.

that it be communicated to many sincere followers of our holy religion...." Such was his letter on this subject: and that which related to the providing of copies of the Scriptures for reading in the churches was to the following purport.[3]

Constantine continued his instruction to Eusebius of Caesarea as he said:

I have thought it expedient to instruct your Prudence to order fifty copies of the sacred Scriptures, the provision and use of which you know to be most needful for the instruction of the Church, to be written on prepared parchment in a legible manner, and in a convenient, portable form, by professional transcribers thoroughly practiced in their art. The catholicus of the diocese has also received instructions by letter from our Clemency to be careful to furnish all things necessary for the preparation of such copies; and it will be for you to take special care that they be completed with as little delay as possible. You have authority also, in virtue of this letter, to use two of the public carriages for their conveyance, by which arrangement the copies when fairly written will most easily be forwarded for my personal inspection; and one of the deacons of your church may be intrusted with this service, who, on his arrival here shall experience my liberality. God preserve you, beloved brother![4]

Eusebius of Caesarea reported that he obeyed the emperor's commands and immediately began the work of producing the ordered manuscripts. Tischendorf believed that both the *Codex Sinaiticus* and *Codex Vaticanus* were produced as part of the fifty Bibles ordered by Constantine.[5] The production of these manuscripts was paid for by the Roman Empire, and overseen by Eusebius of Caesarea.

---

[3] Ibid., p. 549.

[4] Ibid.

[5] William Grady, *Final Authority: A Christian's Guide to the King James Bible* (Schererville, Indiana: Grady Publications, Inc., 1997), p. 109.

Selecting the Manuscripts

Charged by the emperor with the responsibility of producing a new Bible to unite the new official universal Christian religion of the fourth century, Eusebius of Caesarea was faced with a formidable task. Many of the critical manuscripts of the Bible had been destroyed by the reign of terror that had been launched against Christians by Diocletian and others prior to the ascension of Constantine to power. Wishing to please Constantine, Eusebius used the manuscripts of Origen that had been preserved, by whatever means, from destruction. Some believe Constantine preferred the manuscripts of Origen, which were edited by Eusebius, because they reflected a blending of Christianity and Gnosticism. One writer described Constantine's preference this way:

> Quite naturally he preferred the one edited by Eusebius and written by Origen, the outstanding intellectual figure that had combined Christianity with Gnosticism in his philosophy, even as Constantine himself was the political genius that was seeking to unite Christianity with pagan Rome.[6]

As we shall see, the influence of Origen and Eusebius of Caesarea on both the Old and New Testaments of the Fourth Century Bibles was enormous. For the foundation of the Bibles ordered by Constantine, Eusebius of Caesarea selected both Origen's Greek New Testament *and* his Greek Old Testament, which was a revision of the Septuagint.

The Septuagint: The Greek Version of the Old Testament

Its Origin in Alexandria, Egypt

The Septuagint was essentially a Greek translation of the Hebrew Old Testament. Its production was the outcome of the tremendous influence of Alexander the Great (356-323 B.C.). The Macedonian king conquered the Persian Empire and caused the Greek language and philosophy to be spread throughout much of the known world,

---

[6] Benjamin G. Wilkinson, *Our Authorized Bible Vindicated*, In *Which Bible?*, David Otis Fuller, ed. (Grand Rapids, Michigan: Institute for Biblical Textual Studies, 1990), p. 195.

including Egypt. [As we have learned, it was in the great city of Alexandria, Egypt that many Jews and early Christians came under the influence of Greek philosophy.] After the death of Alexander the Great, his empire was divided up among various Greek rulers. Ptolemy I (called Soter or Savior) (about 367-283 B.C.), who was also a Macedonian, seized Egypt. He also gained control of Jerusalem by using deceit. He entered the city on the Sabbath under the pretense of offering a sacrifice to God and then seized the city.[7]

When Ptolemy II (called Philedelphus) (308-245 B.C.) took control of Egypt, he established the great library in Alexandria. His goal was to gather together copies of all of the books on earth into his library. To accomplish his goal, he also needed to include the books of the law in the possession of the Jews. Realizing, however, that these books were written in Hebrew, a language with which most Greeks were unfamiliar, he proposed to have them translated into Greek so that they could be added to the numbers of books in his library.[8]

For Sale: The Name of God

As part of the arrangement for translating the Hebrew books of the law into Greek, the king's friend and advisor, Aristeus, proposed that Ptolemy II set free more than a hundred thousand ("a few more than ten times ten thousand") Jews who were then slaves in Egypt. As a rationalization for translating the books of the Hebrew God, יהוה [YHWH], into the Greek language, Aristeus argued that both the Greeks and the Hebrews actually worshipped the same god. As he explained to Ptolemy:

> ...for both these people and we also worship the same God, the framer of all things. We call him, and that truly, by the name of Ζηνα, [Zena, or life, or Jupiter,] because he breathes life into all men.[9] [Jupiter is the Roman name for the supreme Greek god, Zeus.]

(

---

[7] *The Works of Josephus*, bk. 12, chs. 1 and 2, William Whiston, trans. (Peabody, Massachusetts: Hendrickson Publishers, 1985), pp. 245-246.

[8] Ibid., p. 246.

[9] Ibid.

Convinced of the strategy, King Ptolemy II freed the Jewish slaves. Then one of his advisors recommended that he write a letter to Eleazar, the high priest of the Jews, requesting that he send six elders out of every tribe of Israel to make a translation of the Hebrew laws into Greek that would be suitable for the king. He also informed Eleazar of his release of the Jewish slaves. In addition, the king offered to send the high priest, "fifty talents of gold...and an immense quantity of precious stones...[and] that a hundred talents in money should be sent to the temple for sacrifices, and for other uses." The letter written to the high priest said, "...I have determined to procure an interpretation of your law, and to have it translated out of Hebrew into Greek, and to be deposited in my library." Ptolemy also promised Eleazar that if he would "**do a thing acceptable to me**," then he could let him know what he would further want.[10]

Eleazar responded that, "...we greatly rejoiced at your intentions...when the multitude were gathered together, we read it [the letter] to them.... We also showed them the twenty vials of gold, and thirty of silver...also the hundred talents for the sacrifices...and for the making what shall be needful at the temple...." He continued, "...we will gratify thee in what is for thy advantage, though we do what we used not to do before; for we ought to make a return for the numerous acts of kindness which thou hast done to our countrymen." Therefore, Eleazar said that he chose six elders out of every tribe to do the translation for the king of Egypt.[11, 12]

When the elders came to Alexandria, they brought a book of the law written in golden letters. King Ptolemy II greeted them with a feast and gave them excellent quarters. They reportedly finished the task of translating the Old Testament in seventy-two days. Ptolemy II ac-

---

[10] Ibid., p. 247.

[11] Ibid., p. 247-248.

[12] Note: It would be of interest to find out how these seventy-two elders, consisting of six elders from each of the twelve tribes of Israel, were found. Both the Bible and other historical accounts show that the northern tribes of Israel were captured by Assyria in 722 B.C. and that they never returned to Judah. It is more likely that those chosen were all from the tribes of Judah and Benjamin, along with a remnant of Levites, who made up the House of Judah and were allowed to return to Jerusalem after their Babylonian captivity.

cepted the translation and "... the king rejoiced when he saw that his design of this nature was brought to perfection...." He had the translators read the law to him and he, eventually, paid them significant sums of money, gave them gifts, and sent them home.[13] Thus, the Septuagint was produced.

There are various accounts surrounding the timing and details of the production of the Septuagint. Some say the Greek translation of the Pentateuch, the first five books of the Old Testament, was produced around 285 B.C.[14] Then the balance of the Hebrew Bible was believed to have also been completed in Alexandria, possibly as early as 250 to 200 B.C.[15] By other estimations, however, the entire work took more than 150 years, during the period between 285 and 130 B.C.[16] Regardless of the precise timing required and details of its production, that Greek translation of the Hebrew Bible became known as the Septuagint.

God, Who? Renaming the God of Israel

YHWH or LORD?

God's Word was fulfilled in the Septuagint. Through the prophet Jeremiah, God had said that His name, יהוה, which is translated as YHWH, Yahweh, or Jehovah, would no longer be named in Egypt among the people of Judah. He said:

> So hear the word of **Jehovah [יהוה]**, all Judah who reside in the land of Egypt: Behold, I have sworn by My great name, says **Jehovah [יהוה]**, that My name shall no more be named

---

[13] *The Works of Josephus*, pp. 250-251.

[14] Paul Lamarche, *The Septuagint: Bible of the Earliest Christians*, In *The Bible in Greek Christian Antiquity*, Edited and Translated by Paul M. Blowers, Based on *Bible De Tous Les Temps,* vol. 1, *Le monde grec ancien et la Bible*, C. Mondesert, ed. (Notre Dame, Indiana: University of Notre Dame Press, 1997), p. 18.

[15] Sidney Jellicoe, *The Septuagint and Modern Study* (London: Oxford at the Clarendon Press, 1968), pp. 47-52.

[16] Ira Maurice Price, *The Ancestry of Our English Bible*, 2nd ed. (Philadelphia: The Sunday School Times Company, 1907), p. 52.

in the mouth of any man of Judah in all the land of Egypt, saying, The Lord **Jehovah [יהוה]** lives.

—Jeremiah 44:26 (Green's Literal)[17]

Διατουτο ακουσατε λογον **Κυριου [Lord]**, πας Ιουδα οι καθημενοι εν γη Αιγυπτω, ιδου ωμοσα τω ονοματι μου τω μεγαλω, ειπε **Κυριος [Lord]**, εαν γενηται ετι ονομα μου εν τω στοματι παντος Ιουδα ειπειν, ζη **Κυριος [Lord]** επι παση γη Αιγυπτω

—Jeremiah 44:26 (Septuagint)[18, 19]

When the men of Judah, while in Egypt, translated God's Word into the Septuagint they had replaced the name יהוה (YHWH) with Κυριος (Lord). Just as Jeremiah had prophesied, the men of Judah in the land of Egypt did not name His name, saying the Lord YHWH lives!

Eli-YAH or Eli-hu?

Everyone who utters the name of Elijah proclaims that God (Eli) is YAH (Jah). It means Elohiym (God) is YHWH. It was Elijah who challenged the people of Israel to choose which God they would serve:

And **Elijah [אליהו]** came unto all the people, and said, How long halt ye between two opinions? if the LORD **[יהוה]** *be* God, follow him: but if **Baal [בעל]**, *then* follow him. And the people answered him not a word.

—1 Kings 18:21

The translators of the Septuagint gave Elijah a new name. They wrote:

και προσηγαγεν **ηλιου [Elijah]** προς παντας και ειπεν αυτοις ηλιου εως ποτε υμεις χωλανειτε επ αμφοτεραις

---

[17] Jay P. Green, Sr., *The Interlinear Bible: Hebrew-Greek-English*, 2nd ed. (Lafayette, Indiana: Sovereign Grace Publishers, 1986), p. 622.

[18] Lancelot C. L. Brenton, (Jeremiah 51:26), *The Septuagint with Apocrypha: Greek and English*, Originally published by Samuel Bagster & Sons, Ltd., London, 1851 (Peabody, Massachusetts: Hendrickson Publishers, 1987), p. 969.

[19] The Greek text of this edition of the Septuagint is primarily based on the *Codex Vaticanus. See* Preface to Brenton, *The Septuagint with Apocrypha*.

ταις ιγνυαις ει εστιν **κυριος [LORD]** ο θεος πορευεσθε
οπισω αυτου ει δε ο **βααλ [Baal]** αυτος πορευεσθε οπισω
αυτου και ουκ απεκριθη ο λαος λογον

—1 Kings 18:21 (Septuagint)[20]

Elijah's Hebrew name, אליהו, which is also written as אליה (Alyh or Elyah), means God is YAH. It was translated to the Greek word, ηλιου (Heliou), which, as Helios, is the Greek *sun god*![21] YHWH, through the prophet Malachi, explains the importance of His name:

> For from the rising of **the sun** even unto the going down of the same my name *shall be* great among the Gentiles; and in every place incense *shall be* offered unto my name, and a pure offering: for my name *shall be* great among the heathen, saith the LORD [יהוה] of hosts.
>
> —Malachi 1:11

The Hebrew word for the sun, שמש (shemesh), was translated into the Greek Septuagint as **ηλιου**, which is *also* the word used for Elijah:

> διοτι απ ανατολων **ηλιου [the sun]** εως δυσμων το ονομα μου δεδοξασται εν τοις εθνεσιν και εν παντι τοπω θυμιαμα προσαγεται τω ονοματι μου και θυσια καθαρα διοτι μεγα το ονομα μου εν τοις εθνεσιν λεγει **κυριος [LORD]** παντοκρατωρ
>
> —Malachi 1:11 (Septuagint)[22]

In contrast to the name of Elijah, the name of Elihu, אליהוא, which, for example, is found in Job 32:2, refers to God (or god) without a name. It refers to God in a nonspecific manner, such as a reference to he, she, they, which, or who.[23] In other words, the name "Elihu" refers to *no specific name* for God. As the Septuagint translators translated the name of Elihu into Greek, they left this name as it was in the

---

[20] *LXX Septuagint*, In *Online Bible*, Millennium ed. (Winterbourne, Ontario, Canada: Timathaserah, January 14, 2002).

[21] William Smith, *A New Classical Dictionary of Greek and Roman Biography, Mythology and Geography, partly based upon the Dictionary of Greek and Roman Biography and Mythology* (New York: Harper & Brothers, 1851), p. 349.

[22] *LXX Septuagint*, In *Online Bible*.

[23] Strong, "Hebrew and Chaldee Dictionary," pp. 13, 32.

Hebrew, with a reference to an unspecified God (Eli). They wrote his name as ελιους (elious). With the name of Elijah, however, the translators not only removed reference to name of God (YAH), but they also removed the reference to God (Eli) as they wrote ηλιου (hliou), meaning "the sun" or the "sun god." While the name of the God of Israel, יהוה (YHWH), is translated as κυριος, meaning LORD, in the Septuagint, the name of Baal (בעל), which also means "lord,"[24] is retained as βααλ (Baal).

When the high priest of the Jews, Eleazar, received a great wealth of treasures from King Ptolemy II of Egypt, he said to the king, "Know then that we will gratify thee in what is for thy advantage, though we do what we used not to do before...."[25] As we have learned, the king accepted the Universalist position that all gods are true. Therefore, obscuring the name of the God of Israel, which is יהוה, in the book of the law that was to be placed in the king's library in Alexandria was to his advantage. Might blurring the name of God have been part of the gratification offered to the king by the high priest?

Errors in the Septuagint

Origen, Pamphilus, and Eusebius Revisions

Once the Septuagint was produced, it was still subjected to critical revisions. In his *Hexapla* Bible, for example, Origen attempted to translate the Greek Septuagint back to the Hebrew. In doing so, he was believed to have either obscured or lost many of the superior readings of the Old Testament.[26] We have learned that the meaning of important Hebrew readings, such as the name of Elijah, were obscured in the Septuagint. Because his name was translated as ηλιου (hliou) which meant *both* Elijah and "the sun" or the "sun god" in the Septuagint, an attempt to translate the word back to Hebrew could easily lead one to confusion. Despite Origen's use of this practice of

[24] Strong, "Hebrew and Chaldee Dictionary," p. 22.

[25] *The Works of Josephus*, p. 248.

[26] Eugene Ulrich, *The Old Testament Text of Eusebius: The Heritage of Origen*, In *Eusebius, Christianity, and Judaism*, Harold W. Attridge and Gohei Hata, eds. (Detroit: Wayne State University Press, 1992), p. 557.

reverse translation, his Septuagint revisions, which were later amended by Pamphilus and Eusebius of Caesarea, have received a high level of credibility. Even when the apparent theological biases of Origen and Eusebius of Caesarea are discounted, the practice of accepting a re-troverted translation from the Greek back into the Hebrew can be regarded with suspicion. This is because specific Greek words may carry an imprecise meaning of the Hebrew words.[27]

Notwithstanding the substantive changes Origen made in the Septuagint used by Eusebius of Caesarea in the fourth century Bibles, by some accounts the text also had in it, "...qualitative changes, including transposed word order, not marked, and ineluctably with some copyists' errors."[28] Pamphilus, with the help of Eusebius of Caesarea, produced their revised Septuagint from Origen's Hexapla.[29] After Origen, Pamphilus, and Eusebius worked on the Septuagint, the form in which they found it was lost and no longer available.[30]

Perpetuating the Errors

The changes introduced into the Septuagint by its revisors created interesting challenges for its defenders. Augustine, for example, opposed many of the Origen's heretical teachings. Origen's heresy was considered so grave that in A.D. 400 Pope Anastasius wrote a letter to Simplicianus, bishop of Milan, in which he directly condemned the writings of Origen whose blasphemies had been brought under his notice by Eusebius of Cremona. In that letter, he wrote that:

> ...everything written in days gone by Origen that is contrary to our faith is even by us rejected and condemned.[31]

Despite a belief in Origen's heresy, Augustine attempted to defend the Septuagint, into which Origen, and later, Pamphilus and Eusebius

---

[27] Ibid., p. 70.

[28] Ibid., p. 556.

[29] Edward Backhouse, *Early Church History to the Death of Constantine*, p. 383.

[30] Kenyon, *The Text of the Greek Bible*, p. 25.

[31] *Letter XCV, From Pope Anastasius To Simplicianus,* In *A Select Library of Nicene And Post-Nicene Fathers*, series 2 vol. 6 -- *St. Jerome: Letters and Select Works*, Philip Schaff and Henry Wace, eds. (Grand Rapids: Wm. B. Eerdmans Publishing Company, 1954), p. 186.

of Caesarea, introduced their own editorial influences. Although August-ine attempted to defend the Septuagint and the Latin manuscripts based on it, he acknowledged significant discrepancies in critical areas, espe-cially as it related to the computation of ages. For example, the Latin versions of the Septuagint said that Adam was 230 years old before he begat Seth, whereas the Hebrew manuscripts said that he was only 130 years old. Then, after he begat Seth, the Septuagint-based Latin manu-scripts said Adam lived another 700 years, whereas the Hebrew manu-scripts said he lived another 800 years. The effect of the discrepancy becomes significant in the seventh generation from Adam with Enoch, who was translated without death. The Latin manuscripts based on the Septuagint had Enoch being 100 years older than did the Hebrew manu-scripts before he begat Methuselah.[32]

Augustine believed that the errors were less likely to have occurred in the widely distributed Hebrew manuscripts than in the single manu-script in the possession of the Egyptian king. The essence of this dis-cussion by Augustine concerning the discrepancies in the ages of vari-ous Old Testament men was that a copyist may have introduced an error into the copy first transcribed from the library of Ptolemy II, the king of Egypt, who had ordered the translation of the Septuagint. However, it appeared that the error was perpetuated and that other errors were purposely introduced in order to make various dates work out as they believed they should.[33] In other words, it appeared that, once an error was introduced, it was perpetuated and even knowingly magnified, perhaps to preserve the perceived reliability of the text.

Augustine seemed to take two different positions regarding apparent discrepancies between the Septuagint and the Hebrew texts. On one hand, he said that if the disagreement between the Septuagint and the Hebrew is:

> ...so great that both versions cannot be true, we must take our ideas of the real facts from that text out of which our own version had been translated [the Hebrew].[34]

---

[32] *St. Augustin's City of God*, p. 291.

[33] Ibid., pp. 293-294.

[34] Ibid., p. 295.

While Men Slept...

On the other hand, Augustine suggested that perhaps the Holy Spirit caused the translators of the Septuagint to give a varying version from what was originally written in Hebrew. He said:

> ...if anything is found in the original Hebrew in a different form from that in which these men [the seventy translators under the authority of the Egyptian king Ptolemy] have expressed it, I think we must give way to the dispensation of the Providence which used these men to bring it about...thus it is possible that they translated in such a way as the Holy Spirit, who worked in them and had given them all one voice, thought most suitable for the Gentiles.[35]

Even though there were other significant discrepancies between the Hebrew text and the Septuagint, Augustine said:

> ...any one who pleases has it in his power to correct this version, yet it is not unimportant to observe that no one has presumed to emend the Septuagint from the Hebrew text in the many places where they seem to disagree.[36]

Despite Augustine's conclusion that any deviation of the Greek Septuagint from the original Hebrew must have been by instruction by the Holy Spirit, he asserted that any deviation of the Latin texts from the Greek in the New Testament, must yield to the Greek.[37] Thus, Augustine accepted the Greek as authoritative in both the Old and New Testaments. This posed a problem for Augustine as Jerome (A.D. c.345-420) was considering translating the Old Testament for the Latin Vulgate from the Hebrew, instead of the Septuagint. Fearing that the Hebrew manuscripts would displace the revered Septuagint, Augustine strongly urged Jerome to use the Greek text as the basis for the

---

[35] *On Christian Doctrine*, bk. 2, written 397 A.D., J. F. Shaw, trans., In *A Select Library of the Nicene and Post-Nicene Fathers of the Christian Church*, vol.. 2, *St. Augustin's City of God and Christian Doctrine*, Philip Schaff, ed., 1886 ed. (Grand Rapids, Michigan: Reprinted by Wm. B. Eerdmans Publishing Co., 1979), p. 542.

[36] *St. Augustin's City of God*, p. 295.

[37] Ibid., p. 543.

Latin Vulgate Old Testament. Eventually, Augustine yielded and Jerome used the Hebrew text.[38]

While some believed that the Hebrew text needed to be amended by the text of the Septuagint because they thought the Hebrew text to be in error, such a view posed a problem to those relying upon the Latin Vulgate. As one author explains, to argue that the Septuagint was more reliable than the Hebrew would be:

> "…equal to saying that our Vulgate translation is erroneous, since it was translated from the Hebrew on, which they say is itself erroneous, and with which it accords without comparison better than with the one of the Septuagint.[39]

Jerome wrote that the book of Daniel was so corrupted in the Septuagint that, during his time, it was not read in the church. While Jerome used the Hebrew text as the basis for the Vulgate Old Testament, he defended the use of the Septuagint because by it the Gentiles had heard the prophecy of the coming of Christ.[40] (It should be noted that Daniel, Job, and several other books of the Old Testament were originally written in the language of the Chaldee.)[41]

The Greek New Testament

Challenges by Eusebius of Caesarea

Eusebius of Caesarea thus rejected the Hebrew Old Testament in favor of the Greek Septuagint for the Bibles he prepared for Constantine. He was also critical of the validity of several books of the New

---

[38] Philip Schaff, *History of the Christian Church: Nicene and Post-Nicene Christianity from Constantine the Great to Gregory the Great, A.D. 311-600*, vol. 3 (New York: Charles Scribner's Sons, 1886), p. 975.

[39] Mariana Monteiro, *The Life of Saint Jerome: The Great Doctor of the Church in Six Books from the Original Spanish of the Reverend Father Fray Jose de Siguenza, 1595* (London: Sands and Co., 1907), pp. 311-312.

[40] Monteiro, *The Life of Saint Jerome*, pp. 320-321.

[41] Desiderius Erasmus, *The Life of the Eminent Doctor Jerome of Stridon Composed Mainly from His Own Writings by Desiderius Erasmus of Rotterdam*, In *Collected Works of Erasmus*, James E. Brady and John C. Olin, eds. (Toronto: University of Toronto Press, 1992), pp. 34-35.

Testament. Just as he had oscillated on his Arian views, he also oscillated on his views of which Scriptures were true. Following Origen's lead, Eusebius of Caesarea either disputed or placed doubt on the authenticity of many books of the Bible, including Hebrews, James, 2 Peter, 2 John, 3 John, Jude, and Revelation (the Apocalypse of John).[42] Eusebius rejected the Apocalypse, even though Origen had accepted it.[43] Claiming that the Apocalypse of John had been forged to advance the cause of millenarianism, he outlined his view of the order of the writings of the New Testament, saying:

> After them is to be placed, if it really seem proper, the Apocalypse of John, concerning which we shall give the different opinions at the proper time.[44]

Church historian, Philip Schaff, explained the reason for the dispute. He wrote that the:

> ...Epistle to the Hebrews, the second and third Epistles of John, the second Epistle of Peter, the Epistle of James, and the Epistle of Jude were by many disputed as to their apostolic origin, and the book of Revelation was doubted by reason of its contents.[45]

According to Brooke Foss Westcott (1825-1901), who, as we shall learn, would have a major influence on the language of modern Bibles, Eusebius of Caesarea noticed the challenge to the authenticity of the Book of Hebrews. Because of the Book of Hebrews, doubts were being "...entertained by some on the authority of the Church of Rome."[46] In other words, some have concluded that the Books of

---

[42] Eusebius of Ceasarea, "The Church History of Eusebius," Arthur Cushman McGiffert, trans with Prolegomena and notes, bk. 3, ch. 25, In *A Select Library of Nicene and Post-Nicene Fathers of the Christian Church*, vol. 1, 2nd series, Philip Schaff and Henry Wace, eds. (Grand Rapids, Michigan: Wm. B. Eerdmans Publishing Company, 1979), pp. 154-156.

[43] Robert M. Grant, *Eusebius as Church Historian* (Oxford: Clarendon Press, 1980), p. 126-140.

[44] Eusebius, "The Church History of Eusebius," bk. 3, ch. 25, p. 156.

[45] Schaff, *History of the Christian Church,* vol. 3, p. 608.

[46] Westcott, *The Bible in the Church*, pp. 147-148.

Hebrews and Revelation were disputed because they might have been interpreted as challenging the Roman Church.

The Manuscripts During the Arian Resurgence

As we have learned, the official position of the Roman Church at the Council of Nicea in A.D. 325 concerning the deity of Jesus Christ was soon reversed. Dictated by his desire for unity, Constantine began to waiver within three years of the Council on his sternness against the opposition.[47] The Council did adopt the Nicene Creed, professing that God was expressed in three Persons, the Father, the Son, and the Holy Ghost, and Arius was banished from fellowship. However, there was a complete turnaround from that position within ten years. Arianism was proclaimed to be the truth and Athanasius, condemned as an advocate of error, took his turn in exile in A.D. 335.[48] In other words, just about the time Eusebius of Caesarea was preparing the Greek Bibles ordered by the Roman emperor, Arianism, which denied the deity of Jesus Christ, was becoming the dominant view of the official church.

Consequently, Arian views, especially those promoted by Origen, were particularly attractive. There is also strong evidence to support that Eusebius of Caesarea relied heavily upon the work of Origen to produce his Bibles. For example, Arthur Cushman McGiffert, the translator of *The Church History of Eusebius*, wrote:

> We learn from Jerome (*Praef. in librum Paralip.*) that Eusebius and Pamphilus published a number of copies of Origen's edition of the LXX., that is, of the fifth column of the Hexapla. A colophon found in a Vatican MS., and given in fac-simile in Migne's *Opera*, IV. 875, contains the following account of their labors (the translation is Lightfoot's): "It was transcribed from the editions of the Hexapla, and was corrected from the

---

[47] Archibald Robertson, "Prolegomena," *Select Writings and Letters of Athanasius, Bishop of Alexandria*, Archibald Robertson, ed., In *A Select Library of the Nicene and Post –Nicene Fathers of the Christian Church*, 2nd series, vol. 4, Philip Schaff and Henry Wace, eds. (Grand Rapids: Wm. B. Eerdmans Publishing Company, reprinted 1978; 1891), p. xxxiv.

[48] Nigg, *The Heretics*, pp. 128-129.

> Tetrapla of Origen himself, which also had been corrected and furnished with scholia in his own handwriting; whence I, Eusebius, added the scholia, Pamphilus and Eusebius corrected [this copy]."[49]

Philip Schaff summed up the effect of the Arian influence on Christianity as follows:

> Finally Christ cannot be a proper object of worship, as he is represented in Scripture and has always been regarded in the Church, without being strictly divine. To worship a creature is idolatry....The Arian error is cold and heartless, degrades Christ to the sphere of the creature, and endeavors to substitute a heathen deification of the creature for the true worship of God. For this reason also the faith in the true and essential deity of Christ has to this day an inexhaustible vitality, while the irrational Arian fiction of a half-deity, creating the world and yet himself created, long ago entirely outlived itself.[50]

Origen opened the door to Arianism when he insisted on the subordination of the Son to the Father.[51] Eusebius of Caesarea, as a dedicated follower of Origen, prepared the copies of the Bible ordered by Constantine, while the Roman Church was making resurgence toward Arianism. There is evidence that two of the surviving fourth century Greek manuscripts, the *Codex Vaticanus* (also known as Vaticanus B) and the *Codex Sinaiticus* (also known as Sinaiticus Aleph) manuscipts, were written by Eusebius of Caesarea.[52] The work was apparently based on the work of Origen and performed during a period of Arian resurgence. As we shall learn, the two copies were used as the primary basis for the revision of the Greek New Testament.

---

[49] McGiffert, "Prolegomena. The Life and Writings of Eusebius of Caesarea, The Life of Eusebius," p. 38.

[50] Schaff, *History of the Christian Church,* vol. 3, pp. 662-663.

[51] "De Decretis or Defence of the Nicene Definition," In *Select Writings and Letters of Athanasius, Bishop of Alexandria*, Robertson, ed., p. 174.

[52] Pamphilus, "The Life of the Blessed Emperor Constantine," p. 549n.

Section 2. The Method

While Men Slept...

Chapter 5. Redefining Global Christianity

> **...if it is a duty, to say that Eternity in relation to God has nothing to do with time or duration, are we not bound to say that also in reference to life or to punishment, it has nothing to do with time or duration?[1]**
>
> —F. D. Maurice

Unitarian Universalism and Christianity

The Sixteenth Century "Unitarian" Resurgence

A return to many of the values defined by the early Neo-Platonists and Arians was critical to defining a new universal Christianity. As we have learned, the teachings of Origen had a major influence on fourth century Arianism, which taught the denial of the divinity of Jesus Christ. In the sixteenth century, a resurgence of Unitarian thought developed in Eastern Europe, out of Transylvania, which is in the eastern region of modern Romania and bordering Hungary. In 1565, Transylvania was the location of active preaching against the doctrine of the Trinity.[2] It was Fausto Sozzini (1539-1604) who led the "Socinists," as they were called, in expounding the Unitarian doctrine. He outwardly conformed to the Roman Church and lived in Basel, Switzerland. However in his major published work, *De Jesu Christo servatore*, Sozzini rejected the "natural" deity of Christ, claiming that the Father made Him God's righteous, suffering Servant.[3]

Socinianism applied a rationalist interpretation of Scripture, reduced the role of Jesus from that of Savior to that of "One" teaching by good moral example, and advocated a wide tolerance for believers of all creeds. The Socinianists openly preached against the doctrine of

---

[1] Frederick Denison Maurice, *Theological Essays*, First Published in 1853, Introduced by Edward F. Carpenter (New York: Harper & Brothers, Publishers, 1957), p. 307.

[2] Walker et al., *A History of the Christian Church*, p. 535.

[3] Ibid., p. 536.

the Trinity.[4] Those who held the Socinian views were frequently called Unitarians.[5] Sozzini went to Transylvania and to Poland where he continued his teaching on the anti-Trinitarian doctrine. Although Socinianism was banished from Poland in 1658, "...it found supporters in Holland and even more in England, where it was to have considerable influence."[6]

Unitarians in England

As Socinianism moved into England, it influenced such well-known Englishmen as John Milton, John Locke, and Isaac Newton. They adopted the Arian view, denying the deity of Jesus Christ.[7] During the eighteenth century, the movement also significantly influenced Joseph Priestley (1733-1804), who became known as "the first great English Unitarian."[8] Priestley saw John Locke's beliefs as the precursor to his own Unitarian beliefs.[9] The liberal theology Priestley promoted in England, and later in America, was commonly called Unitarianism.[10] Eighteenth and nineteenth century Unitarians clarified their position in rejecting the Bible as the source of authority and in denying the divinity of Jesus Christ.[11] Unitarianism was distinguished by the conviction that reason was supreme over all church organizations and over all books.[12] [A description of many widely held Unitarian beliefs is presented in Appendix A.]

---

[4] Ibid., p. 535.

[5] Gerard Reedy, *The Bible and Reason: Anglicans and Scripture in Late Seventeenth-Century England* (Philadelphia: University of Pennsylvania Press, 1985), p. 119.

[6] Walker et al., *A History of the Christian Church,* p. 538.

[7] John White Chadwick, *Old and New Unitarian Belief* (Boston: Geo. H. Ellis, 1894), pp. 9-10.

[8] Ibid., p. 11.

[9] Young, *Religion and Enlightenment in Eighteenth-Century England*, p. 2.

[10] Wright, *The Beginnings of Unitarianism in America*, p. 200.

[11] David Robinson, *The Unitarians and Universalists* (Westport, Connecticut: Greenwood Press, 1985), p. 5.

[12] John Fletcher Hurst, *History of Rationalism Embracing A Survey of the Present State of Protestant Theology* (New York: Eaton Mains, 1901), p. 559.

Powerful Unitarian Influences

Joseph Priestley and Michael Maurice

Joseph Priestley was a well-known chemist who is known for the discovery of oxygen. It was as a Unitarian minister, however, that he exerted an enormous influence for the cause of Unitarianism on both sides of the Atlantic Ocean. While in England during 1792, Priestley was the morning preacher in a church in which the twenty-six year old Michael Maurice was appointed to be the afternoon preacher.[13] During the course of their relationship, Priestley, who was called "the lawgiver of the Unitarians," became the personal friend of Michael Maurice.[14]

Michael Maurice, born in 1766, attended the Hoxton Academy where he first came under the influence of professors who were either openly or secretly Unitarian. As a result of these influences, Michael emerged in 1786 as a Unitarian and as a political Liberal.[15] By 1787 Michael Maurice had become "zealous" in his Unitarian opinions."[16]

Michael Maurice and Priestley preached in the same church for two years. Priestley frequently spoke about the nature of religious rights and civil liberties. As his theological and political views became more controversial, however, he was forced to emigrate from England. [Priestley's expulsion occurred at a time of great political uncertainty amidst the French Revolution. In 1794, Michael Maurice helped Priestley pack up his books and scientific instruments to make his journey to the United States of America.[17, 18] [As we shall learn, Michael Maurice was to greatly influence the direction of global theology through his later influence on his son, Frederick Denison Maurice.]

[13] Frederick Maurice, ed., *The Life of Frederick Denison Maurice: Chiefly Told in His Own Letters*, vol. 1 (New York: Charles Scribner's Sons, 1884), p. 6.

[14] Ibid, pp. 9-10.

[15] Ibid., pp. 6-7.

[16] Ibid., p. 7.

[17] Gibson, *Church, State, and Society*, p. 51.

[18] Maurice, *The Life of Frederick Denison Maurice*, vol. 1, p. 8.

While Men Slept...

Priestley: Unitarianism from England to America

While in America, Priestley exerted a powerful Unitarian influence on American churches. During the latter part of the eighteenth century, Priestley founded Unitarian societies in Philadelphia. These societies were direct English transplants.[19] He also found that he had much in common with the liberal theology of key political leaders of the new nation of the United States of America. A characteristic of their liberal theology was a belief in freedom from the bonds of any specific doctrine.[20] Thomas Jefferson (1743-1826), one of the founding fathers and the third president of the United States, shared many of Priestley's Unitarian views, including his objection to the divinity of Jesus Christ.[21]

Such views by Jefferson and others were viewed as heresy under the acts of Parliament. Until that time, heresy was defined as follows:

> ...if a person brought up in the Christian religion denies the being of a God, or the Trinity, or asserts there are more gods than one, or denies the Christian religion to be true, or the scriptures to be of divine authority...Reason and free inquiry are the only effectual agents against error.[22]

According to Thomas Jefferson, the Virginia Convention of May 1776 declared that the exercise of religion in the State of Virginia should be free. By October 1776, all acts of Parliament that had rendered any opinions concerning religion were repealed.[23] Jefferson was convinced that freedom of inquiry concerning religion would have prevented the establishment of Christianity in the first place. He wrote:

---

[19] Jerry Wayne Brown, *The Rise of Biblical Criticism in America, 1800-1870: The New England Scholars* (Middletown, Connecticut: Wesleyan University Press, 1969), p. 60.

[20] Wright, *The Beginnings of Unitarianism in America*, p. 3.

[21] Thomas Jefferson, *The Writings of Thomas Jefferson*, Saul K. Padover, ed. (Lunenburg, Vermont: The George Macy Companies, Inc, 1967), p. 322.

[22] Ibid., pp. 300-301.

[23] Ibid., p. 300.

Had the Roman government permitted free inquiry, Christianity could never have been introduced. Had not free inquiry been indulged at the era of the reformation, the corruptions of Christianity could not have been purged away. If it be restrained now, the present corruptions will be protected, and new ones encouraged.[24]

So convinced was Jefferson that freedom of religion would bring people to a belief in Unitarianism, that he believed the entire country of the United States would soon be brought to a Unitarian belief. He wrote on June 26, 1822 that:

> ...I trust that there is not a young man now living in the United States who will not die a Unitarian.[25]

Emerson: Unitarianism from America back to England

Of course Jefferson was mistaken on the timing of the conversion of the United States toward Unitarianism. Influential Americans, however, picked up the Unitarian cause and articulated it on both sides of the ocean. One such influential American was Ralph Waldo Emerson (1803-1882). His theology reflected the pervasive thought by enlightened Unitarians in America that God can only be defined by reason. Well known as a writer, Emerson was also a Unitarian minister who preached Unitarianism throughout New England. Many of his sermons were based on individual verses, taken out of context. Nevertheless, Emerson effectively used them as the starting point from which to embark upon a discourse of his Unitarian views. For example, he used the following Scripture:

> But the natural man receiveth not the things of the Spirit of God: for they are foolishness unto him: neither can he know *them*, because they are spiritually discerned.
>
> —1 Corinthians 2:14

---

[24] Ibid., p. 301.
[25] Ibid., p. 360.

While Men Slept...

Using that Scripture, Emerson concluded that if we study the New Testament, we will find that most men do not listen to their "own inward Teacher." Instead, he said, they:

> ...will find that they are looking for heaven and for hell in an outward condition, instead of receiving that word of our Lord, "the kingdom of God is within you." We sit still and hope that our salvation will be wrought out for us, instead of working out our own...the time will come when we shall see as we are seen, we shall know as we are known, and shall become wise unto eternal life (1 Corinthians 13:12).[26] [Scripture reference and parenthesis is in the original.]

The implication in the conclusion of this sermon by Emerson, arrived at through partial references to selected Scriptures, was that we would become wise from within, from our own reason, and that this wisdom would be "eternal life." If one were to look at one of the referenced Scriptures more carefully and completely, it would be read as follows:

> For now we see through a glass, darkly; but then face to face: now I know in part; but then shall I know even as also I am known.
>
> —1 Corinthians 13:12

In other words, when we read the entire verse, it is learned that the Scripture is not directed to our own reason, but that it appears to be directed to Jesus Christ who will reveal hidden things to us. The Scripture says that, "...now we see through a glass darkly, but **then face to face....**" When we finally come face to face with Jesus Christ, the things that were a mystery to us will be seen clearly and understood.

Equipped with his Unitarian theology and excellent communication capabilities, Emerson left the United States in 1832 for Europe. After

---

[26] *The Complete Sermons of Ralph Waldo Emerson*, Ronald A. Bosco, ed. (Columbia and London: Ralph Waldo Emerson Memorial Association, University of Missouri Press, 1991), p. 194.

a visit to Rome, Emerson traveled to England where he made the acquaintance of John Stuart Mill (1806-1873), Thomas Carlyle (1795-1881), the poet-philosopher Samuel Taylor Coleridge (1772-1834), and others with whom he shared his Unitarian theological views.[27, 28]

F. D. Maurice: The Unitarian Anglican Priest

Building Upon Plato and Alexandrian Christianity

A key figure in moving the world toward a new universal Christianity was John Frederick Denison Maurice (1805-1872). F. D. Maurice was born as the son of Michael Maurice, the Unitarian minister who, as we have learned, had been associated with Joseph Priestley, and Priscilla (Hurry) Maurice in Normanstone near Lowestoft, England on August 29, 1805.[29] Throughout much of his life he dropped the use of his first name, John, and was known as Frederick Denison, or F. D. Maurice.[30] Building upon the teachings of Plato and Alexandrian Christianity, he influenced the minds that laid the foundations of most modern day versions of the Bible and set a course for merging the religions and governments of the world into a single system under the banner of Socialism. During his lifetime, F. D. Maurice had many roles that enabled him to be an important influence on the lives of those with whom he came in contact.

Although he frequently confused others concerning his true theology by using a circular writing style and by redefining words to suit his purposes, he espoused a definite Universalist and Unitarian theology. While maintaining what many believed to be heretical theological views, he was also an Anglican priest, a politically active Socialist, a university professor, a scholar of Greek philosophy, a scholar of early church history, and an author. Perhaps his most profound mark on the

---

[27] James Elliot Cabot, *A Memoir of Ralph Waldo Emerson* (Boston and New York: Houghton, Mifflin and Company, 1888), pp. 176-204.

[28] Gay Wilson Allen, *Waldo Emerson: A Biography* (New York: The Viking Press, 1981), p. 211.

[29] Maurice, *The Life of Frederick Denison Maurice*, vol. 1, pp. 1-8.

[30] Ibid., p. 1.

world, however, was left through his personal, and sometimes secretive, influence on the theological beliefs and lives of his young students and his colleagues. It was through this "behind the scenes" influence that he was able to deeply plant the seeds of Unitarian theology and global Socialism into post-Enlightenment Christian thought.

A Childhood Home with Theological Confusion

Like Joseph Priestley, F. D. Maurice was very fond of John Locke, who had been a strong proponent of Unitarian theology. Maurice prided himself on having the honor of being born on Locke's birthday, which was 173 years earlier on August 29, 1632.[31] Beyond any other writer, Locke was said to have been "the moving spirit of the eighteenth century."[32]

F. D. Maurice had three older sisters, Elizabeth, Mary, and Anne, and an older brother, William, who died before F. D. Maurice was born. He also had four younger sisters, Emma, Priscilla, and twins, Esther and Lucilla. After F. D. Maurice's birth his orphan cousins, Edmund and Anne Hurry, also lived in the Maurice household.[33]

The household of F. D. Maurice's early childhood was filled with dissent and confusion concerning religion. During the first years of F. D. Maurice's life, his mother, who had been raised in a Unitarian home, was apparently supportive of his father's Unitarian views.[34] However, as time progressed, the theological views of many of the members of the household underwent a significant change. They went from a Unitarian theology to one that believed in the death and resurrection of Jesus Christ for forgiveness of sins and everlasting life. That is, they believed in the deity of Jesus Christ.

---

[31] Ibid., pp. 14-15.

[32] Gerald R. Cragg, *Reason and Authority in the Eighteenth Century* (Cambridge: Cambridge University Press, 1964), pp. 5-6.

[33] Maurice, *The Life of Frederick Denison Maurice*, vol. 1, pp. 8, 27.

[34] Ibid., pp. 10-11.

Ironically, the event that triggered the change occurred on Easter Sunday in 1814 when F. D. Maurice's orphaned cousin, Edmund Hurry, became ill from a broken blood vessel. He eventually died several months later. Anne Hurry, while caring for her brother during his long illness, became convinced of the need for personal salvation, which the Unitarians did not teach.[35, 36]

Gradually, F. D. Maurice's sisters, Elizabeth, Anne, Mary, and Emma followed in rejecting Unitarianism. As such, they were influenced by the teachings of John Wesley. Gradually, their beliefs moved toward Calvinism, which was most offensive to the Unitarians, including Michael Maurice. Adding to Michael Maurice's grief, many in his family underwent a second baptism, seeming to cut themselves off entirely from their childhood. Gradually, Priscilla Maurice also rejected her husband's views.[37, 38, 39]

The revolt of his family against the Unitarian doctrine greatly distressed Michael Maurice.[40] As a result, he took charge of F. D. Maurice's education and forbade his older daughters from talking to his son about religion. As the religious differences in the household intensified, Mrs. Maurice wrote her husband a letter in 1821, when F. D. Maurice was sixteen years old, telling him that she could no longer worship with him.[41] She first became a Baptist and then a Calvinist. As a Baptist, she refused to allow her youngest daughter to be baptized until she reached sufficient age to make her own decision concerning baptism. The religious controversies in the family caused years of "moral confusion and contradictions" for young F. D. Maurice.[42]

---

[35] Ibid., p. 11.

[36] Ibid., p. 22.

[37] Ibid., p. 20.

[38] Ibid., p. 20.

[39] Ibid., p. 31.

[40] Ibid., p. 23.

[41] Ibid., p. 26.

[42] Ibid., pp. 20-21.

The confusion was fueled as Priscilla Maurice moved farther toward the Calvinist belief of salvation for a select body of believers, known as the "elect." This belief was diametrically opposed to the Universalist belief held by Michael Maurice, which was that the whole world was already saved. To add to the religious turmoil, Priscilla was convinced that, even though her older daughters would be saved, she was not among the "elect" and, therefore, would not receive salvation. F. D. Maurice's understanding that his mother believed she had not been selected for salvation while others in his family were chosen was to be remembered by him as an important influence on his early life.[43]

There remained, however, no middle ground between the Calvinistic beliefs of Priscilla and the Unitarian views of Michael. These great differences of opinion between his parents had a serious impact on F. D. Maurice's life. His mother's decision to openly separate from his father's Unitarian beliefs directly impacted Maurice's career choice. Both his father and mother wanted him to be a minister. His father wanted him to be a Unitarian minister, like himself, whereas his mother, even though she did not believe she was one of the "elect," expressed her hope that her son would become a minister of the "'everlasting Gospel.'"[44, 45] In order to avoid creating additional turmoil in his family, F. D. Maurice did not go to college to study for the ministry at all. Instead, he decided to study civil law at Cambridge University in 1823.[46]

German Influences through Julius Hare

Frederick Denison Maurice entered Cambridge University in 1823 with a mind that was confused about God. Those whom he loved in his family adhered to a "multiplicity of earnest creeds."[47] Soon after beginning his studies at the University, Maurice wrote to his mother

---

[43] Ibid., p. 29.

[44] Ibid., p. 19.

[45] Ibid., p. 30.

[46] Ibid., pp. 42-44.

[47] Ibid., p. 45.

telling her that he enjoyed a certain Baptist preacher, whom he had apparently heard often.[48] It was not long, however, before other influences led him away from the Baptist preacher and back toward the Unitarian roots of his father. One of Maurice's lecturers at Trinity College of Cambridge University, Julius Charles Hare (1795-1855), was destined to become a major influence in his life.[49] It was Hare who would help shape F. D. Maurice's Socialist, Unitarian, and Universalist thinking, as well as his entire personal and professional life.

Hare wrote of the tremendous influence that William Wordsworth and Samuel Taylor Coleridge had on his life in the dedication of his book, *Guesses at Truth*.[50] Like both Wordsworth and Coleridge, Hare spent time in Germany where he learned of the lives and philosophies of such influential Germans as Johann Wolfgang von Goethe (1749-1832) and Freidrich Schiller (Johann Cristoph Friedrich Schiller) (1759-1805). The writings of both Goethe and Schiller demonstrated their beliefs in religious universalism. For a time, Goethe boarded with a Swedenborgian and Schiller's thinking was heavily influenced by Kant (who as we have learned was influenced by Swedenborg's teachings on the divinity of human reason.)[51]

Hare later attended Trinity College at Cambridge in 1812 and, after success with his college examinations, took his place among the Fellows of Trinity in October 1818.[52] After spending some time traveling abroad, Hare studied law and began lecturing at Trinity College in 1822.[53]

---

[48] Ibid., p. 47.

[49] Ibid., p. 48.

[50] Julius Charles Hare, *To William Wordsworth*, In [*Augustus William and Julius Charles* Hare], *Guesses at Truth by Two Brothers*, new ed. (London: Macmillan and Co., 1876), pp. ix-xi.

[51] Hjalmar H. Boyesen, *Goethe and Schiller: Their Lives and Works, Including a Commentary on Goethe's Faust* (New York: Charles Scribners Sons, 1901), pp. 4, 12, 386, 409.

[52] Hare, *To William Wordsworth*, pp. xx-xxi.

[53] Ibid., p. xxiii.

While Men Slept...

During Hare's travels and studies, German philosophers and theologians who were challenging biblical Christianity influenced him toward anti-evangelical beliefs. Those influences were similar to those that had affected Samuel Taylor Coleridge, of whom Hare became a loyal disciple. Through Hare, the German anti-evangelical philosophy and theology of Coleridge was introduced to students at Cambridge University.

In particular, Hare's greatest success in promoting Coleridge's positions was through two of his brilliant students, F. D. Maurice and John Sterling (1806-1844). By 1824, both of these young men had become Hare's favorite students.[54] Coleridge was the guide for Hare, Maurice, and those who pioneered the new ways of understanding Christianity.[55]

Those "new ways" of understanding Christianity were actually void of the central biblical doctrines of Christianity. Speaking of Hare, James H. Rigg wrote:

> Yet it must not be forgotten in reading his writings, that Hare, with all his excellences and accomplishments, with all his wisdom and eloquence and Christian feeling, *was* seriously defective in his views of those doctrines which constitute the very heart of Christianity.[56]

Heavily influenced by German writers and theologians, Hare developed a significant interest in German textual criticism as it related to the Bible. He demonstrated that interest when he translated Schleiermacher's *Critical Essay on the Gospel of St. Luke*. Subjected to similar German influences as Samuel Taylor Coleridge, it was quite natural for Hare to also have a very high reverence for Coleridge. Hare was quoted as saying that Coleridge was the "true sovereign of modern English thought."[57]

---

[54] Distad, *Guessing at Truth: The Life of Julius Charles Hare*, p. 39.

[55] Bernard M.G. Reardon, *From Coleridge to Gore: A Century of Religious Thought in Britain* (London: Longman Group Ltd., 1971), p. 159.

[56] Rigg, *Modern Anglican Theology*, p. 241.

[57] Reardon, *From Coleridge to Gore*, p. 61.

According to Daniel Macmillan (1813-1857), Hare always spoke of Coleridge:

> ... in the most affectionate manner. He knew him well, and I fancy all who knew him personally think far more of him than those who knew him through his writings. Great as his writings are, it would appear that his best things were spoken. There seems to have been something in a company of men which raised him higher than he could ever rise with merely paper before him. The melody of his voice when delivering one of his long discourses must have been enchanting....[58]

Hare, who was ordained as a minister in 1826, taught Maurice the teachings of Plato. He somehow left a tremendous impression on his student about the concept of "unity" that was to occupy him throughout his lifetime.[59, 60] Although Maurice was not in the classes on the Greek New Testament that Hare had apparently taught, Hare's lectures on Sophocles and Plato had a lasting impact on the young student. Maurice relayed his perception of the influence of Hare's lectures on him this way:

> But to his lectures on Sophocles and Plato I can trace the most permanent effect on my character, and on all my modes of contemplating subjects, natural, human, and divine.[61]

Maurice understood that the "enlightened men in Germany, France, and England" were greatly indebted to Plato who taught them to seek wisdom from within their own hearts.[62]

---

[58] Thomas Hughes, *Memoir of Daniel Macmillan* (London: Macmillan and Co., 1882), p. 141.

[59] Charles R. Sanders, *Coleridge and the Broad Church Movement: Studies in S. T. Coleridge, Dr. Arnold of Rugby, J. C. Hare, Thomas Carlyle, and F. D. Maurice* (New York: Octagon Books, 1972), p. 123.

[60] Maurice, *The Life of Frederick Denison Maurice*, vol. 1, pp. 53-54.

[61] Ibid., pp. 53-54.

[62] Maurice, *The Life of Frederick Denison Maurice,* vol. 1, p. 81.

While Men Slept...

It appears that it was Hare who affirmed to Maurice the underlying concepts of Universalism and Socialism. Among the teachings of Hare was that Jesus' death on the cross was not one endured for sinners but, instead, it was His own self-sacrifice by which He gave character to his whole life.[63] According to Maurice's son, Frederick, his father attributed to Hare:

> ...first, the setting before his pupils of an ideal not for a few "religious" people, but for all mankind, which can lift men out of the sin which "assumes selfishness as the basis of all actions and life," and secondly, the teaching them [sic] that "there is a way out of party opinions which is not a compromise between them, but which is implied in both, and of which each is bearing witness." "Hare did not tell us this....Plato himself does not say it; he makes us feel it."[64]

Maurice understood the importance of Plato's teachings and the Alexandrian School and their influence on the Arian controversy. In a letter to Charles Kingsley in 1851 on the matter, Maurice said:

> To understand the Platonists of the fourth century I conceive you should read the Enneads of Plotinus, who belongs to the third. He is, I apprehend, immeasurably the greatest and the lawgiver of the rest. The life of Apollonius of Tyana by Philostratus will give you a notion of their efforts to combine miracle-working and a semi-divine person with philosophy....The Christian Alexandrian School is worthy to be thoroughly restudied, I should think; its influence on Athanasius and the Arian controversy was very great indeed.[65]

While encountering Julius Hare's teaching, studies on Plato and Greek philosophy, and issues of current events, Maurice insisted that he was

---

[63] Rigg, *Modern Anglican Theology,* p. 230.

[64] Maurice, *The Life of Frederick Denison Maurice*, vol. 1, p. 56.

[65] Frederick Maurice, ed., *The Life of Frederick Denison Maurice: Chiefly Told in His Own Letters*, vol. 2 (New York: Charles Scribner's Sons, 1884), pp. 56-57.

neither a Calvinist nor a Unitarian.[66] He asserted that he took neither of the two extreme positions. However, through the influence of Hare and others on his life, Maurice began to get a clearer picture of his own beliefs. By 1826, Maurice had confirmed in his mind that he did not want to be a *bona fide* member of the Church of England. However, he felt that he could not tell his family of his feelings without inflicting pain on them.[67]

Nevertheless, as the time approached for him to graduate from Cambridge University, Maurice came to a moment of decision. A requirement for receiving his degree was that he had to subscribe to the 36th Canon, which said he would support the doctrines of the Church of England. Even though he passed all of his examinations in 1827, Maurice was not offered a law degree because he refused to consent and adhere to the doctrines of the Church of England.[68] Therefore, Maurice left Cambridge without a degree. John Sterling, who was under the same influences as Maurice, also left Cambridge University in 1827.[69]

In 1828, Hare returned to Germany. While visiting Bonn, he contacted and met with German writers.[70] During that same year Julius Hare came to Maurice's aid and provided financial support to help him, and other members of a group known as the "Apostles Club," purchase the *Athenaeum* magazine. Maurice then became its editor and Sterling one of its major writers.[71, 72]

In addition to his influence on Maurice, Hare was creating significant controversy at Cambridge University because he favored admitting nonconformists to the University. He also favored abolishing the re-

---

[66] Ibid., p. 64.

[67] Ibid., p. 70.

[68] Ibid., pp. 71-73.

[69] *John Sterling,* In *Catholic World*, vol. 7, issue 42, Sept. 1868, p. 813.

[70] David Young, *F. D. Maurice and Unitarianism* (Oxford: Clarendon Press; New York: Oxford University Press, 1992), p. 111.

[71] Ibid., p. 102.

[72] *John Sterling,* In *Catholic World*, vol. 7, issue 42, Sept. 1868, p. 813.

quirement by the University that students attend chapel lectures on divinity.[73] Amidst this controversy, however, Maurice consulted Hare on the most critical decision facing him at this point in his life, which was whether to study theology at Oxford University.[74]

The Interconnected Lives of Hare, Maurice, and Sterling

During the following years, the lives of Hare, Maurice, and Sterling became interconnected by marriage. In 1837, Maurice married Anna Barton, with John Sterling as the officiating clergyman.[75] Since Sterling was married to Anna's sister, Susannah Barton, he and Maurice were brothers-in-law.[76, 77] On November 12, 1844, Hare married Maurice's sister, Esther.[78] Thus, Hare and Maurice were also brothers-in-law. Anna took ill with tuberculosis and died in March 1845.[79, 80] On July 4, 1849 Maurice married Hare's half-sister, Georgina.[81, 82] Thus, Maurice and Hare became double brothers-in-law. Hare further demonstrated the depth of their relationship by naming Maurice to be the executor of his estate upon his death.[83]

Maurice was totally involved with Hare. He described their relationship in a letter to Daniel Macmillan on January 24, 1855, the day after Hare's funeral:

> You will, I am sure, be grieved to hear that the battle is over with my dear brother Julius Hare. He died yesterday morning.

---

[73] Latourette, *Christianity in a Revolutionary Age*, vol. 2, p. 300.

[74] Maurice, *The Life of Frederick Denison Maurice*, vol. 1, pp. 99-104.

[75] Ibid., p. 234.

[76] Young, *F. D. Maurice and Unitarianism*, p. 101.

[77] James Anthony Froude, *Thomas Carlyle: A History of His Life in London, 1834-1881*, vol. 1 (New York: Charles Scribner's Sons, 1910), p. 33.

[78] Maurice, *The Life of Frederick Denison Maurice*, vol. 1, pp. 385-386.

[79] Ibid., p. 405.

[80] Young, *F. D. Maurice and Unitarianism*, p. 177.

[81] Maurice, *The Life of Frederick Denison Maurice*, vol. 1, p. 552.

[82] Young, *F. D. Maurice and Unitarianism*, p. 124.

[83] Rigg, *Modern Anglican Theology*, p. 169.

My whole life for the last eighteen years had been closely bound up with his, and nearly every joy or sorrow I have had has been connected with his home and with him.[84]

Founding the "Apostles Club"

Although members of Saint John's College founded the "Apostles Club" in 1820, it soon became centered at Trinity College. Consistent with its name, as after the Apostles of Christ, the club's membership was limited to twelve. F. D. Maurice joined the club in 1823 or 1824 while he was a student at Trinity College at Cambridge University. He then effectively reorganized it into a new club and led its reconstituted membership to such a high degree of intellectualism, introspection, soul-searching, and self-revelation that its members claimed they received metaphysical powers of spiritual regeneration.[85]

By 1830, the Apostles Club and F. D. Maurice had already become somewhat of a legend at Cambridge. A nineteen-year-old student summed up his awe of Maurice as follows:

I do not myself know Maurice, but I know well many whom he has known, and whom he has moulded like a second nature, and those, too, men eminent for intellectual powers, to whom the presence of a commanding spirit would, in all other cases, be a signal rather for rivalry than reverential acknowledge-ment.[86]

More significant than the fact that Maurice was credited with founding the Apostles Club is the impact that the club had on the minds of its members. The young student went on to say of Maurice:

The effect which he has produced on the minds of many at Cambridge by the single creation of the Society of the Apostles (for the spirit, though not the form, was created by him) is far

---

[84] Maurice, *The Life of Frederick Denison Maurice*, vol. 2, p. 255.

[85] Distad, *Guessing at Truth: The Life of Julius Charles Hare*, pp. 45-46.

[86] Maurice, *The Life of Frederick Denison Maurice*, vol. 1, p. 110.

greater than I can dare calculate, and will be felt, both directly and indirectly, in the age that is upon us.[87]

Julius Hare had a powerful influence on the Apostles Club during its early years. In particular, he helped instill into the Apostles a near god-like devotion to Samuel Taylor Coleridge and William Wordsworth.[88]

The legendary contributions of Maurice to the Apostles Club were so important that at the 1834 annual dinner of the Club he was toasted three times. Maurice's son read the following from a letter:

> "...they this year toasted him in his [Maurice's] absence three times; first as the author of the Club itself; second, as having taken orders since the last meeting; third, as the author of "Eustace Conway.""[89]

In 1849, the year after he had cofounded the Christian Socialist Movement, which we shall study further, Maurice had dinner at the Apostles Club expressing his fondness for the Club by writing, "...the bonds which connect me with them [the Apostles] are very sacred. I owe very much to them, more than anyone can tell."[90]

During the 1850s the members of The Apostles Club referred to it as "the Society." It then went underground and maintained itself with a long-prevailing secrecy.[91] The secret society was constantly changing and the selection of new members was made with the utmost care. When a name was brought forward for possible membership, each of the other members was required to become acquainted with the nominee before bringing him forward for a vote. During the years between 1855 and 1875, the society's members had major impacts on theological, scientific, and political changes that impacted the world. Dem-

---

[87] Ibid., p. 110.

[88] Distad, *Guessing at Truth: The Life of Julius Charles Hare*, p. 46.

[89] Maurice, *The Life of Frederick Denison Maurice*, vol. 1, p. 165.

[90] Ibid., p. 547.

[91] Distad, *Guessing at Truth: The Life of Julius Charles Hare*, p. 45.

onstrating the depth of the impact, the members included such names as Mill, Comte, Spencer, Strauss, Renan, Carlyle, Matthew Arnold, George Elliott, and Charles Darwin.[92] Henry Sidgwick (1838-1900), who served as the first president of the Psychical Research Society, said the Apostles' Club continually debated the "gravest subjects" and:

> ...the tie of attachment to the society is much the strongest corporated bond which I have known in life.[93]

Redefining the Meaning of "Eternal"

One of the key skills Maurice developed during his association with the Apostles Club was how to study words. Maurice's son said that Hare had trained his father in the skill. As such, Maurice was able to determine the "finer shades of meaning" associated with words. In doing so, Maurice was able to define words so they had meanings that were significantly different from those that almost everyone else attached to them. In writing of his father, F. D. Maurice, Frederick Maurice wrote, "He never believed in an absolute dictionary sense of a word."[94] He taught his students to make their own definitions of words by understanding the mind of the author.

A key example of Maurice's application of his skill in redefining words was in his treatment of the word "eternal," as translated from the Greek word "αιωνιος." He sought to distinguish the meaning "eternal" from that of the word "everlasting." He used his revised definition of the word to deny the concepts of "eternal life" in heaven and of "eternal damnation" in hell. Maurice said that the word "eternal" had nothing to do with duration. Instead, he insisted, it only meant having the knowledge of God. Thus, it appeared that Maurice had actually given a Gnostic meaning to the word "eternal." He said that if his unique definition of the word "eternal" were right with refer-

---

[92] Arthur Sidgwick and Eleanor Mildred Sidgwick, *Henry Sidgwick: A Memoir by A. S. and E. M. S.* (London: Macmillan and Co., Ltd., 1906), pp. 29-32.

[93] Arthur Sidgwick and Eleanor Mildred Sidgwick, *Henry Sidgwick: A Memoir*, p. 35.

[94] Maurice, *The Life of Frederick Denison Maurice*, vol. 2, p. 541.

ence to removing the duration dimension from eternal life, then it could also be used to remove the duration dimension with reference to punishment also. He stated:

> ...if it is a duty, to say that Eternity in relation to God has nothing to do with time or duration, are we not bound to say that also in reference to life or to punishment, it has nothing to do with time or duration?[95]

Thus, to Maurice, the word "eternal" required a new definition, which he was willing to supply. It was Maurice's conclusion that:

> ...eternal life is the knowledge of God who is Love, and eternal death the loss of that knowledge....[96]

F. D. Maurice's son went on to say that his father believed that the ability to carefully establish the meaning of words, which he cultivated at the Apostles Club, was one of the most important experiences of his life:

> I think, as he himself has in fact suggested, that Hare's training tended to this habit; but far more important in fixing it was that practical training in his meeting at first with Cambridge Undergraduates, especially with the members of the "Apostles Club,"...to which he habitually declared that he was more indebted than to almost any other experience in his life.[97]

The skills that Maurice had learned through Hare and the Apostles Club enabled him to give new meanings to words. He based his meanings on his subjective interpretation of words as he believed he understood the mind of the author. Therefore, if he could know the mind of God, as he believed, then he could give the words of God new meanings, based on his own reason. Thereby, it was possible to redefine the meaning of global Christianity, paving the way for the new Universal Christianity.

---

[95] Maurice, *Theological Essays*, p. 307.

[96] Ibid., p. 314.

[97] Maurice, *The Life of Frederick Denison Maurice*, vol. 2, p. 541.

Chapter 6. The Anglo-Catholic Path

The Catholic Church, I think, has established itself in the East and in the West, and is acknowledged by God as His kingdom upon earth.[1]

—F. D. Maurice

The Anglo-Catholic Oxford Movement

Maurice Goes to Oxford

As we have learned, Roman Catholicism had been suppressed in England since 1534. Although banned from England since their formation and from the entire world by the Roman Catholic Church from 1773 to 1814, the Jesuits did much to keep Roman Catholicism alive in England. As religious freedom was granted to the Roman Catholics of England through the Emancipation Act of 1829,[2] the Jesuits, who had a long connection with Oxford, were drawn toward the University.[3] Consequently, Oxford University became the center of a developing movement, which had the goal of moving the Anglican Church, and, through it, the Protestant churches, toward the Roman Catholic Church. During the year of the passage of the Catholic Emancipation Act, F. D. Maurice, with the consultation of Julius Hare, developed a strong attraction to what was becoming the center of a major Anglo-Catholic movement. By the fall of 1829 he had decided that he should enroll in Oxford University.[4, 5, 6]

---

[1] Maurice, *The Life of Frederick Denison Maurice*, vol. 1, p. 307.

[2] Rene Fulop-Miller, *The Power and Secret of the Jesuits*, F. S. Flint and D. F. Tait, trans. (New York: Viking Press, 1930), p. 118.

[3] Edwards, *The Jesuits in England: From 1580 to the Present Day*, p. 184.

[4] Maurice, *The Life of Frederick Denison Maurice*, vol. 1, p. 99.

[5] Latourette, *Christianity in a Revolutionary Age,* vol. 2, p. 264.

[6] R. W. Franklin, *Nineteenth-Century Churches: A History of a New Catholicism in Wurttemberg, England, and France*, In *Modern European History: A Garland Series of Outstanding Dissertations*, William H. McNeill, Gen. Ed. (New York and London: Garland Publishing, Inc., 1987), p. 5.

While Men Slept...

While much Anglo-Catholic activity was progressing at Oxford, John Henry Newman (1801-1890) identified the official beginning of the Oxford Movement with a sermon preached on July 14, 1833 by John Keble (1792-1866) entitled "National Apostasy."[7] The Oxford Movement represented the Roman Catholic revival within the Church of England. Ironically, July 14 was also Bastille Day, which marked the beginning of the 1789 French Revolution!

Maurice's Oxford Bonds

The bonds which F. D. Maurice developed at Oxford were strong. Arthur Maurice reflected upon the words of his father, F. D. Maurice, as he spoke about the influence of the "Oxford school" on those who became associated with it:

> He [F. D. Maurice] always spoke of it with a kind of shudder, as it were, of an escape from a charmed dungeon. "They never have allowed any one who has once come within their meshes to escape," was often his last sentence on the subject.[8]

Even before F. D. Maurice arrived at Oxford, he was well known by some of his future close associates. William Ewart Gladstone (1809-1898), who would later become the prime minister of England, was already very impressed by the accounts of Maurice's activities at Cambridge. Gladstone even founded the Essay Society, which was modeled after the Apostles Club that Maurice had effectively founded at Cambridge. After Maurice arrived at Oxford, he was admitted into the Essay Society and he became well acquainted with Gladstone.[9, 10]

---

[7] Horton Davies, *Worship and Theology in England from Watts and Wesley to Maurice, 1690-1850* (Princeton, New Jersey: Princeton University Press, 1961), p. 259.

[8] Maurice, *The Life of Frederick Denison Maurice*, vol. 1, p. 186.

[9] Ibid., pp. 108-109.

[10] John Morley, *The Life of William Ewart Gladstone*, 3 vols. in 2, vol. 1, new ed. (New York: The Macmillan Company, 1911), p. 54.

While at Oxford, Maurice also came in close contact with many other key men who were working toward establishing a new universal form of Christianity. While part of the Anglo-Roman Catholic movement, they became Maurice's lifelong friends and associates. They achieved international prominence in key positions either within the Church of England or within the Roman Catholic Church.

John Henry Newman, who later became a Roman Catholic cardinal, helped pave the way for the Anglo-Roman Catholic movement by his conversion to the Roman Catholic Church. Henry Edward Manning (1808-1892), whose father was a Member of Parliament, would also convert to the Roman Catholic Church, become an archbishop, become the leading proponent of the declaration of papal infallibility at the First Vatican Council, and be elected as a Roman Catholic cardinal. Samuel Wilberforce (1805-1873) would remain in the Church of England as the bishop of Oxford and then as the bishop of Winchester. Samuel Wilberforce's two brothers, Henry and Robert, would convert to the Roman Catholic Church. Arthur Penrhyn Stanley (1815-1881) would also remain in the Church of England and become the Dean of Westminster.[11, 12, 13, 14, 15]

Maurice's Theological "Conversion"

In addition to the reputation Maurice had made at Cambridge University through his involvement with the Apostles Club, he was also known as the nonconformist who had refused to submit to Creeds of the Church of England as a condition for receiving his law degree. Now that Maurice was going to Oxford to study for the priesthood of the Church of England, it appeared that he had reconsidered his theological position and was now ready to submit himself to the authority

[11] Maurice, *The Life of Frederick Denison Maurice*, vol. 1, p. 533.

[12] Walker et al., *A History of the Christian Church*, p. 643.

[13] David Newsome, *The Wilberforces and Henry Manning: The Parting of Friends* (Cambridge, Massachusetts: The Belknap Press of Harvard University Press, 1966), p. 67.

[14] Purcell, *Life of Cardinal Manning*, vol. 1, p. 1.

[15] Ibid., pp. 503, 595.

of the Church of England and its creeds. What had caused his "conversion?"

With the enactment of the Catholic Emancipation Act and the resulting increase in Anglo-Roman Catholic activity at Oxford, Maurice saw an opportunity to help move the Church of England toward the Roman Catholic Church. He became convinced that the Roman Catholic Church was the vehicle, which already existed, through which men could be brought together.[16] In his view, it was the means through which men could establish the earthly Kingdom of Christ. On the day before his ordination, F. D. Maurice wrote to his Unitarian father, Michael Maurice, of his desire to be a minister of the "Catholic and universal" church:

> I feel that the minister of the Gospel of peace, the minister of a Church which is called Catholic and universal, is bound to have a much lower opinion of himself than I have practically and habitually of myself, and also to feel a much more perfect and unlimited love towards all and each than has yet ever been shown forth in me.[17]

On August 8, 1841 F. D. Maurice wrote concerning his belief in the universal importance of the Catholic Church:

> The Catholic Church, I think, has established itself in the East and in the West, and is acknowledged by God as His kingdom upon earth.[18]

In Maurice's discussions concerning the "Catholic Church," he did not necessarily mean the "Roman Catholic Church," as most Catholics or Protestants understand it. Instead, he envisioned it as:

---

[16] Alec R. Vidler, *The Church in an Age of Revolution: 1789 to the Present Day* (Harmondsworth, Middlesex: Penguin Books Ltd, 1961), p. 84.

[17] Maurice, *The Life of Frederick Denison Maurice*, vol. 1, p. 158.

[18] Ibid., p. 307.

...a part, the highest part of that spiritual constitution of which the nation and the family are lower and subordinate parts....[19]

While at Oxford, Maurice appeared to have been "converted" because he accepted the requirements of the Church of England as he became ordained as an Anglican priest in 1834. Maurice's son, Frederick, obtained copies of his father's examination papers which were the basis for his admission as a priest of the Church of England. As a condition for his admission into the Anglican priesthood, F. D. Maurice's examination papers showed that he was required to:

> Specify some of those erroneous and strange doctrines which on your admission to the priesthood, you promise to "banish and put away." [Maurice listed eight of these doctrines, including]...The doctrine that the Father, Son, and Holy Ghost are not "in glory equal, in majesty co-eternal."[20]

As a condition for his admission as a priest in the Church of England, Maurice was required to promise that he would reject false doctrines, including his denial of the Trinity. However, as one looks more closely at Maurice's views on this subject, it is clear that he was able to say he agreed with the Trinitarian doctrines because he did not believe they meant what nearly everyone else thought they meant. It was his Unitarian belief that helped Maurice to understand that the unity of God is the grounds for unity of all men.[21]

Redefining Trinitarian Doctrine

In reality, Maurice had merely redefined his view of the Trinitarian doctrine to suit his Unitarian theology. He appeared to define his position with reference to his ability to accept "*a* Trinity" even though he rejected *the* Trinity. He wrote that:

---

[19] Ibid., p. 306.

[20] Ibid., pp. 159-160.

[21] Young, *F. D. Maurice and Unitarianism*, p. 207.

Many Unitarians still think as their fathers did, that the idea of a Trinity involves an utter contradiction—that every rational man must reject it. Many of them are aware that some of the deepest minds in the world have felt that the acknowledgement of a Trinity was necessary to their reason. But they are careful to observe that *this* is not the Trinity of which we speak; if they should ever come to accept *a* Trinity as a portion of their belief they would still, they say, not be stooping to a creed. That act would be a sign of Progress, not retrogression; they would welcome a discovery of philosophy, not surrender themselves to a religious tradition.[22]

Maurice had an exchange with Henry Solly, a Unitarian minister, which demonstrated his perspective on this topic. Solly explained to Maurice that he had rejected the Athanasian Creed because it asserted the equality of the Son and the Father. Solly wrote of Maurice's response:

"Well," replied Maurice, "that, you know, was the ground on which Coleridge rejected it, but for my own part, I do not see that it does."[23]

Maurice had his own definition of the Trinitarian doctrine. He defined it differently than both the Trinitarians and Unitarians. He acknowledged that, even though he may have pretended to do so, he did not believe in the doctrine of the Trinity as conventionally defined. He said in his *Theological Essays* that if a Unitarian did not accept his unique definition of a Trinity, then:

Let him cling to his belief in a One God; let him hold fast to the name of the Father. I do not dread his zeal, but his indifference; not his grasp of his own convictions, but his inclination to use them as weapons against other men. While *we* use the doctrine of the Trinity in that way, I am certain we shall not believe it, whatever we may pretend.[24]

---

[22] Maurice, *Theological Essays*, p. 295.

[23] Solly, *These Eighty Years, vol. 2*, p. 108.

[24] Maurice, *Theological Essays*, p. 299.

Maurice's "Kingdom"

Unity of Church and State

In his book, *The Kingdom of Christ*, F. D. Maurice challenged the doctrines of the Protestant churches in a series of letters directed toward the Society of Friends (Quaker) Church. He sharply criticized George Fox, the founder of the Quakers, whom he called "…the shoemaker of the seventeenth century…who hated Greek and Philosophy most cordially…." He also criticized Fox for taking Scripture literally rather than metaphorically.[25]   Maurice especially challenged Fox's belief that the Kingdom of God is spiritual and not physical.

Maurice was profoundly influenced by Derwent Coleridge (1800-1883), the second son of Samuel Taylor Coleridge.[26] In dedicating the Second Edition of *The Kingdom of Christ* to Derwent Coleridge, Maurice explained that his own system of theological and ecclesiastical idealism was a further development of the ideas of Samuel Taylor Coleridge. Those ideas were related to God and man, mind and matter, philosophy and morals, and to church and state. Influenced by the ideas of Samuel Taylor Coleridge, who had been significantly influenced by the ideas of the French Revolution, Maurice argued that politics and religion were inseparable and that Socialism was the better alternative to individualistic and competitive capitalism.[27, 28]

Maurice may have "borrowed" the title and the underlying concept of his book, *The Kingdom of Christ*, from Augustine, who wrote, "...the Church even now is the kingdom of Christ, and the kingdom of heaven."[29] However, Augustine's view included the heavenly dimen-

---

[25] Frederick Denison Maurice, *The Kingdom of Christ or Hints to a Quaker Respecting the Principles, Constitution and Ordinances of the Catholic Church*, vol. 1, new ed. based on the 1842 2nd ed. of, Alec R. Vidler, ed. (London: SCM Press Ltd, 1958), pp. 56-57.

[26] Rigg, *Memoir of Canon Kingsley*, In Rigg, *Modern Anglican Theology,* p. 26.

[27] Ibid., p. 48.

[28] Reardon, *From Coleridge to Gore*, p. 61.

[29] *St. Augustin's City of God*, p. 430.

sion whereas Maurice's view was only physical and earthly. Augustine continued speaking of the church as he wrote:

> For they reign with Him who do what the apostle says, "If ye
> be risen with Christ, mind the things which are above, where
> Christ sitteth at the right hand of God. Seek those things which
> are above, not the things which are on the earth." [Scripture
> reference- Colossians 3:1-2, version is not stated.][30]

Maurice took the basic concept as presented by Augustine that the
Kingdom of Christ was the church. Then, however, Maurice took it
out of heaven and placed it only on the physical earth, to be made by
the efforts of man. He argued not only that the "Kingdom of Christ"
was physical and not spiritual, but also that it was earthly and not
heavenly. Maurice insisted that the "Kingdom of Christ" already existed on earth and that it was the Catholic Church.[31]

Maurice taught that the church and state must be in unity. His view
was that a unified church and state would work together to establish
the ideal society. Even though Maurice held Unitarian views and the
Roman Catholic Church had, since its formation during the time of
Constantine, officially embraced Trinitarianism, he maintained that
the moral authority of the world belonged to the papacy. Maurice
wrote:

> Once separate the belief of Christ's kingdom from this sys-
> tem, once believe that they are not necessary to each other,
> and the moral power of the papacy is gone. What signifies it,
> then, if all the physical power in the universe should for a time
> be granted to it, if kings should send presents to it, if all forms
> of infidelity and false worship should combine themselves with
> it? The Church may then with confidence take up the lan-
> guage of the prophet, "Associate yourselves, and ye shall be
> broken in pieces; gird yourselves, and ye shall be broken in

---

[30] Ibid., p. 430.

[31] Maurice, *The Kingdom of Christ*, 1958, vol. 1, p. 282.

pieces; take counsel together, and it shall come to nought, for GOD IS WITH US."[32]

The Church of England: The Universal Church Unifier

Maurice did not like the term "Protestant Church" and rejected the concept of a church united merely because of the profession of a certain doctrine.[33] Instead, he promoted a "Catholic" world in which the universal church and the state would be unified. Maurice saw the English Church (the Anglican Church) as the unifier of the universal church. He said:

> I then proceed to consider the position of the English Church as enabling us, if we will, to unite ourselves with any part of the Eastern or Western Church which will meet us on the ground of our Catholic institutions, provided it recognises the true Centre of Unity; as enabling us, on the other hand, to unite with any Protestants on the ground of our recognition of that true centre, provided they do not refuse to adopt the Catholic institutions which connect us with that centre, and with each other.[34]

But how could such a universal Christianity be established? Maurice was encouraged to learn in 1841 that the king of Prussia had entered into negotiations with the "Heads of the English Church," which reportedly said:

> All parties agreed in the conviction that the diversities of Christian worship according to languages and nations, and according to the peculiarities and historical development of each nation—that is to say, in the Protestant Church—are upheld by a superior unity, the Head of the Church Himself, and that in this unity, to which all the diversities refer, as to their centre, is the foundation of true Christian toleration. By a cordial

---

[32] Ibid. vol. 2, 1958, p. 287.

[33] Maurice, *The Life of Frederick Denison Maurice*, vol. 1, p. 325.

[34] Ibid., p. 326.

co-operation directed in this spirit, a distinct bishopric has been founded in Jerusalem, in which all Protestant Christians may find a common support and point of union in respect of the Turkish government, and in all cases when their representation as one Church may be necessary.[35]

Christianity Without the Sacrifice for Sin

While embracing a new universal Christianity, Maurice strongly supported the Unitarian position of denying the atoning sacrifice of Jesus Christ. Maurice explained that:

The Unitarians were the great assertors of the absolute unqualified love of God, in opposition to all mythologies and theologies which had preceded. And Unitarianism was the first of all theologies or mythologies which *denied* that the Almighty had, in his own person, by some act of condescension and sacrifice, interfered to redress the evils and miseries of his creatures![36]

---

[35] Ibid., pp. 324-325.

[36] Maurice, *The Kingdom of Christ*, vol. 1, 1958, p. 136.

Chapter 7. Christian Socialism: The Earthly Heaven

> **The idea of Christian Communism has been a most vigorous and generative one in all ages, and must be destined to a full development in ours.**[1]
>
> —F. D. Maurice

Heaven on Earth

Garden of Eden

Ever since the episode in the Garden of Eden when men and women lost their right to live in harmony with God and His creation, man has been searching for a way to regain that which he lost. In Eden , the LORD God (יהוה אלהים) (YHWH Elohiym) provided everything that was needed. According to the Book of Genesis:

> And the LORD God planted a garden eastward in Eden; and there he put the man whom he had formed. And out of the ground made the LORD God to grow every tree that is pleasant to the sight, and good for food; the tree of life also in the midst of the garden, and the tree of knowledge of good and evil.
>
> —Genesis 2:8-9

The only thing man had to do to continue to live in the Garden was to obey God. It seemed like a pretty simple task. Everything in the entire Garden could be eaten except for the fruit that came from one tree, the tree of knowledge of good and evil:

> And the LORD God commanded the man, saying, Of every tree of the garden thou mayest freely eat: But of the tree of the knowledge of good and evil, thou shalt not eat of it: for in the day that thou eatest thereof thou shalt surely die.
>
> —Genesis 2:16-17

---

[1] Maurice, *The Life of Frederick Denison Maurice*, vol. 2, p. 7.

While Men Slept...

The LORD was asking man to trust Him. He said He would let the man, whom He called Adam, freely eat of every tree of the Garden, except one. This tree that God told the man not to eat of was one that contained a certain kind of knowledge. In Hebrew, the word is דעת, or *da'ath*. In Latin, the word is *scientiae*, and is the basis for the modern English word, *science*. In Greek, the word is γνωσις, or *gnosis*. To put the command of God into modern English, He did not want man to eat of the tree that contained a certain kind of *science*, *gnosis*, or *knowledge*. It was His will that man be limited in that certain knowledge. That kind of knowledge was reserved for God and was not for man.

But there was a great temptation given to the woman to eat of the forbidden tree. That temptation was to have her eyes opened, or to be *enlightened*. Once *enlightened* she and the man would become like a god, knowing good and evil. They would then depend upon their own reason rather than upon the wisdom of God.

> For God doth know that in the day ye eat thereof, then your eyes shall be opened, and ye shall be as gods, knowing good and evil.
>
> —Genesis 3:5

But they willfully disobeyed the LORD God. They ate of the forbidden tree and had their eyes opened, knowing good and evil. It might be said that they were *enlightened*. But the cost was great. They descended to a fallen state. Because Adam had listened to his wife and disobeyed God, he was destined to till the ground and was removed from the presence of the tree of life that, should he also eat of it, would give him everlasting life:

> And the LORD God said, Behold, the man is become as one of us, to know good and evil: and now, lest he put forth his hand, and take also of the tree of life, and eat, and live for ever: Therefore the LORD God sent him forth from the garden of Eden, to till the ground from whence he was taken.
>
> –Genesis 3:22-23

If man had both the knowledge of good and evil *and* everlasting life, then he would indeed compete directly with God forever. It was unacceptable to God to let the fallen man live forever. Because of disobedience to His Word, God sent man out of the place of perfect order. Ever since, mankind has been trying to get back to that state of order on his own terms, without God. Using enlightened reason, being like a god in the sense of knowing good from evil, man is still trying to get back to the Garden. He is trying to create his own Garden, his own heaven on earth, where all things are in perfect order.

Platonic Socialism

It is this desire of man to create a world in which all people would live in ordered harmony, provide for the needs of each other, and be ruled by the "Enlightened Ones" that underlies the global Socialist movement. In teaching the foundations for modern Socialism, Plato taught that human reason could attain truth and certainty. He also stated that a genuine philosopher, without personal prejudices, could ascend to the home of the gods in which the essence of all things that are true and beautiful dwell. He held that the purified soul of the true philosopher could attain that supercelestial sphere.[2]

When one achieves this higher level of knowledge, he is said to be "enlightened" and like the gods because he has obtained the secret and mystical knowledge that unlocks the secrets of the universe. Plato believed, however, that this level of knowledge could only be obtained by some. The masses, he believed, were incapable of comprehending it. Therefore, only those who are enlightened with this level of knowledge should be allowed to rule the masses.

Plato taught that the classes of people in this world could be categorized into three groups. They are the philosophers or enlightened ones, the guardians or enforcers, and the workers or producers. He taught that the philosophers must direct the state (or city), the enforcers or warriors must defend the state, and the workers or producers must produce the things needed by the state. As such, Plato taught that

---

[2] Rigg, *Modern Anglican Theology,* p. 127.

man could create an ideal state where all would dwell in ordered harmony.[3] The ordered harmony that Plato described was actually that of a Communistic society, where all things are held in common. Plato described it this way:

> If a city is to achieve the height of good government, wives must be in common, children and all their education must be in common, their way of life, whether in peace or war, must be in common....[4]

Plato's pupil, Aristotle (384-322 B.C.), played a major role in spreading Greek philosophy. As the teacher of Alexander the Great, his philosophies were rapidly spread throughout the vast regions of the known world, which had been swiftly conquered by the young leader of the Greek Empire.[5] Through Alexander's conquests, he spread Greek culture and philosophy, as taught by Plato and Aristotle, throughout the empire, including Alexandria, Egypt.

While some, such as the Alexandrian theologian, Origen, readily accepted and taught the philosophies of Plato, others thought his proposals seemed idealistic and unachievable. Thomas More, for example, satirically presented a society such as that proposed by Plato in his 1516 book, *Utopia*.[6] He told of a mythical island where all would live in Socialistic harmony. However, he presented it as a fantasy that could never be achieved. He even gave the island the name "Utopia," which was derived from the Greek, ου τοποσ, meaning, "no place." Others, however, have taken Plato's teachings very seriously and have picked up both the word and concept of "Utopia" as a realistically achievable goal.

---

[3] Plato, *The Republic*, In *Plato: Complete Works*, John M. Cooper and D. S. Hutchinson, eds. (Indianapolis, Indiana: Hackett Publishing Company, 1997), pp. 971-1223.

[4] Ibid., p. 1155.

[5] Charles Anthon, *A Manual of Greek Literature from the Earliest Authentic Periods to the Close of the Byzantine Era* (New York: Harper & Brothers, 1853), pp. 329-330.

[6] Thomas More, *Utopia*, with an Introduction by Jenny Mezciems (New York and Toronto: Alfred A. Knopf, 1992).

Hegel and Coleridge: The Bridge to England

The Evangelical Christian Revival of the eighteenth century, called the Great Awakening, led by the preaching of John Wesley (1703-1791) and others, brought a revitalization to Christianity through a renewed faith in Jesus Christ.[7] Shortly, however, there was a resurgence of Plato-styled thinking that went back to the concept that everything in nature could be explained through science, or knowledge. Behind this thinking was the belief that once one was "enlightened" there was nothing that could not be achieved.

Two thinkers emerged in the late 1700's who were to have significant influences on philosophies that would lead to great global changes in the nineteenth and twentieth centuries. They were Georg Hegel (1770-1831), a German philosopher, and Samuel Taylor Coleridge, an English poet and philosopher.[8, 9] Both were able to exert a tremendous influence on the minds of nineteenth century theologians and philosophers which led to their rejecting orthodox Christian beliefs as well as biblical authority. Once these underlying principles of belief were rejected, the foundation was laid for working toward a blended system of universal religion and of global Socialism.

Hegel intended to pursue a life in the ministry and, therefore, attended the Protestant Seminary in Tubingen, Germany.[10] As he progressed in his studies, however, Hegel became more convinced that it was through philosophy and not religion that truly important issues could be addressed. In his view, philosophy, rather than religion or art, was the medium through which absolute issues concerning nature, society, and God could be reconciled.[11]

Much like the Alexandrian Neo-Platonists in the early centuries of Christianity, Hegel believed reason governed the world. He defined

---

[7] Latourette, *A History of Christianity*, vol. 2, p. 827.

[8] Ibid., p. 1124.

[9] Ibid., p. 1172.

[10] John E. Toews, *Hegelianism: The Path Toward Dialectical Humanism, 1805-1841* (Cambridge: Cambridge University Press, 1980), p. 13.

[11] Ibid., p. 51.

God as being the absolute reason, who is everlastingly developing Himself in history.[12] Therefore, according to Hegel's perspective, reason became the basis for the absolute. As one writer explains it, Hegel believed that the "...ultimate reconciliation of man and God was achieved only when religious consciousness comprehended itself in the activity of absolute knowledge."[13] Hegel considered the historical sequence of philosophical ideas as crucial and promoted the idea of a new concept emerging out of two opposing concepts. Using the terms, "thesis," "antithesis," and "synthesis," he proposed that a new alternative is born out of two opposing alternatives in a dialectical process.[14] The philosophy of Hegel and its derivations is at the core of the philosophy of Marxism.[15]

As with many of the eighteenth and nineteenth century philosophers, Samuel Taylor Coleridge's earliest beliefs were also traditional and Christian. His father, who was a clergyman in the Church of England, died when Samuel was eight years old. Thereafter, Coleridge attended a school for the orphans of clergymen.[16] In 1791, during the French Revolution, Samuel Taylor Coleridge went to Jesus College, Cambridge. There he progressed toward a theology that led him to plan on becoming a Unitarian minister.[17, 18] Coleridge developed a deep interest in Platonic mysticism and German philosophy.[19]

---

[12] *Georg Wilhelm Friedrich Hegel's Leben, beschrieben durch* Karl Rosenkranz, Berlin, 1844, Review Art. IV. In *The Princeton Review*, October 1848, pp. 586-587.

[13] John E. Toews, *Hegelianism,* p. 66.

[14] Latourette, *A History of Christianity*, vol. 2, p. 1124.

[15] G. N. G. Orsini, *Coleridge and German Idealism: A Study in the History of Philosophy with Unpublished Materials from Coleridge's Manuscripts* (Carbondale: Southern Illinois University Press, 1969), p. 239.

[16] Ibid., p. 4.

[17] H. M. Margoliouth, *Wordsworth and Coleridge 1795-1834* (London: Oxford University Press, 1953), p. 1.

[18] Latourette, *A History of Christianity*, vol. 2, p. 1172.

[19] Kenneth Scott Latourette, *Christianity in a Revolutionary Age, A History of Christianity in the Nineteenth and Twentieth Centuries,* vol. 2, *The Nineteenth Century in Europe-The Protestant and Eastern Churches* (New York: Harper & Brothers, Publishers, 1959), p. 262.

Coleridge met William Wordsworth (1770-1850) in 1795 and the two visited Germany in 1798. While in Germany, they sought to learn German philosophy, acquire the language, study the natural sciences, and study the great authors of that country.[20, 21] There, Coleridge became enamored with Transcendentalist and Neo-Platonistic philosophies. He became more acquainted with the masters of German literature as well as with the thought of German philosophers, such as Immanuel Kant.[22, 23] Coleridge's thinking was significantly influenced by the writings of Kant. Neo-Platonic mysticism became the core of Coleridge's philosophical Pantheism.[24, 25]

Under the influence of the Alexandrian Neo-Platonists, such as Plotinus, Coleridge embraced the mystical doctrine that reason was a beam of the Uncreated Light, or a Divine Spark in the soul.[26] According to Coleridge, "...Reason is the supreme reality, the only true Being in all things visible and invisible...."[27] He further stated that:

> ...Reason is Being, the Supreme Being contemplated objectively, and in abstraction from the personality. The Word, or Logos, is life and communicates life; is light and communicates light. Now this light, contemplated *in abstracto*, is reason...when we speak of ourselves as possessing reason; and this we can no otherwise define than as the capability with which God had endowed man of beholding, or being conscious of, the Divine Light. But this very capability is itself that light, not as the Divine light, but as the life or indwelling

---

[20] Margoliouth, *Wordsworth and Coleridge*, p. 2.

[21] Ibid., pp. 41-48.

[22] *Review of the Works of S. T. Coleridge*, In *The Princeton Review*, vol. 20, No. 2, April 1848, p. 152.

[23] Walker et al., *A History of the Christian Church*, p. 640.

[24] Orsini, *Coleridge and German Idealism*, p. 34.

[25] Rigg, *Modern Anglican Theology*, p. 146.

[26] William Kaye Fleming, *Mysticism in Christianity* (New York and Chicago: Fleming H. Revell Company, 1913), pp. 252-253.

[27] Samuel Taylor Coleridge, *Dialogue between Demosius and Mystes, Church and State*, 1852 ed., p. 221, Quoted In Rigg, *Modern Anglican Theology*, p. 146.

of the living Word [Logos], which is our light; that is a life whereby we are capable of the light, and by which the light is present to us, a being which we may call ours, but which I cannot call *mine*; for it is the life that we individualise, while the light, as its correlative opposite, remains universal.[28]

Coleridge, like Emerson and others of similar mind, eclectically used the manipulation of Scripture to make it fit his purpose. For example, Coleridge perverted the meaning of Paul's letter to the Corinthians in which Paul said that the natural man cannot understand spiritual things:

> For what man knoweth the things of a man, save the spirit of man which is in him? even so the things of God knoweth no man, but the Spirit of God. Now we have received, not the spirit of the world, but the spirit which is of God; that we might know the things that are freely given to us of God. Which things also we speak, not in the words which man's wisdom teacheth, but which the Holy Ghost teacheth; comparing spiritual things with spiritual. But the natural man receiveth not the things of the Spirit of God: for they are foolishness unto him: neither can he know *them*, because they are spiritually discerned. But he that is spiritual judgeth all things, yet he himself is judged of no man. For who hath known the mind of the Lord, that he may instruct him? But we have the mind of Christ.
>
> —1 Corinthians 2:11-16

Coleridge interpreted the above Scripture to say that the "natural man" meant one who had logical understanding, which was the "spirit of the world." He saw the "spiritual man" as meaning one who had the "mind of Christ," who was none other than the one who understands truth by the light of the "intuitive Reason." Thus, by his interpretation, Reason or the Logos are made to be the discoveries of the Holy Spirit to the soul of man.[29] Thus, like Hegel, Coleridge subjected

---

[28] Samuel Taylor Coleridge, *Lay Sermons*, 1827, p. 73, Quoted in Rigg, *Modern Anglican Theology,* p. 147.

[29] Rigg, *Modern Anglican Theology,* p. 148.

faith to reason. Coleridge used the German terms for reason (*Vernunft*) and for understanding (*Verstand*) to try to make a distinction between the two. Using reason, one might accept a multitude of facts and principles that he might otherwise reject with his understanding. Everything depended on one's ability to make this distinction.[30]

Much more can be said of Coleridge's Neo-Platonic and Transcendental philosophies. However, much of his philosophy can be confusing. Perhaps that is because during much of Coleridge's life he seemed to be in a state of confusion. His writing was extemporaneous, containing whatever entered his mind at the moment. Many felt, however, that there was a "strange enchantment" associated with his conversation.[31] He suffered greatly throughout much of his life because of his dependency on alcohol and opium.[32] This dependency was believed by some to have weighed against the probability that he possessed the faculty of a clear and steadfast vision, or the ability to exercise wise judgment, especially in areas of religion and morality.[33]

Socialism in England

Nevertheless, Coleridge was an important bridge between the philosophy of the Germans, such as Kant, and the philosophers and theologians in England who were ready to embrace the Neo-Platonic philosophy. After Coleridge brought German philosophy to England, the concept of changing the order of society spread very rapidly. In 1795, Coleridge promoted the revolutionary nature of Christianity by speaking of Christ as a reformer and by emphasizing the poverty of the apostles.[34]

Robert Owen (1771-1858), influenced by the emerging popularity of Plato and the "enlightened" thinking of Coleridge and Hegel, pro-

---

[30] *John Sterling*, In *Catholic World*, vol. 7, issue 42, Sept. 1868, p. 812.

[31] *Review of the Works of S. T. Coleridge*, In *The Princeton Review*, vol. 20, No. 2, April 1848, p. 160.

[32] Ibid., pp. 155-156.

[33] Rigg, *Modern Anglican Theology*, p. 123.

[34] Gibson, *Church, State, and Society*, p. 50.

posed that "villages of cooperation" be built where everyone would work together in harmony, for the good of all. So convinced was Owen that the Socialist concept would work, that he moved to Indiana in 1825 to set up "New Harmony," a model community to demonstrate how an ideal community should operate.[35] However, Owen's efforts failed by 1835, partly because he had initiated a campaign of antireligious propaganda.[36]

Those who agreed with and were followers of Owen were called "Owenites." They believed that industrial wealth should be owned in common. The first use of the terms "Socialism" or "Socialists" in English occurred in November 1827 in the "Cooperative Magazine" to describe the views of Robert Owen.[37] After the introduction of these terms, Owen's supporters who accepted the principles of Communism were called "Socialists." These converts of Owen were the source of the Chartist Movement in England.[38]

1848: The Year of the Socialist Revolutions

The New Order from France

Interest intensified in movements toward Socialism and in changing the existing order of nations. In 1848, revolutions shook much of Europe. In France, for example, the 1848 Revolution was used as a basis to re-establish the new order that had been created by the 1789 French Revolution. The French proposed that they should serve as a model for the rest of the world. As one writer explained:

> Frenchmen, it is for you to give to the world the example which Paris has given to France; prepare yourselves by order

---

[35] *Introduction to Utopianism and Education*, John F. C. Harrison, ed. (New York: Teachers College Press, Teachers College, Columbia University, 1968), p. 4.

[36] John C. Cort, *Christian Socialism: An Informal History* (Maryknowll, NY: Orbis Books, 1988), p. 141.

[37] Cort, *Christian Socialism: An Informal History*, p. 141.

[38] Mark Hovell, *The Chartist Movement*, T. F. Tout, ed. (Manchester: Manchester University Press and London: Longmans, Green & Co., 1918), p. 47.

and by confidence in your destiny for the firm institutions which you are about to be called upon to establish.[39]

Sparked by a revolt in Paris in February, revolts spread throughout Austria, Prussia, Hungary, Bohemia, and parts of Italy. Rebellion in Rome led to the assassination of Pellegrino Rossi, the prime minister who had only recently been appointed to that position by Pope Pius IX. The pope fled Rome in the disguise of a simple priest.[40]

The "Communist Manifesto"

While in 1848 bloody revolutions were raging throughout Europe, Russia and England were conspicuously isolated from the revolts. There was, however, another kind of revolution taking place in England, which laid the foundation for the 1917 bloody revolution that occurred within seventy years in Russia. It was in England in 1848 that the Germans Karl Marx (1818-1883) and Friedrich Engels (1820-1895) issued the *Communist Manifesto*, advocating a revolutionary struggle between classes as a means for achieving Socialism.[41] The Communist philosophy behind the Russian revolution was then spread to places like China, North Korea, Cuba, and Albania.

Marx was born as a Jew but was raised as a Christian. His philosophy of history was largely shaped by the influence of Hegel. Engels, who was also born as a Jew, was the son of a cotton industrialist in Manchester, England. Significantly, the Marxist form of Socialism denounced the church. They believed that the church, as well as the bourgeoisie, which was the class of people owning property and the means for industrial production, would eventually be eliminated as the proletariat, which was the working class, was brought into power.[42]

---

[39] *Documents of the Revolution of 1848 in France*, J. H. Robinson, ed., Readings in European History (Boston: Ginn, 1906; Hanover Historical Texts Project February, 1997), 2: 559-562 .

[40] Coppa, *Pope Pius IX*, pp. 87-91.

[41] Louis Atlhusser, *For Marx*, Ben Brewster, translator (New York: Pantheon Books, 1969), p. 221.

[42] Latourette, *A History of Christianity*, vol. 2, pp. 1066-1067.

While Men Slept...

A seventy-year experiment in Russia began in 1917 and was based on the blueprint provided by Marx and Engels. The Czar was overthrown in the Bolshevik Revolution and the people were controlled with an iron hand. The economy was also controlled, and God was removed from the lives of the people. The experiment, which demonstrated significant flaws in the Marxist form of Socialism, publicly ended in Russia in 1991.

Christian Socialism

Consistent with Hegel's teaching that a new concept would emerge out of two opposing concepts, an alternative plan for global Socialism was proposed. It was also in 1848 England that contemporaries of Karl Marx and Friedrich Engels were developing another plan for global Socialism. The Englishmen Frederick Denison Maurice (1805-1872), Charles Kingsley (1819-1875), and John Malcom Forbes Ludlow (1821-1911) founded the Christian Socialist Movement. It appears significant that both plans for global Socialism were announced in England and in 1848![43]

As Ludlow was in France during the 1848 French Revolution, he saw a Socialistic revolution. He became convinced, however, that Socialism must be made "Christian" in order to benefit the rest of the world. Upon his return to England, Ludlow contacted F. D. Maurice, telling him of his belief that Socialism must be made "Christian."[44] According to Henry Solly (1813-1903), who was a Unitarian minister, the Christian Socialist Movement actually came from John Malcom Ludlow who, while in Paris during the 1848 revolution, was greatly influenced by the movement in France. Ludlow then influenced F. D. Maurice, who took up the banner and became a leader of the movement in England. As a result, Maurice, along with Ludlow, Kingsley, and others, conducted a series of evening meetings for organizing working men. Thus, they established Christian Socialism in the form

---

[43] N. Merrill Distad, *Guessing at Truth: The Life of Julius Charles Hare* (Shepherdstown: The Patmos Press, 1979), p. 184.

[44] John Ludlow, *The Autobiography of a Christian Socialist*, A. D. Murray, ed. and intro. (London: Frank Cass and Company Ltd., 1981), pp. 112-114.

138

of Cooperative Workshops.[45] These workshops were held with working men with the goal of putting Socialist ideas into action.

Use of the term "Christian" as part of this Socialist movement did not necessarily have the same meaning that most traditional Christians would infer from the word. Instead of confirming a belief in the saving sacrifice of Jesus Christ, the term really implied implementing the *moral teachings* of Christ in a movement toward Secularism. Christian teachings were embraced, except where they seemed to contradict what were believed to be moral truths established by the rationality of reason. This also meant that the parts of the Bible that did not contradict rationality were accepted. As Edward Royle described the approach:

> Christian teaching was therefore to be judged by the dual standards of morality and utility, and this latter was to replace the standard of traditional Christianity.[46]

Robert Owen, the Socialist, had advocated what he called a "Rationalist Religion." One of Owen's followers, George Holyoake (1817-1906), was a well-known atheist who was convicted in England of atheism. Holyoake renamed the "Rationalist Religion" of Owen. He chose the new name, "Secularism" in order to symbolically break away from such labels as atheism and infidelity.[47, 48]

The Christian Socialist Movement was seen as one responding to the needs of the times. New philosophical ideas were being accepted:

> ...some clergymen were even prepared to tolerate and listen to Holyoake...Biblical scholars, geologists and biologists were

---

[45] Henry Solly, *These Eighty Years Or, The Story of an Unfinished Life*, vol. 2 (London: Simpkin, Marshall, & Co., Ltd., 1893), pp. 53-54.

[46] Edward Royle, *Victorian Infidels: The Origins of the British Secularist Movement, 1791-1866* (Manchester: Manchester University Press, 1974), pp. 148-150.

[47] David Berman, *A History of Atheism in Britain: From Hobbes to Russell* (London, New York, and Sydney: Croom Helm, 1988), pp. 207-208.

[48] Royle, *Victorian Infidels*, p. 3.

beginning to convince Christian opinion that the views of the atheists were respectable.[49]

Holyoake, however, was opposed to the concept of mixing up Christianity with Socialism.[50] Whether under the name of "Christian Socialism" or "secularism," clearly the movement had the aim of changing the order of both Christian and social thought. The firmly entrenched atheistic Socialists, Marx and Engels, were blunt about their perception of the motives behind attaching the word "Christian" to this Socialist movement when they said:

> Christian Socialism is nothing but the holy water with which the priest consecrates the heart-burnings of the aristocrate.[51]

The New Moral World

Subtle Promotion of Christian Socialism

Julius Hare, who helped provide the financial support for the Christian Socialist Movement, was also a major participant in the activities of the movement.[52] He participated in the Christian Socialist meetings conducted by Maurice, even though other participants were often unaware of his presence. Henry Solly, for example, described one of those meetings:

> In the course of the evening, I was asked to speak to one of the resolutions, and in touching on the self-sacrificing spirit in which the movement they were then inaugurating must be carried out if it was to be successful, I referred to a sermon by an Archdeacon of the English Church (whom I spoke of as one of its brightest ornaments), on the "Law of Self Sacri-

---

[49] Ibid., p. 145.

[50] Ludlow, *The Autobiography of a Christian Socialist*, p. 191.

[51] Karl Marx and Friedrich Engels, *Manifesto of the Communist Party*, In *Karl Marx and Friedrich Engels On Religion*, Introduced by Reinhold Niebuhr (New York: Schocken Books, 1964), p. 89.

[52] Distad, *Guessing at Truth: The Life of Julius Charles Hare*, p. 187.

fice." I had thought it one of the very finest that had ever been penned, and I said it might be taken as a guiding star in their enterprise because it was so grand and beautiful an exposition of the meaning of the "Cross." When I sat down, I was rather puzzled by the way in which the young men on the platform came round me, thanking me for what I had said, and asking eagerly who the Archdeacon was. On answering "Julius Hare," they were immensely delighted—one or two of them exclaiming: "Did you know he was sitting just in front of you?" (which I certainly did not)....[53]

It seems that the other participants at the meeting were also uninformed about the relationship between Hare and Maurice and their Unitarian views. As Solly related further:

But afterwards I guessed that their enthusiasm was excited partly because they were so surprised and pleased to hear "a Unitarian parson" [Solly] speak thus highly of a Church of England clergyman [Hare], and partly because, like their leader [Maurice], they were filled with a sort of chivalrous desire to give a heretic Dissenting minister [Solly] a kindly welcome.[54]

Thus, the participants in the Christian Socialist meetings were often unaware of the true relationships that the leaders of the movement had with each other. Because they were unaware of Maurice's true Unitarian position, they were impressed that he would welcome a known Unitarian, Solly, to their meetings. Often unaware that Maurice's brother-in-law, Hare, was present at the meetings and that Maurice and Hare shared similar theological and political views, they were surprised that a Unitarian would speak so highly of Hare. It appeared that many who were embracing the Christian Socialist Movement did not understand the dynamics of the relationships nor comprehend the underlying agenda of those who were advocating the movement.

---

[53] Solly, *These Eighty Years*, vol. 2, p. 55.

[54] Ibid., p. 56.

While Men Slept...

Christian Communism

Following the publication of the *Communist Manifesto* by Marx and Engels and the introduction of Christian Socialism by Maurice and his associates, it was clear to Maurice that "Christian Socialism" would be the far more palatable of the two proposals to the general public in England. Thus, Maurice proposed the concept of "Christian Communism" in the "New Moral World" in a letter to Ludlow:

> I think they should be made to feel that Communism, in whatever sense it is a principle of the New Moral World, is a most important principle of the old world, and that every monastic institution—properly so called—was a Communist institution to all intents and purposes. The idea of Christian Communism has been a most vigorous and generative one in all ages, and must be destined to a full development in ours.[55]

It appears that a key difference between Maurice's position relative to that of Marx and Engels on Communism was on whether it should be implemented by the church or by the state. Maurice, convinced that the church should bring forth Communism, said that although he did not have power to act on the minds of statesmen:

> ... I do not think myself the least absolved from the duty of helping all I can to give the Communist principle a fair trial....The State, I think, cannot be Communist; never will be; never ought to be. It is by nature and law Conservative of individual rights, individual possessions..... But the Church, I hold, is Communist in principle; Conservative of property and individual rights only by accident; bound to recognise them, but not as its own special work; not as the chief object of human society or existence. The union of Church and State, of bodies existing for opposite ends, each necessary to the other, is, it seems to me, precisely that which should accomplish the fusion of the principles of Communism and of property.[56]

---

[55] Maurice, *The Life of Frederick Denison Maurice*, vol. 2, p. 7.

[56] Ibid., pp. 8-9.

According to Maurice, the church and Communism are inseparable. He asserted that the very existence of the church implies Communism because it is based on Communism. Maurice described the relationship this way:

> ...we want the Church fully to understand her own foundation, fully to work out the Communism which is implied in her existence.[57]

In an 1848 letter, Maurice had said this of Plato's impact on the universal church and on Communism:

> The republic of Plato is, in its highest aspect, the dream of an universal Church, in its lowest it touches upon French Communism. It is very wonderful in both respects, and will not at all disengage you from present interests, but rather will help you to contemplate them from a higher point of view.[58]

Maurice, who was one of the great contributors to the change in English religious life, has also been praised as a supporter of "Christian Platonism."[59]

Writing to J. M. Ludlow on September 24, 1852, F. D. Maurice announced that the realization of an earthly Kingdom of Heaven was the basic principle on which he was to base his life. He said:

> I wish very earnestly to be understood on this point, because all my future course must be regulated on this principle, or on no principle at all. The Kingdom of Heaven is to me the great practical existing reality which is to renew the earth and make it a habitation for blessed spirits instead of for demons.[60]

---

[57] Ibid., p. 9.

[58] Maurice, *The Life of Frederick Denison Maurice.*, vol. 1, pp. 465-466.

[59] Raymond Chapman, *Faith and Revolt: Studies in the Literary Influence of the Oxford Movement* (London: Weidenfeld and Nicolson, 1970), p. 275.

[60] Maurice, *The Life of Frederick Denison Maurice*, vol. 2, p. 137.

While Men Slept...

Maurice was promoting the concept of a one-world religious, economic and political system. The concept which he was promoting was similar to the views held by the preterists, who believed that biblical prophecy has been fulfilled and that Christ has already returned, those of the postmillennialists, who believed Christ would return to rule a Kingdom that was set up by man, or those of the amillennialists, who believed that biblical references to the return of Christ are only figurative and not literal.[61, 62] Similar to the thinking of Swedenborg,[63] for example, Maurice believed that man would establish the Kingdom of Christ on earth. He strongly advocated a blend of "Christianity," Socialism, and reason, which he called "Christian Socialism."

Maurice explained the basis for selecting the name of the movement as "Christian Socialism." In a letter to Ludlow he wrote:

> ...it [Christian Socialism] seems to me, [to be] the only title which will define our object, and will commit us at once to the conflict we must engage in sooner or later with the unsocial Christians and the unchristian Socialists.[64]

In summarizing his view of the relationship between Christianity and Socialism, Maurice stated:

> I seriously believe that Christianity is the only foundation of Socialism, and that a true Socialism is the necessary result of a sound Christianity.[65]

---

[61] Robert Jamieson, A.R. Fausset, and David Brown, *A Commentary, Critical and Explanatory on the Old and New Testaments*, vol. 2 (New York: S.S. Scranton and Company, 1873), p. 549.

[62] Timothy P. Weber, *Living in the Shadow of the Second Coming: American Premillennialism, 1875-1925* (New York and Oxford: Oxford University Press, 1979), p. 9.

[63] Swedenborg, *On the New Jerusalem and Its Heavenly Doctrine*, pp. 85-88.

[64] Maurice, *The Life of Frederick Denison Maurice*, vol. 2, p.35.

[65] Percy Dearmer, *Socialism and Christianity*, Pub. Fabian Society, Fabian Tract No. 133, 1907, page 3. (Referenced by Bernard Mends, "John Trevor - The Labour Church And Socialist Sunday Schools," http://www.qbradley.freeserve.co.uk/labourchurch.html, 1999.)

Chapter 8. Maurice: An Author of Confusion

Let the Christians of England be aware of this new and complex heresy, which is little better than a modern Gnosticism in a refined character.[1]

—James H. Rigg

Unveiling Maurice's Theology

Confirming Suspicions

After being politically active through various publications that he had either written or edited, F. D. Maurice became a professor at King's College of London in 1846.[2] Up to that time in his life, no one suspected Maurice of heresy, except those who knew him well at Oxford.[3] As he became more politically involved in 1848, however, his principal at the College, Richard William Jelf (1798-1871), developed growing suspicions that Maurice held unorthodox political and theological views. Maurice's public association with Christian Socialism, his membership in the Sterling Club, as well as his friendship with Sterling and Hare, added to his growing conflict with Jelf.[4]

After Maurice published his *Theological Essays* in 1853, he revealed his religious views more clearly. Jelf and others became convinced of Maurice's heresy. A special meeting of a disciplinary council at King's College concluded that Maurice's teachings were "calculated to unsettle the minds of the theology students of King's College." While Maurice's book revealed much about his unorthodox theology, the specific reason cited in support of disciplinary action against him was that he rejected the doctrine of eternal punishment. Among the specific conclusions made by the Council as it reached its decision to dismiss Maurice from his position at King's College was that:

---

[1] Rigg, *Modern Anglican Theology,* p. 333.

[2] Maurice, *The Life of Frederick Denison Maurice*, vol. 1, p. 422.

[3] Janet E. Courtney, *Freethinkers of the Nineteenth Century* (London: Chapman & Hall, Ltd., 1920), p. 32.

[4] Distad, *Guessing at Truth: The Life of Julius Charles Hare*, p. 188.

...the opinions set forth and the doubts expressed in the said essay, and re-stated [sic] in the said answer as to certain points of belief regarding the future punishment of the wicked and the final issues of the day of judgement, are of dangerous tendency, and calculated to unsettle the minds of the theological students of King's College.[5]

Friends to His Defense

Maurice's longtime friend, William Gladstone, who was among those serving on the Council, unsuccessfully attempted to block the Council's decision to expel him.[6] In response to Maurice's dismissal, many of his closest associates rushed to his defense. His longtime mentor and brother-in-law, Julius Hare, defended Maurice's *Theological Essays*. He said:

To me it seems a most noble book, worthy of Luther in its dauntless bravery, and fitted to deliver the Church from divers notions, offensive to reason & conscience, w[hi]ch have become attacht [sic] to some of the primary doctrines of faith.[7]

As we shall learn, Maurice was forced in 1853 to leave his position as a professor at King's College and he started a Working Men's College in 1854. He invited a group of men who had previously attended the Working Men's meetings to come to a meeting to discuss his plans. Henry Solly, who was among those invited, wrote that Maurice's dismissal from King's College was the impetus behind the formation of this new college.[8] (Maurice started the Working Men's meetings in 1849, where working men gathered to receive his teachings concerning Socialism.)[9]

---

[5] Maurice, *The Life of Frederick Denison Maurice*, vol. 2, pp. 191.

[6] Morley, *The Life of William Ewart Gladstone*, vol. 1, pp. 454-455.

[7] *Hare to Thirwall, 22 Aug. 1853*, Quoted in: Distad, *Guessing at Truth: The Life of Julius Charles Hare*, p. 188.

[8] Henry Solly, *These Eighty Years*, vol. 2, pp. 93-94.

[9] John Ludlow, *The Autobiography of a Christian Socialist*, pp. 146-147.

Unsettling the Mind of Fenton Hort

Hort's Journey to Cambridge

An example of the kind of influence F. D. Maurice had on the minds of theological students in England can be found in Fenton John Anthony Hort (1828-1892). Born in Dublin, Ireland, Hort had a strong-willed mother who also had "strong and deep religious feelings."[10] As an Evangelical, she studied and knew her Bible well and raised her children with a close study of the Bible.[11] As a boy, Hort excelled in school, but had a "somewhat overbearing" personality with other boys.[12] At the age of seventeen, while at boarding school, he wrote to his mother and father on Easter Sunday April 12, 1846 of his desire to enter into the ministry.[13]

Just a week later, Fenton Hort wrote his father again, with an almost ominous foreshadowing of the kind of belief system into which he would enter. In it, he displayed his understanding of the union that was occurring between the Roman Catholic Church and the philosophy of "reason." At this time in his life, he said:

> I cannot help thinking it is a very fearful sign of these latter days, that godlessness has taken such a strange form; it began with persecution open and undisguised, then came Popery, then (to omit minor forms) in the last century the philosophy of "reason," not one perishing in the meantime, but each springing up by the side of the other. But now such is the spirit of the age, it is driven to take a new shape, the shape of Christianity and religion itself. For I cannot regard in any better light this widely-spread system of assuming the name of the Gospel to wrong principles.[14]

---

[10] Arthur Fenton Hort, *Life and Letters of Fenton John Anthony Hort*, vol. 1, (London: Macmillan & Co., 1896), p. 7

[11] Hort, *Life and Letters,* vol. 1, pp. 7-9.

[12] Ibid., p. 10.

[13] Ibid., pp. 34-37.

[14] Ibid., pp. 37-38.

While Men Slept...

In October 1846, Hort went to Trinity College at Cambridge University, but was unsuccessful in his competition for a scholarship. Therefore, he did not enroll as a scholar. Since he had come from an evangelical Christian family, Hort sought to find his place among other Evangelicals at Cambridge University. He read widely, as he continued to compete for scholarships. Through his reading and associations, Hort came under nonevangelical influences within the University community.[15] The next two and one-half years proved to be a time of great change in the thinking and theology of Fenton Hort.

By 1847, Hort had such an interest in Samuel Taylor Coleridge, as did Julius Hare and F. D. Maurice before him, that, as his son Arthur later described it, he had "come under the spell of Coleridge." This was evident in his diary, where he recorded the dates of Coleridge's birth and death. He soon began to question his early Christian training and "outgrew" the Evangelical teaching.[16] By January 1848, Hort had come under major Anglo-Catholic influences, including that of Julius Hare and, especially, F. D. Maurice.[17]

The Influence of Maurice

The anti-evangelical influences on Fenton Hort intensified during 1848. At the age of nineteen, he became engrossed in the writings of Maurice. As he carefully studied Maurice's book, *The Kingdom of Christ*, Hort commented that "...everyday seems to bring out more clearly in my mind the truth, beauty, wisdom, scripturality, and above all unity of Maurice's baptismal scheme." Speaking of Maurice, Hort said, "I love him more and more every day." In the same paragraph, he continued, "I am carefully reading Derwent Coleridge's *Sermons on the Church*; they are truly excellent and beautiful, though the tone is occasionally perhaps rather too ecclesiastical instead of Catholic."[18]

Ironically, Hort was coming under the very theological influences that he had previously rejected and that his mother had feared. She had

---

[15] Ibid., pp. 40-41.

[16] Ibid., pp. 41-42.

[17] Ibid., p. 64.

[18] Ibid., p. 67

148

dreaded the potential influence that the Oxford Movement, and its rejection of evangelical teachings, might have on her son.[19] By rejecting his evangelical background, Hort was embracing a wholly different set of values and basis for his theology. In defining Evangelicalism, one writer described it as:

> ...that version of Christianity which affirms the salvation of sinners by grace alone in Christ alone through faith alone, as against any thought of salvation by effort and merit on the one hand or by the working of ecclesiastical mechanisms, institutional and sacramental, on the other. But evangelicalism, viewed methodologically, must be defined as that version of Christianity which determines its teaching, attitudes, worship style, and practical priorities by expounding and applying Holy Scripture, which it receives as authoritative instruction from God the Creator, the God who speaks.[20]

As Hort's son further described it, the progression of Hort's theology was natural:

> From Coleridge to Maurice the passage was natural. Maurice's teaching was the most powerful element in his religious development...[21]

Hort soon believed that Maurice's Unitarianism provided a stronger basis for his emerging theology than he had received from the Evangelical teachers. Hort's son, Arthur, described his father's position this way:

> ... he was led to seek firmer foundations than he could find in the Evangelical position; with all the earnestness which inspired the teaching of the best of that school, he could not discover the religious philosophy which he desiderated. In this

---

[19] Ibid., p. 7.

[20] J. I. Packer, *Beyond the Battle for the Bible* (Westchester, Illinois: Cornerstone Books, 1980), pp. 37-38.

[21] Hort, *Life and Letters,* vol. 1, p. 42

search for a definite *locus standi* he was attracted by the writings of F. D. Maurice. Here he found a religious teacher who seemed to bring the doctrines and sacraments of the Church into relation with the needs of individual and social life. In Maurice, moreover, there was not that distrust of the human reason which, so far as it characterised the "anti-Liberalism" of the Oxford Movement, made it impossible for Hort to be in complete sympathy with the leaders of that school.[22]

Maurice's Influence on Hort's Emerging Beliefs

Seeking Doctrine from Maurice

The tremendous impact that Maurice had on shaping the beliefs of young theological students is clearly demonstrated by the example of Fenton Hort. By 1848, which was the same year in which Maurice and his associates started the Christian Socialist Movement, Hort found himself supporting many of Maurice's key theological beliefs.[23] However, it took Hort more than a year to write his first letter to Maurice. Hort was twenty-one years old when he mustered up enough nerve to ask Maurice to expound upon his Unitarian and Universalist views. Specifically, on November 16, 1849, Hort asked for Maurice's advice on such doctrinal questions as hell, infinite punishment, atonement for sins, universal salvation, the devil, remission of sins without the shedding of blood, and others.[24] Hort wrote to Maurice:

> ...surely the aid you have already given is a pledge of your willingness to assist us again in discerning the eternal order among all the confusions that beset us, and to bear with the perverseness which more than anything blinds our eyes.[25]

As a result of their communication, Maurice apparently influenced Hort's views on such basic issues as eternal punishment, eternal life

---

[22] Hort, *Life and Letters,* vol. 1, p. 61.

[23] Ibid., p. 64.

[24] Ibid., pp. 116-123.

[25] Ibid., p. 116.

and heaven, original sin, believer's baptism, diligent Bible study, Mary worship, the devil as evil, and substitutional atonement for sin.

Eternal Punishment

Maurice's views on eternal punishment were at the core of the reason for his expulsion from his King's College professorship in 1853. In a November 16, 1849 letter to Maurice, Hort wrote:

> I have therefore resolved to ask you to guide me, if you can, to a satisfactory solution of a question which has long been tormenting me...I mean the question whether any man will be hereafter punished with never-ending torments, spiritual or physical.[26]

Before waiting to receive a response from Maurice concerning the issue of everlasting punishment, Hort had already concluded in his same letter that such a concept was not rational and therefore could not be true. He said:

> Nor do I see how to dissent from the equally common Universalist objection, that finite sins cannot deserve an infinite punishment.... So that the way to defend what is presumed to be an essential doctrine of Christianity is by denying the fact of a revelation, in any living sense of the word! for what is the revelation of Hell?[27]

Eternal Life and Heaven

Maurice responded with a letter to young Hort on November 23, 1849. In explaining his view of eternal life and everlasting punishment as Jesus described in Matthew 25:46, Maurice argued that eternal life was nothing more than the knowledge of God and eternal punishment is nothing more than the loss of the knowledge of God. In his letter to Hort, Maurice said this:

---

[26] Ibid.

[27] Ibid., p. 118.

> I am bound to believe that the eternal life into which the righteous go is that knowledge of God which *is* eternal life; I am bound to suppose that the eternal punishment into which those on the left hand go, is the loss of that eternal life- what is elsewhere called "eternal death."[28]

In 1845 Maurice asserted that he had a special interpretation of the meaning of "eternal life." His view was not that which was held by any "Doctor of the Church" or by any council. He confessed that he did not believe the Reformers would have agreed with him on his interpretation. He said the following:

> ...I take the words *aeterna vita* [eternal life] not as they are explained by any Doctor of the Church, by any council, provincial or oecumenical, but as they are explained by the Lord Himself in His last awful prayer, "This is life eternal, that they may know Thee, the only true God, and Jesus Christ.".... But I am by no means certain that the Reformers would have given that precise force to the words "eternal life," upon which my construction of the Article turns. I do not feel sure that they might not have been willing to take the words "future state," as a synonym of the words "eternal life."[29]

This argument of Maurice's to redefine eternal life might be accepted, except that he used the verse outside of the overall context in which it was presented. Just as Maurice said, John wrote the words wherein Jesus said:

> And this is life eternal, that they might know thee the only true God, and Jesus Christ, whom thou hast sent.
>
> —John 17:3

However, the verse was written in the context of Jesus' prayer to the Father, *who is in Heaven*:

---

[28] Maurice, *The Life of Frederick Denison Maurice*, vol. 2, p. 18.
[29] Ibid., vol. 1, p. 397-398.

> These words spake Jesus, and lifted up his eyes to heaven, and said, Father, the hour is come; glorify the Son, that thy Son also glorify thee:
>
> —John 17:1

Simply put, F. D. Maurice said that Hell is ignorance and Heaven is knowledge. He wrote:

> How I long to be telling myself and telling every one that the Hell we have to fly is ignorance of the perfect goodness and separation from it, and the Heaven we have to seek is the knowledge of it and participation in it.[30]

On April 29, 1870, F. D. Maurice hinted of his position that the Father is *not* in Heaven and that there is *no* Heaven. He wrote:

> If these men are right we must give up saying the Lord's Prayer. Our Father is *not* in Heaven; there is no Heaven; all is of the earth, earthly. I have felt this feebly for a long time; now it comes to me with a tremendous demonstration.[31]

According to Maurice:

> The whole New Testament is for me a revelation of eternal life, the life of God....If I preached that there could be no deliverance from eternal death, I should be preaching that no sinner can be raised from darkness to light, from the power of Satan to God. That this deliverance can only take place before the grave closes upon us I am told is the doctrine of Scripture. When I ask for the passages, I am referred to those very words, "eternal" and "everlasting," against the contraction and perversion of which I am protesting.[32]

---

[29] Ibid., p. 364.

[31] Ibid., vol. 2, p. 614.

[32] F. D. Maurice, *The Claims of the Bible and of Science: Correspondence Between a Layman and the Rev. F. D. Maurice on Some Questions Arising Out of the Controversy Respecting the Pentateuch* (London and Cambridge: Macmillan and Co., 1863), p. 133.

While Men Slept...

In a letter written on May 12, 1850, Hort made it clear that Maurice had convinced him of his position concerning the issue of the duration of future punishment:

> I think Maurice's letter to me sufficiently showed that we have no sure knowledge respecting the duration of future punishment, and that the word "eternal" has a far higher meaning than the merely material one of excessively long duration; extinction always grates against my mind as something impossible....[33]

In Maurice's view, it was not about duration at all. Instead, it was about having a knowledge of God. Although many may view the words "eternal" and "everlasting" as synonymous and, therefore, interchangeable, the use of the word "eternal" by Maurice, Hort, and their associates had nothing to do with duration.

Original Sin

In a letter dated January 19, 1848, Hort agreed strongly with Maurice in rejecting the Calvinistic training that his mother had given him during his youth. Hort wrote that Maurice had "...dealt a manly blow at the central *lie* of Calvinism, viz. that man's natural state is diabolical...."[34] In other words, nineteen-year old Hort already agreed with Maurice in rejecting the notion of the sinful nature of man, who was in need of salvation.

At the age of twenty, Hort continued his new thinking by also denying the existence of the Garden of Eden and that the fall of Adam imparted sin to anyone but himself. In his continued discourse he further revealed Coleridge's influence on his thinking by saying:

> ...I am inclined to think that no such state as "Eden" (I mean the popular notion) ever existed, and that Adam's fall in no degree differed from the fall of each of his descendents, as

---

[33] Hort, *Life and Letters,* vol. 1, p. 149.
[34] Ibid., p. 64.

> Coleridge justly argues that in each individual man there must have been a primal apostasy of the will, or else sin would not be guilty, but merely a condition of nature.[35]

This belief was consistent with that of Maurice, who totally rejected the concept of the Fall, which included the whole human race that stood under God's judgement.[36]

Believer's Baptism

Fenton Hort confessed that, in his view, the Evangelical position on baptism, which may be called a believer's baptism, was false and that the thinking of Maurice on the subject was true. He wrote in a letter dated July 6, 1848 that:

> ...nothing so frequently engages my attention as thinking what my theological position must be. Now, looking at the doctrinal question, I think we shall avoid much disquietude by laying it down as a preliminary axiom that we must not expect ever to get to the bottom of the meaning of baptism. One of the things, I think, which shows the falsity of the Evangelical notion of the subject, is that it is so trim and precise....I never expect to get completely round, to comprehend the idea of baptism. But I believe we agree in thinking that Maurice's view, so far as we enter into it, is the true one....[37]

In Maurice's opinion, baptismal regeneration was not based on the "individual faith of men."[38] Hort agreed with Maurice and emphasized that the Roman Catholic position on baptism was, to him, more nearer to the truth than that of the Evangelicals. In his own words:

---

[35] Ibid., p. 78.

[36] J. W. Rogerson, *The Bible and Criticism in Victorian Britain: Profiles of F. D. Maurice and William Robertson Smith,* In *Journal for the Study of the Old Testament, Supplement Series 201* (Sheffield, England: Sheffield Academic Press, 1995), p. 18.

[37] Hort, *Life and Letters,* vol. 1, pp. 75-76.

[38] Maurice, *The Life of Frederick Denison Maurice,* vol. 1, p. 236.

Is the Holy Spirit given only in baptism? (I mean of course, not till baptism) or given before, but increased in baptism, or lastly, is it given to every human creature, and is baptism only its seal and assurance? This is a point on which I should like to have a long talk with Maurice himself ...we maintain 'Baptismal Regeneration' as the most important of doctrines. Almost all Anglican statements are a mixture of the true and the Romish view: ...the pure Romish views seems to me nearer and more likely to lead to truth than the Evangelical....[39]

As Hort wrestled with the issue of baptism, he continued to look to Maurice to help him establish his theology. However, he proposed that, in public, he would *appear* to publicly accept the Evangelical position on baptism, even though he did not believe it. If, however, he were forced to state his true position, he would confess the Roman Catholic position on baptism.[40]

In other words, both Maurice and Hort rejected a believer's baptism. Clear support from the Scriptures for a believers' baptism is found in the exchange between Philip and the eunuch in the Book of Acts:

And as they went on *their* way, they came unto a certain water: and the eunuch said, See, *here is* water; what doth hinder me to be baptized? **And Philip said, If thou believest with all thine heart, thou mayest. And he answered and said, I believe that Jesus Christ is the Son of God.** And he commanded the chariot to stand still: and they went down both into the water, both Philip and the eunuch; and he baptized him.

—Acts 8:36-38 [Bold type shows verse 37.]

[The Revised Greek New Testament, which Hort was to coauthor, omits verse 37, reflecting Maurice's theological position concerning baptism. Various readings of the verse are shown in Appendix B.]

---

[38] Hort, *Life and Letters,* vol. 1, p. 76.
[40] Ibid., p. 76.

Diligent Bible Study

Twenty-year old Hort was critical of Luther for opening up the Bible, which had been closed during medieval times. He was also critical of the "absurd manner" in which some were trying to defend the Bible from attacks by the "Rationalists." Seeing little difference between diligent Bible study and saying the rosary, Hort described dedicated Bible study as the "fanaticism of the bibliolaters:"

> ...the Bible was then closed, but now, thanks to Luther, it is open, and no power (unless it be the fanaticism of the bibliolaters, among whom reading so many "chapters" seems exactly to correspond to the Romish superstition of telling so many dozen beads on a rosary) can close it again; a curious proof of which is afforded by the absurd manner in which the "Anglo-Catholics" defend, as they think, the Bible from "Rationalists"....[41]

The use of the term "bibliolaters" by Hort demonstrated the influence that Samuel Taylor Coleridge, perhaps through Julius Hare and F. D. Maurice, had on his theological beliefs. Samuel Taylor Coleridge was fond of using the term "bibliolatry" to stigmatize the high reverence some had for the Bible.[42] Some viewed his protest against the "bibliolatry" of popular religion as the single most important accomplishment of his religious teaching.[43]

Mary-Worship

Mary-worship, or Mariolatry, reached a new level among Roman Catholics in 1854 as Pope Pius IX declared the dogma of the Immaculate Conception of Mary, which was that Mary was conceived

---

[41] Ibid., p. 77.

[42] *Review of the Works of S. T. Coleridge*, In *The Princeton Review*, vol. 20, no. 2, April 1848, p. 178.

[43] Arthur Kenyon Rogers, *English and American Philosophy Since 1800: A Critical Survey* (New York: The Macmillan Company, 1922), p. 112.

without sin.[44, 45] As Hort's unsettled theology continued to evolve, some of his positions became Unitarian and some of them became Roman Catholic. The concept of Mary-worship, seemed to be a blend of both. As Mary was brought nearer in worship, Jesus was removed to a more distant and less accessible location. Without denying Jesus' divinity, His role was reduced, as was done by fourth century semi-Arians. By reducing His role, one is easily moved toward an Arian, or a Unitarian, position.

By the time Hort was thirty-seven years old, he supported Mariolatry. Taking an Arian position, he viewed Mary as more real and nearer than Jesus. In Hort's opinion, Jesus seemed to have "retired to a distant cloud" where He was compared to the Greek god Apollos. In a letter to Brooke Foss Westcott during October 1865, Hort wrote of his attraction toward Mary-worship:

> In Romish countries the Virgin is a nearer and more attractive object, not rejected by the dominant creed; and the Divine Son retires into a distant cloud-world with the Father, the whole speculative tendencies of Latin theology (and much of the later Greek from Ephesus onwards) aiding in the result, being Apollinarian in spirit. Another idea has lately occurred to me: is not Mariolatry displacing much worship of scattered saints, and so becoming a tendency towards unity of worship?[46]

Hort's emerging position on Mariolatry was coming into agreement with that which Westcott had expressed many years prior as he had written to his fiancée on January 2, 1847:

---

[44] Pope Pius IX, "Letters Apostolic of Our Most Holy Lord Pius IX, by Divine Providence Pope, Concerning the Dogmatic Definition of the Immaculate Conception of the Virgin Mother of God," In *Life of the Blessed Virgin, Mother of God; with the History of the Devotion to Her*, J. Sadlier, trans. (New York: D. & J. Sadlier & Co., 1854), pp. xiii-xxviii.

[45] James Cardinal Gibbons, *The Faith of Our Fathers: Being a Plain Exposition and Vindication of the Church Founded by Our Lord Jesus Christ* (Rockford, Illinois: Tan Books and Publishers, Inc., 1980 [Originally published: Baltimore: The John Murphy Company, 1876]), pp. 107,141.

[46] Hort, *Life and Letters,* vol. 2, pp. 49-50.

After leaving the monastery we shaped our course to a little oratory which we discovered on the summit of a neighboring hill…Fortunately we found the door open. It is very small, with one kneeling-place; and behind a screen was a 'Pieta' the size of life (i.e. a Virgin and dead Christ)…I could not help thinking on the grandeur of the Romish Church, on her zeal even in error, on her earnestness and self-devotion, which we might, with nobler views and a purer end, strive to imitate. Had I been alone I could have knelt there for hours.[47]

Hort continued his discussion of Mary worship. He confessed he had been persuaded that it was very similar to "Jesus" worship. He wrote of the topic in a letter to Westcott on October 17, 1865:

I have been persuaded for many years that Mary-worship and 'Jesus'-worship have very much in common in their causes and their results.[48]

The Devil

Responding to Hort's question about the devil, Maurice said that:

The Word upholds his existence, not his evil. That is in himself; that is the mysterious, awful possibility implied in his being a will. I need scarcely say that I do not mean by this acknowledgement of an evil *spirit* that I acknowledge a *material* devil. But does any one?[49]

In giving his advice to Hort, Maurice ignored the instructions that John gave concerning the devil, who committed sin from the very beginning. Jesus was manifested in the flesh for the express purpose of destroying the works of the devil, which was sin:

---

[47] Westcott, *Life and Letters*, vol. 1, p. 81.

[48] Hort, *Life and Letters,* vol. 1, p. 50.

[49] Maurice, *The Life of Frederick Denison Maurice*, vol. 2, p. 21.

> He that committeth sin is of the devil; for the devil sinneth from the beginning. For this purpose the Son of God was manifested, that he might destroy the works of the devil.
>
> —1 John 3:8

Substitutional Atonement

The belief that Jesus offered Himself as a sacrifice for the sin of those who accept it through belief was central to first-century Christianity. When Paul was edifying the Christian church in Corinth, he found himself dealing with Greeks who were sophisticated in worldly philosophies. Therefore, he was determined to focus on the most central doctrine to Christianity: the crucifixion of Jesus Christ. Paul put it this way:

> And I, brethren, when I came to you, came not with excellency of speech or of wisdom, declaring unto you the testimony of God. For I determined not to know any thing among you, save Jesus Christ, and him crucified.
>
> —1 Corinthians 2:1-2

During his long and close association with Maurice, Hort had clearly developed strong Unitarian beliefs that undermined the very essence of biblical Christian belief. On the issue of the atoning sacrifice of Jesus Christ, Hort had this to say in a letter to Westcott on October 15, 1860:

> I entirely agree - correcting one word - with what you there say on the Atonement, having for many years believed that "the absolute union of the Christian (or rather, of man) with Christ Himself" is the spiritual truth of which the popular doctrine of substitution is an immoral and material counterfeit....Certainly nothing can be more unscriptural than the modern limiting of Christ's bearing our sins and sufferings to His death; but indeed that is only one aspect of an almost universal heresy.[50]

---

[50] Hort, *Life and Letters,* vol. 1, p. 430.

In 1871, while Hort was in the process of helping rewrite the English Bible, he clarified his belief that the sacrifice of Jesus Christ was not complete. In his opinion, it did not replace all other sacrifices. Instead, he believed that it gave power and meaning to the other sacrifices that were still required. He explained his position this way:

> So also the uniqueness of the great Sacrifice seems to me not to consist in its being a substitute which makes all other sacrifices useless and unmeaning, but in its giving them the power and meaning which of themselves they could not have.[51]

Other Influences of Maurice on Hort

Instilling the Dream of the Socialist Universal Church

Maurice became the lifelong mentor of Hort. It can be readily observed from studying Hort's own letters that Maurice was the single most influential person on his theology and life. In further correspondence, Maurice urged Hort to study Plato and Aristotle as a means toward gaining a better appreciation for Socialism:

> ...on the whole I should hold fast to Plato and Aristotle, and make the other books of the course illustrative of them. Our modern Socialist questions which, as you say, must press more and more upon us will, I conceive, present themselves to you again and again while you are busy with these ancients.[52]

Secret Clubs

The year of 1851 was a busy and exciting time for Hort. In June, he "...joined the mysterious company of the 'Apostles.' "[53] Ironically, when he was considering membership into the Club, Hort consulted Maurice, who was its effective founder many years prior. According to Arthur Hort, his father:

---

[51] Ibid., vol. 2, p. 158.
[52] Maurice, *The Life of Frederick Denison Maurice*, vol. 2, p. 39.
[53] Hort, *Life and Letters,* vol. 1, p. 170

...remained always a grateful and loyal member of the secret Club, which has now become famous for the number of distinguished men who have belonged to it. In his time the Club was in a manner reinvigorated, and he was mainly responsible for the wording of the oath which binds the members to a conspiracy of silence....That he considered his membership as a great responsibility is shown by the fact that, before consenting to join, he asked Maurice's advice.[54]

Hort was the "moving spirit" in starting a small choral music club and another called the "Ghostly Guild," which dealt with psychical phenomena. According to Hort, a group at Cambridge University, including Westcott and others started the society for:

...the investigation of ghosts and all supernatural appearances and effects, being all disposed to believe that such things really exist, and ought to be discriminated from hoaxes and mere subjective delusions; we shall be happy to obtain any good accounts well authenticated with names.[55]

Brooke Foss Westcott, a contemporary of Hort, was the secretary of The Ghost Society, as others called it, until 1860. The Society was concerned with the investigation of ghost stories and with "Psychical Research." Henry Sidgwick joined the "Ghost Society" while he was an undergraduate at Cambridge University.[56, 57] Sidgwick continued the work and in 1874 helped start an association that soon became known as the Psychical Research Society, becoming its first president.[58]

B. F. Westcott also studied at Cambridge and became an original member of "The Philogical Society," which was later known as

---

[54] Ibid., p. 171.

[55] Ibid., p. 211.

[56] Arthur Sidgwick and Eleanor Mildred Sidgwick, *Henry Sidgwick: A Memoir*, p. 43.

[57] C. D. Broad, *Religion, Philosophy and Psychical Research* (New York: Harcourt, Brace & Company, Inc., 1953), p. 89.

[58] Ibid., pp. 91-94.

"Hermes."[59] Hermes was a Greek-Egyptian god who, among other things was considered to be:

> ...the founder of astrology, alchemy, or magic, the revealer of occult correspondences...European attempts at practicing astrology, alchemy, or magic, often called the "Hermetic sciences." ...the philosophical position of the Hermetica, with its doctrine that matter is evil and to be escaped, can be paralleled by the Gnostics.[60]

Reason as Revelation from God

On reviewing manuscripts in 1852 that Hort had written, Maurice asked him to rethink certain issues to present them more clearly. Specifically, Maurice told Hort that man's reason is really the revelation of God to man. Therefore, that revelation is in an endless flux which has its source in the "creature energy of man." Maurice explained:

> The Living and True God reveals Himself to the Reason; that is the Mesothesis of the external and internal. The idea of Revelation in the seventeenth and eighteenth centuries was the announcement of certain decrees, imperative Laws enacted by God. In the nineteenth it is the discovery of an endless flux, of which the source is in the creature energy of man. The gospel of God concerning Himself in His Son is, as you have so happily indicated, the reconciliation of two ideas each of which by itself tends to Atheism and to superstition.[61]

In 1863, Maurice argued that a word given once is not an accurate description of divine revelation, as many had supposed the Bible to be. Instead, he asserted that there is a gradual unveiling and unfolding of the truth. In Maurice's words:

---

[59] Arthur Westcott, *Life and Letters of Brooke Foss Westcott*, vol. 1 (London: Macmillan & Co., 1903), p. 47.

[60] James Webb, *The Occult Underground* (LaSalle, Illinois: Open Court Publishing Company, 1974), pp. 198-199.

[61] Hort, *Life and Letters,* vol. 1, p. 176.

While Men Slept...

> I repeat it, with the Bible in my hands, I cannot interpret the struggles of the scientific man in any other way than this. Whilst, therefore, a "word once given" seems to me a very inaccurate description of a divine Revelation, in so far as it denies that to be a gradual unveiling and unfolding of Truth, I can imagine a sense of that phrase which a student of physical science would not consider inapplicable to his experience.[62]

By 1868, Hort had demonstrated that he understood and agreed with the instruction of Maurice. The worshipper in this world must worship the God in this world (reason), not the God of heaven. In a letter to B. F. Westcott, he explained that:

> It is doubtless true that false religion (of Christian origin) usually arises (when it is not idolatrous) from an effort to extricate the worshipper from the world, and God from the world; whereas such effort, if consistently successful, could only end in reducing the worshipper to a pin-point of nothingness and destroying the medium through which alone God can be known. The world must therefore "assist" at all religion, and true religion will welcome its presence.[63]

Maurice's Universalism

By the time Fenton Hort was forty-three years old, he had been under the influence of F. D. Maurice for twenty-three years. As we have seen, Maurice challenged the most basic doctrines of orthodox Christianity with great success among the thinkers of his day. He even argued that the phrase, "people of God," as used in the Bible had been distorted to be only those who believe in Him. Consistent with Universalist theology, Maurice argued against the concept of salvation only for *those who believe*. Instead, he argued that this "cruel exclusion" of nonbelievers was not fair. He explained his position this way:

---

[62] F. D. Maurice, *The Claims of the Bible and of Science*, p. 23.
[63] Hort, *Life and Letters,* vol. 2, pp. 99-100.

There are certain evidences in certain persons that they truly believe—believe things which other men do not believe—believe in a way that other men do not believe. These persons are said to be the people of God. Their belief invests them with that character. *They* are loved with an everlasting love. *Their* transgressions are blotted out. *They* are to be brought to an endless felicity. Devout men become aware of the contradictions which this theory involves, of its dangerous permissions, of its cruel exclusions, of the security which it holds out to insincere profession, of the despair which it causes to humble Christians…They become impatient of it. They long to overthrow barriers which it has set up between them and their fellow-creatures. **But they never dream that they might recover a sounder position by reconsidering the language of the book from which theirs has been adopted.**[64] [Bold type is shown for emphasis.]

Jesus said that believing in Him was a condition for everlasting life:

For God so loved the world, that he gave his only begotten Son, that whosoever believeth in him should not perish, but have everlasting life.

–John 3:16

Maurice, on the other hand, suggested that the *language* of the book, which was used as the basis for such a belief, should be reconsidered.

Maurice's Global Impact

A Prophet or Heretic?

Whether one sees F. D. Maurice as a prophet or a heretic has much to do with whether he agrees with Maurice's unorthodox form of Christianity, which is really in strong agreement with the beliefs of many Unitarians and Universalists. As we have learned, the officials at King's College in London saw in Maurice's *Theological Essays* sufficiently

---

[64] F. D. Maurice, *The Claims of the Bible and of Science*, pp. 129-130.

clear evidence of heresy to dismiss the professor from his position at the College. Young Fenton Hort was sufficiently persuaded by Maurice to abandon the evangelical faith, which he had brought with him to Cambridge University, and to accept Maurice's new universal Christian teachings called Christian Socialism.

Maurice's teachings were contrary to the accepted positions of the Church of England, but in line with those teachings he had received through his Unitarian upbringing. Specifically, he took the Unitarian position by rejecting the doctrines of eternal punishment and of substitutionary Atonement.[65] Maurice's teaching on denying everlasting punishment was very consistent with the thinking of other Unitarians. For example, after listening to a sermon on eternal damnation, Henry Solly remarked to his wife that "...salvation means being saved from sin, not from punishment...."[66]

F. D. Maurice acknowledged that the Unitarian influence he received from his father, Michael, played a major role in shaping the direction of his life. At the age of sixty-one, he recollected his father's Unitarian influence on his life:

> My ends have been shaped for me, rough hew them how I would, and shape has been given to them by my father's function and this name "Unitarian" more than by any other influences....[67]

Maurice's fond admirers, such as Ludlow, were so enamoured by him that they called him "The Prophet." Ludlow said that when the spirit was on Maurice:

> His face was radiant with a solemn beauty, the tones of his voice pealed upon your ear as those of a magnificent organ.[68]

---

[65] D.G. Wigmore-Beddoes, *How the Unitarian Movement Paid its Debt to Anglicanism*, In *Transactions of the Unitarian Historical Society*, vol. 13, no. 2, October, 1964, pp. 69-79.

[66] Henry Solly, *These Eighty Years*, vol. 2, p. 12.

[67] Maurice, *The Life of Frederick Denison Maurice*, vol. 1, p. 13.

[68] Ludlow, *The Autobiography of a Christian Socialist*, pp. 117-118.

Ludlow almost worshipped Maurice. He described his feelings toward Maurice this way:

> ...I had towards Mr. Maurice a feeling of reverence which I have never had towards any other man. I have no doubt known many a greater man than myself, and yet none who did not, so to speak, stand on the same level with myself, and whom I could not thus measure myself. Mr. Maurice stood on an altogether higher level; him I could not measure.[69]

Widening Influence

The global impact of F. D. Maurice cannot be underestimated. His thinking changed the course of governments, churches, and the modern view of the role of the Bible in Christian theology. Frequently operating behind the scenes, Maurice both swayed thinking and motivated action. When Philip Schaff, the noted theologian who would head the American Committee to Revise the Bible, came to London in 1844, he met with Maurice, the "author of the *Kingdom of Christ*," on several occasions.[70] During his trip, Schaff also met with Maurice's friend, Arthur Stanley, who was to become the Dean of Westminster during the Revision of the English Bible.[71]

Schaff again visited Maurice in 1854. Much had transpired since their previous meetings: Maurice had started the Christian Socialist Movement and he had been expelled from King's College for heresy. As will be shown, his students had undertaken a revision of the Greek New Testament; the pope had established an official hierarchy of the Roman Catholic Church in England; two of Maurice's close friends, Henry Manning and John Newman, had become Roman Catholics; and the pope was declaring the Immaculate Conception of the Virgin Mary. Schaff attended a worship service, with Maurice officiating, and the two directed their attention to discussing the role of the Catholic Church in England.[72]

---

[69] Ibid., pp. 118-119.

[70] Schaff, *The Life of Philip Schaff*, p. 84.

[71] Ibid., p. 327.

[72] Ibid., p. 174.

While Men Slept...

According to John Stuart Mill, it was F. D. Maurice who, along with John Sterling, aided him in the process of humanizing his philosophy.[73] As part of Maurice's widening influence, he attended the meetings of the Metaphysical Society, which met nine times a year, to discuss and debate theological issues with various dignitaries.[74] In 1866 Maurice became Professor of "Casuistry, Moral Theology and Moral Philosophy" at Cambridge University.[75] F. D. Maurice died in 1872, but his cause did not die with him. His work as a strong advocate of Unitarianism and Socialism had a tremendous influence on theology and Socialist thought, and remained an inspiration to the Christian Socialists, long after his death.[76]

Confusing the Minds

Poisonous Insincerity

The minds of theology students throughout the world have been greatly affected and unsettled by the teachings of Maurice. To his followers, Maurice was a brilliant orator and world-changing thinker who blended Socialism, Unitarianism, and Catholicism in a unique relationship between the church and state and a new order for the world. To others, Maurice was inconsistent. Many orthodox churchmen viewed him as a "dangerous liberal, even a heretic" for his views on eternal punishment, yet also as someone who believed in God.[77] Because of his many inconsistencies and subtle but careful use of redefined meanings of words, the extent of Maurice's heresies have been difficult for all but the most careful scholars to clearly delineate. James H. Rigg (1821-1909) was a scholar who believed that it was his business to:

---

[73] John Stuart Mill, *Autobiography*, In *The Harvard Classics*, vol. 25, Charles Elliott, ed. (New York: P. F. Collier & Son Corporation, 1937), p. 3.

[74] A. N. Wilson, *God's Funeral* (London: John Murray, 1999), p. 198.

[75] Maurice, *The Life of Frederick Denison Maurice*, vol. 2, p. 542.

[76] Paul T. Phillips, *A Kingdom on Earth: Anglo-American Social Christianity, 1880-1940* (University Park, Pennsylvania: The Pennsylvania State University Press, 1996), pp. 1-2.

[77] Wilson, *God's Funeral*, p. 45.

...find out Mr. Maurice's system and principles,—to discover the root of all his heresies,—the πρωτον ψευδος [first false] of all his errors...I have thought it most proper to aim, not so much at showing into how many errors and inconsistencies Mr. Maurice had fallen (this, I repeat, would have been an endless task), as at giving a clear and decisive reply to whatever seem most plausible and most like truth in what he teaches.[78]

Thus Rigg saw Maurice's errors and inconsistencies as being so numerous that he could not address them all. Instead, he focused upon exposing those positions of Maurice that seemed most like the truth to all but the most careful readers of his work.

One example of Maurice's techniques of misleading uncritical readers of his writings was to carefully place dual meanings upon words. He could, for example, use the word "Christ" in the term "Christian Socialism" without compromising either his Unitarian beliefs or the Trinitarian beliefs held by most Christians. While most Christians believed he was talking about the promised Messiah, Jesus Christ, who died for our sins, he actually meant:

> Christ the actual foundation of the universe; **not Christ a Messiah** to those who received Him and shaped Him according to some notion of theirs; the head of a body, not the teacher of a religion, was the Christ of St. Paul.[79] [Bold type shown for emphasis.]

In other words, Maurice denied the purpose of Jesus Christ was the promised Messiah who offered Himself as the Sacrifice for sin:

> By the which will we are sanctified through the offering of the body of Jesus Christ once *for all*.
>
> —Hebrews 10:10

---

[78] Rigg, *Modern Anglican Theology,* p. 121.

[79] Maurice, *The Life of Frederick Denison Maurice,* vol. 2, p. 138.

Maurice also denied the fact that Jesus Christ came to bear witness to the truth:

> Pilate therefore said unto him, Art thou a king then? Jesus answered, Thou sayest that I am a king. To this end was I born, and for this cause came I into the world, that I should bear witness unto the truth. Every one that is of the truth heareth my voice.
>
> —John 18:37

Instead, Maurice seemed to take a position similar to that of Pilate in focusing on the positional role of Christ, as a king or a head of a body, while denying His purpose.

Maurice's lengthy, multi-phrased complex sentences took his readers on journeys of vague and often contradictory theology. Rigg said he felt compelled to abridge Maurice's words:

> ...for to transcribe all the needless words which Mr. Maurice employs in that profluent and redundant style of over-simple talk, which (of late years more than formerly) he affects in preaching to the common people, would be most tedious penance.[80]

Maurice's theological beliefs remained so elusive that his Unitarian critics said that he was worshipping in his own imaginary church and his orthodox critics called him a heretic.[81, 82] After thoroughly reviewing Maurice's most important works, James H. Rigg offered this caution:

> Let the Christians of England be aware of this new and complex heresy, which is little better than a modern Gnosticism in a refined character.[83]

But to those who studied him more closely, he seemed confused. For example, Thomas Carlyle, who knew Maurice, esteemed him, and

---

[80] Rigg, *Modern Anglican Theology,* p. 345.

[81] Young, *F. D. Maurice and Unitarianism,* p. 108.

[82] Rigg, *Modern Anglican Theology,* p. 333.

[83] Ibid.

personally liked him just as others liked him, had some very telling observations of his beliefs. According to Carlyle's biographer:

> ...[Carlyle] found him confused, wearisome, and ineffectual; and he thought no better of the whole business in which he was engaged. An amalgam of "Christian verities" and modern critical philosophy was, and could be nothing else but, poisonous insincerity.[84]

Moving Faith into Doubt

During his major involvement in rewriting the Greek New Testament of the English Bible, of which we shall learn, Hort wrote in 1871 about the influence that Maurice had on his life and on his theology. It was through the influence of Maurice that Hort had been led to doubt the adequacy of the Christian faith as expressed in the accepted Christian doctrines:

> ...Mr. Maurice has been a dear friend of mine for twenty-three years, and I have been deeply influenced by his books. To myself it seems that I owe to them chiefly a firm and full hold of the Christian faith; but they have led me to doubt whether the Christian faith is adequately or purely represented in all respects in the accepted doctrines of any living school.[85]

Maurice's thinking was to especially manifest itself throughout the world through his activities with his Oxford associates through secret clubs and by his mentoring of brilliant young undergraduate students, such as Fenton John Anthony Hort and his contemporaries. These young men were philosophically and theologically prepared by Maurice and his closest associates to undertake a critical rewriting of the Greek New Testament and then the English Bible that would have a subtle and vast impact on the the world for a movement toward a new universal Christianity.

---

[84] James Anthony Froude, *Thomas Carlyle: A History of His Life in London, 1834-1881*, vol. 1 (New York: Charles Scribner's Sons, 1910), p. 34.

[85] Hort, *Life and Letters,* vol. 2, p. 155.

While Men Slept...

Chapter 9. The Bold Publishing Plan

> **I have read the Old and New Testament very carefully through more than once, and cannot for the life of me find anything about endless punishment. I don't think God does anything *endlessly*....**[1]
>
> **—Alexander Macmillan**

Developing the Publishing Company

The Macmillan Brothers: Bringing the Message to the World

F. D. Maurice, supported by his friend, brother-in-law, and mentor, Julius Hare, had helped to prepare the minds of his students and colleagues for the new universal Christianity that he was promoting. We have already learned of Hare's significant influence on both John Sterling and F. D. Maurice since their early days at Cambridge. It was Hare, for example, who first introduced Maurice to the writings of the great Greek philosopher, Plato.[2] Hare, Maurice, and Sterling, having very close personal ties, were all under the steadily growing influence of Samuel Taylor Coleridge. The influence of German philosophers and textual critics, along with that of Coleridge, was so significant that John Stuart Mill called Cambridge University the "Germano-Coleridgean School."[3]

The foundations had already been forged for a new universal Christianity. It was now necessary to get the message of the coming changes in Christianity to the rest of the world. A publisher was needed that was sympathetic to the cause. Two brothers, Daniel (1813-1857) and Alexander Macmillan (1818-1896), were found to fulfill this publish-

---

[1] Charles L. Graves, *Life and Letters of Alexander Macmillan* (London: Macmillan and Co., Ltd., 1910), p. 406.

[2] H. G. Wood, *Frederick Denison Maurice* (Cambridge: Cambridge University Press, 1950), p. 30.

[3] Nigel Leask, "Coleridge and the Idea of a University," *Queens' College Record 1998*, http://www.quns.cam.ac.uk/Queens/Record/1998/Academic/coleridge.html, 1998.

ing role. Both, having limited formal education, worked for Seeley's printing shop where they learned dealing in books.[4]

Daniel Macmillan's Correspondence with Julius Hare

Julius Hare was instrumental in launching the Macmillan brothers into a publishing business that was to help change the course of the world. He forged the relationship between F. D. Maurice and Daniel Macmillan. As Daniel read Hare's book, *Guesses at Truth*, he wrote to Hare, telling him of the need for someone to provide spiritual guidance for young men, such as himself.[5]

In September of 1840, Julius Hare forwarded one of those letters to F. D. Maurice. According to Maurice's son, Frederick, the letter expressed, among other things, that the working class of men was dissatisfied with "current theology in all its forms, and their craving for some outspoken utterance that should put before them what they could believe."[6] Hare replied to Daniel that Maurice was "...the man in all London who had devoted himself most to studying the difficulties of the class question."[7] Hare, in turn, forwarded to F. D. Maurice the letters he had received from Daniel Macmillan.[8]

By June 1842, Daniel Macmillan continued his correspondence with Archdeacon Hare, forwarding to him tracts. Hare soon told Daniel of F. D. Maurice's work on the book, *The Kingdom of Christ*.[9] On July 25, 1842, Daniel wrote to Hare that he had:

> "'...attended their religious and political meetings, the Chartist meetings and Socialist meetings; and ...knows how they often laught at the ineptitudes of the public spouters who pre-

---

[4] Graves, *Life and Letters of Alexander Macmillan*, p. 9.

[5] Distad, *Guessing at Truth: The Life of Julius Charles Hare*, pp. 152-153.

[6] Maurice, *The Life of Frederick Denison Maurice*, vol. 1, p. 288.

[7] Ibid.

[8] Ibid., pp. 328-329.

[9] Graves, *Life and Letters of Alexander Macmillan*, p. 23.

tend to lead them; [and knows] how little faith they have in all existing churches and spiritual guides...."[10]

Daniel continued his correspondence with Hare and wrote on to him on August 14, 1842 with suggestions on how to reach the working class with the message they were promoting. He suggested that they use publications that included nonthreatening tracts which acknowledged their intended audience as:

> ...reasonable creatures, really desirous to know what is true, and as already having thoughts and feelings on subjects in which we are interested.[11]

Daniel Macmillan was becoming enamored with the prospects of implementing the concepts which Maurice had proposed in his book, *The Kingdom of Christ*. On August 31, 1842, wrote to Rev. D. Watt of his excitement over Maurice's book:

> You may remember that in the first letter Hare sent me (which you saw), he mentioned a book by Mr. Maurice, on *The Kingdom of Christ*....I looked in to this part, and then into that, and in a very short time found that he was no common man, that he dwelt in a higher, purer, clearer region than that of party. I found it to be a book that I could not live without. I have learnt [sic] much from it, but don't expect to master it for many a day. It is a most extraordinary book....He expounds on the *idea* of the Holy Catholic Church; and answers all the objections of the Quaker, the pure Protestant, the Rationalist, the Philosopher, the Romanist, severally.[12]

On the recommendation of Julius Hare, F. D. Maurice wrote to Daniel Macmillan on August 31, 1842 requesting to meet him.[13]

---

[10] Maurice, *The Life of Frederick Denison Maurice*, vol. 1, p. 329.
[11] Ibid., pp. 330-331.
[12] Hughes, *Memoir of Daniel Macmillan,* pp. 103-104.
[13] Maurice, *The Life of Frederick Denison Maurice*, vol. 1, p. 331.

While Men Slept...

The Growing Influence of Hare and Maurice

During September of 1842, Daniel spent three days with Archdeacon Hare discussing the works of Wordsworth, Coleridge, and others. Daniel found himself in entire agreement with Hare on issues pertaining to social justice and religious matters, including his vision for the Catholic Church.[14] Daniel Macmillan found himself changed. Although he had joined the Baptist community at Cambridge in 1833 and attended Dr. Binney's congregation at the Weigh House Chapel for several years, it was while he was staying at the house of Archdeacon Hare during those three days in September that the change in direction of his faith came to a head.[15]

Daniel soon rejected his participation in the Baptist community in favor of the Church of England. Admittedly, it was Maurice's book, *The Kingdom of Christ* that brought about his decision. In a letter to the Rev. Dr. Binney on September 7, 1842, Daniel Macmillan expressed his interest in the work of F. D. Maurice:

> By and by, have you ever read Mr. Maurice's book called *The Kingdom of Christ*? I think it a most noble work. It is the second edition which I have read. Some parts are perhaps rather hastily written, but, take it as a whole, it is the fairest and most candid work I ever read on the subject.[16]

From that time forward, Hare and Maurice were to have a growing influence on both of the Macmillan brothers.[17] The more Daniel studied Maurice's works, the more impressed with Maurice he became. It was Daniel's habit with the books that influenced his own mind, such as those of Maurice, to bring them to the attention of other readers.[18] By November 12, 1842, Maurice expressed to Hare that he had been increasingly interested in Macmillan each time he met with him. He said that Macmillan:

---

[14] Graves, *Life and Letters of Alexander Macmillan*, p. 24.
[15] Hughes, *Memoir of Daniel Macmillan*, pp. 76-77.
[16] Ibid., p. 75.
[17] Graves, *Life and Letters of Alexander Macmillan*, p. 24.
[18] Hughes, *Memoir of Daniel Macmillan*, pp. 225-226.

...is anxious to see some book written which shall point out an orderly course of reading, and he ingeniously pitched upon me as the person fit to undertake it, upon the same principle which, according to Sidney Smith, makes the opening of St. Paul's so important to young architects, that it contains every imaginable contradiction and anomaly which they can be required to avoid.[19]

Financing the Endeavor

Now that Daniel Macmillan had been "converted" to a new way of thinking, Archdeacon Hare loaned him the money in the spring of 1843 to help him purchase a publishing shop in Cambridge. Thus, the brothers set out upon their new publishing business "...much to the patronage and support of Archdeacon Hare and his friends, but still more to the ability and personality of the senior partner."[20] Established with the financial help of Julius Hare, the new publishing business was the beginning of a long and fruitful relationship between the Macmillan brothers and F. D. Maurice, along with his friends, family, and like-minded associates.[21]

As F. D. Maurice and Daniel Macmillan continued to be actively engaged with each other, Maurice expressed the need for specific publications that would be targeted to the various social classes in England. He said that the poor must see a sense of reality. Religion should not just be about abstractions. In an expression of the plight of the poor to Macmillan on June 28, 1844, Maurice said:

> And the specific for all this evil is some evangelical discourse upon the Bible being the rule of faith, some High Church cry for tradition, some liberal theory of education.[22]

---

[19] Maurice, *The Life of Frederick Denison Maurice*, vol. 1, p. 331.

[20] Graves, *Life and Letters of Alexander Macmillan*, pp. 25-26.

[21] Hughes, *Memoir of Daniel Macmillan*, p. 302.

[22] Maurice, *The Life of Frederick Denison Maurice*, vol. 1, p. 370.

While Men Slept...

Soon Hare was exerting an increasing amount of influence on the fledgling publishing company by bringing influential Unitarian writers to the Macmillan brothers. In November 1844 Hare requested that Wordsworth call upon Daniel Macmillan. That visit was followed by several more in which Wordsworth discussed his spiritual views.[23]

By 1847, Maurice had a tremendous influence on Daniel Macmillan. According to Thomas Hughes (1822-1896), the author of Daniel Macmillan's Memoir:

> The growing influence of Mr. Maurice's works on Daniel Macmillan becomes now very apparent. The more he studied them the more they impressed him; and, as was his habit in the case of all books which had influenced his own mind, he lost no opportunity of pressing them on the attention of readers.[24]

Other influences on Daniel Macmillan included John Henry Newman, whose Anglo-Catholicism was seen to him as a "blinding ray of light."[25]

Like Daniel, Alexander Macmillan also had very close associations with the leaders of the Christian Socialist Movement. During Alexander's association with these leaders, who included Maurice, Hughes, Kingsley, and Ludlow, he produced previously unpublished writings promoting the Socialist movement.[26] Among the topics of great interest to Alexander were More's *Utopia* and Plato's *Republic*. Concerning Plato's work, Alexander believed that the philosopher's ideas could actually be realized in England. Alexander's biographer, Charles L. Graves, quoted him as writing:

> Plato's ideal *Republic* is to a great extent capable of being realised by us here in England, and much of the true blessedness which he promises us can be obtained without straying

---

[23] Graves, *Life and Letters of Alexander Macmillan*, pp. 28-29.

[24] Hughes, *Memoir of Daniel Macmillan*, pp. 226-227.

[25] Alistair Horne, *Harold Macmillan, 1894-1956*, vol. 1 (New York: Viking Penguin Inc., 1988), p. 7.

[26] Graves, *Life and Letters of Alexander Macmillan*, p. 46.

beyond the bounds of our own towns or away from the circle of our own duties or our own family life.[27]

During a period between October 1849 and January 1853, the Macmillan brothers participated in the Sunday night meetings of a small society known as "The Synagogue."[28] "Smoking all the time," the participants of these meetings disputed over manuscript differences in the Greek New Testament, had supper, drank "audit ale," and discussed some difficult sermon until midnight.[29] All the while, the Macmillan brothers were staunch defenders of Maurice and Hare against adverse criticism. In March 1849, Alexander called a critical article a "declaration of war."[30]

Frederick and Maurice Macmillan: Maurice's Legacy

Daniel Macmillan demonstrated his great personal affection for F. D. Maurice by making him the godfather of his children and naming them after him. Frederick Macmillan was born in 1851 and Maurice Macmillan was born in 1853.[31] Maurice Macmillan was destined to become the father of the future prime minister of England, Harold Macmillan (1894-1986).[32]

In an 1856 letter, Daniel Macmillan quoted other admirers of Maurice in a manner that demonstrates the significant impact that Maurice had on the publisher:

> As one knows that such a man as John Stuart Mill says that Mr. Maurice is the ablest and most subtle logician in Europe, one would be surprised to see him charged with being dreamy,

---

[27] Ibid., p. 50.

[28] Ibid., pp. 34-35.

[29] W. H. Thorton, *Reminiscences of an old West Country Clergyman* (Privately Printed) pp. 71-73, quoted in Graves, *Life and Letters of Alexander Macmillan*, pp. 34-35.

[30] Graves, *Life and Letters of Alexander Macmillan*, p. 40.

[31] Hughes, *Memoir of Daniel Macmillan*, p. 193.

[32] Alistair Horne, *Harold Macmillan, 1894-1956*, vol. 1 (New York: Viking Penguin Inc., 1988), p. 7.

only it is frequently done. A very learned man who had read and thought as few have, and was a perfect Cambridge scholar, once said to my brother that Mr. Maurice has the most subtle intellect that had been on the face of this earth since Plato. Another man, as calm and clear as Aristotle, said to me, "The world has only had three great theologians, Augustine, Luther, Maurice, and the greatest of these is Maurice."[33]

The Macmillans' Influence on Hort and his Associates

The Macmillan publishing company became a rendezvous spot for Cambridge faculty and students, many of whom were "intimate personal friends of the brothers." Included among these were Westcott, Lightfoot, and, especially, Hort.[34] During this time, Hort developed an "intimate and lifelong" friendship with the Macmillan brothers.[35] Fenton Hort first met Daniel Macmillan in 1849. At about that time, Macmillan was thirty-six and Hort was twenty-one years old.[36] Hort was quoted as describing his introduction to Daniel Macmillan this way:

> When I began to reside as a freshman...My tutor put down his name for me by way of recommendation, but without comment...I do not in the least remember how I first got into conversation with him, but it must have been very soon, before the end of my first term. I was reading away at Maurice, of whom I had heard from John Ellerton, the present Rector of Barnes, and this as a matter of course led to frequent conversations as time went on.[37]

Although Fenton Hort had been significantly influenced by the writings of Maurice, he had not, as of April 8, 1849, personally met him. Hort wrote that Daniel Macmillan had promised to introduce him to

---

[33] Hughes, *Memoir of Daniel Macmillan*, p. 284.

[34] Graves, *Life and Letters of Alexander Macmillan*, p. 33.

[35] Ibid.

[36] Hort, *Life and Letters,* vol. 1, p. 91.

[37] Hughes, *Memoir of Daniel Macmillan*, pp. 213-214.

Maurice, as well as to Kingsley. Macmillan, who had already been significantly influenced by F. D. Maurice and Julius Hare, now had a direct influence on Hort's thinking.[38]

For the next eight years, until Daniel Macmillan died in 1857, he became one of Hort's chief Cambridge friends. Upon his death, he left Hort valuable first edition writings of Maurice, including *The Kingdom of Christ*, which had previously belonged to John Sterling and contained many notes written by Sterling.[39]

It was Macmillan who in 1849 introduced Hort to the writings of George Sand (1804-1876) (the pseudonym of Aurore Dupin). Sand was a renowned French feminist and Socialist writer. She advocated a "Christian Communism," which was farther to the left and more militant than "Christian Socialism."[40] According to a letter written by Hort on the matter, "At Macmillan's persuasion, I at last read *Consuelo* and its sequel, *La Comtesse de Rudolstadt*, and am most truly grateful for him making me read them."[41] Hort went on to explain the theme of the books:

> The Communistic idea appears quite in the bud, scarcely separating itself from the true idea of brotherhood which it mimics. There are most strange accounts of medieval German heretics (for who G. Sand has a great affection, as a sort of anticipator of Communism), chiefly Hussites, worshippers of "Satan," whose chief formula of benediction was, *Que celui a qui l'on a fait tort, te salue*, meaning thereby that beforementioned worthy....It is full of strange mysterious incidents, much connected with the Rosicrucians, Freemasons, and "Invisibles," a sort of secretest society to which the Masons formed a sort of outer court, Communism being the grand secret and object of it all....But she is most relentless to "the

---

[38] Hort, *Life and Letters*

[39] Ibid., vol. 1, pp. 357-358.

[40] Joseph Barry, *Infamous Woman: The Life of George Sand* (Garden City, New York: Anchor Press/Doubleday, 1978), p. 266.

[41] Hort, *Life and Letters,* vol. 1, pp. 111-112.

Church" for having been the enemy of humanity, for crushing what it ought to have educated.[42]

Hort had frequent exchanges with both Daniel and Alexander Macmillan. The topics of their interactions were mainly on theological and literary subjects. According to Arthur Hort, Fenton Hort's son:

> On theological and literary subjects he [Hort] exchanged opinions freely by post with Daniel and Alexander Macmillan. The former gave him an interesting piece of advice with regard to the writing of prize essays...[43]

By 1850, Fenton Hort was in regular communication with the Macmillans. Alexander relayed Hort's great admiration for Maurice when he wrote on April 10, 1850 of their interactions:

> I had a long chat with our friend Fenton Hort last night. He wants to know all about Mr. Maurice—what he thinks on this, that and the other thing.... A truly Catholic nature. He is terribly set upon having Mr. Kingsley to preach before the University here. Could Mr. Maurice do anything towards it?[44]

Alexander Macmillan shared with Fenton Hort his great admiration for Maurice and Kingsley, who were both key leaders of the Christian Socialist Movement. This admiration by Alexander Macmillan made him a "willing recruit" to their cause.[45] On August 8, 1850, Alexander Macmillan explained his position on Socialism to Hort:

> About converting you to Socialism I am not solicitous. Believing in my deepest soul that the center principle is right, I am yet by no means cocksure about many details which I yet accept.[46]

---

[42] Ibid., pp. 111-112

[43] Ibid., pp. 94-95.

[44] Graves, *Life and Letters of Alexander Macmillan*, pp. 42-43.

[45] Ibid., p. 44.

[46] Ibid., pp. 44-45.

During 1850, Alexander Macmillan was actively engaged with Socialist philosophy. Having studied in detail More's *Utopia* and Plato's *Republic*, he recorded in his notes on the *Republic* that it is:

> ...one of the most wonderful utterances that has ever proceeded from the mind and pen of man beyond the influence of direct Christian Revelation....[47]

In 1851, Alexander Macmillan continued his correspondence and interaction with Fenton Hort. He praised Hort for defending Maurice and Kingsley against attacks that had been made against them in publications. In particular, Macmillan showed his keen interest in the accusations by the Council of King's College that had questioned the orthodoxy of Maurice's publications on Christian Socialism.[48]

Hort continued to be subjected to the influences of Socialism. He wrote on June 21, 1851 that Maurice had had discussions with him on Socialism and had asked him to read Kingsley's lecture on agriculture. In the same letter, Hort discussed his interactions with Kingsley, who had asked him to read a letter Maurice had written in the *Christian Socialist*.[49] During 1851, the young Hort saw Maurice frequently. It was also in that year that Maurice introduced Hort to Archdeacon Julius Hare.[50]

The Macmillans went on to produce publications that actively promoted the cause of Socialism. After Daniel's death in 1857, Alexander founded *Macmillan's Magazine* in 1859.[51] The publication became a forum for Socialist and utopian ideologies. For example, the concept of total State control of the very foundations of families was promoted in 1865:

> Let us, then, give reins to our fancy, and imagine a Utopia - or a Laputa, if you will - in which a system of competitive exami-

---

[47] Ibid., p. 50.

[48] Ibid., pp. 52-53.

[49] Hort, *Life and Letters,* vol. 1, pp. 195-196.

[50] Ibid., p. 173.

[51] Graves, *Life and Letters of Alexander Macmillan*, p. 115.

nation for girls, as well as for youths, had been so developed as to embrace every important quality of mind and body, and where a considerable sum was yearly allotted to the endowment of such marriages as promised to yield children who would grow into eminent servants of the State.[52]

At the same time, Alexander Macmillan continued to have a major influence on Brooke Foss Westcott and Joseph Barber Lightfoot (1828-1889). According to Westcott's son, Arthur, Macmillan approached his father and told him that it was "...clear that the need of a scholarly Biblical Commentary was very well felt. My father entered into Macmillan's plan, and wrote to him..." on November 24, 1859, detailing his interest in also getting Lightfoot involved in the project.[53] As an undergraduate, Lightfoot had been a student of Westcott's.[54] Westcott wrote to Lightfoot on December 7, 1859 that Macmillan "...seems to be open to any scheme on which we could agree, so that for the present time we may theorise safely."[55]

Alexander Macmillan reaffirmed the position of Maurice and Hort on the question of Eternal Punishment. In August 1863, he wrote:

> The record of God's guidance and teaching of His chosen people for some thousands of years contains not one distinct allusion to a hereafter at all.... I have read the Old and New Testament very carefully through more than once, and cannot for the life of me find anything about endless punishment. I don't think God does anything *endlessly*....[56]

As young Hort continued to be influenced by those around him, he showed that he was moving toward the Unitarian doctrine when he wrote:

---

[52] Francis Galton, *Imagining a Utopia - or Laputa*, *MacMillan's Magazine*, vol. 11 (November, 1864-April, 1865), pp. 157-166, 318-327, referenced in http://www.cimm.jcu.edu.au/hist/stats/galton/macm9.htm.

[53] Westcott, *Life and Letters*, vol. 1, p. 205.

[54] Latourette, *Christianity in a Revolutionary Age*, vol. 2, p. 306.

[55] Westcott, *Life and Letters*, vol. 1, p. 205.

[56] Graves, *Life and Letters of Alexander Macmillan*, p. 406.

And I am likewise persuaded that practically men gain this seemingly impossible reconciliation in and through that same Spirit in whom the Son and the Father are (I do not *now* say *one*- that is another question) *equal.*[57]

Since his early days, Alexander Macmillan "had strong leanings towards Socialism," and he was especially attracted to the Christian Socialism of Maurice.[58] As Hort wrote about discussions that he had with Maurice and Alexander Macmillan on Socialism, he explained how he could see no difference between the "Christian Socialism" that Maurice advocated and any other Socialism:

> I have never been able to ascertain from any of you wherein the Socialistic par, i.e. the machinery of "Christian Socialism," differs from that of other Socialism; the moral principle of co-operation I fully recognise, but think that Maurice makes his definition deceptive and arbitrary by including it.[59]

Close associates of Hort's, such as Brooke Foss Westcott, also expressed their Socialist views. Westcott clearly declared the influence of Socialism on his thinking when he said on July 18, 1871:

> I suppose I am a communist by nature; but surely dress and jewels cannot be tolerated even in this world for ever.[60]

A Mission to Enlighten the World

By 1853, the Christian Socialist Movement was already five years old. There had been numerous discussions and many meetings by the promoters of the movement, some of which were held under the shroud of secrecy, as had become the practice of the elite Apostles Club.[61] According to one member of the Apostles Club, Charles Merivale (1808-1893), the members began to think they had:

---

[57] Hort, *Life and Letters,* vol. 1, p. 136.

[58] Graves, *Life and Letters of Alexander Macmillan*, p. 407.

[59] Hort, *Life and Letters,* vol. 1, p. 163.

[60] Westcott, *Life and Letters*, vol. 1, p. 309.

[61] Distad, *Guessing at Truth: The Life of Julius Charles Hare*, p. 45.

> ...a mission to enlighten the world upon things intellectual and spiritual. We held established principles, especially in poetry and metaphysics, and set up idols for our worship. Coleridge and Wordsworth were our principle divinities, and Hare and Thirlwall were regarded as their prophets.[62]

In order to accomplish the perceived mission of the "Apostles" to "enlighten the world" to the ideology they had been secretly studying, it was becoming necessary to take bold steps to affect the minds of the public. Daniel Macmillan had the means to make the new theology known to the world through the publishing company that he and his brother Alexander owned.

Publishing Plans

Maurice: the Center of Controversy

As Maurice continued to strongly advocate Socialism, in a form that he called "Christian Socialism," there arose growing suspicion concerning the orthodoxy of his theology. As we have learned, the leadership of King's College, where Maurice served as a professor, was especially concerned about his theology. By January 15, 1851, Alexander Macmillan wrote of the decision by the Council of King's College to form a sub-committee for the purpose of examining Maurice's theology:

> I was in town the other day and had a complete account of the matter between Maurice and the Council of King's College...It was finally settled that a sub-committee of enquiry should be appointed to determine the question of Maurice's orthodoxy.[63]

Maurice had not yet directly published concrete proof of his unorthodox theology. Therefore, the sub-committee at that time did not find sufficient evidence to condemn Maurice. They did say, however, that:

[62] Charles Merivale, *Autobiography and Letters* (Oxford, 1898), pp. 97-99, Quoted in Distad, *Guessing at Truth: The Life of Julius Charles Hare*, p. 46.
[63] Graves, *Life and Letters of Alexander Macmillan*, p. 52.

...they could not help regretting that Mr. Maurice's name had been connected with publications and people of questionable character and orthodoxy.[64]

Those who suspected Maurice's unorthodoxy found it difficult to prove his views based upon his own writings. This was mainly because he wrote in a subtle and circular dialectic style, similar to that used by Plato.[65]

Indeed, in 1852 the Macmillan brothers were actively involved in publishing works of both Maurice and Plato. Those works included Plato's *Republic*, Maurice's *Prophets and Kings*, Kingsley's *Phaethon*, and others.[66] On December 31, 1852, Maurice wrote two letters to Daniel Macmillan which were apparently a response to a letter that Daniel had forwarded to him charging Maurice with heresy. In one of the letters, Maurice strongly objected to the Calvinist doctrine and vowed to fight against those who held such views. He wrote of universal righteousness, without faith in the atoning sacrifice of Jesus Christ, as he quoted his own thoughts that:

> "All men are righteous so far as they confess a calling from the righteous God and yield to it." From which I deduce, or rather find in Scripture this further doctrine deduced for me, "That all false religion proceeds from the notion that man is to make his way up to God by certain acts or by a certain faith of his, instead of receiving God's witness of Himself and yielding to His government."
>
> It is just because I find the teaching and the practice of religious men—not Calvinists only, but Calvinists more formally, theoretically, consistently than others—in deadly contradiction with these principles, that I fight against them, and by God's grace will fight against them....[67]

---

[64] Ibid., p. 53.

[65] Hughes, *Memoir of Daniel Macmillan*, p. 284.

[66] Ibid., p. 246.

[67] Maurice, *The Life of Frederick Denison Maurice*, vol. 2, p. 152.

While Men Slept...

By 1853, it became clear that F. D. Maurice was planning to publicly reveal more about his theological views. In a letter to his dying sister, Priscilla, on February 12, 1853, F. D. Maurice proposed his plan to write "a book for Unitarians:"

> I have been much grieved, among other neglects which press heavily on me, by reflecting that I have never really performed Miss Harker's dying wish about a book for Unitarians, though I have tried to make my sermons bear upon them. I have felt I must do it, however much else I may have to do....[68]

Within a few days, Fenton Hort also knew of Maurice's plans to write a book on Unitarianism. Hort wrote on February 20, 1853 that: "Maurice is going to preach sermons and make a book on Unitarianism....""[69]

The book for Unitarians that Maurice spoke of was his controversial *Theological Essays*. It was adapted from his sermons and was published in 1853 by Daniel Macmillan. Although written from the perspective of an Anglican priest, it was clearly for Unitarians. With the publication of that book the world then received a much better understanding of F. D. Maurice's true theology. This publication served as a vehicle for Maurice to present his Socialist Unitarian views to the public.

Since Maurice was a priest of the Church of England and a professor at King's College, the publication, which was strongly supported by his close friends, was destined to create a significant amount of public outrage and controversy. Showing strong support for the book he was publishing for Maurice, Daniel Macmillan wrote:

> I saw Mr. Maurice, and had rather lengthy chats with him. The last time I took up and put into his hand ℥100 to pay for the first edition of his *Theological Essays*. I never paid money with such pleasure in my life.[70]

---

[68] Ibid., pp. 155-156.

[69] Hort, *Life and Letters,* vol. 1, p. 248.

[70] Hughes, *Memoir of Daniel Macmillan*, p. 248.

In 1884, about thirty years after Maurice's *Theological Essays* were published, Alexander Macmillan reflected upon the impact of the book and upon the warnings that he and Daniel Macmillan had received against publishing it. He wrote:

> What changes in these thirty years since Maurice's *Theological Essays* were published have we seen! People then shuddered at the very look of the book, and Daniel and I were warned by friends, who were attached to us, that we were doing vast harm to religion—and to ourselves!—in publishing such a book.[71]

Upon its publication, Maurice's *Theological Essays* exposed his theological views, which were branded as heresy by traditional Christians. The controversy, as we have learned, centered on Maurice's definition of the meaning of the word "eternal" and on his denial of the eternity of punishment. As Daniel Macmillan praised the publication, Maurice was dismissed from his position as a professor at King's College for public heresy.[72] Following Maurice's dismissal, Daniel wrote to his brother, Alexander, saying of Maurice:

> He is not even allowed to lecture to-day....He is a grand man! And must endure like other prophets. The good people of the next age will build his tomb.[73]

Hort responded to the news of Maurice's expulsion in a letter to John Ellerton on October 31, 1853. He defended Maurice against the charges of Richard William Jelf, the Principal of King's College:

> ...I must write you a line to tell you, if you do not know it already, that Maurice was expelled from King's College by a vote of the Council on Thursday last....Jelf would not allow him even to lecture on English literature the next day. He was condemned exclusively on the last Essay, Jelf's charges being—(1) that he "threw a cloudiness about the

---

[71] Graves, *Life and Letters of Alexander Macmillan*, p. 371.

[72] Hughes, *Memoir of Daniel Macmillan*, p. 251.

[73] Ibid., p. 251.

meaning of the word "eternal""; and (2) that he seemed to tend towards the belief that the wicked might perhaps find mercy at last,—or words to that effect....My own feeling is that a considerable number of High Churchmen will support him. On the first head [sic] he only repeats Plato's doctrine, which Augustine lays down in the most emphatic terms in the *Confessions*; on the second he goes no further than is implied in prayers for the dead.[74]

Still troubled by Maurice's expulsion, on November 4, 1853, Hort wrote to Gerald Blunt:

...First of all I must give you some details of the sad event which is haunting my mind incessantly. All the long Maurice and Jelf have been having correspondence about the former's Essay on Eternal Life and Death....These two documents [stating the positions of Jelf and Maurice on issues relating to eternal life and death] were placed in the hands of the King's College Council....The result of the meeting was a vote for Maurice's expulsion from both his Professorships....On the receipt of the minutes of the Council, Maurice wrote to the secretary to ask whether the Council wished him to continue at his post till a successor should be appointed; Jelf sent back a message that he would never be allowed to deliver another lecture at King's College....I ought to add that Jelf (and, I believe, the Council) urged Maurice to resign quietly, but he positively refused, denying that a professor at King's College could be subjected to any test of orthodoxy beyond the Creeds, Prayerbook, and Articles, all of which he cheerfully accepted. Maurice desires every one to know, therefore, that it was an *expulsion*....A letter from Sir J. Stephen to Macmillan says it has caused no small stir in London....My own feeling is that a large proportion of high Churchmen will stand by him: I am sure they will mainly agree with him. If they speak out, an immense good will indeed arise out of this present evil, and we shall have one more proof how the ancient Catholic faith

---

[74] Hort, *Life and Letters,* vol. 1, pp. 260-261.

is the only one really capable of meeting the wants of the age. Meanwhile, it is a time of great anxiety for us all....I think every one who is grateful to Maurice ought to send him a line of sympathy privately.[75]

Response to the Controversy

Notable among the seventeen theological topics that Maurice addressed in his controversial book, *Theological Essays*, is the one on the inspiration of the Bible. Using his characteristic writing style in which the reader is twisted through a labyrinth of phrases, Maurice displayed his Unitarian tendencies toward the Bible. In trying to lightly disguise his Unitarian position, he described his theories as "Semi-Unitarian" as he explained to the "Unitarian listener" that:

> I have appeared to protest against current theories of Inspiration, because they *fail* to assert the actual presence of that Spirit, whom it has been one of the standing articles of his creed *not* to confess.
>
> I cannot deny the charge. I do think that our theories of Inspiration, however little they may accord with Unitarian notions, have a semi-Unitarian character; that they are derived from that unbelief in the Holy Ghost which is latent in us all, but which was developed and embodied in the Unitarianism of the last century.[76]

Instead of believing in the verbal inspiration of the Bible, Maurice believed that God reveals Himself to man through Science. He said:

> ...He has in a wonderful and orderly history enabled us to see what He is, and what He is to us, what those eternal laws and principles are which dwell in Himself and which determine His dealings with us, is to believe that there is a divine and human *Science*, that we are not left to the anticipations or guesses of one age or of another.[77]

---

[75] Ibid., pp. 261-263.

[76] Frederick Denison Maurice, *Theological Essays*, p. 242.

[77] Ibid., p. 244.

While Men Slept...

The "New Testament Scheme"

Much was happening in 1853. Daniel Macmillan had published and praised Maurice's *Theological Essays*, which resulted in Maurice's expulsion as a heretic from his professorship at King's College. Daniel and Alexander Macmillan's efforts with their fledgling publishing business were still "...sorely hampered by their reliance on their partners." Clearly their unidentified "partners" were having a significant influence in the operation of the publishing business. According to Charles L. Graves, Alexander's biographer, "These partners had to be constantly consulted, and were frequently obstructive."[78] At least one of the people who had a financial interest in the publishing business was Julius Hare.[79]

The insecurity caused by this relationship, as well as by Daniel's physically unhealthy condition, was frequently a source of anxiety and dissatisfaction for Daniel.[80] Daniel wrote to his brother during October 1853 that:

> _____ [the predominant partner of the moment] is our master and holds the money bags.[81]

While Daniel Macmillan was lamenting to his brother about being under the control of "our master," the partner who held "the money bags," he was making plans to publish a rewritten Greek New Testament. It is not clear whether the project was conceived by the "master" or by Macmillan. Nevertheless, Daniel Macmillan approached Fenton Hort, Brooke Westcott, and Joseph Lightfoot asking them to undertake a secretive joint project that was called an "...interesting and comprehensive "New Testament Scheme""[82] The 1853 invitation to these young men, who then ranged from twenty-four to twenty-seven years of age, would change their lives and would also help redefine the course of global Christianity.

---

[78] Graves, *Life and Letters of Alexander Macmillan*, p. 56.

[79] Ibid., p. 25.

[80] Ibid., p. 56.

[81] Ibid.

[82] Hort, *Life and Letters,* vol. 1, p. 240.

Chapter 10. Conquering the Bible with Reason

For Germany, the criticism of religion has been essentially completed, and the criticism of religion is the prerequisite of all criticism.[1]

—Karl Marx

The Challenge Against Biblical Authority

Rejecting Verbal Inspiration

The issue of overthrowing all authority except that of reason was the basis of the Enlightenment. However, even after the revolutionary periods of the late eighteenth century and the mid-nineteenth century, the Scriptures remained a source of authority. As long as people continued to believe that the Scriptures were given by the verbal inspiration of God, the writings could not be placed under the authority of human reason.

Therefore, the central question regarding the authority of Scripture remained: "Was Scripture verbally inspired by God or was it conceived and written by man?" If God verbally inspired it, then man had no authority to rewrite it to suit his reason. If, however, it could be reasoned that the Scriptures were conceived and written by man, then they would be subject to the authority of man and his reason. The Scriptures would, in effect, be part of the natural world. Therefore, man could subject them to the same kind of scientific principles that he had learned to apply to all other aspects of nature.

Thus, the first step in carrying out the plan to rewrite the Greek New Testament was to challenge the verbal inspiration of the existing Scriptures. F. D. Maurice questioned the notion that inspiration was unique

---

[1] Karl Marx, A *Contribution To The Critique Of Hegel's Philosophy Of Right*, Introduction, In *Deutsch-Franzosische Jahrbucher*, February, 1844, Annette Jolin and Joseph O'Malley, trans., Joseph O'Malley, ed. (Cambridge: Cambridge University Press, 1970), p. 131.

to Scripture. Instead, it was his view that whatever a man wrote, spoke, or thought was inspired. He wrote that:

> According to the principle of a spiritual kingdom, as we have considered it, inspiration is not a strange anomalous fact; it is the proper law and order of the world; no man ought to write, or speak, or think, except under the acknowledgement of inspiration; no man can speak, or write, or think, if he have not really an inspiration.[2]

Using this view, F. D. Maurice rejected the belief that the very words of Scripture were inspired by God. He said that he:

> ...must reject as monstrous and heretical the notion of a *dictation*...and that it remains for him [the Rationalist] to show how the discovery of different readings in MSS. [manuscripts], or the rejection of books as not genuine, which are now esteemed to be parts of the Canon, or even the detection of historical inconsistencies and mistakes in the inspired writers, would affect our belief."[3]

F. D. Maurice saw the Bible as a book like all other books, which should be submitted to the tests of reason. According to him, it is neither practical nor reasonable for us to submit our judgements to the authority of the Bible. He said:

> I perfectly agree, therefore, with the Rationalist, that to talk as some do of our right to sit in judgement upon all other books, and of the duty of submitting our judgments to the Bible, is not practical or reasonable.[4]

---

[2] Frederick Denison Maurice, *The Kingdom of Christ*, vol. 2, 1959 reprint, p. 148.

[3] Ibid., pp. 149-150.

[4] Ibid., p. 153.

Support from Darwin

Charles Darwin (1809-1882) was a student at Cambridge University studying to be a clergyman in 1829 when he began to doubt his spiritual fitness for a religious vocation.[5] He soon set out on a course of study that provided the support needed in order to mount a credible challenge to the authority of the Scriptures. In 1859, Darwin published his book, *The Origin of the Species.* In what became known as the "Theory of Evolution," Darwin's work suggested that all species evolved from lower forms, without divine intervention. This, of course, was a direct challenge to Scripture. John gave a clear account of the role of the Word in the creation of all things. According to the Gospel of John, the Word, who was God, made all things:

> In the beginning was the Word, and the Word was with God, and the Word was God. The same was in the beginning with God. All things were made by him; and without him was not any thing made that was made.
>
> —John 1:1-3

Somebody was wrong. Either John was wrong or Darwin was wrong. If Darwin's theory were true, then the words John wrote are not true and are not the Word of God. Therefore, it could be concluded that the Bible is not the Word of God. In other words, Darwin's theory provided the necessary component to enable one to use reason to challenge the authority of God and His Word.

Darwin's book caused quite a stir. During the year of 1860, there was great excitement about *The Origin of the Species.* The book was especially exciting to many people who had been looking for some evidence that could be used to support their desire to overthrow the authority of Scripture, including those who were already secretly working on rewriting the Greek New Testament.

---

[5] Frank Burch Brown, *The Evolution of Darwin's Religious Views*, National Association of Baptist Professors of Religion Special Studies Series, No. 10 (Macon, Georgia: Mercer University Press, 1986), p. 9.

While Men Slept...

Seven years after Fenton Hort and his colleagues embarked on the plan to rewrite the Greek New Testament, he was especially excited about Darwin's new book. Hort wanted to openly support it but knew that such public action would brand him with suspicion at a time when he was engaged in the potentially controversial rewriting of the Greek New Testament. Arthur Hort said that his father:

> ...combined with his devotion to theology an ever-fresh enthusiasm for science and criticism, the year 1860, in which fell the controversies aroused by the publication of *The Origin of Species* and of *Essays and Reviews*, was to a very high degree exciting. Discussion of these two books fills a large part of his letters for some months, and on the subjects of both he burned to speak openly; yet here again speech failed him.[6]

Although Hort did not feel free to publicly state his views about Darwin's work on evolution, he was privately ecstatic. He excitedly wrote to Westcott, his coauthor of the rewritten Greek New Testament, on March 10, 1860:

> ...Have you read Darwin? How I should like a talk with you about it! In spite of difficulties, I am inclined to think it unanswerable. In any case it is a treat to read such a book.[7]

Continuing to show his enthusiasm for Darwin, Hort wrote to John Ellerton on April 3, 1860:

> But the book which has most engaged me is Darwin. Whatever may be thought of it, it is a book that one is proud to be contemporary with. I must work out and examine the argument in more detail, but at present my feeling is strong that the theory is unanswerable.[8]

---

[6] Hort, *Life and Letters,* vol. 1, p. 374.

[7] Ibid., p. 414.

[8] Ibid., p. 416.

Hort was still excited about Darwin on May 10, 1860 as he wrote to the one who was to publish the rewritten Greek New Testament, Alexander Macmillan. He told Macmillan:

> I shall be glad to know whether an article on Darwin, if I can manage one, would do for your Magazine...for some reasons I should like to write, only I would not spend time on it unless I were pretty sure that it would serve your purpose.[9]

While Hort worked on rewriting the Greek New Testament, it was Darwin who occupied his mind. In another letter to Alexander Macmillan, which he had apparently written over a two day period, on May 10 and 11, 1860, Hort demonstrated his main preoccupation with the natural sciences, botany and geology:

> ...About Darwin, I have been reading and thinking a good deal, and am getting to see my way comparatively clearly, and to be also desirous to say something....The subject [of Darwin] will be none the worse churning in my mind through the summer. Except some Greek Testament (and perhaps Plato), I am going to give myself in the Alps to botany and geology.[10]

By October 15, 1860, Hort remained occupied with Darwin. He expressed his shock when Westcott said that he "...had seen no facts..." to support Darwin's theory on evolution. Hort's letter to Westcott demonstrated that he was willing to accept the theory as true, without facts. He was encouraged because the Socialist, Robert Owen, had also discussed the concept of the "upward" development [evolution from a lower form to a higher form] of all the species. Arguing in favor of evolution, Hort wrote:

> It certainly startles me to find you saying you have seen no facts which support such a view as Darwin's....But it seems to me the most probable *manner* of development, and the reflexions suggested by his book drove me to the conclusion

---

[9] Ibid., p. 415.

[10] Ibid., pp. 424-425.

that some kind of development must be supposed. Owen's view I found to be precisely the same, except that he prefers the *Vestiges* to Darwin without having any certainty as to either. He has no doubt in his own mind of the upward development of all species, though he thinks it not yet capable of being scientifically proved, and is very angry with Darwin for rushing prematurely in the face of the bigoted and unprepared public.[11]

While continuing to work on rewriting the Greek New Testament, Hort was still preoccupied by Darwin. On November 9, 1860 he wrote again to Alexander Macmillan:

Another last word on Darwin. ...to discuss this matter properly, one must go in for a thorough theological discussion, less popular even than the *Essays and Reviews*. However, I shall not let the subject drop in a hurry, or, to speak more correctly, it will not let me drop. It has completely flung me back into Natural Science. Not that I had ever abandoned it either in intention or altogether in practice. But now there is no getting rid of it any more than of a part of oneself.[12]

Seventeen years later, while finishing both the rewritten Greek New Testament and the English Revised Version of the Bible, Hort was still excited by Darwin. Hort was included among those who gathered to honor Charles Darwin in 1877 as he received an honorary degree from Cambridge. According to Arthur Hort, his father "...dined in the evening with the Philosophical Society, to meet a distinguished gathering of scientific men, including Huxley, Tyndall, Rae, Prof. Burdon Sanderson, and Mr. Francis Galton."[13]

For Hort, Westcott, and Lightfoot the work of Darwin was the key to undermining the doctrine of the inerrancy of the Scriptures. One au-

---

[11] Ibid., p. 431.

[12] Ibid., pp. 433-434.

[13] Hort, *Life and Letters,* vol. 2, p. 186.

thor described the effect of the theory of evolution on the three re-writers of the Greek New Testament this way:

> Evolution was made a leading *motif* in their philosophy and the doctrine of biblical inerrancy was frankly jettisoned.[14]

Rejecting Scriptural Infallibility

Hort, Westcott, and Lightfoot demonstrated in their interactions with each other the role of Darwin's theory of evolution in shaping their belief in the fallibility of Scripture. While Hort was occupied with the study of Darwin, the work toward rewriting the Greek New Testament continued. As the rewriting was in progress, Hort and his colleagues were faced with a major dilemma. If a perfect God inspired the Scriptures and God does not err, then the Scriptures could not be in error. Therefore, the Scriptures would be infallible. If, however, the Scriptures were written by men and not by the inspiration of God, they would be fallible. If the Scriptures were fallible, then there would be little concern with applying the principles of reason to edit and rewrite them.

As the rewriting work progressed, it was inevitable that the question of the infallibility of Scripture would arise. To be sure that each person involved in rewriting the Greek New Testament was working in unity with regard to rejecting the infallibility of the Scriptures, they exchanged letters confirming the position of each on the topic. In Hort's letter to Lightfoot on May 4, 1860, he made clear his understanding that the two were in agreement:

> ...I am also glad that you take the same provisional ground as to infallibility that I do.[15]

On the very next day, Westcott wrote a letter to Hort confirming that all three were in full agreement in rejecting the infallibility of Scripture:

---

[14] Reardon, *From Coleridge to Gore,* pp. 19-20.

[15] Hort, *Life and Letters,* vol. 1, p. 424.

> I am very glad to have seen both your note and Lightfoot's—glad too that we have had such an opportunity of openly speaking. For I too "must disclaim setting forth infallibility" in front of my convictions. All I hold is, that the more I learn, the more I am convinced that fresh doubts come from my own ignorance, and that at present I find the presumption in favour of absolute truth—I reject the word infallibility—of Holy Scripture overwhelming.[16]

Almost two years later, Hort continued to rationalize away the issue of Scriptural infallibility. In a letter on April 30 and May 1, 1862, Hort described the many books he had been reading. One of them included "Maurice's thick new volume of his philosophy," which Alexander Macmillan had given to him. Hort felt that it:

> ...seems to be clearly and broadly directed to maintaining that the English clergy are not compelled to maintain the absolute infallibility of the Bible. And, whatever the truth may be, this seems just the liberty required at the present moment, if any living belief is to survive in the land.[17]

Maurice took a strong stand against the inspiration of Scripture by God. In a letter to John Hodgkin on July 31, 1865, after reading his son's pamphlet on inspiration, Maurice had this to say:

> When 1100 clergymen declared eighteen months ago that the Bible not only contains, but *is*, the Word of God, the position struck me not as an exaggeration, but as a perilous *denial* of the truth.[18]

Using his characteristic Platonic style of logical discourse, Maurice used a member of the Society of Friends (the Quakers) as the target of his argument against the Divine inspiration of Scripture:

---

[16] Westcott, *Life and Letters*, vol. 1, p. 207.

[17] Hort, *Life and Letters,* vol. 1, pp. 452-454.

[18] Maurice, *The Life of Frederick Denison Maurice*, vol. 2, pp. 499-500.

Now what I should have craved of a member of the Society of Friends, writing on the inspiration of Scripture, would have been especially an exposure of our unbelief on this subject, and a vindication of the doctrine which may at times have been used negatively to diminish the reverence for the Scriptures, but which may also be the great restorer of that reverence, which may do more than any other to connect it with the demands of the human conscience and reason. Again and again I said to myself, as I read Mr. Hodgkin's essay, "What strength it would give to that and that assertion and argument, and how the missing link in it would be supplied, if the writer would speak as the Bible itself speaks of the Divine Word, if he would bear witness to his readers that he has a Teacher with him continually, whether he reads the letters of the book or cannot spell out one of them." It seems, I know, to many, as if this were an advanced lore to which we must arrive through the previous reception of the volume, and of all the uninspired and unauthoritative evidences which are supposed to establish its inspiration and authority.[19]

Maurice adopted the view of the rational inspiration of Scripture. Those who accept that perspective believe that inspiration is the "illumination of the rational consciousness." They believe that the sayings and teachings of Jesus are similar to those of Socrates and that the writings of Paul and of John are on the same plane as those of Plato and Aristotle.[20] This, of course, leaves the Scriptures without any final or binding authority.

Maurice saw little difference between reading the Bible and making scientific inquiry. The way he saw it, Darwin, Huxley, and others were revealing the truth of God as they uncovered the natural truths that had been put upon the earth. In other words, the discovery of nature

---

[19] Ibid., p. 500.

[20] Charles Elliott, *Subjective Theory of Inspiration*, In *The Princeton Review* (New York: July-December, 1881), p. 198.

was the discovery of God. Once the inspiration of Scripture by God, and the resultant need for acceptance of its infallibility, were rejected, then man was free to say that the Bible says whatever he wanted it to say. As one writer put it:

> Beyond expression is the sense of relief with which some theologians have freed themselves from the "straitjacket" of an infallible Bible, as they have substituted for it their own reasonings.[21]

The concept of challenging the authority of God's Word was really not new. The serpent mounted the first challenge in Genesis 3:1 when he said to the woman, "Yea, hath God said...?" The remnant of the Jews who escaped the Babylonian captivity and fled into Egypt demonstrated their defiance against the authority of God's Word when they told Jeremiah:

> *As for* the word that thou hast spoke unto us in the name of the Lord, we will not harken unto thee.
> —Jeremiah 44:16

Questions regarding the authority and reliability of Scripture had existed for centuries. The beginning of the nineteenth century, against the backdrop of the Age of Enlightenment, brought new attacks on Scripture. Heavy attacks were mounted against the historical reliability, apologetic value, and even moral authority of the Scriptures.[22]

Rescinding the Greek New Testament

The "Vile" Textus Receptus

Having rejected the belief of verbal inspiration, Scriptural infallibility, and, therefore, Scriptural authority, Hort, Westcott, and their col-

---

[21] Pache, *The Inspiration and Authority of Scripture*, pp. 314-315.

[22] Claude Welch, *Protestant Thought in the Nineteenth Century*, vol. 1, *1799-1870* (New Haven and London: The Bross Foundation, Yale University Press, 1972), p. 59.

leagues were ready to set their sights on unseating the traditionally accepted Greek New Testament, the *Textus Receptus*, upon which the Authorized Bible was based. By 1851, when he was just twenty-three years of age, Hort had already rejected the *Textus Receptus*. In a letter to John Ellerton, Hort explained:

> I had no idea till the last few weeks of the importance of texts, having read so little Greek Testament, and dragged on with the villainous *Textus Receptus*.... Think of that vile *Textus Receptus* leaning entirely on late MSS. [manuscripts]; it is a blessing there are such early ones.[23]

Admittedly, without having even read much of the Greek New Testament, Hort's mind had already been conditioned by influences, such as those received from Daniel Macmillan, Hare, and Maurice, to reject the *Textus Receptus*. He reached this conclusion after he had been subjected to influences that he never could have expected when he left his evangelical home to enter Trinity College at Cambridge.

Then in 1853, Daniel Macmillan proposed a plan that would make the dream of getting rid of the "vile" *Textus Receptus*, which was based on the Byzantine majority manuscripts, a reality. Hort wrote a letter to John Ellerton on April 19, 1853 to tell him of the plan:

> He [Westcott] and I are going to edit a Greek text of the N.T. some two or three years hence, if possible. Lachmann and Tischendorf will supply rich materials, but not nearly enough; and we hope to do a good deal with Oriental versions. Our object is to supply clergymen generally, schools, etc., with a portable Gk. Test., which shall not be disfigured with Byzantine corruptions. But we *may* find the work too irksome.[24]

In a letter he wrote on November 4, 1853, after he had agreed to undertake the task of rewriting the Greek New Testament and closely

---

[23] Hort, *Life and Letters,* vol. 2, p. 211.

[24] Ibid., vol. 1, p. 250.

following Maurice's expulsion as a professor at King's College for heresy, Hort wrote:

> ...I don't know any really plain *subjects* in the Bible: the plainness should lie in the treatment. I can't now discuss Maurice's doctrine about the Resurrection, etc. Much seems to me good....[25]

Before the ancient manuscripts had been reviewed and the newly developed science of textual criticism had been applied, the details of the plan to rewrite the Greek New Testament were established:

> We came to a distinct and positive understanding about our Gk. Test. and the details thereof. We still do not wish it to be talked about, but are going to work at once, and hope we may perhaps have it out in little more than a year. This, of course, gives me good employment.[26]

Hort saw the Bible and the church as the obstacles preventing people from being "led to the fulness of truth." He wrote to Maurice:

> Thousands, I suspect, who might easily be led into the fulness of truth, would be stopped at the threshold by anything which seemed to interfere with their devotion to their Bible or their Church, as the case might be.[27]

The Plan

There was a plan to "rescind" the commonly accepted Greek New Testament text and to replace it with another text, which would be placed in schools throughout the world. The strategy was to not *completely* replace the Received Text but, instead, to introduce only "*certain* emendations" that would not be readily detected. In places where the changes would appear to be noticeable, the plan was to use mar-

---

[25] Ibid., p. 264.

[26] Ibid.

[27] Ibid., p. 245.

ginal notes or footnotes in which they would apply their "own ingenuity or principles" in order to overcome the most likely objections to the changes. On October 12, 1853, Westcott wrote a letter to Hort detailing the proposed plan:

> ...As to our proposed recension of the New Testament text, our object would be, I suppose, to prepare a text for common and general use—in schools, for instance. With such an end in view, would it not be best to introduce only *certain* emendations into the received text, **and to note in the margin such as seem likely or noticeable—after Griesbach's manner?** Such a book would, I think, do great good...I feel most keenly the disgrace of circulating what I feel to be falsified copies of Holy Scripture, and am most anxious to provide something to replace them. This cannot be any text resting solely on our own judgement, even if we were not too inexperienced to make one; but it must be supported by a clear and *obvious* preponderance of evidence. **The margin will give ample scope for our own ingenuity or principles. In the arrangement of paragraphs I think we might follow our own judgement entirely.**...[28] [Bold type is shown for emphasis.]

While putting alternative readings into the footnotes or margins may seem helpful to the casual reader, it has the overall effect of causing him to doubt the reliability and, therefore, the authority of the Scripture. He also loses the ability to distinguish between what God says and what men wrote. The effect of using marginal notes is to leave the decision to the reader to accept the reading of preference or to reject the entire Scripture. In other words, it would then be up to the reader, perhaps believing that both readings are of equal value, to accept or reject whichever reading he preferred.

The translators of the 1611 Authorized Bible were apparently well aware of the danger of this practice of using marginal readings. Among the rules that were set forth to be observed in the translation of the Bible was the following:

---

[28] Westcott, *Life and Letters*, vol. 1, p. 228.

6. **No Marginal Notes at all to be affixed**, but only for the Explanation of the *Hebrew* or *Greek* Words, which cannot without some circumlocution, so briefly and fitly be express'd in the Text. [29] [Bold type is shown for emphasis.]

John Burgon (1813-1888) was also well aware of the problem that was created by executing the proposed nineteenth century plan in rewriting the English Bible. He expressed his concerns this way:

For, the ill-advised practice of recording in the margin of an English Bible certain of the blunders-such things cannot by any stretch of courtesy be styled "Various Readings"- which appear in the margin as "some" or "many" "ancient authorities," can only result in hopelessly unsettling the faith of millions. It cannot be defended on the plea of candor, the candor which is determined that men shall "know the worst." The worst had NOT been told; and it were dishonesty to insinuate that it has. If all the cases were faithfully exhibited where "a few," "some," or "many ancient authorities" read differently from what is exhibited in the actual Text, not only would the margin prove insufficient to contain the record, but the very page itself would not nearly suffice.[30]

According to Burgon, these alternative readings that were put in the margins "...are specimens *arbitrarily selected* out of an immense mass."[31]

While Hort was rewriting the New Greek New Testament, he was preoccupied with lamenting over the expulsion of Maurice from King's College. In a letter to Westcott on January 3, 1854, he said that the events surrounding Maurice's expulsion were keeping him busy enough to:

---

[29] Alfred W. Pollard, *Records of the English Bible*, p. 54.

[30] John William Burgon, *The Revision Revised: A Critique of the English Revised Version of 1881, with Application to the Modern Translations*, In *Unholy Hands on the Bible*, vol. 1, Jay P. Green, ed. (Lafayette, Indiana: Sovereign Grace Trust Fund, 1990), p. D-31.

[31] Ibid., p. D-35.

...take up my time and prevent me from making much progress toward the Greek New Testament. But what I have done has been pretty efficiently done.[32]

Five days later, on January 8, 1854, Maurice explained that he believed that the Bible should be treated like all other books:

> But I have said *a posteriori* that I believed the Bible did serve as a key book which enabled us to understand the histories and legends of various nations, to justify the true beliefs which were in them, to show what false beliefs or unbeliefs had mingled with these, to explain how they had become confounded. I have called for the application of the most severe test to its records; I have said that they ought to bear it if the book is what it assumes to be, and the Christians have wronged and degraded it by severing it from all other books instead of manfully evincing their own confidence in its veracity and its strength by trying whether it will not throw light upon all.[33]

George Holyoake, a well-known atheist, also expressed his view of the relationship between secularism and the Bible. In Holyoake's view, Christian morality had failed:

> ...because the Christian constantly holds up the Bible as the only source of morals, and that, consequently, all who do not believe in the Bible as a divine book are without morality.[34]

In 1858 Hort continued his work on rewriting the underlying basis for the New Testament of the Bible. During the course of his work, he declined to publicly state his views on the Bible in a proposed publication called *Essays*. He knew that his views against the Evangelical doctrines and his rejection of biblical authority would be viewed as false by most of those who would participate in that publication:

---

[32] Hort, *Life and Letters,* vol. 1, p. 266.

[33] Maurice, *The Life of Frederick Denison Maurice,* vol. 2, p. 229.

[34] Royle, *Victorian Infidels,* p. 151.

While Men Slept...

> The positive doctrines even of the Evangelicals seem to me perverted rather than untrue. There are, I fear, still more serious differences between us on the subject of authority, and especially the authority of the Bible; this alone would make my position among you sufficiently false in respect to the great questions which you will be chiefly anxious to discuss.[35]

In a letter to Lightfoot, who was also a collaborator in rewriting the Greek New Testament, Westcott wrote in 1859:

> The prospect of a common work on the New Testament is one so delightful in every respect that the differences in our plans must be very great if I, at least, do not yield far enough to make common work possible. Macmillan's letter reached me this morning. He seems open to any scheme on which we could agree, so that for the present we may theorise safely.
>
> The peculiarities of your plan seem, then, as far as it is distinguished from that which had occurred to me— 1. The printing of a Greek text. 2. The addition of select various readings. 3. The printing of the English Version....[36]

Biblical Criticism

Submitting God's Word to the Standard of Reason

German thought had a tremendous influence on the development of modern textual criticism. The Prussian philosopher Immanuel Kant, by teaching analytical and synthetic critical thinking skills, had already laid the foundation for applying reason to the evaluation of the Bible in the form of textual criticism. Johann Wolfgang von Goethe and Georg Hegel also had a great influence on the thought of young theologians. Friedrich Ernst Daniel Schleiermacher, for example, was one of these young theologians who had a major impact on textual criticism as it would be adopted by the rewriters of the English Bible.

---

[35] Hort, *Life and Letters*, vol. 1, p. 400.

[36] Westcott, *Life and Letters*, vol. 1, p. 205.

Schleiermacher studied these great German philosophers while in seminary at Barby, in the context of a secret club. He read and debated the writings of German philosophers and soon came to question his own Christian beliefs. As was described by one writer, he:

> ...became skeptical about whether the one who called himself "Son of Man, was the true eternal God," and whether "his death was a vicarious atonement, because he never expressly said so himself," and continued by saying that he could not believe Christ's death was necessary, "because God, who evidently did not create men for perfection, but of the pursuit of it, cannot possibly intend to punish them eternally, because they have not attained it." An inability to obtain answers to these religious doubts led to severe disillusionment, a painful exchange of views with his father ("written with trembling hands and tears"), and his removal to the University of Halle.[37]

After entering the University of Halle in 1787, he further studied the philosophies of Plato, Aristotle, and Immanuel Kant. As he became a leader in textual criticism, Schleiermacher made clear his views on Scripture:

> You are right to despise the paltry imitators who derive their religion wholly from someone else or cling to a dead document by which they swear and from which they draw proof. Every holy writing is merely a mausoleum of religion, a monument that a great spirit was there that no longer exists; for if it still lived and were active, why would it attach such great importance to the dead letter that can only be a weak reproduction of it? It is not the person who believes in a holy writing who has religion, but only the one who needs none and probably could make one for himself.[38]

---

[37] Richard Crouter, In the Introduction to *Friedrich Schleiermacher On Religion: Speeches to Its Cultured Despisers,* Richard Crouter, intro., trans., and notes (Cambridge: Cambridge University Press, 1988), p. 4.

[38] Friedrich Schleiermacher, *On Religion: Speeches to Its Cultured Despisers,* pp. 134-135.

While Men Slept...

Schleiermacher believed that the Bible was nothing more than a collection of religious books written by ordinary Christians.[39] He eliminated the supernatural element from the Bible. Samuel Taylor Coleridge chiefly introduced this theory of the absence of supernatural guidance or control from Germany into England. There, Julius Hare, Maurice, and others embraced and disseminated it.[40]

By the efforts of Schleiermacher and others in textual criticism, the authority of the Bible came under intensifying attacks with the dawn of the new Enlightenment. The beginning of modern textual criticism is attributed to another German textual critic, Johann Jakob Griesbach (1745-1812), who was a close friend of Goethe. As part of his comprehensive work on textual criticism, J. J. Griesbach attacked the orthodox position that the text of the New Testament Scriptures was inspired by God. Thus, he attacked the doctrine of *theopneustia*, which says that individual words were God-inspired.[41] According to Griesbach, Mark used the Gospels of Matthew and Luke from which to extract and record the acts of Jesus that were written in the Gospel of Mark.[42] Other German theologians, including Schleiermacher, defended this hypothesis of Griesbach.[43]

Griesbach was the first editor of the Greek New Testament who used Greek manuscripts other than those that had been based on the work of Erasmus.[44] Carolus Lachmann (1793-1851) also took the position

---

[39] Charles Elliott, *Subjective Theory of Inspiration*, In *The Princeton Review* (New York: July-December, 1881), p. 193.

[40] Ibid., p. 194.

[41] Gerhard Delling, *Johann Jakob Griesbach: His Life, Work and Times*, Ronald Walls, trans., In *J. J. Griesbach: Synoptic and Text-critical Studies, 1776-1976*, Bernard Orchard and Thomas R. W. Longstaff, eds. (Cambridge: Cambridge University Press, 1978), pp. 5-11.

[42] Bo Reicke, *Griesbach's Answer to the Synoptic Question*, Ronald Walls, trans., In *J.J. Griesbach: Synoptic and Text-critical Studies, 1776-1976*, pp. 53-54.

[43] Ibid., p. 60.

[44] J.J. Griesbach, *Commentatio qua Marci Evanelium totum e Matthaei et Lucae commentariis decerptum esse monstratur,* Bo Reicke, intro., In *J. J. Griesbach: Synoptic and Text-critical Studies, 1776-1976*, p. 69.

of referring to a few manuscripts to the exclusion of the many.[45] Although Griesbach departed from the readings of the *Textus Receptus* considerably, his departure was not nearly as consistent as that of subsequent editors, such as Fenton Hort.[46] Generally, Griesbach printed the *Textus Receptus* and indicated the readings, based on other manuscripts, that he preferred in the footnotes. Hort, on the other hand, printed his own text and, therefore, decided for himself what reading he wanted at each point.[47]

As Coleridge studied in Germany, he came into contact with some of the early essays on biblical criticism. These caused him to question whether the conventional assumptions that existed in England regarding the Bible could be tolerated. At that time, the Bible was still widely accepted by nearly all Christians in England to be a collection of writings that was equally inspired and authoritative in all of its parts. It was seen as the place where the external evidence of the truth of Christianity was stored.[48]

The modern school of biblical criticism was largely centered at the Tubingen School of Divinity, which had been greatly influenced by Hegel's ideas and his belief that religion manifested itself in a myth. It was this critical approach to the Scriptures that had been the one phenomenon most responsible for the destruction of the Christian faith in the nineteenth century.[49] Ferdinand Christian Baur (1792-1860) was the pioneer of the Tubingen school's theories in textual criticism. Heavily influenced by Hegel, Baur applied Hegel's dialectic philosophies to the New Testament and to the history of Christianity.[50]

---

[45] Burgon, *The Revision Revised*, p. D-10.

[46] G. D. Kilpatrick, *Griesbach and the Development of Text Criticism*, In *J. J. Griesbach: Synoptic and Text-critical Studies, 1776-1976*, p. 137.

[47] Ibid., p. 138.

[48] Alec R. Vidler, *The Church in an Age of Revolution: 1789 to the Present Day* (Harmondsworth, Middlesex: Penguin Books Ltd, 1961), p. 80.

[49] Wilson, *God's Funeral*, p. 48.

[50] Latourette, *A History of Christianity*, vol. 2, p. 1127.

While Men Slept...

On November 21, 1842, Maurice expressed his concern about the ability of the poor to use their intellect to reason spiritual truths. He said that:

> ...it is the intellect, which meddles with propositions, that is wanting or only exists very feebly in the poor (so however that the exercise of the higher power will be a means of cultivating the lower); that if we do not touch that [the intellect], but endeavour to make our appeal to the senses as the great helpers to the *reason* and as supplying *it* with its materials, we are able at once to provide a richer and simpler lore for the poor man than is commonly the portion of the rich.[51]

Maurice, who, along with Hare, studied the works of Schleiermacher,[52] did not accept the Bible as a solitary fact, being its own independent authority. Instead, he tried to show that a connection actually exists between the church, creeds, and Bible.[53] In the light of historical criticism, the Bible was losing its authority among those who relied on reason as their guide. The critics became more and more convinced that, although God may have had a hand in the work, it was really the work of fallible men.[54]

Biblical Confusion

Biblical criticism, such as that taught at the Tubingen school was central to using reason as a tool to overcome the Bible. The German theologians of the Tubingen school, who had been influenced by Hegel, accepted that Christianity contained many deep truths but that it was, in reality, a mythology.[55] They believed that the Gospels were not a literal or a historical account of miracles that had actually happened. Instead, they believed them to be an account of "religio-mythical be-

---

[51] Maurice, *The Life of Frederick Denison Maurice*, vol. 1, p. 334.

[52] Ibid., p. 453.

[53] *Toward the Recovery of Unity: The Thought of Frederick Denison Maurice*, John F. Porter and William J. Wolf, eds. (New York: The Seabury Press, 1964), p. 25.

[54] Reardon, *From Coleridge to Gore*, p. 18.

[55] Wilson, *God's Funeral*, p. 72.

lief systems" that happened to be focused on a first century prophet. The application of biblical criticism was seen by key historical figures as a tool to be used to bring confusion into the minds of believers. Gorky, an advisor to the former Soviet Union dictator, Joseph Stalin, explained the usefulness of the biblical criticism of the Tubingen school when he wrote in a letter to Stalin that:

> We cannot do without an edition of the "Bible" with critical commentaries from the Tubingen school and books on criticism of biblical texts, which could bring a very useful "confusion into the minds" of believers.[56]

Successful challenge of the Word of God is fundamental to all other challenges. Karl Marx summarized the progress in this area of challenge or criticism as follows:

> For Germany, the criticism of religion has been essentially completed, and the criticism of religion is the prerequisite of all criticism.[57]

---

[56] Maxim Gorky, *Letter from Gorky to Stalin*, (lcweb@loc.gov Library of Congress, posted November 13, 1995).

[57] Karl Marx, A *Contribution To The Critique Of Hegel's Philosophy Of Right*, p. 131.

While Men Slept...

Chapter 11. The Fourth Century Influence on the New Greek Text

> ...a text, issued by men already known for what will un-
> doubtedly be treated as dangerous heresy, will have great
> difficulties in finding its way to regions which it might
> otherwise hope to reach...[1]
>
> —Fenton Hort

Subjective Inquiry

Before a revision of the Greek New Testament could be made, the revisors needed something to revise. Since key participants in the plan to rewrite the Greek New Testament had already decided that the *Textus Receptus*, known as the Received Text, and the majority of the available manuscripts did not adequately pass the tests of enlightened reason, alternative Greek texts were needed. Erasmus compiled his Greek text on which the *Textus Receptus* was based in 1516.[2] Martin Luther made his famous challenge to the authority of the Roman Catholic Church the following year, marking the beginning of the Protestant Reformation. As we have learned, German theologians, such as Schleiermacher, Griesbach, and Lachmann, mounted significant challenges against the traditional Greek New Testament text, which had been used as the basis for Protestant Bibles for more than three hundred years. It was at the height of these challenges that Fenton Hort and Brooke Foss Westcott began to theorize and work on developing a new Greek New Testament.[3] Before they even started their work, they had already concluded that the *Textus Receptus* could not be accepted.

In other words, the revisors had a preconceived bias against the *Textus Receptus*. As we have learned, Hare, Maurice, the Macmillans, Hort,

---

[1] Hort, *Life and Letters,* vol. 1, p. 445.
[2] Miller, *Introduction* to John William Burgon, *The Traditional Text of the New Testament*, p. 2.
[3] Burgon, *The Traditional Text of the New Testament*, p. 3.

While Men Slept...

Westcott, Lightfoot, and others who were to influence the direction of the rewritten Greek New Testament, already had clearly established their theological positions before the rewriting began in 1853. They knew which of their key desired readings differed from those of the traditional Bible. They even knew who in the early centuries of Christianity agreed with their position on these Scriptures. This pre-established position became an obstacle to finding objective textual evidence to support the changes that were desired in the traditional Bible text.

Knowing certain fourth century manuscripts, such as the Eusebius-Origen Bibles previously discussed, tended to support their preconceived theological positions, the revisors set out to rationally justify their argument in favor of using those manuscripts. It might be reasoned, for example, that older Greek manuscripts are more reliable. Since they would have undergone fewer generations of hand copying, there would have been fewer opportunities for either willful or accidental changes to be made in them. Some might argue that the copiers embellished later manuscripts because they were trying to promote certain doctrines. Using this visible logic, the promoters of the new Greek New Testament put forward a strong argument in favor of using certain fourth century manuscripts.[4]

Many would agree with their rational arguments, unless they knew that those fourth century texts relied heavily upon manuscripts that were known to either contain critical errors or that were subjected to clearly known heretical influences. As we have learned, the corruption of manuscripts certainly goes back much farther than the fourth century after Christ. In addition the fourth century itself was a time of great heresy and a time of significant critical challenges to the belief in the divinity of Jesus Christ.

F. D. Maurice, who took strong Unitarian theological positions, was the mentor of those who were to undertake rewriting the Greek New Testament. Trained as a lawyer (although he did not receive his law degree), Maurice used the skills of subjective advocacy rather than

---

[4] Miller, *Witness of the Early Fathers, The Involuntary Evidence Given by Dr. Hort*, In *The Traditional Text of the New Testament*, pp. 41-48.

those of objective scientific inquiry. Thus, Maurice was in a position to develop a case for manuscript selection from a perspective of biased argument in a secretive manner in order to minimize the opposition's ability to prepare a counter argument.

A Conspiracy of Secrecy

Having already established the plan and being well equipped with an understanding of the underlying Unitarian theology that they wished to promote, the rewriters of the Greek New Testament began the work of finding supporting Scriptures. In order to achieve acceptance of the newly proposed Unitarian-oriented Bible, a vigorous search was made for supporting manuscripts that could be used to replace the existing Greek authority, the *Textus Receptus*. A chief criticism of the Authorized Version was that it is based on "inferior" original manuscripts that came from the "Byzantine" type of Greek Text. It was argued that this manuscript type "...represents a revision made in the fourth century A.D. and later; it is farther removed from text-types which have been distinguished in more recent times."[5]

The Socinians, who were Unitarians, maintained that the church fathers in the first three centuries after Christ did not teach the Trinity. Thus, the Unitarians argued that their beliefs, and not those of the Trinitarians, maintained the traditions of the church that were the oldest and most authentic.[6] Therefore, it was natural that the Unitarians sought to find evidence developed in the first three centuries by the Arians to support their proposed changes in the Scriptures.

The nineteenth century scribes set out to find textual evidence to support the proposed rewriting of the Greek text of the New Testament. Although their work was not authorized by any visible authority, Hare, Maurice, and the Macmillans promoted their cause. Each of these men, as we have learned, shared documented Unitarian theological and a Socialist economical and governmental positions.

[5] F.F. Bruce, *History of the Bible in English From the Earliest Versions* (New York: Oxford University Press, 1978), p. 127.
[6] Gerard Reedy, *The Bible and Reason: Anglicans and Scripture in Late Seventeenth-Century England* (Philadelphia: University of Pennsylvania Press, 1985), p. 122.

217

While Men Slept...

In order to avoid premature suspicion, the rewriters worked secretly and subtly. In defending his decision to avoid publicity on their work, Hort explained the value of doing the work in secret. It was his position that making changes in the Scriptures without the knowledge of evangelical Christians would avoid confrontation with them. Hort believed that publicly writing of his views on the Bible and theology would cause a problem because:

> It is surely likely to bring on a crisis; and that I cannot think desirable on any account. The errors and prejudices, which we agree in wishing to remove, can surely be more wholesomely and also more effectually reached by individual efforts of an indirect kind than by combined open assault. At present very many orthodox but rational men are being unawares acted on by influences which will assuredly bear good fruit in due time, if the process is allowed to go on quietly; but I cannot help fearing that a premature crisis would frighten back many into the merest traditionalism.[7]

Hort explained to Westcott the need for the conspiracy to surround rewriting the Bible. He reasoned that it was important that the new text be published before it was found out that the views they represented would be considered heresy to most Christians. In his letter on April 12, 1861, Hort put it this way:

> Also - but this may be cowardice - I have a sort of craving that our text should be cast upon the world before we deal with matters likely to brand us with suspicion. I mean, **a text, issued by men already known for what will undoubtedly be treated as dangerous heresy, will have great difficulties in finding its way to regions which it might otherwise hope to reach**, and whence it would not be easily banished by subsequent alarms.[8] [Bold type is used for emphasis.]

In 1865, the plan of secrecy for rewriting the Greek New Testament continued to be evident as Hort wrote to Westcott:

---

[7] Hort, *Life and Letters,* vol. 1, p. 400.
[8] Ibid., p. 445.

218

But it is even more important not to break silence with anything crude.[9]

While working in "silence," the rewriters of the Greek New Testament needed manuscripts that could be used to support their positions and to replace the majority manuscripts that contained the basis for the Authorized King James Version of the Bible.

Replacing the Majority Manuscripts

It was fortunate for those who were rewriting the Greek New Testament that they were able to gain access to the two fourth century Alexandrian manuscripts. They relied on them to give support for the "recension" of the *Textus Receptus*, known as the "Received Text." Desiderius Erasmus had written the basis for this Greek New Testament from the Majority Manuscripts. The two fourth-century Alexandrian manuscripts that were of the same "type" were called the *Codex Vaticanus* and the *Codex Sinaiticus*. B. F. Westcott believed the history of the *Codex Vaticanus* to be unknown. However, he agreed that it had been in the Vatican Library from the close of the fifteenth century.[10] According to Tischendorf, the *Codex Vaticanus* appeared in the first catalog of the Vatican Library collection, which was dated to 1475.[11] Others have noted that the manuscript was first brought to Rome in 1448 by Pope Nicholas V and that it was entered into the first catalog of the Vatican Library in 1475. The manuscript was first made known outside the Vatican in 1533, when it was brought to the attention of Erasmus.[12]

It appears that the manuscript arrived at the Vatican while the Medici family had significant influence in the Roman Catholic Church, as has been previously explained. The *Codex Vaticanus* was carefully guarded

---

[9] Ibid., p. 50.

[10] Westcott, *The Bible in the Church*, p. 305.

[11] Constantine Tischendorf, *Introduction*, In *The New Testament: the Authorized English Version; with Introduction, and Various Readings from the Three Most Celebrated Manuscripts of the Original Greek*, Tauchnitz ed., vol. 1000 (Leipzing: Bernard Tauchnitz, 1869), p. x.

[12] Price, *The Ancestry of Our English Bible,* p. 150.

and not generally accessible to those outside the Vatican. In 1843, however, Tischendorf was allowed to look at it for six hours. Then, in 1866 he was again able to view it, but then for only three hours per day. Even though he had agreed not to make copies of the manuscript as a condition for his access to the manuscript, Tischendorf hand-copied twenty pages of the text.[13]

According to B. F. Westcott, the Vatican manuscript may be::

> ...pronounced to be the most correct copy of the Greek Bible, though it is not free from grave faults. It is mutilated both at the beginning and at the end, and consequently has no table of contents like that in the Alexandrine MS.; nor is there any-thing to show whether it originally included the *Apocalypse*....[14]

A third manuscript, the *Codex Alexandrinus*, was given to King Charles I in 1628 by Cyril Luca, the Patriarch of Constantinople, who had brought it from Alexandria. The German biblical researcher, Constantine von Tischendorf (b. 1815), believed this manuscript to be dated in the fifth century.[15] It was Tischendorf in 1844 who found the *Codex Sinaiticus*, which was in a wastebasket at St. Catherine's Monastery at Mount Sinai. According to a review written by Charles Hodge (1797-1878), Tischendorf found it as:

> ...he was there rummaging in a basket of torn and mutilated fragments of manuscripts which had been thrown away as useless, and were destined to the flames, he drew forth sev-eral pages of a very ancient copy of the Septuagint.[16]

Westcott recognized the need for the newly found *Codex Sinaiticus* text to provide support for rewriting the Greek New Testament that

---

[13] Ibid., pp. 150-151.

[14] Westcott, *The Bible in the Church*, p. 305.

[15] Tischendorf, *Introduction*, In *The New Testament: the Authorized English Version*, Tauchnitz ed., p. xi.

[16] Charles Hodge, ed., *The Biblical Repertory and Princeton Review for the Year 1861*, vol. 33 (Philadelphia: Peter Walker, 1861), p. 160.

was in progress. The manuscript differed from the Alexandrine and Vatican manuscript in both the Old and New Testaments.[17] Of the need for the new Tischendorf Greek text, Westcott wrote to Hort in 1865 that:

> I hope to send to-morrow the last two chapters of St. Matthew. The work grows somewhat easier, I think, as it goes on, but it always brings its characteristic headache. I must have the new Tischendorf. The advertisement which I saw gave me the same idea of the book which you give. His changes show, what is abundantly evident elsewhere, that he really has no very clear ideas about the Text. I am more and more struck with the phenomena of distinct recensions, or whatever else they may be called. But indeed it is very long since D. made me give expression to the belief in the existence of co-existent types of Text at the earliest period to which we can descend.[18]

Alterations in the Fourth Century Manuscripts

Many scholars argue that, because these Alexandrian manuscripts apparently date back to the fourth century, they are more likely to be free of corruption than more recent copies would be. Unfortunately, the manuscript considered by many to be the best available from the fourth century, the *Codex Sinaiticus*, appeared to be the work of careless and, perhaps, malicious scribes. According to a critical Greek Concordance of the New Testament, which was revised and completed in 1871 by the Unitarian scholar, Ezra Abbott, the *Codex Sinaiticus:*

> ... is regarded as a genuine document of the fourth century, of the same age as the Vatican manuscript, the readings of which it often confirms, while it is evidently independent of it. And though in its frequent omissions occasioned by the similar ending of words, and otherwise, it shows some carelessness

---

[17] Westcott, *The Bible in the Church,* p. 308.
[18] Westcott, *Life and Letters,* vol. 1, p. 288.

of the scribe, it is still deemed a most important witness of the early state of the text.[18]

The *Codex Sinaiticus* manuscript contained 110,000 lines. Tischendorf himself, along with two of his colleagues, noted more than 12,000 changes in the manuscript by *later hands*.[19] The editions of the *Codex Sinaiticus* prepared by Tischendorf also changed significantly over time. There were reportedly at least 3,572 changes made by Tischendorf in the manuscript between the 1859 and 1872 editions.[20] Despite the thousands of changes that Tischendorf found in the *Codex Sinaiticus* and the thousands of additional changes he made in the manuscript between 1859 and 1872, he believed that, because of its age, it was more reliable than the later manuscripts, such as those used by Erasmus.[21]

Erasmus had access to numerous manuscripts, *including* the *Vatican Codex* (*Codex Vaticanus*) of the fourth century,[22] which is one of the two manuscripts that were reported to "have been distinguished in more recent times." The other "distinguished" manuscript was the *Sinaitic Codex* (*Codex Sinaiticus*). Erasmus affirmed that he used the oldest and most correct manuscripts in preparation of his Greek New Testament.[23] He, however, rejected the use of manuscripts that had readings differing from the majority of those he had available to him.

Tischendorf edited both the *Codex Sinaiticus,* in 1862, and the *Codex Vaticanus,* in 1867. Many modern scholars refer to these two manu-

---

[18] Charles Frederic Hudson, *A Critical Greek and English Concordance of the New Testament, Prepared by Charles F. Hudson under the Direction of Horace L. Hastings... Revised and Completed by Ezra Abbott*, 2nd ed., rev. (Philadelphia: J. B. Lippincott & Co., 1871), p. xix.

[19] Price, *The Ancestry of Our English Bible*, p. 145.

[20] Burgon, *The Traditional Text of the New Testament*, p. 4.

[21] Tischendorf, *Introduction*, In *The New Testament: the Authorized English Version*, Tauchnitz ed., p. viii.

[22] Price, *The Ancestry of Our English Bible,* p. 150.

[23] Jack Finegan, *Encountering New Testament Manuscripts: A Working Introduction to Textual Criticism* (Grand Rapids, Michigan: William B. Eerdmans Publishing Company, 1974), p. 56.

scripts as being "oldest and best."[24] Tischendorf said that in 1828 Pope Leo XII had authorized Angelo Mai, who was later made a cardinal, to prepare an edition of the *Codex Vaticanus*. It appeared in 1857, but was extremely inaccurate. Therefore, Tischendorf said he corrected its "many hundreds" of errors, which he presented in his 1867 edition. Even more corrections were made for the 1869 edition![25]

These manuscripts, with the thousands of changes that had been made in them, were truly different from the thousands of other manuscripts and from the references that had been made by early scholars to manuscripts which have since been destroyed. Because many modern scholars believed both the *Codex Vaticanus* and the *Codex Sinaiticus* to be reliable, they really believed that God's Word was lost and then rediscovered. They believed that the *Codex Vaticanus* was lost for more than 1000 years, somewhere in Alexandria, and that the *Codex Sinaiticus* was lying in the trash at Mt. Sinai for nearly 1500 years.

Speaking of the *Codex Sinaiticus*, Dean Burgon expressed his unbelief that the Holy Spirit would have kept the truth of His Word from believers for hundreds of years by hiding it in an obscure wastebasket. Burgon put it this way:

> I am utterly disinclined to believe—so grossly improbably [sic] does it seem—that at the end of 1800 years 995 copies out of every thousand, suppose, will prove untrustworthy; and on the contrary that one, two, three, four, or five remain whose contents were until yesterday as good as unknown should be found to have retained the secret of what the Holy Spirit originally inspired. I am utterly unable to believe that God's promise has had in point of fact to be picked by a German critic out of a waste-paper basket in the convent at St. Catherine, and that the entire text had to be remodeled after the pattern set by a couple of copies which had remained in neglect during fifteen centuries, and had probably owed their survival to that

---

[24] Tischendorf, *Introduction*, In *The New Testament: the Authorized English Version*, Tauchnitz ed., p. xii.
[25] Ibid., p. xi.

neglect while hundreds of others had been thumbed to pieces, and had bequeathed their witness to copies made from them.[26]

Even J. B. Lightfoot, one of the three who would use the Alexandrian manuscripts as the basis for rewriting the Greek New Testament, had this to say about Christianity in Alexandria:

> In Alexandria, when at length the curtain rises, Christianity is seen enthroned between Greek philosophy and Gnostic speculation, while Judaism is far in the background.[27]

Lightfoot clearly recognized the problems that Christianity had experienced in Alexandria. Yet he attacked those who had rejected the Alexandrian Greek manuscripts in favor of what they considered to be the more reliable majority manuscripts. He said of Tyndale and implied of Erasmus:

> It was not the fault, it was the misfortune, of the scholars from Tyndale downward, to whom we owe our English Bible, that the only text accessible to them was faulty and corrupt.[28]

The Rewritten Greek Not Ready For English Translation

As the work on rewriting the Greek New Testament continued, there was a general feeling among many of the Socialist Unitarian theologians that there should soon be "revision" of the Authorized Version of the English Bible. Brooke Foss Westcott resisted the timing of the "revision," believing that it should wait until a replacement for the *Textus Receptus* Greek New Testament was developed. By 1868, Westcott had determined that the translators of the Authorized Version of the Bible had:

---

[26] Burgon, *The Traditional Text of the New Testament,* p. 7.

[27] J. B. Lightfoot, *Dissertations on the Apostolic Age* (London: Macmillan and Co., 1892), p. 92.

[28] Joseph Barber Lightfoot, *On A Fresh Revision of the English New Testament* (London: Macmillan and Co., 1891), p. 21.

...suffered most from the corrupt form in which the Greek text of the New Testament was presented to them.[29]

He further expressed his views that a rewritten Greek New Testament was the essential foundation for a rewritten English Bible. He wrote in 1868 that:

> One question however in connexion (sic) with the Authorised Version I have purposely neglected. It seemed useless to discuss its revision. The revision of the original texts must precede the revision of the translation, and the time for this, even in the New Testament, has not yet fully come.[30]

According to Westcott's son, Arthur:

> His own view at the time was that the text of the New Testament needed to be more accurately determined before an improved translation could be profitably undertaken.[31]

Others were in agreement with Westcott on this matter. In 1871, after the English "revision" had commenced, Charles Hodge recognized that the very foundation upon which the "revisors" wanted to base the new version was still unsettled. He said:

> Many of the principles of criticism are still in dispute. Surely the time is not ripe for a final emendation of the text. And until that has been obtained there cannot be a final revision of the authorized version...The question is, are these results sufficiently secure to be trusted as final?* What does fidelity to truth demand? Is it not best not to be too hasty in deciding on such a matter? Should not critical principles and facts be al-

---

[29] Westcott, *A General View of the History of the English Bible*, 1st ed., p. 337.
[30] Brooke Foss Westcott, *A General View of the History of the English Bible* 3rd ed., rev. by William Aldis Wright (London: Macmillan and Co., Ltd., 1905), p. vii.
[31] Westcott, *Life and Letters*, vol. 1, pp. 389-390.

lowed more time for settlement, and is it well to presume upon them when, as now, the most important results are so recent, and when every year adds to the sources of correction.

*The controversy between the authority of the oldest manuscripts and the greater mass of more recent manuscripts is still going on. Mr. Schrivener would give more authority to the latter than others are willing to do. And Tragelles is criticized for excessive adherence to the former, so restricting the range of his authorities as to assimilate his text to Lachmann's, though from different principles. Ellicott himself has changed in this respect since he began to publish on the New Testament—*Saturday Review*, October 1, 1870.[30]

Even without a settled replacement Greek New Testament to serve as the basis for the English revision, the revisors proceeded anyway!

---

[30] Charles W. Hodge, *Proposed Revision of the English Bible*, In *The Biblical Repertory and Princeton Review*, Charles Hodge and Lyman H. Atwater, eds. (New York: Charles Scribner & Co., 1871), p. 45.

Chapter 12. The Roman Connection to the New Bible

> I believe that it [the Society of Jesus, the Jesuits] was a creation of God by St. Ignatius, raised up for a special work, that is, to react against the heresy and schism of the Lutheran reformation. This it accomplished. [1]
>
> —Cardinal Henry Edward Manning

Infallible Pope and the Defective Bible

The Fruit of the Oxford Movement

As we shall learn, the key participants in the Oxford Movement reached two climatic milestones in 1870. They announced that the pope was infallible and that the Bible was in error. These major achievements were central to their efforts to return the Church of England and, through it, the Protestant churches to the authority of the Roman Catholic Church. These goals were achieved through the pivotal figures in the Oxford Movement, who had established lasting personal bonds and were placed in key positions within the Church of England, the Roman Catholic Church, and the government of England.

Among these influential friends and, sometimes, relatives were Frederick Denison Maurice, the cofounder of Christian Socialism, William Ewart Gladstone, the prime minister of England, Arthur Penrhyn Stanley, the Anglican Dean of Westminster, Henry Edward Manning, the Roman Catholic archbishop of Westminster, and Samuel Wilberforce, the Anglican bishop of Winchester. Their strong influences were prominent at the highest levels among Anglicans, Roman Catholics, and within the British government. The strong personal relationships among these influential friends provided a network through which to accomplish the objectives of the Oxford Movement.

---

[1] Quoted in Edwards, *The Jesuits in England: From 1580 to the Present Day*, p. 300.

While Men Slept...

Manning and Wilberforce: The Visible Keys

Henry Manning's brother-in-law was Samuel Wilberforce. Manning married Caroline Sargent, the sister of Samuel Wilberforce's wife, Emily.[2] Wilberforce, as one of Manning's closest friends, officiated at his wedding.[3,4] (Caroline died after four years of marriage.) Later, the two were also to play the most visible roles of those who were part of the Oxford Movement in the declaration in Rome of papal infallibility and in London of biblical errancy.

If one were not aware of the relationship between Manning and Samuel Wilberforce, he might think that the incredible timing of the events in Rome and in London was nothing short of miraculous. On February 9, 1870, Manning led the effort within the Roman Catholic Church that set the decree of papal infallibility before the First Vatican Council. Then, on February 10, 1870, Samuel Wilberforce's proposal to the Church of England Convocation was passed that the Church of England revise the Authorized Version of the English Bible because it contained "erroneous passages." The two long-time friends and family members, who had been part of the Oxford Movement, had reached key leadership positions within the Roman and English Churches. Roman Catholic Archbishop Manning, who had previously been an Anglican, served as the whip of the majority party on the committee to declare papal infallibility. Samuel Wilberforce, on the other hand, had remained in the Church of England and, as the bishop of Winchester, had achieved sufficient influence to successfully call for a revision of the English Bible.[5,6]

---

[2] Newsome, *The Wilberforces and Henry Manning*, p. 24.

[3] Ibid., p. 199.

[4] Ibid., p. 150.

[5] James Hennesey, *The First Council of the Vatican: The American Experience* (New York: Herder and Herder, 1963), p. 13.

[6] Reginald G. Wilberforce, *Life of the Right Reverend Samuel Wilberforce, D. D., Lord Bishop of Oxford and Afterwards of Winchester with Selections from His Diaries and Correspondence*, vol. 3 (London: John Murray, 1882), p. 346.

Manning's Rise to Power

Manning, the Anglicans, and the Pope

Henry Manning had a special relationship with Pope Pius IX who, until he was elected pope in 1846 was known as Bishop Giovanni Maria Mastai-Ferretti.[7] By 1847, Pope Pius IX found himself in the middle of significant controversy because of his sympathy with the Jesuits.[8] During that year, Manning, who was still a member of the Church of England, traveled to Rome along with John Newman. Both Manning and Newman had been key movers in the Oxford Movement and Newman had recently converted to Roman Catholicism. They were also in Rome with John Sterling, who was a rationalist and founder of the "Eclectic Club" in London, also known as the "Sterling Club," of which Manning was a member.[9, 10] [We recall that Sterling and his brother-in-law, F. D. Maurice, were strongly influenced by Julius Hare since their years at Cambridge University.]

Manning was in Rome from November 27, 1847 to May 11, 1848,[11] during which time the seeds of revolution were germinating throughout much of Europe. The public harbored increasing suspicion that the Jesuits were exerting influences on the pope.[12] To reduce the perceived Jesuit influence on the Roman Catholic Church, demonstrations against the Jesuits were held throughout Italy and the popular pressure mounted to expel them from Rome. Pope Pius IX "clung desperately to the Jesuits," thereby creating a major impasse. Eventually, however, the pope agreed to a "compromise" whereby the Jesuits would leave Rome voluntarily.[13]

---

[7] Robert Gray, *Cardinal Manning: A Biography* (New York: St. Martin's Press, 1985), p. 121.

[8] Coppa, *Pope Pius IX,* p. 68.

[9] Purcell, *Life of Cardinal Manning*, vol. 1, p. 362.

[10] Ibid., p. 273.

[11] Ibid., p. 362.

[12] Coppa, *Pope Pius IX*, p. 72.

[13] Ibid., pp. 78-79.

While Men Slept...

Manning was meticulous in keeping a diary in which he recorded the details of daily events. However, it is very curious to note that he made no entries into his diary concerning his meeting with the pope or with John Newman while he was in Rome.[14] Although his diary did not document the significant events, Henry Manning had at least two audiences with Pope Pius IX.[15] The reasons for the absence of any details concerning these important meetings in Rome can only be the subject of speculation.

By 1849, Manning had gained the respect of Maurice for the influence that he was now able to exert in the church. In F. D. Maurice's view, Manning had more power with the clergy than any other living man! Maurice put it this way:

> ...there was one man in that room who can save the Church from its confusion if he has it in his mind to do so. That was Manning...His power with the clergy is very great, greater certainly than that of any man living.[16]

During 1849, Manning's secret meetings were with Julius Hare, F. D. Maurice, Samuel Wilberforce, William Gladstone, and other influential figures in both church and state as members of the "Sterling Club." The club, which had received its name in honor of John Sterling, whom many considered to be an "avowed infidel," met at the Freemason's Tavern.[17, 18, 19]

Some viewed the members of the Sterling Club as proof that there were infidels within the very bosom of the church.[20] A publication called the *Record* fiercely attacked the Sterling Club, declaring that it

---

[14] Purcell, *Life of Cardinal Manning*, vol. 1, pp. 414-415.

[15] *Biographical Note on Henry Edward Manning (1808-1892) Collection,1826-1891, Manuscript No. 002* (Atlanta, Georgia: Archives & Manuscripts, Pitts Theology Library, Emory University) http://www.pitts.emory.edu/text/mss002.html

[16] Maurice, *The Life of Frederick Denison Maurice*, vol. 1, p. 545.

[17] Hughes, *Memoir of Daniel Macmillan*, p. 231.

[18] Maurice, *The Life of Frederick Denison Maurice*, vol. 1, p. 516.

[19] Purcell, *Life of Cardinal Manning*, vol. 1, p. 275.

[20] Distad, *Guessing at Truth: The Life of Julius Charles Hare*, p. 181.

was founded in honor of the Rationalistic unbelief of John Sterling.[21] As awareness of the activities of the Sterling Club grew among the public, some members became concerned about the impact that the revelation of their membership could have on their public image. Consequently, some of the members, including Samuel Wilberforce and Henry Manning, resigned after careful deliberation.[22]

While Manning had a very close relationship with the pope, even before his conversion to Roman Catholicism, he also continued to maintain close ties with his friends from Oxford University, including many who were well-known Socialists. Manning, who had been labeled a Socialist by his opponents, never rejected or accepted the description.[23, 24]

Manning's Move to the Roman Catholic Church

In 1850, Pope Pius IX reestablished the Roman Catholic diocesan episcopate in England, which had been absent since the Reformation, and Manning converted to Roman Catholicism the following year.[25] The pope appointed Cardinal Wiseman as the first archbishop of Westminster. Wiseman maintained a cordial understanding with the Jesuits and eagerly helped to promote the special work that he saw for their Society in England.[26, 27]

A Jesuit received Manning into the Church of Rome on April 6, 1851. By April 15 (Tuesday of Holy Week), Manning wrote that he was living near and attending the Jesuits' Church.[28] As a Catholic, Manning used Jesuit confessors and considered the Jesuits to be among

---

[21] Purcell, *Life of Cardinal Manning*, vol. 1, p. 276.

[22] Distad, *Guessing at Truth: The Life of Julius Charles Hare*, p. 181.

[23] Gray, *Cardinal Manning*, p. 302.

[24] Purcell, *Life of Cardinal Manning*, vol. 1, p. 174.

[25] Walker et al., *A History of the Christian Church*, p. 643.

[26] *Religious Controversies of the Nineteenth Century: Selected Documents*, A. O. J. Cockshut, ed. (Lincoln: University of Nebraska Press, 1966), p. 10.

[27] Purcell, *Life of Cardinal Manning*, vol. 1, p. 673.

[28] Ibid., pp. 620-621.

his friends.[29, 30] Still maintaining his close relationship with members of the Sterling Club, Manning also visited the ailing Julius Hare at the beginning of April 1851.[31]

Within ten weeks of entering the Roman Catholic Church, Manning received Holy Orders as a priest from Wiseman on June 14, 1851. Upon completion of the ceremony, Wiseman embraced Manning and said to him:

> I look to you as one of the first-fruits of the restoration of the Hierarchy by our Holy Father Pius IX. Go forth, my son, and bring your brethren and fellow-countrymen by thousands and tens of thousands into the one true Fold of Christ.[32]

Two days later, Manning gave his first mass as a newly ordained priest in the Church of the Jesuits. He was assisted by a well-known French Jesuit priest.[33]

Manning's Relationship with Pope Pius IX

The relationship between Manning and the pope progressed. Even in the face of serious problems, including the 1848 revolutions, the pope took the time to regularly see Manning as the two became close personal friends. They became so close, that Manning could see the pope anytime he desired. Manning described their relationship this way to Robert Wilberforce, who was the brother of Samuel Wilberforce:

> "I had free access at any moment to the Pope," Manning told Robert Wilberforce in 1854, "who treated me as a father treats a son, with an affection and playfulness of kindness, as well as with a confidence greater than I ever had from an Anglican bishop." [34]

---

[29] Cornish, *The English Church in the Nineteenth Century, Part I*, p. 334.

[30] Edwards, *The Jesuits in England: From 1580 to the Present Day*, pp. 199-200.

[31] Distad, *Guessing at Truth: The Life of Julius Charles Hare*, p. 193.

[32] Purcell, *Life of Cardinal Manning*, vol. 1, p. 633.

[33] Ibid.

[34] Quoted in Gray, *Cardinal Manning*, p. 152.

While Manning maintained his special relationship with the pope, he also took the opportunity to meet with other key contemporary theologians. For example, during 1854 Manning met with Philip Schaff, who would later head the American Committee for revising the Bible. They discussed issues concerning the reconciliation between Protestantism and Catholicism and the comparative merits of personal and social morality in Roman Catholic and Protestant countries. During Schaff's visit to London, Manning also took him to meet with Roman Catholic Cardinal Nicholas Wiseman.[35] Schaff was not a stranger to Catholicism since he had taken an opportunity to have an audience with Pope Gregory XVI during a visit to Rome twelve years earlier.[36] During that visit to Rome, Schaff also described attending the church of the Jesuits, where he heard a sermon on forbidden reading.[37]

In addition to Schaff's relationship with Manning as a Roman Catholic, he took the occassion of his visit to meet with key Anglican leaders. While meeting with Manning's brother-in-law, Samuel Wilberforce, who was then the bishop of Oxford, Schaff also met with Archdeacon Wilberforce.[38] Schaff also had an opportunity to renew his acquaintance with F. D. Maurice and to meet with Julius Hare.[39]

The pope rapidly promoted Manning to positions of authority within the Roman Catholic Church, over the heads of those that had been born into the faith and with years of service to the church. By 1857, the pope suddenly appointed Manning as head of the Westminster Chapter.[40] Thus, Manning became very unpopular with some members of the English Catholic Church who suspected him of having "disguised intentions and objects."[41] In a rare move, the pope overruled the normal channels of recommendation for the archbishop of Westminster and personally appointed Manning to the post in 1865.[42]

---

[35] Schaff, *The Life of Philip Schaff*, pp. 193-194.

[36] Ibid., pp. 53-54.

[37] Ibid., p. 45.

[38] Ibid., p. 174.

[39] Ibid., p. 176.

[40] Gray, *Cardinal Manning*, p. 163.

[41] Ibid., p. 169.

[42] Ibid., pp. 199-200.

While Men Slept...

Manning's Role on Papal Infallibility

On June 29, 1868, Pope Pius IX called the First Vatican Council, which began on December 8, 1869.[43, 44] However, from the beginning, there was a feeling among many Catholic bishops that something wrong was about to happen at the Council. The official historian of the First Vatican Council, Theodor Granerath, wrote this account of some of the circumstances surrounding the Council:

> From the first moment it met until it dissolved, the general Council was occupied almost exclusively with an issue which had never appeared in any of the numerous preliminary proposals, an issue which no one in Rome had wanted to lay before the council fathers for debate. Today one point stands clear and beyond all doubt: The matter of infallibility was brought into the Council's deliberations from the *outside*.[45]

Although the issue of papal infallibility had not been placed on the January 21, 1870 agenda, Archbishop Henry Edward Manning was the leader of extensive behind-the-scenes discussions on the subject. Manning, who as we have learned, had a close personal relationship with the pope, was the whip of the majority party in favor of declaring papal infallibility.[46] Manning's position on the issue was that the pope was infallible on *both* spiritual and temporal matters. In his role as archbishop, Manning was the key proponent of the dogma of papal infallibility at the First Vatican Council in 1870. Then on February 9, 1870 in the Vatican Palace, Manning made a strong argument in favor of the immediate presentation of the question of papal infallibility to the Council for approval. Although the committee was divided, Manning's proposal passed.[47, 48]

---

[43] Lillian Parker Wallace, *The Papacy and European Diplomacy: 1869-1878* (Chapel Hill: The University of North Carolina Press, 1948), p. 55.

[44] Hasler, *How the Pope Became Infallible*, pp. 74-75.

[45] Quoted in: Hasler, *How the Pope Became Infallible*, p. 67.

[46] Hennesey, *The First Vatican Council*, p. 13.

[47] Ibid., p. 116.

[48] Ibid., pp. 172-173.

Manning sought the universal recognition of the infallibility of the Holy See.[49] Some Roman Catholic archbishops also thought this was an opportunity for the Church of England to move toward reunification with the Roman Catholic Church.[50] On July 13, 1870, which was the day before Bastille Day, which commemorated the beginning of the 1789 French Revolution, Pope Pius IX formally defined the dogma of the Infallibility of the Roman Pontiff! Upon this action by the pope, the bishops opposing the dogma acknowledged their defeat. The formal vote for adopting the dogma of papal infallibility was taken on July 18, 1870.[51] The effect of the dogma was to make the pope the supreme authority, accountable to no one. Even the Council of Trent left the pope and his judgements to be accountable to the assembled representatives of the Christian world.[52]

The Role of Gladstone

Affection of Newman and Manning

William Ewart Gladstone was the key participant in the Oxford Movement who did not take an active role as either an Anglican or Roman Catholic clergyman. Instead, Gladstone positioned himself within the political area of England, eventually becoming its prime minister. Gladstone, however, was no stranger to the most influential clergy of the Anglo-Catholic movement within both the Anglican and the Roman Catholic Churches. John Henry Newman, for example, was, along with Manning, one of the two most important defectors from the Anglican to the Roman Catholic Church. Nevertheless, he remained Gladstone's very close friend thoughout his life. In 1888, Cardinal John Newman demonstrated the depth of his life-long friendship with the former prime minister of England when he wrote:

---

[49] Newsome, *The Wilberforces and Henry Manning*, p. 410.

[50] Francis Warre Cornish, *The English Church in the Nineteenth Century, Part II* (London: Macmillan and Co., 1910), p. 342.

[51] Purcell, *Life of Cardinal Manning*, vol. 2, pp. 450-451.

[52] Morley, *The Life of William Ewart Gladstone*, vol. 2, p. 516.

> "My dear Gladstone, I cannot let this opportunity pass by without writing to you; I am very ill: God bless you.
> —Yours very affectionately, John H. Card. Newman."[53]

Manning's friendship with Gladstone was one of the most cherished and valued of his life.[54] Although Manning destroyed much of the correspondence between himself and Gladstone before he died, it is well known that the two men had a long and intimate relationship.[55] Their friendship began in about 1830, while they were at Oxford University together. Demonstrating the strength of their personal relationship, Gladstone selected Manning to be the godfather of his eldest son, William.[56]

Several years before his death, Manning recalled his reaction to the March 1850 Gorham Judgment, which was concerning a dispute between two groups within the Church of England. One group called itself Protestant and rejected the sacramental system and saw the state as the authority to decide matters of the church. The other group called itself Catholic and believed in the spiritual efficacy and divine origin of the sacraments and believed that a supreme authority of the head of the church and not the civil powers should decide matters related to the church.[57]

The decision by the highest court in England was in favor of George C. Gorham and against Manning. The court rejected baptismal regeneration and affirmed Royal supremacy in matters of faith. When Manning heard the decision, he went directly to Gladstone's home, where he was in bed with the flu. Despite Gladstone's illness, he joined Manning and others in drawing up a petition against the decision. Manning quoted one of their group as saying:

---

[53] Quoted in: Purcell, *Life of Cardinal Manning*, vol. 1, p. 44.

[54] Purcell, *Life of Cardinal Manning*, vol. 2, p. 531.

[55] Ibid., vol. 1, p. 569.

[56] Ibid., vol. 2, p. 530.

[57] Ibid., vol. 1, pp. 522-529.

"I suppose we are all agreed that if the Church of England does not undo this we must join the Church of Rome."[58]

Although the meeting of thirteen protesters was held at Gladstone's home, in the end he did not sign the petition because of his position as a "Privy Councillor." Gladstone was torn between his obligations with the state and on how he could serve the church when he wrote to Manning on April 4, 1850 that his:

> ...best way of serving the Church is by working not *in* the State, but *on* the State, you will comprehend all that the change of the single letter implies.[59]

Gladstone and Stanley to Rome

Prior to his election as the prime minister of England in 1868 and prior to the convening of the First Vatican Council in 1869, William Ewart Gladstone paid a visit to Rome. During the winter of 1866 to 1867, Arthur Stanley, who was the Dean of Westminster, accompanied Gladstone to Rome, where they shared a house together during their stay.[60, 61] While in Rome, Gladstone repeatedly met with Archbishop Henry Manning, whom he had known since their days together at Oxford.[62, 63] F. D. Maurice had commented almost thirty years earlier in 1839 about how pleased he was that Gladstone was getting along well with Manning.[64]

In addition to his numerous meetings with Manning, Gladstone met with ten of the Roman Catholic cardinals and had at least two audiences with Pope Pius IX. His other colleagues, which presumably included Arthur Stanley, also met with the pope. Later, Gladstone

---

[58] Ibid.

[59] Ibid., pp. 530-536.

[60] Morley, *The Life of William Ewart Gladstone*, vol. 2, p. 222.

[61] Ibid., p. 252.

[62] Ibid., p. 215.

[63] Morley, *The Life of William Ewart Gladstone*, vol. 1, p. 55.

[64] Maurice, *The Life of Frederick Denison Maurice*, vol. 1, p. 257.

"...used to tell with much glee in what diverse fashion they impressed the pontiff..." during their "open and free" conversation.[65]

After Gladstone's election as the prime minister of England, his close friend Roman Catholic Archbishop Henry Manning saluted him on his victory.[66] Gladstone had knowledge of the papal infallibility plan, even before the opening of the First Vatican Council. On November 24, 1869, Lord Acton wrote to Prime Minister Gladstone:

> Everything is in readiness here for the proclamation of papal infallibility and the plan of operation has already been agreed on in a way that reveals a careful study of Sarpi's history of the Council of Trent.[67]

Positioning Samuel Wilberforce

By some accounts, the Anglo-Catholic movement had in Gladstone its most important political ally and in Samuel Wilberforce its most important clerical ally.[68] Following Gladstone and Stanley's visit to Rome and their associated meetings with Manning and with Pope Pius IX, Wilberforce remained in close correspondence with Gladstone on matters concerning newly proposed methods of conducting rituals as part of public worship in the Anglican Church. On matters such as the details of worship within the Church of England, Wilberforce told Gladstone on March 12, 1867, "I agree entirely with every word you say."[69] Wilberforce both communicated and met frequently and informally with Gladstone on numerous occasions between the time of Gladstone's meeting with the pope and the year of 1869.[70]

---

[65] Morley, *The Life of William Ewart Gladstone*, vol. 2, pp. 216-218.

[66] Ibid., p. 255.

[67] Quoted in: August Bernhard Hasler, *How the Pope Became Infallible: Pius IX and the Politics of Persuasion* (Garden City, NY: Doubleday & Co., Inc., 1981) p. 67.

[68] John Shelton Reed, *Glorious Battle: The Cultural Politics of Victorian Anglo-Catholicism* (Nashville: Vanderbilt University Press, 1996), p. 7.

[69] Wilberforce, *Life of the Right Reverend Samuel Wilberforce,* vol. 3, pp. 208-209.

[70] Ibid., pp. 205-306.

After the November 23, 1868 election, Gladstone became the prime minister of England.[71] He was then in a strategic position to have significant influence on the Church of England. Notably, after Gladstone took office, a bill was passed in 1869 called the Bishop's Resignation Bill. This new legislation made it possible for the bishops of the Church of England to resign their positions so that replacements could be appointed. After passage of the bill, a large number of vacancies were created in the upper levels of the Church of England. In 1869 alone seven new bishops were appointed and one bishop was transferred.[72]

It is notable that in 1869 Samuel Wilberforce was already the bishop of Oxford, where he had been for many years. However, in 1869 his long-term friend, Gladstone, recommended to the queen of England that Wilberforce be transferred to the position of bishop of Winchester. Gladstone wrote to Wilberforce on September 28, 1869 saying:

> ...that I now personally propose to you, with the Queen's sanction, that you should be translated from Oxford to Winchester.[73]

The only problem was that the position of bishop of Winchester was already occupied! Therefore, Gladstone added to his letter:

> If you obtain any more exact information as to the time when Winchester will be vacant, please let me know.[74]

After the resignation of the former bishop, Samuel Wilberforce began his work as the bishop of Winchester on December 1, 1869.[75] That

---

[71] Morley, *The Life of William Ewart Gladstone*, vol. 2, p. 249.

[72] G. I. T. Machin, *Politics and the Churches in Great Britian in 1869 to 1921* (Oxford: Clarendon Press, 1987), p. 21.

[73] Wilberforce, *Life of the Right Reverend Samuel Wilberforce*, vol. 3, pp. 304-307.

[74] Ibid., pp. 304-307.

[75] Ibid., p. 317.

was one week prior to the opening of the First Vatican Council, in which his brother-in-law, Henry Manning, was to play a key role.

Rejecting The Catholic Bishops' Plea for Help

While Manning was involved in behind-the-scenes negotiations at the First Vatican Council to adopt the dogma of papal infallibility, some Roman Catholic bishops had apparently contacted Samuel Wilberforce for help. They requested that the Church of England intervene on behalf of Catholic bishops who were dissatisfied with the plans of the papacy. In his letter of January 22, 1870, Wilberforce conceded that he would go along with Gladstone on matters related to the clergy *and* the papacy! He wrote:

> The Bishop of Gibraltar writes for my advice on a suggestion from the American Bishops there that we should send one of *our* body to meet an American Bishop and endeavour together to open conferences and negotiations with the Italian clergy dissatisfied with the Papacy as to their interior reformation. I am *not* much inclined to such a movement, but would attempt anything which you thought desirable in this matter.[76]

The Roman Catholic bishops may have been appealing for help in dealing with the papal infallibility proposal that was surfacing at the ongoing First Vatican Council. Since that proposal was being led by Manning, who was a former Anglican, the brother-in-law of Wilberforce, and a close friend of Prime Minister Gladstone, the bishops may have believed that England could have some influence on the matter. Gladstone's response to Wilberforce on January 24, 1870 was that:

> I should think any question of dealing with dissatisfied Italian clergy could not yet be ripe for handling by any English Bishop, and that it had better remain, as you seem to think, in other hands.[77]

---

[76] Wilberforce, *Life of the Right Reverend Samuel Wilberforce*, vol. 3, p. 340.
[77] Ibid., p. 341.

The Roman Connection to the New Bible

Wilberforce's Role in Rewriting the English Bible

The Motion

The work of Archbishop Manning caused a significant controversy in England. After the First Vatican Council adopted the decree of papal infallibility, some English members of the church thought it was right that the decree should also be taken by the Church of England. Others within the Church of England argued, however, that the church should reject the decree of papal infallibility because it was contrary to Holy Scripture and the judgment of the ancient church.[78]

Samuel Wilberforce, who was well known for his contributions to the Anglo-Catholic trend in the Church of England, had just been named the bishop of Winchester in 1869.[79] Bishop Wilberforce, who, as we know, was also Roman Catholic Archbishop Manning's brother-in-law, made a resolution on February 10, 1870 calling for a revision of the Authorized Version of the New Testament because of errors contained in it.[80]

Wilberforce's resolution to challenge the authority of the Authorized Version of the English Bible was made on the day following Henry Manning's successful placement before the First Vatican Council of the proposal to declare the universal authority of the pope with the declaration of papal infallibility! The resolution, made in the Upper House of Convocation of the Province of Canterbury, was that a committee would be appointed to consider and report upon the desirability of revising the *erroneous passages* in the New Testament of the Authorized Version of the Bible.[81] Charles John Ellicott, who was then the bishop of Gloucester and Bristol, seconded the motion.[82]

---

[78] Cornish, *The English Church in the Nineteenth Century, Part II*, p. 344.

[79] Latourette, *Christianity in a Revolutionary Age,* vol. 2, pp. 272-273.

[80] Wilberforce, *Life of the Right Reverend Samuel Wilberforce*, vol. 3, p. 346.

[81] Newsome, *The Wilberforces and Henry Manning*, p. 411.

[82] *The Bible in its Ancient and English Versions*, H. Wheeler Robinson, ed. (London: Oxford at Clarendon Press, 1940), p. 240.

While Men Slept...

Samuel Wilberforce was the person who in 1870, while the First Vatican Council was in progress, made the motion to "revise" the Authorized Bible.[83]

The Plan for the English Revision

Samuel Wilberforce privately made clear to Prime Minister Gladstone on February 22, 1870 the subtlety of the revision strategy that he envisioned. He said that the process should involve one of making marginal notes that would gradually migrate into the text. He said:

> My own impression is that it will be best to keep the *text* unaltered and put any corrections into the margin. Thence by slow degrees they may migrate into the text.[84]

Continuing in the same letter to Gladstone, Wilberforce wrote that the *new* Authorized Version should be adopted under the authority of the church, and not under the authority of the state. He then added:

> It is quite another matter for the Pope *authoritatively* to fix a text.[85] [Italics are in the original.]

By March 24, 1870, the committee issued a report that said:

I. That it is desirable that a Revision of the Authorized Version of the Holy Scriptures be undertaken. II. That the Revision be so conducted as to comprise both marginal renderings, and such emendations as it may be found necessary to insert in the text of the Authorized Version. III. That in the above Resolutions we do not contemplate any new translation of the Bible, or any alteration of the language, except where in the judgment of the most competent scholars such change is necessary. IV. That in such necessary changes, the style of the language employed in the existing Version be closely followed. V. That it is desirable that Convocation should nominate a

---

[83] Wilberforce, *Life of the Right Reverend Samuel Wilberforce*, vol. 3, p. 346.

[84] Ibid., p. 350.

[85] Ibid.

body of its own Members to undertake the work of Revision, who shall be at liberty to invite the co-operation of any eminent for scholarship, to whatever nation or religious body they may belong.[86]

The report, which had been brought before the Convocation of Canterbury by a committee of eight bishops, including Dean Stanley, was accepted by both the Upper and Lower Houses on May 6, 1870.[87]

On July 7, 1870, a resolution was also passed that invited cooperation of Americans in the work. It was arranged that Philip Schaff would select those Americans who would participate. There were eleven members of the American Old Testament Company and fifteen members of the American New Testament Company, including Philip Schaff and Ezra Abbott, a Unitarian.[88] Abbott was the librarian of Harvard University. Demonstrating his close friendship with Abbott, Philip Schaff was a pallbearer at his funeral. Speaking of Abbott, David Schaff, Philip's son said:

> No one took a deeper interest in the Revision movement or left the work of the committee with more profound respect of the Revisers than he.[89]

The Leadership Switch

Bishop Samuel Wilberforce attended the first meeting and was appointed as the permanent chairman, with Bishop Ellicott of Gloucester and Bristol as vice chairman. Wilberforce was unable to participate in the work of the Committee, reportedly because of his pressing workload. He was only present with the Committee for one day and

---

[86] *The Bible in its Ancient and English Versions*, p. 241.

[87] Philip Schaff, *Introduction on the Revision of the English Bible*, In J. B. Lightfoot, Richard Chenevix Trench, and C. J. Ellicott, *The Revision of the English Version of the New Testament*, J. B. Lightfoot, Richard Chenevix Trench, and C. J. Ellicott (New York: Harper & Brothers, Publishers, 1873), p. ix.

[88] *The Bible in its Ancient and English Versions*, p. 248.

[89] Schaff, *The Life of Philip Schaff*, p. 340.

then only for a short time. After that, vice chairman Ellicott, assumed the responsibilities as the chairman of the Committee.[90] The first meeting of the English Revision Committee of the New Testament was held on Bastille Day, which was July 14, 1870.[91] As we have learned, the pope had assured victory of the dogma of the Infallibility of the Roman Pontiff on the *previous day*!

Ellicott had been trying to revise the Authorized Version of the Bible since at least 1856, when he was one of five people who were brought together to revise the Gospel of John. That work was followed by revisions of other New Testament books.[92] Following those efforts, Ellicott and Henry Alford, the Dean of Canterbury, closely monitored public opinion to determine when a more comprehensive revision could be undertaken. Meeting frequently on the subject, they concluded in 1869 that they should undertake the revision. Therefore, they "...at length obtained the hearty aid and support of Samuel Wilberforce." It was Wilberforce who was instrumental in getting "definitive and authoritative sanction" for the plan.[93]

Other Behind-the-Scenes Influences

Maurice and Hare

While not a publicly visible participant in either declaring biblical errancy or papal infallibility, F. D. Maurice was an important player in the Anglo-Catholic activities surrounding the Oxford Movement.[94]

---

[90] Wilberforce, *Life of the Right Reverend Samuel Wilberforce,* vol. 3, p. 351.

[91] The day, July 14, was Bastille day which marked the beginning of the French Revolution in 1789, it was also the day that signaled the beginning of the Anglo-Catholic Oxford Movement, and it was the first day after Pope Pius IX formally defined the dogma of the Infallibility of the Roman Pontiff at the First Vatican Council, signaling the defeat of the opposition!

[92] [American Bible Revision Committee], *Documentary History of the American Committee on Revision: Prepared by Order of the Committee for the Use of the Members* (New York: Printed, Not Published, 1885), p. 5.

[93] Ibid., p. 6.

[94] Chapman, *Faith and Revolt: Studies in the Literary Influence of the Oxford Movement*, p. 92.

Recall, for example, Maurice's teaching that the Christian Socialist Movement was to establish the "Kingdom of Christ" on earth, through the vehicle of the Catholic Church. Julius Hare, Maurice's teacher and brother-in-law, privately supported his position on this matter. While helping to finance both the Christian Socialist Movement *and* the Macmillan Publishing Company, Hare had key influences in both England and Rome. While we have already learned of Hare's many important influences in England, it should also be noted that he was the intimate friend of one of the two most influential converts to the Roman Catholic Church in the nineteenth century, Henry Manning.[95]

The Jesuits and the Papal Infallibility Dogma

Exactly where the idea for the declaration of papal infallibility came from is not clear. Some believed that the idea came from the Jesuit Order, which had always strongly advocated such a doctrine. They suggested that the Jesuits used Pope Pius IX to accomplish their own purpose.[96] Others might believe that the pope was in opposition to the Jesuits since he "expelled" them from Rome in 1848. Manning recorded some of the reasons for expelling the Jesuits. The first was that they, "...incorporate the doctrine of the Canonists upon the Pope's absolute sovereignty, opposing constitutional liberty."[97] In other words, Manning said the pope expelled the Jesuits because they supported the pope's absolute sovereignty, or infallibility!

In reality, the Jesuits did not operate within the normal channels of the Roman Catholic Church. Even as Henry Manning was serving as the Catholic archbishop of Westminster in England, the Jesuits were not under the rule of the bishop of the diocese in which they worked. Instead, they were under the direct authority of the Father-General in Rome, who was the head of the Jesuit Order and referred to as "the Black Pope."[98, 99] While Archbishop Manning displayed public an-

---

[95] Purcell, *Life of Cardinal Manning*, vol. 1, pp. 166-176.

[96] Wallace, *The Papacy and European Diplomacy*, pp. 52-53.

[97] Purcell, *Life of Cardinal Manning*, vol. 1, p. 386.

[98] Ibid., vol. 2, p. 505.

[99] Ibid., vol. 1, p. 371.

tagonism toward the Jesuits, his relationship with them appears to have involved much more than that which was publicly shown. Manning's biographer, Edmund Sheridan Purcell, acknowledged that:

> A veil of mystery, for instance, seemed to hang over his [Manning's] relations not only with the Jesuits, but with Cardinal Newman; and mystery, like the shadowless night, magnifies every object it touches.[100]

Demonstrating his views of the Jesuits, Pope Pius IX issued as many as one hundred thirty-two briefs and bulls, each of which conferred some favor upon the Jesuits. Furthermore, he beatified seventy-seven and canonized three Jesuits. In addition, he built colleges for and gave colleges to the Jesuits.[101]

While the role of the Jesuits in influencing Pope Pius IX to enact the papal infallibility dogma may never be known, it is clear that he attempted to enforce doctrine which the people attributed to the Jesuits, including that of maintaining the temporal power of the pope as an article of faith.[102] Wherever the source of the idea originated, the result of the papal infallibility dogma was the triumph of declaring all past, present, and future popes to be infallible.[103] [The infallibility dogma, however, apparently did not extend to Pope Clement XIV, who had banned the Jesuits in 1773.]

The Goal Was Accomplished

The aftermath of the First Vatican Council left the world with an infallible pope and with a fallible Bible, which was then opened up for countless revisions. Henry Manning was made a Roman Catholic cardinal in 1875. As such, he maintained his extensive contacts with many of his colleagues in England who were overseeing the Anglo-Catho-

---

[100] Ibid., vol. 2, p. 770.

[101] Thomas Campbell, *The Jesuits, 1534-1921: A History of the Society of Jesus from Its Foundation to the Present Time*, vol. 2. (New York: The Encyclopedia Press, 1921), p. 899.

[102] Thompson, *The Footprints of the Jesuits*, p. 310.

[103] Ibid., pp. 478-479.

lic revival. For example, shortly after Alexander Macmillan published the new Greek New Testament, it was clear that he continued to be in contact with Manning. On February 14, 1882, Macmillan wrote to Manning telling him that he was conveying the cardinal's comments concerning certain books to their respective authors.[104, 105] Bishop Ellicott, who had acted as chairman of the New Testament Revision Committee in place of Samuel Wilberforce, also continued to maintain a relationship with Rome, well after the publication of the Revised Version of the Bible. In 1887, Ellicott wrote to Cardinal Henry Manning offering him his new commentary on 1 Corinthians.[106]

In a 1993 debate in the British House of Commons, Ian Paisley repeated a quote that was attributed to Manning, concerning the goal of the Church of Rome in England. He said:

> In 1928 a Scottish Member, Mr. Rosslyn Mitchell, reminded the House [of Commons] of the aim of the Church of Rome in this country, in the words of one Cardinal Manning. Cardinal Manning said :

> "It is good for us to be here in England. It is yours, right reverend fathers, to subjugate and subdue the mind and break the will of an imperial race, a will which, as the will of Rome of old, rules over nations and peoples, invincible and inflexible. It is the head of Protestantism, the centre of its movements and the stronghold of its power. Weakened in England, Protestantism is paralysed everywhere. Conquered in England, it is conquered throughout the world. Once overthrown here it is but a war of detail."—[Official Report, 13 June 1928 ; Vol. 218, c. 1126.] [107]

---

[104] Graves, *Life and Letters of Alexander Macmillan*, p. 360.

[105] Hughes, *Memoir of Daniel Macmillan*, p. 231.

[106] Purcell, *Life of Cardinal Manning*, vol. 1, p. 708.

[107] Hansard Volume (House of Commons Debates), Session 1993-94, vol. 248, 17th October 1994 - 3rd November 1994, http://www.parliament.the-stationery-office.co.uk/pa/cm/cmse9394.htm.

While Men Slept...

Manning later explained the role of the Jesuits in what had been accomplished.[108, 109] On April 19, 1889, he said:

> I wish to put down carefully my judgement as to the Society of Jesus, because I have often been thought and said to be opposed to it. I believe that it was a creation of God by St. Ignatius, raised up for a special work, that is, to react against the heresy and schism of the Lutheran reformation. This it accomplished.[110]

---

[108] Walker et al., *A History of the Christian Church*, p. 643.

[109] Latourette, *A History of Christianity*, vol. 2, p. 1170.

[110] Quoted in Edwards, *The Jesuits in England: From 1580 to the Present Day*, p. 300.

Chapter 13. Unitarian Influences on the New English Bible

> Ah yes, decidedly the Fourth Gospel [the Gospel of John] does teach the doctrine of the Pre-existence of Christ; but then we do not accept the authority of that Gospel as conclusive. [1]
>
> —G. Vance Smith

The Unitarian Victory

Election to Biblical Revision Committee

During the early stages of the English New Testament Revision Committee, Fenton Hort tried to dispel the charge made by some that the revision was "...in the hands of a clique...."[2] Despite his public efforts to show otherwise, a minority of those who were serving on the Committee frequently made key decisions. One of those key decisions was that a Unitarian would be made a member of the Committee. This decision was met by strong opposition from the church and from other members of the Committee. In a bold move, a well-known Unitarian, G. Vance Smith, was accepted to the Revision Committee under very curious circumstances. He was appointed to the Revision Committee when only nine of the twenty-four members were present and, even then, he was elected by a majority of only one.[3,4] Apparently, it was Westcott, Hort, Lightfoot, perhaps Ellicott, and one other, who voted in favor of putting the Unitarian on the Committee.

It is significant that Smith was placed on the New Testament Revision Committee, even though he did not accept the authority of the Scriptures, maintaining that Jesus Christ and the Apostles taught erroneous ideas:

---

[1] Henry Solly, *These Eighty Years*, vol. 2, p.100.

[2] Hort, *Life and Letters*, vol. 2, p. 55.

[3] Wilberforce, *Life of the Right Reverend Samuel Wilberforce,* vol. 3, p. 351.

[4] *The Bible in its Ancient and English Versions*, pp. 242-247.

While Men Slept...

> In Christ's own teachings and those of the Apostles, as time has ample shown, erroneous ideas were not wanting.[5]

Smith accepted whatever part of the Scripture suited him and rejected those parts that did not suit him. His view of the Gospel of John was described by Henry Solly, a fellow Unitarian minister, who wrote of an encounter with Smith at a ministers' conference:

> ...I remember Dr. Vance Smith, who had a deservedly high reputation among Unitarian divines for Biblical learning, saying, in reply to a question I put to him, "Ah yes, decidedly the Fourth Gospel [the Gospel of John] does teach the doctrine of the Pre-existence of Christ; but then we do not accept the authority of that Gospel as conclusive."[6]

In considering the views of Unitarians, Solly went on to consider their problems:

> ...but their denial of the authenticity and authority of the Fourth Gospel is one of those facts in theological science which the more one reads and studies appears the more unintelligible, and all the more so, because they do not deny the authenticity of Paul's principal epistles—only when they find him holding and expressing his belief in our Lord's "Pre-existence" they simply observe, "Yes, but that is where we differ from Paul." For my own part I cannot help thinking Paul was in a position to know the truth on this subject more accurately than the learned men now mentioned.[7]

Hort believed that a Unitarian position on the Revision Committee was an important requirement for the acceptance of the Revised Bible by the laity because in England there were few people left who ac-

---

[5] G. Vance Smith, *Christianity: What It Is Not, and What It Is,* In *Christianity and Modern Thought* (Boston: American Unitarian Association, 1873), p. 267.

[6] Henry Solly, *These Eighty Years,* vol. 2, p. 100.

[7] Ibid., p. 101.

cepted the Trinity as anything more than the "merest dogma." In a letter to Westcott in August 1870 he wrote:

> Are you sure that in the turn things are now taking it is right to keep total silence? There is the strangest blindness about the Unitarian position, and the moral damage that would have been done to the acceptance of the Revision by the laity if Unitarians had been outlawed as such. Also, is it not amazing to see people who suppose themselves to be good Church-men abandoning the Catholic position and setting up a "Trinitarian" Alliance? There is some real faith in the Incarnation left in various quarters, but in England the Trinity seems to have become the merest dogma. It has been killed, one fears, by that hapless *Quicunque vult* [Athanasian Creed] and its substitution of geometry for life.[8]

After G. Vance Smith was accepted to the Revision Committee, Hort confirmed his belief that the action would contribute to the acceptance of the Revised Version of the Bible. He wrote to Lightfoot on September 1, 1870 that:

> ...It is, I think, difficult to measure the weight of acceptance won beforehand for the Revision by the single fact of our welcoming an Unitarian, if only the Company perseveres in its present serious and faithful spirit.[9]

At the age of forty-two, after the plan to rewrite the English Bible had become a reality, Hort reassured Maurice on November 2, 1870 that he agreed with his mentors views, which, as we have learned, were Unitarian, Universalist, and Socialist:

> You must often feel as if you were uttering words in a strange tongue; and now you will have the certainty of at least one coadjutor whose ears are opened.[10]

---

[8] Hort, *Life and Letters,* vol. 2, p. 140.

[9] Ibid.

[10] Ibid., p. 143.

Now that Hort's ears had been opened to Maurice's teachings, he had become Maurice's "coadjutor," meaning "one who works together with another."[11]

The Unitarian Celebration of Holy Communion

Putting G. Vance Smith onto the English Bible Revision Committee was not sufficient for those who were exerting the strongest influences on the operations of the Committee. Indeed, Westcott wrote to Dean Arthur Stanley requesting that they all celebrate Holy Communion together before the first meeting of the Revision Committee. On June 10, 1870, Westcott told Lightfoot about the plan and sought his support. Then, on June 17, 1870, Westcott told Lightfoot that Stanley had "heartily" accepted his proposal, provided *all* of the members were invited to participate. Acting behind the scenes, Westcott saw the move as an opportunity to "celebrate" a Communion that included all, including the Unitarian, without assuming any of the responsibility for the action. He wrote it this way:

> ...Stanley heartily accepts the proposal of Holy Communion if the *notice* is sent to all. To this I see no objection. He will celebrate, and with him all the responsibility rests. We at least (and, I think, *Scotch* Presbyterians) can have no scruple in availing ourselves of the offered service.[12] [Italics are in the original.]

The acceptance of the Unitarian scholar onto the English Bible Revision Committee was sealed with an unprecedented act of his receiving Communion along with the other revisors. According to the plan, Dean Arthur Stanley of Westminster sent G. Vance Smith an invitation to the Communion, along with the other revisors.[13] On June 22, 1870, G. Vance Smith participated in Holy Communion, with the other

---

[11] *Webster's Seventh New Collegiate Dictionary* (Springfield, Massachusetts: G. & C. Merriam Company, 1969), p. 158.

[12] Westcott, *Life and Letters*, vol. 1, p. 391.

[13] Cornish, *The English Church in the Nineteenth Century, Part II*, p. 175.

members of the Revision Committee, in what was later called the "Westminster scandal."[14]

Samuel Wilberforce, who was absent and did not participate in the Communion, publicly stated his sadness that such an action was permitted to have occurred:

> ...I deeply lament that any one professing not only to hold but to be the teacher of a doctrine so dishonouring Our Lord and Saviour as the denial of His Godhead, joined in the act of Holy Communion of our Church, with the Bishops of that Church. I do most deeply lament that such should have been the case.[15]

On July 16, 1870, he also expressed his frustration over what he viewed as the "evil" that had been done:

> So, though my heart is sick about it, I see nothing to do. The Dean of Westminster is the real offender and cause of the evil.[16]

This strong response suggested that Wilberforce viewed this as a blasphemous act on the part of Dean Stanley. It is significant that the act was committed under the authority of the Dean and in preparation for the revision of the English New Testament. Some might see the act as one of profaning the holy things of God as described in Ezekiel:

> Her priests have violated my law, and have profaned mine holy things: they have put no difference between the holy and profane, neither have they shewed difference between the unclean and the clean, and have hid their eyes from my sabbaths, and I am profaned among them.
>
> –Ezekiel 22:26

---

[14] Wilberforce, *Life of the Right Reverend Samuel Wilberforce,* vol. 3, p. 351.

[15] Ibid., p. 352.

[16] Ibid.

Maurice, on the other hand, had quite a different view of Smith having received Holy Communion at Westminster. According to Maurice's son:

> The Dean had administered the Communion to the whole body of the Revisers of the New Testament, including a Unitarian; my father's delight at his having done so is expressed in many letters.[17]

In expressing the significance of this event, Maurice wrote to his son on July 23, 1870 that he had met with Dean Stanley that day and that:

> He [the Dean of Westminster] is in spirits about the Revision, and is not much disturbed by the attacks on him for the Westminster Abbey Communion, which I think was a greater event than most which have happened in our day.[18]

Hort viewed the event as one that marked a point in his life as he said:

> The Communion in Henry VII's Chapel was one of those few great services which seem to mark points in one's life.[19]

Despite the wholehearted support of Maurice and Hort, the controversy continued among those who believed in the deity of Jesus Christ over the acceptance of G. Vance Smith onto the Revision Committee and into Holy Communion. At the Convocation in February 1872, Samuel Wilberforce offered a resolution which passed in the Upper House, that:

> "...no person who denies the Godhead of our Lord Jesus Christ ought to be invited to join either company to which is committed the revision of the Authorised Version of Holy Scrip-

---

[17] Maurice, *The Life of Frederick Denison Maurice*, vol. 2, p. 617.
[18] Ibid.
[19] Hort, *Life and Letters,* vol. 2, p. 136.

ture, and that any such person now on either company should cease to act herewith."[20]

When that resolution, however, was sent to the Lower House, it was met with strong opposition from Dean Stanley. Because of Stanley's "vigorous rhetoric" and his "strong personality" the resolution failed in the Lower House.[21] Because Dean Stanley prevailed, Unitarians were permitted to directly influence the Revision of the English Bible. He believed this would help accomplish the goal of bringing about a closer union of the different denominations of English-speaking Christians.[22]

Dean Stanley: Evidence of His Theology

Maurice's Influence

As early as 1844, F. D. Maurice was in close correspondence with Arthur Stanley concerning doctrinal issues.[23] Stanley looked up to F. D. Maurice who, as we have learned, had strong Unitarian positions on many doctrinal issues and was also a cofounder of the Christian Socialist Movement, as a "leader of thought." Frederick Maurice explained that his father was:

> ...an older man, to whom the Dean confessed many obligations as a leader of thought; that my father had borne the brunt of many fights in behalf of fairness and justice, and that the Dean had himself brought many men under my father's influence....[24]

By 1846, Stanley had gained a reputation by 1846 for being a leader of the "Oxford Liberals," who had petitioned Parliament in a move-

---

[20] Quoted in Cornish, *The English Church in the Nineteenth Century, Part II*, p. 177.

[21] Cornish, *The English Church in the Nineteenth Century, Part II*, p. 177.

[22] Schaff, *The Life of Philip Schaff*, p. 328.

[23] Maurice, *The Life of Frederick Denison Maurice,* vol. 1, p. 391.

[24] Ibid., vol. 2, p. 601.

ment to open universities to "non-conformists."[25] These nonconformists included the Unitarians, who rejected the deity of Jesus Christ.

In addition to being under F. D. Maurice's influence, Arthur Stanley also maintained a very close relationship with Maurice's brother-in-law, Julius Hare. As a final demonstration of the very close relationship that existed between him and Julius Hare, Stanley served as a pallbearer upon Hare's death. He helped lay Hare's body to rest on January 30, 1855.[26] Maurice and Stanley had taken the train together to Hare's funeral.[27]

Following Hare's death, Maurice and Stanley continued to be closely involved in each other's lives. In 1862, Maurice was elated when Stanley was appointed to be the Dean of Westminster. Stanley brought his fiancee, who was the sister of Maurice's college friend, to meet Maurice.[28] In 1864, Maurice wrote to Stanley on John Newman's conversion to Roman Catholicism:

> I do believe that Newman loves truth in his heart of hearts, and more now than when he was an Anglican.[29]

Stanley was well acquainted with the movement of Anglicans toward the Roman Catholic Church, since his sister was also a Roman Catholic.[30]

Maurice and Stanley on the "Trinitarian" Creed

While praising Newman's love for the truth as a Roman Catholic, Maurice also wrote to Stanley in 1864 that they were in agreement that subscriptions to the Athanasian Creed have been "bits in the mouths of religious parties."[31] The Athanasian Creed, which, among

---

[25] Cornish, *The English Church in the Nineteenth Century, Part I*, p. 306.

[26] Distad, *Guessing at Truth*, pp. 196-197.

[27] Maurice, *The Life of Frederick Denison Maurice*, vol. 2, p. 255.

[28] Ibid., p. 436.

[29] Ibid., pp. 478-479.

[30] Hort, *Life and Letters*, vol. 2, p. 147.

[31] Maurice, *The Life of Frederick Denison Maurice*, vol. 2, p. 492.

other things, was an exposition of the doctrines of the Trinity and of the incarnation, had been recited by Maurice as a confession of faith as part of his taking orders as an Anglican priest.

However, many years later, Maurice made it clear that his recitation of the Creed should not be misinterpreted. He said that if he had meant his reading of the Creed as others meant it, he would have considered that to be a sin, from which he would need to repent for the rest of his life. On September 24, 1870, Maurice wrote about an article he had written concerning the Athanasian Creed:

> ....I have written an article for the next "Contemporary" about the Athanasian Creed. It is pretty sure to be banished from our service now, and I wish that it should. But I wish also to explain what I have meant by reading it while I have read it; since if I had meant what some seem to do, or what the interpreters of the Royal Commission impute, I should be bound to confess it as a sin and repent of the act all the rest of my life. The article will please few people; but it has been a great relief to my own conscience.[32]

As an Anglican priest, it appears that he effectively deceived his parishioners who undoubtedly thought he meant what he was reading. Stanley recommended that the use of the Creed be relaxed in the church services, "for avoiding of controversy and quieting of conscience."[33] Stanley was a prominent as a broad churchman, which included many Unitarians. Many high churchmen, which included Anglo-Catholics and evangelicals, however, objected to his appointment as the Dean of Westminster. Arthur Russell reportedly wrote to Gladstone on November 9, 1863 warning that having Stanley as the dean would mean having a dean who believed that the New Testament contained no doctrine.[34]

---

[32] Ibid., p. 618-619.

[33] Quoted in: Cornish, *The English Church in the Nineteenth Century, Part II*, p. 162.

[34] G.I.T. Machin, *Politics and the Churches in Great Britain in 1832 to 1868* (Oxford: Clarendon Press, 1977), p. 300.

While Men Slept...

Stanley on the Inspiration of Scripture

In July 1864, Stanley clarified his position on many doctrinal issues. In his assessment of recent controversies concerning the inspiration of Scripture, Stanley wrote:

> It is now declared to be no doctrine of the Church of England that "every part of the Bible is inspired, or is the Word of God."[35]

If there had ever been any doubts as to whether Stanley utterly rejected the notion that the Scriptures were inspired by God, he erased them during his visit to America in 1878. In an address presented in Boston to the clergy of the Protestant Episcopal Church of Massachusetts and Rhode Island on September 23, 1878, Stanley made his position clear. He said:

> First, as regards the Bible. The crude notions which prevailed twenty years ago on the subject of inspiration have been so completely abandoned, as to be hardly anywhere maintained by theological scholars. Of the eleven thousand English clergy who set their hands to a declaration in favour of those crude notions fifteen years ago, there are probably not fifty who would now do it again.
>
> As regards the interpretation of the sacred books, questions of criticism and authorship which were formerly considered to be entirely closed are now fully and freely discussed...The Biblical criticism, begun so admirably at Oxford by Professor Jowett, and continued in a more cautious spirit, though with more visible results, at Cambridge, by Professor Lightfoot, is full of promise for the future.[36]

---

[35] A. P. Stanley, *Judgement on "Essays and Reviews," "Edinburgh Review," July 1864*, In *Religious Controversies of the Nineteenth Century*, Cockshut, ed., p. 207.

[36] Arthur Penrhyn Stanley, "The Prospects of Liberal Theology," *Addresses and Sermons Delivered During a Visit to the United States and Canada in 1878*, ch. 2 (New York: Macmillan & Co., 1879), pp. 9-10.

Philip Schaff's assessment of Stanley was summarized in a note written during 1872 in which he said:

> Stanley calls the pope the head of our profession and speaks of Rainy's reply to his laudation of Scotch moderation as "delightful and wonderful for so short preparation." This is truly broad. His unmarried sister is Roman Catholic. He admires the pope and Sakya-Muni as a religious prophet to the Hindoos. His liberality is as broad as the universe.[37]

It is curious that, while Schaff possessed such a view of Stanley, he still carried on his correspondence concerning his work on the American Committee to Revise the Bible through Dean Stanley and Bishop Ellicott.[38]

Hort and Westcott: Evidence of Their Theology

Public Orthodoxy and Private Heresy

While publicly appearing to be an orthodox Christian, Hort privately subscribed to the Socialist and Unitarian teachings of Maurice. As he worked toward rewriting both the Greek and English versions of the New Testament in 1871, Hort had the full knowledge that his theological views were not acceptable to those who accepted mainline Christianity. He, therefore, refused to put himself in a situation in which his true views would become known, such as that of examining chaplain. His reason was because:

> My fear is that, partly in views, and still more in sympathies, I do not sufficiently conform to any of the recognized standards of a fit person for the special post which you offer me....[39]

Hort went on to give specific examples of his controversial views that would place him in a "false" position as the examining chaplain. Among

---

[37] Quoted in: David S. Schaff, *The Life of Philip Schaff* (New York: Charles Scribner's Sons, 1897), p. 266.

[38] David S. Schaff, *The Life of Philip Schaff* (New York: Charles Scribner's Sons, 1897), p. 358.

[39] Hort, *Life and Letters,* vol. 2, p. 155.

his unorthodox beliefs were those on the Atonement, the need for continuing sacrifices, the Immaculate Conception of Mary, and the purpose of the death of Jesus Christ on the cross which, rather than being the complete sacrifice, he believed gave power and meaning to other sacrifices. Citing his confidence that Maurice would be supportive of his views, Hort explained:

> I feel entirely with you that a fundamental difference on the subject of Atonement, if it existed, would place me in a false position as your examining chaplain....But it does not seem to me any disparagement to the sufferings and death of the Cross to believe that they were the acting out and manifestation of an eternal sacrifice, even as we believe that the sonship proceeding from the miraculous birth of the Virgin Mary was acting out the manifestation of the eternal Sonship. So also the uniqueness of the great Sacrifice seems to me not to consist in its being a substitute which makes all other sacrifices useless and unmeaning, but in its giving them the power and meaning which of themselves they could not have....I have thought it best to speak for myself without reference to the views of any other. But you will, I am sure, forgive me for expressing a belief that Mr. Maurice would assent entirely to what I have said... he may have failed to make clear the Sacrifice is not the only way of conceiving Atonement....[40]

Like Hort, Westcott also challenged the concept of the Atonement. On Good Friday in 1855 he wrote a letter to his wife in response to hearing a sermon on the Atonement. Westcott said of the minister:

> All he said was very good, but then he did not enter into the great difficulties of the notion of sacrifice and vicarious punishment. To me it is always most satisfactory to regard the Christian as in Christ—absolutely one with Him, and then he does what Christ has done: Christ's actions become his, and Christ's life and death in some sense his life and death. Don't

---

[40] Ibid., pp. 157-158.

you think this is the answer to the real difficulties? or do I not make myself clear?[41]

Westcott did not sway from his view on his challenge to the atoning sacrifice of Jesus Christ for our sins. On December 5, 1894, several years after the publication of the Revised Version of the English Bible, Westcott said that the Church had never laid down any authoritative theory of the Atonement.[42]

In contrast to Hort and Westcott, who rejected the importance of the sacrifice of Jesus Christ, the Apostle Paul writes that He is the one:

> In whom we have redemption through his blood, *even* the forgiveness of sins:
> —Colossians 1:14

Ignoring Doctrine

Despite the unorthodox views of Hort and Westcott on the basic Christian doctrine preached by Paul, they were the keys to rewriting both the Greek New Testament and the English Bible. Even though the Greek New Testament version that Hort and Westcott were developing was still secret and would not be ready for publication for eleven more years, there was great pressure in 1870 to use it as the basis to immediately undertake a rewriting of the English Bible. Using his influence on the Revision Committee, Westcott proposed a plan to acting chairman Ellicott that they prepare their proposed changes *before* their first meeting. This was apparently in response to finding that discussions of the impact of changes on doctrine had taken place at a previous meeting. Westcott wrote to Hort on July 1, 1870 that:

> This [discussing anything doctrinally or on doctrine] seems to me to be wholly out of our province. We have only to determine what is written and how it can be rendered. Theologians may deal with the text and version afterwards.[43]

---

[41] Arthur Westcott, *Life and Letters of Brooke Foss Westcott*, vol. 1 (London: Macmillan & Co., 1903), p. 231.

[42] Ibid., vol. 2, p. 226.

[43] Ibid., p. 393.

While Men Slept...

Even though Westcott did not want to openly discuss the impact of the proposed changes on doctrinal questions, he was well trained in the field and it is likely that he understood the impact. In the same letter, Westcott went on to tell Hort that the rendering of πνευμα αγιον as "the Holy Ghost" was not satisfactory to him.[44] He preferred to translate it as "the Holy Spirit."[45]

The Trinitarian Scripture

Erasing it from the Bible

The views of John Locke and Isaac Newton concerning the Trinitarian Scriptures, 1 John 5:7 and 1 Timothy 3:16, were well known. In letters written to each other on November 14, 1690, each presented to the other fuel for an argument in favor of Unitarian-acceptable changes to both Scriptures.[46, 47] It took about 180 years for the opportunity to present itself that would make those changes in the Bible possible.

F. D. Maurice celebrated the fact that he shared a common date of birth with John Locke.[48] Maurice's affection for Locke and its subsequent influence on Fenton Hort, however, went much further than that. On January 21, 1870, Maurice explained to Hort that John Locke was the starting point of Modern English philosophy.[49] Hort responded

---

[44] Ibid.

[45] The word "πνευμα" does, of course, mean "spirit" and can easily be interpreted as meaning a spirit that is not associated with a person. The word "πνευμα" may also mean, "ghost," which often means a specific kind of spirit in that it has some connection with a body or a person. Therefore, the term "Holy Ghost" suggests a spirit of a Person, whereas the term "Holy Spirit" does not necessarily suggest an association with a Person.

[46] E. S. De Beer, ed., *The Correspondence of John Locke*, vol. 4 (Oxford: Clarendon Press, 1979), pp. 164-165.

[47] H. W. Turnbull, ed., *The Correspondence of Isaac Newton, 1688-1694*, vol. 3 (Cambridge: Cambridge University Press for the Royal Society of London, 1961), pp. 84-129.

[48] Maurice, *The Life of Frederick Denison Maurice*, vol. 1, pp. 14-15.

[49] Ibid., vol. 2, p. 598.

to Maurice on February 2, 1870 that, as far as he was able to judge, Maurice's assessment of Locke was true.[50] In view of Hort's agreement with Maurice concerning his affection for Locke's philosophy, it was quite natural for him to look to Locke's correspondence with Isaac Newton concerning his desire to remove the Trinitarian Scripture from the Bible. Hort now had the opportunity to challenge the passage, 1 John 5:7, that is commonly referred to as the *Jonannine Comma*. The verse reads:

> For there are three that bear record in heaven, the Father, the Word, and the Holy Ghost: and these three are one.
> —1 John 5:7

Even before the English Bible Revision Committee met, Hort had already decided to remove the most Trinitarian of all Scriptures from the Bible. On May 14, 1870, Hort specifically targeted 1 John 5:7 for removal. This Scripture was the strongest witness in the Bible in favor of the three Person nature of God, as the Father, the Word, and the Spirit. Hort's strategy was to make the changes slowly. If he could get rid of 1 John 5:7, he thought he should wait before challenging other key Scriptures. He knew that a rapid rewriting of the traditional text would be rejected. Slow actions were apparently needed in order to reduce an anticipated resistance to the change. This is the way Hort said it:

> No rational being doubts the need of a revised Bible; and the popular practical objections are worthless. Yet I have an increasing feeling in favour of delay. Of course no revision can be final, and it would be absurd to wait for perfection. But the criticism of both Testaments, in text and interpretation alike, appears to me to be just now in that chaotic state (in Germany hardly if at all less than in England), that the results of immediate revision would be peculiarly unsatisfactory.... I John v. 7 might be got rid of in a month; and if that were done, I should prefer to wait a few years.[51]

---

[50] Hort, *Life and Letters,* vol. 2, p. 119.

[51] Ibid., p. 128.

Many modern scholars concur with Hort's view that 1 John 5:7 should be removed from the Bible.[52] They argue that Erasmus relied on late manuscripts for including it in his Greek New Testament and that he did not have sufficient early Greek manuscripts to support including that critical Scripture in the Bible.[53] Hort's friend and colleague, Joseph Barber Lightfoot, for example, tried to make a strong argument against the authenticity of that verse because it was not quoted by the writers in the fourth and fifth centuries. Lightfoot wrote:

> Indeed the very fact that it is nowhere quoted by the great controversial writers of the fourth and fifth centuries has been truly regarded as the strongest evidence against its genuineness.[54]

Then, however, Lightfoot continued and showed his bias toward the Unitarian movement with which he and his colleagues had been so intimately involved. He said:

> And in more recent times, when the [Trinitarian] doctrine began to be challenged, the text was challenged also; so that at this stage the doctrine did not gain, but lose, by the advocacy of a witness whose questionable character threw discredit upon it.[55]

Lightfoot, however, failed to mention that, as we have already learned, the fourth and fifth centuries marked a period of Arian resurgence. Thus, it was a time when the Scripture would have been strongly opposed by those in control of the Roman Church. As we have also learned, the more recent times to which he was referring were marked by the work of Newton, Locke, Priestley, Emerson, and Maurice. The efforts of these men and others helped to move England and America toward Unitarianism.

---

[52] Wright, *The Beginnings of Unitarianism in America*, p. 203.

[53] Carson, D. A., *The King James Version Debate: A Plea for Realism* (Grand Rapids, MI: Baker Book House, 1992), pp. 34-35.

[54] Joseph Barber Lightfoot, *On A Fresh Revision of the English New Testament* (London: Macmillan and Co., 1891), p. 28.

[55] Ibid., p. 28.

Defense of the Scripture

On the surface, the argument against the Trinitarian Scripture appears to be credible. However, it is essential to weigh the evidence, as Erasmus did, before making a hasty decision on that Scripture. It is true that there are many manuscripts that do not contain the essence of 1 John 5:7-8. A review of this issue has shown that 498 of 5000 Greek manuscripts are hostile to 1 John 5:7-8. However, of those 498 that are hostile to the Scripture, only 14 were written in the first eight centuries of Christianity! In other words, only 14 of 498, or 2.8 percent, of all of the hostile manuscripts date from within those centuries. All of the rest (97.2 percent of the hostile manuscripts) are dated to the tenth century or later![56] Thus, more than 97 percent of the evidence against the Scripture is found in *late* instead of in *early* manuscripts.

John Wesley (1703-1791) addressed the controversy over 1 John 5:7 before a packed house on May 7, 1775.[57] When he considered the issue of the authenticity of 1 John 5:7, he asked the question, "Is the text genuine?" Wesley concluded:

> I would insist only on the direct words, unexplained, just as they lie in the text: "There are three that bear record in heaven, the Father, the Word, and the Holy Ghost: And these three are one." ..."As they lie in the text :" — but here arises a question: Is that text genuine? Was it originally written by the Apostle, or inserted in later ages? Many have doubted of this; and, in particular, the great light of the Christian church, lately removed to the Church above, Bengelius, — the most pious, the most judicious, and the most laborious, of all the modern Commentators on the New Testament. For some time he stood in doubt of its authenticity, because it is wanting in many of the ancient copies. But his doubts were removed by three con-

---

[56] Michael Maynard, *A History of the Debate Over 1 John 5, 7-8: A Tracing of the Longevity of the Comma Johanneum With Evaluations of Arguments Against its Authenticity* (Tempe, AZ: Comma Publications, 1995), p. 285.

[57] *The Journal of the Rev. John Wesley, A. M.*, vol. 6, Nehemiah Curnock, ed. (London: Charles H. Kelly, 1779), p. 63.

siderations: (1.) That though it is wanting in many copies, yet it is found in more; and those copies of the greatest authority: — (2.) That it is cited by a whole gain of ancient writers, from the time of St. John to that of Constantine. This argument is conclusive: For they could not have cited it, had it not been in the sacred canon: — (3.) That we can easily account for its being, after that time, wanting in many copies, when we remember that Constantine's successor was a zealous Arian, who used every means to promote his bad cause, to spread Arianism throughout the empire; in particular the erasing this text out of as many copies as fell into his hands. And he so far prevailed, that the age in which he lived is commonly styled, *Seculum Aranium,*— "the Arian age;" there being then only one eminent man who opposed him at the peril of his life. So that it was a proverb, *Athanasius contra mundum*: "Athanasius against the world."[58]

If, as Wesley stated, as many traces as possible of 1 John 5:7 were destroyed by the zealous Arian who succeeded Constantine, then it is important to look to other early writings which referenced the text. These early writings offer conclusive proof of the essence of the Scripture from the earliest centuries of Christianity. For example, as early as A.D. 177, Athenagoras wrote:

> Who, then, would not be astonished to hear men who speak of God the Father, and of God the Son, and of the Holy Spirit, and who declare both their power in union and their distinction in order, called atheists?[59]

Other references to the essence of the Scripture have been attributed to Tertullian in A.D. 215, Cyprian in A.D. 250, Priscillian in A.D.

---

[58] John Wesley, *On The Trinity Advertisement, Sermon LV,* In *The Works of John Wesley,* vol. 6, (Albany, Oregon: The Sage Digital Library Collected Works, Sage Software, 1996), p. 228.

[59] Athenagoras, *Writings of Athenagoras,* B. P. Pratten, trans. In *The Anti-Nicene Fathers the Writings of the Fathers Down to A.D. 325, The Ante-Nicene Fathers,* vol. 2, ch. 10, Alexander Roberts and James Donaldson, eds. (Albany, Oregon: Sage Software, 1996, American Reprint of the Edinburgh ed., July, 1975), p. 266.

380, Gregory of Nazianzus in A.D. 385, a North African Author in A.D. 450, Victor Vitensis in A.D. 485, in the *Codex Freisingensis* in about A.D. 500, Fulgentius in A.D. 527, Cassiodorus in A.D. 570, Isidore of Seville in A.D. 636, as well as many others.[60] This Scripture has been hotly contested for centuries, with Unitarians arguing most vocally that it be eliminated from the Bible. Ignoring the early citations of the Scripture, Unitarians rejoice in believing that it was successfully removed from the Bible. According to a publication of the British and Foreign Unitarian Association:

> In the Authorised Version of the Bible there is one Trinitarian text: "There are three in heaven that bear record, the Father, the Word, and the Holy Ghost, and these three are one"...This text was at one time regarded as a scriptural refutation of Unitarianism, but it has proved that it was introduced by a later hand. It does not occur in the earliest manuscripts, and out of simple honesty it had to be omitted from the Revised Version of the New Testament.[61]

Because of the success in removing 1 John 5:7 from the Revised Version, and subsequent versions based on similar premises, the Unitarians boasted in 1910 that:

> There are few scholars of repute belonging to any branch of the Christian Church in the present day who would contend that the New Testament contains any clear or explicit statement of the doctrine of the Trinity.[62]

Following Origen: The Father of Unitarianism

Westcott, along with Lightfoot, made major contributions to a Dictionary of Christian Antiquites and assumed the "...editorship of the sections devoted to Literature and Biography, to Sects and Heresies, and to the History of Doctrine."[63] According to Arthur Westcott, his

---

[60] Maynard, *A History of the Debate Over 1 John 5, 7-8*, pp. 37ff.

[61] Hall, *Fifty Points in Favour of Unitarianism*, p. 24.

[62] Ibid., p. 25.

[63] Westcott, *Life and Letters*, vol. 2, p. 319.

father's most important contributions were "...his articles on the Alexandrian divines, including Clement, Demetrius, Dionysius, and,
greatest of all, Origen."[64] Arthur Westcott wrote of an account of a
sermon in which the preacher referred to B. F. Westcott:

> ...as "this good man, this great scholar, this dear friend, this
> abiding glory of our College," pronounced Origen to have
> been "a man after his own heart," and said, "I have been read-
> ing again lately his fine essay on the great "Origen and the
> Beginnings of Christian Philosophy." Not a word in it, nor
> yet a silence, that breathes suspicion against that gracious name.
> Nothing to decry, to cramp, to fetter thought. Throughout,
> spoken or unspoken, we hear the lofty prayer for light—light
> from the Father of lights, light through the Eternal Spirit, who
> "in all ages, entering into holy souls, maketh them friends of
> God and prophets."[65]

While displaying great admiration for the teachings of Origen, Westcott
was also actively engaged with Maurice in promoting the social gospel as a key dimension of Christianity. According to one account:

> He wrote to Professor F. D. Maurice in 1871 that without
> some such application of theology to life, our scheme will be
> very imperfect, and it will be an inestimable gain to the stu-
> dents preparing for Holy Orders if they can from the first be
> taught to feel that Social Morality is one side of the doctrine
> of the Church.[66]

Maurice's Deathbed Confession on the Trinity

Maurice had successfully planted the seeds of Socialism and Unitarianism into the minds of key men who were destined to change the
course of modern Christianity. While the rewriting of the English Bible

---

[64] Ibid., pp. 319-320.

[65] Ibid., vol. 1, pp. 320-321.

[66] Paul C. Hullyer, "A Short History Of The Cambridge Clergy Training School
And Westcott House, 1881-1996," http://www.ely.anglican.org/westcott/
history.htm, 1999.

was in its early stages, Maurice's health began to slow him down. Wanting to be near Maurice while he worked on the Bible Revision Committee, Fenton Hort moved to Cambridge in March 1872. According to Hort's son, Arthur, "One of the great attractions of the change had been the prospect of being a near neighbor to Professor Maurice."[67] Ironically, on the very day of Hort's arrival, Maurice left Cambridge, never to return.

As Maurice was on his deathbed in 1872, his wife sat at his side reading Scriptures to him. There were two great ironies in the life of the almost lifelong Unitarian, Frederick Denison Maurice. They were the day of his death and the last words that he ever uttered. As Mrs. Maurice recorded in her diary, it was on the night of Easter Sunday April 1, 1872 when:

> He went on speaking, but more and more indistinctly, till suddenly he seemed to make a great effort to gather himself up, and after a pause he said slowly and distinctly, "The knowledge of the love of God- the blessing of God Almighty, the Father, the Son, and the Holy Ghost be amongst you- amongst us- and remain with us for ever." He never spoke again.[68]

He died on Easter Sunday, the day celebrated as the day of the resurrection of Jesus Christ from the dead. As previously noted, Maurice had believed that the fact that he had been born on the same day as John Locke was significant. He might have also agreed that the fact that he died on Easter Sunday was also significant. In his last words, Maurice professed the Trinitarian doctrine and an everlasting belief in God when he said, "...the blessing of God Almighty, the Father, the Son, and the Holy Ghost...remain with us forever...." Were the last words of his life based on some definition that he had newly created within his own mind, as he had freely redefined so many words throughout his lifetime? Or were the last words of F. D. Maurice really a sincere confession of the faith that he had so vigorously opposed throughout his lifetime? Only God knows.

---

[67] Hort, *Life and Letters,* vol. 2, p. 172.

[68] Maurice, *The Life of Frederick Denison Maurice*, vol. 2, p. 641

While Men Slept...

Carrying the Mantle

On the day after Maurice's death, Hort lamented of his regret over having missed the opportunity to live as a near neighbor of Maurice:

> ...This is a heavy day with us. We heard this morning of the death of our very dear friend Mr. Maurice. Almost the brightest hope for our life at Cambridge was the prospect of having him for a near neighbour; three doors off. But it seems selfish to dwell on these thoughts in the presence of the great public loss.[68]

Despite (and perhaps without the knowledge of) Maurice's Trinitarian deathbed confession of God as the Father, the Son, and the Holy Ghost, those whom he had trained with his philosophies continued with their work. Hort, Westcott, and Lightfoot continued rewriting the Bible, equipped with Maurice's powerful influence and well trained in his belief in the power of words.[69] The work went on.

The prime minister of England, Gladstone, and soon to be Roman Catholic Cardinal Manning continued to participate in the Metaphysical Society, of which Maurice had been an active participant. Boasting that it represented those of "every faith and of no faith," it discussed every aspect of the foundations of human creeds. In 1875, after papal infallibility had been proclaimed by Rome and while the prospect of a rewritten Bible was a reality, Gladstone presided over one of the Society's meetings and Manning was in attendance.[70, 71] Maurice had made his contribution, in the name of Christian Socialism, toward achieving the new universal Christianity, but the work was not done.

---

[68] Hort, *Life and Letters,* vol. 2, p. 193.

[69] Reardon, *From Coleridge to Gore*, p. 346.

[70] Morley, *The Life of William Ewart Gladstone*, vol. 2, p. 524.

[71] Ibid., p. 504.

Chapter 14. New Bibles for the New Universal Christianity

> **Textual criticism, as applied to the Greek New Testament, forms a special study of much intricacy and difficulty, and even now leaves room for considerable variety of opinion among competent critics.[1]**
> **—Preface to The English New Testament, 1881 Revision**

The Scheme

"We Three:" The Revision Triad

Thus, after more than seventeen years of work on a new Greek New Testament, Brooke Foss Westcott, Fenton Hort, and Joseph Lightfoot were invited in 1870 to take part in the Revision of the English Bible. The two activities, rewriting the Greek New Testament and the English Bible, were to be performed nearly simultaneously! Things were moving rapidly. It was no time for hesitation. Suddenly, the opportunity to make major changes in the Bible had developed. Although the timing was not what those who were rewriting the Bible had planned, the opportunity was ripe. After agreeing to take part in the "revision" of the English Bible, Westcott wrote to Hort:

> ...though I think that Convocation is not competent to initiate such a measure, yet I feel that as "we three" are together it would be wrong not to "make the best of it" as Lightfoot says. Indeed, there is a very fair prospect of good work, though neither with this body nor with any body likely to be formed now could a complete textual revision be possible. There is some hope that alternative readings might find a place in the margin. But this is one of the details on which it will be necessary for us to confer before the first meeting....Even if we fail

---

[1] *The New Testament of Our Lord and Saviour Jesus Christ Translated Out of the Greek: Being the Version Set Forth A.D. 1611 Compared with the Most Ancient Authorities and Revised A.D. 1881* (Oxford University Press, 1881), p. xii.

greatly we shall not fail from unwillingness to co-operate with others....How rapidly things move now. This scheme seems like a dream.[2]

As part of a planned conspiracy among three of the Revision Committee participants, Westcott wrote to Lightfoot in 1870:

Ought we not to have a conference before the first meeting for Revision? There are many points on which it is important that we should be agreed. The rules though liberal are vague, and the interpretation of them will depend upon decided action at first.[3]

In 1872 Westcott wrote: "The experience of the work of the New Testament Revision during the last two years has shewn me that I was wrong in this opinion [that the Greek Text had to be completed before the English text could be written]."[4]

Maurice's "Word of God"

In 1870, the year that the decision was made to proceed with the Revised English Bible, Hort was still in very close contact with F. D. Maurice. On January 21, 1870, Maurice wrote a letter to Hort in which he expressed his thankfulness to Westcott for his favorable review of an article on national morality. He also expressed his gratitude to the editors of the article for "...forcing us to ask ourselves what we mean by Humanity and how we connect it with Theology."[5] In the same letter, Maurice praised the philosophy of Kant and told Hort that he had accepted his suggestion that he give private lessons on John Locke and on modern English philosophy.

Maurice challenged the belief that the Bible was the "Word of God." In addressing the question in 1863, Maurice responded that:

---

[2] Westcott, *Life and Letters*, vol. 1, p. 390.

[3] Ibid., p. 391.

[4] Westcott, *A General View of the History of the English Bible*, p. vii.

[5] Maurice, *The Life of Frederick Denison Maurice*, vol. 2, p. 598.

On the other hand, I have spoken at some length on the expression *"Word of God."* It seems to me that we clergymen should very seriously apply ourselves to the question, "What sense does this expression convey to us when we read the Scriptures? Have what we call the different senses of it no relation to each other? Is the use of it by St. John a mere figurative accidental use; or does that interpret all the other applications of it? Has it found its meaning till we come to that meaning?"[6]

In other words, Maurice said the Scripture is not the Word of God until human reason is applied to it. Thus, the argument might follow, that the Word of God is placed under and is subject to the authority of reason. Using such reasoning, when considered in the context of Paul's writings, one might declare human reason to *be* the Spirit of God. Paul wrote:

> For what man knoweth the things of a man, save the spirit of man which is in him? even so the things of God knoweth no man, but the Spirit of God.
> —1 Corinthians 2:11

On March 12, 1870, Maurice continued by saying that Martin Luther's study of the writings of Paul:

> …showed him [Luther] that there was a direct access for him to a God of righteousness and truth. And thus was born that kind of affection for the scriptures which has characterised the people, far more than the learned, of the Protestant nations.[7]

Maurice's son said that his father referenced Luther's influence on the Thirty-Nine Articles when he went on to:

> ...speak of the Articles as composed under this influence, and therefore everywhere appealing to the Living Word, rever-

---

[6] Maurice, *The Claims of the Bible and of Science*, 1863, pp. 120-121.

[7] Maurice, *The Life of Frederick Denison Maurice*, vol. 2, pp. 602-603.

encing the scriptures in so far as they helped to reveal Him. He contrasted with this appeal the tendency shown by the clergy, who had attributed to the scriptures the title of the Word of God- an expression not to be found in any passage of the Bible in which the name Scripture could be substituted for it.[8]

Subtle Subjectivity: Undermining Biblical Authority

A major criticism that was widely put forth concerning the beliefs of F. D. Maurice and those who subscribed to his teachings was their lack of objectivity. As one author put it:

The root of Maurice's error was the complete subjectivity which was his only standard or authority.[9]

It was Maurice's view that the Bible was a useful historical document. But by adding his subjectivity to its study, it can be argued that even its historical reliability is severely diminished. According to one reviewer of the problem, textual criticism has destroyed the reliability of the Bible as a chronicle. The techniques used by Maurice tended to confuse all but the most discerning readers. He made his points in a conflicting manner that caused the reader to get lost in a maze of argumentative and alternative statements. One of Maurice's great admirers, Arthur Michael Ramsey (1904 -1988), known as Michael Ramsey who was later to become the archbishop of Canterbury, seemed to agree. Describing Maurice's confusing style of discourse, Ramsey wrote:

The points which Maurice was making were lost in the fog of battle. The orthodox thought that they saw things crystal clear: either the Bible was true or it was not; and those questions of Maurice, "what do you mean by true?", "what do you mean by history?", were not being faced. And, while Maurice abhorred the theological outlook of Colenso, his abhorrence of

---

[8] Ibid., p. 603.

[9] Olive J. Brose, *Frederick Denison Maurice: Rebellious Conformist* (Athens, Ohio: Ohio University Press, 1971), p. 227.

the proceedings against him, his belief that critical studies ought to be pursued and his inability to call the Bible the "Word of God" put him alongside the Radicals in current estimation.[10]

Maurice mastered the subtle approach to undermining the authority of the Bible as the Word of God. To Maurice, those who were direct and open in espousing views that were very similar to his were too controversial. For example, John William Colenso (1814-1883), the first bishop of Natal, South Africa and a close friend of Maurice, wrote a critical review of the Pentateuch and book of Joshua of the Old Testament. While translating the Bible into Zulu, Colenso also declared that the Bible was not God's Word. In addition, he indicated that Paul's letter to the Romans suggested universal salvation.[11] After the religious press and the church hierarchy condemned Colenso's views as heresy, Colenso made a direct appeal to the Privy Council in London where he was vindicated. Charles Darwin helped pay his legal fees.[12]

Prior to the great controversy, Colenso had communicated frequently with Maurice. Colenso had even written to tell Maurice of his intentions to publish the book discrediting the Pentateuch.[13] However, after the controversy became public, Maurice tried to distance himself from Colenso and the direct approach he used in rejecting the Old Testament.

Maurice was much too tactful and subtle to be involved in such a public display of heresy. He wrote to a South African clergyman on March 21, 1865 that the laity of the church would be suspicious of someone who they thought was trying to take the Bible from them. Even though Maurice had rejected it as the Word of God, he advised the clergyman to, "...show that you have no sympathy with any depreciation of the Old Testament, that you claim it as the Divine au-

---

[10] Arthur M. Ramsey, *F. D. Maurice and the Conflicts of Modern Theology: The Maurice Lectures, 1948* (Cambridge: Cambridge University Press, 1951), p. 90.

[11] Latourette, *Christianity in a Revolutionary Age*, vol. 2, p. 296.

[12] Wilson, *God's Funeral*, p. 110.

[13] Maurice, *The Life of Frederick Denison Maurice,* vol. 2, p. 421.

thority for the true life of our nation at home...."[14] He then concluded his advice as follows:

> They will always suspect you if they think you are taking the Bible from them. They will love you in time, if not at first, if you restore the Bible to them; its professed worshippers as well as the ecclesiastics have been stealing it from them.[15]

The Strategy

Subtle Revision Instead of Open Destruction

Consistent with the philosophy of F. D. Maurice, the revisors recognized the need for subtle revision rather than open destruction of the Bible. Having been convinced that the Bible is not the Word of God, it would seem reasonable to rewrite it as the word of man. However, attempts to destroy God's written Word have failed even from the earliest of times. Even after King Jehoiakim had burned the Word of God, the Lord had a simple solution to the problem. He simply told His prophet, Jeremiah, to write it again:

> Take thee again another roll, and write in it all the former words that were in the first roll, which Jehoiakim the king of Judah hath burned.
> —Jeremiah 36:28

When the Word of God was blatantly destroyed, God gave the words back to Jeremiah and his scribe to write all of the former words. Throughout history when Bibles were burned, God preserved copies through people who lost their lives in the process of saving God's Word. The revisors of the Bible learned that its open destruction would not be tolerated. Therefore, a new strategy was required. It was that of making what appeared to be *subtle* or *trifling* alterations.

---

[14] Ibid., p. 491
[15] Ibid.

Make "What Appear To Be Trifling Alterations"

As Hort explained on July 19, 1870, which was shortly after the first meeting of the Revision Committee, their strategy was to make what appeared to be "trifling alterations" in the Bible. Taken individually, the alterations would seem trivial to the undiscerning reader, but when taken in total, they would have a major impact on what the Bible says. Each change, he added, needed to be meticulously considered so that it would also have a "truth of tone." He put it this way:

> It is quite impossible to judge the value of what appear to be trifling alterations merely by reading them one after another. Taken together, they have often important bearings which few would think of at first. There is but one safe rule, to be as scrupulously exact as possible, remembering, of course, that there is a truth of tone as well as of grammar and dictionary. The difference between a picture say of Raffaelle and a feeble copy of it is made up of a number of trivial differences.[16]

Hort continued on July 19, 1870 saying:

> We have successfully resisted being warned off dangerous ground, where the needs of revision required that it should not be shirked . . . It is, one can hardly doubt, the beginning of a new period in Church history. So far the angry objectors have reason for their astonishment.[17]

The New Greek New Testament: The New Foundation

By 1878, Alexander Macmillan had become frustrated at the delays of Westcott and Hort in the publication of their New Greek New Testament. Hort had been hesitating on its publication and Macmillan was applying pressure to get it out. Macmillan wrote to Westcott on May 21, 1878:

---

[16] Hort, *Life and Letters,* vol. 2, p. 138.

[17] Ibid., p. 139.

> I wish you could persuade our friend Hort to let the text, that
> you and he have elaborated so thoroughly, come out…. I can
> see no sense in which his delay is right. He seeks a perfection
> that would lead to no existence before it reached to possible
> fault. He is getting to be a critical Buddhist. We practical En-
> glish would think of him as trying to catch his shadow.[18]

Macmillan was concerned that they were going to be beaten to publication by another reviser of the Greek New Testament. Determined
to get his new Greek New Testament on the market first, Macmillan
ordered its publication before Hort was ready to have it published.
He wrote his concerns in a letter to Hort on June 6, 1878:

> You probably have seen that the Pitt Press is going to publish
> an edition of the *Greek Testament* with a new text by Profes-
> sor Perowne…it therefore becomes of vital importance that
> not a moment should be lost in issuing ours. As Dr. Westcott
> has the same interest and responsibility as you and does not in
> the least approve of the delay, and we have the strongest rea-
> sons for speedy publication, it does not seem to me reason-
> able that you should any longer impose your judgment on your
> two equal partners against their strong judgment and interest.
> You have had your way now for several years, to our serious
> loss, and deference to your judgment has been already carried
> beyond due limits. I therefore am ordering paper to go to Clay,
> with orders to print an edition of 1250 copies, and mean to
> publish the book in time for the opening of the public schools
> in August.[19]

Part of the reason for Hort's delay in his publication of the new Greek
New Testament was that he knew it would be subjected to significant
criticism. He was especially concerned about critics that included Birch
and Burgon. Macmillan wrote to Hort on June 12, 1878 saying:

---

[18] Graves, *Life and Letters of Alexander Macmillan*, p. 344.

[19] Ibid., p. 345.

> I have read all your arguments with amazement. They can only be meant to convince yourself, and is that needful? What on earth has Professor Birch's criticism to do with the case— or Burgon's, or any of the same sort? If you wrote fifteen volumes of vindication or explanation it won't be read by such, or if read not appreciated….I am sure your text will justify itself *pro tem.* You can smash gainsayers afterwards.[20]

By 1881, Hort and Westcott succeeded in producing a rewritten Greek New Testament based on totally different manuscripts than had been previously used. The new publication was the result of subjecting the Scriptures to reason using the new "science" of textual criticism.

The Depth of the Changes Was Never Anticipated

When Samuel Wilberforce made the resolution to revise the Authorized Version of the New Testament, he thought the changes would be in the form of notes in the margin that would eventually make their way into the text. He had no idea of the extent and the depth of the changes that were being planned for the new English version of the Bible. According to his son, Reginald Wilberforce:

> The alterations which have been made are so various and manifold that it is well to record the words used by the Bishop in moving the above resolution, to show what changes he contemplated, and how jealously he would have excluded those alterations which, to use his own words, destroyed the "ring of familiarity" to the ordinary reader.[21]

The key point to the resolution was that it specifically stated that the revision was to be based on the Greek text originally adopted by the translators of the Authorized Version, which was the *Textus Receptus*! The only changes that were to be made were in:

---

[20] Ibid., pp. 345-346.

[21] Wilberforce, *Life of the Right Reverend Samuel Wilberforce,* vol. 3, p. 347.

> ...all those passages where plain and clear errors, whether in the Greek text originally adopted by the Translators or in the translation made by the same, shall, on due investigation, be found to exist.[22]

In reality, the changes were enormous. By at least one count, the Revised Greek Text had no less than 5,788 readings that differed from the text on which the Authorized Bible was based, about a quarter of which were held to have modified the subject-matter.[23] The Unitarians claimed that since a quarter, or more than 1400, of those changes affected the subject matter of the Bible, there was sufficient cause to reject the concept of the infallibility of Scripture:

> The deathblow was given to this theory [of infallibility of Scripture] by the publication of the Revised Version. The Revisers made 36,191 alterations in the text, translation, and punctuation of the New Testament alone. In the text 5,788 changes were introduced, though only a quarter of these were regarded as affecting the subject matter.[24]

Samuel Wilberforce was killed by a fall from a horse in 1873.[25] Consequently, Wilberforce was never able to learn the full extent to which the rewriters boldly reached beyond the authority of the resolution he had made for its revision. Instead of being a "revision," the English Bible became an entirely new text, which was based on a secretly produced Greek New Testament that the world had not even seen. It was produced under the authority of reason, rather than of God. Thus, the English Bible was not "revised." Instead, it was rewritten!

The New English Bible: Either the Best or the Worst

During the course of rewriting the English Bible, there were 27 members of the Old Testament Committee (new members were added be-

---

[22] Ibid., p. 347.

[23] Frederic Kenyon, *Our Bible and the Ancient Manuscripts* (London: Eyre & Spottiswoode, 1948), pp. 238-239.

[24] Hall, *Fifty Points in Favour of Unitarianism*, pp. 34-35.

[25] Wilberforce, *Life of the Right Reverend Samuel Wilberforce,* vol. 3, p. 423-425.

cause seven died and three resigned) and 24 members of the New Testament Committee (new members were added because three died and one resigned). The New Testament was completed on November 11, 1880 and the Old Testament completed on June 20, 1884.[26] The Revised Version of the New Testament was published on May 17, 1881 and the Old and New Testaments together were published on May 19, 1885.[27] (Dean Arthur Stanley died on July 18, 1881.[28] This was shortly after the Revised Version of the New Testament, which was published on May 17, 1881.)[29]

The authors of the rewritten English New Testament insisted in the preface that it was simply a revision of the 1611 Authorized Version. They stated it this way:

> The English Version of the New Testament here presented to the reader is a Revision of the Translation published in the year of Our Lord 1611, and commonly known by the name of the Authorised Version.[30]

Although the authors of the new English Version said that it was simply a "revision," they acknowledged that it was really built upon a new and totally different foundation from the Authorized Version:

> A revision of the Greek text was the necessary foundation for our work...[31]

---

[26] *The Bible in its Ancient and English Versions*, H. Wheeler Robinson, ed. (London: Oxford at the Clarendon Press, 1940), pp. 242-247.

[27] Ibid., p. 250.

[28] Cornish, *The English Church in the Nineteenth Century, Part II*, p. 346.

[29] *The Bible in its Ancient and English Versions*, Edited by H. Wheeler Robinson, Oxford at the Clarendon Press, London, 1940, p. 250.

[30] *The New Testament of Our Lord and Saviour Jesus Christ Translated Out of the Greek: Being the Version Set Forth A.D. 1611 Compared with the Most Ancient Authorities and Revised A.D. 1881* (Oxford: Oxford University Press, 1881), p. v.

[31] Ibid., p. xi.

While Men Slept...

After thoroughly reviewing the "revisions" of the Bible that were made by Westcott and Hort, Dean William Burgon concluded that there could be no middle ground concerning the rewritten text. It was either the very best or it was the very worst. It was either the most accurate or the least accurate. He put it this way:

> The Text of Drs. Westcott and Hort is either the very best which has ever appeared, or else it is the very worst; the nearest to the sacred Autographs, or the furthest from them. There is no room for both opinions; and there cannot exist any middle view.[32]

The arguments against accepting the Revised Bible by persons such as John Burgon were sufficient to cause many to reject the new Bible Version. However, Unitarians further fueled the fire by publicly claiming that the new version strongly favored Unitarian doctrines.[33]

Submitting the Scripture to the Test of Reason

Faith in the literal word of the Bible used to be held as a surer guide on how to conduct one's life than the light of reason or conscience. But then, as described by the Unitarian Alfred Hall, things changed:

> In 1836 James Martineau said in his "Rationale of Religious Enquiry" that all questions of religion must finally be submitted to the judgment (sic) of the *reason*, "to the test of which even scripture must be brought." It was a bold assertion for those days, and was condemned by some of his own brother ministers. But for many years past Unitarians have accepted this position without question.[34]

Using a new method of applying reason, which was called "textual criticism," the Word of God was placed under the authority of man.

---

[32] John William Burgon, *The Secret Spanking of Westcott and Hort,* In *Unholy Hands on the Bible*, vol. 1., Jay P. Green, Sr., ed. (Lafayette, Indiana: Sovereign Grace Trust Fund, 1990), pp. G-62-G-63.

[33] *The Bible in its Ancient and English Versions*, H. Wheeler Robinson, ed. (London: Oxford at Clarendon Press, 1940), pp. 262-263.

[34] Hall, *Fifty Points in Favour of Unitarianism*, p. 14.

New Bibles for the New Universal Christianity

The critical approach to the Bible was built upon the philosophical background of Kant, Hegel, Schleiermacher, and others.[35] Textual criticism is the study of differences in wording among several copies of any written document. It presumably involves three main kinds of activity: (1) observation of these differences; (2) recording these differences with clarity and precision; and (3) the establishment of criteria by which these differences may be explained.[36] (Prayerfully seeking the guidance of the Holy Spirit is not necessarily a component in modern textual criticism.)

The method of textual criticism proposed by Hort was not universally accepted. Dean Burgon wrote, for example, that Hort's theory was "...too devoid of anything like proof, ever to win universal acceptance."[37] He went on to say that the Bible is different from all other books because it is Divine:

> That which distinguishes Sacred Science from every other science which can be named is that it is Divine; it has to do with the Book which is inspired, one whose true Author is God.[38]

Whether we have the authority to subject Scripture to "textual criticism" has been a key issue that has been debated for more than a century. According to Arthur M. Ramsey who was the future archbishop of Canterbury:

> There was first the need to assert the rights of critical study, and here Maurice did much to kindle the temper in which Hort and his Cambridge colleagues did their work. Then there came the gradual awareness that criticism could have its own wrong presuppositions and could lose the key to the Bible. And more

---

[35] Earle E. Cairns, *Christianity Through the Centuries,* 3rd ed. (Grand Rapids, Michigan: Zondervan Publishing House, 1996), p. 419.

[36] J. Neville Birdsall, *Textual Criticism and New Testament Studies* (Birmingham, England: University of Birmingham, 1984), p. 2.

[37] Burgon, *The Traditional Text of the New Testament,* pp. 4-5.

[38] Ibid., p. 5.

recently there came the violent reactions in which a theological approach to the Bible has been recovered, and the labours of historical criticism have sometimes been disparaged in the supposed interests of the transcendental Word of God.[39]

According to the authors of the rewritten English New Testament, the art of textual criticism was far from an objective science as many had presumed. They acknowledged that:

Textual criticism, as applied to the Greek New Testament, forms a special study of much intricacy and difficulty, and even now leaves room for considerable variety of opinion among competent critics.[40]

Accountable to No One

Hort confessed his arrogance and unwillingness to submit his decisions concerning various readings of the Greek text to others for accountability when he stated that there was no one of sufficient competence to challenge his selection of textual readings. In a letter to Lightfoot on May 18, 1860, Hort put it this way:

It sounds an arrogant thing to say, but there are very many cases in which I would not admit the competence of nay one to judge a decision of mine on a textual matter, who was only an amateur, and had not had considerable experience in *forming* a text. And it seems to me worse than delusive to appear to submit our decision to the verdict of persons whose jurisdiction we challenge.[41]

Using his arrogance to put forward techniques which others did not successfully challenge, Hort built upon the work of Griesbach and others and succeeded in accomplishing his goal. He dethroned the Syrian majority texts, together with the *Textus Receptus*. Some, how-

---

[39] Ramsey, *F. D. Maurice and the Conflicts of Modern Theology*, p. 97.

[40] *The New Testament, Revised A.D. 1881,* p. xii.

[41] Hort, *Life and Letters,* vol. 1, p. 425.

ever, who may agree with his overall approach, believed that Hort went too far in denying all value to readings that were found only in the Syrian manuscripts.[42] To many others, Hort's system of distinguishing between what he called "Neutral" and "Alexandrine" manuscripts seemed artificial. Using Hort's approach, too much emphasis was believed to have been placed on their preferred manuscripts, especially on the *Codex Vaticanus*.[43] Some believed that much of the textual criticism approach used by Hort may have been used as "window-dressing" in order to accomplish his objective:

> If we find it unconvincing, then Hort's parade of the genealogical method may seem just so much window-dressing, fashionable to the extent that in general it has retained its place in scholarly esteem.[44]

When Westcott and Hort published their rewritten Greek New Testament five days before the release of the rewritten English New Testament, they viewed it as a major victory. Having sworn the Revision Committee to secrecy, the world would not know that their "revisions" of the King James Version were based on a new Greek text, based on the minority Alexandrian manuscripts instead of the majority Syrian manuscripts. Even their supporters, acknowledged that "…Westcott and Hort's devotion to the text of the Vatican and Sinaitic codices was excessive…."[45] Nevertheless, the Revision Committee voted by a three to one margin to accept the new Greek manuscript as the foundation for the new English Bible that it presented to the world.

Universal Bibles

The World Council of Churches and the National Council of Churches of Christ had already embraced the Revised Versions of the English Bible prior to the commencement of the Second Vatican Council. To help support the global Ecumenical Movement, the National Council

---

[42] Kilpatrick, *Griesbach and the Development of Text Criticism*, p. 139.

[43] Gordon D. Fee, *Modern Text Criticism and the Synoptic Problem*, In *J. J. Griesbach: Synoptic and Text-critical Studies, 1776-1976*, p. 155.

[44] Kilpatrick, *Griesbach and the Development of Text Criticism*, p. 139.

[45] Bruce, *History of the Bible in English*, p. 139.

of Churches of Christ obtained the rights to the Revised Versions of the Bible, made revisions in them, and then offered them to the world as the Revised Standard Version.[46] Luther Allan Weigle was the chairman of the committee that produced the Revised Standard Version. Weigle, like Coleridge, Maurice, Schleiermacher, Hort, and many others who had major influences on biblical revision, was a student of the Prussian philosopher, Immanuel Kant. After four years of classical Greek studies, Weigle wrote his dissertation at seminary on Kant.[47]

Many of the changes in the Revised Standard Version were met with opposition among conservative Christians. Most significant among these changes were those that seemed to some to undermine the virgin birth and divinity of Jesus Christ. Significant among these was Isaiah 7:14, where the well-known prophecy of the virgin birth of "Immanuel" was changed from "...a virgin..." to "...a young woman..." shall conceive.[48] Other controversial texts included Psalm 2:11-12, which removed the reference to "the Son."[49] The comparative renderings are shown as follows:

> Serve the LORD with fear, and rejoice with trembling. **Kiss the Son**, lest he be angry, and ye perish *from* the way, when his wrath is kindled but a little. Blessed *are* all they that put their trust in him.
> —Psalms 2:11-12 (KJV) [Bold type is shown for emphasis.]

> Serve the LORD with fear, with trembling **kiss his feet**, lest he be angry, and you perish in the way; for his wrath is quickly kindled. Blessed are all who take refuge in him. .
> —Psalms 2:11-12 (RSV) [Bold type is shown for emphasis.]

---

[46] *The Holy Bible, Revised Standard Version: Containing the Old and New Testaments*, (New York: Thomas Nelson & Sons, 1952; Copyright by National Council of Churches of Christ: New Testament, 1946, Old Testament, 1952).

[47] Peter J. Thuesen, *In Discordance with the Scriptures: American Protestant Battles over Translating the Bible* (New York and Oxford: Oxford University Press, 1999), pp. 73-75.

[48] Ibid., p. 95.

[49] Ibid., p. 107.

Whereas the last twelve verses of Mark had been set apart with blank lines in the 1881-85 Revised Version, the Revised Standard Version dropped the entire passage into a footnote. Among the other controversial passages is Luke 24:6, comparatively shown in Appendix B in several Bible versions, which removed the famous reference to the resurrection of Jesus.[50] The comparison with the King James Version is as follows:

> **He is not here, but is risen:** remember how he spake unto you when he was yet in Galilee,
> —Luke 24:6 (KJV) [Bold type is shown for emphasis.]

> Remember how he told you, while he was still in Galilee,
> —Luke 24:6 (RSV)

Following the opening of the Second Vatican Council, the movement toward ecumenical Bibles intensified. Using the groundwork that had already been laid during the rewriting of the Greek New Testament by Brooke Foss Westcott and Fenton Hort, members of the United Bible Societies and the Roman Catholic Church met in 1964 at the Driebergen Conference. There they approved the preparation of a new common translation of the Bible. The Second Vatican Council ratified the proposal in 1965.[51] Members of Weigle's committee presented a Roman Catholic edition of the Revised Standard Version to Pope Paul VI on May 22, 1965. For his effort, Weigle was awarded the papal knighthood of St. Gregory the Great on January 27, 1966.[52]

Jesuit Cardinal Carlo Maria Martini joined the United Bible Societies International Editorial Committee in 1967. Using the Westcott and Hort Greek New Testament as its basis, the Committee continued to make changes in the text. During the three-year interval between the production of the second and third editions of the United Bible Societies' Greek New Testament, the committee of five introduced more than five hundred additional changes. Most modern versions of the

---

[50] Ibid., pp. 108-109.

[51] Michael de Semlyen., *All Roads Lead to Rome? The Ecumenical Movement* (Bucks, England: Dorchester House Publications, 1993), p. 200.

[52] Thuesen, *In Discordance with the Scriptures*, p. 142.

Bible were based on the United Bible Societies/Nestle-Aland Greek New Testament text, which was approved by the Vatican.[53]

By 1968, work commenced on the New International Version. Soon, the Zondervan Corporation, who was a distributor of the Revised Standard Version, also became the primary corporate patron of the New International Version. In an appeal to the Evangelicals, the producers of the New International Version restored some of the controversial readings that had been changed in the Revised Standard Version. The sales of the new Bible soared. In what one author called "The Contemporary Babel of Bibles," more Bibles followed.[54] David P. Gaines, a historian of the World Council of Churches, wrote that:

> Although the Bible remained the "Word of God," it was that in a different sense. Sectarian readings of it slowly lost their authority. Many doctrinal distinctions and denominational demarcations, whatever the occasion for the continued emphasis on them, ceased to be supported by supposedly scriptural sanctions once stoutly maintained. Gradually the spirit triumphed over the letter, and the experience of God through faith and love, however explained theologically, was recognized as the deepest common bond between believers.[55]

Thus, new Roman Catholic-approved versions of the Bible were used to replace the King James Bible, which had been the standard among Protestants since 1611. As what God really said became less clear, because there seemed to be so many conflicting words that supposedly came from Him, reliance upon the Bible as the standard for establishing Christian doctrine gradually became secondary. Instead, the desires of man and spiritual experiences were used to establish global bonds in a new universal Christianity, while compromising the doctrine of salvation by faith in the shed blood of Jesus Christ.

---

[53] de Semlyen., *All Roads Lead to Rome?*, pp. 200-201.

[54] Thuesen, *In Discordance with the Scriptures*, pp. 147-152.

[55] David P. Gaines, *The World Council of Churches: A Study of Its Background and History* (Peterborough, New Hampshire, Richard R. Smith, Noone House, 1966), p. 1097.

Section 3. The Impact

While Men Slept...

Chapter 15. What is Truth?

Those who first *invent their facts,* and then proceed to build their premises on them, do but go astray themselves, and then hopelessly mislead others....

—John Burgon[1]

Lighting Up the Darkness

The Secret Made Known

Since the work to rewrite the Bible was mainly done in secret, there was little known about the details of the kinds of major changes that were occurring until the work had actually been completed. Even after the publication of the Revised Version of the English New Testament in 1881, and the entire Revised Bible in 1885, most people did not feel sufficiently competent to publicly challenge the results of the work. The product was the result of years of toil by those who were believed by many to be the foremost Bible scholars in the world. Even fewer people were aware that there was a hidden agenda that had permeated the very core of the Revised Bible.

Nevertheless, while perhaps not comprehending that there was a conspired plan to instill a Universalist Unitarian slant to the Revised Bible, there were still some who were paying attention. After the contents of the revision became known, John William Burgon strongly voiced his concerns regarding what had been done. Burgon was a contemporary of Maurice, Hort, Westcott, Lightfoot, Macmillan, Hare, and the many others who successfully changed both the Greek and English versions of the Bible to promote the new universal Christianity of Christian Socialism. The first major step toward the cause that had dominated each of their lives was accomplished. It was because of Burgon and others, who clearly saw the willful alterations that were being made in the Bible, that Hort delayed bringing out the rewritten Greek New Testament.[2]

---

[1] Burgon, *The Revised Revision*, p. D-51.

[2] Graves, *Life and Letters of Alexander Macmillan*, pp. 345-346.

While Men Slept...

Exposing the Invented Facts

How can we be sure that the scholars who expounded their Socialist and Unitarian views while they were intimately involved in rewriting the Bible actually allowed those views to affect their work? We must examine the fruit of their labor. From a distance, many trees look about the same. It is only when we look more closely at the fruit of those trees that we are able to discern whether it is a good tree or a corrupt tree. A good tree produces good fruit, whereas a bad tree produces bad fruit. Jesus explained that:

> For a good tree bringeth not forth corrupt fruit; neither doth a corrupt tree bring forth good fruit. For every tree is known by his own fruit. For of thorns men do not gather figs, nor of a bramble bush gather they grapes.
>
> —Luke 6:43-44

Was Jesus God Manifest in the Flesh?

Burgon intensely studied and wrote of the problems that he found with the methods of textual criticism used by the rewriters of the Bible. He also clearly documented why he believed many of the selected readings in the Revised Bible to be incorrect. He provided clear documentation for the validity of key rejected Scriptures of controversy. The point of the "controversy"[3] is summed up in 1 Timothy 3:16. The Authorized Version clearly, and without controversy, states that Jesus Christ was indeed God manifest in the flesh:

> And without controversy great is the mystery of godliness: **God** was manifest in the flesh, justified in the Spirit, seen of angels, preached unto the Gentiles, believed on in the world, received up into glory.
>
> —1 Timothy 3:16 (KJV) [Bold type is shown for emphasis.]

---

[3] James R. White, *The King James Only Controversy: Can You Trust the Modern Translations?* (Minneapolis, Minnesota: Bethany House Publishers, 1995), p. iii.

The Revised Version, on the other hand, denied that Jesus Christ was God manifest in the flesh:

> And without controversy great is the mystery of godliness; **He who** was manifested in the flesh, justified in the spirit, seen of angels, preached among the nations, believed on in the world, received up in glory.
> –1 Timothy 3:16 (RV)[4] [Bold type is shown for emphasis.]

The footnote in the Revised Version read:

> The word *God*, in place of *He who*, rests on no sufficient ancient evidence. Some ancient authorities read *which*.[5] [Italics are in the original.]

What was this "no sufficient ancient evidence" that the authors were referring to in the footnote? Following the publication of the Revised Version of the Bible, Dean William Burgon wrote to Bishop Ellicott concerning the change that had been made to 1 Timothy 3:16. In his lengthy discussion (seventy-six pages), Burgon demonstrated why θεος (God) could not be replaced by ος (he) in the Greek text. The rewriters of the Bible were determined to remove the witness that God was actually manifest in the flesh. Following a lengthy discussion citing ancient authorities and manuscripts, Burgon wrote:

> Permit me, my lord Bishop, as an ordinary writer addressing ordinary readers to respectfully point out that you entirely mistake the problem at hand. The Greek Text of the New Testament is *not* to be settled by *modern opinion*, but by *ancient authority*....And now will you listen while I state for you and my reader the grounds on which I am convinced that your substitution of ος for θεος in 1 Tim. 3:16 is nothing else but a calamitous perversion of Truth?[6]

---

[4] *The New Testament, Revised A.D. 1881*, p. 327.

[5] Ibid., p. 327.

[6] John William Burgon, *Proof of the Genuineness of God Manifested in the Flesh*, In *Unholy Hands on the Bible*, vol. 1., Jay P. Green, Sr., ed. (Lafayette, Indiana: Sovereign Grace Trust Fund, 1990), p. E-24.

But what was the authority on which Burgon based his claim that what Paul actually wrote was θεος and not ος? The issue actually centered upon the presence of the horizontal stroke in O to make it read "θ" in θς, which is an abbreviation for θεος, in the Greek manuscript, the *Codex Alexandrinus*.[7] Tischendorf published an Authorized Version of the New Testament in 1869 in which he noted in the margin the places where the readings in the *Codex Alexandrinus*, *Codex Vaticanus*, or *Codex Sinaiticus* differed from the reading in the Authorized Version. Although he made marginal notations throughout the New Testament, he made no such notation for 1 Timothy 3:16.[8] The reason was that the horizontal stroke *was* there in the Greek manuscript, making it θ!

Those performing textual criticism on the passage *believed that the stroke should not be there* and that it should read O. The manuscript was examined over and over with the naked eye and with powerful lenses. Various arguments were put forth to explain the horizontal stroke: maybe someone added the stroke later or perhaps a letter on the opposing page bled over onto the letter making the O appear to be a θ. Even the presence of a line drawn over the disputed letters to indicate that it was a contraction was unconvincing to the critical reviewers. To add to their plight, there were many other places in the manuscript where the letter was known to be θ and not O but the cross stroke was invisible because it had faded away. No one, however, seemed concerned about those instances.[9]

The critical reviewers looked to Tischendorf and his *Codex Sinaiticus* for support for their cause. *That manuscript also read θς*. Tischendorf, however, reasoned away that obvious support for the use of "God" in the Scripture. He argued that some late corrector of the manuscript must have also added the crossbar to the O, changing it to θ.[10] Even

---

[7] *The Biblical Repertory and Princeton Review for the Year 1861*, vol. 33, Charles Hodge, ed. (Philadelphia: Peter Walker, 1861), p. 153.

[8] Tischendorf, *Marginal Notes*, In *The New Testament: the Authorized English Version,* Tauchnitz ed., p. 334.

[9] *The Biblical Repertory and Princeton Review for the Year 1861*, vol. 33, pp. 153-154.

[10] Ibid., p. 154.

though Tischendorf insisted on the authority of the *Codex Sinaiticus*, this particular passage was so critical to the issue of who Jesus Christ is that he was willing to question the reliability of the manuscript.

While the evidence for error in the Revised Bible was overwhelming, Bishop Ellicott was unmoved. The rewriters of the Bible were determined to remove the clear witness that God was actually manifest in the flesh. This verse was crucial to the movement to deny the deity of Jesus Christ. While Burgon mainly adhered to the discussion on the scholarly level in reviewing the weight of the evidence supporting the traditional reading of the verse, he did hint that he understood the underlying reason for the change that had been made when he cited the following:

> Dr. Henderson (the learned nonconformist commentator) in 1830 published a volume with the following title:
> "The great mystery of godliness incontrovertible—or, Sir Isaac Newton and the Socinians foiled in an attempt to prove a corruption in the text of 1 Tim. 3:16; containing a review of the charges brought against the passage; an examination of the various readings; and a confirmation of that in the Received Text on principles of general biblical criticism."[11]

Do the Differences in Bible Versions Matter?

Even if the minds of those who undertook the laborious task of rewriting the Bible were tainted with what many Christians have branded as heresy, would that have affected their work? Would their denying the deity of Jesus Christ, denying the existence of heaven and hell, denying the complete atonement provided by the sacrifice of Jesus Christ, as well as many other basic doctrines, have affected the way they selected various readings of Scripture? Did their personal beliefs really matter? One might ask the simple question, "Did the Unitarian, Universalist, and Socialist views which they supported have any significant effect on the doctrines of the Bible?" In other words, "Didn't they remove their theology from their work on textual criticism?"

---

[11] Burgon, *Proof of the Genuineness of God Manifested in the Flesh*, p. E-30.

Even a casual observer can see that the changes in the Bible which have occurred since the period of the Enlightenment do, when taken together, challenge the biblical basis for the basic beliefs that many orthodox Christians have long held. A few specific examples of these Scriptures are illustrated in Appendix B, along with a brief statement of the impact that the changes are likely to have on many Christians. As the samples of Scripture are studied, readers with a discerning spirit can see which examples support each belief.

Some Bible scholars insist, however, that there is no difference in the way the above Scriptures address the differing views of Universalists, Unitarians, and Trinitarians. For example, according to one critical review of the topic, it was concluded that:

> In the final analysis, there is no substantial difference between the texts. Their differences are mainly technical and methodological, not doctrinal, for the textual variants are doctrinally inconsequential.[12]

Therefore, there should be no controversy. However, even the statements, "Without controversy" and "godliness," which appeared in both the Authorized Version *and* the Revised Version were removed from some later versions:

> [_____ _____] Great indeed, we confess, is the mystery of **our religion: He** was manifested in the flesh, vindicated in the Spirit, seen by angels, preached among the nations, believed on in the world, taken up in glory.
> —1 Timothy 3:16 (RSV)
> [Bold type is shown for emphasis.]

The Essential Deity of Jesus Christ

Certainly, the question of the deity of Jesus Christ should be without controversy. If, however, one found that there were significant differences in the way different versions of the Bible support the deity of Jesus Christ, why would it matter?

---

[12] Norman L. Geisler and William E. Nix, *A General Introduction to the Bible, Revised and Expanded* (Chicago: Moody Press, 1986), p. 464.

Without His deity, Jesus Christ's sacrifice on the cross becomes insufficient to pay the price required for the sin of the world. When the denial of the deity of Jesus Christ is coupled with a sense of a universal system of justice, then an additional price must be added to His sacrifice to pay for salvation. Striving to achieve justification, one must then contribute human effort to the payment equation. This effort is often in the form of the good works that one does.

Once rejecting the gospel of salvation by the blood of Jesus Christ, other sources for salvation must be sought. These may include the works of social action. Perceived sources of salvation might include such causes as the earth, the society, or some other god. Consequently, the works of the Social Christian are often directed toward environmental responsibility, social equality, economic equality, or another "justifying" principle. Adherence to a form of Social Christianity is an outcome of denying the deity of Jesus Christ.

The problem with trying to continually offer our own payment for sin is that, according to Scripture, we are born into the flesh, which was corrupted by sin. As Jesus explains to Nicodemus the need for being reborn in the Spirit, he says:

> That which is born of the flesh is flesh; and that which is born of the Spirit is spirit. Marvel not that I said unto thee, Ye must be born again.
> —John 3:6-7

The Apostle Paul writes:

> For all have sinned, and come short of the glory of God;
> —Romans 3:23

It would, however, be utterly hopeless to believe that one could perform enough good works to pay for original sin. Consequently, one who denies the deity of Jesus Christ needs to also reject the concept of original sin.

While Men Slept...

Defining Truth

The question of Pilate to Jesus has echoed throughout the earth for nearly two thousand years:

> Pilate saith unto him, What is truth?
>
> —John 18:38a

Jesus demonstrates the high level of importance truth holds when He says that His purpose in this world is to bear witness unto the truth:

> To this end was I born, and for this cause came I into the world, that I should bear witness unto the truth. Every one that is of the truth heareth my voice.
>
> —John 18:37b

The high value that Jesus placed upon truth has been remembered for centuries. The refusal of Martin Luther, for example, to compromise on what he believed to be the truth brought about the Reformation. Since then, human minds have been hard at work in their efforts to redefine truth. Modernists, equipped with the authority of reason, define truth based on human beings.

To the Alexandrian Neo-Platonists, such as Plotinus, truth was very subjective. He said of truth:

> It is within us...It is the agreement of the mind with itself. Consciousness, therefore, is the sole basis of certainty. The mind is its own witness.[13]

Vaclav Havel, the president of the Czech Republic, like Pilate, asked the question, "But what is truth?" He then answered the question much as a Neo-Platonist would by concluding that truth is information avouched for by a human being. He explained in an address, given at the occasion of his receiving an honorary degree at The University of Michigan, how he defined truth:

> I believe that truth is also information, but, at the same time, it is something greater. Truth—like any other information—is information which has been clearly proved, or affirmed, or

---

[13] Muller, *Theosophy or Psychological Religion*, p. 431.

298

verified within a certain system of coordinates or paradigms, or which is simply convincing. But it is more than that—it is information avouched by a human being with his or her whole existence, with his or her reputation and name, with his or her honor.[14]

Havel defined truth as relative to human reason. Jesus, however, defined truth as being the Word of God. He said:

Thy word is truth.

—John 17:17b

The Westminster Confession of Faith, we recall, declared that God is Truth and the author of truth. It explained that truth is the Holy Scripture, which is the very Word of God. Whether truth is the Word of God or information avouched for by a human being, Havel explained what it means to be committed to it. He said:

...genuine commitment to truth means standing firm no matter whether it yields returns or not, whether it meets with universal recognition or universal condemnation, whether a fight for truth leads to success or to absolute scorn and to obscurity.[15]

Beware of the Scribes and the Pharisees

Jesus gave seven warnings in the book of Matthew chapter 23 that were specifically directed to the scribes and the Pharisees whom He called "hypocrites." He said:

Woe unto you, scribes and Pharisees, hypocrites!
—Matthew 23:13a, 14a, 15a, 23a, 25a, 27a, 29a

He called them hypocrites because they were not genuine. They feigned righteousness. Outwardly they *appeared* holy by making long prayers, from which they profited. Jesus said:

---

[14] Vaclav Havel, Quoted in Jane R. Elgass, "Honorary Degree for Vaclav Havel," *Michigan Today*, The University of Michigan, Ann Arbor, vol. 32, no. 3, Fall, 2000.

[15] Ibid.

> Beware of false prophets, which come to you in sheep's cloth-
> ing, but inwardly they are ravening wolves.
>
> —Matthew 7:15

Some scholars and theologians may also act and sound "holy" as they perform textual criticism on God's Word. But in some cases, as we have seen among some of the key scholars and theologians associated with the revision of the Greek New Testament and the English Bible, there was another agenda. The obvious agenda was to submit the authority of God's Word to the authority of reason.

When Jesus declared "woe" to the scribes and Pharisees, He addressed specific things they did by which they attempted to deceive those who were honestly seeking to do God's will. To understand the motives behind the things that people do, we need to study what they said and compare that with what they did. Maurice was so right when he made this observation:

> I always tell my pupils not to read cold, impartial biographies,
> but to study a man's life in the book of someone who loved
> him. Such a person, I tell them, will alone have found out
> what he really was.[16]

As we have studied the lives of the men behind the Greek New Testament and English Bible revisions, especially through the letters and biographies written by their sons or close friends, we should have a better understanding of who they really were. As they said one thing in private, among their trusted friends, and quite another thing in public, it should be clear that they were often not who they represented themselves to be.

Leaving the Issue to Time

Ignore Him

Burgon presented overwhelming evidence to support his view that the truth was being undermined. However, his depth of understanding was too great and his presentation was too thorough to be com-

---

[16] Maurice, *The Life of Frederick Denison Maurice*, vol. 1, p. 531.

prehended by the public. Additionally, many of the theologians who could have helped him were unwilling to invest the amount of energy required to clearly state the facts. In an effort to try to minimize the potential public reaction to an open discussion, Hort adopted the strategy of ignoring the charges, hoping the controversy would subside.

Arthur Hort recognized that there were many people who felt Burgon had some justification in questioning the basis for his father, Fenton's, revision theory. He wrote:

> Westcott and Hort are therein treated as the chief authors of all the mischief of the Revision, and their text is throughout regarded as the work of a picturesque imagination. But it would be unprofitable to quote at length, or in any way to revive unnecessarily a somewhat hopeless controversy. There were some, doubtless, who wished that the two Cambridge Professors had publically defended themselves against the attack. **There were more, perhaps, who felt that Dean Burgon had some justification for the complaint that their exposition of their own theory did not set forth all the facts on which it rested.**[17] [Bold type is used for emphasis.]

Burgon challenged the very facts on which Hort's theory rested. He clearly asserted that they had built a superstructure on something that was really not a foundation at all:

> Those who first *invent their facts,* and then proceed to build their premises on them, do but go astray themselves, and then hopelessly mislead others....I repeat - for I wish it to be distinctly understood and remembered - that what I assert concerning those Critics is - *not* that their superstructure rests upon an insecure foundation; but that it rests *on no foundation at all.* My complaint is - *not* that they are *somewhat and frequently* mistaken; but that they are mistaken *entirely,* and that they are mistaken *throughout.* There is no possibility of approximation between *their* mere assumptions, and the re-

---

[17] Hort, *Life and Letters,* vol. 2, p. 239.

sults of my humble and laborious method of dealing with the Text of Scripture. We shall only *then* be able to begin to reason together with the slightest prospect of coming to any agreement when they have unconditionally abandoned all their preconceived imaginations, and un-reservedly scattered every one of their postulates to the four winds.[18] [Italics are in the original.]

Arthur Hort went on to explain that it was his father, Fenton, to whom Burgon directed the strongest criticism for his role in producing a misleading revision of the Bible. He wrote:

Of the two editors Dean Burgon selected Hort as the most guilty, inasmuch as the "Introduction" was the work of his hand....[on Hort's decision not to respond to Burgon's criticism] If, therefore, an answer to Dean Burgon had been thought advisable, it would have naturally fallen on Hort to write it. That he did not do so was not due to any indolence or indifference to criticism, but to deliberate choice. Dean Burgon's work was not unknown to him. His defence of the genuineness of the last twelve verses of St. Mark's Gospel, published some years before, had been thought to necessitate a fuller treatment of that passage in Westcott and Hort's "Appendix."[19]

Responding with Silence

The criticism put forth by Burgon of the basis for rewriting the English Bible was unanswerable. From Burgon's point of view, many of the changes that had been made in the rewriting were totally wrong and without justification. From Hort's point of view, he had invested the better portion of his life in making the changes, first in the Greek New Testament and then in the English Bible. Much of his work had been done in secrecy. There were too many people involved and too much at stake in rewriting the Bible to put it out for a public debate. Therefore, the strategy of Hort in responding to Burgon was to not respond. According to Arthur Hort:

---

[18] Burgon, *The Revised Revision*, p. D-51.

[19] Hort, *Life and Letters,* vol. 2, p. 240-241.

Still silence seemed best, and it has been justified. The adversary was not, indeed, likely to be silenced by a reply, and would certainly not have been convinced, seeing that his fundamental conceptions of the province of Biblical criticism were hopelessly irreconcilable with those of his opponents. There was no common ground on which Hort could meet a critic who started with the conviction that any reading stood self-condemned which altered a cherished passage; that in deciding a question of reading the traditional printed text should be the starting-point of investigation, instead of the original documents, on an exceedingly meagre selection of which the text was founded; and that, in settling a question between rival readings, the witnessing authorities should be counted, not weighed. That these are no unfair examples of Dean Burgon's views will be evident to any reader of *The Revision Revised*. His quarrel was with the whole school of criticism of which Hort was the latest representative, and from his own point of view he was unanswerable, since the only possible answer would not appeal to him. Apart from these considerations, however, Hort felt it to be useless for him to answer criticism which could not be founded on knowledge equal to his own. It was hardly any disparagement of a critic's attainments to say that he was not qualified to review theories founded on induction from an enormous number of facts, unless he had himself mastered those facts and thought out their meaning.[20]

Hort decided to leave the issue to time. According to Arthur Hort, his father:

> ...did indeed read and annotate carefully his copy of *The Revision Revised*, but decided eventually to leave the issue to time.[21]

The Issue Commended to Almighty God

Dean Burgon had a direct style that many felt to be abusive. Because he stood up for the truth of the power of God's Word against those

---

[20] Ibid., p. 241.

[21] Ibid., p. 242.

who had subjected it to the god of reason, he was severely criticized. The criticism of the Bible continues among scholars who have wholeheartedly adopted this theory of textual criticism. Burgon, not being privy to the "behind the scenes" activities that Hare, Maurice, Macmillan, Hort, Westcott, Lightfoot, and others had been participating in, naively thought the issue was about preserving the Word of God. That is why he addressed the issues of the Word of God directly, without another agenda. He did not see that there was a much larger plan of laying the foundation for global Unitarian Socialism of the new universal Christianity, for which a direct challenge to the Word of God was essential. There are still few who see it.

Following a very detailed discourse by John Burgon, a very learned Christian scholar, in *The Revision Revised*, he summarized his conclusion of the matter:

> The issue of this prolonged contention I now commend, with deep humility, to Almighty God. The Spirit of Truth will (I know) take good care of His own masterpiece, the Written Word. May He have compassion on my ignorance and graciously forgive me, if I shall prove to have anywhere erred in my strenuous endeavor to maintain the integrity of Scripture against the rashness of an impatient and unlearned generation. But if (as I humbly believe and confidently hope) my conclusions are sound throughout, then may He enable men freely to recognize the Truth; and thus, effectually avert from our Church the supreme calamity with which for a few months in 1881 it seemed threatened; namely, of having an utterly depraved Recension of the Greek Text of the New Testament thrust upon it, as the basis of a very questionable 'Revision"... of English.[22]

---

[22] Burgon, *The Revision Revised*, p. D-51.

Chapter 16. Let Us Build Us a City and a Tower

And they said, Go to, let us build us a city and a tower, whose top *may reach* unto heaven; and let us make us a name, lest we be scattered abroad upon the face of the whole earth.

—Genesis 11:4

The City and the Tower

Foundations of Babylon

Nimrod, as we learn from the Book of Genesis, began to be mighty upon the earth and became the first king of Babel, the land which was also called Babylon:

> And Cush begat Nimrod: he began to be a mighty one in the earth. He was a mighty hunter before the LORD: wherefore it is said, Even as Nimrod the mighty hunter before the LORD. And the beginning of his kingdom was Babel, and Erech, and Accad, and Calneh, in the land of Shinar.
>
> —Genesis 10:8-10

At that time, the whole earth was unified and able to communicate with each other:

> And the whole earth was of one language, and of one speech.
>
> —Genesis 11:1

As the people of Babylon set out to build a city and a tower (Genesis 11:4), the LORD (יהוה) saw that being united and having one language enabled the people to do anything they imagined to do. Therefore, He confounded their language and scattered them throughout the earth and they stopped building the City, which was called Babel:

> And the LORD came down to see the city and the tower, which the children of men builded. And the LORD said, Behold, the people *is* one, and they have all one language; and this they begin to do: and now nothing will be restrained from

them, which they have imagined to do. Go to, let us go down, and there confound their language, that they may not understand one another's speech. So the LORD scattered them abroad from thence upon the face of all the earth: and they left off to build the city. Therefore is the name of it called Babel; because the LORD did there confound the language of all the earth: and from thence did the LORD scatter them abroad upon the face of all the earth.

—Genesis 11:5-9

The Need for Restored Unity

Thus, the work was left unfinished. In order to continue building the City and the Tower of Babel, or Babylon, it would first be necessary to restore a common language and to recover the unity of the people throughout the earth. Building the City would require unity of the nations. Building the Tower that could reach to the heavens would also require unity of the religions.

One King and One Kingdom

How can complete unity of the nations and religions of the world be accomplished? It would require that they be under one sovereign authority. In the Bible the highest authority was to be a king who was over other kings. There were only two in the Bible who were called the "king of kings."[1] Both Ezekiel and Daniel called the king of Babylon, who was Nebuchadnezzar, the "king of kings."[2] On the other hand, both the Apostles Paul and John not only called Jesus the "King of Kings," but they also called Him the "Lord of Lords." (This is the title by which YAHWEH (יהוה), the LORD God of Israel, is known.)[3]

---

[1] Artaxerxes, the King of Persia, addressed *himself* as the "king of kings" in his letter to Ezra (Ezra 7:12). There is, however, no record in the Bible that others called him by that title.

[2] Ezekiel 26:7; Daniel 2:37.

[3] 1 Timothy 6:15; Revelation 17:14; Revelation 19:16, and Deuteronomy 10:17.

Let Us Build Us a City and a Tower

King Nebuchadnezzar was impressed by the power of his might. He had conquered and ravaged Jerusalem, and destroyed the temple of God! According to Daniel, the king walked into the palace of the Kingdom of Babylon and began to boast:

> The king spake, and said, Is not this great Babylon, that I have built for the house of the kingdom by the might of my power, and for the honour of my majesty?
>
> —Daniel 4:30

However:

> While the word *was* in the king's mouth, there fell a voice from heaven, *saying*, O king Nebuchadnezzar, to thee it is spoken; The kingdom is departed from thee.
>
> —Daniel 4:31

Isaiah prophetically told about the fate of Lucifer, who was also known as הילל, heylel, or the light-bearer.[4] He was typified by Isaiah as the king of Babylon, who many have historically believed to represent Satan. Lucifer fell after he tried to ascend into heaven and exalt himself on a throne above the stars of God:

> How art thou fallen from heaven, O Lucifer, son of the morning! *how* art thou cut down to the ground, which didst weaken the nations! For thou hast said in thine heart, I will ascend into heaven, I will exalt my throne above the stars of God: I will sit also upon the mount of the congregation, in the sides of the north: I will ascend above the heights of the clouds; I will be like the most High. Yet thou shalt be brought down to hell, to the sides of the pit.
>
> —Isaiah 14:12-15

---

[4] *Online Bible Hebrew Lexicon, English,* 01966, (Winterbourne, Ontario, Canada: Timnathserah Inc., 2001).

While Men Slept...

As Isaiah prophetically described, the king of Babylon's efforts to exalt himself were unsuccessful. Although Lucifer said in his heart, "I will...I will...I will...I will...I will be like the most High," God declared through the prophet that he would be brought down. He tried, by his own will, to assume the position of the Most High. Despite his efforts, only Jesus Christ can reign as both King of Kings and Lord of Lords because only Jesus has all power on heaven and earth:

> And Jesus came and spake unto them, saying, All power is given unto me in heaven and in earth.
>
> —Matthew 28:18

Therefore, only He has the authority to establish the true Kingdom of God, regardless of whether it is also called the Kingdom of Heaven or the Kingdom of Christ. True unity will be restored by the true King in the true Kingdom of God.

The Kingdom of God

The Millennial Reign of Christ

Exactly what the Kingdom of God is and how it will be established has been a topic of great controversy, having a major influence on the world for nearly two thousand years. Part of the controversy has been over what is called the "millennial reign" of Christ, as described by John in the Book of Revelation:

> And I saw thrones, and they sat upon them, and judgment was given unto them: and *I saw* the souls of them that were beheaded for the witness of Jesus, and for the word of God, and which had not worshipped the beast, neither his image, neither had received *his* mark upon their foreheads, or in their hands; and they lived and reigned with Christ a thousand years.
>
> —Revelation 20:4

The "thousand years" that John refers to was frequently called the "millennium," meaning Christ will return and establish His Kingdom on earth and the faithful will reign with Him for a thousand years.

308

There were, however, significantly differing views on how His Millennial Kingdom will be established. Is the timing of Christ's second coming near or distant? Will it be silent or cataclysmic? Will it be gradual or swift?[5] Can man establish the Kingdom of God or can only God establish His Kingdom? The view one holds on each of these questions has a major impact on how he understands Christianity. This, in turn impacts his view of the church in relation to the world.

Two Views of the Millennial Kingdom

While there were many variations in the way people understand the millennium, there were two basic views. One is that the world will continue to degenerate until Jesus Christ returns and establishes His millennial Kingdom. This was called the "premillennial" view, because it states that Jesus Christ will return *before* the millennium. The other basic view is that mankind must first establish the Kingdom of God on earth, after which Christ will come to assume power. This is the "postmillennial" view, which is that Christ will return *after* the millennial Kingdom is established.[6] Those holding the postmillenial view argue that the Kingdom of God will be gradually extended as mankind makes the world better by ordering it with laws and by their subsequent enforcement.

Premillennial View

Premillennialists, however, reminded us that the Kingdom of God is spiritual and cannot, therefore, be inherited by flesh and blood. The Apostle Paul supported this view in his first letter to the Corinthians:

> Now this I say, brethren, that flesh and blood cannot inherit the kingdom of God; neither doth corruption inherit incorruption.
>
> —1 Corinthians 15:50

---

[5] Ernest R. Sandeen, "Millennialism," In *The Rise of Adventism: Religion and Society in Mid-Nineteenth-Century America*, Edwin S. Gaustad, ed. (New York, Evanston, San Francisco, London: Harper & Row, Publishers, 1974), p. 105.

[6] James H. Snowden, *The Coming of the Lord: Will it be Premillennial?*, 3rd ed., rev. (New York: The Macmillan Company, 1922), pp. 4-5.

While Men Slept...

They also believed in the literal and visible Second Coming of Jesus Christ, as supported by the following Scriptures:

> For the Lord himself shall descend from heaven with a shout, with the voice of the archangel, and with the trump of God: and the dead in Christ shall rise first: Then we which are alive *and* remain shall be caught up together with them in the clouds, to meet the Lord in the air: and so shall we ever be with the Lord.
>
> —1 Thessalonians 4:16

> And when he had spoken these things, while they beheld, he was taken up; and a cloud received him out of their sight. And while they looked stedfastly toward heaven as he went up, behold, two men stood by them in white apparel; Which also said, Ye men of Galilee, why stand ye gazing up into heaven? this same Jesus, which is taken up from you into heaven, shall so come in like manner as ye have seen him go into heaven.
>
> —Acts 1:9-11

> Behold, he cometh with clouds; and every eye shall see him, and they *also* which pierced him: and all kindreds of the earth shall wail because of him. Even so, Amen.
>
> —Revelation 1:7

> When the Son of man shall come in his glory, and all the holy angels with him, then shall he sit upon the throne of his glory: And before him shall be gathered all nations: and he shall separate them one from another, as a shepherd divideth *his* sheep from the goats: And he shall set the sheep on his right hand, but the goats on the left. Then shall the King say unto them on his right hand, Come, ye blessed of my Father, inherit the kingdom prepared for you from the foundation of the world:
>
> —Matthew 25:31-34

The premillennialists believe that the Second Coming can occur anytime. They take literally the words of Jesus when He said:

Watch ye therefore, and pray always, that ye may be accounted worthy to escape all these things that shall come to pass, and to stand before the Son of man.

—Luke 21:36

Postmillennial View

Postmillennialists, on the other hand, argued that the premillennialist view was too narrow and that it was based upon a too literal interpretation of Scripture. On the issue of watching for the Second Coming of Jesus, for example, one postmillennialist author wrote:

Premillenarianism is also narrow in its doctrine of watching for the coming of Christ. It confines the duty of watching to the final coming of the Lord and thereby overlooks the duty of watching for other forms of his coming. Its advocates with few exceptions hold to the "any moment" imminence of this event and resolve watching into some kind of expectancy.[7]

While rejecting the literal interpretation of Luke 21:36, many postmillennialists readily embraced the literal reading of Luke 17:20-21. This Scripture says that the coming of the Kingdom of God is without observation. It reads:

And when he was demanded of the Pharisees, when the kingdom of God should come, he answered them and said, The kingdom of God cometh not with observation: Neither shall they say, Lo here! or, lo there! for, behold, the kingdom of God is within you.

—Luke 17:20-21

In his book, *The Kingdom of God is Within You*, Lyof Tolstoi considered Luke 17:21. He defended his reasons for viewing the "…ecclesiastical doctrine commonly called Christianity as erroneous, and to me incredible."[8]   He argued that the Kingdom of God is within us. He

---

[7] Snowden, *The Coming of the Lord: Will it be Premillennial?*, pp. 222-223.

[8] Lyof N. Tolstoi, *The Kingdom of God is Within You*, In *The Complete Works of Lyof N. Tolstoi* (New York: E.R. Dumont, 1899), p.1.

said the reason why no one can know the hour of the "advent of the Kingdom of God" is because it depends on men themselves. He maintained that each of us can bring about our own advent of the Kingdom of God by living according to the "light" that is within us:

> And that we all know; for each one has but to begin to do his duty, each one has but to live according to the light that is within him, to bring about the immediate advent of the promised Kingdom of God, for which the heart of every man yearns.[9]

Tolstoi was really talking about the same thing that so many Unitarians and Universalists were professing. He spoke of "non-resistance" and the principles of global Socialism. His conclusion was that we should let our reason be our guide. He says the "Almighty Power" gave us reason and:

> He demands of us only what is reasonable and possible,—to serve the Kingdom of God, which establishes the unity of mankind, a unity possible only in the truth; to recognize and profess the truth revealed to us, which is always in our power to do.[10]

Taking this logic further, it can be concluded that everything devised in man's mind, through the light of his enlightened reason, is a revelation from God. Emanuel Swedenborg wrote that:

> This light, which enlightens the mind, flows in from no other source than out of heaven from the Lord; and because they who will be of the New Jerusalem will approach the Lord directly, that light flows in by the orderly way, which is through the love of the will into the perception of the understanding.[11]

---

[9] Ibid., p. 254.

[10] Ibid., p. 335.

[11] Emanuel Swedenborg, *The Apocalypse Revealed, Wherein are Disclosed The Arcana There, Foretold, Which Have Hitherto Remained Concealed*, trans. from Latin (Philadelphia: J.B. Lippincott Company, 1887), p. 1061.

Taking a broader interpretation of Scripture than the premillennialists, the postmillennialists emphasized that it is possible to "Christianize" the world. They stressed, however, that the bodily coming, presence, or power of Christ will not establish the Kingdom of God. Instead, they argued that it is now being established by "his spiritual presence in his truth and grace as energized by the Holy Spirit." Therefore, they believed the world will be converted to "Christianity," through various forms of His coming, before the final advent of Christ.[12] Consistent with this postmillennial view, Emanuel Swedenborg argued that the second coming of the Lord was not in the person of Jesus Christ. He said that:

> The reason why he will not appear in person, is, because since his ascension into heaven he is in his glorified humanity, and in that humanity he cannot appear to any man unless the eyes of his spirit be first opened, and this opening cannot be effected in any that are in evils and the falses thence derived, thus not in any of the goats whom he sets on his left hand....[13]

Instead, Swedenborg wrote, the Lord revealed Himself in the Word, which is Divine Truth. Thus, according to Swedenborg, the Lord gave to him the Divine Truth of the New Church, known as the New Jerusalem, which was to be set up on earth by man. The Divine Truth, he said, is not present in the literal Word, but in the spiritual sense of the Word, which is the light.[14] Thus, Swedenborg continued, a new heaven, which is the internal of the church in man, must be formed as a condition for the formation of the New Jerusalem. He wrote:

> It is agreeable to divine order, that a new heaven be formed before a New Church on earth; for the church is both internal and external, and the internal church forms a one with the church in heaven, and consequently with heaven; and that the internal must be formed before the external, and afterwards

---

[12] Snowden, *The Coming of the Lord: Will it be Premillennial?*, pp. 236-240.

[13] Swedenborg, *The True Christian Religion Containing the Universal Theology of the New Church*, p. 765.

[14] Ibid., p. 767.

the external by the internal, is a truth known and acknowledged by the clergy of the world. In proportion as this new
heaven, which constitutes the internal of the church in man,
increases, in the same proportion the New Jerusalem, that is,
the New Church, comes down from that heaven; so that this
cannot be effected in a moment, but in proportion as the falses
of the former church are removed....[15]

A condition for the New Church of Swedenborg was that the things
of heaven and the things of earth must first be put in order. According
to Swedenborg, creating order in the world requires a king that has
governors who are skilled in the law, who are wise, and who obey
truth. There must also be, he said, priests who teach truths and thereby
lead the people to the good life.[16] The evidence of the "conversion"
of the world, postmillennialists say, will be the formation of a better
world of optimism, rather than pessimism. The evidence of the establishment of the Kingdom of God on earth can, they insist, be seen
through the material, intellectual, ethical, social, and religious progress
that is being made in the world.[17]

Therefore, it may be argued, enlightened reason can be used to determine God's purpose for us and for the world. Consequently, it can be
used to determine God's Word. At issue was the concept of authority
of God vs. the authority of man and his reason. Charles Kingsley,
quoting Luke 17:21, also argued that the Kingdom of God is in each
of us.[18] Kingsley, who had from his youth in grammar school studied
Plato and Alexandrian philosophies,[19] expressed views similar to those
of Swedenborg and used similar logic to that of F. D. Maurice to
argue that Jesus Christ has already come back to earth and that He
manifests Himself through man's reason. Therefore, when one devel-

---

[15] Ibid., pp. 770-771.

[16] Swedenborg, *On the New Jerusalem and Its Heavenly Doctrine*, pp. 85-88.

[17] Snowden, *The Coming of the Lord: Will it be Premillennial?*, pp. 240-279.

[18] Charles Kingsley, *Sermons on National Subjects* (London: Macmillan and Co.,
1890), p. 373.

[19] James H. Rigg, *Memoir of Canon Kingsley*, In Rigg, *Modern Anglican Theology*, p. 27.

ops a new invention or makes a new discovery, it is really the Spirit of God who is teaching all men.[20] In reality, many of those who reportedly have a postmillennial view of the Second Coming are actually "amillennialists," believing that there will be no literal Second Coming of Jesus Christ. Instead, they believe that the millennial reign of Christ occurs in the hearts of men.[21]

The New Universal Christianity and the New Order

The essence of the new universal Christianity was that the Kingdom of God, which is sometimes also called the Kingdom of Christ or the Kingdom of Heaven, would be on the physical earth, set up by the reason of man through laws and the enforcement of those laws. Many world leaders have embraced Plato's designs for establishing a global "Republic" for the common good. Plato's outline for such a society required rule by an "enlightened" few who would enact laws of order to be enforced by "enforcers" upon the "workers."[22] These "enlightened ones" were believed to be able to develop such a state of global order that there would be no need to dispute about anything. Some believed that, if people would live by a set of ordered rules that included bountifully sharing the fruits of their labor, our society would be heaven on earth. Instead of being ruled by God, such a society would be ruled by the reason of the "enlightened ones."

This theory really represented a global Socialist movement in which people would be controlled by international laws that would require all to behave in a manner that would be in the best interest of the world. Using combinations of a global economic system, a global political system, and a global religious system, it was believed that a new order could be established that would be unlike any other. B. F. Westcott believed that, while the fellowship of the Kingdom of God on earth must be rational, above all, it must be spiritual.[23]

---

[20] Kingsley, *Sermons on National Subjects*, p. 29.

[21] Weber, *Living in the Shadow of the Second Coming*, p. 9.

[22] Plato, *The Republic*, pp. 971-1223.

[23] Westcott, *Social Aspects of Christianity*, p. 148.

While Men Slept...

Modern global leaders, as a means of achieving a "utopian" New World Order, increasingly accept the need for a critical spiritual dimension. John A. Mackay, who, as we shall learn, was the president of the Princeton Theological Seminary, president of the International Missionary Society, and instrumental in establishing the World Council of Churches, was keenly aware of the relationship between religion and the New World Order. In 1950, he quoted Jesuit theologian John Courtney Murray (1904-1967) as having said:

> Among all the problems relating to a new world order, religious liberty occupies a unique position. The reason is, no other problem so directly and immediately faces an ultimate issue.[24]

Zbigniew Brzezinski (1928-), the former director of the National Security Council of the United States under President Jimmy Carter (1924-), emphasized the necessity for interaction among religious, political, and economic factors. He viewed such interaction as necessary in order to bring about the kind of global changes that were sought in the French Revolution. He said:

> ...the need for an enhanced moral consciousness is not only advocated by religious leaders but also by more reflective political leaders. Even disillusioned Marxist ideologues are recognizing that life cannot be defined meaningfully only on the basis of material criteria.[25]

He went on to emphasize the need for moral guidance. He stressed that the world is in a "global crisis of the spirit" that must be overcome for mankind to control its destiny:

> Moral guidance ultimately has to come from within. The modern age, initiated by the French Revolution, placed a premium on the certainties of the so-called objective truth, spurning

---

[24] Quoted in John A. Mackey, *Christianity on the Frontier* (New York: The Macmillan Company, 1950), p. 143.

[25] Zbigniew Brzezinski, *Out of Control: Global Turmoil on the Eve of the Twenty-First Century* (New York: Simon and Schuster Inc., 1995), p. 229.

subjectivity as irrational....*The global crisis of the spirit has to be overcome if humanity is to assert command over its destiny.*[26] [Italics are in the original.]

Global Religious Unity

The Ecumenical Movement

Overcoming the "global crisis of the spirit" so that the world can achieve an ordered global political, economic, and social plan requires global religious unity. Once achieved, tremendous power will be placed in the hands of a few people who will be able to use their enlightened imagination to accomplish whatever they will:

> And the LORD said, Behold, the people is one, and they have all one language; and this they begin to do: and now nothing will be restrained from them, which they have imagined to do.
> —Genesis 11:6

The Greek word "οικουμενη" (oikoumene), meaning the whole inhabited earth, is the basis for the English word "ecumenical." Although the word had been used in 1900 at a New York City conference, the current usage of the word, "ecumenical," was established at the Oxford Conference of 1937. The movement conceived at the Conference became known as the "The Ecumenical Movement."[27]

With an aim of unifying the entire world into one religion, the goal of the Ecumenical Movement was to establish one church for the whole inhabited earth under the banner of Christianity. This was the vision that F. D. Maurice had expounded in his book, *The Kingdom of Christ*. He envisioned the "Kingdom of Christ" as being the "Kingdom of God" on earth, established on the foundation of "Christian Socialism." As such, Maurice wrote of his conception of a new universal

---

[26] Ibid., p. 230.

[27] John A. Mackay, *Ecumenics: The Science of the Church Universal* (Englewood Cliffs, New Jersey: Prentice-Hall Inc., 1964), pp. 6-7.

Christian church, which the Church of England would play a key role in establishing.[28]

The move toward global Christian Socialism, as it may be called, required the global unification of world religions under one banner. The difficulty of establishing the Kingdom of Christ on earth when most of the world does not profess Christianity is formidable. In a world of Christians, Jews, Moslems, Hindus, Buddhists, and countless other religions and sects, how can spiritual unity be achieved under the banner of Christianity? How can all enter into the Kingdom? *All* must be declared as "righteous."

1893 World's Parliament of Religions

A major step toward this goal was taken at the World's Parliament of Religions, which was convened in Chicago during the 1893 World's Columbian Exposition. Charles Carroll Bonney, a Swedenborgian, conceived the plan for the meeting and served as its president.[29] He appointed the organization committee in 1891. His key appointees were Jenkin Lloyd-Jones, a well-known liberal Unitarian, who served as the executive secretary and John Henry Barrows, a Presbyterian, who served as committee chairman.[30, 31] Lloyd-Jones was the pub-

---

[28] Henry Renaud Turner Brandreth, "Approaches of the Churches Towards Each Other in the Nineteenth Century," In *A History of the Ecumenical Movement, 1517-1948*, ch. 6, Ruth Rouse and Stephen Charles Neill, eds. (Philadelphia: The Westminster Press, 1954), p. 274.

[29] Note: As a Swedenborgian, he was a follower of Emanuel Swedenborg who taught that the Second Coming of Jesus Christ already occurred in 1757 and that He had transferred the Divine Truth to man's reason by which to establish the New Church, or the Church of the New Jerusalem, on Earth.

[30] John Henry Barrows, ed., *The World's Parliament of Religions: An Illustrative and Popular Story of the World's First Parliament of Religions, Held in Chicago in Connection with the Columbian Exposition of 1893*, vol. 1. (Chicago: The Lakeside Press, H. H. Donnelley & Sons, 1893), pp. 6-8.

[31] Richard Hughes Seager, ed., *The Dawn of Religious Pluralism: Voices from the World's Parliament of Religions, 1893* (La Salle, Illinois: Open Court Publishing Company, 1993), p. 4.

lisher of a radical Unitarian journal, known as *Unity*.[32] Although Barrows was reported to represent Presbyterians, the General Assembly of the Presbyterian Church in the United States of America passed a resolution in 1892 "...emphatically disapproving of the Parliament."[33] The attendees to the Parliament represented such diverse beliefs and religions as those claiming Swedenborgism, Universalism, Unitarianism, Christianity, Hinduism, Jainism, Buddhism, Confucianism, Shintoism, Mohammedism, Mazdaism, and Theosophy. The Theosophists summarized their primary purpose as "...to bring about a Universal Brotherhood based upon the essential deity of man."[34, 35, 36]

Expectations were high. The Parliament had received endorsements from religious and civil dignitaries from around the world, including British Prime Minister William Ewart Gladstone.[37] The head of the Roman Catholic Church in America, Cardinal James Gibbons of Baltimore, occupied the chair of state and opened the meeting in prayer.[38]

Cardinal Gibbons' paper, which was read by Bishop John Joseph Keane, pronounced that the most interesting and important aspect of his faith was its system of organized benevolence. He concluded his remarks with a quote from the pagan Cicero:

> There is no way by which men can approach nearer to the gods than by contributing to the welfare of their fellow creatures.[39]

---

[32] Spencer Lavan, *Unitarians and India: A Study in Encounter and Response*, 2nd ed. (Boston: Skinner House, 1984), p. 144.

[33] Barrows, *The World's Parliament of Religions*, vol. 1, p. 19.

[34] Swami Nikhilananda, *Vivekananda: A Biography*, 4th Indian ed. (Calcutta: Advaita Ashrama, 1982), pp. 116-117.

[35] Charles James Ryan, *H. P. Blavatsky and the Theosophical Movement: A Brief Historical Sketch* (Point Loma, California: Theosophical University Press, 1937), pp. 1, 318-319.

[36] Barrows, *The World's Parliament of Religions*, vol. 1, pp. 64-66.

[37] Ibid., p. 12.

[38] Ibid., pp. 62, 80-81.

[39] Ibid., p. 493.

While Men Slept...

Philip Schaff, chairman of the American New Testament Company, was intimately involved in revising the Bible.[40] In his address to the Parliament on the reunion of the Christian churches, namely the Eastern Orthodox and Protestant Churches with the Roman Catholic Church, he made a statement in 1893 foreshadowing events that were to happen in the twentieth century. He said:

> Before the reunion of Christendom can be accomplished, we must expect providential events, new Pentecosts, new reformations—as great as any that have gone before. The twentieth century has marvelous surprises in store for the church and the world.[41]

Schaff stood among those who suggested that the next step toward global unity was to establish a church federation.[42]

At the closing session of the 1893 World's Parliament of Religions, its president, Charles C. Bonney said:

> Fathers of the contemplative East; sons of the executive West— Behold how good and how pleasant it is for brethren to dwell together in unity. The New Jerusalem, the City of God, is descending, heaven and earth chanting the eternal hallelujah chorus.[43]

The Gospel of Universal Righteousness

Thirty representatives from various world religions spoke, reading lengthy papers expounding upon the characteristics of their particular religion. Then a thirty-year old turban-clad Hindu monk from India, Swami Vivekananda (1863-1902), stepped to the podium and the crowd of more than seven thousand attendees broke out in applause.

---

[40] *The Bible in its Ancient and English Versions*, H. Wheeler Robinson, ed. (London: Oxford at Clarendon Press, 1940), p. 248.

[41] Barrows, *The World's Parliament of Religions*, vol. 2, p. 1198.

[42] Phillips, *A Kingdom on Earth*, pp. 18, 184.

[43] Barrows, *The World's Parliament of Religions*, vol. 1, p. 173.

Speaking in the "name of the mother of religions," the Swami excited the crowd as he spoke of toleration and of the belief of Hindus that all religions are true, quoting a hymn and then the Gita that said:

> "As the different streams having their sources in different places all mingle their water in the sea, O Lord, the different paths which men take through different tendencies, various though they appear, crooked or straight, all lead to thee."

> "Whosoever comes to me, through whatsoever form I reach him, they are all struggling through paths that in the end always lead to me."[44]

Position and scholarship notwithstanding, by many accounts Vivekananda made the greatest impact of all the speakers with his addresses at the 1893 World's Parliament of Religions.[45] The world loved his message. He proclaimed that all the religions of the world are true and that they all lead to God. Vivekananda also taught that unity would come out of diversity. He believed that the Hindu religion, based on the teachings of the Vedas, was the appropriate vehicle by which to achieve the synthesis of unity. Suddenly the unknown monk was transformed into a major figure in the religious world.[46] The world was embracing the spirit of unity.

Vivekananda's first visit to America was a phenomenal success. He soon visited England and then returned to America, where he toured extensively giving lectures on various subjects, including Hinduism. Vivekananda traveled to England in 1896 where Canon [Basil] Wilberforce [the son of Samuel Wilberforce] honored him with a reception. Max Muller of Oxford also invited him to the University. Muller, who was German, was a well-known Sanskritist and Indologist. Having published an article on Vivekananda's mentor, Ramakrishna, Muller was eager to meet Vivekananda as a direct disciple of the "Master." [According the Vivekananda, Muller's "reverence for

---

[44] Ibid., pp. 101-102.

[45] Nikhilananda, *Vivekananda: A Biography,* p. 123.

[46] Ibid., pp. 122-123.

While Men Slept...

Ramamkrishna Paramahamsa is extreme."][47] Muller invited Vivekananda to his home on May 28, 1896. There, Vivekananda bowed before Muller and hailed him as a reincarnation of an ancient Rishi.[48] He said of Muller, "He is a saint—a Vedantist through and through."[49] After a brief trip to continental Europe, Vivekananda returned to England where he spent another two months meeting with Muller, Frederick Myers, Edward Carpenter, and Canon Wilberforce, while lecturing on Hinduism.[50] Vivekananda left England on December 16, 1896 and was in Rome for the feast of Christmas. Upon observing the Catholic Liturgy, he was impressed with its similarity to Hindu ceremonies. According to Romain Rolland, a biographer of Vivekananda:

> Everything reminded him [Vivekananda] of India: the tonsure of the priests, the sign of the Cross, the incense, the music. He saw in the Holy Sacrament a transformation of the Vedic Prasada—the offering of food to the gods, after which it is immediately eaten.[51]

Vivekananda returned to India in 1897 where he intensely worshipped the "Divine Mother" as the Terrible Kali.[52] The goddess Kali was a form of the Great Goddess, known as Devi.[53] Upon returning to America in 1899 for his second visit, his followers welcomed him as he traveled westward from New York. He gave his famous lecture, "Christ, the Messenger," at the Universalist Church in Pasadena, California and he spent a month at the "Home of Truth" in Los Angeles.

[47] Swami Vivekananda, In *The Complete Works of Swami Vivekananda*, vol. 6, Swami Tadrupananda, ed., (Calcutta: Advaita Ashrama, 1978), p. 362.

[48] Romain Rolland, *The Life of Vivekananda and the Universal Gospel*, 6th impression, E. F. Malcolm-Smith, trans. (Calcutta: Advaita Ashrama, 1965), p. 91.

[48] Swami Vivekananda, In *The Complete Works of Swami Vivekananda*, vol. 8, Swami Tadrupananda, ed., (Calcutta: Advaita Ashrama, 1977), p. 378.

[50] Rolland, *The Life of Vivekananda and the Universal Gospel*, pp. 98-99.

[51] Ibid., p. 100.

[52] Swami Nikhilananda, *Vivekananda: The Yogas and Other Works*, revised ed. (New York: Ramakrishna-Vivekananda Center, 1953), pp. 90-150.

[53] John Stratton Hawley, "Prologue: The Goddess of India," In *Devi: Goddesses of India*, John S. Hawley and Donna M. Wulff, eds. (Berkeley and Los Angeles: University of California Press, 1996), p. 9.

There, he conducted regular classes and gave public lectures, each attended by more than a thousand people. He gave lectures at the First Unitarian Church in Oakland, and continued lecturing in San Francisco, Chicago, and Detroit before returning to Europe and then to India. Vivekananda died in 1902 at the age of thirty-nine.[54]

Achieving Universal Christianity

Christ: "The Universal Man"

At the 1893 World's Parliament of Religions in Chicago, Christianity was defined to include all religions on earth. At the closing of the meeting, George Dana Boardman proclaimed that the event was:

> ...more august than on Pentecost itself, the memorable prophesy of the one coming, universal religion: "It shall be in the last days, saith God, I will pour forth of my Spirit on all flesh; and your sons and your daughters shall prophesy, and your young men shall see visions, and your old men shall dream dreams. Yea, and on my servants and handmaidens in those days will I pour forth of my Spirit; and they shall prophesy."[55]

Boardman explained the secret to the marvelous unity of the world religions as being Jesus of Nazareth, the one great unifier of mankind because He is "The Son of Man." As the son of human nature, Boardman said that Jesus is:

> Blending in himself all races, ages, sexes, capacities, temperaments, Jesus is the archetypal man, the ideal hero, the consummate incarnation, the symbol of perfected human nature, the sum total of unfolded, fulfilled humanity, the Son of Mankind.[56]

He said that while all other religions are more or less topographical, Christianity is the religion of mankind. Boardman said:

---

[54] Ibid., pp. 150-179.

[55] Barrows, *The World's Parliament of Religions*, vol. 2, p. 1338.

[56] Ibid., p. 1339.

> ... Jesus Christ is the one universal man; and therefore it is
> that the first Parliament of Religions is meeting in a Christian
> land, under Christian auspices. Jesus Christ is the sole bond of
> the human race; the one nexus of the nations; the great verte-
> bral column of the one body of mankind.[57]

As the Swami Vivekananda explained:

> We are all Christians; we are all Mohammedans; we are all
> Hindus; or all Buddhists. No matter if a Buddhist is a Chinaman,
> or is a man from Persia, they think that they are brothers,
> because of their professing the same religion. Religion is the
> tie, the unity of humanity.[58]

At an 1894 conference of Unitarians in Saratoga, New York, the participants publicly accepted the "religion of Jesus," saying that the sum
of practical religion is "Love to God and Love to Man."[59] Thus, Unitarians publicly identified themselves as "Christians" in a Christianity
that is based on "Love." The position the Unitarians adopted was that
of Jabez T. Sunderland, a University of Chicago educated Unitarian
minister who had a twenty-year ministry in Ann Arbor, Michigan.
Sunderland went to India in 1895 to study the openings for Unitarianism in that country.[60]

Christianity had taken on a new meaning. Its purpose was no longer
to accept the sacrifice of Jesus Christ on the cross for sin. Instead, it
was about teaching universalism. Max Muller concisely explained his
view of the concept of the Christian religion, especially as it fit in with
the beliefs of the Neo-Platonists of the early Christianity of Alexandria, Egypt. He said:

> I hope I have made it clear to you that from the very first the
> principal object of the Christian religion has been to make the

---

[57] Ibid., p. 1346.

[58] Swami Vireswarananda, *The Complete Works of Swami Vivekananda*, Part IV,
4th ed. (Mayavati, Almora, Himalayas: Advaita Ashrama, 1932), p. 139.

[59] Lavan, *Unitarians and India*, pp. 144-145.

[60] Ibid., p. 145.

world comprehend the oneness of the objective Deity, call it Jehovah, or Zeus, or Theos, or the Supreme Being, το ον, with the subjective Deity, call it self, or mind, or soul, or reason, or Logos.[61]

Each Having His "Own Christ"

In agreement with the teachings of Muller, Swami Vivekananda explained that all are Christians regardless of their particular religion or beliefs. When the Hindu Keshab Chandar Sen visited England in 1870 he said that, since he arrived in England, he found himself:

> ...incessantly surrounded by various religious denominations, professing to be Christians...When the Roman Catholic, the Protestant, the Unitarian, the Trinitarian, the Broad Church, the Low Church, the High Church, all come round me, and offer me their respective Christs, I desire to say to one and all: "Think you that I have no Christ within me? Though an Indian, I can still humbly say, thank God that I have my Christ."[62]

Vivekananda explained that there are different Christs in different religions, which all should be reverenced. For example, he said:

> I pity the Hindu who does not see the beauty in Jesus Christ's character. I pity the Christian who does not reverence the Hindu Christ.[63]

Through his belief in his Christ or even in the Christian Jesus Christ, Vivekananda could call himself a "Christian." However, Vivekananda's "Christ" was clearly not the Jesus Christ that the Apostle Paul referred to when he wrote.

> But God commendeth his love toward us, in that, while we were yet sinners, Christ died for us. Much more then, being now justified by his blood, we shall be saved from wrath through him. For if, when we were enemies, we were recon-

---

[61] Muller, *Theosophy or Psychological Religion*, p. 447.

[62] Williams, *Religious Thought and Life in India, Part 1*, p. 506.

[63] Vivekananda, In *The Complete Works of Swami Vivekananda*, vol. 8, p. 219.

> ciled to God by the death of his Son, much more, being recon-
> ciled, we shall be saved by his life. And not only *so*, but we
> also joy in God through our Lord Jesus Christ, by whom we
> have now received the atonement.
>
> —Romans 5:6-11

Instead, the Christ of Vivekananda and others had nothing to do with salvation through the blood of Jesus Christ. In a lecture in Detroit, Michigan on February 21, 1894, he said:

> I, for one, would not come to be saved by such a doctrine
> [salvation through Jesus' blood]. If anybody would come and
> say, "Be saved by my blood", [sic] I would say to him, "My
> brother, go away; I will go to hell; I am not a coward to take
> innocent blood to go to heaven; I am ready for hell.[64]

Vivekananda said that salvation is not through the blood of Jesus Christ. His view was similar to that of Emanuel Swedenborg who argued that, because God is love itself, He could not sentence a man to damnation and "...still abide in his own divine essence." He added that, "...men have mistaken the passion of the cross for redemption itself."[65] Instead of believing in the redemptive work performed on the cross by Jesus Christ, Vivekananda said in an address entitled "Way to Salvation," which he gave at the First Unitarian Church in Oakland, California on March 12, 1900, that: "Salvation is in work and love."[66]

Socializing Christianity

Works and Love

With an understanding of Vivekananda's Christianity, which took away the sacrifice of Jesus Christ as the payment for the sin of believers, the world was prepared for a new social global Christianity that was based upon "work and love." Soon after the 1870 decision to rewrite the

---

[64] Ibid., p. 209.

[65] Swedenborg, *The True Christian Religion*, p. 166.

[66] Vivekananda, In *The Complete Works of Swami Vivekananda*, vol. 8, p. 242.

English Bible, a new theological liberalism flourished that became the inspiration for the Social Gospel.[67] The late 1870s and 1880s marked the beginning of a continuous period of Social Christianity.[68] Using philosophy, such as that of Plato, modified to Neo-Platonism for its application to Christianity, the new liberal theology of Christian Socialism was seeded into Christian thought. Essentially, Christian theology was rewritten to submit to the sovereignty of man. As explained by Charles Gregg Singer (1910-1999):

> Christian theology, even among evangelical [sic], was modified to bend with the winds of the new scientific naturalism, posing as humanism and democracy. Once again democracy sought to rewrite theology in terms of the sovereignty of man; many theological leaders were demanding a god who would cooperate with democracy and rejecting the God to whom they must submit.[69]

Whether the term used to describe this "New Christianity" was the "Social Gospel," "Social Christianity," or "Christian Socialism" may have been partly influenced by whether the term was used in Europe or in America.[70] Whatever the label used, however, the movement was essentially one of Socialism blended into a new liberal theology called "Christianity." The work of F. D. Maurice and his colleagues had laid the foundation for the gospel of Social Christianity that emerged in the twentieth century.[71]

Brooke Foss Westcott, the coauthor of the Westcott and Hort Greek New Testament and a member of the English New Testament Revision Committee, remained a leading advocate for the cause of Christian Socialism toward the close of the nineteenth century. As the president of the Christian Social Union, he was the most visible spokes-

---

[67] Charles Gregg Singer, *The Unholy Alliance* (Tyler, Texas: Institute for Christian Economics, 1975), p. 15.

[68] Phillips, *A Kingdom on Earth*, p. xxvi.

[69] Singer, *The Unholy Alliance*, p. 15.

[70] Phillips, *A Kingdom on Earth*, p. xviii.

[71] Ibid., p. xiv.

person for Christian Socialism at that time.[72] Westcott had been a longtime student and behind-the-scenes advocate of Maurice's Christian Socialism. His public participation in those activities became manifest in 1889 when he gave the inaugural address at the founding of the Christian Social Union.[73]

In that address, Westcott excited the listeners toward the cause of Christian Socialism. His son, Arthur Westcott, quoted the response of one of those who heard the address:

> There was a famous address at the founding of the Christian Social Union, delivered to us at Sion College, which none who were present can ever forget. Yet none of us can ever recall, in the least, what was said. No one knows. Only we know that we were lifted, kindled, transformed. We pledged ourselves; we committed ourselves; we were ready to die for the Cause; but if you asked us why, and for what, we could not tell you. There he was: there he spoke: the prophetic fire was breaking from him: the martyr-spirit glowed through him. We, too, were caught up. But words had become only symbols. There was nothing verbal to report or to repeat. We could remember nothing, except the spirit which was in the words: and that was enough.[74]

At times, B. F. Westcott appeared somewhat timid about expressing his true Socialistic goals. In a letter to his daughter on January 24, 1898, for example, he tried to distinguish the "Christian Social Union" from "Christian Socialism."[75] However, as president of the Christian Social Union, Westcott fully endorsed the idea of Socialism and its goals.[76] To achieve those goals, Westcott advocated a National Church that, in compromise, would blur the lines between the secular and the sacred.[77]

---

[72] Ibid., p. 166.

[73] Westcott, *Life and Letters*, vol. 2, p. 15.

[74] Ibid., p. 16.

[75] Ibid., pp. 260-261.

[76] Phillips, *A Kingdom on Earth*, p. 195.

[77] Ibid., pp. 176-177.

Westcott denied that the essential component of Christianity was personal and individual. Instead, he saw Christianity as societal or social. Admitting that he had once "given occasion to it," he declared as false the concept that Christianity concerns a believer's personal life. He said:

> Many who allow that Christianity can deal with individuals deny that it has any message for classes or states. Its virtues, they say, are the petty virtues of private life: its promises, the gratification of the small objects of personal aim: towards the struggles of society, of the nation of the race, it can at the best produce nothing better than a temper of benevolent neutrality. We know that the charge is false, essentially false, but we must admit without reserve that we have given occasion to it.[78]

Instead of believing that Christianity involved a personal relationship between a believer and Jesus Christ, Westcott insisted that the key purpose of faith in Christ was to inspire national policy. As he explained:

> We have not dared, as we should have done, to assert that our Faith in Christ, the Saviour of the world, must be the inspiration of our national policy; that our Faith in the Divine Fatherhood must be the measure of our social obligations.[79]

As Westcott spoke of this fellowship of the entire race encompassing the "whole sum of life," he asserted that the temporal and the spiritual must be united. He said:

> It [the fellowship] must banish the strange delusion by which we suppose that things temporal and spiritual can be separated in human action, or that we can render rightly to Caesar that which is not in the very rendering rendered also to God.[80]

---

[78] Brooke Foss Westcott, *Social Aspects of Christianity* (London and Cambridge: Macmillan and Co., 1887), pp. 141-142.

[79] Ibid., p. 142.

[80] Ibid., p. 147.

Insisting that the fellowship be social, Westcott was apparently speaking of a "Utopian" Socialistic society as he said:

> Every member of it [the fellowship] must hold himself pledged to regard his endowments of character, of power, of place, of wealth, as a trust to be administered with resolute and conscious purpose for the good of men: pledged to spread and deepen the sense of one life, one interest, one hope, one end for all, in the household, in the factory, in the warehouse, in the council-room: pledged to strive as he has the opportunity to bring all things that are great and pure and beautiful within the reach of every fellow-worker: pledged to labour so that to the full extent of his example and his influence toil may be universally honoured as service to the state, literature may be ennobled as the spring and to the substitute of thought, art (too often the minister of luxury) may be hallowed as the interpreter of the outward signs of God's working.[81]

The Social Gospel

The Ecumenical Movement made major strides in the first part of the twentieth century. Soon ecumenical organizations, such as the Federal Council of the Churches of Christ in America, started in 1908, embraced the Social Gospel movement.[82] Walter Rauschenbusch, a leading advocate of the movement, saw the reconstruction of the Bible as a critical component in the realization of the inevitable Social Gospel. He wrote in 1907 that:

> All the biblical sciences are now using the historical method and striving to put us in the position of the original readers of each biblical book. But as the Bible becomes more lifelike, it becomes more social...The Bible hereafter will be "the people's book" in a new sense. For the first time in religious history we

---

[81] Ibid.

[82] Donald Herbert Yoder, "Christian Unity in Nineteenth-Century America," In *A History of the Ecumenical Movement, 1517-1948*, Ruth Rouse and Stephen Charles Neill, eds. (Philadelphia, Westminster Press, 1954), p. 257.

have the possibility of so directing religious energy by scientific knowledge that a comprehensive and continuous reconstruction of social life in the name of God is within the bounds of human possibility.[83]

Rauschenbusch had picked up the banner from F. D. Maurice and B. F. Westcott in declaring Socialism to be the objective of Christianity. This new social Christianity was believed to be the vehicle by which a progressive regeneration of society would occur. He said that Christianity was not to be of personal repentance, but of societal repentance, with a faith in a "higher social order."[84] He saw that "higher social order" as one of returning to Communism. As Rauschenbusch explained it:

> Primitive society was communistic. The most valuable institutions in modern life—the family, the school and church— are communistic. The State, too, is essentially communistic and is becoming increasingly so. During the larger part of its history the Christian Church regarded communism as the only ideal life. Christianity certainly has more affinity for cooperative and fraternal institutions than for competitive disunion. It should therefore strengthen the existing communistic institutions and aid the evolution of society from the present temporary stage of individualism to a higher form of communism.[85]

Rauschenbusch saw the world emerging into a "new age" for which the early Christian Socialists in England, of which F. D. Maurice was the key leader, suffered. He saw the movement toward establishing the earthly "Kingdom of God" as being similar to the miracle that happens in nature during the month of May:

> Last May a miracle happened. At the beginning of the week the fruit trees bore brown and greenish buds. At the end of the

---

[83] Walter Rauschenbusch, *Christianity and the Social Crisis* (New York: The Macmillan Company, 1907, Reprinted in 1912), p. 209.

[84] Ibid., pp. 411-412.

[85] Ibid., pp. 413-414.

week they were robed in bridal garments of blossom. But for weeks and months the sap had been rising and distending the cells and maturing the tissues which were half ready in the fall before. Perhaps these nineteen centuries of Christian influence have been a long preliminary stage of growth, and now the flower and fruit are almost here.[86]

In 1910 the World Missionary Conference was held in Edinburgh, Scotland for the purpose of advancing the Kingdom of Christ on earth.[87] As the participants in the conference voted to move toward global Christian unity, a bishop of the Roman Catholic Church sent a message to the Conference in which he concluded:

> Finally, from the various Churches and religious denominations into which you Christians are divided there arises a new unifying element, a noble aspiration, restraining too great impulsiveness, levelling dividing barriers, and working for the realisation of one Holy Church though all the children of redemption...My desire for you is but the echo of Christ's words, which have resounded through the centuries—"Let there be one flock and one Shepherd."[88]

At the 1928 meeting of the International Missionary Council in Jerusalem the attendees came to a conclusion that a fresh vision of the Kingdom of God was needed. They stated:

> There has always been a tendency, a side-current, in Christian circles to postpone the Kingdom of God to some distant crisis. Sometimes the crisis is death. Sometimes it is the crisis of "a second coming" of Christ. Death, no doubt, will be an event of first importance to each one of us and it will have its own revelation to make to us. "Second comings" have been ex-

---

[86] Ibid., p. 422.

[87] W. H. T. Gairdner, *Echoes from Edinburgh, 1910: An Account and Interpretation of the World Missionary Conference* (New York: Fleming H. Revell Company, 1910), pp. vi-vii.

[88] Gairdner, *Echoes from Edinburgh, 1910*, pp. 212-213.

pected in every century since Christ but they have not so far occurred as expected, and we need to be humble in our predictions. It is wiser meantime to focus attention upon one point which Christ made perfectly clear and which is capable of laboratory demonstration. He declared that the Kingdom of God was something to that could be realized in men: "It is in you," he said...It is a kingdom that "comes on earth" as fast and as far as God's will is done here as it is done in heaven. It is not a dream or a mirage; it is a fact already in some lives—in more perhaps than we suppose or have counted... [Our Christian religion]...must be at the practical task of building the City of God down here where we live.[89]

Throughout history, societal chaos was used as the reason for change. Following the global chaos surrounding World War I and the Great Depression, a new universal Christianity was seen as the religion through which the whole world could be unified into a world-religion. It was seen as "...the only religion that is able to consecrate all human relationships, reaching through family, civic, and national loyalites to the Catholic loyalty of a universal brotherhood of all men in the incarnated manhood of the Son of God."[90]

The National Council of Churches of Christ in the United States was built upon the foundation laid by the Federal Council of Churches. It had the avowed objective of the realization of the Kingdom of God on earth through the proclamation of the Social Gospel. Following the chaos created by World War II, the plan to "Christianize" the world became even clearer.[91]

---

[89] International Missionary Council, *The Jerusalem Meeting of the International Missionary Council, March 24-April 8, 1928* (New York and London: International Missionary Council, 1928), pp. 272-273.

[90] Howard Masterman, *Chapter 4. The Confusion in International Relations*, In *Christianity and the Crisis*, Percy Dearmer, ed. (London: Victor Gollancz Ltd, 1933), p. 154.

[91] Singer, *The Unholy Alliance*, p. 180.

While Men Slept...

Enforcing "Christianity"

In Westcott's eyes, achieving global Social Christianity would require enforcement. To help achieve the kind of Christian fellowship that he envisioned, Westcott saw that soldiers would be needed to "remind others of his obligations." He said:

> The uniform of the soldier is at once a symbol and a safe-guard. It reminds others of his obligations, and supports him in the endeavour to fulfil them.[92]

Three years after the papal infallibility dogma had been adopted and while the rewriting of the English Bible was well underway, the prime minister of England, William Ewart Gladstone, considered how the control of the world might be achieved. According to John Morley, Gladstone's biographer:

> The answer was to be found in the favourite design, hardly a secret design, of restoring by the road of force when any favourable opportunity should arise, and of re-erecting, the terrestrial throne of the popedom, "even if it could only be re-erected on the ashes of the city, and amidst the whitening bones of the people."[93]

---

[92] Ibid., pp. 147-148.

[93] Morley, *The Life of William Ewart Gladstone*, vol. 2, p. 517.

Chapter 17. Seeking a Clean Heart and a Right Spirit

> **Create in me a clean heart, O God; and renew a right spirit within me. Cast me not away from thy presence; and take not thy holy spirit from me.**
> **—Psalms 51:10-11**

Christian Perfection and the Higher Life Movement

Mahan and Finney: Holiness and Pentecostal Pioneers

The role of Asa Mahan (1799-1889) and Charles Finney (1792-1875) in preparing the world for the Holiness and Pentecostal revivals in the late nineteenth and early twentieth centuries should not be underestimated. Both were avid social reformers who taught the perfectionist theology of sanctification. As we shall see, Mahan's writings and work were the key to the new Pentecostal Movement of the nineteenth and twentieth centuries. Finney, through his teachings on revivals, provided the means by which the new Pentecost theology was delivered to large numbers of Christians throughout the world. The two were brought together by the founder of Oberlin College, John Jay Shipherd, and by businessman and abolitionist leader, Arthur Tappan. After being invited to become the first president of Oberlin College in Ohio, Mahan travelled with Shipherd to New York in January 1835, where they helped persuade Charles Finney to come to Oberlin as a professor of theology. Tappan agreed to finance the endeavor.[1,2]

Tappan was well established in the anti-slavery movement, serving as the president of the American & Foreign Anti-Slavery Society. His brother, Lewis, served as the Corresponding Secretary of the Soci-

---

[1] Charles Grandison Finney, *Memoirs of Rev. Charles G. Finney. Written by Himself* (New York: A.S. Barnes & Company, 1876), pp. 332-333.

[2] Norris Edward Kirk, *Lectures on Revivals* (Boston: Congregational Publishing Society, 1875), p. 50.

ety.[3] Lewis Tappan had been a Unitarian and served as the founding Treasurer of the American Unitarian Association after its formation in May 1825.[4] According to Finney, Arthur Tappan was an orthodox Christian. Finney also reported that Lewis was converted to the orthodox Christian belief through his New York revivals.[5]

Finney's New York revivals had a great impact on international revivalism. He used a series of sermons that he preached on revivals as the basis for a book entitled, *Finney's Lectures on Revivals.*[6] According to Finney, the book was a major success throughout the world and, after it was translated into the Welsh language, was later reported to be responsible for the great revival in Wales of 1859.[7, 8] Finney wrote that:

> After they [his lectures in his book on revivals] had been printed in Welsh, the Congregational ministers of the Principality of Wales, at one of their public meetings, appointed a committee to inform me of the great revival that had resulted from the translation of those lectures into the Welsh language. This they did by letter.[9]

Finney focused on offering concrete techniques to excite people, similar to those used in a political rally. Techniques to attract people to the meetings included circulating handbills, pamphlets, and newspaper

---

[3] American & Foreign Anti-Slavery Society, *The Thirteenth Annual Report of the American & Foreign Anti-Slavery Society, Presented at New York, May 11, 1853 with the Addresses and Resolutions* (New York: The American & Foreign Anti-Slavery Society, 1853), p. 191.

[4] John Ware, *Memoir: Life of Henry Ware, Jr.,* vol. 1 (Boston: American Unitarian Association, 1874), p. 187.

[5] Finney, *Memoirs of Rev. Charles G. Finney*, pp. 280-282.

[6] Ibid., p. 330.

[7] Ibid.

[8] Thomas Phillips, *The Welsh Revival: Its Origin and Development* (Edinburgh and Carlisle, Pennsylvania: The Banner of Truth Trust, 1989; reprinted from the 1860 publication), p. 10.

[9] Finney, *Memoirs of Rev. Charles G. Finney*, p. 330.

promotions. Once the people arrived, the strategy was to attack their opponent, the devil.[10]

After Finney accepted the position at Oberlin College, he spent time alternating between his work in Oberlin and in New York. While in New York, he preached sermons on "Christian Perfection."[11] Finney said:

> In those sermons I defined what Christian perfection is, and endeavored to show that it is attainable in this life, and the sense in which it is attainable.[12]

Asa Mahan, while serving as the president of Oberlin College, protested against the Oberlin Calvinism, holding that "a man could be a good man if he had a mind to be." He developed this view into the doctrine of "possible sanctification," in contrast to the doctrine of the "total depravity" of man, which was held by the Calvinists. Finney also "devastated the Calvinism" of New York State by preaching a "freer gospel."[13] Building upon the Methodist doctrine taught by John Wesley of entire sanctification through the cleansing work of grace,[14] Mahan and Finney took the doctrine further, with greater emphasis on natural ability.[15] Both Mahan and Finney carried their doctrinal positions away from the Calvinistic beliefs in human depravity toward a doctrine of achieving human goodness, or perfection. Thus, they found that they were in unity with each other concerning the doctrine of Christian perfection.

---

[10] William G. McLoughlin, "Revivalism," In *The Rise of Adventism: Religion and Society in Mid-Nineteenth-Century America*, Edwin S. Gaustad, ed. (New York, Evanston, San Francisco, and London: Harper & Row, Publishers, 1974), pp. 143-144.

[11] Finney, *Memoirs of Rev. Charles G. Finney*, p. 339.

[12] Ibid., p. 341.

[13] Dan F. Bradley, "Oberlin Theology—From Mahan to Horton," *The Oberlin Alumni Magazine*, vol. 29, no. 6, March 1, 1933 (Oberlin, Ohio: Oberlin College Archives, 1933).

[14] Francis J. McConnell, *The Essentials of Methodism* (New York and Cincinnati: The Methodist Book Concern, 1916), p. 18.

[15] Smith, *Revivalism and Social Reform*, p. 109.

In 1839 Mahan published *The Scripture Doctrine of Christian Perfection*, which had a major influence on the Holiness Movement.[16] Soon, both men began preaching "perfectionism" or "full sanctification." Phoebe Palmer, who would later help Mahan publish some of his work, also began emphasizing perfectionism. Mahan admired her work and was reported to have considered her book, *The Way to Holiness*, published in 1843, to be next in value to the Bible.[17,18] By 1848, Mahan began using the term "sanctification" instead of "perfectionism" to describe the goal of the Christian life.[19] Through the influences of Mahan and Finney, others soon followed in promoting the doctrine of perfectionism, or sanctification. William Edwin Boardman, a Presbyterian from Illinois, made a major impact on the sanctification movement in 1858 through the publication of his book, *The Higher Christian Life*. By using the expression, "Higher Christian Life" instead of "perfectionism" or "sanctification," Boardman hoped to appeal to the many denominations without a direct association with Oberlin or the Methodists.[20] As we shall see, Boardman's "Higher Christian Life" expression was to become the banner under which major revivals would be promoted from England in the nineteenth and twentieth centuries.

Mahan, Global Peace, and England

The 1840's brought promotion of the doctrine of sanctification, or "holiness," which had been preached in England by John Wesley more than a hundred years earlier. While Americans, including Mahan,

---

[16] Edward H. Madden and James E. Hamilton, *Freedom and Grace: The Life of Asa Mahan* (Metuchen, NJ and London: The Scarecrow Press, Inc., 1982), p. 62.

[17] Harold E. Raser, *Phoebe Palmer: Her Life and Thought*, In *Studies in Women and Religion*, vol. 22 (Lewiston, New York and Queenston, Ontario: The Edwin Mellen Press, 1987), p. 292.

[18] Ibid., p. 177.

[19] Barbara Brown Zikmund, *Asa Mahan and Oberlin Perfectionism*, Doctoral Dissertation (Durham, North Carolina: Department of Religion, Duke University, 1969), p. 242.

[20] Timothy L. Smith, *Revivalism and Social Reform In Mid-Nineteenth-Century America* (New York and Nashville: Abingdon Press, 1957), p. 106.

Finney, Palmer, and Boardman, were making great contributions toward various aspects of the doctrine, leading Anglo-Catholics, such as John Henry Newman, were also promoting some forms of sanctification. By 1841, Newman, who was soon to defect from the Church of England to the Roman Catholic Church, wrote:

> It is sanctity of heart and conduct which commends us to God. If we be holy, all will go well with us. External things are comparatively nothing; whatever be a religious body's relation to the State—whatever its regimen—whatever its doctrines—whatever its worship—if it has but the life of holiness within it, this inward gift will, if I may so speak, take care of itself.[21]

Soon after Mahan began using the term "sanctification" rather than "perfectionism," he was drawn to Europe on a mission for "global peace" that left him in England for several months. As we recall, many of the countries of Europe were plagued by revolution in 1848, which ignited from a spark in France. We also recall that during that same year, Ludlow brought the idea for the Christian Socialist Movement from France to F. D. Maurice and his colleagues in England. Consequently, activities for promoting peace intensified. In addition, William Arthur (1819-1901), an Irish-born Methodist minister, was also in France during the 1848 French Revolution.[22] Arthur, who had recently returned from a missionary trip in India, as we shall see, wrote the book, *The Tongue of Fire*, which preceded Mahan's book, *The Baptism of the Holy Ghost*.

Elihu Burritt (1810-1879), who was active in the American Peace Society, conceived an international peace pledge. All men who took

---

[21] John Henry Newman, Quoted In: Davies, *Worship and Theology in England From Watts and Wesley to Maurice, 1690–1850*, pp. 248-249.

[22] Henry C. Fish, *Pulpit Eloquence of the Nineteenth Century: Being Supplementary to the History and Repository of Pulpit Eloquence, Deceased Divines; and Containing Discources of Eminent Living Ministers in Europe and America with Sketches Biographical and Descriptive* (New York: Dodd, Mead & Company, Publishers, 1871), p. 594.

the pledge became members of a new international "League of Universal Brotherhood" for the purpose of abolishing war. Mahan and others at Oberlin had taken the pledge and called themselves the "friends of peace." As a result, Asa Mahan, along with Hamilton Hill, who was the Secretary of the Oberlin College Board of Trustees, traveled to Paris during the summer of 1849 to attend an international peace convention. The ecumenical conference was presided over by Victor Hugo (1802-1885), who called for all to unite as brethren.[23]

Mahan remained in England after the convention, where he spent the next few months preaching and writing among his British friends. While he was promoting the publication of a London edition of his book on Christian Perfectionism, Mahan also led revival meetings in London.[24] Other reports indicated that he also worked in England and in Scotland, advocating "peace, temperance, antislavery, and revivalism."[25] William Arthur also returned to London, where he was appointed as one of the general secretaries of the Mission House.[26] While all that Mahan did while in England is not readily evident, the trip seemed to be a turning point in his life. First, he returned in 1850 from his extended trip to Europe only to find himself pressured to resign from his position as president of Oberlin College.[27] Second, he identified 1850 as the year that he became involved in investigations into spiritualism.[28]

---

[23] [Asa Mahan], "Peace Congress at Paris," *The Oberlin Evangelist*, Oct 10, 1849, p. 166.

[24] Ibid., p. 311.

[25] Richard Carwardine, *Transatlantic Revivalism: Popular Evangelicalism in Britain and America, 1790-1865* (Westport, Connecticut and London: Greenwood Press, 1978), p. 221.

[26] Fish, *Pulpit Eloquence of the Nineteenth Century*, p. 594.

[27] Hamilton Hill and John Keep, "Minutes of the Trustee Meeting of Oberlin College, August 28, 1850, John Keep, Chairman, Hamilton Hill, Secretary (Oberlin, Ohio: Oberlin College Archives, 1850).

[28] Asa Mahan, *Modern Mysteries: Explained and Exposed* (Boston: John P. Jewett and Company; Cleveland: Jewett, Proctor and Worthington; New York: Sheldon, Lamport and Blakeman; London: Trubner and Co., 1855), p. iii.

The Path to the "Baptism of the Holy Ghost"

Mahan submitted his resignation from the presidency of Oberlin College on August 26, 1850 and the Board of Trustees accepted it on August 28, 1850.[29] Mahan's resignation from Oberlin followed significant pressure from the faculty, citing his overbearing behavior.[30] The College faculty had brought ten charges against Mahan, including that:

> ...his self esteem has amounted to self-conceit, and has led him to overrate, both his natural and his moral attainments, and that under the same influence he underrates the ability and character of his brethren...[and his tendency] to assume an attitude and use language unbecoming to a Christian minister, and the President of a religious Institution...He should be careful not to leave his work in the Institution without consultation and arrangement with his brethren, thus embarrassing our operations and burdening the other instructors...He should refrain from committing the Institution to sentiments which he only holds, or which are contrary to the views of his brethren.[31]

After resigning from Oberlin College, Mahan started Cleveland University, which soon failed. He resigned as its president in 1852.[32] While Mahan was still in Cleveland, William Arthur, made his way to Sandusky, Ohio (about fifty miles west of Cleveland) in 1855, where

---

[29] Hamilton Hill and John Keep, "Minutes of the Trustee Meeting of Oberlin College, August 28, 1850."

[30] Asa Mahan, In Asa Mahan (1799-1889) Papers, [1764] 1835-1985, Accession No. 223, Processed by Brian A. Williams (Oberlin, Ohio: Oberlin College Archives, April 1992).

[31] [Anon.] "Basis of Unity and Hearty Co-operation" on the Part of the Faculty with Pres. Mahan, Asa Mahan (1799-1889) Papers, [1764] 1835-1985, Accession No. 223, Processed by Brian A. Williams (Oberlin, Ohio: Oberlin College Archives, April 1992).

[32] Madden and Hamilton, *Freedom and Grace: The Life of Asa Mahan*, pp. 129, 133.

he preached before the Conference of North Ohio on the Pentecostal theme. According to Arthur, that sermon served as the theme of the book he first published in 1856 entitled *The Tongue of Fire*.[33] (While the influence of Mahan and Arthur on each other's Pentecostal theology, if any, is not clear, it appears that both were in France, London, and northern Ohio, prior to each publishing a key book on the subject.)

Mahan soon moved on to Michigan where he pastored a Congregational church in Jackson.[34] While there, Mahan became associated with the Wesleyan college, which was known as the Michigan Union College, in Leoni, a small town east of Jackson. Mahan moved to Adrian, Michigan in 1857, where he pastored the Plymouth Congregational Church. By the fall of 1859, the Michigan Union College was having financial difficulties, so Mahan successfully moved it to Adrian. The name was changed to Adrian College and Mahan became its first president, as well as its Professor of Intellectual and Moral Science.[35]

Mahan believed that his moves from Oberlin to Cleveland to Jackson and then to Adrian were providential. He said that if he had not gone to Adrian College, his book, *The Baptism of the Holy Ghost*, would probably not have been written at all. According to Mahan:

> I will now speak of the origin of the work on "The Baptism of the Holy Ghost" which, in all probability, never would have been written at all, and certainly never in its present form, but for my connection with Adrian College. The origin of this work, which has been and is being read in all Christian and missionary lands, was on this wise: During the latter years of my connection with the college, it became a part of my duty

---

[33] William Arthur, *The Tongue of Fire, or the True Power of Christianity* (New York: Harper & Brothers, Franklin Square, 1880), pp. v-vi.

[34] Madden and Hamilton, *Freedom and Grace: The Life of Asa Mahan*, pp. 127-155.

[35] Margaret Burnham Macmillan, *The Methodist Church in Michigan: The Nineteenth Century* (Grand Rapids: The Michigan Area Methodist Historical Society and William B. Eerdmans Publishing Company, 1967), pp. 195-195.

to deliver before the theological students a course of theological lectures. Prior to this my mind had been very deeply impressed with the importance of the return of the Pentecost, its renewals and enduements of power, to the Churches of Christ. When I came to this subject, two impressions dwelt with overpowering weight upon my mind: that the lectures must, in the first instance, be of such a character as to induce in my students a full understanding of the doctrine, and an absolute conviction of its truth; but, in the next place, and above all, to induce in them an irrepressible desire and determination to become personally possessed in full of the Pentecostal enduements of power.

Under these distinct impressions, and with much prayer, each lecture was written out in full before it was delivered. When I witnessed the result, not only upon my class, but in the flood-tide of revival influence in the college, the thought for the first time possessed my mind, that what I had thus written out the ministry and Churches imperiously needed. Thus was originated "The Baptism of the Holy Ghost."[36]

While in Michigan, Mahan published other books, including *Science of Logic* in 1857 and *Science of Natural Theology* in 1867. However, it was his book *The Baptism of the Holy Ghost*, which was published in 1870 by Phoebe Palmer (1807-1874) of New York, that provided the basis for a new emphasis beyond that of Christian Perfectionism. As such, Mahan was the key figure in shifting the emphasis from that of perfectionism to that of power, which was through the baptism in the Holy Ghost.[37, 38, 39] Demonstrating the importance he placed on power as an outcome of the baptism in the Holy Ghost, later editions

---

[36] Asa Mahan, "Reminiscences and Reflections," *Divine Life*, vol. 13, May 1890, p. 292. In Oberlin College Archives, Asa Mahan (1799-1889) Papers, [1764] 1835-1985, Accession No. 223, Processed by Brian A. Williams (Oberlin, Ohio: Oberlin College Archives, April 1992).

[37] Madden and Hamilton, *Freedom and Grace: The Life of Asa Mahan*, p. 157.

[38] Ibid., p. 166.

[39] Terrence Robert Crowe, *Pentecostal Unity: Recurring Frustration and Enduring Hopes*, p. 113.

of Mahan's book included a treatise by Charles Finney entitled, "The Enduement of Power."[40]

From Adrian College to Oxford University

The year following his publication of *The Baptism of the Holy Ghost*, Asa Mahan resigned as president of Adrian College on June 22, 1871. He continued there until 1872, which, according to Mahan, was the year in which the public in England began reading his book. [41, 42] His life soon took a mysterious turn that brought him back to England. He received news that Mary Chase Mahan, his second wife, was the possible heir to a sizeable estate in England. After asking a long time friend and secretary to the American Missionary Association, to investigate the matter, Mahan found himself on an unplanned trip to England. Following an unfruitful search of records concerning the supposed inheritance, he was received into Christian holiness circles. Mahan then became totally involved in the English Holiness Movement.[43, 44] Mahan's writings were among those largely responsible for preparing the groundwork for the Holiness Movement that was to be promoted from Oxford. In addition to his work on promoting the doctrine of the baptism of the Holy Ghost and scriptural holiness, Mahan's influence on the involvement of key Americans, such as Dwight Lyman Moody and William Edwin Boardman, in England was also notable.

For example, Mahan took much of the responsibility for the evangelistic campaign of Dwight L. Moody and Ira D. Sankey in the United

---

[40] C. G. Finney, "Induement of Power," In Asa Mahan, *The Baptism of the Holy Ghost* (London: Elliott Stock, 1876), pp. 229-254.

[41] Madden and Hamilton, *Freedom and Grace: The Life of Asa Mahan*, pp. 170-171.

[42] Asa Mahan, *The Baptism of the Holy Ghost* (London: Elliot Stock, 1876), p. v.

[43] Madden and Hamilton, *Freedom and Grace: The Life of Asa Mahan*, pp. 192-196.

[44] Asa Mahan, "Reminiscences and Reflections," *Divine Life*, vol. 13, May 1890, p. 293. In Asa Mahan (1799-1889) Papers, [1764] 1835-1985, Accession No. 223, Processed by Brian A. Williams (Oberlin, Ohio: Oberlin College Archives, April 1992).

Kingdom during the early 1870's. Mahan pointed out that Cuthbert Bainbridge, an eminent Wesleyan laymen who was responsible for Moody's coming to England, had been converted to the Holiness Movement through his work. Unfortunately, Bainbridge died before Moody arrived in England on June 17, 1873.[45, 46] This trip by Moody and his singing companion, Sankey, followed Moody's trip in 1872, when he attended the Mildmay Conference in London.[47] In the Spring of 1873, just about the time Moody and Sankey arrived in England, W. E. Boardman, another American who had been under the influence of the teachings of Mahan and Finney, also made his way to England. Boardman, along with the American Quaker, Robert Pearsall Smith, were invited to speak to pastors in London concerning the topic of the Higher Life.[48]

The work soon intensified to establish a major holiness convention in England. During the summer of 1874, a hundred invited guests assembled at the home of W. Cowper-Temple, which was known as "Broadlands." In that meeting, which was chaired by Robert Pearsall Smith, it was proposed that another conference be held at Oxford later that summer.[49] That conference at Oxford became known as the "Oxford Convention for the Promotion of Scriptural Holiness," which was held from August 29 to September 7, 1874. Mahan was invited to that Convention as a key participant, along with W. E. Boardman, Robert Pearsall Smith, and Thomas Dundas Harford-Battersby, the Vicar of St. John's Anglican Church of Keswick, England.[50]

---

[45] Asa Mahan, "Reminiscences and Reflections," *Divine Life*, vol. 13, May 1890, p. 293. In Asa Mahan (1799-1889) Papers, [1764] 1835-1985, Accession No. 223, Processed by Brian A. Williams (Oberlin, Ohio: Oberlin College Archives, April 1992).

[46] William Haven Daniels, *D.L. Moody and his work, by Rev. W.H. Daniels* (Hartford: American Publishing Company, 1876), p. 240.

[47] J. Wilbur Chapman, *The Life and Work of Dwight L. Moody* (Chicago and Philadelphia: International Publishing Co., 1900), p. 128.

[48] Madden and Hamilton, *Freedom and Grace: The Life of Asa Mahan*, pp. 196-197.

[49] Ibid., p. 197.

[50] Ibid., pp. 192-197.

While Men Slept...

The Oxford and Brighton Conferences

Oxford

Robert Pearsall Smith, as chairman of the conferences leading up to the Oxford Convention, continued as chairman of the Oxford Convention. As such, he remained the Convention's most visible leader. Smith's wife, Hannah Whitall Smith, was also a very popular speaker. While Mahan did not occupy the most visible position at the Convention, his influence on the assembly through his preaching and teaching concerning the Holy Ghost and entire sanctification was significant.[51] Mahan said that his books, especially *The Baptism of the Holy Ghost*, had:

> ...prepared the way among the advocates of the higher life, so that labours for the cause at once accumulated upon my hands to the full measure of my power and endurance.[52]

Being the author of the increasingly popular book, *The Baptism of the Holy Ghost*, Mahan spoke at 9:30 AM on the second day of the Conference. As he spoke, Mahan emphasized sanctification *and* power, saying:

> If you want to be sanctified, if you want power, go to Christ for sanctification and power.[53]

Mahan continued in anticipating the outpouring of the Holy Spirit at the Convention by saying:

---

[51] Ibid., pp. 198-200.

[52] Asa Mahan, "Reminiscences and Reflections," *Divine Life*, vol. 13, May 1890, p. 293. In Asa Mahan (1799-1889) Papers, [1764] 1835-1985, Accession No. 223, Processed by Brian A. Williams (Oberlin, Ohio: Oberlin College Archives, April 1992).

[53] Anon, *Account of the Union Meeting for the Promotion of Scriptural Holiness held at Oxford, August 29 to September 7, 1874* (London: S.W. Partridge & Co., c1875; Reprinted in *"The Higher Christian Life: Sources for the Study of the Holiness, Pentecostal, and Keswick Movements*, Donald W. Dayton, ed., New York and London: Garland Publishing, Inc., 1985), p. 51.

Thus I am *waiting, enjoying, expecting*. Christ has loved you as He has loved me. He will pour out His Spirit on you; ye, upon all—on you and on your children.[54]

On the third day of the Conference, Mahan continued stressing receiving the baptism of the Holy Ghost. He emphasized that the power of the Holy Ghost was available and all that the participants needed to do was to ask for it. He said:

> If the Apostle Paul stood here, he would put to us this question:—"Have ye received the Holy Ghost since ye believed?" If Christ came to us what should we most desire? That He should breathe on us and say, "Receive ye the Holy Ghost." Christ *is* here, God is here, and ready to bestow this unspeakable gift upon you and upon me; more ready than we are to give bread to a hungry child. The power of the Holy Ghost is ours when we ask the Father in the name of Christ. Do you realise this?[55]

Day after day at the Conference, Mahan continued to press upon the participants the privilege of being there and that being "filled with the Spirit" was a Scriptural experience, which they should seek. As Mahan continued his efforts to promote the spiritual experience at the Conference, many who attended his conversational meetings reportedly received the baptism of the Holy Ghost. The experience was reportedly characterized by having "...a subdued will, an obedient heart, and deep love to God and man."[56]

The Keswick Anglican, Thomas Dundas Harford-Battersby, became a key participant in the Convention. As he became more involved in the operations of the Convention, he soon realized that it was not like other religious conferences. Instead, Harford-Battersby recognized that the Oxford Convention was characterized by a "definiteness of purpose." The organizers of the Convention were using an ordered

---

[54] Ibid.

[55] Ibid., p. 81.

[56] Ibid., p. 143.

scheme of promoting holiness directly from the Scriptures.[57, 58] Battersby, thankful that he had the opportunity to participate in this new Pentecostal Movement, said of the Conference:

> I feel most thankful to have shared in this Pentecostal season. I have read recent books on the subject now before our minds and hearts, pondered over them, and tried to say a word in defence of them, when I thought myself required; but I felt that I wanted myself the very blessing I had advocated...It is a very difficult thing to speak of my own experience, and very distasteful, yet perhaps for this reason it may be right for one to do so, and to acknowledge the blessing I have received.[59]

Asa Mahan wrote that one of the memorable speakers at the Convention was a man known as Mr. Reade, who had held an important governmental office in India. Reade reported that after returning to London from India, he and his entire family unitedly sought "the promise of the Father" and were all "filled with the Holy Ghost." Then, according to Mahan, Reade reported that:

> Immediately, for the first time in their lives, an ever-burning desire took supreme possession of every one of these minds to devote their entire being to the advancement of the cause of Christ.[60]

Many of those who attended the Oxford Convention reported in letters that they also had received the promise of the baptism of the Holy

---

[57] J. B. Figgis, *Keswick from Within* (London: Marshall Brothers, Ltd., 1914; Reprinted in *"The Higher Christian Life:" Sources for the Study of the Holiness, Pentecostal, and Keswick Movements*, Donald W. Dayton, ed. (New York & London: Garland Publishing, Inc., 1985), p. 21.

[58] J. C. Pollock, *The Keswick Story: The Authorized History of the Keswick Convention* (London: Hodder and Stoughton, 1964), p. 25.

[59] Anon, *Account of the Union Meeting for the Promotion of Scriptural Holiness held at Oxford*, p. 174.

[60] Asa Mahan, *Autobiography: Intellectual, Moral, and Spiritual* (London: T. Woolmer, 1882; reprinted New York: AMS Press, 1979), pp. 425-426.

Ghost.[61] Asa Mahan, the chief promoter of the Pentecostal experience at the Conference, summed up his experience as follows:

> I did believe for it, the promised blessing of the Baptism of the Holy Ghost came, and in that power I intend to walk until He calls me home.[62]

In addition to the main activities at the Oxford Convention, many side meetings were conducted. According to convention participant, J.B. Figgis:

> There were several side meetings held in Oxford, some of them quite private, and there were also meetings very specially public—meetings in the Market Place. Was it at one of these that a countryman was heard to give his idea of the Convention in the words: "It's all the Christian folk in all the world going to be one sect"?[63]

Whatever happened in those private meetings, the outcome was that Keswick was selected as the location for annual camp meetings that promoted the Higher Christian Life.

Brighton

Less than a year after the Oxford Convention and prior to the first Keswick Convention, another ten-day meeting called "The Convention for the Promotion of Scriptural Holiness" was held at Brighton, May 29 to June 7, 1875. As before, Robert Pearsall Smith was again the chairman of the Conference.[64] Asa Mahan, who had promoted the baptism of the Holy Ghost at the Oxford Conference, was the

---

[61] Anon, *Account of the Union Meeting for the Promotion of Scriptural Holiness held at Oxford*, pp. 349-388.

[62] Ibid., p. 192.

[63] Figgis, *Keswick from Within*, p. 32.

[64] Anon., *Record of the Convention for the Promotion of Scriptural Holiness Held at Brighton, May 29th to June 7th, 1875* (Brighton: W.J. Smith and London: S. W. Partridge and Co., c1896; Reprinted in *"The Higher Christian Life: Sources for the Study of the Holiness, Pentecostal, and Keswick Movements*, Donald W. Dayton, ed., New York and London: Garland Publishing, Inc., 1985), pp. 1-7.

president of the sectional meetings on the theme of the baptism of the Holy Ghost.[65] This theme, stressed throughout the Conference, was that the Pentecostal baptism of the Holy Ghost was needed for power for service. Toward the close of the Convention, Mahan's meetings:

> ...on this sacred subject grew more and more into the character of solemn gatherings, with the definite purpose of waiting for, and, as some bore witness, for the receiving of the Spirit. The power of these meetings was varied, some being seasons of remarkable blessing, when souls were bowed in reverence and in consciousness of the sacred baptism of the promised Comforter.[66]

A key outcome of the Brighton Conference was the establishment of a weekly paper advocating the doctrine of the higher life. The paper was started under the name, *The Banner of Holiness*. Mahan was appointed as its editor. Mahan later also became the editor of the publication, *Divine Life*.[67] Looking forward to a new era of "universal illumination," Mahan wrote:

> The era is not distant when the last cloud of darkness will have passed away, and religion and science will become visible to all the world, as having a common source and a common end and aim, the light of each proceeding from the same central sun of universal illumination, the face of Infinity unveiled.[68]

---

[65] Ibid., p. 383.

[66] Ibid., pp. 384-385.

[67] Asa Mahan, "Reminiscences and Reflections," *Divine Life*, vol. 13, May 1890, p. 294. In Oberlin College Archives, Asa Mahan (1799-1889) Papers, [1764] 1835-1985, Accession No. 223, Processed by Brian A. Williams (Oberlin, Ohio: Oberlin College Archives, April 1992).

[68] Asa Mahan, "Theism and Anti-Theism in Their Relations to Science," Lecture no. 4, In *The Ingham Lectures. A Course of Lectures on the Evidences of Natural and Revealed Religion. Delivered before the Ohio Wesleyan University, Delaware, Ohio*, William George Williams, ed. (Cleveland: Ingham, Clarke and Company: New York: Nelson & Phillips, 1873), p. 135.

The Keswick Conventions

Getting Started

Keswick, England was the selected location for the annual conventions on the higher Christian life. It was known for its rich heritage among the forerunners of the new Christian thought. Positioned in the lake country of northwestern England, it had been the home of William Wordsworth and Samuel Taylor Coleridge. As we have learned, Coleridge exerted important influences on Julius Hare and F. D. Maurice, who wrote *The Kingdom of Christ*. Hare demonstrated the depth of that influence by Coleridge when he called him:

> ...the great Christian philosopher, who, through dark and winding paths of speculation was led to the light, in order that others by his guidance might reach that light, without passing through the darkness.[69]

The first Keswick Convention was held in 1875 amid a shroud of confusion within the expected leadership of the meeting. The American Quaker, Robert Pearsall Smith, was considered by many to be a key to the anticipated "higher life" movement. He had chaired the meetings leading up to the present meeting and was expected to again serve as chairman and chief speaker at the Keswick Convention. Canon Thomas Dundas Harford-Battersby, who was Vicar of St. John's Anglican Church in Keswick, was expected to have the second position of leadership. At the last minute, however, Smith, along with his wife, Hannah Whitall Smith, cancelled out of the meeting, citing his health as the reason.[70] Whatever the details of Smith's "health" issues, morals-related rumors were spread and he later was reported to have suffered from a "mental breakdown."[71] In the absence of Smith, Harford-Battersby emerged to the position of leadership of the Keswick Convention.[72]

---

[69] Quoted in Figgis, *Keswick from Within.*, p. 49.

[70] Pollock, *The Keswick Story*, pp. 11-13.

[71] Ibid., p. 35.

[72] Figgis, *Keswick from Within*, p. 58.

While Men Slept...

Harford-Battersby, who had strong Catholic interests, considered his heros to be the two well-known and influential former Anglicans, John Henry Newman and Henry Edward Manning.[73, 74] Harford-Battersby came to St. John's Anglican Church in Keswick as curate in 1849, while the church was experiencing other intense Anglo-Catholic influences. Harford-Battersby's predecessor, Frederic Myers, had been the perpetual curate at St. John's until his death in 1851. Myers was the author of *Catholic Thoughts*, which strongly influenced Harford-Battersby.[75] Fenton Hort wrote of his visit to the church on August 30, 1849, describing the sermon as being "...neither evangelical nor belonging to any other form of ordinary theology." It was only after hearing the sermon that Hort learned that it was given by Arthur Penrhyn Stanley [the future Dean of Westminster].[76]

In addition to the strong Anglo-Catholic influences that Harford-Battersby experienced at St. John's, the church also had ties to psychical research and investigations into spiritualism. Frederic Myers' son, Frederick William Henry Myers (1843-1901), along with Henry Sidgwick and others, was a co-founder of the Society for Psychical Research.[77] That society became involved in the investigation of various spiritualist phenomena.

Upon accepting the leadership position of the Keswick Convention, Harford-Battersby selected another Quaker, Robert Wilson, as his assistant.[78] Wilson was later credited with choosing the motto of the Keswick Conventions: *"All one in Christ Jesus."*[79] The Convention,

---

[73] As we have learned, both of these men were key participants in the Oxford Anglo-Catholic Movement that began in the 1830's. Both also defected from the Church of England to the Roman Catholic Church and moved into international prominence as cardinals.

[74] Pollock, *The Keswick Story*, p. 23.

[75] Ibid., pp. 23-24.

[76] Hort, *Life and Letters*, vol. 1, p. 111.

[77] Boris de Zirkoff, "Compiler's Notes," In *H.P. Blavatsky: Collected Writings, 1883*, Boris de Zirkoff, compiler (Los Angeles: Philosophical Research Society, Inc., 1950), p. 263.

[78] Figgis, *Keswick from Within*, p. 58.

[79] Pollock, *The Keswick Story*, p. 62.

which was for Christians of different backgrounds and centered on teachings of the power of the Holy Spirit, opened on June 28, 1875.[80] The influences of Asa Mahan's work at the preceding conferences were seen at Keswick, as the command presented at the meeting on July 1, 1875 was: "Be filled with the Holy Spirit!"[81]

The Key to the Global Spiritual Movements

Much about the Keswick Conventions and their significant influences on spiritual movements throughout the world remains a public mystery. The known influences are, however, great. Each of the major twentieth-century spiritual milestones can, for example, be traced either directly or indirectly back to Keswick. As we shall see, these included the events in Topeka, Kansas in 1901, in Loughor, Wales in 1904, in Mukti, India in 1905, in Los Angeles, California in 1905, in Pretoria, South Africa in 1936, and in Rome, Italy in 1964. In addition, scores of other spiritual movements throughout the world can be traced back to each of these secondary movements.

The Keswick Influence on Global Revivals

Northeastern America

While the leaders of the Keswick Conventions were praying for a major spiritual movement in India, Keswick influences were also moving in America. D. L. Moody imported Keswick teachings to America in the early 1890's by inviting, for example, Frederick Brotherton Meyer (1847-1929) to his Northfield Conventions. Meyer had attended the 1874 Oxford Conference[82] and was also prominent at the Keswick Conventions.[83] As such, Meyer returned five times within the decade. In addition, Albert Benjamin Simpson (1843-1919), the founder of the Christian and Missionary Alliance in Old Orchard,

---

[80] Ibid., p. 38.

[81] Figgis, *Keswick from Within*, p. 57.

[82] Pollock, *The Keswick Story*, p. 103.

[83] Figgis, *Keswick from Within*, p. 129.

Maine,[84] was considered to be "Keswick" in his teachings.[85] Simpson played a major role in paving the way for the "new Pentecost" of the twentieth century through the two volumes, *The Holy Spirit, or Power from on High* that he produced in 1895 and 1896.[86]

Another spiritual movement launched in 1893 was that of Frank Weston Sandford (1862-1948). He and his wife, Helen, along with Elizabeth Sisson, a returned missionary from India, incorporated the "World Evangelization Crusade on Apostolic Principles." They started the new ministry in Maine on July 5, 1893, just over two years after Frank Sandford returned from a trip that took him to San Francisco, Japan, China, India, Egypt, and Palestine. The trip, which lasted from October 1890 to March 1891, included one month of travel to the interior missions of India.[87, 88]

Sandford, opened a Bible school, named "The Holy Ghost and Us," and built a community called "Shiloh" in 1895. He demanded a commitment from his followers to the degree that his students and others associated with his organization were required to sell their assets and give the money to the community. In 1899, Sandford received national attention because he reportedly raised a woman from the dead. In 1901, Sandford also declared that *he* was Elijah.[89, 90]

Midwestern America

The 1893 Columbian Exposition was a magnetic attraction to the religions of the world. In addition to the organized activities at the World's Parliament of Religions, others with specific ministerial em-

---

[84]Terrence Robert Crowe, *Pentecostal Unity: Recurring Frustration and Enduring Hopes* (Chicago: Loyola University Press, 1993), p. 7.

[85] Donald W. Dayton, *Theological Roots of Pentecostalism* (Grand Rapids, Michigan: Francis Asbury Press of Zondervan Publishing House, 1987), p. 105.

[86] Ibid., p. 107.

[87] Ibid., pp. 145-146

[88] Shirley Nelson, *Fair, Clear, and Terrible: The Story of Shiloh, Maine* (Latham, New York: British American Publishing, 1989), p. 52.

[89] Faupel, *The Everlasting Gospel*, pp. 145-157.

[90] Goff, *Fields White Unto Harvest*, p. 58.

phases were drawn to Chicago. John Alexander Dowie (1847-1907), for example, was a faith healer who was born in Scotland, moved to Australia at the age of fourteen, returned to Scotland to attend New College, and then returned to Australia where he lived until coming to America in 1888. Notably, Dowie was present in Chicago during the 1893 Columbian Exposition, where he set up a tabernacle just outside the entrance to the fairground.[91] His ministry achieved national attention through a string of miracle healings.[92]

In 1896, Dowie formally established the Christian Catholic Church (which was renamed in 1904 as the Christian Catholic Apostolic Church in Zion). By 1900, Dowie announced plans to build a utopian community called Zion on property north of Chicago. In 1901, he *also* declared himself to be Elijah, the "Restorer of All Things." Dowie consecrated himself in 1904 to be the First Apostle of a new apostolic order.[93]

Two key people in the twentieth century "Pentecost" as it came to America were Charles F. Parham (1873-1929) and Agnes Ozman [LaBerge] (1870-1937), both of whom were influenced heavily by Keswick teachings. Parham was influenced by the theologies that came from the annual camp meetings at Keswick, England, which, as we recall, through the influence of Asa Mahan, promoted the emphasis on the "Baptism with the Holy Spirit." Those influences came to Parham through key Christian leaders, including the well-known dispensational evangelist Dwight Lyman Moody, John Alexander Dowie, A. B. Simpson, and especially Frank Weston Sandford.[94] Other influences included the Quaker teachings of David Baker, who was the grandfather of Parham's future wife, Sarah Eleanor Thistlethwaite.[95]

---

[91] D. William Faupel, *The Everlasting Gospel: The Significance in the Development of Pentecostal Thought* (Sheffield, England: Sheffield Academic Press, 1996), pp. 116-118.

[92] James R. Goff, Jr., *Fields White Unto Harvest: Charles F. Parham and the Missionary Origins of Pentecostalism* (Fayetteville: The University of Arkansas Press, 1988), p. 50.

[93] Faupel, *The Everlasting Gospel*, pp. 119-120.

[94] Ibid., pp. 50-57.

[95] Ibid., pp. 35-38.

While Men Slept...

While Moody was very influential in the Keswick Convention movement in England, the healing ministries of Dowie and Sandford, in particular, helped build the foundation upon which Parham built his Apostolic Faith Movement. A visit by two of Sandford's students to Parham in Topeka, Kansas early in 1900 was followed by a visit by Sandford himself in June 1900 on a return from a trip to the west coast of the United States.[96] After meeting with Sandford, Parham decided to leave Topeka with him to enroll in Sandford's Bible college at Shiloh. En route, Parham also stopped at Dowie's ministry in Chicago and at Simpson's Missionary Training Institute in Nyack, New York.[97, 98]

At Shiloh, Sandford taught his doctrine and evangelistic strategies to Parham for six weeks before they embarked together on a missionary trip to Canada. After his trip, Parham returned to Kansas, convinced that God was calling him for a fresh start. He brought the message of the baptism in the Holy Spirit and healing to Topeka. In October 1900, Parham announced the opening of a new Bible school, believing that God would use it to bring in the end-time worldwide revval.[99, 100]

The Holy Ghost in Topeka

It was at Parham's Bethel Bible College in Topeka, Kansas that the gifts of the Holy Ghost, with the evidence of speaking in other tongues, were introduced into the twentieth century. Parham reported that one of the women at the school, Agnes N. Ozman [LaBerge], received the baptism of the Holy Ghost and began speaking in the Chinese language.[101] LaBerge also wrote an account of the occassion. She said

---

[96] Faupel, *The Everlasting Gospel*, 164.

[97] Ibid.

[98] Crowe, *Pentecostal Unity*, p. 11.

[99] Faupel, *The Everlasting Gospel*, pp. 164-169.

[100] Nils Bloch-Hoell, *The Pentecostal Movement: Its Origin, Development, and Distinctive Character* (Halden, Norway: Universitetsforlaget, 1964), p. 19.

[101] Sarah E. Parham, *The Life of Charles F. Parham: Founder of the Apostolic Faith Movement* (Joplin, Missouri: Hunter Print. Co., c1930; reprinted New York and London: Garland Publishing Inc., 1985), pp. 51-55.

that she requested that hands be laid on her at about eleven o'clock on New Year's night to:

> ...fulfill all scripture, that I might receive the baptism which my whole heart longed to have. There as I was praying I remembered in the Bible hands were laid on believers as on me and prayer was offered for me; I began to talk in tongues and had great joy and was filled with glory...I did not know that I would talk with tongues when I received the Baptism, but as soon as I did on that night I spoke in tongues and I knew I had received the promise of the Father, fulfilled. Blessed be God! Hallelujah! Bless the Lord! Amen.[102]

[Some have reported that the date of this occurrence was on New Years Eve 1900. Sarah Parham repeated Ozman's words as follows:

> During the first day of 1901 the presence of the Lord was with us in a marked way stilling our hearts to wait upon Him for greater things. The spirit of prayer was upon us in the evening. It was nearly seven o'clock on the first of January that it came into my heart to ask Bro. Parham to lay his hands upon me that I might receive the gift of the Holy Spirit. It was as his hands were laid upon my head that the Holy Spirit fell upon me and I began to speak in tongues, glorifying God. I talked several languages, and it was clearly manifest when a new dialect was spoken.[103]

Thus, both of these accounts put the date as January 1, 1901, apparently at either eleven or seven o'clock in the evening.]

After the initial report of the twentieth century Pentecost, Parham reported that during January 1901 several others at the school had

---

[102] Agnes N. O. LaBerge, *What God Hath Wrought: Life and Work of Mrs. Agnes N. O. LaBerge, Nee Miss Agnes N. Ozman* (Chicago: Herald Publishing Co. Press, Date Unavailable; reprinted New York and London: Garland Publishing, Inc., 1985), p. 29.

[103] Parham, *The Life of Charles F. Parham*, p. 66.

also received the baptism of the Holy Ghost, each speaking in various languages of the world. Parham said that he spoke Swedish.[104] Parham's Holy Ghost revivals soon moved to a Bible school in Texas, where accounts were made of people speaking in other languages, including an African dialect and Hindu.[105]

The Great 1904 Wales Revival

Prayer Circle Foundations

While Parham was teaching about the baptism of the Holy Ghost in America, another spiritual movement was brewing in India and Wales. Like Parham, the leaders of the movements in both countries were influenced by the annual conventions being held in Keswick, England. In 1902, R. J. Ward, who had been under Keswick influences since his experience at the Keswick Convention of 1891, helped institute a general "prayer circle" in India among missionaries of all denominations to pray for an "outpouring of the Holy Spirit."[106]

Spirit circles were a tool employed by spiritualists as a supposed means of bringing manifestations of spiritual power. Asa Mahan, the first president of Oberlin College in Ohio and also of Adrian College in Michigan,[107] described the use of spirit circles by mediums in seances.[108] According to Mahan, the universality of the spirit circles was that the kind of spirits which were supposedly called forth were dependent upon the particular circles in which they originated. For example, among Buddhists, Hindus, Catholics, or Protestants, the spirits took on the complexion of the circles in which they appeared.[109]

---

[104] Ibid., pp. 51-55.

[105] Ibid., p. 131.

[106] J. Edwin Orr, *The Flaming Tongue: The Impact of Twentieth Century Revivals* (Chicago: Moody Press, 1973), p. 132.

[107] Asa Mahan, *Autobiography: Intellectual, Moral, and Spiritual* (London: T. Woolmer, 1882; reprinted New York: AMS Press, 1979), p. 265.

[108] Asa Mahan, *The Phenomena of Spiritualism: Scientifically Explained and Exposed* (New York, Chicago, and New Orleans: A.S. Barnes and Co., 1876), p. 193.

[109] Ibid.

Jessie Penn-Lewis, who played a key role in initiating the Wales revival, recalled that at the 1902 Keswick Convention stories were also being circulated about "home prayer circles" in Melbourne, Australia for a "Pentecost" and that:

> Just one month earlier, in faraway India the Divine Spirit laid the same burden upon the servants of God, and guided them— without any conscious connection with the prayer movement in other lands—to form a prayer circle of those who would unite to plead for the outpoured Spirit upon that dark and needy land.[110]

Upon hearing these reports, the "Keswick Circle of Prayer" was inaugurated at the 1902 Keswick Convention.[111] The forty-year-old Jessie Penn-Lewis gave addresses at the Ladies' Meetings at the 1902 Keswick Convention, where two Welsh ministers approached her about conducting "Keswick" in Wales.[112] She agreed to help organize a 1903 convention in Llandrindod Wells in central Wales. To facilitate the arrangements, she obtained the help of F. B. Meyer's assistant, who had recently organized a series of meetings in the town.[113]

Connections in India

At the close of 1902, a woman who was unknown to Jessie Penn-Lewis wrote her a letter saying, "God has shown me you are to go to India."[114] In obedience to the message in the letter, Penn-Lewis sailed for India by January 7, 1903.[115] Penn-Lewis said that in 1903 in India

---

[110] Jessie Penn-Lewis, *The Awakening in Wales: and Some of the Hidden Springs* (Originally Published in England by The Overcomer Literature Trust, Ltd.; Fort Washington, Pennsylvania: Christian Literature Crusade, 1993), p. 34.

[111] Pollock, *The Keswick Story*, p. 120.

[112] Ibid., pp. 121-122.

[113] Mary N. Garrard, *Mrs. Penn Lewis* (London: The Overcomer Book Room; Reprinted and Web Published by Toni Cauchi, Architech Information Designs, Inc., http://revival-library.org/catalogues/world6/garrard/foreshadowings.ihtml, 2001), p. 11.

[114] Garrard, *Mrs. Penn Lewis*, p. 1.

[115] Ibid., p. 11.

the "...Spirit of God unveiled to one of his honored servants the cross of Calvary in new and vivid power...."[116]

While Penn-Lewis was in India, a spiritual movement was forming in the Khasi Hills of northeastern India. In early 1903, prayer meetings were announced at a church in the Khasi Hills to specifically seek an outpouring of the Holy Spirit there and throughout the entire world.[117] Ironically, there had been a spiritual connection between India and Wales ever since 1888 when Welsh Presbyterian missionaries established what became known as the Cherrapunjee Theological College in the Khasi Hills area of northeastern India.[118] The Khasi tribes-people have been described as, "...head-hunters, with human sacrifices persisting in obscure cults...."[119]

At approximately the same time that the Welsh influence was being felt among the Khasi tribes-people, there was a Unitarian movement also manifesting itself in the area. Through correspondence with a Khasi tribesman named Hajjom Kissor Singh, the Ann Arbor, Michigan Unitarian minister, Jabez Sunderland, who was also the editor of *The Unitarian* magazine, began supplying tracts to the tribe in 1888. Sunderland continued his relationship with the Khasi Unitarian movement for forty eight years.[120]

The Wales "Keswick" Conventions

In addition to Penn-Lewis, F. B. Meyer was key to the August 1903 convention in Wales.[121] After the first convention, another "Keswick-like" convention was organized and held in Wales during August 1904. Through testimonies, some of the attendees to the previous convention revealed that their spiritual lives had been deeply affected. Soon

---

[116] Penn-Lewis, *The Awakening in Wales*, p. 39.

[117] Orr, *The Flaming Tongue*, p. 133.

[118] Anon., Khasi Hills, 2001, http://www.newdelhi.net/india/DiscoverIndia/Meghalaya/khasi.html.

[119] Orr, *The Flaming Tongue*, p. 133.

[120] Lavan, *Unitarians and India*, pp. 149-150.

[121] Brynmor Pierce Jones, *An Instrument of Revival: The Complete Life of Evan Roberts (1878-1951)* (South Plainfield, New Jersey, 1995), p. xvii.

Penn-Lewis reported that the: "The Spirit of God broke forth again in glorious power that momentous week in 1904...."[122]

Anticipating a move of the Spirit in Wales, a young Welsh coal miner and blacksmith who was studying for the ministry, was brought to the forefront in September 1904. Twenty-six year old Evan Roberts (1878-1951) had been intensely praying for a move of the Spirit.[123, 124] On October 31, 1904 Roberts returned to his hometown of Loughor by train and obtained permission to hold a spiritual revival meeting in the Moriah Church and its chapel.[125]

Roberts immediately began holding meetings and preaching the importance of being filled with the Spirit. One of the characteristics of the Wales revival was that it was rapidly chronicled to the public through newspapers and other publications. On Friday, November 4, 1904, Roberts wrote that: "We are on the eve of a great and grand revival, the greatest the world has ever seen. Do not think the writer is a madman."[126] Another characteristic of the Welsh revival was the eruptions of hour-long songs and the occurrence of "Hywl," which were half-sung and half-spoken prayers.[127] Evangelist Gipsy Rodney Smith (1860-1947), who attended some of the Welsh revival meetings, reportedly described the meetings as beginning with two-and-a-half hours of praise and exhortation, in which anybody, even a little child, would sing.[128] As Roberts continued with nightly meetings, Jessie Penn-Lewis wrote columns in the weekly publication of the Keswick Movement, which was published on November 9, 1904 in London, telling about the events that were happening in Wales. By November 11, 1904, other newspapers picked up the stories of the meetings in Wales, giving them wide circulation.[129]

---

[122] Penn-Lewis, *The Awakening in Wales*, pp. 55-56.

[123] Pollock, *The Keswick Story*, pp. 121-122.

[124] Orr, *The Flaming Tongue*, p. 5.

[125] Ibid., pp. 6-7.

[126] Quoted in Ibid., p. 8.

[127] Crowe, *Pentecostal Unity*, p. 16.

[128] Orr, *The Flaming Tongue*, p. 15.

[129] Ibid., p. 10.

While Men Slept...

A "new Pentecost" in Wales

By Monday, November 14, 1904, the quick publicity drew a thousand people to the meeting. The following day, Roberts announced that a great awakening was coming to all of Wales.[130] Soon, a powerful revival did break out in Wales! Roberts travelled about from place to place, as the Spirit led him, exhorting words of knowledge calling out specific individuals for repentance.[131] As the events in Wales were extensively publicized throughout the world, the spiritual movement was being spread to India and Los Angeles. Frank Bartleman (1871-1935) who, as we shall learn, was the key behind-the-scenes advocate and chronicler of the Azusa Street, Los Angeles revival, confirmed that the worldwide Pentecostal revival did indeed come from Wales as he wrote:

> And history repeats itself. Let the Pentecostal people beware! The present world-wide revival was rocked in the cradle of little Wales. It was 'brought up' in India, following; becoming full grown in Los Angeles later.[132]

The 1905 Revival in India

Keswick Influences in India

The influences of the Keswick Conventions were felt among the people of India long before the 1905 revival. During the spring of 1883, before the start of the the eighth annual Keswick Convention, a twenty-four year old widow and her young daughter made their way from India to England. Pandita Ramabai (1858-1922), a high caste Hindu, lived at the Anglican Community of St. Mary the Virgin in Wantage (located about 15 miles southwest of Oxford). Although she had insisted that she would not become a Christian, Ramabai was baptized into Christianity as an Anglican in September 1883 and accepted the

---

[130] Ibid., p. 11.

[131] Jones, *An Instrument of Revival*, pp. 80-82.

[132] Bartleman, *How Pentecost Came to Los Angeles.*, p. 21.

name, Mary Rama.[133, 134] During her time in England, Ramabai made key contacts with influential Englishmen, including Max Muller, the renowned Indian studies professor at Oxford. Muller, who became an authority on Ramakrishna, also later developed a very positive relationship with the Swami Vivekananda.[135]

Ramabai first visited Muller's home in Oxford in 1883, soon after arriving in England from India. After that, she maintained a very cordial relationship with Muller and his family, visiting their home often.[136] Among the other influential Englishmen who took an interest in Ramabai was William Ewart Gladstone,[137] the prime minister of England. Gladstone, as we recall, was the long-time associate of F. D. Maurice, Henry Manning, John Newman, the Wilberforces and other key participants in the Oxford Movement. Gladstone, who helped fund the work of Ramabai, had taken a strong interest in psychical research, such as that which Fenton Hort, Brooke Foss Westcott, and their colleagues had participated in as members of the "Ghostly Guild."[138] Gladstone provided earnest support for psychical research endeavors. He considered psychical research to be the most important research that was going on in the world.[139]

Early in her Christian experience, Ramabai also came under such liberal influences as the teachings of Brooke Foss Westcott and, although she had been baptized into the Anglican Church, rejected a belief in

---

[133] Shamsundar Manohar Adhav, *Pandita Ramabai: Confessing the Faith in India Series—No. 13* (Madras, India: The Christian Literature Society, 1979), p. 11.

[134] Meera Kosambi, In *Pandita Ramabai Through Her Own Words: Selected Works*, Meeri Kosambi, ed. (Oxford: Oxford University Press, 2000), p. 9.

[135] Nikhilananda, *Vivekananda: The Yogas and Other Works*, pp. 90-150.

[136] Adhav, *Pandita Ramabai: Confessing the Faith in India Series—No. 13*, pp. 12-13.

[137] A. B. Shah, *The Letters and Correspondence of Pandita Ramabai*, compiled by Sister Geraldine (Bombay: Maharashtra State Board for Literature and Culture, 1977), p. 30.

[138] Hort, *Life and Letters,* vol. 1, p. 172.

[139] Aland Gauld, *The Founders of Psychical Research* (London: Routledge & Kegan Paul, 1968), p. 140.

Trinitarian Christianity.[140] She soon rejected both the miraculous birth and the deity of Jesus Christ.[141] She wrote on September 1, 1885 that:

> ...I shrink from calling Christ the Supreme God, and from worshipping Him as God. To give the title and worship which belongs only to the God of gods to a man, and a created being is to my understanding nothing but idolatry.[142]

In addition to her contacts in England, Ramabai also traveled in the United States, where she sought funding for her work in women's missions.[143] By December 1887, Ramabai's popularity in the United States had increased to the degree that the American Ramabai Association was formed in Boston, with a subsidiary association opening later in San Francisco. Ramabai wrote *The High-caste Hindu Woman*, which was a book on Indian feminism, as part of her fund-raising effort. Consequently, the Association pledged ten years of financial support for a secular school for Hindu widows in India. She returned to India in February 1889 and opened the "Sharada Sadan" [Home of the Goddess of Learning] in Bombay, which she later moved to Poona for economic reasons.[144] Unitarians were very interested in Ramabai's school in Poona. Jabez Sunderland, the noted Unitarian missionary from Ann Arbor, Michigan, for example, made the school his first stop when he attended the meeting of the Indian National Congress and National Social Conference in Poona during 1895.[145]

In 1893, following his American debut at the World's Parliament of Religions, the Swami Vivekananda was invited to speak at the Ladies Club in Boston, which was helping to fund the work of Ramabai.[146]

---

[140] Shah, *The Letters and Correspondence of Pandita Ramabai*, pp. 108-112.

[141] Kosambi, *Pandita Ramabai Through Her Own Words*, p. 15.

[142] Adhav, *Pandita Ramabai*, p. 158.

[143] Uma Chakravarti, *Rewriting History: The Life and Times of Pandita Ramabai* (New Delhi: Kali for Women, 1998), p. 325.

[144] Meera Kosambi, "Multiple Contestations: Pandita Ramabai's Educational and Missionary Activities in Late Nineteenth-Century India and Abroad," *Women's History Review*, vol. 7 no. 2, 1998, pp. 193-208.

[145] Lavan, *Unitarians and India*, p. 148.

[146] Swami Vivekananda, In *The Complete Works of Swami Vivekananda*, vol. 5, Swami Tadrupananda, ed., (Calcutta: Advaita Ashrama, 1978), pp. 17-19.

On the heels of the Swami Vivekananda's triumphant return to India in 1897 from America and England, where he had just met with Max Muller at Oxford and with such dignitaries as Canon Basil Wilberforce [the son of Samuel Wilberforce], there was a call for a new move of the Spirit in India.[147] Vivekananda responded with intense worship of Kali as the "Terrible Mother." During October 1898, Vivekananda withdrew himself alone in Kashmir to a Kali sanctuary, from which he reportedly came out "transfigured," submitting as a child to the authority of Kali.[148, 149]

The leaders of the various Indian missionary agencies responded by issuing a special call to prayer for some "...special manifestation of the life and power of God the Holy Ghost."[150] Despite Ramabia's confession of a Unitarian belief, her personal appeal to the 1898 Keswick Convention in England resulted in a prayer for two hundred thousand Christian evangelists for India.[151]

Influences from Wales

In 1899 Ramabai moved her school from Poona to the nearby village of Kedagon, where it became known as the Ramabai Mukti [Salvation] Mission, which was operated as a Christian mission.[152] After Ramabai learned of the revival in Wales, she instituted "special prayer circles," as had been used in Wales and at the Keswick Convention, at the beginning of 1905.[153] A "new Pentecost" came to the girls living

---

[147] David Miller, "Modernity in Hindu Monasticism: Swami Vivekananda and the Ramakrishna Movement," *Journal of Asian and African Studies*, vol. 34, February 1999, pp. 111ff.

[148] Nikhilananda, *Vivekananda*, pp. 90-150.

[149] Romain Rolland, *The Life of Vivekananda and the Universal Gospel*, 6th impression, E.F. Malcolm-Smith, trans. (Calcutta: Advaita Ashrama, 1965), p. 115.

[150] Gary B. McGee, "Pentecostal Phenomena and Revivals in India: Implications for Indigenous Church Leadership," *Internationaal Bulletin of Missionary Research*, vol. 20, no. 3, July 1996, pp. 112-116.

[151] Gary B. McGee, "'Latter Rain' Falling in the East: Early-Twentieth-Century Pentecostalism in India and the Debate over Speaking in Tongues," *Church History*, vol. 68 no. 3, September 1999, pp. 648-665.

[152] Kosambi, "Multiple Contestations...," pp. 193-208.

[153] Orr, *The Flaming Tongue*, p. 132.

in her Indian mission. On June 29, 1905, one of the girls in the dormitory of the Mukti Mission in Kedgaon in south India reportedly was baptized with the Holy Spirit and with "fire."[154] Bartleman referenced an undocumented quote of the event:

> The girls in India so wonderfully wrought upon and baptized with the Spirit (in Ramabai's mission), began by terrifically beating themselves, under pungent conviction of their need. Great light was given them. When delivered they jumped up and down for joy, for hours without fatigue, in fact were stronger for it. They cried out with the burning that came into and upon them...About twenty girls went into a trance at one time and became unconscious of this world for hours; some for three or four days...The Spirit was poured out upon one of the seeking girls in the night. Her companion sleeping next to her awoke, and seeing fire envelop her, ran across the dormitory and brought a pail of water to dash upon her.[155]

According to Meera Kosambi, Professor and Director of the Research Center for Women's Studies at SNDT Women's University in Mumbai, India, one of the effects of the revivals was that it enabled Ramabai a means to control the lower caste women who were at the school. She wrote that:

> This mob of unruly and uneducated rural women, so different from the strictly disciplined upper-caste widows, was indeed controlled through large-scale conversions to Christianity and frequent "Revivals." These visitations from the Holy Spirit were akin to the phenomenon of "possession" by Hindu deities with which these women were familiar; however, they were treated with scepticism by Ramabai's Christian friends.[156]

Pandita Ramabai explained the similarities between Hinduism and Christianity. For example, she compared a prayer to the sun-god as

---

[154] McGee, "Latter Rain' Falling in the East," pp. 648-665.

[155] Bartleman, *How Pentecost Came to Los Angeles*, p. 37.

[156] Kosambi, "Multiple Contestations...," p. 199.

being similiar to the "Hail Mary" of the Roman Catholics, in that it was frequently repeated, at least thirty times per day. She explained:

> It is quite clear that when hymns in praise are addressed to several divinities, the worshipper thinks of them as different manifestations of the same Omnipresent Spirit.[157]

The Welsh had been a significant influence in India long before the outbreak of the March 1905 Indian revival, which occurred on the heels of the 1904 revival in Wales. The revival began among the tribal peoples in the Khasi Hills at stations staffed by Welsh Presbyterian missionaries.[158] As we have learned, Jessie Penn-Lewis made a trip to India just before she helped initiate the conventions that lead to the great Wales revival. Even after the Wales revival, Welsh influences continued in India. Sidney Evans, the close friend and brother-in-law of Wales revival leader Evan Roberts, served for twenty-five years as the Head of the College among the Khasi Hills tribal people in India.[159]

The 1906 Azusa Street Revival in Los Angeles

Influences from Wales and Keswick

The Englishman, Frederick Brotherton Meyer (1847-1929), who attended the 1874 Oxford Conference,[160] was prominent at the Keswick Convention,[161] was key to the Wales Convention in August 1903 that brought about the 1904 Wales revival,[162] and was also instrumental in

---

[157] Pandita Ramabai, Quoted in *Pandita Ramabai Through Her Own Words: Selected Works*, Meeri Kosambi, ed. (Oxford: Oxford University Press, 2000), pp. 122-123.

[158] Gary B. McGee, "'Latter Rain' Falling in the East: Early-Twentieth-Century Pentecostalism in India and the Debate over Speaking in Tongues," *Church History*, vol. 68 no. 3, September 1999, pp. 648-665.

[159] Anon., "Moriah C. M. Chapel: Evan Roberts-The Man-What was He Like?," 2001, http://www.moriah1904.ukgateway.net/evan.htm.

[160] Pollock, *The Keswick Story*, p. 103.

[161] Figgis, *Keswick from Within*, p. 129.

[162] Brynmor Pierce Jones, *An Instrument of Revival: The Complete Life of Evan Roberts (1878-1951)* (South Plainfield, New Jersey, 1995), p. xvii.

the 1906 Los Angeles spiritual revival. Prior to his work in Wales and in Los Angeles, Meyer had spent time in India. He reported the details of his trip to India at the 1899 Keswick Convention.[163] [Ironically, that was the same year that Swami Vivekananda returned from India to Los Angeles and the year that Pandita Ramabai moved the location of her mission in India.]

A few months after the Wales revival began, Meyer brought the news of the event to Los Angeles. On April 8, 1905, he told about the Great Wales Revival. Frank Bartleman responded to the news by distributing a "little tract" and a "little book" describing the events in Wales.[164] Bartleman, the son of a Roman Catholic father and a Quaker mother, had come to Los Angeles for the specific purpose of helping to promote an anticipated spiritual revival. He had been in Los Angeles since December 22, 1904, having been invited to the city in anticipation of the new spiritual movement.[165, 166]

As Bartleman's interest concerning the spiritual movement in Wales intensified, he actively promoted the occurrence of a similar revival in Los Angeles and in Pasadena, California. Joseph Smale (1867-1926), a Baptist preacher from Los Angeles, was also among those who had visited the Evan Roberts revival in Wales. After Bartleman learned that Smale had just returned from the Wales revival, he was excited to attend his church. By June 17, 1905, Bartleman started attending the Baptist church of Joseph Smale, whom Bartleman described as being "...on fire to have the same visitation and blessing come to his own church in Los Angeles." Bartleman soon wrote and distributed his own tract about the revival in Wales.[167]

---

[163] Figgis, *Keswick from Within*, p. 135.

[164] Frank Bartleman, *From Plow to Pulpit; From Maine to California* (Los Angeles: Frank Bartleman, 1924; Reprinted in *Witness to Pentecost: The Life of Frank Bartleman, with a Preface by Cecil M. Robeck, Jr.* (New York and London: Garland Publishing, Inc., 1985)), pp. 11-14.

[165] Ibid., pp. 5-6.

[166] Frank Bartleman, *How Pentecost Came to Los Angeles: As It Was in the Beginning*, 2nd ed. (Los Angeles: Frank Bartleman, 1925; Reprinted in *Witness to Pentecost: The Life of Frank Bartleman, with a Preface by Cecil M. Robeck, Jr.* (New York and London: Garland Publishing, Inc., 1985)), p. 5.

[167] Ibid., pp. 5-16.

Soon Bartleman wrote to Evan Roberts, establishing a personal link with him and the Welch movement. In response to Bartleman's correspondence, Roberts encouraged him to "Congregate the people together who are willing to make a total surrender. Pray and wait. Believe God's promises. Hold daily meetings." During June 1905, Bartleman was writing articles in which he was anticipating an expected "Pentecost."[168]

Throughout the summer and fall, Bartleman continued to correspond with Roberts, who responded in November 1905 by saying, "May the Lord bless you with a mighty outpouring." Roberts added, "We are teaching no sectarian doctrine, only the wonder and beauty of Christ's love."[169] Roberts continued with a prophetic statement about the anticipated global spiritual movement:

> Wonderful things have happened in Wales in a few weeks, but these are only a beginning. The world will be swept by His Spirit as a rushing, mighty wind. Many who are now silent Christians will lead the movement. They will see a great light, and will reflect this light to thousands now in darkness. Thousands will do more than we have accomplished, as God gives them power.[170]

Thus, Roberts told Bartleman to anticipate a worldwide spiritual movement wherein the participants would receive power. However, the movement would *not be based on the teaching of doctrine*. Instead, it would be based on *love*.

On the heels of Roberts' correspondence, Bartleman continued producing the publications which were key to laying the foundations on which the Azusa Street movement was to be built and which would make a significant contribution to the growth of the movement.[171] On November 16, 1905 Bartleman wrote such writings of anticipation as:

---

[168] Ibid., pp. 18-19.

[169] Ibid., pp. 33-36.

[170] Ibid., p. 36.

[171] Goff, *Fields White Unto Harvest*, p. 114.

'Pentecost' is knocking on our door...Wales will not stand alone in this glorious triumph for our Christ. The spirit of reviving is coming upon us, driven by the breath of God, the Holy Ghost...Los Angeles, Southern California, and the whole continent shall surely find itself ere long in the throes of a mighty revival, by the Spirit and power of God.[172]

Bringing Pentecost to Los Angeles

Much has been written about the events surrounding the outpouring of the Holy Spirit at Azusa Street in Los Angeles. In brief, one of the students from Charles Parham's Texas Bible school, William J. Seymour, was invited to Los Angeles to preach the Pentecostal message that he had received from Parham. Accepting the invitation, Seymour, who was African-American, traveled to Los Angeles. After a spiritual revival occurred on Bonnie Bray Street, a larger place was needed for the increased numbers of people who attended the meetings. Seymour then opened a mission on Azusa Street in Los Angeles in 1906.[173, 174]

According to the account of Agnes Ozman LaBerge, someone paid Seymour to travel to Los Angeles for the anticipated revival. LaBerge described her understanding of the early events of the Azusa Street spiritual movement this way:

Parties hearing of the Holy Ghost being here [in Texas], sent him [William Seymour] money to come to Los Angeles, California. They supposed he had its [the Holy Ghost's] fulfillment, but he received it later. He went to Los Angeles, California, and meetings were started and as hungry hearts prayed God mightily poured out the Holy Ghost and many received the Holy Spirit and spoke in tongues and great joy and glory was given. On the evening of April 9, 1906 on Bonnie Bray Street, it was where the Spirit first fell in Los Angeles. After-

---

[172] Bartleman, *How Pentecost Came to Los Angeles*, p. 39

[173] Parham, *The Life of Charles F. Parham*, pp. 161-162.

[174] Vinson Synan, *The Holiness-Pentecostal Tradition: Charismatic Movements in the Twentieth Century*, 2nd ed. (Grand Rapids, Michigan and Cambridge, U.K.: William B. Eerdmans Publishing Company, 1997), p. 97.

wards because of the need of more room, they moved to Azusa Street Mission at 312 Azusa Street.[175]

That They All May Be One

The message at Azusa Street was summarized by a tract written by Bartleman entitled, "That They All May Be One."[176] According to Asa Mahan, one of the outcomes of the baptism of the Holy Ghost is the promotion of Christian unity and love. Quoting Jesus, Mahan used the following Scriptures to support his point concerning unity:[177]

> That they all may be one; as thou, Father, *art* in me, and I in thee, that they also may be one in us: that the world may believe that thou hast sent me... I in them, and thou in me, that they may be made perfect in one; and that the world may know that thou hast sent me, and hast loved them, as thou hast loved me.
>
> —John 17:21, 23

Jesus, however, was praying to the Father for unity in Him and that those who are in Him would be sanctified through the truth, which is the Word of God:

> Sanctify them through thy truth: thy word is truth. As thou hast sent me into the world, even so have I also sent them into the world. And for their sakes I sanctify myself, that they also might be sanctified through the truth.
>
> —John 17:17-19

Jesus, who is the living Word of God, is Himself the Truth, through whom believers are sanctified. He declared that He is the Truth and the Life and that He is the *only* way to the Father:

> Jesus saith unto him, I am the way, the truth, and the life: no man cometh unto the Father, but by me.
>
> —John 14:6

---

[175]LaBerge, *What God Hath Wrought*, p. 34.

[176] Ibid., p. 27.

[177] Mahan, *The Baptism of the Holy Ghost*, pp. 53-54.

While Men Slept...

The Apostle Paul wrote that we should walk worthy of the vocation to which we are called:

> Endeavouring to keep the unity of the Spirit in the bond of peace.
>
> —Ephesians 4:3

Paul further wrote, however, that we should continue to work in our calling for the purpose of helping to edify the Body of Christ:

> Till we all come in the unity of the faith, and of the knowledge of the Son of God, unto a perfect man, unto the measure of the stature of the fulness of Christ: That we *henceforth* be no more children, tossed to and fro, and carried about with every wind of doctrine, by the sleight of men, *and* cunning craftiness, whereby they lie in wait to deceive; But speaking the truth in love, may grow up into him in all things, which is the head, *even* Christ:
>
> —Ephesians 4:13-15

Jesus promised that the Spirit of Truth, would not speak of Himself, but would guide us to all truth, which is in Jesus Christ.

> Howbeit when he, the Spirit of truth, is come, he will guide you into all truth: for he shall not speak of himself; but whatsoever he shall hear, *that* shall he speak: and he will shew you things to come. He shall glorify me: for he shall receive of mine, and shall shew *it* unto you.
>
> —John 16:13-14

As the Spirit of Truth points us toward Jesus Christ, He reminds us that we come to unity with the Father through the *doctrine* of the shed blood of Jesus Christ:

> But now in Christ Jesus ye who sometimes were far off are made nigh by the blood of Christ.
>
> —Ephesians 2:13

Thus, the Holy Ghost, who is the Spirit of Truth brings us to unity as He directs us to Jesus Christ and His redemptive work on the cross.

372

Chapter 18. Believe Not Every Spirit

Beloved, believe not every spirit, but try the spirits whether they are of God: because many false prophets are gone out into the world.

—1 John 4:1

The Spirit of Error: Counterfeiting Spirits

Taking Our Eyes Away from Jesus and the Cross

The Holy Ghost pointed those who were present on the day of Pentecost toward Jesus Christ. As Peter explained the purpose of the gift of the Holy Ghost, he concluded:

> Therefore let all the house of Israel know assuredly, that God hath made that same Jesus, whom ye have crucified, both Lord and Christ.
>
> —Acts 2:36

As the Spirit of Truth directs us toward Jesus Christ and His atoning sacrifice on the cross, so the Spirit of Error points us away from His work on the cross. The Spirit of Error is a distracting spirit. While perhaps outwardly speaking of Jesus Christ, this spirit seeks to call attention to itself.

As Asa Mahan discussed "Temptations and Errors" in his book, *The Baptism of the Holy Ghost*, his first caution was about the "Temptation to Spiritual Pride." He wrote that:

> It is proper, and a duty, to tell others what the Lord has done for us, provided the supreme motive is not to glorify self, but to magnify the grace, and love, and saving power of Christ. When the mind begins to revolve about self as its center, it ceases, to the same extent, to revolve about Christ; and when it glories in self, it ceases to glory in the cross of Christ, and will soon be the object of Divine reprobation.[1]

---
[1] Mahan, *The Baptism of the Holy Ghost*, p. 129.

While Men Slept...

Another major deception which Mahan described among some who have received the Holy Ghost was that they undervalued any knowledge that was not spiritually revealed to them. Thus, they would neglect study, claiming that they were only taught by God. Mahan described the outcome for such people as he wrote:

> We have known individuals who have attained to the highest forms of the higher life afterwards "make shipwreck of the faith," by assuming that they were infallibly taught all forms of revealed truth, and then bitterly denouncing as unspiritual, worldly, sensual, and devilish, all who questioned any of their nudest absurdities. We have known individuals, once deeply spiritual, by imperiously placing themselves above all need of human teaching, under the claim that they were taught of God, manifest the most proud, boastful, fanatical, and hateful spirit and character of which we can conceive.
>
> We have known ministers of bright promise, and who were once "full of faith and of the Holy Ghost," become empty and void in their own hearts, and utterly powerless with the Church and world, and that because they relied upon Divine teaching to the neglect of study, inquiry, watching unto prayer, and the diligent use and cultivation of their own faculties.[2]

As we shall learn, the Great Wales Revival of 1904 had a tragic outcome, with the presence of deceiving spirits. Following their disastrous encounter with false spirits, the two people who were key to starting the Revival, Jessie Penn-Lewis and Evan Roberts, pointed out that after one receives a filling with the Holy Ghost, he becomes open to the spiritual world. As the work of the Spirit occupies the attention of the believer, an opportunity comes for:

> ... the arch-deceiver to commence his wiles under a new form. If the man is untaught in the Scriptural statements of the work of the Triune God, to "obey the Spirit" is now his supreme purpose; and to counterfeit the guidance of the Spirit, and the Spirit Himself, is now the deceiver's scheme; for he must some-

---

[2] Ibid., pp. 130-131.

how regain power over this servant of God, so as to render him useless for aggressive warfare against the forces of darkness, drive him back into the world, or in some way side-track him from active service for God.[3]

Pointing Us to Other Gods

Throughout the history of Israel, there was a struggle between the worshippers of pagan gods and goddesses and those descendants of Abraham, Isaac, and Jacob who worshipped God, who was known as יהוה (YHWH).[4] Many of the people of Israel also often found themselves worshipping the gods and goddesses of the pagans. Even the great King Solomon, the son of David, struggled between his love for YHWH and the worship of the pagan gods and goddesses of his wives. After Solomon married the daughter of Pharaoh, the King of Egypt, he compromised his love for YHWH by sacrificing to pagan gods:

> And Solomon loved the LORD, walking in the statutes of David his father: only he sacrificed and burnt incense in high places.
>
> —1 Kings 3:3

What other gods did Solomon worship? As explained in I Kings, they were Ashtoreth, Milcom, Chemosh, and Molech:

> For Solomon went after Ashtoreth the goddess of the Zidonians, and after Milcom the abomination of the Ammonites. And Solomon did evil in the sight of the LORD, and went not fully after the LORD, as *did* David his father. Then did Solomon build an high place for Chemosh, the abomination of Moab, in the hill that *is* before Jerusalem, and for Molech, the abomination of the children of Ammon.
>
> —1 Kings 11: 5-7

---

[3] Jessie Penn-Lewis, with Evan Roberts, *War on the Saints*, unabridged ed. (1st ed. published in 1912; New York: Thomas E. Lowe, Ltd., 10th printing of 9th ed., 1994), p. 52.

[4] As we have learned, His name has also been translated as YAHWEH and as JEHOVAH. Many English Bibles also replace YHWH with "the LORD."

While Men Slept...

Worshipping the Goddess

Ashtoreth, the goddess of the Zidonians, was the first of the gods mentioned among those that Solomon worshipped. This female deity has been known by many names, including Astarte and Ishtar.[5] As Ishtar, the Babylonian goddess was known by titles that included the "Mother of gods and of men" and the "Queen of Heaven." She was believed to be the source of all life on earth.[6] Even though the LORD (יהוה) clearly cautioned against worshipping the "queen of heaven" through the prophet Jeremiah, the people of Judah were determined to ignore the warnings and do whatever they wanted to do:

> The children gather wood, and the fathers kindle the fire, and the women knead *their* dough, to make cakes to the queen of heaven, and to pour out drink offerings unto other gods, that they may provoke me to anger.
>
> —Jeremiah 7:18

> *As for* the word that thou hast spoken unto us in the name of the LORD, we will not hearken unto thee. But we will certainly do whatsoever thing goeth forth out of our own mouth, to burn incense unto the queen of heaven, and to pour out drink offerings unto her, as we have done, we, and our fathers, our kings, and our princes, in the cities of Judah, and in the streets of Jerusalem: for *then* had we plenty of victuals, and were well, and saw no evil.
>
> —Jeremiah 44:16-17

Why were the people of Judah so determined to worship the "queen of heaven?" It appears that they believed the goddess brought them both peace and prosperity. They believed the goddess had power over these things.

---

[5] C. Kerenyi, *The Gods of the Greeks* (London: Thames and Hudson, 1951), p. 67.

[6] Lewis R. Farnell, *Greece and Babylon: A Comparative Sketch of Mesopotamian, Anatolian, and Hellenic Religions* (Edinburgh: T. & T. Clark, 1911), p. 120.

Who is the Goddess?

Whoever the goddess is, there has been a strong desire to worship her as god for thousands of years throughout the world. Some believe the concept of the goddess goes back to Eve and her encounter with the serpent in the Garden of Eden. Some Roman Catholics taught that the ancient goddess was really a representation of the Virgin Mary, known to them as the "Mother of God," who would crush the serpent under her feet. According to Mathieu Orsini, for example, in his *History of the Blessed Virgin, Mother of God*:

> A daughter of Eve, a woman of *masculine* courage, was to crush the head of the serpent beneath her feet, and to regenerate for ever a guilty race; that woman was Mary.[7] [Italics are in the original.]

Orsini's account of the role of the woman as the conquerer of the serpent was consistent with the account given in the Roman Catholic Douay-Rheims Bible. It says that the *woman* shall crush the head of the serpent, which will then lie in wait for her heel. It reads:

> I will put enmities between thee and the woman, and thy seed and her seed: **she** shall crush thy head, and thou shalt **lie in wait for her heel.**
>
> —Genesis 3:15 (Douay-Rheims)[8]
> [Bold type is shown for emphasis.]

A similar account of the role of the woman in relation to the serpent, however, is not found in most other versions of the Bible. According to the Authorized Version, for example, the Conqueror of the ser-

---

[7] Mathieu Orsini, *Life of the Blessed Virgin, Mother of God; with the History of the Devotion to Her*, J. Sadlier, trans. (New York: D. & J. Sadlier & Co., c1854), p. 1.

[8] *The Holy Bible Translated from the Latin Vulgate: Diligently Compared with the Hebrew, Greek, and Other Editions, in Divers Languages: The Old Testament First Published by the English College, at Douay, A.D. 1609; and the New Testament First Published by the English College at Rheims, A.D. 1582* (New York: Edward Dunigan & Brother, 1850), p. 7.

pent, which represents Satan, is masculine, rather than feminine. It says that her *seed* shall bruise the head of the serpent, which will bruise *his* heel. It reads:

> And I will put enmity between thee and the woman, and be-tween thy seed and her seed; **it** shall bruise thy head, and thou shalt **bruise his heel**. [Bold type is shown for emphasis.]
> —Genesis 3:15

So who is the Conqueror of Satan, the *woman* or the *seed* of the woman? Recall that the Apostle Paul explained that the promises of God were made to Abraham and his seed, which is Jesus Christ:

> Now to Abraham and his seed were the promises made. He saith not, And to seeds, as of many; but as of one, And to thy seed, which is Christ.
> —Galatians 3:16

According to Orsini, however, since the most ancient time of history it was believed that a woman, whom he thought to be the Virgin Mary, would repair the evil that had been done by another. He wrote that this tradition kept up the hopes of a fallen race as they were dispersed on the "plains of Sennaar." (This area is often called "Shinar," which was the location of ancient Babylon.) He claimed that a belief in the Virgin and the Messiah survived the flood and manifested itself through different cultures, including those of Japan, India, China, Egypt, Babylon, and other regions throughout the world.[9]

Alexander Hislop, in his book, *The Two Babylons*, also believed that the ancient goddess was first recognized in the land of Shinar.[10] According to Hislop, Semiramis, who was both the wife *and mother* of Nimrod, was the first queen of Babylon and a builder of towers. Nimrod, was the son of Cush, who was the son of Ham, who was the

---

[9] Orsini, *Life of the Blessed Virgin, Mother of God*, pp. 1-6.

[10] Alexander Hislop, *The Two Babylons* (Ontario, California: Chick Publica-tions, no date; first published as a pamphlet in 1853 and greatly expanded in 1858), pp. 21-30.

son of Noah, whose family survived the flood (see Genesis 9 and 10). We learn of Nimrod's might in the Book of Genesis:

> And Cush begat Nimrod: he began to be a mighty one in the earth.
>
> —Genesis 10:8

According to Hislop, Semiramis was worshipped under the names of Rhea or Cybele (known as Kybele to the Greeks) as the great goddess "Mother." Nimrod, under the name Ninus, was worshipped as "The Son." Representing Semiramis, who was a builder of towers, Cybele wore a turreted, or towered, crown.[11] Cybele was known as the "Great Mother, or as "Mother," or as "Mother Goddess."[12] There were more than one thousand names for the "Mother Goddess."[13] Among these names were Aphrodite, Athena, Gaia, and Minerva to the Greeks. They also included Venus to the Romans and Cyprians, Astarte to the Phoenicians, Ceridwan to the Celts, Diana to the Ephesians, Isis to the Egyptians, Ishtar to the Babylonians, Juno to the Romans, Sophia to the Gnostics, Kali to the Indians, and Mary to the [Roman Catholic] Christians.[14, 15, 16] These various symbols and names represented the archetype, or the pattern, of the goddess, which was also known as the "Great Mother.[17]"

Throughout history, the specific names used for the "Mother Goddess," or "Great Mother," largely depended upon the times and cul-

---

[11] Ibid.

[12] Lynn E. Roller, *In Search of God the Mother: The Cult of Anatolian Cybele* (Berkeley: University of California Press, 1999), p. 1

[13] Monier Williams, *Religious Thought and Life in India, Part 1: Vedism, Brahmanism, and Hinduism* (London: John Murray, 1883), p. 187.

[14] Hislop, *The Two Babylons*, p. 75.

[15] Alex Jack, *The New Age Dictionary* (Brookline, Massachusetts: Kanthaka Press, 1976), pp. 135-136.

[16] Nikhilananda, *Vivekananda: A Biography,* p. 214.

[17] Erich Neumann, *The Great Mother: An Analysis of the Archtype*, Ralph Manheim, trans., Bollingen Foundation, Inc., Series 47, (New York:., Pantheon Books Inc., 1954), p. 11.

tures of the worshippers. Those who recognized the importance of calling the goddess by another name in different cultures were able to appeal to worshippers by simply honoring her by a different name. For example, when Alexander the Great (356-323 B.C.) conquered Egypt for Greece, he was careful to honor both the gods and goddesses of Egypt as well as those of Greece. When he marked out the ground plan for the City of Alexandria, he laid out temples that were to be built for both the Greek gods and for the Egyptian goddess, Isis. As a result of Alexander's actions, the Egyptian cult of Isis, Osiris, and Horus was also spread throughout much of the Greek world.[18]

A major deity to the Greeks in Ephesus was Artemis, who was known to the Romans as Diana. The goddess, like Cybele, was known as the virgin "Mother of the gods" and also wore a tower-bearing crown.[19] Alexander Hislop believed the tower-bearing goddess to be the "God of forces" that Daniel wrote about while he was a captive in Babylon. Daniel described a king who would rise up and, without regard for the God of his fathers, would honor the "God of forces," as he wrote:

> Neither shall he regard the God of his fathers, nor the desire of women, nor regard any god: for he shall magnify himself above all. But in his estate shall he honour the God of forces: and a god whom his fathers knew not shall he honour with gold, and silver, and with precious stones, and pleasant things.
> —Daniel 11:37-38

The word "forces" is from the Hebrew word מָעוֹז, "maowz" and related derivations, meaning "a fortified place."[20] Who is this "God of forces" that Daniel wrote about? As the tower-bearing goddess, Hislop thought that Semiramis, Cybele, Diana, and related goddesses

[18] Irad Malkin, *Religion and Colonization in Ancient Greece* (Leiden, The Netherlands: E. J. Brill, 1987), p. 106.

[19] Hislop, *The Two Babylons*, pp. 21-30.

[20] James Strong, "Hebrew and Chaldee Dictionary," In *The Exhaustive Concordance of the Bible: Showing Every Word of the Text of the Common English Version of the Canonical Books and Every Occurrence of Each Word in Regular Order, Together with Dictionaries of the Hebrew and Greek Words of the Original, with References to the English Words* (Peabody, Massachusetts: Hendrickson Publishers, undated; a reprint of the original), p. 69.

represented the "goddess of fortifications," which he believed to be the "God of forces."[21]

Worshipping the goddess as Diana was common in Asia and throughout the world during the early years of Christianity. Through the controversy created by the Apostle Paul as he challenged the worship of man made images, such as those of Diana in Ephesus, it is clear that such worship was considered by him to be false and not compatible with Christianity. After Paul had persuaded people that these images were not even gods, Demetrius, the silversmith, complained:

> Moreover ye see and hear, that not alone at Ephesus, but almost throughout all Asia, this Paul hath persuaded and turned away much people, saying that they be no gods, which are made with hands: So that not only this our craft is in danger to be set at nought; but also that the temple of the great goddess Diana should be despised, and her magnificence should be destroyed, whom all Asia and the world worshippeth.
> —Acts 19:26-27

Those who depended upon the worship of the images of Diana for their livelihood had much to fear. Christianity was displacing Diana worship. Their fears were realized as Christianity gained dominance in the Roman Empire and Emperor Theodosius repressed the worship of Diana in A.D. 380. Being deprived of their goddess, the people of Ephesus soon turned to Mary, who was an alternative that was acceptable to Christianity.[22] In Ephesus, Mary was no longer recognized as being the mother of Jesus, James, Joses, Juda, and Simon, as well as of Jesus' sisters, as Mark had written:

---

[21] Hislop, *The Two Babylons*, pp. 21-30.

[22] "Historical Introduction, The Third Ecumenical Council: The Council of Ephesus, The Seven Ecumenical Councils of the Undivided Church," Henry R. Percival, ed., In *A Select Library of the Nicene and Post-Nicene Fathers of the Christian Church*, series 2, vol. 14, Philip Schaff and Henry Wace, eds. (Grand Rapids, Michigan: Wm. B. Eerdmans Publishing Company, Reprinted 1979), pp. 192-195.

> Is not this the carpenter, the son of Mary, the brother of James, and Joses, and of Juda, and Simon? and are not his sisters here with us? And they were offended at him.
>
> —Mark 6:3

Instead, the "Virgin Mary" replaced the Mary of the New Testament. The status of the Virgin Mary was soon increased from the mother of Jesus and His brothers and sisters to that of being the "Mother of God." The decision to elevate the status of the Virgin Mary occurred at a council in Ephesus in A.D. 431 in the midst of a heated political battle between Cyril, the Patriarch of Alexandria, and Nestorius, the Patriarch of Constantinople. Cyril supported the new title while Nestorius and the Syrian bishops, including John, the Patriarch of Antioch, opposed it. To repress the controversy, Cyril called Ephesian council to order and excommunicated Nestorius, even though he was not present.[23]

The Virgin Mary was said to have taken possession of numerous goddess temples, including those of Ceres and Venus in Sicily, of Isis at Soisseons in France, and of Athena at the Parthenon in Greece. Soon, she shared common feast days with other goddesses. For example, the feast day for the goddess Diana, August 15, also became the day for celebrating the feast of Dormition, or Falling Asleep of the Virgin, around A.D. 600 and, later, the feast day for the Assumption of the Virgin Mary into heaven.[24, 25, 26] [In 1 Kings 12:32-33, we learn that Jeroboam, the first king of the northern house of Israel, devised in his own heart a feast in the "eighth month, on the fifteenth day of the month" in which he sacrificed to golden calves.] There is also evidence to suggest that the cult of the Virgin Mary in the early centuries of Christianity had strong links to that of the pagan Celtic mother-goddesses among the Irish and the Welsh. For example, the Chartres Cathedral was built on the site of a subterranean sanctuary of a Celtic

---

[23] Ibid.

[24] Anne Baring and Jules Cashford, *The Myth of the Goddess: Evolution of an Image* (London: Penguin Books Ltd., 1993), p. 551.

[25] Ibid.

[26] Patrichia Monaghan, *The New Book of Goddesses and Heroines* (St. Paul, Minnesota: Llewellyn Publishers, 1998), p. 103.

mother-goddess. The shrine was called "Our Lady under the Ground." Mary was associated with the healing properties of water. Sacred wells with alleged curative properties were dedicated to her throughout Wales.[27] Shrines to the Virgin Mary have also arisen in many of the places where the goddess Cybele was worshipped.[28]

Although not officially recognized as a goddess, Roman Catholic Church dogma has continually elevated Mary, whose birth and death are not mentioned in the Scriptures. Increased attention was given to Mariology after the formation of the Jesuits in the sixteenth century. For example, in 1577 a Jesuit named Peter Canisius (1521-1597) published *De Maria Virgine Incomparabili*. A Spanish Jesuit, Francis Suarez (1548-1617), developed a systematic theology on Mary.[29] Her titles were increased from that of the mother of Jesus Christ to the "Mother of God," "Perpetually Virgin," "Immaculately Conceived," and "Assumed into Heaven," where she is called its "Queen."[30] According to Lawrence S. Cunningham, a professor of theology at Notre Dame University, the 1950 proclamation of the dogma of the Assumption of Mary into heaven by Pope Pius XII was:

> ...the only infallible pronouncement made by any pope after the doctrine of papal infallibility was proclaimed at the First Vatican Council in 1870.[31]

A Hindu View of the Goddess

As with many cultures and religions throughout history, the Hindus also believe the supreme god to be feminine. Even the Word, or *Logos*, which is masculine in Christianity is the feminine word, *Vak*, in San-

---

[27]Miranda Green, *Celtic Goddesses: Warriors, Virgins and Mothers* (London: British Museum Press, 1995), p. 189.

[28] Maarten J. Vermaseren, *Cybele and Attis: the Myth and the Cult* (London: Thames and Hudson, 1977), p. 182.

[29] Lawrence S. Cunningham, "Mary in Catholic Doctrine and Practice," *Theology Today*, vol. 56, no. 3, October, 1999, pp. 313-314.

[30] Anne Baring and Jules Cashford, *The Myth of the Goddess*, p. 549.

[31] Lawrence S. Cunningham, "Mary in Catholic Doctrine and Practice," *Theology Today*, vol. 56, no. 3, October, 1999, pp. 314-315.

skrit.[32] Thus, the Christian book of John expresses the Word of creation as masculine as it says:

> In the beginning was the Word, and the Word was with God, and the Word was God. The same was in the beginning with God. All things were made by **him**; and without him was not any thing made that was made. [Bold type is shown for emphasis.]
>
> —John 1:1-3

The Hindu Tandya Maha Brahmana, on the other hand, expresses the Word as being feminine:

> This, [in the beginning] was the only Lord of the Universe. His Word was with him. This Word was his second. He contemplated. He said, "I will deliver this Word so that **she** will produce and bring into being all this world." [Bold type is shown for emphasis.]
>
> —TMB [Tandya Maha Brahmana] 20, 14, 2[33]

The Hindu goddess, Devi, of which Kali is one form, is believed in Hindu India to be the one true goddess, from which all other goddesses are expressed.[34] In 1962, Swami Budhananda described the one true goddess as the "Mother Supreme of the Universe" who has all power. He said:

> She is surpassingly beautiful. She is again surprisingly fearful. The aspirant must adore her in both these aspects. She is the lover of sacrifice of blood ("*balipriya*," "*rudhira-priya*"), again She is the giver of boons ("*varada*"). She is the force of good and She is the force of evil. The Ahriman of the Persians and the Satan of the Bible are all She.[35]

---

[32] Francis Vineeth, "Theology of Adisabda and OM," ch. 15, In *Indian Christian Spirituality*, D. S. Amalorpavadass, ed. (Bangalore, India: National Biblical Catechetical and Liturgical Centre, 1982), p. 125.

[33] Ibid.

[34] Monaghan, *The New Book of Goddesses & Heroines*, p. 177.

[35] Swami Budhananda, *Worship of God as Mother*, *The Vedanta Kesari* (Madras-4, India: Sri Ramakrishna Math), vol. 49 (6), October, 1962, pp. 250-251.

Thus, according to Swami Budhananda's account, the worship of the goddess is the worship of Satan.

Goddess Worship as Spirit Worship

In addition to the Hindu belief that a goddess is the creative force of the universe, goddess worship is also closely tied with spiritualism or spirit worship. Scholars of the occult claim that the Holy Spirit or Holy Ghost, although appearing masculine in name or title, was believed by some early "Church Fathers," such as Origen and Jerome, to be a feminine cosmic force or influence.[36] In the Hindu Vedanta, "the Holy Mother" is believed to be a spiritual force, called Sakti or Force or Energy. Ramakrishna, who was the teacher of Vivekananda, believed there was no difference between Brahman and Kali, except that it was Kali when engaged in activities. Thus, the supreme god of power was believed to be Kali, who was a form of Devi, or "the Mother."[37] The Latin goddess, Diana, which, as we have learned, was known to the Greeks as Artemis, was also closely connected with the spirit world. Diana was the female deity of the sun who also became known as the "resort of ghosts and fays."[38]

According to Hindu Swami Budhananda, the worship of God as Mother makes a connection with the primordial energy of the universe. He said:

> And when that connection is discovered we can become all powerful, realizing the fact that at our back is the surging ocean of power, the limitless Sakti, of which we are but waves.[39]

---

[36] G. de Purucker, *Fountain-Source of Occultism*, Grace F. Knoche, ed. (Pasadena, California: Theosophical University Press, 1974), pp. 311, 657-658.

[37] Nirod Baran Chakraborty, "The Holy Mother as a Spiritual Force," In *Bulletin of the Ramakrishna Mission Institute of Culture*, vol. 27, no. 12 (Calcutta: Ramakrishna Mission Institute of Culture, December 1976), pp. 243-248.

[38] Anon., "Spiritualism, Chapter 2," *The Catholic World*, vol. 18, no. 105, December, 1873, pp. 318-337.

[39] Budhananda, *Worship of God as Mother*, p. 255.

While Men Slept...

Goddess-worship, or Saktism, is ultimately the worship of divine energy or power.[40] Monier Williams (1819-1899), professor of Sanskrit at Oxford University, concluded in 1883 that:

> ...Saktism is Hinduism arrived at its worst and most corrupt stage of development.[41]

After offering a graphic translation of a description of Kali, Williams continued saying:

> It is this goddess who thirsts for blood, and especially for human blood; and if the blood of animals is not offered to her, she takes that of men. In [sic] one of the Tantras kings are directed to appease her by the sacrifice of human beings (narabali). The blood of a tiger is said to satisfy her for 100 years, and that of a man for 1000 years.
>
> It might have been expected that a creed like this, which admits of an infinite multiplication of female deities and makes every woman an object of worship, would be likely to degenerate into various forms of licentiousness on the one hand and witchcraft on the other. But if such consequences might have been anticipated, the actual fact has been worse than the most gloomy pessimist could possibly have foretold. In Saktism we are confronted with the worst results of the worst superstitious ideas that have ever disgraced and degraded the human race.[42]

The "Mystic Circle" and Spirit Worship

Williams continued by graphically describing Saktism, or goddess-worship, the details of which initiates are forbidden to reveal to the "uninitiated." He said that, while education and the spread of Christianity throughout India were:

---

[40] Williams, *Religious Thought and Life in India, Part 1*, p. 187.

[41] Ibid., pp. 184-185.

[42] Ibid., p. 190.

...gradually operating to abolish all the grosser forms of Saktism, as they have already helped to do away with Sati, female infanticide, human sacrifices, and other monstrous evils. Still it is well known that even in the present day, on particular occasions, the adherents of the sect go through the whole ceremonial in all its revolting entirety. When such occasions occur, a circle is formed composed of men and women seated side by side without respect of caste or relationship. [according to the doctrine of one of the Tantras, where Siva, the male god, addresses his wife] ...and says "All men have my form and all women thy form; any one who recognizes any distinction of caste in the mystic circle (Cakra) has a foolish soul."[43]

The participants in the "mystic circle" then proceed to drink alcoholic beverages, eat (meat, fish, and grain), and perform sexual acts.[44] These goddess worshippers worship a "mighty mysterious Force" and are called "left-handed worshippers" because they worship the female, or left-handed, side of the deity.[45] The worship of Kali is the worship of the demon that instills evil thoughts into men's hearts.[46] Thus, the worship of Devi as Kali is to worship that which is on the left side of the male deity, which is known as Siva. Hindus who worship the goddess as Mother believe that she has control over magical powers.[47]

Are There False Spirits?

Spritualism: The Work of Spirits or the Mind?

As we have learned, Asa Mahan, through his book entitled *The Baptism of the Holy Ghost*, provided the foundation for the Keswick Convention higher life theology, which led to the slogan on July 1, 1875: "Be filled with the Holy Spirit!"[48] For at least twenty years

---

[43] Ibid., pp. 191-192.

[44] Ibid., p. 192.

[45] Ibid., p. 185.

[46] Ibid., p. 238.

[47] Ibid., p. 229.

[48] Figgis, *Keswick from Within*, p. 57.

prior to writing this book, Mahan had been very deeply involved in investigating the phenomenon known as spiritualism. He wrote:

> Since the year 1850, our residence has been in several of the grand centres of this movement [spiritualism], and where, consequently, the mysterious phenomena were continuously forced upon our attention.[49, 50]

Mahan published the above quote in his book, *Modern Mysteries Explained and Exposed*, in 1855. He then repeated the quote twenty years later in the London edition of *The Phenomena of Spiritualism*, during the year of the first Keswick Convention. After being forced to resign his position as president of Oberlin College following his return from England in 1850, his principal place of residency until 1855 was Cleveland, Ohio (1850-1855). He then moved on to Jackson, Michigan (1855-1858), Adrian, Michigan (1858-1874), and London, England (1874-1875).[51, 52] [Mahan lived in London until 1884 and then moved to Eastbourne where he lived until his death in 1889.][53] The list of Mahan's residences prior to 1875 undoubtedly included those "grande centres" of spiritualism that he described.

Mahan made his 1849-50 trip to England in the midst of significant revivalist, spiritualist, and ecclesiastical activity within the country. While Mahan was in England, his close friend and colleague from Oberlin College, Charles Finney, was also there conducting revivals in meetings which were attended by large numbers of nonconformists. Finney was particularly impressed with an interaction he had with an unnamed Unitarian minister.[54] The Russian-born spiritualist, Helena Petrovna Blavatsky (1831-1891), also embarked on travels in

---

[49] Asa Mahan, *Modern Mysteries: Explained and Exposed* (Boston: John P. Jewett and Company; Cleveland: Jewett, Proctor and Worthington; New York: Sheldon, Lamport and Blakeman; London: Trubner and Co., 1855), p. iii.

[50] Mahan, *The Phenomena of Spiritualism* [London, 1875], p. v.

[51] Madden and Hamilton, *Freedom and Grace: The Life of Asa Mahan*, pp. 99, 106, 150.

[52] Ibid, pp. 129, 147, 152, 209.

[53] Ibid., p. 209.

[54] Finney, *Memoirs of Rev. Charles G. Finney*, p. 396.

1849 that took her to, among other places, England, America, and India. Her work on spiritualism was supported by money from an "unknown source."[55] Also, as we recall, during 1849, Henry Manning participated in secret meetings with influential figures in both church and state as members of the "Sterling Club."[56] As we have learned, he converted to Roman Catholicism the year following Pope Pius IX's re-establishment of the Roman Catholic Church in England in 1850.[57]

Whether these events of 1849 and 1850 in England affected Mahan's decision to become involved in spiritualism investigations is not clear. What is clear, however, is his statement that he had been involved in spiritualism research since 1850.[58] Mahan published his work on spiritualism, *The Phenomonena of Spiritualism: Scientifically Explained and Exposed,* in England in 1875 and then in America in 1876.[59, 60] Also, during 1875, the first year of the Keswick Convention, Mahan published *The Baptism of the Holy Ghost* in England.[61] (As already stated, the book had previously been published in America in 1870.)

Many of the examples Mahan reported in *The Phenomonena of Spiritualism* occurred either in Adrian, Michigan or in Blissfield, Michigan. Blissfield was a small town located ten miles east of his home in Adrian.[62] Since Mahan left Adrian in 1874 for England, never to return, it appears that some of his work on spiritualism was accomplished while he was at Adrian College between 1859 and 1874 while he prepared his book, *The Baptism of the Holy Ghost.*

---

[55] *H. P. Blavatsky: Collected Writings, 1874-1878*, vol. 1, Boris de Zirkoff, compiler (Wheaton, IL: The Theosophical Press, 1966), pp. xxv-lii.

[56] Maurice, *The Life of Frederick Denison Maurice*, vol. 1, p. 516.

[57] Walker et al., *A History of the Christian Church*, p. 643.

[58] Mahan, *Modern Mysteries: Explained and Exposed*, p. iii.

[59] Asa Mahan, *The Phenomena of Spiritualism: Scientifically Explained and Exposed* (London: Hodder and Stoughton, 1875), p. iii.

[60] Asa Mahan, *The Phenomena of Spiritualism: Scientifically Explained and Exposed* (New York, Chicago, and New Orleans: A. S. Barnes and Co., 1876), p. iii.

[61] Asa Mahan, *The Baptism of the Holy Ghost* (London: Elliot Stock, 1876).

[62] Mahan, *The Phenomena of Spiritualism* [London, 1875], pp. 42-60.

While Men Slept...

In his book on *The Phenomena of Spiritualism*, Mahan concluded that the manifestations attributed to spiritualism, as witnessed in spirit-circle seances, were indeed real! He reasoned that the occurrence of strange events must be accepted, otherwise Christian miracles could not be accepted. He said:

> We found, then, that we had to admit the facts, or take the ground that no strange events can be established by testimony. How, then, could we ask the world to believe in Christian miracles? We found equally valid evidence for the reality of the facts of Spiritualism, as far as the intelligent communications are concerned.[63]

After a series of experiments on the manifestations that occurred in spirit circles, Mahan concluded that a force existed in the minds of the participants that produced results which many believed to be caused by spirits. He reasoned that:

> ...the action of the force developed in these circles is, when the proper conditions are fulfilled, controlled by mental states; an absolute accordance being obtained here between the most secret thought and visible and audible effects...The mental states where here controlled the action of this force existed in the minds, or a mind, within the circle, and not in those of spirits from another sphere...The fundamental error of Spiritualism is a misapprehension in regard to the *location* of the mental states which control the action of this force in the production of these phenomena.[64]

Mahan continued by assuring his readers that he had scientifically proven the mundane origins of the manifestations that spiritualists claimed were caused by spirits.[65] He made his point in six key conclusions, which he had presented in the 1855 edition of his *Modern Mysteries* and then repeated in the 1876 American edition of his *The Phenomena of Spiritualism*. [The 1875 London edition of the same book

---

[63] Ibid., p. vii.

[64] Ibid., pp. 255-256.

[65] Ibid., p. 256.

390

contained two fewer pages in the Preface than did the 1876 American edition.] In his 1855 and 1876 books, Mahan clearly stated that *all spiritual phenomena, including witchcraft, necromancy, fortune-telling, and other similiar phenomena, had no spiritual dimension.* He concluded that *all* manifestations previously believed to be caused by spirits were the result of a physical phenomenon, known as the "Odylic Force." Other terms used for this phenomenon of mental force were the odylic, odic, or psychic force. Mahan wrote that:

1. There is in nature...which we denominate the Odylic Force.
2. This force is identical with the cause of all the mesmeric and clairvoyant phenomena, on the one hand, and with the immediate cause of these manifestations, on the other.
3. By a reference to the properties and laws of this force as developed in the spirit-circles, and to its relations to the minds constituting the same, we can account most fully for all the spirit-phenomena, of every kind, without the supposition of the presence or agency of disembodied spirits. Consequently, the hypothesis of Spiritualism is wholly unsustained by any valid evidence whatever.
4. The entire real facts of Spiritualism demand the supposition that this force in the production of these communications is controlled exclusively, for the most part unconsciously, by the minds in the circles, and not by disembodied spirits out of the same.
5. We finally found, what we did not at first expect, that we had developed facts and principles which gave an equally ready and satisfactory explanation of the phenomena of witchcraft, necromancy, fortune-telling, etc., etc., phenomena which from time to time have been the wonder and terror of mankind in all ages.
6. Other consequences of equal and far greater importance seemed undeniably to follow from our facts and deductions.[66, 67]

---

[66] Mahan, *Modern Mysteries Explained And Exposed*, pp. vi-vii.

[67] Mahan, *The Phenomena of Spiritualism* [New York, Chicago, and New Orleans, 1876], pp. ix-x.

While Men Slept...

In his 1855 *Modern Mysteries*, Mahan rejected Emanuel Swedenborg's claims that he had supernatural visions and communicated with the spirits of the dead. Mahan wrote of Swedenborg:

> We agree with the public generally, in regarding the latter [Swedenborg] as honestly supposing himself a divinely commissioned revelator, while he was utterly deceived in that supposition.[68]

While Swedenborg may have been deceived into believing that he communicated with the dead and that the voices and visions he received were from God, Mahan rejected the prospect that they could have been manifestations of supernatural phenomena. Instead, Mahan insisted that all manifestations that might be attributed to false spirits are mental and not spiritual. On April 27, 1875, which was about a month before the Brighton Conference where he was president of the sectional meetings on the Baptism of the Holy Ghost, Mahan calmed the public fears about false spirits. He wrote that the "ghosts" had been exposed and "the spirits" had been caught:

> Facts of recent occurrence have fully prepared the public mind, as we judge, to receive a scientific explanation of the real phenomena of Spiritualism, the impositions of the system having been so fully exposed. Since the following treatise was put into the printer's hands, in every remaining place not therein referred to, where ghosts have been professedly exhibited-in the United States, for example-the impositions have been fully exposed, "the spirits" having been caught, and demonstrated to be men or women in the flesh. With these suggestions the work before us is commended to the careful and candid examination of the reader.[69]

The phenomena that Mahan said he had "scientifically" attributed to Odylic, or mental, forces, the Word of God, however, attributes to familiar spirits, which are an abomination to the LORD (YHWH):

---

[68] Mahan, *Modern Mysteries Explained And Exposed*, p. 465.

[69] Mahan, *The Phenomena of Spiritualism* [New York, Chicago, and New Orleans, 1876], p. x.

There shall not be found among you *any one* that maketh his son or his daughter to pass through the fire, *or* that useth divination, *or* an observer of times, or an enchanter, or a witch, Or a charmer, or a consulter with familiar spirits, or a wizard, or a necromancer. For all that do these things *are* an abomination unto the LORD: and because of these abominations the LORD thy God doth drive them out from before thee.

—Deuteronomy 18:10-12

If one were to accept Mahan's conclusion, he would believe that the "Odylic Force," rather than false spirits, explains biblical accounts of the supernatural phenomena that are opposed by God, as seen in the following examples:

Regard not them that have familiar spirits, neither seek after wizards, to be defiled by them: I *am* the LORD your God.

— Leviticus 19:31

And Saul disguised himself, and put on other raiment, and he went, and two men with him, and they came to the woman by night: and he said, I pray thee, divine unto me by the familiar spirit, and bring me *him* up, whom I shall name unto thee. And the woman said unto him, Behold, thou knowest what Saul hath done, how he hath cut off those that have familiar spirits, and the wizards, out of the land: wherefore then layest thou a snare for my life, to cause me to die?

—1 Samuel 28:8-9

And when they shall say unto you, Seek unto them that have familiar spirits, and unto wizards that peep, and that mutter: should not a people seek unto their God? for the living to the dead?

—Isaiah 8:19

And certain women, which had been healed of evil spirits and infirmities, Mary called Magdalene, out of whom went seven devils,

—Luke 8:2

> For unclean spirits, crying with loud voice, came out of many that were possessed *with them*: and many taken with palsies, and that were lame, were healed.
>
> —Acts 8:7

> Now the Spirit speaketh expressly, that in the latter times some shall depart from the faith, giving heed to seducing spirits, and doctrines of devils;
>
> —1 Timothy 4:1

Theosophy and Psychical Research

While as early as 1855 Mahan concluded that he had disproved that spiritualism was associated with spirits, the Spiritualist Movement was making major progress. By 1875, Madam Blavatsky had become a well-known "spiritualist" who on September 7, 1875 helped form the Theosophical Society in New York.[70] Meanwhile, the Psychical Research Society, whose president was the son of the former vicar of St. John's Anglican Church in Keswick, who was followed in that position by the leader of the Keswick Convention, was also making great progress.

The Psychical Research Society, as we have learned, had common roots with the Ghost Society of Cambridge University, which had such well-known members as Hort, Westcott, and Sidgwick. The Psychical Research Society also had much in common with Madame Blavatsky, who was offered a membership in 1883.[71] In 1884, the Society appointed a committee to study the "marvelous phenomena" that was reported to have taken place in India in connection with Madame Blavatsky and members of the Theosophical Society.[72] The Psychical Research Society came to the conclusion that the spiritual phenomena in India were not caused by spirits.

---

[70] *H. P. Blavatsky: Collected Writings, 1874-1878*, vol. 1, pp. 122-123.

[71] *H. P. Blavatsky: Collected Writings, 1883*, Boris de Zirkoff, compiler (Los Angeles: Philosophical Research Society, Inc., 1950), p. 358.

[72] C. D. Broad, *Religion, Philosophy and Psychical Research* (New York: Harcourt, Brace & Company, Inc., 1953), p. 94.

While both Mahan and the Psychical Research Society questioned the validity of spiritual manifestations, key leaders in England considered the research to be of vital importance. William Ewart Gladstone, for example, who was the prime minister of England during the First Vatican Council and who was a close associate of the leaders of the Anglo-Catholic Oxford Movement, such as Henry Edward Manning and John Henry Newman, also took a strong interest in psychical research. He was quoted as saying that psychical research was: "The most important work, which is being done in the world. By far the most important."[73]

Spirits of India

Source of Vivekananda's Spirit of Unity

Swami Vivekananda's success in bringing the message of global unity of religions to the 1893 Chicago World's Parliament of Religions meeting was overwhelming. He brought a spirit of unity. From where did this spirit of unity come that he so successfully expounded? What was the spirit behind Vivekananda?

Vivekananda was trained at the feet of the "God-man" Ramakrishna (1836-1886) who, as a priest in the Kali temple, worshipped the deity as the "Divine Mother." When Ramakrishna felt the presence of the spirit of Kali, he "...dropped unconscious on the floor, experiencing within himself a constant flow of bliss."[74] His experiences of "deep spiritual emotions" and "apparent insanity" were described by one of his teachers as being "the result of an agonizing love for God." As he turned to Christianity and Islam, he became convinced that these religions, like Hinduism, were ways to realize "God-consciousness." He then began to worship his own wife as the "Divine Mother." He believed the "Divine Mother" would found a new religious order of those who would accept the doctrine of the "Universal Religion."[75]

---

[73] Quoted from *Journal of the Society for Psychical Research*, vol. 8, p. 260, 1898, In Aland Gauld, *The Founders of Psychical Research* (London: Routledge & Kegan Paul, 1968), p. 140.

[74] Nikhilananda, *Vivekanada: A Biography,* pp. 18-19.

[75] Ibid., pp. 20-22.

While Men Slept...

Vivekananda, who was known as Narendranath in his youth, received a British education and developed an appreciation for poets such as Wordsworth and Shelley, the works of John Stuart Mill, the universal reason of Hegel, and the "gospel of Liberty, Equality, and Fraternity of the French Revolution." Under the leadership of Ramakrishna, Vivekananda also became a devoted worshipper of the goddess Kali. He accepted Kali as the "Divine Mother of the universe," who "embodied in Herself creation and destruction, love and terror, life and death."[76]

The worship of Kali, who was also known as the "Terrible Mother," was a gruesome form of goddess worship. The temple of Kali in Calcutta, with its famous blood sacrifices, has been described as one of the "bloodiest temples on earth." The goddess required only blood offerings, so the sacrificial animals were beheaded, their blood drained, and the heads were offered to the goddess idols as trophies.[77] In a description of the "hideous aspect" of the "Goddess," Kali:

> ...the "dark one," raises the skull full of seething blood to her lips; her devotional image shows her dressed in blood red, standing in a boat floating on a sea of blood: in the midst of the life flood, the sacrificial sap, which she requires that she may, in her gracious manifestation (*sundara-murti*) as the World Mother (*jagad-amba*), bestow existence upon new living forms in a process of unceasing generation, that as world nurse (*jagad-dhatri*) she may suckle them on her breasts and give them the good that is "full nourishment" (*anna-purna*).[78]

Vivekananda's biographer quoted him in his worship of Kali as the Terrible Mother saying:

> I love terror for its own sake, despair for its own sake, misery for its own sake. Fight always. Fight and fight on, though

---

[76] Ibid., pp. 33-47.

[77] Neumann, *The Great Mother: An Analysis of the Archtype*, pp. 150-152.

[78] Zimmer, *Die indische Weltmutter*, pp. 179ff, Quoted in Erich Neumann, *The Great Mother*, p. 152.

always in defeat. That's the ideal! ...Worship the Terrible!
Worship Death! All else is in vain. All struggle is vain....[79]

Realizing that Kali worship would not be understood by universal
humanity, Vivekananda did not preach about Kali in public.[80] He did,
however, say:

> ...the Divine Mother Herself [Kali] willed the Parliament [of
> the World's Religions in 1893] in order to give him an oppor-
> tunity to present the Eternal Religion of the Hindus before the
> world at large, and that the stage was set for him to play his
> important role, everything else being incidental.[81]

Thus, Vivekananda believed that Kali, the "Divine Mother," willed
the Parliament of World's Religions so that he could bring the message of global unity of all religions to the world.

Imitators at the Mukti Revival

As part of his 1910 worldwide trip, Frank Bartleman traveled to both
India and Wales in the aftermath of the spiritual revivals in both countries which had been the forerunners to the revival which he had helped
bring to Asuza Street in Los Angeles in 1906. While in India, Bartleman
visited the Mukti home for orphaned and widowed girls run by Pandita
Ramabai. Many of the girls at the school had been part of a major
spiritual outpouring that occurred in 1905. Bartleman was excited to
meet Ramabai, who was then a renowned leader of Christian women's
causes. Like Bartleman, upon learning of the 1904 revival in Wales,
Ramabai had also sought a similar outpouring of the Holy Spirit in
India.[82, 83]

---

[79] Nikhilananda, *Vivekanada: A Biography,* p. 290.

[80] Ibid., pp. 36-47.

[81] Ibid., p. 117.

[82] Frank Bartleman, *Around the World by Faith: With Six Weeks in the Holy Land*
2nd ed. (Los Angeles: Frank Bartleman, undated; Reprinted in *Witness to Pentecost: The Life of Frank Bartleman, with a Preface by Cecil M. Robeck, Jr.* (New
York and London: Garland Publishing, Inc., 1985))., p. 68.

[83] Nicol Macnicol, *Builders of Modern India: Pandita Ramabai* (Calcutta: Association Press, 1930), pp. 116-117.

While Men Slept...

In response to concerns others had about the work of false spirits at the Mukti revival in India, Pandita Ramabai wrote of a man:

> ...I know that God gave him the power of the Holy Spirit to preach to sinners and bring them to repentance. He was a blessing to many people. But there came a time when flesh got the better of him, and he came under the power of the devil. What is the duty of his fellow-Christians toward him, and toward all of us, poor weak sinners, who find the devil too much for us? Let the Bible speak:
>> Brethren, if a man be overtaken in a fault, ye which are spiritual, restore such an one in the spirit of meekness; considering thyself, lest thou also be tempted. (Gal. 6:1) [Galatians 6:1]
>
> I do not want to argue the point. I do not say there are no imitators and no scoundrels among us. There are many, let it be confessed with great grief and humiliation.[84]

The Spirits at Azusa Street

Covering Up the Work of the False Spirits

Among the characteristic spiritual manifestations that Frank Bartleman reported from the Azusa Street revival was what he called "singing in the Spirit." He said that this "...peculiar 'gift' seemed to accompany the work wherever it broke out."[85] He also reported of the "spontaneous composition of hymns" as being a curious feature of some of the spiritual meetings that were occurring in India.[86] In Wales, a related phenomenon was called "Hywl."[87]

While Bartleman reported the presence of the Holy Spirit at Azusa Street, he also reported the presence of false spirits. Bartleman said the great news of the spiritual revival spread rapidly, drawing large

---

[84] Adhav, *Pandita Ramabai*, pp. 222-223.

[85] Bartleman, *How Pentecost Came to Los Angeles*, p. 101.

[86] Ibid., p. 37.

[87] Crowe, *Pentecostal Unity*, p. 16.

crowds to the meetings. While there were outside influences trying to attack the work, he said:

> We had the most fear from the working of evil spirits within. Even spiritualists and hypnotists came to investigate, and to try their influence. Then all the religious sore-heads and crooks and cranks came, seeking a place in the work. We had the most to fear from these. But this is always the danger to every new work. They have no place elsewhere. This condition cast a fear over many which was hard to overcome. It hindered the Spirit much. Many were afraid to seek God, for fear the devil might get them.[88]

The situation at Azusa Street eventually got out of control. By 1909, occult groups became the dominant factor in the meetings. Manifestations, including jerking and barking like a pack of dogs to "tree the devil," were reported.[89] Although Bartleman recognized the presence of false spirits at Azusa Street, he wanted to keep the spiritual movement going. Therefore, he sought to not call the attention of the people to the evil that he knew was also working in their midst. He said:

> We found early in the "Azusa" work that when we attempted to steady the Ark the Lord stopped working. We dared not call the attention of the people too much to the working of the evil.[90]

Exposing the Work of False Spirits

As the news of the outbreak of a spiritual movement at Azusa Street reached Parham he became concerned about the reports that the movement included a spirit of error, prompting him to visit the Azusa Street Mission during October 1906.[91] After he arrived, Parham sought to give biblical teaching against what he considered to be manifestations

---

[88] Bartleman, *How Pentecost Came to Los Angeles*, p. 49.

[89] Crowe, *Pentecostal Unity*, p. 20.

[90] Bartleman, *How Pentecost Came to Los Angeles*, p. 49.

[91] Ibid., p. 102.

of false spirits. It soon became clear to him that there were two spirits at work in Los Angeles. According to Parham:

> I hurried to Los Angeles, and to my utter surprise and aston-
> ishment I found conditions even worse than I had anticipated.
> Brother Seymour came to me helpless, he said he could not
> stem the tide that had arisen. I sat on the platform in Azusa
> Street Mission, and saw the manifestations of the flesh, spiri-
> tualistic controls, saw people practicing hypnotism at the al-
> tar over candidates seeking the baptism; though many were
> receiving the real baptism of the Holy Ghost.
>
> After preaching two or three times, I was informed by two of
> the elders, one who was a hypnotist (I had seen him laying his
> hands on many who came through chattering, jabbering and
> sputtering, speaking in no language at all) that I was not wanted
> in that place.[92]

Critics of the Azusa Street revival reported such extrabiblical spiritual manifestations as the "jerks," the "holy laugh," the "holy dance,"
and "singing in the Spirit."[93]

Sarah Parham wrote of her husband's encounter with an "unteach-
able spirit and spiritual pride." She wrote:

> Those who have had experience with fanaticism know that
> there goes with it an unteachable spirit and spiritual pride,
> which makes those under the influences of these false spirits
> feel exalted and think that they have a greater experience than
> any one else and do not need instruction or advice.[94]

Parham cautioned that, he too, came under the control of a false spirit
during a period of his life. He said that it:

---

[92] Parham, *The Life of Charles F. Parham*, p. 163.

[93] Synan, *The Holiness-Pentecostal Tradition*, p. 100.

[94] Parham, *The Life of Charles F. Parham*, p. 163

...came as a seducing, flattering spirit, but when it gained the supremacy of our lives it used the lash.... Yet it has been a school to us and we come to you, one and all, and beg you to be careful, for when your confidence is betrayed by one of these false seducing spirits, you feel like a poor betrayed girl in a strange city; you have not the courage to return and face your father and you just throw away your life. To those who have had their spiritual power prostituted in this or similar manner, we ask you to come home to Father's house. God bless you! To those nibbling at the [tidbits] of the devil's seductive artifices and bouquets of flattering poppy flowers, beware! The devil as an angel of light is imitating every phase of Christianity today.[95]

Parham's wife, Sarah Eleanor Parham, echoed the need to discern between the two spirits as she wrote:

As Mr. Parham used to say, even a crow could tell the difference between a real man and a scare-crow in the corn field, and a goose could pick out the grains of corn from among the little stones. So we as God's children should be able to tell the real from the counterfeit, and be able to take the wheat and leave the chaff, if we will "try the spirits." As Mr. Parham had tried the spirits, and discerned between the two; he condemned fanaticism in no uncertain way and warned the people of this danger. This brought him bitter persecution from those who were under the influence of this power....[96]

Consequences for Exposing the Work of False Spirits

Thus, both Bartleman and Parham reported the working of false spirits at Azusa Street. Their responses, however, were quite different. Not wanting to quench the spiritual movement, Bartleman avoided calling attention to the presence of false spirits. Parham, on the other hand, actively preached about the importance of discerning the spirits in light of Scripture. Within a month of arriving at Azusa Street, Charles

---

[95] Ibid., pp. 164-165.
[96] Ibid., p. 165.

While Men Slept...

Parham was no longer part of the leadership of what became known as "The Apostolic Faith Movement."[97] (See Appendix C for his warning about the Azusa Street experience.) Parham soon found himself in the middle of a major controversy that created an early division in the twentieth-century Pentecostal Movement. He had created enemies at Azusa Street and, just prior to his trip to Los Angeles, he had also made enemies in Zion, Illinois.

Before he came to Azusa Street in October 1906, Parham mounted an unsuccessful challenge for control over the work of Dowie in Zion, Illinois. In September 1906, Parham challenged Wilbur Glenn Voliva, who was attempting to overthrow Dowie for control of the community. As a result, Voliva mounted a full-scale attack against Parham, accusing him of trying to destroy the City of Zion and of "being full of the devil." Voliva rented all available public buildings in the city to prevent Parham from holding large gatherings. He even threatened to dismiss anyone from the Christian Catholic Apostolic Church who was seen at one of Parham's meetings. However, instead of holding large meetings, Parham's strategy was to hold small meetings in homes throughout the community.[98] However, before Parham could establish control in Zion, he saw the critical need to travel to Azusa Street in Los Angeles.

Because of Parham's efforts in Zion and in Los Angeles, he found himself facing two groups who had an interest in discrediting him. Soon, he stood accused of moral failure and racism. By January 1907, the month following his "Note of Warning" about false spirits at Azusa Street, rumors of immorality began circulating about Parham. A charge was made against him in July 1907, but no verifiable factual evidence was ever presented in the case. Parham believed that the charge was the work of Wilbur Viola, who was trying to protect his control of the Christian Catholic Apostolic Church in Zion, Illinois. After Viola helped publicize the morality charge in Zion, he effectively blocked Parham's ability to mount a serious challenge to his authority over the community.[99]

---

[97] Bloch-Hoell, *The Pentecostal Movement*, p. 48.

[98] Faupel, *The Everlasting Gospel*, pp. 180-181.

[99] Goff, *Fields White Unto Harvest*, pp. 136-137.

As a result of Parham's unwillingness to ignore what he believed to be the work of false spirits at Azusa Street, Seymour's supporters attempted to discredit him and elevate Seymour as the founder of Pentecostalism using the issue of race. They claimed that Parham, who was white, brought forward his defense of biblical doctrine to challenge the leadership of Seymour, who was an African-American. Citing Parham's obedience of the Texas law, where Seymour was required to monitor his teaching from outside rather than inside the classroom, his theories on Anglo-Israelism, and his alleged sympathies with the Ku Klux Klan, some have made racist claims against Parham. Therefore, they reason, Azusa Street and Seymour, instead of Parham, deserve the credit for founding the Pentecostal Movement.[100]

Others, however, confirm that, despite Parham's obedience of local customs and race-related laws in Texas and his apparent racial ideology, he was inclusive of all races in his ministry. They say that based on available evidence, in the context of the conditions that existed in the early 1900's, Parham could "hardly be considered a 'racist.'"[101] In reality, Parham included African-Americans in important positions as part of his ministry.[102] Factual evidence not withstanding, Parham was discredited in the eyes of many. They then pointed to Seymour as the founder and Azusa Street as the beginning of the twentieth-century Pentecostal Movement.[103]

The Spirits in Wales

The Darkness of this World

In 1906, Evan Roberts attended the Keswick Convention. On the last day of the Convention F. B. Meyer, a key instrument in bringing the spiritual movement to Wales in 1903 and to Los Angeles in 1905,

---

[100] Walter J. Hollenweger, *Pentecostalism: Origins and Developments Worldwide* (Peabody, Massachusetts: Hendrickson Publishers, Inc., 1997), pp. 22-23.

[101] Goff, *Fields White Unto Harvest*, p. 108.

[102] Ibid., pp. 108-109.

[103] Walter J. Hollenweger, *The Pentecostals: The Charismatic Movement in the Churches*, 2nd print. (Minneapolis: Augsburg Publishing House, 1973), p. 22.

rose to speak. Evan Roberts also rose and publicly prayed for Meyer.[104]
There soon were disputes over whether the meetings at Keswick should
be controlled by the Spirit or by the trustees. Some advised visitors
that they should not look for special sensations at Keswick. As a
result, a rift developed between Roberts' friends and the Convention
leaders.[105] Clearly the Welsh spiritual enthusiam was not welcome on
the English ground from which it was spawned. J. B. Figgis wrote of
the Welsh as follows:

> They *were* troubled, the torrent from the Welsh hills meeting
> the sluggish stream of English propriety threatened tumult.
> No doubt this was in the hope of extending to England the
> revival which had blessed Wales. That that hope might not be
> quenched one or two further meetings were arranged in which
> our Welsh friends had free play for enthusiasm. Still it is to be
> feared that some disappointed feeling remained amongst them,
> for the attendance at the Convention in 1906 was three hun-
> dred less, being just the number that came from Wales in 1905,
> and this is sadly significant—a revival in England still remains
> conspicuous by its absence.[106]

Clearly, something had happened. The brief revival that was rapidly
broadcast throughout the world was coming to an end. Evan Roberts, who a few short months earlier felt he was on fire with the Spirit,
was becoming discouraged. He began to question the spirits that were
working among the converts. Among the physical manifestations he
observed were barking at the devil, dancing and swooning, and following after healers and prophetesses.[107] Said to have suffered from a
nervous breakdown, young Roberts was whisked away into "retire-
ment" in 1906 by Jessie Penn-Lewis. He had reportedly become broken, both mentally and physically, and was unable to stand or walk for
almost twelve months.[108]

---

[104] Pollock, *The Keswick Story*, p. 129.

[105] Jones, *The Complete Life of Evan Roberts*, pp. 163-164.

[106] Figgis, *Keswick from Within*, p. 151.

[107] Jones, *The Complete Life of Evan Roberts*, p. 158.

[108] Ibid., pp. 165-167.

The Wiles of the Enemy

When Frank Bartleman visited Wales as part of his 1910 worldwide trip, he went to Evan Roberts' hometown of Loughor. While there, he visited the Moriah Chapel, which was where the revival of 1904 broke out. During his visit to Wales, he apparently struggled with spiritual issues, of which he wrote:

> Suffered much from the cold and rain. Fought with demon powers all night one night. Both God and the Devil seemed to be claiming Wales.[109]

Roberts finally wrote something of his struggle with the powers of Satan in December 1913 when he said:

> Now during the revival in Wales, I, in my ignorance, did not escape the wiles of the enemy, who does not leave even the elect to escape him. According to Rev. 13:7, it is said that "it was given unto the beast to overcome the saints." This is only for a period, then even all the united power of hell cannot prevail against God's elect.[110]

What had gone wrong in Wales? Why had the renowned 1904 revival that served as the model for the worldwide Pentecostal Movement suddenly disappeared, leaving in its wake a leader with a mental breakdown?

Jessie Penn-Lewis, a key ochestrator of the revival knew the answer. She had learned it before the revival began. While she was in India, Jessie Penn-Lewis on March 29, 1903 wrote of the spiritual confusion that arises from preaching about an "experience" rather than about the work of Jesus Christ:

> I feel most deeply that the "experimental" side has hidden the power of the Divine side, and prevented the Holy Spirit from showing the work of Christ alone as the basis of faith. In every soul I have dealt with I have seen the disastrous confusion

---

[109] Bartleman, *Around the World by Faith,* pp. 13-14.
[110] Quoted in Ibid., p. 168.

and despair produced by preaching an experience instead of the work of Christ.[111]

Uncovering the Counterfeiter

As we recall, Evan Roberts boasted in his letters to Frank Bartleman, who was promoting the Azusa Street revival in Los Angeles, that he preached total surrender and no sectarian *doctrine*. After his brief encounter with international fame, Evan Roberts found himself trying to recuperate from emotional destruction in the aftermath of the great Wales revival of 1904. While Jessie Penn-Lewis aided him in his long-term recovery, she reflected upon what went wrong in the Wales and in other great revivals. In her book, *War on the Saints,* which she wrote in 1912 in cooperation with Evan Roberts, Penn-Lewis concluded that great deception awaits many in the aftermath of great revivals. She wrote that:

> In the hour and power of God in Revival, the "Tempter" appears to be absent, but he is present as the Counterfeiter. Men say "there is no devil," and yet it is his greatest harvest. He is netting his victims, mixing his workings with the workings of God, and beguiling the saints more effectively than he was ever able to do before with his temptations to sin. As a counterfeiter, and deceiver, the ever watchful foe uses his old methods of deception and guile on new converts who, having victory over known sin, think the Tempter has left them, not knowing his new ways. His absence is only apparent and not real. Satan was never more active among the sons of God.[112]

Based on the hard lessons of experience, Penn-Lewis, Roberts, and many others learned that the Spirit of God is real, but all supernatural things are not of God. Those who teach that it is possible for believers to be deceived into accepting the counterfeit as real offend many who reject the possiblity that Satan is copying the true things of God.

---

[111] Garrard, *Mrs. Penn Lewis*, pp. 3-4.

[112] Jessie Penn-Lewis, with Evan Roberts, *War on the Saints*, unabridged ed. (1st ed. published in 1912; New York: Thomas E. Lowe, Ltd., 10th printing of 9th ed., 1994), p. 282.

Denying the Cross

We need only to look at Peter to see how easily a believer can be deceived. He, like us, was deceived when he looked at the world through the eyes of the flesh, rather than with spiritual eyes. After he had confessed his belief that Jesus was the Christ, the Son of the living God, Peter fell into a fleshly trap causing him to try to undermine the great sacrifice that Jesus was about to make on the cross. Clearly, Peter was deceived into not trusting Jesus when He said He must be killed and be raised again on the third day. Jesus responded:

> But he turned, and said unto Peter, Get thee behind me, Satan: thou art an offence unto me: for thou savourest not the things that be of God, but those that be of men.
>
> —Matthew 16:23

After Peter tried to deny the cross, Jesus brought him and the other disciples back to the cross:

> Then said Jesus unto his disciples, If any *man* will come after me, let him deny himself, and take up his cross, and follow me.
>
> —Matthew 16:24

Penn-Lewis explained that a key test for detecting deceiving spirits is to see what they teach concerning the Scriptures, sin, the Saviour, and the Cross. She wrote that:

> All "truth" is in harmony with the only channel of revealed truth in the world—the written Word of God. All "teachings" originating from deceiving spirits—
> (1) Weaken the authority of the Scriptures;
> (2) Distort the teaching in the Scriptures;
> (3) Add to the Scriptures the thoughts of men; or
> (4) Put the Scriptures entirely aside.
> The ultimate object being to hide, distort, misuse, or put aside the revelation of God concerning the Cross of Calvary, where Satan was overthrown by the God-Man and where freedom was obtained for all his captives.

The test of all "thought" and "belief" therefore is its
>   (1) Harmony with the written Scriptures in its full body
>   of truth.
>   (2) The attitude to the Cross, and sin.
>
> *In the Christianised world*, some doctrines of demons, *tested*
> *by these two primary principles*, may be mentioned as...
> New Theology: no *sin*, no Saviour, no Cross.[113]
>
> > [Italics are in the original.]

In other words, a clear understanding of the *doctrine* of Jesus Christ
and His sacrifice on the cross helps us separate truth from error. We
need to try the spirits. John made the caution clear when he wrote:

> Beloved, believe not every spirit, but try the spirits whether
> they are of God: because many false prophets are gone out
> into the world.
>
> > —1 John 4:1

Isaiah confirmed that:

> They also that erred in spirit shall come to understanding, and
> they that murmured shall learn doctrine.
>
> > —Isaiah 29:24

---

[113] Ibid., pp. 21-22.

Chapter 19. The Universal Spirit for Global Unity

And he doeth great wonders, so that he maketh fire come down from heaven on the earth in the sight of men, And deceiveth them that dwell on the earth by *the means of* those miracles which he had power to do in the sight of the beast;

—Revelation 13:13-14a

Spirit of Unity of Rome

The Spirit in South Africa

The spiritual movement that Asa Mahan had written about in Adrian, Michigan in 1870 in *The Baptism of the Holy Ghost* was adopted by the Keswick Convention in 1875, brought to Wales in 1904, and then taken to Azusa Street in Los Angeles in 1906. In April 1904, which was *before* the second Wales "Keswick-like" Convention, the evangelist, Gipsy Smith, arrived in South Africa with news of the Wales Revival. The message from Azusa Street was then carried to South Africa in 1908 by John G. Lake (1870-1935) and Tom Hezmelhalch (1845-1934). They had been associated with John Alexander Dowie's ministry in Zion, Illinois and had also worshipped at Seymour's mission on Azusa Street.[1,2]

The Azusa Street spiritual movement, in which both Frank Bartleman and Charles Parham reportedly saw the manifestations of both true and false spirits, was now in South Africa. Notably, the Charismatic Movement, as it was to be called, was introduced into the Roman Catholic Church through a South African named David Du Plessis (1905-1987) from the Apostolic Faith Mission.[3] In 1915, soon after David Du Plessis' father came under the Pentecostal influence, a missionary from England named David Fisher brought a further British

---

[1] David Du Plessis, as told to Bob Slosser, *A Man Called Mr. Pentecost* (Plainfield, New Jersey: Logos International, 1977), p. 105.

[2] Hollenweger, *Pentecostalism*, pp. 41-42.

[3] Du Plessis, *A Man Called Mr. Pentecost*, pp. 212-213.

influence to the small church the Du Plessis family attended.[4] By 1918, young David Du Plessis earnestly sought after the gifts of the Holy Spirit. He described his experience in receiving his spiritual baptism this way:

> The joy overwhelmed me, and I said, "Hallelujah." But that was no good; it didn't express what I was feeling. "Praise the Lord" was no better. It sounded silly in comparison to the sheer joy surging through me. "How can I express it?" I thought. But before I could go any further, I began to laugh. And I laughed, on and on, "Ha ha ha ha, ho ho ho ho, he he he he, ha ha ha ha...." I felt I couldn't laugh any more. Nobody stopped me. Some of them laughed a bit with me, obviously because I was laughing so hard, harder than anyone I'd ever heard. But no one seemed upset. I held my stomach and said, "Lord, I can't take it any more. Help me...help me to release what I'm feeling," and I started to shout hallelujah again. I got as far as "ha-a-a...," but the "lelujah" wouldn't come.[5]

The laughing spirit Du Plessis had received would not allow him to say "HALLELUJAH," which is "הלליה" or "Praise YAH" or "Praise the LORD!"

The Personal Prophecy

Sixteen years after David Du Plessis began working for the Apostolic Faith Mission in 1920, another memorable event happened in his life. Du Plessis received a personal prophecy concerning his role in the Ecumenical Movement. As with so many other spiritual manifestations of the twentieth century, this prophecy was linked to the Wales Revival of 1904, which was generated through a Keswick oriented convention.

The vicar of the All Saints' Parish Anglican Church in Sunderland, England, Alexander Boody, was among those who had traveled to Wales during the 1904 revival. After standing with Evan Roberts and

---

[4] Ibid., pp. 12-15.
[5] Ibid., p. 34.

witnessing the spiritual manifestations of the revival, Boody returned to Sunderland where he and a small group of his parishioners sought a similar outpouring of the Holy Spirit. He continued to research the spiritual movement as it directly and indirectly spread from Wales. Finally, he became convinced that England was ready for the new Pentecost and published a pamphlet entitled *Pentecost in England*, which he distributed at the 1907 Keswick Convention.[6]

In September 1907, soon after the Keswick Convention, Boody and some of the parishioners at the All Saints' Parish Anglican Church reportedly experienced what marked the beginning of the Pentecostal Movement in England.[7] By October 25, 1907, a healing evangelist named Smith Wigglesworth (1859-1947) found himself in the All Saints' Parish Church, where he sought the baptism of the Holy Spirit. While he reported having significant spiritual experiences, Wigglesworth did not speak in other tongues until Boody's wife laid hands on him and he then felt the "fire-power" of the Holy Spirit.[8]

About nineteen years later, following an extensive career as a Pentecostal evangelist, Smith Wigglesworth made a trip to Rome in 1936 at the invitation of the Italian Pentecostal Church. Soon after his visit to Rome, Wigglesworth traveled to Johannesburg, South Africa as a guest of the Apostolic Faith Mission. While there, he stayed in the home of the General Secretary of the Mission, David Du Plessis. The two travelled extensively together while Wigglesworth was conducting meetings in South Africa.[9]

Then, one morning in December 1936, Wigglesworth reportedly walked into Du Plessis' office and gave him a personal prophecy.[10, 11] Wigglesworth told of a major revival through the "old-line denominations" that would:

---

[6] Jack Hywel-Davies, *The Life of Smith Wigglesworth: One Man, One Holy Passion* (Ann Arbor, Michigan: Servant Publications, 1988), pp. 64-65.

[7] Ibid., p. 65.

[8] Ibid., pp. 67-68.

[9] Ibid., pp. 151-152.

[10] Hollenweger, *Pentecostalism*, p. 350.

[11] Du Plessis, *A Man Called Mr. Pentecost*, pp. 1-2.

...eclipse anything we have known throughout history. No such things have happened in times past as will happen when this begins.... It will eclipse the present-day, twentieth-century Pentecostal revival that already is a marvel of the world, with its strong opposition from the established church. But this same blessing will become acceptable to the established churches as they will go on with this message and this experience beyond what the Pentecostals have achieved. You will live to see this work grow to such dimensions that the Pentecostal movement itself will be a light thing in comparison with what God will do through the old churches. There will be tremendous gatherings of people, unlike anything we've seen, and great leaders will change their attitude and accept not only the message but also the blessing...[the Lord said]...He is going to use you in this movement. You will have a very prominent part....[12]

Within a year of the prophecy by the Englishman, Wigglesworth, the plans were laid in Oxford, England to establish the World Council of Churches.

Building the Bridge from England to Rome

The foundation for the bridge from England to Rome had already been laid when Englishmen working in both locations successfully replaced the Protestant Bible with one that was more acceptable to Rome and, almost simultaneously, implemented the dogma of papal infallibility. B. F. Westcott, who played a key role in the biblical revision process, insisted that England was the key to a universal fellowship of the human race. He said, "The nation is to the race what the family is to the nation."[13] In his view, England alone had the power to achieve a comprehensive fellowship of the entire race. He said the comprehensive fellowship "...must not deal with opinion, or feeling, or action only, but with the whole sum of life."[14]

---

[12] Ibid., pp. 2-3.

[13] Westcott, *Social Aspects of Christianity*, p. 146.

[14] Ibid., p. 146.

While England may have had the power to achieve the global fellow-ship that Westcott wrote about, only Rome had the structure and mechanism to accomplish the goal. Therefore, it was critical to move the power of England to the structure of Rome. This was done through a continuation of the movement that had begun at Oxford more than a century earlier.

The Oxford Ecumenical Conference of 1937 was pivotal in the for-mation of the World Council of Churches, which became the vehicle through which world religions moved toward unification into Social Christianity.[15] A key to the Conference was John A. Mackay (1889-1983), who became the president of the International Missionary Council, the organization from which the World Council of Churches grew.[16] In 1938, a provisional structure for the World Council of Churches was prepared in Utrecht, the Netherlands, and in 1948 in Amsterdam, the Council was formally organized.[17]

Mackay, described the 1937 Oxford Ecumenical Conference, which was known as the "Conference on Church Community and State," as a "crucial event in the contemporary history of Christianity."[18] It dealt with five themes: Church and Community; Church and State; Church, Community, and State in relation to the Economic Order; Church Community, and State in Relation to Education; the Universal Church and the World of Nations.[19]

Indeed, Mackay stressed the relationship between the World Council of Churches and the International Missionary Council when he wrote:

---

[15] Phillips, *A Kingdom on Earth*, pp. 189-191.

[16] Anon., "Memorial Minute: John Alexander Mackay, *1889-1983*," *Theology Today*, vol. 40, no. 4, http://theologytoday.ptsem.edu/jan1984/v40-4-editorial2.htm, January 1984.

[17] Walker et al., *A History of the Christian Church*, pp. 690-691.

[18] John A. Mackay, *Ecumenics: The Science of the Church Universal* (Englewood Cliffs, New Jersey: Prentice-Hall Inc., 1964), p. 3.

[19] Nils Ehrenstrom, "Movements for International Friendship and Life and Work, 1925-1948," In *A History of the Ecumenical Movement, 1517-1948*, ch. 12, Rouse and Neill, eds., p. 592.

Upon the official letterhead of the World Council one now reads, "The World Council of Churches, in association with The International Missionary Council."[20]

John Mackay, a Presbyterian, was the president of Princeton Theological Seminary when David Du Plessis came under his influence. Du Plessis said that he was attracted to Mackay because of a newspaper article that reported Mackay's description of the Pentecostal Movement as "...the greatest blessing that had come to Christianity this century." This was particularly interesting because, according to Du Plessis, Mackay had "...previously said the Pentecostals in America were the 'fly in the ointment of Protestantism.'" Upon meeting each other, Mackay told Du Plessis that he had changed his mind. From then on, according to Du Plessis, Mackay's "...advice and guidance were immeasurably helpful as I moved carefully along the path the Lord was opening for me."[21]

The path that Mackay led the Pentecostal Du Plessis down was toward the Roman Catholic Church by way of the World Council of Churches. In Mackay's view:

Evangelical catholicity, therefore, embraces all those, whatever their name or sign, who pledge their loyalty to Jesus Christ and manifest the fruits of the Spirit. All such are members of the Holy Catholic Church and are invited to form part of the ecumenical fellowship of Christian believers.[22]

Mackay opened the door for Du Plessis to be the key Pentecostal in the World Council of Churches Ecumenical Movement. He described the significance of his personal and ecumenical relationship with Du Plessis this way:

One of the significant moments in my personal life in recent years was when I first became acquainted with the world Pen-

---

[20] John A. Mackay, *Christianity on the Frontier* (New York: The Macmillan Company, 1950), p. 204.

[21] Du Plessis, *A Man Called Mr. Pentecost*, p. 172.

[22] Mackay, *Christianity on the Frontier*, p. 136.

tecostal leader, David du Plessis; one of the most significant moments in his life was when I subsequently introduced him to the Ecumenical Movement.[23]

The Post-Pentecostal and Pre-Charismatic Spirit

During 1947, the most significant meeting of ecumenically minded Christians since the end of World War II was held in the small Canadian town of Whitby (located a few miles east of Toronto, Ontario). The meeting of the International Missionary Council challenged the attendees to consider the "Unity of Mankind" in a world that was divided. This meeting, among other things, emphasized the "...reality of the Holy Spirit who makes Himself manifest in "Proclamation" and in "Fellowship"" in what was called the "..beginning of a new era."[24] Also in 1947 Donald Gee (1891-1966), a Pentecostal leader from the United Kingdom, and David Du Plessis organized the first Pentecostal world conference, which was held in Zurich.[25]

The following year was marked by the official organization of the World Council of Churches and by a new outpouring of the Holy Spirit in Canada.[26, 27] The 1948 Holy Spirit revival began among students at the Sharon Orphanage and Schools in North Battleford, Saskatchewan, Canada. The new movement, which became known as a "New Order of the Latter Rain," was characterized by the practice of imparting specific gifts of the Holy Spirit by the laying on of hands, by mass singing in tongues, and the use of detailed personal prophecies. As the leaders of the movement challenged established Pentecostal Churches to return to their spiritual roots, the established churches rejected the movement for what was perceived to be errors and excesses. Hundreds of congregations that were part of the move-

---

[23] Mackay, *Ecumenics: The Science of the Church Universal*, p. 198.

[24] Ibid., p. 11.

[25] Walter Hollenweger, "Two Extraordinary Pentecostal Ecumenists," *The Ecumenical Review*, vol. 52, July 2000, pp. 391ff.

[26] Ehrenstrom, "Movements for International Friendship and Life and Work, 1925-1948," p. 595.

[27] Synan, *The Holiness-Pentecostal Tradition*, p. 212.

ment made major contributions to the Neo-Pentecostal and Charismatic Movements that developed in the 1960's.[28]

As of 1948, the World Council of Churches provided a single global organization of non-Roman Catholic Churches which could work in harmony with the Roman Catholic Church to re-establish the ecumenical religion that had been founded by the Roman Emperor Constantine in A.D. 312.

The Secretariat for Christian Unity

As we have learned, during the 1830's, the Oxford Movement was highly successful in moving the Church of England toward the Catholic Church, with key converts such as John Newman and Henry Manning. Many of the main players in the Oxford Movement were also instrumental in either revising the English Bible or in implementing the dogma for papal infallibility at the First Vatican Council. Now the success found with the Anglo-Catholic movement in England was to be built upon in order to move the rest of the world toward Rome.

More than twelve years before the start of the Second Vatican Council, John Mackay said that Protestants were longing for an "authoritative Ecumenical Council" that would formulate a new ecumenical theology.[29] In 1959, Pope John XXIII (Angelo Giuseppe Roncalli (1881-1963)) announced plans to convoke the Twenty-first Ecumenical Council, known as the Second Vatican Council, or Vatican II. A goal of the Council was to invite the "separated brethren" to search for the unity of Christians. On the advice of Lorenz Jaeger (1892-1975), the archbishop of Paderborn, Germany, and German-born Jesuit, Augustin Bea (1881-1968), who among other positions, served as Rector of the Pontifical Biblical Institute, the pope established the Secretariat for Promoting Christian Unity. The pope announced the Secretariat June 1960 and appointed Bea as its first president.[30]

---

[28] Ibid., pp. 212-213.

[29] Mackay, *Christianity on the Frontier*, p. 139.

[30] William Purdy, *The Search for Unity: Relations between the Anglican and Roman Catholic Churches from the 1950s to the 1970s* (London: Geoffrey Chapman, 1996), pp. 25-26.

416

The Anglican Archbishop's Visit to Rome

In anticipation of the Second Vatican Council, preparation was made for Geoffrey Fisher, the archbishop of Canterbury, to visit Pope John XXIII. Before the visit, Cardinal Bea's Secretariat for Promoting Christian Unity requested information from Jesuit priest and theologian Bernard Leeming of Oxford concerning Fisher, the history of Anglicanism, and the current position of Anglicanism. Leeming responded that he personally knew Fisher and that he "was not much of a theologian." However, Leeming added that Fisher was a "sincere man" and that he travelled a lot.[31]

Leeming, however, followed his lukewarm endorsement of Fisher's abilities with an assessment of the importance of his position as the archbishop of Canterbury. He wrote that:

> The position of the Archbishop gives possibilities of considerable influence. He has direct access to the sovereign, he is usually consulted by the Prime Minister, he presides at the Lambeth Conference and at many Anglican societies. He has considerable influence on educational matters.[32]

Amidst rumors that Fisher's visit to Rome had originated at a World Council of Churches assembly, he arrived in Rome on December 1, 1960. Upon meeting Pope John XXIII, Archbishop Fisher's first words were, "Your Holiness, we are making history." After the two entered into a new dialogue, the pope arranged for Fisher to also meet with Cardinal Bea on December 2 for ecumenical discussions. The selection of the Church of England observers who were to attend the upcoming Second Vatican Council was among the matters they discussed.[33]

---

[31] Purdy, *The Search for Unity*, p. 27.

[32] Ibid., pp. 27-28.

[33] Ibid., pp. 25-32.

While Men Slept...

Changing the Anglican Archbishop

Shortly after Fisher's visit to the Vatican as the archbishop of Canterbury, he was asked to appear in a television broadcast discussing Church unity. He declined the invitation and was replaced on the program by [Arthur] Michael Ramsey, the archbishop of York. In Ramsey's television appearance, he proclaimed "the end of bigotry."[34] Indeed, Ramsey was inclusive. He disturbed his conventional critics, for example, by saying that a belief in God was not a precondition to going to heaven.[35] Ramsey said, "I expect to meet some present-day atheists there."[36]

It soon became clear that there were vast differences between Fisher and Ramsey in their theology and in their perception of what the relationship should be between the Roman Catholic Church and the Anglican Church. Fisher was a "low churchman," who had little appreciation for the traditions of the Roman Catholic Church. Ramsey, on the other hand, was an Anglo-Catholic, or "high churchman," who, having wanted to become a monk himself, was of Catholic devotion. He loved the daily eucharist and the traditions of the Roman Catholic Church.[37]

Ramsey represented the tradition of the Anglo-Catholic Oxford Movement.[38] That Movement, as we recall, endorsed the concept of bringing the Anglican Church back under the authority of Rome. According to Ramsey's biographer, Owen Chadwick, Ramsey's:

> Principles were very strong, that the Church of England is a Catholic Church and must never compromise its Catholic principles.[39]

---

[34] Ibid., pp. 29, 35.

[35] Owen Chadwick, *Michael Ramsey: A Life* (Oxford: Clarendon Press, 1990), p. 44.

[36] Quoted in Ibid., p. 198.

[37] Ibid., p. 314.

[38] Ibid., p. 104.

[39] Ibid., p. 86.

418

Thus, Ramsey's views were similar to those of the Christian Socialist, F. D. Maurice, who believed that the Catholic Church should be the center of unity.[40] As such, Ramsey, whose mother was also a Socialist, promoted the teachings of Maurice.[41] His 1948 King's College lectures on F. D. Maurice were published in 1951.[42]

Ramsey had become known for his work at the Lambeth Conference in 1958 as the chairman of the commission on the theme of the Bible. Ramsey seemed to be in agreement with the teachings of F. D. Maurice concerning the Bible. Ramsey thus concluded that the Bible had to be subjected to modern biblical criticism, which he believed had shown, among other things, that it was not historically true in all its parts. With his belief in the unreliability of parts of the Bible, Ramsey promoted the use of the coming modern translations.[43] Few understood the implications of Ramsey's encouragement of the use of modern Bible translations. As Owen Chadwick, Ramsey's biographer, explained:

> Those who encouraged new translations did not yet imagine what would happen. The bishops expected the hallowed Authorized Version to maintain its mastery because it was sanctified in everyone's affections and moral sentiments. They had no idea, as yet, that the coming of modern translations, and the making of English into an international language, would destroy the commonness of a single text of the Bible which was the property of the simple as of the sophisticated.[44]

By January 17, 1961, Fisher had resigned from his position as the archbishop of Canterbury.[45] He did not, however, appear to have an in-depth appreciation for Prime Minister Harold Macmillan's Anglo-

---

[40] Maurice, *The Life of Frederick Denison Maurice*, vol. 1, p. 326.

[41] Chadwick, *Michael Ramsey: A Life*, p. 63.

[42] Ibid., p. 409. (See Arthur M. Ramsey, *F. D. Maurice and the Conflicts of Modern Theology: The Maurice Lectures, 1948* (Cambridge: Cambridge University Press, 1951)).

[43] Chadwick, *Michael Ramsey: A Life*, pp. 98-99.

[44] Ibid., 99-100.

[45] Purdy, *The Search for Unity*, p. 35.

Catholic heritage. Therefore, Fisher tried to warn the prime minister about Ramsey's strong Catholic leanings. He cautioned Macmillan that Ramsey was too Catholic to succeed him as the archbishop of Canterbury. Macmillan, however, was unmoved and even felt a rapport with Ramsey.[46] Consequently, despite Fisher's advice, Macmillan appointed Michael Ramsey as the new archbishop of Canterbury. As such, he became the new head of the Anglican and Episcopal Church.[47]

The decision of Harold Macmillan to appoint the very pro-Catholic Ramsey as the new archbishop of Canterbury was consistent with Macmillan's long family heritage of Anglo-Catholicism. Harold's grandfather, Daniel Macmillan, had, as we have learned, been a great admirer of Frederick Denison Maurice who was an Anglican priest and one of the founders of the Christian Socialist Movement. Although having Unitarian beliefs, F. D. Maurice envisioned the world as one of Socialism, using the structure of the Catholic Church operating in unity with the State. We also recall that Daniel Macmillan initiated the revision of the Greek New Testament in 1853 and that he demonstrated his great admiration for F. D. Maurice when he named his two sons, Frederick and Maurice. Harold Macmillan, the prime minister of England who was playing a critical role in deciding the direction of the Anglican and Episcopal Churches toward Catholicism, was Maurice Macmillan's son.[48]

Having been appointed as the archbishop of Canterbury by Daniel Macmillan's grandson, Ramsey agreed with Cardinal Bea in 1962 that it would be good to have Anglicans attend the Second Vatican Council, as observers. Ramsey said he would send one from the Church of England, one from the Episcopal Church of the United States, and one from the missionary field.[49] During the months preceding the opening of the Second Vatican Council, the Anglicans and Roman Catholics held a series of meetings in England on "ecumenism."[50]

---

[46] Chadwick, *Michael Ramsey: A Life*, p. 105.

[47] Purdy, *The Search for Unity*, p. 39.

[48] Alistair Horne, *Harold Macmillan, 1894-1956*, vol. 1 (New York: Viking Penguin Inc., 1988), p. 6.

[49] Purdy, *The Search for Unity*, pp. 42-43.

[50] Ibid., pp. 43-48.

The World Council of Churches in New Delhi

Ramsey's theological positions were highly compatible with those of the World Council of Churches. In 1961, he was elected president of the World Council of Churches assembly in New Delhi, India.[51] Delegates to the Assembly in New Delhi included key representatives from the Keswick Conventions. Among those were the Convention Chairman, A. T. Houghton, Archbishop Gough, and Keswick speakers Billy Graham and Paul Rees.[52] In addition, the well-known Pentecostal David Du Plessis was invited as an observer. (The Pentecostal leader, Donald Gee, was also invited but he cancelled his acceptance of the invitation.)[53]

The World Council of Churches invited the Roman Catholic Church to send observers to its meeting of the Faith and Order Commission. One of those observers was a Jesuit priest from Oxford, England named Bernard Leeming. He was one of five observers sent by the Roman Catholic Church to the 1961 World Council of Churches Assembly in New Delhi, India.[54] The General Secretary of the World Council of Churches, W. A. Visser't Hooft, recognized the importance of the roles of individual Roman Catholics at the Assembly, and especially noted the importance of the useful relationship with the Secretariat for Christian Unity that had been set up by the pope.[55] The report of the Committee on the Bossey Ecumenical Institute included the recommendation that the Institute should:

---

[51] Chadwick, *Michael Ramsey: A Life*, p. 401.

[52] Pollock, *The Keswick Story*, pp. 171-172.

[53] Hollenweger, "Two Extraordinary Pentecostal Ecumenists," *The Ecumenical Review*, vol. 52, July 2000, pp. 391ff.

[54] Lukas Vischer, *The Ecumenical Movement and the Roman Catholic Church*, In *The Ecumenical Advance: A History of the Ecumenical Movement*, vol. 2: 1948-1968, Harold E. Fey, Editor (Philadelphia: The Westminster Press, 1970), pp. 326-327.

[55] [The World Council of Churches], *The New Delhi Report: The Third Assembly of the World Council of Churches, 1961* (New York: Association Press, 1962), p. 6.

...explore the meaning for the whole ecumenical movement of the Pentecostal groups within the life of the whole Church, and their relation to what one may call the Catholic and Protestant streams of Christianity.[56]

The Second Vatican Council

The Second Vatican Council opened in October 1962. According to Cardinal Bea, the pope saw the Second Vatican Council as a means of fostering a closer brotherhood of all Christians. He saw it as:

"...a more definite and more universal gesture towards the unity of all Christians, so that universal human brotherhood might be better fostered through a closer brotherhood of all those who profess to follow Christ."[57]

Cardinal Bea was a key figure behind Pope John XXIII and perhaps the most productive person in the Ecumenical Movement.[58] In an address on March 8, 1962 to the members of the Second Vatican Council's Secretariat for Christian Unity, of which Bea was the president, Pope John XXIII said that he created the new Secretariat:

...to show his good will toward separated Christians and "to give them the opportunity of following the work of the Council and of finding more easily the path of unity."[59]

Bea recognized that the quest for unity required minimizing the importance of doctrinal differences between Roman Catholics and non-Roman Catholics. Specific among the major doctrinal disagreements were such extrabibilical dogmas of the Roman Catholic Church as the Immaculate Conception of "the Mother of God," the bodily Assump-

---

[56] [The World Council of Churches], *The New Delhi Report*, p. 219.

[57] Augustin Cardinal Bea, *Unity in Freedom: Reflections on the Human Family* (New York and Evanston: Harper & Row, Publishers, 1964), pp. 70-71.

[58] Walker et al., *A History of the Christian Church*, p. 697.

[59] Pope John XXIII, *The Council and the Separated Brethren*, In *The Pope Speaks*, vol. 8, No. 1, 1962, pp. 27-28.

tion of "the Mother of God," the primacy of the bishop of Rome, and the infallibility of the bishop of Rome, known as Papal Infallibility.[60] Instead of discussing doctrinal disagreements, the pope emphasized the importance of "private and social justice" and that the aim of all:

> ...must be to establish more equitable relationships in domestic, national, and international affairs, and so to make a decisive and increasing contribution to the welfare of the whole human race.[61]

Planning for the Spirit

As unity was being established between Roman Catholics and Protestants on the revised Word, further unifying forces were sought as the means to complete the Counter Reformation. The Secretariat for the Promotion of Christian Unity, the Jesuit Cardinal Bea drew up a "Schema," which was approved by the Second Vatican Council but kept from the public. The "Schema" was pervasive and forceful on uniting issues, while giving little prominence to the divisive elements between the Roman Catholic Church and most Protestant churches. One of those uniting issues was seen as the "gifts of the Holy Spirit." Cardinal Bea stressed that the "Schema" was not addressed to the "separated brethren." Instead, it was:

> ...directed to Catholics, who are already convinced of the truth of their faith, who are aware of the rejection of much Catholic teaching by non-Catholics, but who may not be so well aware of the true Christian elements, and of the gifts of the Holy Spirit existing among them, doubtless as part of the grace of their baptism.[62]

In anticipation of a "new Pentecost," the pope summoned Cardinal Leo Joseph Suenens to play a key role in what became known as the

---

[60] Bea, *Unity in Freedom*, pp. 152-153.

[61] Pope John XXIII, *Meditations for the Council*, In *The Pope Speaks*, vol. 8, no. 1, 1962, p. 135.

[62] Bea, *Unity in Freedom*, pp. 176-177.

While Men Slept...

"Charismatic Renewal." In preparation for his role in the Second Vatican Council, Suenens enlisted the help of leading professors from the Jesuit school of theology at Louvain.[63]

John A. Mackay explained the significance of the Pentecostal experience to the Ecumenical Movement:

> What lies at the heart of the Pentecostal movement of today must be given due attention by all Christians who are concerned about Christian unity, and who would help the Churches to fulfill their *unitive function*.[64]

Praying to the "Queen of Heaven" for the Spirit

The Roman Catholic Virgin Mary played a very important role in the introduction of the Charismatic Spirit to the Second Vatican Council. Just as Ignatius of Loyola, the founder of the Jesuits, was said to have written his *Spiritual Exercises* under the inspiration and dictation of the Virgin Mary,[65] the pope also saw the importance of praying to her for the Second Vatican Council and for the new Pentecost he was expecting to become manifest at the Council. During his 1962 preparation for the Second Vatican Council, Pope John XXIII called for special prayers to Mary during the month of May, saying:

> We come invoking Mary's name—the Mystic Rose—begging her who is Jesus' Mother and ours to pray for us and look on us with gentleness and love. [He called upon]...the faithful everywhere [to] unite in their endeavor to show special love and veneration for Mary, God's Virgin Mother...Our fervent prayer, then, is that every Christian shall spend this month [May 1962] on terms of intimacy and friendship and in com-

---

[63] James S. Torrens, "Admiring Cardinal Suenens (Leo Joseph Cardinal Suenens, 1904-1996) (Obituary)," In *America*, vol. 174 no. 20, June 22, 1996, pp. 3ff.

[64] Mackay, *Ecumenics: The Science of the Church Universal*, p. 198.

[65] Joseph de Guibert, *The Jesuits: Their Spiritual Doctrine and Practice*, William J. Young, trans. and George E. Ganss, ed. (Chicago: The Institute of Jesuit Sources in cooperation with Loyola University Press, 1964), p. 166.

munion with the Virgin Mary. May she be their guide and companion as, with her, they make their way to the mount of Christ's ascension.[66]

Reminiscent of the "new Pentecost" that Philip Schaff had spoken of in 1893 at the World's Parliament of Religions in Chicago, the pope called for a "new Pentecost." He called upon the priests for a "fervent and fruitful celebration of Mary's month" and:

> ...to pray, that is, that this great event [the Second Vatican Council] may prove a new Pentecost, in which the Holy Spirit will once again lavish upon the Church the riches of His heavenly gifts.[67]

The pope added that the achievement of the resolutions of the Second Vatican Council was dependent upon the achievement of a new outpouring of the Holy Spirit and that the Council would be "a new Pentecost." He said:

> But to be able to put these resolutions into practice and to give a generous response to the inspirations of heaven, we all need to be imbued with the power of the Holy Spirit. And there can be no doubt that the forthcoming Council will indeed be a new Pentecost—that new and marvellous outpouring of grace that We confidently expect—provided only that all Our dearest sons will give proof of their ardent sincerity.[68]

After Pope John XXIII died in 1963, Pope Paul VI (Giovanni Montini (1897-1978)) resumed the Second Vatican Council. As his predecessor had done, the new pope appealed to the Virgin Mary for special blessings on the Council. On September 13, 1963 he addressed the Marian Congregations saying:

---

[66] Pope John XXIII, *Meditations for the Council*, In *The Pope Speaks*, vol. 8, no. 1, 1962, p. 132.

[67] Ibid., p. 133.

[68] Ibid., p. 136.

This meeting arouses in Our mind a pleasant memory from the distant years of Our adolescence and youth, namely that of Our membership in the Marian Congregation of the Jesuit Fathers...We have the happy opportunity of greeting all of this magnificent assembly surrounding Us, which has met under the august and familiar name of Virgin Mary. What a joy it is for Us to see so many men and women celebrating the glory of the Mother of God; what sweet emotion it is for Us to listen to your resounding voices blending in a single prayer, a single song destined for the Queen of Heaven![69]

Bringing in the Charismatic Spirit

Stressing the commonality of the "gifts of the Holy Spirit," while minimizing doctrinal differences between Roman Catholics and the "separated brethren," was seen by Bea as one of the important tools to help accomplish his goal of the unity of all Christians with the Roman Catholic Church. To accomplish his objective of using the "gifts of the Holy Spirit" as a tool for bringing the "separated brethren" back to the Roman Catholic Church, Cardinal Bea actively sought out a "Pentecostal" to help implement his plan. He found David Du Plessis.

Du Plessis, who had received a prophecy from Smith Wigglesworth almost thirty years earlier, had become well known among Bible-based Pentecostal organizations, such as the Church of God of Cleveland, Tennessee and the Assemblies of God of Springfield, Missouri. To facilitate his international activities, Du Plessis became ordained through the Assemblies of God. However, as he became increasingly involved in the World Council of Churches and with mainline Social Gospel Churches, there was an increasing suspicion among Pentecostal organizations of Du Plessis' motives. By 1958, major international Pentecostal conferences were ignoring Du Plessis. One conference official explained to him the reason why he was being ignored.

---

[69] Pope Paul VI, *Marian Devotion for the Modern Christian: An Address of Pope Paul VI to Marian Congregations*, In *The Pope Speaks*, vol. 9, 1963, p. 164.

He said, "You are so interested in the ecumenical movement in the liberal churches; you seem obsessed by it."[70]

David Du Plessis attended that New Delhi World Council of Churches assembly. While there, Bernard Leeming approached him and asked about the baptism of the Holy Spirit.[71] During the conference Du Plessis became more acquainted with Leeming, learning that he was a professor at the Roman Catholic seminary in Oxford, England. Du Plessis also learned that Leeming was the personal representative of Pope John XXIII. The two became good friends.[72]

Du Plessis continued his active role in ecumenism with the liberal churches of the National Council of Churches and the World Council of Churches. As his activities became increasingly well known and controversial, the Assemblies of God suggested that Du Plessis resign his credentials with their organization. He wrote them a letter assuring them that he neither wished to resign or withdraw. Finally in 1962, Du Plessis received a letter from the Assemblies of God Headquarters saying:

> It is the decision of the Executive Presbytery that your relationship with the Assemblies of God as an ordained minister is now terminated.[73]

Thus, Du Plessis, who had been banished in 1962 from fellowship with the Pentecostal churches of the Assemblies of God for his part in the World Council of Churches Ecumenical Movement, quickly turned toward the Roman Catholic Church. He met again with his Jesuit priest friend, Leeming. This time, during a meeting in Oxford, England, Leeming invited Du Plessis to Rome.

---

[70] Du Plessis, *A Man Called Mr. Pentecost*, pp. 1-192.

[71] Note: Leeming, as was noted earlier, was the Jesuit priest and theologian from Oxford who had reviewed the abilities of Geoffrey Fisher, the Archbishop of Canterbury, on behalf of the Vatican. Shortly after his visit to Rome and Leeming's lukewarm assessment of his abilities, Fisher resigned his position.

[72] Du Plessis, *A Man Called Mr. Pentecost*, pp. 199-204.

[73] Ibid., p. 195.

While Men Slept...

In Rome, Du Plessis was invited to the Vatican where he learned that the pope had sent representatives to the World Council of Churches in Geneva asking where they "could find a Pentecostal." They were then told of Du Plessis, who relayed the words of the Vatican's Tom Strandsky, who served as the secretary for Promoting Christian Unity under Cardinal Bea:

> And when we asked about your status, we were told, "He has no status. He once did, but he lost it." So I figured, "That's our man. If we invite him to the Vatican, nobody can object." Therefore, Mr. Pentecost, here we are![74]

Thus, the Vatican had sought out Du Plessis to help them accomplish their purpose. Soon, Du Plessis was introduced to Cardinal Bea. Du Plessis explained that because Bea was a Jesuit, he was not supposed to have been elevated to the rank of cardinal, "...but Pope John had broken that tradition...."[75]

Subsequently, Cardinal Bea arranged for a special pass for David Du Plessis to attend the September, 1964 session of the Second Vatican Council.[76] On September 29, 1964, Pope Paul VI addressed the observers of the Council who had been invited by Cardinal Bea. Speaking about a "new *modus operandi*" that was bringing about a new spirit of friendship, the pope said:

> Praised be the Lord, who—our faith tells us—has given us the gift of His Holy Spirit.[77]

However, the pope emphasized to the observers, of which David Du Plessis was one:

---

[74] Ibid., p. 211.

[75] Ibid., p. 212.

[76] Ibid., p. 215.

[77] Pope Paul VI, *A New Spirit of Friendship: Address of Pope Paul VI to Christian Observer Delegates Attending the Third Session of the Ecumenical Council*, In *The Pope Speaks*, vol. 10, no. 1, p. 127, 1964.

...although the Catholic Church cannot depart from certain doctrinal requirements to which she must remain faithful in Christ, she is quite ready to consider how she might overcome difficulties and dispel misunderstandings; how she might show respect for the authentic treasures of truth and spirituality which you possess, and expand and adapt certain canonical forms in order to facilitate reunion with the great and henceforth time-honored Christian communities still separated from Us.[78]

Indeed, in 1964 the Second Vatican Council adopted a decree on ecumenism. As such, a new name was given to the separated "Christian communities," especially the Eastern Orthodox Churches and the Anglican Church. The Vatican no longer called them "Churches." Instead, they were called "Communions." The Anglican Communion was named as such because it had preserved the structure and traditions of Catholicism.[79]

Dedicated to the Virgin Mary

Pope Paul VI closed the Third Session of the Second Vatican Council in November of 1964, commending the whole Roman Catholic Church and the Second Vatican Council to the Virgin Mary as he prayed:

O Virgin Mother of God, most august Mother of the Church, We commend the whole Church and the Ecumenical Council to thee...Finally, grant the universal Church that, in celebrating this great Ecumenical Council, it succeed in raising up a solemn hymn of praise and thanksgiving to God, a hymn of joy and exultation, for He that is mighty has done great things for thee, O clement, O loving, O sweet Virgin Mary.[80]

---

[78] Ibid., p. 129.

[79] Chadwick, *Michael Ramsey*, p. 317.

[80] Pope Paul VI, *Exploring the Mystery of the Church: Address of Pope Paul VI at the Close of the Third Session of the Second Vatican Ecumenical Council*, vol. 10, no. 1, p. 141, 1964.

While Men Slept...

The Charismatic Movement was birthed in the Roman Catholic Church during the Second Vatican Council. Then, in closing the Second Vatican Council on December 8, 1965, the feast day of the Immaculate Conception of Mary, Pope Paul VI committed all to her. He said:

> But note what is taking place here this morning. While we close the ecumenical council, we are honoring Mary Most Holy, the mother of Christ, and consequently, as we declared on another occasion, the mother of God and our spiritual mother. We are honoring Mary Most Holy, the Immaculate One, therefore innocent, stupendous, perfect.[81]

To Pope Paul VI, there was a special relationship between the Virgin Mary and the Spirit of God. In February 1974, more than eight years after the close of the Second Vatican Council, the pope issued the *Marialis Cultus*, which explained Marian devotion to the bishops of the Roman Catholic Church. The pope wrote that deeper study and meditation of the whole doctrine concerning the Holy Spirit will:

> ...bring out in particular the *hidden relationship* between the Spirit of God and the Virgin of Nazareth, and show the influence they exert on the Church.[82] [Italics is added for emphasis.]

The pope declared that Mary is the "true Ark of the Covenant and the true Temple of God." She is, he said, "the permanent dwelling of the Spirit of God," who is "...adorned with gifts of the Spirit granted to no one else." The pope added his hope for a "...salutary increase of devotion to Mary with undoubted profit for the Church and for society...."[83]

---

[81] Pope Paul VI, In *Second Vatican Council II Closing Speeches and Messages*, December 8, 1965, http://listserv.american.edu/catholic/church/papal/paul.vi/p6closin.txt.

[82] Pope Paul VI, In *Marialis Cultus: Apostolic Exhortation for the Right Ordering and Development of Devotion to the Blessed Virgin Mary*, February 2, 1974, http://www.ewtn.com/library/PAPALDOC/P6MARIAL.HTM

[83] Ibid.

The Fruit of the Ecumenical Charismatic Spirit

Submission to Authority

The Charismatic Movement promoted the concentration of authority into the hands of its leaders. One speaking under a spiritual anointing, believed to be from God, was able to require others to submit to his leadership. Using a technique in which submission to authoritative leadership was equated with submission to God, believers were brought into submission to His appointed messengers. The effect was that the people in such groups became docile, which ensured conformity and obedience.[84]

In a ten-year study of the effects of speaking in tongues among Neo-Pentecostals, deeply trusting and submissive relationships were created. The study found that:

> ...speakers in tongues develop deeply trusting and submissive relationships to the authority figures who introduced them to the experience...[they] have a strong need for external guidance from some trusted authority—someone "more powerful" than themselves to give them security and direction, even peace and relaxation in their lives. [They] ...tend to "overinvest" their feelings in their leaders to the point of "idealizing them as nearly perfect parents."[85]

Thus, the outcome of the Charismatic Movement that was promoted by Cardinal Bea through the Roman Catholic Church at the Second Vatican Council was to promote submissive relationships to the authority figures. After first submitting to the Spirit, there was a strong tendency to then submit to certain people within the Christian com-

---

[84] David Martin, "The Political Oeconomy of the Holy Ghost," In *Strange Gifts? A Guide to Charismatic Renewal*, David Martin and Peter Mullen, eds. (Oxford: Basil Blackwell Publisher Ltd., 1984), p. 64.

[85] John P. Kildahl, *The Psychology of Speaking in Tongues* (New York: Harper & Row, 1972), pp. 50-51, Cited in Quebedeaux, *The New Charismatics*, pp. 75-76.

munity, especially those who possessed certain spiritual gifts. It was believed that they were representatives of the Spirit and submission to them was therefore believed to be submission to the Spirit.[86] Among the dangers in the submissive relationships created in the Charismatic Movement is the development of a hierarchy of submission among Christians that can lead to authoritarianism.[87]

One example of the application of an authoritative structure created through the Charismatic Movement was in what became known as the Shepherding-Discipleship Movement, which was closely identified with a group in Fort Lauderdale, Florida. They tried to achieve a tighter system of accountability among Charismatics by gaining control over their behavior. The intent was to perfect Christian discipleship through an organized nationwide network based on strict submission in a pyramidal structure with rigid lines of authority.[88]

Universal Fatherhood

What greater authority can one perceive than that of the authority of one who would call himself the "universal father?" Ultimately, as Pope Paul VI clearly stated, the fruit of the Ecumenical Movement is to expand the "fatherhood" of the pope to include the whole world. On return from a pilgrimage, he said on January 25, 1964 that:

> We seemed to feel Our fatherhood expanding to the dimensions of this expectant world. And just as Rome's greeting on Our return intensified Our understanding of the mysterious bond uniting the Pope to his diocese, so the ovations of the crowds encountered in Our pilgrimage made Us experience with inexpressible emotion another dimension of Our vested charge: that universal fatherhood which the coronation lit-

---

[86] Paul S. Fiddes, "The Theology of the Charismatic Movement," In *Strange Gifts? A Guide to Charismatic Renewal*, David Martin and Peter Mullen, eds. (Oxford: Basil Blackwell Publisher Ltd., 1984), p. 37.

[87] Ibid., pp. 35-36.

[88] Crowe, *Pentecostal Unity*, pp. 44-45.

urgy expresses in hieratic language when proclaiming the new pope "guide of the world—*rectorem mundi*."[89]

The pope continued:

> ...We Ourself have just witnessed a vast manifestation of popular approval which thrilled the innermost fibre of Our being.
> In contact with those populations which share Our faith in the one all-powerful God, We felt the attraction exercised on souls by the ideal which the Catholic Church represents. And from the bottom of Our heart We thanked God for thus bringing these men, Our brothers, closer to Us, and for making Us experience so intensely the feeling of universal fatherhood.[90]

The plans of Pope Paul VI for the universal fatherhood of the pope deviated significantly from the teachings of Jesus Christ, as he said:

> And call no *man* your father upon the earth: for one is your Father, which is in heaven.
>
> —Matthew 23:9

Devotion to the Virgin Mary

Consistent with the "hidden relationship" between the Virgin Mary and the "Spirit of God" that Pope Paul VI described, acceptance of the Charismatic spirit among Roman Catholics had the effect of increasing their devotion to the Virgin Mary. Edward D. O'Connor, a Charismatic Roman Catholic priest and theologian from Notre Dame University in South Bend, Indiana, wrote of an experience in a Charismatic prayer meeting:

> One of the women declared that she had always felt a great repugnance for devotion to Mary, but that since receiving the baptism in the Spirit, she had become much more open to

---

[89] Pope Paul VI, "The Universal Fatherhood of the Pope," *The Pope Speaks*, vol. 10, no. 1, 1964, pp. 292-293.

[90] Ibid., p. 293.

it...Some who had been devoted to Mary found their devotion deepened and intensified.[91]

O'Connor continued, speaking of the Charismatic (which he then called Pentecostal) Movement's effect on Marian devotion, not only at Notre Dame but also in the rest of the country, by saying:

> Devotion to Mary has been strengthened by the Pentecostal movement...Some people, who had always been devoted to her, have rejoiced to find that the Holy Spirit has made her dearer than ever before. Many, whose devotion had been perfunctory or lukewarm, have become much more earnest about it, and in some cases have even become zealous promoters.[92]

As O'Connor wrote in 1958, before the Charismatic Movement was introduced to the world through the Second Vatican Council:

> The "child of Mary" is imbued with the spirit of Mary; and the Immaculate Conception is a prime root of this spirit, whether it be considered in her or in him—in the source, or in the derivative.[93]

"Experience," But Not Doctrine

The Charismatic Movement, while resembling the classical Pentecostal Movement of the early 1900's, has been characterized by some very significant differences. Perhaps the most notable difference was that Charismatic Catholics emphasized the spiritual experience, whereas the classical Pentecostals put greater emphasis on biblical doctrine, especially that of personal salvation. Consequently, while classical Pentecostals believed that the baptism in the Holy Ghost occurred *after* conversion and a believer's water baptism, the Catho-

---

[91] Edward D. O'Connor, *The Pentecostal Movement in the Catholic Church* (Notre Dame, Indiana: Ave Maria Press, 1971), pp. 58-59.

[92] Ibid., pp. 167-168.

[93] Edward D. O'Conner, "The Immaculate Conception and the Spirituality of the Blessed Virgin," In *The Dogma of the Immaculate Conception: History and Significance*, Edward Dennis O'Conner, ed. (Notre Dame, Indiana: University of Notre Dame Press, 1958), p. 444.

lic Charismatics said that neither was needed or desired. Consequently, many classical Pentecostals expressed confusion over the combination of spirituality and worldly behavior that they observed among Charismatics.[94, 95]

Many classical Pentecostals believed that preaching the Word of God from the Bible must be of higher priority than personal testimonies of individual experiences. The Charismatic Movement, on the other hand, placed a greater emphasis on description of personal experiences.[96] While some in the Charismatic Movement have been known for embracing extra-biblical manifestations of spiritual power, classical Pentecostals, such as Charles Parham, characterized these as "manifestations of the flesh."[97] Edward O'Connor summarized the Roman Catholic view of the Charismatic, or Neo-Pentecostal, Movement saying that it was about experience and not about theology:

> ...Pentecostalism is *not a theology*, but an experience...[and that the] true Pentecostal, therefore, is not concerned primarily with spreading doctrine, but with leading others to experience for themselves the life and power which he has experienced.[98] [Italics is in the original.]

This was the early position of Evan Roberts in the Wales Revival of 1904. He wrote to Frank Bartleman, that the move of the Spirit was being brought about by teaching no "sectarian doctrine."[99] Soon, Roberts, as he collaborated with Jessie Penn-Lewis in the book, *War on the Saints*, realized that the deceiver wants us to teach no doctrine. He specifically wants us to deny the presence of sin, the Saviour, and the work of salvation accomplished by His sacrifice on the Cross. They wrote that in the Christian Church:

---

[94] O'Connor, *The Pentecostal Movement in the Catholic Church*, pp. 243-246.

[95] Hollenweger, *Pentecostalism*, pp. 9-13.

[96] Julian Ward, "Pentecostal Theology and the Charismatic Movement," In *Strange Gifts? A Guide to Charismatic Renewal*, David Martin and Peter Mullen, eds. (Oxford: Basil Blackwell Publisher Ltd., 1984), p. 195.

[97] Parham, *The Life of Charles F. Parham*, p. 163.

[98] O'Connor, *The Pentecostal Movement in the Catholic Church*, pp. 241-242.

[99] Bartleman, *How Pentecost Came to Los Angeles*, pp. 33-36.

Countless "thoughts" and "beliefs," which are opposed to the truth of God, are injected into the minds of Christians by teaching spirits, rendering them ineffective in the warfare with sin and Satan, and subject to the power of evil spirits, although they are saved for eternity through their faith in Christ, and accept the authority of the Scriptures, and know the power of the Cross. All "thoughts" and "beliefs" should therefore be tested by the truth of God revealed in the Scripture, not merely by "texts" or portions of the Word, but by the principles of truth revealed in the Word. Since Satan will endorse his teachings by "signs and wonders"..., "power" and "signs," are no proof of "teaching" being of God... for Satan's "ministers can be "ministers of righteousness" (2 Cor. xi. 13-15).[100]

Rejecting Salvation by Faith

In 1971, O'Connor cautioned against adopting "alien beliefs and practices" as part of the Catholic "Pentecostal," which was later named the "Charismatic," experience. He cautioned, for example, against accepting:

...a doctrine or doctrinal attitude that is sometimes taken over by Catholics illegitimately [that] has to do with what is called the "salvation experience." This notion derives ultimately from Luther's concept of faith, but seems to have originated with the Puritans, and through the Methodist and Holiness traditions was transmitted to the main-line Pentecostals. It refers to an experience of the saving power of Christ, which occurs before the baptism in the Spirit. It gives a man the knowledge that he is *saved*... However, the doctrine that this is the only mode in which Christ's saving grace can be received, that it is necessary for salvation, and that it gives a man certitude about his state of grace (justification) and even about his ultimate salvation, besides being quite unscriptural is in contradiction with a firm and unanimous Catholic tradition, and with the formal teaching of the Council of Trent.[101]

---

[100] Penn-Lewis, with Evan Roberts, *War on the Saints*, p. 22.

[101] O'Connor, *The Pentecostal Movement in the Catholic Church*, pp. 245-246.

O'Connor's caution against accepting the doctrine of salvation by faith was not accepted by many Christians who believed in the authority of the Scriptures. That which O'Connor labeled as being "quite unscriptural," the Apostle Paul clearly stated:

> For by grace are ye saved through faith; and that not of yourselves: *it is* the gift of God: Not of works, lest any man should boast.
>
> —Ephesians 2:8-9

The New "New Pentecosts"

Third Wave

New spiritual movements that followed the Roman Catholic Charismatic Movement sought to bring spiritual manifestations into mainline denominations, transcending denominational boundaries. One example of such a movement was called a "third wave" spiritual movement because it was considered by some to be a successor to the classical Pentecostals and the Charismatics. The movement was recognized in 1983, with certain notable key leaders being associated with the Fuller Theological Seminary in Pasadena, California. The "third wave" position avoided labels, rejected the concept that baptism in the Holy Spirit was received after the "new birth" of a believer, and did not view "speaking with other tongues" as evidence of the baptism in the Spirit."[102]

Laughing Revival

By the mid-1990's what was called a "new movement," referred to as the "laughing revival," manifested itself in South Africa and soon moved to a church in Toronto, where it became known as the "Toronto Blessing." In reality, the movement was very reminiscent of the experience of David Du Plessis when he received the "Spirit" in South Africa in 1918.[103] The "holy laughter" in the church soon moved into

---

[102] Synan, *The Holiness-Pentecostal Tradition*, pp. 271-276.

[103] Du Plessis, *A Man Called Mr. Pentecost*, p. 34.

other extrabiblical spiritual manifestations, including that of making animal sounds such as those of lions, dogs, and chickens. These were often accompanied by prophecies of a final worldwide revival before the current age ended. Toronto Church had been associated with the Vineyard Churches of John Wimber (1934-1997), who later withdrew his endorsement from the movement because of the exotic extrabiblical manifestations.[104, 105] Some have insisted that the style of "self-centered" worship, which some similar churches promoted, became an end in itself. They maintained that the focus of the worship shifted from being God or Christ-centered to a preoccupation with self-gratification. In other words, the message shifted from emphasis of redemption through Jesus Christ to the "Blessing."[106]

In addition to the extrabiblical manifestation of the spirit, some have brought into question the techniques that were used in Toronto in an effort to elicit a spiritual response. One Pentecostal church pastor, for example, observed the use of extrabiblical gestures in an effort to achieve certain desired spiritual responses. He wrote that the prayer techniques he witnessed were similar to those of the common practices of Hindu gurus. For example, he observed:

> One minister stood behind a couple who wanted prayer for their struggle with infertility. He held his hands above their heads, palms downward, and began pumping vigorously up and down, as if pushing something into them.

> Another minister stood in front of a man desiring prayer, resting his left hand on the man while scooping the air in a sideways motion with his right hand, as if pulling something out of the air and into the man's body.

---

[104] Simon Coleman, *The Globalisation of Charismatic Christianity: Spreading the Gospel of Prosperity* (Cambridge: Cambridge University Press, 2000), pp. 22-23.

[105] Synan, *The Holiness-Pentecostal Tradition*, pp. 275-277.

[106] Wendy J. Porter, "The Worship of the Toronto Blessing?" In *The Toronto Blessing—or Is It?*, Stanley E. Porter and Philip J. Richter, eds. (London: Darton, Longman and Todd Ltd., 1995), pp. 127-128.

Eventually, this man and others fell to the floor to "rest in the Spirit." As the minister moved on, he occasionally looked back at those on the floor and scooped his hand through the air again, lightly throwing "something" toward them.

Other ministers blew on those being prayed for with a series of quick breaths...[107]

A reported characteristic of the "Toronto Blessing" was that it was spread from person to person as it spread globally to other churches. In one example, the wife of a former Anglican vicar named Ellie Mumford reportedly passed the blessing on to Nicky Gumbel of the Holy Trinity Brompton Anglican Church near London. Holy Trinity Brompton adapted the "Holy Spirit" experience into a format for global distribution that became known as the Alpha course.[108, 109]

The Globalization of Charismatic Ecumenism

Spreading the Charismatic Spirit

The Charismatic Movement spread to the United States of America through Roman Catholic universities such as Duquesne University in Pittsburgh in 1966 and then to Notre Dame University in South Bend, Indiana in 1967.[110] The movement then spread to public universities such as Michigan State University in East Lansing, Michigan.[111] By 1972, the movement was thriving in Ann Arbor, Michigan, the home of The University of Michigan, where the International Communications Office (ICO) of the Catholic Charismatics was first established. The office was later moved to Brussels and finally made the circle

---

[107] George Byron Koch, "Pumped and Scooped?" *Christianity Today*, vol. 39, no. 10 (11 September 1995), p. 25.

[108] Synan, *The Holiness-Pentecostal Tradition*, pp. 275-276.

[109] Gene Preston, "The Toronto Wave: Holy Laughter is Contagious," *The Christian Century*, vol. 111 no. 33 (16 November 1994), pp. 1068-1069.

[110] Kevin and Dorothy Ranaghan, *Catholic Pentecostals* (Paramus, New Jersey and New York, New York, 1969), pp. 6, 38.

[111] Ibid., p. 44.

back to Rome, where it became known as the International Catholic Charismatic Renewal Office (ICCRO).[112] By 1973 Cardinal Suenens (1904-1996) of Belgium was appointed by Pope Paul VI as advisor on charismatic developments.[113]

By January 1974 many of the thousand people who attended a service at the National Cathedral in Washington, D.C. spoke in tongues. Then at a 1975 gathering of 10,000 Roman Catholics at St. Peter's in Rome under the eyes of Pope Paul VI, some prayed in unknown tongues. Soon, the movement spread into mainline Protestant denominations.[114]

The Masters of Dialogue

As we have learned, Plato used the "dialogue" technique in *The Republic* whereby he offered the blueprint for an ideal society. Georg Hegel brought the technique forward as a tool for critical thinking and persuasion. F. D. Maurice employed modifications of the technique to challenge the accepted norms of Christianity in his controversial *Theological Essays*. It was, however, the Swami Vivekananda at the 1893 World's Parliament of Religions who successfully applied the technique to bring all of the world's religions toward the path for unity.[115]

Continuing in the spirit of the interreligious dialogue introduced at the 1893 World's Parliament of Religions, Pope Paul VI used the Second Vatican Council as the forum in which he called for "spiritual ecumenism" to be the "soul of the whole ecumenical movement." In doing so, he called for Catholics to have dialogue with the separated

---

[112] de Semlyen., *All Roads Lead to Rome?*, p. 25.

[113] Synan, *The Holiness-Pentecostal Tradition*, p. 250.

[114] Harvey Cox, *Fire from Heaven: The Rise of Pentecostal Spirituality and the Reshaping of Religion in the Twenty-First Century* (Reading, Massachusetts: Addison-Wesley Publishing Company, 1995), p. 107.

[115] M. Darrol Bryant and Frank Flinn, *Introduction, Scouting the Frontier*, In *Interreligious Dialogue: Voices from a New Frontier*, M. Darrol Bryant and Frank Flinn, eds., (New York: Paragon House, 1989), p. xi.

brethren as a means to get a better understanding of their minds and so that "...our belief will be better explained to them."[116]

Cardinal Bea insisted that the Roman Catholic Church use the "dialogue" technique as a tool for promoting Christian unity. Thus, he offered the technique for Roman Catholics to use with non-Roman Catholics, since it would be seen as a nonthreatening encounter. Cardinal Bea said that dialogue does not mean:

> ... an effort to persuade others of the truth of one's faith; nor does it mean an effort to "convert" the other partner or partners [in the dialogue] to one's own allegiance.[117]

As a result of the Second Vatican Council, a new outpouring of the "Holy Spirit" was brought to the world through the Roman Catholic Church. The dialogue technique was used to help many classical Pentecostals accept the new Charismatic Movement. David Du Plessis, while he was disenfranchised from the Bible-based organizations of the Pentecostal Movement, was the key to the Roman Catholic/classical Pentecostal dialogue.[118]

By 1974, the Roman Catholic spiritual movement had abandoned the term "Pentecostal" and adopted the term "Charismatic" in order not to be confused with the older Pentecostals.[119] Du Plessis was among those who believed unity could be found in experience rather than in doctrine. Those who agreed with him readily embraced the "neo-Pentecostal renewal."[120] Du Plessis reportedly concluded that the Holy Spirit was also in unbelievers and that they also have "charismata,"

---

[116] Pope Paul VI, *Vatican II: The Decree on Ecumenism*, vol. 10, no. 1 (1964), pp. 179-180.

[117] Bea, *Unity in Freedom*, p. 187.

[118] Kilian McDonnell, "The Death of Mythologies: The Classical Pentecostal/Roman Catholic Dialogue," *America*, vol. 172, no. 10 (25 March 1995), pp. 14-19.

[119] Synan, *The Holiness-Pentecostal Tradition*, p. 250.

[120] Edith Waldvogel Blumhofer, *The Assemblies of God: A Popular History* (Springfield, Missouri: Gospel Publishing House, 1985), p. 115.

but may not know how to use them correctly.[121] Thus, Charismatics moved outside the belief held by many classical Pentecostals that the Holy Spirit would not inhabit an unclean temple. Jesus said:

> Neither do men put new wine into old bottles: else the bottles break, and the wine runneth out, and the bottles perish: but they put new wine into new bottles, and both are preserved.
> —Matthew 9:17

However, as the Charismatic Movement spread, some Pentecostal organizations recognized that there was a spiritual movement manifesting itself outside of normally recognized Pentecostal bodies. As a consequence, the Assemblies of God restored the minister's credentials of David Du Plessis in 1980.[122] For his contributions to the movement as the chairman of the Roman Catholic-Pentecostal Dialogue team, Pope John Paul II in 1983 awarded Du Plessis the golden "Good Merit" medal. Du Plessis was the first non-Catholic in history to receive such an honor.[123]

Encouraged by his new relationship with the Roman Catholic Church and the successful introduction of the Charismatic Movement into mainline denominational churches, Du Plessis invited the Pentecostal leader, Bishop Paul E. Paino, the founder of Calvary Ministries International in Fort Wayne, Indiana, to accompany him in Rome. Believing that David Du Plessis was compromising biblical positions on doctrine, Paino declined to make the journey to Rome.[124]

The Anglican Communion and Charismatic Ecumenism

Through such dialogue, the goal of the Roman Catholic Church was to restore unity among those who profess Christianity. Ignoring the presence of hundreds of demonstrators near Lambeth Palace in England on March 18, 1966 and efforts by leaders such as Ian Paisley to

---

[121] Hollenweger, *Pentecostalism*, pp. 352-353.

[122] Blumhofer, *The Assemblies of God*, p. 116.

[123] Synan, *The Holiness-Pentecostal Tradition*, p. 226.

[124] Paul E. Paino, personal communication with author, November 22, 2000.

prevent the reunion of the Anglican Church with Rome, the archbishop of Canterbury, Michael Ramsey, offered the Anglican Church
in a submissive reunion with the Roman Catholic Church.[125] On March
24, 1966 Pope Paul VI and the archbishop entered into a common
declaration regarding unity, whereby the Anglican Church became
known as the Anglican Communion. Pope Paul VI wrote that:

> They affirm their desire that all those Christians who belong
> to these two Communions may be animated by these same
> sentiments of respect, esteem and fraternal love, and in order
> to help these develop to the full, they intend to inaugurate
> between the Roman Catholic Church and the Anglican Com-
> munion a serious dialogue which, founded on the Gospels and
> on the ancient common traditions, may lead to that unity in
> truth, for which Christ prayed.[126]

The Anglican-based Alpha course used the dialogue technique as a
means of teaching the acceptance of the gifts of the "Spirit" across
denominational lines throughout the world.[127] English Roman Catholic Bishop Ambrose Griffiths said of the incredible success of the Alpha course:

> This is the first time ever, you know, that the very same course
> is being used by every Christian church in pretty well every
> country in the world... It's very hard to think that it is other
> than a work of the Spirit in which we should rejoice.[128]

To many, such programs appeared to be the solution for spiritually
dying churches. Some supporters of the Alpha course were encour-

---

[125] Chadwick, *Michael Ramsey*, p. 318.

[126] Michael Cantuariensis and Paulus PP. VI, "The Common Declaration by Pope
Paul VI and the Archbishop of Canterbury: Rome, Saint Paul Without-the-Walls,
Thursday, 24 March 1966," In *Anglican/Roman Catholic Dialogue: The Work of
the Preparatory Commission*, Alan C. Clark and Colin Davey, eds. (London:
Oxford University Press, 1974), p. 2.

[127] Clive Price, *Spiritual Renewal Around the World: How the British Rediscovered the Bible, Charisma* (August, 1999) pp. 58-100.

[128] *Alpha for Catholics: UK Bishop on Alpha's "Incredible Achievement," Alpha
News*, USA ed., No. 6 (April-July, 2000), p. 6.

aged because they saw it as a means of duplicating the movement of the "Holy Spirit" throughout the world. A supporter of the Alpha course compared the duplicating principles used in the course to those that were so successfully applied by McDonalds to spread hamburgers throughout the world.[129] Some church leaders believed that the packaged course was a narrow expression of Christianity too strongly driven by a personal charismatic experience.[130] Nevertheless, the new movements of the "Spirit" have been successfully brought into Protestant churches through the efforts of the Roman Catholic, Anglican, and Episcopal Churches.[131, 132]

Notes of Caution

The Charismatic Movement, which was sometimes called the "Neo-Pentecostal" Movement, emphasized that the effect of the gift of the Holy Spirit was that it produced such a religious enthusiasm that it rendered doctrinal differences insignificant.[133] As many ecumenical leaders embraced the introduction of the Anglo-Catholic Charismatic Movement into denominational Protestant churches, classical Pentecostals continued to emphasize the need to avoid compromises with scriptural principles.[134] Because of a belief that there have been compromises in biblical doctrine within the ecumenical spiritual movement, some Bible-based Pentecostal leaders have attempted to distance themselves from the Charismatic Movement. Paul E. Paino, for example, said, "I think the Charismatics did severe damage to the Pentecostal testimony."[135]

[129] Price, *Spiritual Renewal Around the World*, pp. 58-100.

[130] Timothy C. Morgan, "The Alpha-Brits are Coming: a British Course for non-Christians Aims to Transform North American Evangelistic Outreach," *Christianity Today*, vol. 42, no. 2 (9 February 1998), pp. 36-39.

[131] Edward D. O'Connor, *The Pentecostal Movement in the Catholic Church* (Notre Dame, Indiana: Ave Maria Press, 1971).

[132] John Gunstone, *Pentecostal Anglicans* (London: Hodder and Stoughton, 1982).

[133] Richard Quebedeaux, *The New Charismatics: The Origins, Development, and Significance of Neo-Pentecostalism* (Garden City, New York: Doubleday & Company, Inc., 1976), p. 8.

[134] Blumhofer, *The Assemblies of God*, p. 116.

[135] Paul E. Paino, personal communication with author, November 22, 2000.

John prophetically cautioned the world of three unclean spirits coming from the mouths of the dragon, the beast and the false prophet:

> And I saw three unclean spirits like frogs *come* out of the mouth of the dragon, and out of the mouth of the beast, and out of the mouth of the false prophet. For they are the spirits of devils, working miracles, *which* go forth unto the kings of the earth and of the whole world, to gather them to the battle of that great day of God Almighty.
>
> —Revelation 16:13-14

The Greek word John used to describe the whole "world," which would be gathered by the spirits of devils to the "battle of the great day of God Almighty, was οικουμενης ("oikoumenes"). We recall that the word, "oikoumene," is the basis for the word, "ecumenical."

After experiencing the manifestations of false spirits in Los Angeles, Charles Parham wrote "A Note of Warning" on December 1, 1906 in which he warned that we must try the spirits because they are not all from God (See Appendix C). Jesus clearly cautioned us concerning false Christs and false prophets who show great signs and wonders:

> For there shall arise false Christs, and false prophets, and shall shew great signs and wonders; insomuch that, if *it were* possible, they shall deceive the very elect.
>
> —Matthew 24:24

The One World Religion of Universalism

Seventy years after the 1893 World's Parliament of Religions meeting in Chicago, U Thant (1909-1974), the Secretary General of the United Nations from 1961 to 1971, demonstrated that Vivekananda's message of universalism was still echoing loudly around the world as he quoted the Swami's message saying:

> In this country I do not come to convert you to a new belief. I want you to keep your own belief. I want to make the Methodist a better Methodist, the Presbyterian a better Presbyterian, the Unitarian a better Unitarian...I accept all religions that were in the past, and worship them all. I worship God

with every one of them, in whatever form they worship Him. I shall go to the mosque of the Mohammedan; I shall enter the Christian church and kneel before the Crucifix; I shall enter the Buddhist temple, where I shall take refuge in Buddha and his Law. I shall go into the forest and sit down in meditation with the Hindu, who is trying to see the Light which enlightens the hearts of everyone. Not only shall I do these things, but I shall keep my heart open for all that may come in the future.[136]

U Thant, a Buddhist, commented on the Hindu Swami Vivekananda's words on the occasion of celebrating the centennial of the Swami's birth, saying:

Those were very wise words and, friends, on this auspicious occasion when we are doing honour to one of the greatest men of all time, let us dedicate ourselves anew to this pledge: to make Christians better Christians, Hindus better Hindus, Muslims better Muslims, Buddhists better Buddhists, and Jews better Jews.[137]

As we have learned, the Swami Vivekananda did accept all religions as being true, except one. He rejected that which holds the doctrine that Jesus Christ shed His blood for our sins. He said:

I, for one, would not come to be saved by such a doctrine [salvation through Jesus' blood]. If anybody would come and say, "Be saved by my blood", [sic] I would say to him, "My brother, go away; I will go to hell; I am not a coward to take innocent blood to go to heaven; I am ready for hell.[138]

Jesus took offence to the workers of iniquity, even though they pray, prophesy, cast out devils, or even perform miracles in His name. Although they say "Lord, Lord" and claim that they used His name to

---

[136] Swami Vivekananda, quoted in U. Thant, *Swami Vivekananda—The Spiritual Ambassador of India, The Vedanta Kesari* (Madras-4, India: Sri Ramakrishna Math), vol. 50 (4), August 1963, p. 307.

[137] Ibid., p. 307.

[138] Vivekananda, In *The Complete Works of Swami Vivekananda*, vol. 8, p. 209.

accomplish manifestations of supernatural power, He will tell them that He never knew them:

> Not every one that saith unto me, Lord, Lord, shall enter into the kingdom of heaven; but he that doeth the will of my Father which is in heaven. Many will say to me in that day, Lord, Lord, have we not prophesied in thy name? and in thy name have cast out devils? and in thy name done many wonderful works? And then will I profess unto them, I never knew you: depart from me, ye that work iniquity.
>
> —Matthew 7:21-23

He Shall Increase with Glory the "God of forces"

The Apostle Paul cautioned:

> Let no man deceive you by any means: for *that day shall not come*, except there come a falling away first, and that man of sin be revealed, the son of perdition; Who opposeth and exalteth himself above all that is called God, or that is worshipped; so that he as God sitteth in the temple of God, shewing himself that he is God.
>
> —2 Thessalonians 2:3-4

The "son of perdition" whom Paul warned about was reminiscent of the king described by Daniel:

> And the king shall do according to his will; and he shall exalt himself, and magnify himself above every god, and shall speak marvellous things against the God of gods, and shall prosper till the indignation be accomplished: for that that is determined shall be done.
>
> —Daniel 11:36

Daniel continued describing this king:

> Neither shall he regard the God of his fathers, nor the desire of women, nor regard any god: for he shall magnify himself above all.
>
> —Daniel 11:37

While Men Slept...

The king would magnify himself above every god, including the God of gods, who is the Lord of lords, the God of Israel, who revealed Himself to man through Jesus Christ. However, this king whom Daniel described would still honor *one* god. Daniel called this god the "God of forces," which, as we have learned, some believed to be the "goddess of fortresses." The Hebrew word for "forces" was מעוז, or "maowz," which was the same word used for "strong" in the "strong holds" of the king's "estate," where *he will* honor and *he will* increase with glory this god or goddess:

> But in his estate shall he honour the God of forces: and a god whom his fathers knew not shall he honour with gold, and silver, and with precious stones, and pleasant things. Thus shall he do in the most strong holds with a strange god, whom he shall acknowledge *and* increase with glory: and he shall cause them to rule over many, and shall divide the land for gain.
>
> —Daniel 11:38-39

As we see this "king," much like the one whom Paul called the "man of sin," who opposes the God of gods and puts himself above every god, while he honors the "God of forces," Paul said:

> Remember ye not, that, when I was yet with you, I told you these things?
>
> —2 Thessalonians 2:5

We would also do well to remember Isaiah's words of caution:

> ...Watchman, what of the night? Watchman, what of the night? The watchman said, The morning cometh, and also the night....
>
> —Isaiah 21:11b-12a

448

Chapter 20. Take Heed!

Take heed unto thyself, and unto the doctrine; continue in them: for in doing this thou shalt both save thyself, and them that hear thee.

—1 Timothy 4:16

Hold Fast to Sound Doctrine

The Apostle Paul believed the doctrine of salvation through Jesus Christ and Him crucified to be central to the Christian faith. As he wrote to the Corinthians, many of whom were highly educated with Greek philosophy, Paul made a humble, but very convincing, statement. He said:

> And I, brethren, when I came to you, came not with excellency of speech or of wisdom, declaring unto you the testimony of God. For I determined not to know any thing among you, save Jesus Christ, and him crucified.
>
> —1 Corinthians 2:1-2

Paul made his point. The gospel of Christianity is not about excellency of speech or wisdom of man. Instead, it is about Jesus Christ, and Him crucified. The writer of Hebrews, which some claim to be Paul, also clearly made the point that the sacrifice of Jesus Christ on the cross was sufficient for the sins of the world. After it was accomplished, He sat down at the right hand of God because the work was finished. No further offering was required for sin:

> But this man, after he had offered one sacrifice for sins for ever, sat down on the right hand of God;
>
> —Hebrews 10:12

> Now where remission of these *is, there is* no more offering for sin. Having therefore, brethren, boldness to enter into the holiest by the blood of Jesus, By a new and living way, which he hath consecrated for us, through the veil, that is to say, his flesh;
>
> —Hebrews 10:18-20

While Men Slept...

As Jesus rested after making the final offering for sins, so must we also rest if we accept by faith that He gave that final offering:

> For he that is entered into his rest, he also hath ceased from his own works, as God *did* from his. Let us labour therefore to enter into that rest, lest any man fall after the same example of unbelief.
>
> —Hebrews 4:10-11

Therefore, our attempts to attain salvation by continually offering the body and blood of Jesus Christ, or by doing good works, demonstrate our unbelief that Jesus Christ gave the complete sacrifice for our sins. Thus, such actions undermine our faith, through which we are saved by the blood of Jesus Christ. Recall that Paul emphasized:

> For by grace are ye saved through faith; and that not of yourselves: it is the gift of God: Not of works, lest any man should boast.
>
> —Ephesians 2:8-9

Another Gospel

The Apostle Paul was amazed at how quickly the people in the churches of Galatia turned to another gospel besides that which he preached. He sternly rebuked those who put aside the gospel that he brought to them, which was that we are saved through the blood of Jesus Christ, by the grace of God, through faith, and not by our own works. Paul wrote to the Galatians:

> I marvel that ye are so soon removed from him that called you into the grace of Christ unto another gospel: Which is not another; but there be some that trouble you, and would pervert the gospel of Christ. But though we, or an angel from heaven, preach any other gospel unto you than that which we have preached unto you, let him be accursed. As we said before, so say I now again, if any man preach any other gospel unto you than that ye have received, let him be accursed.
>
> —Galatians 1:6-9

Despite Paul's clear warning, the gospel of the new universal Christianity is *not* the same gospel that Paul preached. It is a gospel of universal salvation, without the blood of Jesus Christ sacrificed on the cross. It is a gospel which says that the whole world will be saved without believing in Jesus Christ, being justified instead by good works. It is, as we have learned, a social gospel.

Paul warned that in the latter times some would depart from the faith because they would pay heed to seducing spirits and doctrines of devils:

> Now the Spirit speaketh expressly, that in the latter times some shall depart from the faith, giving heed to seducing spirits, and doctrines of devils;
>
> —1 Timothy 4:1

The doctrines of devils are those opposed to the central doctrine that Paul preached, which was that Jesus Christ was God manifest in the flesh and was, therefore, the acceptable sacrifice for all sin. The Scriptures are clear:

> And without controversy great is the mystery of godliness: God was manifest in the flesh, justified in the Spirit, seen of angels, preached unto the Gentiles, believed on in the world, received up into glory.
>
> —1 Timothy 3:16

> In whom we have redemption through his blood, *even* the forgiveness of sins: Who is the image of the invisible God, the firstborn of every creature: For by him were all things created, that are in heaven, and that are in earth, visible and invisible, whether *they be* thrones, or dominions, or principalities, or powers: all things were created by him, and for him: And he is before all things, and by him all things consist.
>
> —Colossians 1:14-17

> For every house is builded by some *man*; but he that built all things *is* God.
>
> —Hebrews 3:4

451

> Moreover, brethren, I declare unto you the gospel which I preached unto you, which also ye have received, and wherein ye stand; By which also ye are saved, if ye keep in memory what I preached unto you, unless ye have believed in vain. For I delivered unto you first of all that which I also received, how that Christ died for our sins according to the scriptures;
>
> —1 Corinthians 15:1-3

Who would deny this gospel, which is so clearly stated in the Scriptures? John called them liars! He also said that anyone denying that Jesus Christ is come in the flesh is not of God, but is a deceiver and an antichrist:

> Who is a liar but he that denieth that Jesus is the Christ? He is antichrist, that denieth the Father and the Son.
>
> —1 John 2:22

> And every spirit that confesseth not that Jesus Christ is come in the flesh is not of God: and this is that *spirit* of antichrist, whereof ye have heard that it should come; and even now already is it in the world.
>
> —1 John 4:3

> For many deceivers are entered into the world, who confess not that Jesus Christ is come in the flesh. This is a deceiver and an antichrist.
>
> —2 John 1:7

Deceiving and Being Deceived

All that Seems Right is Not Right

King Solomon reminded us that:

> There is a way which seemeth right unto a man, but the end thereof *are* the ways of death.
>
> —Proverbs 14:12

That which seems good to the flesh, such as seemingly easy-to-read Bibles or powerful spiritual manifestations, may lull us into accepting

452

another doctrine. After Jesus warned His disciples about the leaven of the Pharisees and Sadducees, it finally dawned on them that He was actually cautioning them about more than that which fed the flesh. Indeed, they realized that the warning was about the *doctrine* of the Pharisees and of the Sadducees:

> Then understood they how that he bade them not beware of the leaven of bread, but of the doctrine of the Pharisees and of the Sadducees.
>
> —Matthew 16:12

Make no mistake. Those who hold fast to the doctrine of salvation by the blood of Jesus Christ will suffer persecution. They will be hated by the world which has been deceived into believing that all religions are true and that all will be saved through their own works. Those who have been deceived want to deceive others. Paul cautioned that we must continue in the things which we have learned:

> Yea, and all that will live godly in Christ Jesus shall suffer persecution. But evil men and seducers shall wax worse and worse, deceiving, and being deceived. But continue thou in the things which thou hast learned and hast been assured of, knowing of whom thou hast learned *them*; And that from a child thou hast known the holy scriptures, which are able to make thee wise unto salvation through faith which is in Christ Jesus.
>
> —2 Timothy 3:12-15

Refusing to continue in the things they have learned, been assured of, and knowing from whom they have learned them, many will accept the Social Gospel instead of the Salvation Gospel. They will be deceived because:

> ...they received not the love of the truth, that they might be saved. And for this cause God shall send them strong delusion, that they should believe a lie:
>
> —2 Thessalonians 2:10b-11

While Men Slept...

Using the Name of Jesus

The deceivers will use all cunningness and craftiness to deceive under the label of "Christianity." They will even come in the *name of Jesus* to accomplish their objective:

> And Jesus answered and said unto them, Take heed that no man deceive you. For many shall come in my name, saying, I am Christ; and shall deceive many.
>
> —Matthew 24:4-5

Despite the warnings, Satan will deceive the world. John wrote:

> And the great dragon was cast out, that old serpent, called the Devil, and Satan, which deceiveth the whole world: he was cast out into the earth, and his angels were cast out with him.
>
> —Revelation 12:9

Using Signs and Wonders

The Lord God, Yahweh, used signs and wonders to demonstrate His power so that people would believe that He is the one true God. He used them in Egypt where He said:

> And I will harden Pharaoh's heart, and multiply my signs and my wonders in the land of Egypt.
>
> —Exodus 7:3

God used signs and wonders in Babylon to convince Nebuchadnezzar the king of His great power. Nebuchadnezzar said:

> I thought it good to shew the signs and wonders that the high God hath wrought toward me. How great *are* his signs! and how mighty *are* his wonders! his kingdom *is* an everlasting kingdom, and his dominion *is* from generation to generation.
>
> —Daniel 4:2-3

Jesus knew that signs and wonders were required for some to believe:

> Then said Jesus unto him, Except ye see signs and wonders, ye will not believe.
>
> —John 4:48

Signs and wonders convince people of the presence of supernatural power, which many believe to be only from God. Therefore, when Satan uses counterfeit miracles, it will be so convincing that almost everyone will believe that the one who performed them is of God. Jesus warned that false Christs and false prophets would use these tools in their efforts to even seduce believers into deception! He said:

> For false Christs and false prophets shall rise, and shall shew signs and wonders, to seduce, if *it were* possible, even the elect.
>
> —Mark 13:22

Paul cautioned:

> *Even him*, whose coming is after the working of Satan with all power and signs and lying wonders,
>
> —2 Thessalonians 2:9

John cautioned:

> And deceiveth them that dwell on the earth by *the means of* those miracles which he had power to do in the sight of the beast; saying to them that dwell on the earth, that they should make an image to the beast, which had the wound by a sword, and did live.
>
> —Revelation 13:14

Escaping the Universal Deception

The Bondage of Universal Salvation

The gospel of universal salvation is preached on the basis of offering liberty from the bondage of accepting and believing any specific doctrine. The promise, by those who deny salvation through the blood of Jesus Christ, that we can be made free from the guilt of sin through our social works, only leads us back into the bondage that accompanies unrepented and unredeemed sin. Peter explained:

> While they promise them liberty, they themselves are the servants of corruption: for of whom a man is overcome, of the

> same is he brought in bondage. For if after they have escaped
> the pollutions of the world through the knowledge of the Lord
> and Saviour Jesus Christ, they are again entangled therein,
> and overcome, the latter end is worse with them than the be-
> ginning.
>
> —2 Peter 2:19-20

Paul cautioned that once we find liberty through Jesus Christ, we
must be careful not to again allow ourselves again to be put under the
yoke of bondage:

> Stand fast therefore in the liberty wherewith Christ hath made
> us free, and be not entangled again with the yoke of bondage.
>
> —Galatians 5:1

A Remnant Will Escape

While the whole world will be deceived, there is strong biblical evidence that a remnant of God's people will be spared from the deception that leads to bondage. When the question was asked of Jesus
whether a few would be saved, he replied that many who will strive
for salvation will not find it:

> Then said one unto him, Lord, are there few that be saved?
> And he said unto them, Strive to enter in at the strait gate: for
> many, I say unto you, will seek to enter in, and shall not be
> able.
>
> —Luke 13:23-24

> Because strait *is* the gate, and narrow *is* the way, which leadeth
> unto life, and few there be that find it.
>
> —Matthew 7:14

> For many are called, but few *are* chosen.
>
> —Matthew 22:14

The Old Testament prophets, Isaiah and Jeremiah, said that God would
save a remnant of Israel:

For though thy people Israel be as the sand of the sea, *yet* a remnant of them shall return: the consumption decreed shall overflow with righteousness.

—Isaiah 10:22

For thus saith the LORD; Sing with gladness for Jacob, and shout among the chief of the nations: publish ye, praise ye, and say, O LORD, save thy people, the remnant of Israel.

—Jeremiah 31:7

And it shall come to pass in that day, *that* the remnant of Israel, and such as are escaped of the house of Jacob, shall no more again stay upon him that smote them; but shall stay upon the LORD, the Holy One of Israel, in truth.

—Isaiah 10:20

The "Ekklesia," the Called Out from the World

Jesus said that the ekklesia (εκκλησια, meaning "called out" ones and often translated as "the church")[1] of Philadelphia, who had kept His Word and had not denied His name would be spared from the hour of temptation which shall come upon the oikoumene (οικουμενη [the basis of the word "ecumenical"], said by James Strong to mean the "the Roman empire" and often translated as "the world"):[2]

Because thou hast kept the word of my patience, I also will keep thee from the hour of temptation, which shall come upon all the world, to try them that dwell upon the earth.

—Revelation 3:10

Many will not see or understand the significance of the new universal Christianity. By not knowing, not watching, and not praying, the "snare" that will come upon the whole earth will take them who are not worthy to *escape*:

For as a snare shall it come on all them that dwell on the face of the whole earth. Watch ye therefore, and pray always, that

---

[1]Strong, *A Concise Dictionary of the Words in The Greek Testament*, pp. 26, 39
[2] Ibid., p. 51.

457

> ye may be accounted worthy to escape all these things that
> shall come to pass, and to stand before the Son of man.
> —Luke 21:35-36

Why They Cannot See

God Shut Their Eyes and Hearts

In the face of clear and documented biblical and historical evidence of
the goals of the new universal Christianity, many still can neither see
nor understand its implications. Isaiah explained that God has shut
their eyes *and* their hearts so that they cannot understand:

> They have not known nor understood: for he hath shut their
> eyes, that they cannot see; and their hearts, that they cannot
> understand.
> —Isaiah 44:18

Because they cannot understand, they cannot believe. Even though
Jesus performed many miracles, there were still those who did not
believe on Him. Repeating the words of Isaiah, John explained:

> Therefore they could not believe, because that Esaias said
> again, He hath blinded their eyes, and hardened their heart;
> that they should not see with their eyes, nor understand with
> their heart, and be converted, and I should heal them.
> —John 12:39-40

Much of the world, including many fine leaders of Christian churches,
organizations, and colleges have accepted the ecumenical doctrine of
the Socialists, Unitarians, and Universalists, leading to the new universal Christianity.

A Spirit of Deep Sleep

The underlying motives of those who deny that Jesus Christ has come
in the flesh is clear to *some* of those who studied the Word of God.
Many others, however, are looking toward the leaders of large religious organizations for the answers concerning truth and deception.

458

God, however, makes it clear to us that even the prophets, the rulers, and the seers may not be able to understand.

> In whom the god of this world hath blinded the minds of them which believe not, lest the light of the glorious gospel of Christ, who is the image of God, should shine unto them.
>
> —2 Corinthians 4:4

That is because He has poured out upon them a spirit of deep sleep:

> For the LORD hath poured out upon you the spirit of deep sleep, and hath closed your eyes: the prophets and your rulers, the seers hath he covered. And the vision of all is become unto you as the words of a book that is sealed, which men deliver to one that is learned, saying, Read this, I pray thee: and he saith, I cannot; for it is sealed: And the book is delivered to him that is not learned, saying, Read this, I pray thee: and he saith, I am not learned. Wherefore the Lord said, Forasmuch as this people draw near me with their mouth, and with their lips do honour me, but have removed their heart far from me, and their fear toward me is taught by the precept of men: Therefore, behold, I will proceed to do a marvellous work among this people, even a marvellous work and a wonder: for the wisdom of their wise men shall perish, and the understanding of their prudent men shall be hid.
>
> —Isaiah 29:10-14

Even the prophet Daniel could not understand the things which the LORD had not yet opened his eyes to see:

> And I heard, but I understood not: then said I, O my Lord, what *shall be* the end of these *things*? And he said, Go thy way, Daniel: for the words *are* closed up and sealed till the time of the end.
>
> —Daniel 12:8-9

Whether they wake or whether they sleep, we must faithfully bear witness unto the truth, knowing that, in the LORD's time, the wise shall understand:

While Men Slept...

> So, as much as in me is, I am ready to preach the gospel to you that are at Rome also.
>
> —Romans 1:15

> Many shall be purified, and made white, and tried; but the wicked shall do wickedly: and none of the wicked shall understand; but the wise shall understand.
>
> —Daniel 12:10

How Long Halt Ye Between Two Opinions?

Paul told the Corinthians not to be unequally yoked with unbelievers. He then asked them a series of questions which we, if our hearts are open, must also each ask ourselves:

> Be ye not unequally yoked together with unbelievers: for what fellowship hath righteousness with unrighteousness? and what communion hath light with darkness? And what concord hath Christ with Belial? or what part hath he that believeth with an infidel? And what agreement hath the temple of God with idols?
>
> —2 Corinthians 6:14-16a

John, speaking of the false church, then wrote:

> And I heard another voice from heaven, saying, Come out of her, my people, that ye be not partakers of her sins, and that ye receive not of her plagues.
>
> —Revelation 18:4

As Ahab gathered four hundred fifty prophets of Baal and four hundred prophets of the groves, who ate at Jezebel's table, Elijah stood alone. His name itself stood as a witness to the one true God, יהוה (YHWH, known as YAH or Yahweh), proclaiming that God is YAH. In the presence of the people of Israel and the prophets of Baal, Elijah asked the people to choose whom they would follow, the LORD (Yahweh) or Baal:

And Elijah came unto all the people, and said, How long halt ye between two opinions? if the LORD *be* God, follow him: but if Baal, *then* follow him. And the people answered him not a word.

–1 Kings 18:21

Paul wrote:

But what saith the answer of God unto him? I have reserved to myself seven thousand men, who have not bowed the knee to *the image of* Baal. Even so then at this present time also there is a remnant according to the election of grace.

—Romans 11:4-5

Paul was quoting from the words that the LORD (Yahweh) had given to a very discouraged Elijah, who was hiding in a cave. When the LORD asked Elijah what he was doing in the cave, Elijah stood at its entrance and responded:

And he said, I have been very jealous for the LORD God of hosts: because the children of Israel have forsaken thy covenant, thrown down thine altars, and slain thy prophets with the sword; and I, *even* I only, am left; and they seek my life, to take it away.

—1 Kings: 19:14

Elijah felt that he was the only one left who had not forsaken the covenant with the LORD (Yahweh). He was discouraged. The other prophets had already been slain and now Jezebel sought to slay him. The LORD, however, reminded Elijah that he was not alone. Although there were few, the LORD had still preserved a remnant. He said:

Yet I have left *me* seven thousand in Israel, all the knees which have not bowed unto Baal, and every mouth which hath not kissed him.

—1 Kings 19:18

How long halt *ye* between two opinions?

While Men Slept...

Appendix A: Basic Unitarian Universalist Beliefs

By the twentieth century, Unitarians became known as Unitarian Universalists because, in America, the American Unitarian Association and the Universalist Church of America merged to form the Unitarian Universalist Association in 1961.[1] While the religious views of these two merged groups were not necessarily identical, they were similar. For example, both Unitarians and Universalists were at odds against a common theological view, known as Calvinism.[2] In other words, they rejected the Calvinist doctrine that salvation was for an "elect," or chosen, group. Instead, Unitarians and Universalists believed in a "universal" salvation that was not dependent upon believing a specific theological doctrine.

Although Unitarians and Universalists could be discussed as a particular kind of modern-day congregation, *this discussion is not about any particular organization*. Instead, it is directed mainly toward a kind of theology that may broadly be referred to as Unitarianism and Universalism. It represents the fruit of a system of beliefs that openly denies the deity of Jesus Christ, one that functionally denies His deity, or one that de-emphasizes the completeness of the sacrifice of Jesus on the cross. In some cases, many who would not call themselves Unitarians or Universalists might demonstrate similar theologies by offering alternative persons or images as objects of worship in place of or in addition to Jesus Christ, thus reducing His status.

While there is no set of specific doctrinal beliefs that all Unitarians or Universalists must adhere to, most would consider their beliefs to be part of the liberal movement in theology.[3] Even though Unitarians and Universalists, which we may generally refer to as Unitarians, profess that they represent no particular belief, they do have many things in common. They do not accept Jesus Christ as their "Lord and Sav-

---

[1] Robinson, *The Unitarians and Universalists,* p. 3.

[2] Ibid.

[3] Conrad Wright, *The Beginnings of Unitarianism in America* (Hamden, Connecticut: Reprint by Archon Books of Starr King Press 1955 ed., 1976), p. 3.

ior."[4] They also deny that He is part of the Triune Godhead, which is commonly referred to as the "Trinity."[5] An essential concept of Unitarian belief is that Jesus Christ had no pre-existence before He was born as a man. As such, they believe that He is not divine and, therefore, is not included as part of the Godhead as Trinitarians believe: the Father, Son, and Holy Ghost (Holy Spirit). Therefore, most Unitarians deny the deity of Jesus Christ, His atoning sacrifice for sin, and His resurrection from the dead.

Because of a broad diversity in specific beliefs among Unitarians and Universalists, an outline of common beliefs should be considered to be generally, but not always, accepted by those professing to be Unitarians and/or Universalists. Nevertheless, the Committee of the British and Foreign Unitarian Association published *Fifty Points in Favour of Unitarianism* in 1910 which summarized many of the key points of Unitarian belief. In it, they also listed the seven Affirmations of Unitarianism as follows:

1. God has made reason to be man's guide to truth.
2. God from the beginning has created men according to a good plan which has never been frustrated by the devil nor broken by a fall.
3. God brings men into the world as his children, imperfect and ignorant, but partakers of the divine life.
4. God incarnates his life and love in humanity, and in testifying to this fact Jesus gave pre-eminent revelation of a universal truth.
5. God is the eternal Father, the manifestations of whose manifold energies take many forms, but he is the central unity of all.
6. God forgives sin without the need of blood sacrifice to propitiate him.
7. God possesses resources of wisdom and love by which men shall receive discipline, instruction, and opportunity

---

[4] *Religions of America, Ferment and Faith in an Age of Crisis: A New Guide and Almanac*, Leo Rosten, ed. (New York: Simon and Schuster, 1963), p. 265.

[5] Hurst, *History of Rationalism*, p. 559.

to the end that all shall become partakers of the divine nature, and participate in the divine joy of eternal love and life.[6]

The basic philosophy of Unitarianism is that "love" is more important than "faith." Essentially, Unitarians have argued that there is a "higher Reformation" dawning. In contrast to the "Reformation of Faith," which aimed at individual redemption, the "Reformation of Love" is aimed at universal redemption and will move toward establishing the Kingdom of God, proclaiming love, throughout the world.[7] In other words, many Unitarians would agree that we are in the process of establishing the physical and earthly Kingdom of God.

Unitarians profess to believe in a vaguely defined God but believe that it is the "…duty of each man to be diligent in his search for truth and faithful to the light God reveals in *him*."[8] Because an essential component of the Unitarian belief is that Jesus Christ is not deity, it follows that His death was not a worthy sacrifice for sin. Once it is denied that Jesus Christ was God manifest in the flesh, then it follows that the Atonement is also denied. According to Hall:

> But the whole efficacy of the Atonement surely depends on the notion that it was not as man but as God that Jesus died on the cross.[9]

They do believe, however, that Jesus, just as all men do, had "divine potentialities." Therefore, the divinity of all men, including Jesus, is one of degree, and not of kind. Thus, Unitarians believe that Jesus is:

> …the ideal man, whose life bears witness to the loftiness of human nature, and whose achievements assure us of the advance towards Godlikeness the race will gradually make.[10]

---

[6] Alfred Hall, *Fifty Points in Favour of Unitarianism* (London: British and Foreign Unitarian Association, 1910), pp. 9-10.

[7] Ibid., pp. 12-13.

[8] Ibid., p. 15.

[9] Ibid., p. 22.

[10] Ibid., p. 23.

While Men Slept...

While Unitarians reject the doctrine of the Trinity, they assert that the only Trinitarian Scripture in the Bible, 1 John 5:7, was rightly removed from the Revised Version of the New Testament. After that Scripture was removed, they asserted that:

> There are few scholars of repute belonging to any branch of the Christian Church in the present day who would contend that the New Testament contains any clear or explicit statement of the doctrine of the Trinity.[11]

According to Unitarians, because of the "Infinite Love of God" no soul will be lost to God. Thus, Unitarians renounce the doctrine of an eternal hell and reject the notion that there is a devil.[12] Unitarians also believe that the Word of God is not limited to the Bible. Instead, all things must pass the tests of reason and appeal to the mind as being true. They hold that the works of man that are under divine inspiration include:

> ...the work of all faithful workmen, artists, architects, sculptors, engineers, musicians, poets, and others, which makes for the progress of the race...Charles Darwin's account of the origin of man is doubtless nearer the truth than that contained in the first chapter of Genesis.[13]

Unitarians believe truth is continually revealed to man in progressive order, as he "ascends Godward." While acknowledging that the Bible contains valuable truth, they insist that it is an "intensely human book." It is not, however, all of equal importance or value. According to Hall:

> Modern students are now agreed that "The Bible contains the word of God, but it is not all the word of God."[14]

---

[11] Ibid., pp. 24-25.

[12] Ibid., pp. 26-27.

[13] Ibid., p. 30.

[14] Ibid., p. 33.

Appendix A. Basic Unitarian Universalist Beliefs

Because of the belief of Unitarians that Jesus was the natural son of Joseph and his wife Mary, they reject the supernatural virgin birth of Jesus.[15] Unitarians also reject the belief that God performs miracles and that Jesus was resurrected from the dead.[16,17] To Unitarians, true salvation is found in "perfection of character." They believe that heaven is not a place but, instead, it is a condition of the soul.[18] To the Unitarian, heaven means an:

> ...opportunity for gaining greater beauty of character, a nearer approach to God, the pure heart, the consecrated will, the reverent soul. Into such a heaven we can all in some measure begin to enter here and now.[19]

The position of Unitarians and Universalists is that authority in religion lies in personal experience, conscience, and reason and may be summed up as follows:

> We believe that personal experience, conscience and reason should be the final authorities in religion, and that in the end religious authority lies not in a book or person or institution, but in ourselves.[20]

---

[15] Ibid., p. 44.

[16] Ibid., pp. 50-51.

[17] Ibid., pp. 54-57.

[18] Ibid., p. 72.

[19] Ibid., p. 91.

[20] Quoted in Excerpts from *"We Are Unitarian Universalists"*, *pamphlet #3047*, In *Unitarian Universalism in Brief* (Boston: Unitarian Universalist Association, 1995), http://uua.org/uubrief.html.

While Men Slept...

Appendix B: Impact of the Changing Scriptures

This Appendix contains several sample verses of Scripture in two versions of the Greek Text and in six versions of the English text. There are scores of copyrighted versions of the Bible and it is not possible to succinctly present all of the possible variations contained in these versions. Therefore, the versions presented below were selected only as illustrations showing some of the variations in alternative texts.

A statement that many Bible-based Christians accept precedes each set of Scriptures. A note then follows the set of Scriptures indicating the possible impact that the variations in the readings might have on one's belief. Depending on which variations are accepted as being true, some of the Scriptures could be used to support either a Trinitarian Salvation Gospel position or a Unitarian Social Gospel.

Sometimes the changes made in a Greek version were then translated into the English version. Sometimes the Greek changes were not seen in any English version. To some readers, the overall effect of the information presented below is that confusion is created about the reliability of the Scriptures. The evidence indicates that subtle changes in the Scripture have occurred. The changes create doubt concerning several foundational beliefs in the minds of believers.

The Greek Scriptures are taken from the *Textus Receptus* Greek (TR)[1] and the Westcott and Hort Greek (WH).[2] The English Scriptures were grouped into two groups, depending on whether they were based on the Received Text (Group R), which was the *Textus Receptus*, or a critical text (Group C), such as the Westcott and Hort or some other critical text. Group R includes the Authorized King James Version

---

[1] *1550 Textus Receptus Text*, In *Online Bible*, Version 8.11 (Winterbourne, Ontario, Canada: Timnathserah, Inc., 2000).

[2] *1881 Westcott Hort Greek Text*, In *Online Bible*, Version 8.11 (Winterbourne, Ontario, Canada: Timnathserah, Inc., 2000).

(KJV),[3] the New King James Version (NKJV),[4] and the Modern King James Version (MKJV).[5] Group C includes the Revised Version (RV),[6] Revised Standard Version (RSV),[7] and New International Version (NIV).[8] The Scripture references to each of these seven versions are designated as TR, WH, KJV, NKJV, MKJV, RV, RSV, or NIV, respectively. The older Greek Text of the two presented was the TR and the oldest English text of the six presented was the KJV. Therefore, the TR and the KJV were presented as the baseline for comparing the other versions. Obvious differences in the versions are in bold type. When text is omitted from that found in the two baseline versions, then the spaces are underlined to show the difference.

Many of the Bible versions based on the critical texts have extensive footnotes that often have reference to possible alternate readings. Sometimes, multiple options are presented in the footnotes, giving the reader a choice for the preferred reading. The Scripture references presented below are the ones actually contained in the text, which is apparently the preferred reading selected by the editors of each particular version. Therefore, references to the footnotes are not included because the footnotes are not part of the text and because it is cumbersome and confusing to include all possible alternate readings. Italics in some of the versions, such as KJV, NKJV, MKJV, and RV are used to distinguish words that were in not in the Greek manuscript, but were inserted into the English to help readability. In the RSV and NIV versions, such distinctions are not made. Also,

---

[3] *1769 Authorized Version*, In *Online Bible*, Version 8.11 (Winterbourne, Ontario, Canada: Timnathserah, Inc., 2000).

[4] *1982 New King James Version*, In *Online Bible*, Version 8.11 (Winterbourne, Ontario, Canada: Timnathserah, Inc., 2000).

[5] *Modern King James Version of the Holy Bible* (Lafayette, Indiana: Jay P. Green, Sr., Sovereign Grace Publishers, 1999).

[6] *The New Testament of Our Lord and Saviour Jesus Christ Translated Out of the Greek: Being the Version Set Forth A.D. 1611 Compared with the Most Ancient Authorities and Revised A.D. 1881* (Oxford: Oxford University Press, 1881).

[7] *The Holy Bible, Revised Standard Version*

[8] International Bible Society, *The Holy Bible, New International Version* (Grand Rapids, Michigan: The Zondervan Corporation, 1984).

470

Appendix B. Impact of the Changing Scriptures

since biblical "revision" is an ongoing process for many versions, it must be recognized that specific verses in a certain version may vary, depending upon the specific revision of that version being referenced.

Jesus is the Only Begotten Son of God

Greek (TR: Received Text; WH: a Critical Text)	John 3:16
ουτως γαρ ηγαπησεν ο θεος τον κοσμον ωστε τον υιον αυτου τον μονογενη εδωκεν ινα πας ο πιστευων εις αυτον μη αποληται αλλ εχη ζωην αιωνιον	-TR
ουτως γαρ ηγαπησεν ο θεος τον κοσμον ωστε τον υιον ____ τον μονογενη εδωκεν ινα πας ο πιστευων εις αυτον μη αποληται αλλ εχη ζωην αιωνιον	-WH

English: Based on Received Greek Text	John 3:16
For God so loved the world, that he gave **his only begotten Son**, that whosoever believeth in him should not perish, but have **everlasting life**.	-KJV
For God so loved the world that He gave **His only begotten Son**, that whoever believes in Him should not perish but have **everlasting life**.	-NKJV
For God so loved the world that He gave **His only-begotten Son**, that whoever believes in Him should not perish but have **everlasting life**.	-MKJV

English: Based on Critical Greek Texts	John 3:16
For God so loved the world, that he gave **his only begotten Son**, that **whosoever** believeth on him should not perish but have **eternal** life.	-RV
For God so loved the world that he gave **his only** ____ **Son**, that **whoever** believes in him should not perish but have **eternal** life.	-RSV
For God so loved the world that he gave **his one and only** ____ **Son**, that **whoever** believes in him shall not perish but have **eternal** life.	-NIV

Impact: The only begotten Son is uniquely of the very essence of God. This is contrasted with those who are not uniquely begotten of God but are as many sons of God as in examples in Genesis 6:2, Job 2:1; and John 1:12. The critical text changes subtly diminish the claim of the deity of Jesus

While Men Slept...

Christ and also reflect Maurice's redefinition of the distinction between "everlasting" and "eternal" life. In Maurice's view, "eternal" did not refer to duration in time. Instead, he said that it meant having knowledge of God.

Greek (TR: Received Text; WH: a Critical Text)	John 1:14
και ο λογος σαρξ εγενετο και εσκηνωσεν εν ημιν και εθεασαμεθα την δοξαν αυτου δοξαν ως μονογενους παρα πατρος πληρης χαριτος και αληθειας	-TR
και ο λογος σαρξ εγενετο και εσκηνωσεν εν ημιν και εθεασαμεθα την δοξαν αυτου δοξαν ως μονογενους παρα πατρος πληρης χαριτος και αληθειας	-WH

English: Based on Received Greek Text	John 1:14
And the Word was made flesh, and **dwelt** among us, (and we beheld his glory, the glory as of **the only begotten of the Father**,) full of grace and truth.	-KJV
And the Word became flesh and **dwelt** among us, and we beheld His glory, the glory as of **the only begotten of the Father**, full of grace and truth.	-NKJV
And the Word became flesh, and **tabernacled** among us. And we beheld His glory, the glory as of **the only begotten of *the* Father**, full of grace and of truth.	-MKJV

English: Based on Critical Greek Texts	John 1:14
And the Word was made flesh, and **dwelt** among us, (and we beheld his glory, the glory as **of the only begotten from the Father**,) full of grace and truth.	-RV
And the Word became flesh and **dwelt** among us, full of grace and truth; we have beheld his glory, glory as of **the only _____ Son from the Father**.	-RSV
The Word became flesh and made his **dwelling** among us. We have seen his glory, the glory of **the ___ _____ One and Only, who came from the Father**, full of grace and truth.	-NIV

Impact: The subtle implications of the changes in the critical text-based English are discussed above with John 3:16. The use of "One and Only" tends to move the reader away from the specific Person, Jesus, to a non-specified Christ. It moves the reader toward the Neo-Platonic concept of "the One" of pantheism.

Appendix B. Impact of the Changing Scriptures

Greek (TR: Received Text; WH: a Critical Text)	John 1:18
θεον ουδεις εωρακεν πωποτε **ο** μονογενης υιος ο ων εις τον κολπον του πατρος εκεινος εξηγησατο	-TR
θεον ουδεις εωρακεν πωποτε _ μονογενης θεος ο ων εις τον κολπον του πατρος εκεινος εξηγησατο	-WH

English: Based on Received Greek Text	John 1:18
No **man** hath seen God at any time, **the only begotten Son**, which is in the bosom of the Father, he **hath declared** *him*.	-KJV
No **one** has seen God at any time. **The only begotten Son**, who is in the bosom of the Father, He **has declared** *Him*.	-NKJV
No **one** has seen God at any time; **the Only-begotten Son**, who is in the bosom of the Father, He **has declared** *Him*.	-MKJV

English: Based on Critical Greek Texts	John 1:18
No **man** hath seen God at any time; **the only begotten Son**, which is in the bosom of the Father, he hath **declared** *him*.	-RV
No **one** has ever seen God; **the only** _____ **Son**, who is in the bosom of the Father, he has **made him known**.	-RSV
No **one** has ever seen God, _____ ___ **but God the One and Only**, who is at the Father's side, has **made him known**.	-NIV

Impact: See the comment for John 1:14. In addition, the lead taken in the WH Greek by saying God has seen God was not taken in the RV or RSV but was taken in the NIV. The clear implication in the Received Greek text is that no man has seen God but His only begotten Son, who was not just a man, has declared Him. Using the expression "the One" is suggestive of the Neo-Platonic pantheistic deity.

While Men Slept...

Jesus Christ is God Manifest in the Flesh

Greek (TR: Received Text; WH: a Critical Text)	1 Timothy 3:16
και ομολογουμενως μεγα εστιν το της ευσεβειας μυστηριον θεος εφανερωθη εν σαρκι εδικαιωθη εν πνευματι ωφθη αγγελοις εκηρυχθη εν εθνεσιν επιστευθη εν κοσμω ανεληφθη εν δοξη	-TR
και ομολογουμενως μεγα εστιν το της ευσεβειας μυστηριον ος εφανερωθη εν σαρκι εδικαιωθη εν πνευματι ωφθη αγγελοις εκηρυχθη εν εθνεσιν επιστευθη εν κοσμω ανελημφθη εν δοξη	-WH

English: Based on Received Greek Text	1 Timothy 3:16
And without controversy great is the **mystery of godliness: God was manifest in the flesh, justified in** the Spirit, seen of angels, preached unto the **Gentiles,** believed on in the world, **received** up into glory.	-KJV
And without controversy great is the **mystery of godliness: God was manifested in the flesh, Justified in** the Spirit, Seen by angels, Preached among the **Gentiles,** Believed on in the world, **Received** up in glory.	-NKJV
And without controversy great is the **mystery of godliness: God was manifest in the flesh, justified in** the Spirit, seen by angels, preached among **nations,** believed on in *the* world, and **received** up into glory.	-MKJV

English: Based on Critical Greek Texts	1 Timothy 3:16
And without controversy great is the **mystery of godliness; He who was manifested in the flesh, justified in** the spirit, seen of angels, preached among the **nations,** believed on in the world, **received** up into glory.	-RV
___ _____ _____**Great indeed, we confess**, is the **mystery of our religion: He was manifested in the flesh, vindicated in** the Spirit, seen by angels, preached among the nations, believed on in the world, **taken** up in glory.	-RSV
Beyond all question, the mystery of godliness is great: He appeared in a body, was vindicated by the Spirit, was seen by angels, was preached among the **nations,** was believed on in the world, was **taken** up in glory.	-NIV

Impact: This verse has been the subject of great debate. It, of course, is a definite statement affirming of the deity of Jesus Christ if God was manifest

474

Appendix B. Impact of the Changing Scriptures

in the flesh. The rewriters of the Bible claim that the θ in the Greek may have been tampered with and should have been an O, instead. This is a very important verse for those who would like to deny the deity of Jesus Christ. The subtle difference of whether He was "taken up" or "received up" into glory could be used to enhance or diminish one's belief in the power of Jesus Christ.

Greek (TR: Received Text; WH: a Critical Text)	1 John 4:3
και παν πνευμα ο μη ομολογει τον ιησουν χριστον εν σαρκι εληλυθοτα εκ του θεου ουκ εστιν και τουτο εστιν το του αντιχριστου ο ακηκοατε οτι ερχεται και νυν εν τω κοσμω εστιν ηδη	-TR
και παν πνευμα ο μη ομολογει τον ιησουν _____ __ _____ _____ εκ του θεου ουκ εστιν και τουτο εστιν το του αντιχριστου ο ακηκοατε οτι ερχεται και νυν εν τω κοσμω εστιν ηδη	-WH

English: Based on Received Greek Text	1 John 4:3
And every spirit that **confesseth not that Jesus Christ is come in the flesh** is not **of** God: and this is that *spirit* of antichrist, whereof ye have heard that it should come; and **even** now already is it in the world.	-KJV
and every spirit that does **not confess that Jesus Christ has come in the flesh** is not **of** God. And this is the *spirit* of the Antichrist, which you have heard was coming, and is ____ now already in the world.	-NKJV
and every spirit that **does not confess that Jesus Christ has come in** *the* **flesh** is not **of** God. And this is the antichrist you heard is coming, and even now is already in the world.	-MKJV

English: Based on Critical Greek Texts	1 John 4:3
and every spirit which **confesseth not Jesus** _____ __ _____ __ ____ _____ is not **of** God: and this is the *spirit* of **the** antichrist, whereof ye have heard that it _____ cometh; and ____ now it is in the world already.	-RV
and every spirit which does **not confess Jesus** _____ __ _____ __ ____ _____ is not **of** God. This is the spirit of antichrist, of which you heard that it was coming, and ____ now it is in the world already.	-RSV
but every spirit that does **not acknowledge Jesus** _____ __ _____ __ ____ _____ is not **from** God. This is the spirit of **the** antichrist, which you have heard is coming and **even** now is already in the world.	-NIV

475

While Men Slept...

Impact: Those who would want to deny the deity of Jesus Christ would not want to confess that He has come in the flesh. They who would deny this are not of God, but are of the spirit of antichrist.

Only God is Good and Jesus is Good

Greek (TR: Received Text; WH: a Critical Text)	Matthew 19:16-17	
και ιδου εις προσελθων ειπεν αυτω διδασκαλε αγαθε τι αγαθον ποιησω ινα εχω ζωην αιωνιον ο δε ειπεν αυτω τι με λεγεις αγαθον ουδεις αγαθος ει μη εις ο θεος ει δε θελεις εισελθειν εις την ζωην τηρησον τας εντολας	-TR	
και ιδου εις προσελθων αυτω ειπεν διδασκαλε _____ τι αγαθον ποιησω ινα σχω ζωην αιωνιον ο δε ειπεν αυτω τι με _____ ερωτας περι του αγαθου εις εστιν ο αγαθος ει δε θελεις _____ εις την ζωην εισελθειν τηρει τας εντολας	-WH	

English: Based on Received Greek Text	Matthew 19:16-17	
And, behold, one came and said unto him, **Good Master,** what good **thing** shall I do, that I may have eternal life? And he said unto him, **Why callest thou me good?** *there* is none good but one, ***that is,*** God: but if thou wilt enter into life, **keep** the commandments.	-KJV	
Now behold, one came and said to Him, "**Good Teacher,** what good **thing** shall I do that I may have eternal life?" So He said to him, "**Why do you call Me good?** No one *is* good but One, ***that is,*** God. But if you want to enter into life, **keep** the commandments."	-NKJV	
And behold, one came and said to Him, **Good Master,** what good **thing** shall I do that I may have eternal life? And He said to him, **Why do you call Me good?** *There is* none good but one, **that is, God.** But if you want to enter into life, **keep** the commandments.	-MKJV	

Appendix B. Impact of the Changing Scriptures

English: Based on Critical Greek Texts	Matthew 19:16-17	
And behold, one came to him and said, ____ **Master**, what good **thing** shall I do, that I may have eternal life? And he said unto him, **Why askest thou me concerning that which is good? One there is which is good** _____: but if thou wouldest enter into life, **keep** the commandments.	-RV
And behold, one came up to him, saying, "____ **Teacher**, what good **deed** must I do, to have eternal life?" And he said to him, **"Why do you ask me about what is good? One there is who is good** _____. If you would enter life, **keep** the commandments."	-RSV
Now a man came up to **Jesus** and asked, "____ **Teacher**, what good **thing** must I do to get eternal life?" **"Why do you ask me about what is good?"** Jesus replied. **"There is only One who is good** _____. If you want to enter life, **obey** the commandments."	-NIV

Impact: Only God is good. Therefore, if Jesus is called "good," then He is, by implication, God. The rewritten Bibles do not call Him "good" and they do not confess that God is "good." Universalists who believe that all are good would, by inference, also believe that all are God.

God Created All Things by Jesus Christ

Greek (TR: Received Text; WH: a Critical Text)	Ephesians 3:9	
και φωτισαι παντας τις η κοινωνια του μυστηριου του αποκεκρυμμενου απο των αιωνων εν τω θεω τω τα παντα κτισαντι δια ιησου χριστου	-TR
και φωτισαι _____ τις η οικονομια του μυστηριου του αποκεκρυμμενου απο των αιωνων εν τω θεω τω τα παντα κτισαντι ___ _____ _____	-WH

English: Based on Received Greek Text	Ephesians 3:9	
And to make all *men* see what *is* the **fellowship** of the mystery, which from **the beginning of the world** hath been hid in God, who created all things **by Jesus Christ**:	-KJV
and to make all see what *is* the **fellowship** of the mystery, which from the **beginning of the ages** has been hidden in God who created all things **through Jesus Christ**;	-NKJV
and to bring to light what *is* the **fellowship** of the mystery which from **eternity** has been hidden in God, who created all things **by Jesus Christ**;	-MKJV

While Men Slept...

English: Based on Critical Greek Texts	Ephesians 3:9
and to make all men see what is the **dispensation** of the mystery which **from all ages** hath been hid in God who created all things ___ ___ ___ ;	-RV
and to make all men see what is the **plan** of the mystery **hidden for ages** in God who created all things ___ ___ ___ ;	-RSV
and to make plain to everyone the **administration** of this mystery, which **for ages past** was kept hidden in God, who created all things ___ ___ ___ .	-NIV

Impact: If God created all things by Jesus Christ, then Jesus Christ was in the beginning. This would, therefore, affirm John 1:1-3. The change in the rewritten versions weakens the affirmation that the Word was in the beginning and that all things were made through Him. If left unchanged, then those, such as many Unitarians, who would try to discredit John would also have to discredit Paul.

The change in the Greek word "κοινονια" in the TR to "οικονομια" in the WH resulted in a change in the translation of the English word from "fellowship" in the KJV to "dispensation" in the RV, "plan" in the RSV, and "administration" in the NIV. The fellowship of the mystery, which is direct access to God through Jesus Christ, is changed to suggest access to God through an administrative structure.

Jesus Christ has Risen from the Dead

Greek (TR: Received Text; WH: a Critical Text)	Luke 24:6
ουκ εστιν ωδε αλλ ηγερθη μνησθητε ως ελαλησεν υμιν ετι ων εν τη γαλιλαια	-TR
[[ουκ εστιν ωδε αλλα ηγερθη]] μνησθητε ως ελαλησεν υμιν ετι ων εν τη γαλιλαια	-WH

English: Based on Received Greek Text	Luke 24:6
He is not here, but is risen: remember how he spake unto you when he was yet in Galilee,	-KJV
"He is not here, but is risen! Remember how He spoke to you when He was still in Galilee,	-NKJV
He is not here, but has risen. Remember how He spoke to you when He was still in Galilee,	-MKJV

478

Appendix B. Impact of the Changing Scriptures

English: Based on Critical Greek Texts	Luke 24:6
He is not here, but is risen: remember how he spake unto you when he was yet in Galilee,	-RV
__ __ __ ___ __ __ __ ____ Remember how he told you, while he was still in Galilee,	-RSV
He is not here; he has risen! Remember how he told you, while he was still with you in Galilee:	-NIV

Impact: The Scripture was challenged, being placed in parenthesis, in the WH Greek text. However, it was included in RV, deleted in the RSV, and then restored in the NIV. This confusion about what Luke had written concerning the resurrection could cause one to question the promise of everlasting life through the living Jesus Christ.

Jesus is the Christ and is the Son of God

Greek (TR: Received Text; WH: a Critical Text)	Mark 1:1
αρχη του ευαγγελιου ιησου χριστου υιου του θεου	-TR
αρχη του ευαγγελιου ιησου χριστου ____ ___ ___	-WH

English: Based on Received Greek Text	Mark 1:1
The beginning of the gospel **of** Jesus Christ, the Son of God;	-KJV
The beginning of the gospel **of** Jesus Christ, the Son of God.	-NKJV
The beginning of the gospel **of** Jesus Christ, *the* Son of God:	-MKJV

English: Based on Critical Greek Texts	Mark 1:1
The beginning of the gospel **of** Jesus Christ, the Son of God.	-RV
The beginning of the gospel **of** Jesus Christ, the Son of God.	-RSV
The beginning of the gospel **about** Jesus Christ, the Son of God.	-NIV

Impact: The WH dropped off the confession that Jesus Christ is the Son of God. However, the rewritten English versions retained it.

479

While Men Slept...

Greek (TR: Received Text; WH: a Critical Text)	Acts 4: 26-27
παρεστησαν οι βασιλεις της γης και οι αρχοντες συνηχθησαν επι το αυτο κατα του κυριου και κατα του χριστου αυτου συνηχθησαν γαρ επ αληθειας επι τον αγιον παιδα σου ιησουν ον εχρισας ηρωδης τε και ποντιος πιλατος συν εθνεσιν και λαοις ισραηλ	-TR
παρεστησαν οι βασιλεις της γης και οι αρχοντες συνηχθησαν επι το αυτο κατα του κυριου και κατα του χριστου αυτου συνηχθησαν γαρ επ αληθειας εν τη πολει ταυτη επι τον αγιον παιδα σου ιησουν ον εχρισας ηρωδης τε και ποντιος πιλατος συν εθνεσιν και λαοις ισραηλ	-WH

English: Based on Received Greek Text	Acts 4: 26-27
The kings of the earth **stood up**, and the rulers **were gathered** together against the Lord, and against his **Christ.** For of a truth against thy holy **child** Jesus, whom thou hast anointed, both Herod, and Pontius Pilate, with the Gentiles, and the people of Israel, were gathered together,	-KJV
The kings of the earth **took their stand**, And the rulers **were gathered** together Against the LORD and against His **Christ.**' "For truly against Your holy **Servant** Jesus, whom You anointed, both Herod and Pontius Pilate, with the Gentiles and the people of Israel, were gathered together	-NKJV
The kings of the earth **stood up**, and the rulers **were gathered** together against the Lord and against His **Christ."** For truly, against Your holy **child** Jesus, whom You have anointed, both Herod and Pontius Pilate, with the nations, and *the* people of Israel, were gathered together	-MKJV

480

Appendix B. Impact of the Changing Scriptures

English: Based on Critical Greek Texts	Acts 4: 26-27
The kings of the earth **set themselves in array**, And the rulers **were gathered** together, Against the Lord, and against his **Anointed:** for of a truth **in this city** against thy holy **Servant** Jesus, whom thou didst anoint, both Herod and Pontius Pilate, with the Gentiles and the peoples of Israel, were gathered together,	-RV
The kings of the earth set themselves in array, and the rulers **were gathered** together, against the Lord and against his **Anointed'** --for truly **in this city** there **were gathered** together against thy holy **servant** Jesus, whom thou didst anoint, both Herod and Pontius Pilate, with the Gentiles and the peoples of Israel,	-RSV
The kings of the earth take their stand and the rulers **gather** together against the Lord and against his **Anointed One.** Indeed Herod and Pontius Pilate **met** together with the Gentiles and the people of Israel **in this city to conspire** against your holy **servant** Jesus, whom you anointed.	-NIV

Impact: The word χριστου (Christos), is clearly written in both Greek sources. Changing the word that clearly says "Christ" to "Anointed" or to his "Anointed One" and then selecting the word "servant" instead of "child," only serves to confuse and not clarify who Jesus is. It dilutes His identity and familial standing.

Greek (TR: Received Text; WH: a Critical Text)	Matthew 8:29
και ιδου εκραξαν λεγοντες τι ημιν και σοι ιησου υιε του θεου ηλθες ωδε προ καιρου βασανισαι ημας	-TR
και ιδου εκραξαν λεγοντες τι ημιν και σοι _____ υιε του θεου ηλθες ωδε προ καιρου βασανισαι ημας	-WH

English: Based on Received Greek Text	Matthew 8:29
And, **behold**, they cried out, saying, What have **we** to do with **thee, Jesus**, thou Son of God? art thou come hither to torment us before the time?	-KJV
And **suddenly** they cried out, saying, "What have **we** to do with **You, Jesus**, You Son of God? Have You come here to torment us before the time?"	-NKJV
And **behold**, they cried out, saying, What *have* **we** to do with **You, Jesus**, Son of God? Have You come here to torment us before the time?	-MKJV

While Men Slept...

English: Based on Critical Greek Texts	Matthew 8:29
And **behold**, they cried out, saying, What have **we** to do with **thee**, _____thou Son of God? art thou come hither to torment us before the time?	-RV
And **behold**, they cried out, "What have **you** to do with **us**, _____O Son of God? Have you come here to torment us before the time?"	-RSV
What do **you** want with **us**, _____ Son of God?" they shouted. "Have you come here to torture us before the **appointed** time?"	-NIV

Impact: The Received Text-based versions clearly state that Jesus is the Son of God. The rewritten versions reduce the certainty that Jesus is the Son of God.

Greek (TR: Received Text; WH: a Critical Text)	Acts 8:37
ειπεν δε ο φιλιππος ει πιστευεις εξ ολης της καρδιας εξεστιν αποκριθεις δε ειπεν πιστευω τον υιον του θεου ειναι τον ιησουν χριστον	-TR
Verse Omitted from Text	-WH

English: Based on Received Greek Text	Acts 8:37
And Philip said, If thou believest with all thine heart, thou mayest. And he answered and said, I believe that Jesus Christ is the Son of God.	-KJV
Then Philip said, "If you believe with all your heart, you may." And he answered and said, "I believe that Jesus Christ is the Son of God."	-NKJV
Philip said, If you believe with all your heart, it is lawful. And he answered and said, I believe that Jesus Christ is the Son of God.	-MKJV

English: Based on Critical Greek Texts	Acts 8:37
Verse Omitted from Text	-RV
Verse Omitted from Text	-RSV
Verse Omitted from Text	-NIV

Impact: This powerful verse addresses two major doctrinal issues. First is the confession that Jesus Christ is the Son of God. The second, is that of a believer's baptism. It is made clear by this passage that believing that Jesus Christ is the Son of God is a condition for baptism. If the verse were included in the rewritten Bibles, it would be more difficult to justify the concept of infant, rather than believer's, baptism.

Appendix B. Impact of the Changing Scriptures

Greek (TR: Received Text; WH: a Critical Text)	John 9:35
ηκουσεν ο ιησους οτι εξεβαλον αυτον εξω και ευρων αυτον ειπεν αυτω συ πιστευεις εις τον υιον του θεου	-TR
ηκουσεν _ ιησους οτι εξεβαλον αυτον εξω και ευρων αυτον ειπεν ____ συ πιστευεις εις τον υιον του ανθρωπου	-WH

English: Based on Received Greek Text	John 9:35
Jesus heard that they had cast him out; and when he had found him, he said **unto him**, Dost thou believe **on** the Son of **God**?	-KJV
Jesus heard that they had cast him out; and when He had found him, He said **to him**, "Do you believe **in** the Son of **God**?"	-NKJV
Jesus heard that they had cast him out; and finding him, He said **to him**, Do you believe on the Son of **God**?	-MKJV

English: Based on Critical Greek Texts	John 9:35
Jesus heard that they had cast him out; and finding him, he said ____ ___, Dost thou believe **on** the Son of **God**?	-RV
Jesus heard that they had cast him out, and having found him he said ____ ___, "Do you believe **in** the Son of **man**?"	-RSV
Jesus heard that they had thrown him out, and when he found him, he said ____ ___, "Do you believe **in** the Son of **Man**?"	-NIV

Impact: True, Jesus is the Son of God and the Son of Man. Our salvation from our sins requires that we believe that He is the Son of God. The RV agreed with the TR, rather than with the WH. The later critical versions, however, accepted the WH rendering of the Scripture. This poses an interesting question about whether, in general, one would accept older or newer English versions as more reliable.

Greek (TR: Received Text; WH: a Critical Text)	1 Corinthians 16:22
ει τις ου φιλει τον κυριον ιησουν χριστον ητω αναθ-εμα μαραν αθα	-TR
ει τις ου φιλει τον κυριον _____ _____ ητω αναθ-εμα μαρανα θα	-WH

While Men Slept...

English: Based on Received Greek Text	1 Corinthians 16:22
If any man love not the Lord **Jesus Christ**, let him be **Anathema Maranatha**.	-KJV
If anyone does not love the Lord **Jesus Christ**, let him be **accursed. O Lord, come!**	-NKJV
If anyone does not love the Lord **Jesus Christ**, let him be **accursed. The Lord comes!**	-MKJV

English: Based on Critical Greek Texts	1 Corinthians 16:22
If any man loveth not the Lord _____ _____, let him be **anathema. Marinatha**.	-RV
If any one has no love for the Lord _____ _____, let him be **accursed. Our Lord, come!**	-RSV
If anyone does not love the Lord _____ _____**--a curse be on him. Come, O Lord!**	-NIV

Impact: Which Lord must we love? Is it the Lord Jesus Christ or some other Lord?

Greek (TR: Received Text; WH: a Critical Text)	John 6:69
και ημεις πεπιστευκαμεν και εγνωκαμεν οτι συ ει ο χριστος ο υιος του θεου του ζωντος	-TR
και ημεις πεπιστευκαμεν και εγνωκαμεν οτι συ ει ο _____ _ ____ ___ αγιος του θεου _____	-WH

English: Based on Received Greek Text	John 6:69
And we **believe and are sure that thou art that Christ,** the Son of the living God.	-KJV
"Also we **have come to believe and know that You are** the **Christ, the Son of the living God.**"	-NKJV
And we **have believed and have known that You are the Christ, the Son of the living God**.	-MKJV

English: Based on Critical Greek Texts	John 6:69
And we **have believed** and **know** that thou art the _____ __ __ __ __ _____ **Holy One of God.**	-RV
and **we have believed**, and **have come to know**, that you are the **Holy One of God.**	-RSV
We **believe** and **know** that __ __ __ __ __ __ __ __ __ _____ you are the **Holy One of God.**	-NIV

Impact: The strong statement of believing that Jesus is the Christ and the Son of the living God is severely weakened in the WH and in the rewritten English versions. The change in the tenses in the various versions also adds confusion about whether they still believe or had only previously believed.

484

Appendix B. Impact of the Changing Scriptures

Greek (TR: Received Text; WH: a Critical Text)	Acts 2:30
προφητης ουν υπαρχων και ειδως οτι ορκω ωμοσεν αυτω ο θεος εκ καρπου της οσφυος αυτου το κατα σαρκα αναστησειν τον χριστον καθισαι επι του θρονου αυτου	-TR
προφητης ουν υπαρχων και ειδως οτι ορκω ωμοσεν αυτω ο θεος εκ καρπου της οσφυος αυτου __ ____ ____ _____ ___ _____ καθισαι επι τον θρονον αυτου	-WH

English: Based on Received Greek Text	Acts 2:30
Therefore being a prophet, and **knowing** that God had sworn with an oath to him, that of the fruit of his **loins, according to the flesh**, he would **raise up Christ to sit** on his throne;	-KJV
"**Therefore**, being a prophet, and **knowing** that God had sworn with an oath to him that of the fruit of his **body, according to the flesh**, He would **raise up the Christ to sit** on his throne,	-NKJV
Therefore being a prophet, and **knowing** that God had sworn with an oath to him that of *the* fruit of his **loins, according to the flesh**, He would **raise up Christ to sit** upon his throne,	-MKJV

English: Based on Critical Greek Texts	Acts 2:30
Being therefore a prophet, and **knowing** that God had sworn with an oath to him, that of the fruit of his **loins** _____ __ ___ _____ he would _____ __ _____ **set** *one* upon his throne;	-RV
Being therefore a prophet, and **knowing** that God had sworn with an oath to him that ____ __ ___ ___ ___ __ ___ _____ _____ __ ___ _____ he would _____ __ _____**set one of his descendants** __ ___ upon his throne,	-RSV
But he was a prophet and **knew** that God had promised him on oath __ ___ ____ ___ __ ___ ____ __ ___ ___ _____ __ ___ _____ that he would _____ __ ____ _____ **place one of his descendants** __ ___ on his throne.	-NIV

Impact: The promise was specific. It was Christ who was to sit on the throne. The rewritten versions omit this fact and leave open the possibility that it could be someone else.

While Men Slept...

Jesus Christ is Lord

Greek (TR: Received Text; WH: a Critical Text)	1 Corinthians 15:47	
ο πρωτος ανθρωπος εκ γης χοικος ο δευτερος ανθρωπος ο κυριος εξ ουρανου		-TR
ο πρωτος ανθρωπος εκ γης χοικος ο δευτερος ανθρωπος _ _____ εξ ουρανου		-WH

English: Based on Received Greek Text	1 Corinthians 15:47	
The first man **is of** the earth, **earthy**: the second man is **the Lord from** heaven		-KJV
The first man *was* **of** the earth, *made* **of dust**; the second Man *is* **the Lord from** heaven.		-NKJV
The first man *was* **out of** earth, **earthy**; the second Man *was* **the Lord from** Heaven.		-MKJV

English: Based on Critical Greek Texts	1 Corinthians 15:47	
The first man **is of** the earth, **earthly**: the second man is __ ____ **of** heaven.		-RV
The first man **was from** the earth, _____ a man of **dust**; the second man is ___ ____ **from** heaven.		-RSV
The first man **was of the dust** of the earth, _____ the second man __ ___ ____ **from** heaven.		-NIV

Impact: Who is this second man who came from heaven? He is the Lord.

Greek (TR: Received Text; WH: a Critical Text)	Acts 9:6
τρεμων τε και θαμβων ειπεν κυριε τι με θελεις ποιησαι και ο κυριος προς αυτον αναστηθι και εισελθε εις την πολιν και λαληθησεται σοι τι σε δει ποιειν	-TR
_____ __ __ _____ ____ ____ __ __ _____ ____ __ _ ____ ____ ____ αλλα αναστηθι και εισελθε εις την πολιν και λαληθησεται σοι ο τι σε δει ποιειν	-WH

Appendix B. Impact of the Changing Scriptures

English: Based on Received Greek Text	Acts 9:6
And he trembling and astonished said, Lord, what wilt thou have me to do? And the Lord *said* unto him, Arise, and go into the city, and it shall be told thee what thou must do.	-KJV
So he, trembling and astonished, said, "Lord, what do You want me to do?" Then the Lord *said* to him, "Arise and go into the city, and you will be told what you must do."	-NKJV
And trembling and being astonished, he said, Lord, what will You have me to do? And the Lord *said* to him, Arise and go into the city, and you shall be told what you must do.	-MKJV

English: Based on Critical Greek Texts	Acts 9:6
___ __ _____ __ _____ ____ __ ____ _____ _____ _____ but rise, and enter into the city, and it shall be told thee what thou must do.	-RV
___ __ __ __ __ __ _____ ___ ___ _____ but rise and enter the city, and you will be told what you are to do."	-RSV
___ __ __ __ __ __ ___ ____ ____ ____ ___ Now get up and go into the city, and you will be told what you must do.	-NIV

Impact: When Paul confessed that Jesus was the Lord, it was the turning point in his life. After his confession, Paul sought to do the will of the Lord Jesus Christ. In an act of submission and obedience to the authority of the Lord Jesus Christ, Paul asked for clear direction in his life. This is all lost in the rewritten texts.

Greek (TR: Received Text; WH: a Critical Text)	Matthew 13:51
λεγει αυτοις ο ιησους συνηκατε ταυτα παντα λε-γουσιν αυτω ναι κυριε	-TR
_____ _____ _ _____ συνηκατε ταυτα παντα λε-γουσιν αυτω ναι _____	-WH

While Men Slept...

English: Based on Received Greek Text	Matthew 13:51
Jesus saith unto them, Have ye understood all these things? They say unto him, Yea, **Lord**.	-KJV
Jesus said to them, "Have you understood all these things?" They said to Him, "Yes, **Lord**."	-NKJV
Jesus said to them, Have you understood all these things? They said to Him, Yes, **Lord**.	-MKJV

English: Based on Critical Greek Texts	Matthew 13:51
____ ____ ____ ____ Have ye understood all these things? They say unto him, Yea ____ .	-RV
" ____ ____ ____ ____ Have you understood all this?" They said to him, "Yes ____ ."	-RSV
"Have you understood all these things?" **Jesus asked**. "Yes ____ ," they replied.	-NIV

Impact: Here the confession that Jesus is Lord is removed in the WH Greek. Both His name and his position were removed in the WH, RV, and RSV. His position but not his name was removed by NIV.

Greek (TR: Received Text; WH: a Critical Text)	Luke 23:42
και ελεγεν τω ιησου μνησθητι μου κυριε οταν ελθης εν τη βασιλεια σου	-TR
και ελεγεν __ ιησου μνησθητι μου _____ οταν ελθης εις την βασιλειαν σου	-WH

English: Based on Received Greek Text	Luke 23:42
And he said unto Jesus, **Lord**, remember me when thou comest into thy kingdom.	-KJV
Then he said to Jesus, "**Lord**, remember me when You come into Your kingdom."	-NKJV
And he said to Jesus, **Lord**, remember me when You come into Your kingdom.	-MKJV

English: Based on Critical Greek Texts	Luke 23:42
And he said, Jesus, ____ remember me when thou comest in thy kingdom.	-RV
And he said, "Jesus, ____ remember me when you come into your kingdom."	-RSV
Then he said, "Jesus, ____ remember me when you come into your kingdom."	-NIV

488

Appendix B. Impact of the Changing Scriptures

Impact: The confession that Jesus is Lord is lost in the rewritten texts.

Greek (TR: Received Text; WH: a Critical Text)	2 Timothy 4:22
ο κυριος ιησους χριστος μετα του πνευματος σου η χαρις μεθ υμων αμην	-TR
ο κυριος _____ _____ μετα του πνευματος σου η χαρις μεθ υμων ____	-WH

English: Based on Received Greek Text	2 Timothy 4:22
The Lord **Jesus Christ** be with thy spirit. Grace be with you. Amen.	-KJV
The Lord **Jesus Christ** be with your spirit. Grace be with you. Amen.	-NKJV
May the Lord **Jesus Christ** *be* with your spirit. Grace *be* with you. Amen.	-MKJV

English: Based on Critical Greek Texts	2 Timothy 4:22
The Lord _____ _____ be with thy spirit. Grace be with you.	-RV
The Lord _____ _____ be with your spirit. Grace be with you.	-RSV
The Lord _____ _____ be with your spirit. Grace be with you.	-NIV

Impact: Which Lord? Paul is talking about the Lord Jesus Christ.

Greek (TR: Received Text; WH: a Critical Text)	Ephesians 1:10
εις οικονομιαν του πληρωματος των καιρων ανακε-φαλαιωσασθαι τα παντα εν τω χριστω τα τε εν τοις ουρανοις και τα επι της γης	-TR
εις οικονομιαν του πληρωματος των καιρων ανακε-φαλαιωσασθαι τα παντα εν τω χριστω τα επι τοις ουρανοις και τα επι της γης	-WH

489

While Men Slept...

English: Based on Received Greek Text	Ephesians 1:10
That in the dispensation of the fulness of times **he might gather together in one all things in Christ, both** which are in **heaven**, and which are on earth; *even* in him:	-KJV
that in the dispensation of the fullness of the times **He might gather together in one all things in Christ, both** which are in **heaven** and which are on earth----in Him.	-NKJV
for an administration of the fullness of times, **to head up all things in Christ**, both the things in **Heaven**, and the things on earth, *even* in Him,	-MKJV

English: Based on Critical Greek Texts	Ephesians 1:10
unto a dispensation of the fulness of the times, **to sum up all things in Christ**, the things in **the heavens**, and the things upon the earth; in him,	-RV
as a plan for the fulness of time, to unite all things **in him** _____, things in **heaven** and things on earth.	-RSV
to be put into effect when the times will have reached their fulfillment—to bring all things in **heaven** and on earth together **under one head, even Christ**.	-NIV

Impact: All things in heaven and earth will be gathered together in Christ. The RSV omits Christ, even though it is in both of the Greek texts.

God is One, but He is in the Godhead of Three Persons

Greek (TR: Received Text; WH: a Critical Text)	1 John 5:7-8
οτι τρεις εισιν οι μαρτυρουντες εν τω ουρανω ο πατηρ ο λογος και το αγιον πνευμα και ουτοι οι τρεις εν εισιν και τρεις εισιν οι μαρτυρουντες εν τη γη το πνευμα και το υδωρ και το αιμα και οι τρεις εις το εν εισιν	-TR
οτι τρεις εισιν οι μαρτυρουντες __ __ _____ _ _____ _ _____ ___ το _____ _____ __ __ _____ __ _____ ___ _____ ___ __ _____ __ __ __ πνευμα και το υδωρ και το αιμα και οι τρεις εις το εν εισιν	-WH

490

Appendix B. Impact of the Changing Scriptures

English: Based on Received Greek Text	1 John 5:7-8
For there are three that bear record in heaven, the Father, the Word, and the Holy Ghost: and these three are one. And there are three **that bear witness in earth**, the Spirit, and the water, and the blood: and these three agree in one.	-KJV
For there are three that bear witness in heaven: the Father, the Word, and the Holy Spirit; and these three are one. And there are three **that bear witness on earth**: the Spirit, the water, and the blood; and these three agree as one.	-NKJV
For there are three that bear record *in Heaven, the Father, the Word, and the Holy Spirit, and these three are one. And there are three that bear witness in the earth*, the Spirit, and the water, and the blood; and the three are to the one.	-MKJV

English: Based on Critical Greek Texts	1 John 5:7-8
___ ____ ___ ___ ____ __ ___ __ ____ __ ___ ____ ___ ___ ____ __ ___ __ ___ __ ___ ___ **And it is the Spirit that beareth witness, because the Spirit is the truth. For** there are three **who bear witness** __ ____, the Spirit, and the water, and the blood; and these three agree in one.	-RV
___ ____ ___ ___ ____ __ ___ __ ____ __ ___ ____ ___ ___ ____ __ ___ __ ___ ____ ___ ___ **And the Spirit is the witness, because the Spirit is the truth.** ___ There are three **witnesses** __ ____, the Spirit, the water, and the blood; and these three agree __ __.	-RSV
___ ____ ___ ___ ____ __ ___ __ ____ __ ___ ____ ___ ___ ____ __ ___ __ ___ ___ ___ ___ For there are three that **testify** __ ____: the Spirit, the water and the blood; and the three are in agreement __ __.	-NIV

Impact: This is the most Trinitarian and the most vigorously attacked of all passages in the Bible. All of the critical texts reject it. The MKJV weakens it with the use of italics. The changes remove the heavenly witnesses. The RV and RSV place emphasis on the Spirit, rather than the Word, as the truth. As has been discussed in the main text, it has been removed from so many manuscripts that, even though numerous ancient witnesses quote it, most modern theologians are willing to let it go.

While Men Slept...

Greek (TR: Received Text; WH: a Critical Text)	Acts 17:29
γενος ουν υπαρχοντες του θεου ουκ οφειλομεν νο-μιζειν χρυσω η αργυρω η λιθω χαραγματι τεχνης και ενθυμησεως ανθρωπου το θειον ειναι ομοιον	-TR
γενος ουν υπαρχοντες του θεου ουκ οφειλομεν νο-μιζειν χρυσω η αργυρω η λιθω χαραγματι τεχνης και ενθυμησεως ανθρωπου το θειον ειναι ομοιον	-WH

English: Based on Received Greek Text	Acts 17:29
Forasmuch then as we are the offspring of God, we ought not to think that the **Godhead** is like unto gold, or silver, or stone, graven by art and man's device.	-KJV
"Therefore, since we are the offspring of God, we ought not to think that the **Divine Nature** is like gold or silver or stone, something shaped by art and man's devising.	-NKJV
Then being offspring of God, we ought not to think that the **Godhead** is like gold or silver or stone, engraved by art and man's imagination.	-MKJV

English: Based on Critical Greek Texts	Acts 17:29
Being then the offspring of God, we ought not to think that the **Godhead** is like unto gold, or silver, or stone, graven by art and device of man.	-RV
Being then God's offspring, we ought not to think that the **Deity** is like gold, or silver, or stone, a representation by the art and imagination of man.	-RSV
Therefore since we are God's offspring, we should not think that **the divine being** is like gold or silver or stone -- an image made by man's design and skill.	-NIV

Impact: This is a subtle change from the Godhead, which suggests the Trinity, to Deity or divine being, which does not suggest the Trinity. The RV footnoted the Godhead with "Or, that which is divine." This left the door open for removing the Godhead from subsequent versions. The NKJV uses the term "Divine Nature."

Appendix B. Impact of the Changing Scriptures

Greek (TR: Received Text; WH: a Critical Text)	Colossians 1:2
τοις εν κολασσαις αγιοις και πιστοις αδελφοις εν χριστω χαρις υμιν και ειρηνη απο θεου πατρος ημων και κυριου ιησου χριστου	-TR
τοις εν κολοσσαις αγιοις και πιστοις αδελφοις εν χριστω χαρις υμιν και ειρηνη απο θεου πατρος ημων ___ _____ ____ _____	-WH

English: Based on Received Greek Text	Colossians 1:2
To the saints and faithful brethren in Christ which are at Colosse: Grace *be* unto you, and peace, from God our Father **and the Lord Jesus Christ**.	-KJV
To the saints and faithful brethren in Christ *who are* in Colosse: Grace to you and peace from God our Father **and the Lord Jesus Christ**.	-NKJV
to the saints and faithful brothers in Christ at Colosse. Grace to you, and peace from God our Father **and from** *the* **Lord Jesus Christ**.	-MKJV

English: Based on Critical Greek Texts	Colossians 1:2
to the saints and faithful brethren in Christ *which are* at Colossae: Grace to you and peace from God our Father ___ ___ ____ _____ ____ _____ .	-RV
To the saints and faithful brethren in Christ at Colossae: Grace to you and peace from God our Father ___ ___ ____ _____ _____ .	-RSV
To the holy and faithful brothers in Christ at Colosse: Grace and peace to you from God our Father ___ ___ ____ _____ .	-NIV

Impact: Grace and peace come from God our Father and the Lord Jesus Christ. The rewritten versions deny the reference that identifies the Lord Jesus Christ in the reference to God.

Greek (TR: Received Text; WH: a Critical Text)	Phillipians 2:6
ος εν μορφη θεου υπαρχων ουχ αρπαγμον ηγησατο το ειναι ισα θεω	-TR
ος εν μορφη θεου υπαρχων ουχ αρπαγμον ηγησατο το ειναι ισα θεω	-WH

English: Based on Received Greek Text	Phillipians 2:6
Who, being in the form of God, **thought it not robbery to be equal with God**:	-KJV
who, being in the form of God, **did not consider it robbery to be equal with God,**	-NKJV
who, being in the form of God, **thought *it* not robbery to be equal with God,**	-MKJV

English: Based on Critical Greek Texts	Phillipians 2:6
who, being in the form of God, **counted it not a prize to be on an equality with God,**	-RV
who, though he was in the form of God, **did not count equality with God a thing to be grasped,**	-RSV
Who, being in very nature God, **did not consider equality with God something to be grasped,**	-NIV

Impact: The Greek is unchanged. In the Received Text versions, the fact that Jesus is equal with God did not in any way diminish who God is. The passage in the RSV and NIV was rewritten from a whole different perspective. That is, that Jesus did not consider that He could ever be equal with God. Therefore, He was a lower being.

Wisdom Comes from God and not from Reason

Greek (TR: Received Text; WH: a Critical Text)	James 3:17
η δε ανωθεν σοφια πρωτον μεν αγνη εστιν επειτα ειρηνικη επιεικης ευπειθης μεστη ελεους και καρπων αγαθων αδιακριτος και ανυποκριτος	-TR
η δε ανωθεν σοφια πρωτον μεν αγνη εστιν επειτα ειρηνικη επιεικης ευπειθης μεστη ελεους και καρπων αγαθων αδιακριτος ___ ανυποκριτος	-WH

Appendix B. Impact of the Changing Scriptures

English: Based on Received Greek Text	James 3:17
But the wisdom that is from **above** is first pure, then **peaceable**, gentle, *and* **easy to be intreated**, full of mercy and good fruits, without **partiality**, and without **hypocrisy**.	-KJV
But the wisdom that is from **above** is first pure, then **peaceable**, gentle, **willing to yield,** full of mercy and good fruits, without **partiality** and without **hypocrisy**.	-NKJV
But the wisdom that is from **above** is first truly pure, then **peaceable**, gentle, **easy to be entreated**, full of mercy and good fruits, without **partiality** and without **hypocrisy**.	-MKJV

English: Based on Critical Greek Texts	James 3:17
But the wisdom that is from **above** is first pure, then **peaceable**, gentle, **easy to be intreated**, full of mercy and good fruits, without **variance**, without **hypocrisy**.	-RV
But the wisdom from **above** is first pure, then **peaceable**, gentle, **open to reason**, full of mercy and good fruits, without **uncertainty or insincerity**.	-RSV
But the wisdom that comes from **heaven** is first of all pure; then **peace-loving**, **considerate**, **submissive**, full of mercy and good fruit, **impartial and sincere**.	-NIV

Impact: The RSV suggests that wisdom, which is from God, is open to reason.

Our Body and Spirit Belong to God

Greek (TR: Received Text; WH: a Critical Text)	1 Corinthians 6:20
ηγορασθητε γαρ τιμης δοξασατε δη τον θεον εν τω σωματι υμων και εν τω πνευματι υμων ατινα εστιν του θεου	-TR
ηγορασθητε γαρ τιμης δοξασατε δη τον θεον εν τω σωματι υμων ___ __ __ _____ ____ _____ _____ ___ ____	-WH

495

While Men Slept...

English: Based on Received Greek Text	1 Corinthians 6:20
For ye are bought with a price: therefore **glorify** God in your body, **and in your spirit, which are God's.**	-KJV
For you were bought at a price; therefore **glorify** God in your body **and in your spirit, which are God's.**	-NKJV
for you are bought with a price. Therefore **glorify** God in your body **and in your spirit, which are God's.**	-MKJV

English: Based on Critical Greek Texts	1 Corinthians 6:20
for ye were bought with a price: **glorify** God therefore in your body ___ __ __ __ __ __ __ ___.	-RV
you were bought with a price. So **glorify** God in your body ___ __ __ __ __ __ ___.	-RSV
you were bought at a price. Therefore **honor** God with your body ___ __ __ __ __ __ ___.	-NIV

Impact: We do not only live in a physical world but also a spiritual world. Both our body and our spirit belong to God. The rewritten versions diminish this understanding.

Truth through the Spirit and Love with a Pure Heart

Greek (TR: Received Text; WH: a Critical Text)	1 Peter 1:22
τας ψυχας υμων ηγνικοτες εν τη υπακοη της αληθειας δια πνευματος εις φιλαδελφιαν ανυποκριτον εκ καθαρας καρδιας αλληλους αγαπησατε εκτενως	-TR
τας ψυχας υμων ηγνικοτες εν τη υπακοη της αληθειας ___ _____ εις φιλαδελφιαν ανυποκριτον εκ _____ καρδιας αλληλους αγαπησατε εκτενως	-WH

English: Based on Received Greek Text	1 Peter 1:22
Seeing ye have purified your souls in obeying the truth **through the Spirit** unto unfeigned love of the brethren, *see that ye* love one another with a **pure** heart fervently:	-KJV
Since you have purified your souls in obeying the truth **through the Spirit** in sincere love of the brethren, love one another fervently with a **pure** heart,	-NKJV
Purifying your souls in the obedience of the truth **through the Spirit** to unfeigned love of the brothers, love one another fervently out of a **pure** heart,	-MKJV

496

Appendix B. Impact of the Changing Scriptures

English: Based on Critical Greek Texts	1 Peter 1:22
Seeing ye have purified your souls in your obedience to the truth _____ ___ _____ unto unfeigned love of the brethren, love one another ____ _ ____ **from** the heart fervently:	-RV
_____ __ Having purified your souls by your obedience to the truth _____ ___ _____ for a sincere love of the brethren, love one another ____ _ ____ **earnestly from the** heart.	-RSV
_____ Now that you have purified yourselves by obeying the truth _____ ___ _____ so that you have sincere love for your brothers, love one another ____ _ ____ **deeply, from the** heart.	-NIV

Impact: The rewritten versions diminish the role of the Spirit and the importance of a pure heart.

Avoid Even the Appearance of Idol Worship

Greek (TR: Received Text; WH: a Critical Text)	1 Corinthians 10: 28
εαν δε τις υμιν ειπη τουτο ειδωλοθυτον εστιν μη εσθιετε δι εκεινον τον μηνυσαντα και την συνειδησιν του γαρ κυριου η γη και το πληρωμα αυτης	-TR
εαν δε τις υμιν ειπη τουτο ιεροθυτον εστιν μη εσθιετε δι εκεινον τον μηνυσαντα και την συνειδησιν ___ __ _____ __ ___ __ _____ _____	-WH

English: Based on Received Greek Text	1 Corinthians 10: 28
But if any **man** say unto you, This **is offered in sacrifice unto idols, eat not** for his sake that **shewed** it, and for conscience sake: **for the earth** *is* **the Lord's, and the fulness thereof:**	-KJV
But if **anyone** says to you, "This **was offered** __ _____ **to idols," do not eat it** for the sake of the one who **told you**, and for conscience' sake; **for "the earth** *is* **the LORD'S, and all its fullness."**	-NKJV
But if **anyone** says to you, This is **slain in sacrifice to idols, do not eat** for the sake of him who **showed** *it*, and for conscience' sake; **"for the earth** *is* **the Lord's, and the fullness of it";**	-MKJV

While Men Slept...

English: Based on Critical Greek Texts	1 Corinthians 10: 28
But if any **man** say unto you, This hath been offered in sacrifice ____ _____, **eat not** for his sake that **shewed** it, and for conscience sake: ___ ___ _____ __ ___ _____ ___ __ _____	-RV
(But if some **one** says to you, "This **has been** offered in sacrifice ____ _____," **then** ___ ___ out of consideration for the man who **informed you**, and for conscience' sake-- - __ __ __ ___ __ __ __ ___ __ ___ _____.	-RSV
But if anyone says to you, "This has been offered in sacrifice ____ _____," then **do not eat it**, both for the sake of the man who **told you** and for conscience' sake--- ___ ___ ___ __ __ __ ___ __ ___	-NIV

Impact: All that is belongs to the Lord and is not, of itself, unclean. However, when someone tells us that something has been offered to idols, we should not eat it. The critical English texts make no mention of idols.

We Have an Inheritance in Heaven

Greek (TR: Received Text; WH: a Critical Text)	Hebrews 10:34
και γαρ τοις δεσμοις μου συνεπαθησατε και την αρπαγην των υπαρχοντων υμων μετα χαρας προσεδεξασθε γινωσκοντες εχειν εν εαυτοις κρειττονα υπαρξιν εν ουρανοις και μενουσαν	-TR
και γαρ τοις δεσμιοις ___ συνεπαθησατε και την αρπαγην των υπαρχοντων υμων μετα χαρας προσεδεξασθε γινωσκοντες εχειν _ εαυτους κρειττονα υπαρξιν __ _____ και μενουσαν	-WH

English: Based on Received Greek Text	Hebrews 10:34
For ye had compassion of **me** in **my** bonds, and took joyfully the **spoiling** of your goods, knowing in yourselves that ye have **in heaven** a better and an **enduring substance**.	-KJV
for you had compassion on **me** in **my** chains, and joyfully accepted the **plundering** of your goods, knowing that you have a better and an **enduring possession** for yourselves **in heaven**.	-NKJV
For you both sympathized with ___ ___ **my** bonds and took joyfully the **spoiling** of your goods, knowing in yourselves that you have **in Heaven** a better and an **enduring substance**.	-MKJV

498

Appendix B. Impact of the Changing Scriptures

English: Based on Critical Greek Texts	Hebrews 10:34
For ye both had compassion on **them** that were in bonds, and took joyfully the **spoiling** of your possessions, knowing that ye yourselves have __ _____ a better possession and an **abiding one.**	-RV
For you had compassion on **the prisoners**, and **you** joyfully accepted the **plundering** of your property, since you knew that you **yourselves had** __ _____ a better possession and an **abiding one.**	-RSV
You sympathized with **those** in prison and joyfully accepted the **confiscation** of your property, because you knew that you yourselves **had** __ _____ better and **lasting possessions.**	-NIV

Impact: Those who only believe in the physical earth and who deny the existence of heaven do not confess that we have a better and more enduring substance in heaven.

Our Father is in Heaven

Greek (TR: Received Text; WH: a Critical Text)	Luke 11:2
ειπεν δε αυτοις οταν προσευχησθε λεγετε πατερ ημων ο εν τοις ουρανοις αγιασθητω το ονομα σου ελθετω η βασιλεια σου γενηθητω το θελημα σου ως εν ουρανω και επι της γης	-TR
ειπεν δε αυτοις οταν προσευχησθε λεγετε πατερ ____ __ ___ _____ αγιασθητω το ονομα σου ελθετω η βασιλεια σου _____ __ ____ ___ __ __ ___ __ __ ___	-WH

English: Based on Received Greek Text	Luke 11:2
And he said unto them, When ye pray, say, **Our** Father **which art in heaven**, Hallowed be thy name. Thy kingdom come. **Thy will be done, as in heaven, so in earth.**	-KJV
So He said to them, "When you pray, say: **Our** Father _____ ___ **in heaven**, Hallowed be Your name. Your kingdom come. **Your will be done On earth as** *it is* **in heaven.**	-NKJV
And He said to them, When you pray, say: **Our** Father, **who** *is* **in Heaven**, hallowed be Your name. Your kingdom come, **Your will be done, as in Heaven, so also on the earth.**	-MKJV

While Men Slept...

English: Based on Critical Greek Texts	Luke 11:2
And he said unto them, When you pray, say: ___ Father ___ ___ __ _____, Hallowed be thy name. Thy king-dom come. ___ ___ __ ___ __ __ ___ _ ___	-RV
And he said to them, "When you pray, say: "___ Father ___ ___ __ _____, hallowed be thy name. Thy king-dom come. ___ ___ __ __ __ __ __ _ ___	-RSV
___ He said to them, "When you pray, say: "'___ Father ___ ___ __ _____, hallowed be your name, your king-dom come. ___ ___ __ ___ __ __ ___ _ ___	-NIV

Impact: Our Father is in heaven. We ask for His will to be done on earth, as it is done in heaven.

Heavenly Angels, not Eagles, are God's Messengers

Greek (TR: Received Text; WH: a Critical Text)	Revelation 8:13
και ειδον και ηκουσα ενος αγγελου πετωμενου εν μεσουρανηματι λεγοντος φωνη μεγαλη ουαι ουαι ουαι τοις κατοικουσιν επι της γης εκ των λοιπων φωνων της σαλπιγγος των τριων αγγελων των μελ-λοντων σαλπιζειν	-TR
και ειδον και ηκουσα ενος αετου πετομενου εν μεσουρανηματι λεγοντος φωνη μεγαλη ουαι ουαι ουαι τους κατοικουντας επι της γης εκ των λοιπων φωνων της σαλπιγγος των τριων αγγελων των μελ-λοντων σαλπιζειν	-WH

Appendix B. Impact of the Changing Scriptures

English: Based on Received Greek Text	Revelation 8:13
And I beheld, and heard an **angel** flying through the **midst of heaven**, saying with a loud voice, Woe, woe, woe, to the inhabiters of the earth by reason of the other voices of the trumpet of the three angels, which are yet to sound!	-KJV
And I looked, and I heard an **angel** flying through the **midst of heaven**, saying with a loud voice, "Woe, woe, woe to the inhabitants of the earth, because of the remaining blasts of the trumpet of the three angels who are about to sound!"	-NKJV
And I saw and I heard one **angel** flying in **mid-heaven**, saying with a loud voice, Woe! Woe! Woe to the inhabitants of the earth, from the rest of the voices of the trumpet of the three angels being about to sound!	-MKJV

English: Based on Critical Greek Texts	Revelation 8:13
Then I saw, and I heard an **eagle, flying in mid heaven**, saying with a great voice, Woe, woe, woe, for them that dwell on the earth, by reason of the other voices of the trumpet of the three angels, who are yet to sound.	-RV
Then I looked, and I heard an **eagle** crying with a loud voice, as it flew in **midheaven**, "Woe, woe, woe to those who dwell on the earth, at the blasts of the other trumpets which the three angels are about to blow!"	-RSV
As I watched, I heard an **eagle** that was flying in **midair** call out in a loud voice: "Woe! Woe! Woe to the inhabitants of the earth, because of the trumpet blasts about to be sounded by the other three angels!"	-NIV

Impact: Angels are in heaven. Eagles are in the air. The rewritten versions say the scene is physical and not spiritual, earthly and not heavenly. Origen wrote "And I saw an **angel** flying in the midst of **heaven**"[9] in the third century, well before Eusebius of Caesarea was commissioned to provide Bibles for Emperor Constantine.

---

[9] Origen, *Origen's Commentary on the Gospel of John, Book I* (translated by Allan Menzies), In *The Ante-Nicene Fathers,* vol. 10, A. Roberts and J. Donaldson, eds. (Albany, Oregon: The Sage Digital Library Collections, Sage Software, 1996), p. 512.

While Men Slept...

An Angel and A Great Voice Out of the Temple of Heaven

Greek (TR: Received Text; WH: a Critical Text)	Revelation 16:17	
και ο εβδομος αγγελος εξεχεεν την φιαλην αυτου εις τον αερα και εξηλθεν φωνη μεγαλη απο του ναου του ουρανου απο του θρονου λεγουσα γεγονεν	-TR	
και ο εβδομος _____ εξεχεεν την φιαλην αυτου επι τον αερα και εξηλθεν φωνη μεγαλη εκ του ναου απο του _____ __ __ θρονου λεγουσα γεγονεν	-WH	

And the seventh **angel** poured out his vial **into** the air; and there came a great voice out of the temple **of heaven**, from the throne, saying, It is done.	-KJV
Then the seventh **angel** poured out his bowl **into** the air, and a loud voice came out of the temple **of heaven**, from the throne, saying, "It is done!"	-NKJV
And the seventh **angel** poured out his vial **into** the air. And a great voice came out of the temple **of Heaven**, from the throne, saying, It is done!	-MKJV

English: Based on Critical Greek Texts	Revelation 16:17
And the seventh _____ poured out his bowl **upon** the air; and there came forth a great voice out of the temple __ _____, from the throne, saying, It is done:	-RV
The seventh **angel** poured his bowl **into** the air, and a loud voice came out of the temple __ _____, from the throne, saying, "It is done!"	-RSV
The seventh **angel** poured out his bowl **into** the air, and out of the temple __ _____ came a loud voice from the throne, saying, "It is done!"	-NIV

Impact: WH and RV omitted the role of the angel, which was restored in the later versions. Again, the scene is either heavenly or earthly. By omitting heaven, the implication is that the temple is earthly. The temple of heaven, from which the great voice came, is the Lord God Almighty and the Lamb (See Revelation 21:22).

Appendix B. Impact of the Changing Scriptures

Jesus Ascended Back into Heaven

Greek (TR: Received Text; WH: a Critical Text)	John 3:13
και ουδεις αναβεβηκεν εις τον ουρανον ει μη ο εκ του ουρανου καταβας ο υιος του ανθρωπου ο ων εν τω ουρανω	-TR
και ουδεις αναβεβηκεν εις τον ουρανον ει μη ο εκ του ουρανου καταβας ο υιος του ανθρωπου _ _ _ _ _	-WH

English: Based on Received Greek Text	John 3:13
And no man hath ascended up to heaven, but he that came **down** from heaven, *even* the Son of man **which is in heaven.**	-KJV
"No one has ascended to heaven but He who came **down** from heaven, *that is*, the Son of Man **who is in heaven**.	-NKJV
And no one has ascended up to Heaven except He who came **down** from Heaven, the Son of man **who is in Heaven.**	-MKJV

English: Based on Critical Greek Texts	John 3:13
And no man hath ascended into heaven, but **he** that descended **out of** heaven, *even* the Son of man, **which is in heaven.**	-RV
No one has ascended into heaven but **he** who descended _____ from heaven, the Son of man _____ _ _ _____.	-RSV
No one has ever gone into heaven except **the one** who came _____ from heaven--the Son of Man _____ _ _ _____.	-NIV

Impact: To declare that the Son of man is in heaven supports His deity. Although the WH did not say, "ο ων εν τω ουρανω," meaning "which is in heaven," the phrase was left in the RV. But, by using a footnote to suggest that the reference to heaven could be omitted, the RV provided the opportunity for it to be omitted in subsequent re-writings of the Bible. The rewriters do not say that He is in heaven.

Greek (TR: Received Text; WH: a Critical Text)	John 16:16
μικρον και ου θεωρειτε με και παλιν μικρον και οψεσθε με οτι εγω υπαγω προς τον πατερα	-TR
μικρον και ουκετι θεωρειτε με και παλιν μικρον και οψεσθε με __ __ _____ _____ _ _____	-WH

503

While Men Slept...

English: Based on Received Greek Text	John 16:16
A little while, and ye shall not see me: and again, a little while, and ye shall see me, **because I go to the Father.**	-KJV
"A little while, and you will not see Me; and again a little while, and you will see Me, **because I go to the Father.**"	-NKJV
A little *while* and you will not see Me; and again a little *while*, and you will see Me, **because I go to the Father.**	-MKJV

English: Based on Critical Greek Texts	John 16:16
A little while, and ye behold me no more: and again, a little while, and ye shall see me _____ _ __ __ __ _____ .	-RV
A little while, and you will see me no more; again a little while, and you will see me _____ _ __ __ _____ .	-RSV
In a little while you will see me no more, and then after a little while you will see me _____ __ __ __ .	-NIV

Impact: If it is acknowledged that Jesus goes to the Father and it is believed that the Father is in heaven, then the conclusion would be that Jesus is in heaven also. This supports His deity and is excluded from the rewritten versions.

Trading a Soul or Trading a Life for the World?

Greek (TR: Received Text; WH: a Critical Text)	Matthew 16:26
τι γαρ ωφελειται ανθρωπος εαν τον κοσμον ολον κερδηση την δε ψυχην αυτου ζημιωθη η τι δωσει ανθρωπος ανταλλαγμα της ψυχης αυτου	-TR
τι γαρ ωφεληθησεται ανθρωπος εαν τον κοσμον ολον κερδηση την δε ψυχην αυτου ζημιωθη η τι δωσει ανθρωπος ανταλλαγμα της ψυχης αυτου	-WH

Appendix B. Impact of the Changing Scriptures

English: Based on Received Greek Text	Matthew 16:26
For what is a man be profited, if he shall gain the whole world, and lose his own **soul**? or what shall a man give in exchange for his **soul**?	-KJV
"For what profit is it to a man if he gains the whole world, and loses his own **soul**? Or what will a man give in exchange for his **soul**?	-NKJV
For what is a man be profited if he shall gain the whole world and lose his own **soul**? Or what shall a man give in exchange for his **soul**?	-MKJV

English: Based on Critical Greek Texts	Matthew 16:26
For what shall a man be profited, if he shall gain the whole world, and forfeit his **life**? or what shall a man give in exchange for his **life**?	-RV
For what will it profit a man, if he gains the whole world and forfeits his **life**? Or what shall a man give in return for his **life**?	-RSV
What good will it be for a man if he gains the whole world, yet forfeits his **soul**? Or what can a man give in exchange for his **soul**?	-NIV

Impact: The use of the term "soul" implies a spiritual dimension whereas the term "life" implies a physical dimension. The confusion is over whether the exchange is for one's soul or for one's life.

Hell is a Place of Eternal Damnation

Greek (TR: Received Text; WH: a Critical Text)	Mark 9:45-46
και εαν ο πους σου σκανδαλιζη σε αποκοψον αυτον καλον εστιν σοι εισελθειν εις την ζωην χωλον η τους δυο ποδας εχοντα βληθηναι εις την γεενναν εις το πυρ το ασβεστον οπου ο σκωληξ αυτων ου τελευτα και το πυρ ου σβεννυται	-TR
και εαν ο πους σου σκανδαλιζη σε αποκοψον αυτον καλον εστιν σε εισελθειν εις την ζωην χωλον η τους δυο ποδας εχοντα βληθηναι εις την γεενναν ___ __ __ __ _____ ___ __ _ ____ ____ __ ____ __ ___ ___ _____	-WH

While Men Slept...

English: Based on Received Greek Text	Mark 9:45-46
And if thy foot **offend thee**, cut it off: it is better for thee to enter halt into life, than having two feet to be cast into hell, **into the fire that never shall be quenched: Where their worm dieth not, and the fire is not quenched.**	-KJV
"And if your foot **causes you to sin**, cut it off. It is better for you to enter life lame, rather than having two feet, to be cast into hell, **into the fire that shall never be quenched----"where `Their worm does not die, And the fire is not quenched.'**	-NKJV
And if your foot **offends** you, cut it off. It is better for you to enter into life lame than to have two feet to be cast into hell, **into the fire that never shall be quenched where their worm dies not, and the fire is not quenched.**	-MKJV

English: Based on Critical Greek Texts	Mark 9:45-46
And if thy foot **cause thee to stumble**, cut it off: it is good for thee to enter into life halt, rather than having thy two feet to be cast into hell ___ ___ ___ ___ ___ ___ ___ ___ ___ ___ ___ ___ ___ ___ ___ ___ ___ .	-RV
And if your foot **causes you to sin**, cut it off; it is better for you to enter life lame than with two feet to be thrown into hell ___ ___ ___ ___ ___ ___ ___ ___ ___ ___ ___ ___ ___ ___ ___ ___ ___ .	-RSV
And if your foot **causes you to sin**, cut it off. It is better for you to enter life crippled than to have two feet and be thrown into hell ___ ___ ___ ___ ___ ___ ___ ___ ___ ___ ___ ___ ___ ___ ___ ___ ___ .	-NIV

Impact: The last portion of this passage tells of everlasting punishment in fire. It is strong and objectionable to many. It is omitted from both the re-written Greek and English versions.

Greek (TR: Received Text; WH: a Critical Text)	Mark 3:29
ος δ αν βλασφημηση εις το πνευμα το αγιον ουκ εχει αφεσιν εις τον αιωνα αλλ ενοχος εστιν αιωνιου κρισεως	-TR
ος δ αν βλασφημηση εις το πνευμα το αγιον ουκ εχει αφεσιν εις τον αιωνα αλλα ενοχος εστιν αιωνιου αμαρτηματος	-WH

506

Appendix B. Impact of the Changing Scriptures

English: Based on Received Greek Text	Mark 3:29
But he that shall blaspheme against the Holy Ghost hath never forgiveness, but is **in danger of eternal damnation**.	-KJV
"but he who blasphemes against the Holy Spirit never has forgiveness, but is **subject to eternal condemnation**" ----	-NKJV
But he who blasphemes against the Holy Spirit never shall have forgiveness, but is **liable to eternal condemnation**.	-MKJV

English: Based on Critical Greek Texts	Mark 3:29
but whoever shall blaspheme against the Holy Spirit hath never forgiveness, but is **guilty of an eternal sin**:	-RV
but whoever blasphemes against the Holy Spirit never has forgiveness, but is **guilty of an eternal sin**"	-RSV
But whoever blasphemes against the Holy Spirit will never be forgiven; **he is guilty of an eternal sin**.	-NIV

Impact: Again, the rewriters rejected the concept of eternal damnation.

Greek (TR: Received Text; WH: a Critical Text)	John 5:29
και εκπορευσονται οι τα αγαθα ποιησαντες εις αναστασιν ζωης οι δε τα φαυλα πραξαντες εις αναστασιν κρισεως	-TR
και εκπορευσονται οι τα αγαθα ποιησαντες εις αναστασιν ζωης οι __ τα φαυλα πραξαντες εις αναστασιν κρισεως	-WH

English: Based on Received Greek Text	John 5:29
And shall come forth; they that have done good, unto the resurrection of life; and they that have done **evil**, unto the resurrection of **damnation**.	-KJV
"and come forth----those who have done good, to the resurrection of life, and those who have done **evil**, to the resurrection of **condemnation**.	-NKJV
and shall come forth, those who have done good to the resurrection of life, and those who have practiced **evil** to the resurrection of **condemnation**.	-MKJV

507

While Men Slept...

English: Based on Critical Greek Texts	John 5:29
and shall come forth; they that have done good, unto the resurrection of life; and they that have done **ill**, unto the resurrection of **judgement**.	-RV
and come forth, those who have done good, to the resurrection of life, and those who have done **evil**, to the resurrection of **judgment**.	-RSV
and come out---those who have done good will rise to live, and those who have done **evil** will rise to be **condemned**.	-NIV

Impact: The word "evil" was replaced with "ill" in the RV but restored in the later versions. The rewriters softened the concept of damnation.

Jesus Came to Save the Lost

Greek (TR: Received Text; WH: a Critical Text)	Matthew 18:11
ηλθεν γαρ ο υιος του ανθρωπου σωσαι το απολωλος	-TR
Verse Omitted from Text	-WH

English: Based on Received Greek Text	Matthew 18:11
For the Son of man is come to save that which was lost.	-KJV
"For the Son of Man has come to save that which was lost.	-NKJV
For the Son of man has come to save that which was lost.	-MKJV

English: Based on Critical Greek Texts	Matthew 18:11
Verse Omitted from Text	-RV
Verse Omitted from Text	-RSV
Verse Omitted from Text	-NIV

Impact: This is a clear statement that Jesus came to save the lost. It is omitted from the rewritten versions.

Appendix B. Impact of the Changing Scriptures

Greek (TR: Received Text; WH: a Critical Text)	Luke 9:55-56
στραφεις δε επετιμησεν αυτοις και ειπεν ουκ οιδατε οιου πνευματος εστε υμεις ο γαρ υιος του ανθρωπου ουκ ηλθεν ψυχας ανθρωπων απολεσαι αλλα σωσαι και επορευθησαν εις ετεραν κωμην	-TR
στραφεις δε επετιμησεν αυτοις ___ ___ ___ _____ ___ _____ ____ __ __ ___ ___ __ _____ __ _____ _____ _____ _____ __ ____ και επορευθησαν εις ετεραν κωμην	-WH

English: Based on Received Greek Text	Luke 9:55-56
But he turned, and rebuked them, **and said, Ye know not what manner of spirit ye are of. For the Son of man is not come to destroy men's lives, but to save them.** And they went to another village.	-KJV
But He turned and rebuked them, **and said, "You do not know what manner of spirit you are of. "For the Son of Man did not come to destroy men's lives but to save them."** And they went to another village.	-NKJV
But He turned and rebuked them **and said, You do not know of what spirit you are. For the Son of man has not come to destroy men's lives, but to save.** And they went to another village.	-MKJV

English: Based on Critical Greek Texts	Luke 9:55-56
But he turned, and rebuked them. ___ ___ __ ___ ___ ____ __ __ __ __ __ __ __ __ __ __ ___ _____ __ __ __ __ __ ____ And they went to another village.	-RV
But he turned and rebuked them. ___ ___ __ ___ ___ ____ __ __ __ __ __ __ __ __ __ __ ___ _____ __ __ __ __ __ ____ And they went on to another village.	-RSV
But Jesus turned and rebuked them, ___ ___ __ ___ ___ ____ __ __ __ __ __ __ __ __ __ __ ___ _____ __ __ __ __ __ ____ and they went to another village.	-NIV

Impact: Jesus came to save us.

509

While Men Slept...

Jesus Calls Sinners to Repentance

Greek (TR: Received Text; WH: a Critical Text)	Matthew 9:13
πορευθεντες δε μαθετε τι εστιν ελεον θελω και ου θυσιαν ου γαρ ηλθον καλεσαι δικαιους αλλ αμαρτωλους εις μετανοιαν	-TR
πορευθεντες δε μαθετε τι εστιν ελεος θελω και ου θυσιαν ου γαρ ηλθον καλεσαι δικαιους αλλα αμαρτωλους ___ _____	-WH

English: Based on Received Greek Text	Matthew 9:13
But go ye and learn what *that* meaneth, **I will have** mercy, and not sacrifice: for I am not come to call the righteous, but sinners **to repentance**.	-KJV
"But go and learn what *this* means: `I desire` mercy and not sacrifice.' For I did not come to call the righteous, but sinners, **to repentance**."	-NKJV
But go and learn what *this is*, **I will have** mercy and not sacrifice. For I have not come to call the righteous, but sinners **to repentance**.	-MKJV

English: Based on Critical Greek Texts	Matthew 9:13
But go ye and learn what *this* meaneth, **I desire** mercy, and not sacrifice: for I came not to call the righteous, but sinners ___ _____	-RV
Go and learn what this means, '**I desire** mercy, and not sacrifice.' For I came not to call the righteous, but sinners ___ _____."	-RSV
But go and learn what this means: `I desire` mercy, not sacrifice.' For I have not come to call the righteous, but sinners ___ _____."	-NIV

Impact: The call is for sinners to repent.

Greek (TR: Received Text; WH: a Critical Text)	Mark 2:17
και ακουσας ο ιησους λεγει αυτοις ου χρειαν εχουσιν οι ισχυοντες ιατρου αλλ οι κακως εχοντες ουκ ηλθον καλεσαι δικαιους αλλα αμαρτωλους εις μετανοιαν	-TR
και ακουσας ο ιησους λεγει αυτοις οτι ου χρειαν εχουσιν οι ισχυοντες ιατρου αλλ οι κακως εχοντες ουκ ηλθον καλεσαι δικαιους αλλα αμαρτωλους ___ _____	-WH

Appendix B. Impact of the Changing Scriptures

English: Based on Received Greek Text	Mark 2:17
When Jesus heard *it*, he saith unto them, They that are whole have no need of the physician, but they that are sick: I came not to call the righteous, but sinners **to repentance.**	-KJV
When Jesus heard *it*, He said to them, "Those who are well have no need of a physician, but those who are sick. I did not come to call *the* righteous, but sinners, **to repentance.**"	-NKJV
When Jesus heard, He said to them, They who are strong have no need of a physician, but the ones who have illness. I did not come to call the righteous, but sinners **to repentance.**	-MKJV

English: Based on Critical Greek Texts	Mark 2:17
And when Jesus heard it, he saith unto them, They that are whole have no need of a physician, but they that are sick: I came not to call the righteous, but sinners __	-RV
And when Jesus heard it, he said to them, "Those who are well have no need of a physician, but those who are sick; I came not to call the righteous, but sinners __ ."	-RSV
On hearing this, Jesus said to them, "It is not the healthy who need a doctor, but the sick. I have not come to call the righteous, but sinners __ ."	-NIV

Impact: Again, the call is for sinners to repent.

We are Redeemed by the Blood of Jesus

Greek (TR: Received Text; WH: a Critical Text)	Colossians 1:14
εν ω εχομεν την απολυτρωσιν δια του αιματος αυτου την αφεσιν των αμαρτιων	-TR
εν ω εχομεν την απολυτρωσιν __ __ _____ ____ την αφεσιν των αμαρτιων	-WH

While Men Slept...

English: Based on Received Greek Text	Colossians 1:14
In whom we have redemption **through his blood**, *even* the forgiveness of sins:	-KJV
in whom we have redemption **through His blood**, the forgiveness of sins.	-NKJV
in whom we have redemption **through His blood**, the remission of sins.	-MKJV

English: Based on Critical Greek Texts	Colossians 1:14
in whom we have our redemption _____ ___ _____, the forgiveness of **our** sins:	-RV
in whom we have redemption _____ ___ _____, the forgiveness of sins.	-RSV
in whom we have redemption _____ ___ _____, the forgiveness of sins.	-NIV

Impact: We are redeemed through the blood of Jesus Christ.

All Will Not Be Saved

Greek (TR: Received Text; WH: a Critical Text)	Revelation 21:24
και τα εθνη των σωζομενων εν τω φωτι αυτης περιπατησουσιν και οι βασιλεις της γης φερουσιν την δοξαν και την τιμην αυτων εις αυτην	-TR
και __ ____ __ __ __ __ ____ _____ περιπατησουσιν τα εθνη δια του φωτος αυτης και οι βασιλεις της γης φερουσιν την δοξαν __ __ _____ αυτων εις αυτην	-WH

English: Based on Received Greek Text	Revelation 21:24
And the nations **of them which are saved shall** walk in the light of it: and the kings of the earth **do** bring their **glory and honour** into it.	-KJV
And the nations **of those who are saved shall** walk in its light, and the kings of the earth __ bring their **glory and honor** into it.	-NKJV
And the nations **of those who are saved will** walk in the light of it; and the kings of the earth __bring their **glory and honor** into it.	-MKJV

Appendix B. Impact of the Changing Scriptures

English: Based on Critical Greek Texts	Revelation 21:24
And the nations __ ____ _____ __ ____ **shall** walk amidst the light thereof: and the kings of the earth **do** bring their **glory** ___ _____ into it.	-RV
By its light **shall** the nations __ ___ ____ __ ____ walk; and the kings of the earth **shall** bring their **glory** ____ __ _____ into it,	-RSV
The nations **will** walk by its light, and the kings of the earth **will** bring their **splendor** ___ ____ _____ into it.	-NIV

Impact: Universalists teach that all are saved. The Received Text-based versions clearly state that all are not saved because the nations "of them that are saved" will walk in the light of it. The rewritten versions omit the qualification and, therefore, imply that all are saved.

Greek (TR: Received Text; WH: a Critical Text)	Matthew 20:16
ουτως εσονται οι εσχατοι πρωτοι και οι πρωτοι εσχατοι πολλοι γαρ εισιν κλητοι ολιγοι δε εκλεκτοι	-TR
ουτως εσονται οι εσχατοι πρωτοι και οι πρωτοι εσχατοι ____ ___ ____ _____ ___ __ ____	-WH

English: Based on Received Greek Text	Matthew 20:16
So the last **shall** be first, and the first last: **for many be called, but few chosen.**	-KJV
"So the last **will** be first, and the first last. **For many are called, but few chosen.**"	-NKJV
So the last **shall** be first, and the first last, **for many are called, but few are chosen.**	-MKJV

English: Based on Critical Greek Texts	Matthew 20:16
So the last **shall** be first, and the first last ___ ____ __ _____ .	-RV
"So the last **will** be first, and the first last ___ ____ __ _____ ."	-RSV
"So the last **will** be first, and the first will be last ___ ____ _____ ."	-NIV

Impact: This is a clear statement against universal salvation and it is clearly omitted by the rewriters. The change supports Universalism.

513

While Men Slept...

He that Believes on Jesus has Everlasting Life

Greek (TR: Received Text; WH: a Critical Text)	John 6:47
αμην αμην λεγω υμιν ο πιστευων εις εμε εχει ζωην αιωνιον	-TR
αμην αμην λεγω υμιν ο πιστευων ___ ___ εχει ζωην αιωνιον	-WH

English: Based on Received Greek Text	John 6:47
Verily, verily, I say unto you, He that believeth **on me** hath **everlasting** life.	-KJV
"Most assuredly, I say to you, he who believes **in Me** has **everlasting life.**	-NKJV
Truly, truly, I say to you, he who believes **on Me** has ev-erlasting life.	-MKJV

English: Based on Critical Greek Texts	John 6:47
Verily, verily, I say unto you, He that believeth ___ ___ hath **eternal** life.	-RV
Truly, truly, I say to you, he who believes ___ ___ has **eter-nal** life.	-RSV
Truly, truly, I say to you, he who believes ___ ___ has **ev-erlasting** life.	-NIV

Impact: Everlasting life comes not just from believing. It comes from believing on Jesus Christ. The use of the word "eternal" in the RV and RSV was likely done in consideration for the word study that F. D. Maurice had done in trying to define the word as a state of having a "knowledge" of God and not as having an everlasting life.

Greek (TR: Received Text; WH: a Critical Text)	Revelation 22:14
μακαριοι οι ποιουντες τας εντολας αυτου ινα εσται η εξουσια αυτων επι το ξυλον της ζωης και τοις πυλωσιν εισελθωσιν εις την πολιν	-TR
μακαριοι οι πλυνοντες τας στολας αυτων ινα εσται η εξουσια αυτων επι το ξυλον της ζωης και τοις πυλωσιν εισελθωσιν εις την πολιν	-WH

Appendix B. Impact of the Changing Scriptures

English: Based on Received Greek Text	Revelation 22:14
Blessed *are* they that **do his commandments**, that **they may have right to** the tree of life, and may enter in through the gates into the city.	-KJV
Blessed *are* those who **do His commandments**, that **they may have the right to** the tree of life, and may enter through the gates into the city.	-NKJV
Blessed *are* they who **do His commandments**, that **their authority will be over** the Tree of Life, and they may enter in by the gates into the city.	-MKJV

English: Based on Critical Greek Texts	Revelation 22:14
Blessed are they that **wash their robes**, that **they may have the right** *to come* to the tree of life, and may enter in by the gates into the city.	-RV
Blessed are those who **wash their robes**, that **they may have the right to** the tree of life and that they may enter the city by the gates.	-RSV
Blessed are those who **wash their robes**, that they **may have the right to** the tree of life and may go throught the gates into the city.	-NIV

Impact: The rewritten version concept of "wash their robes" suggests that our works can be used to earn our right to the tree of life.

We Should Not Trust in Our Riches

Greek (TR: Received Text; WH: a Critical Text)	Mark 10:21
ο δε ιησους εμβλεψας αυτω ηγαπησεν αυτον και ειπεν αυτω εν σοι υστερει υπαγε οσα εχεις πωλησον και δος τοις πτωχοις και εξεις θησαυρον εν ουρανω και δευρο ακολουθει μοι αρας τον σταυρον	-TR
ο δε ιησους εμβλεψας αυτω ηγαπησεν αυτον και ειπεν αυτω εν σε υστερει υπαγε οσα εχεις πωλησον και δος *τοις* πτωχοις και εξεις θησαυρον εν ουρανω και δευρο ακολουθει μοι	-WH

English: Based on Received Greek Text	Mark 10:21
Then Jesus beholding him loved him, and said unto him, One thing thou lackest: go thy way, sell whatsoever thou hast, and give to the poor, and thou shalt have treasure in heaven: and come, **take up the cross**, and follow me.	-KJV
Then Jesus, looking at him, loved him, and said to him, "One thing you lack: Go your way, sell whatever you have and give to the poor, and you will have treasure in heaven; and come, **take up the cross**, and follow Me."	-NKJV
Then Jesus, beholding him, loved him and said to him, One *thing* you lack. Go, sell whatever you have and give it to the poor, and you shall have treasure in Heaven. And come, **take up the cross** and follow Me.	-MKJV

Greek (TR: Received Text; WH: a Critical Text)	Mark 10:21
And Jesus looking upon him loved him, and said unto him, One thing thou lackest: go, sell whatsoever thou hast, and give to the poor, and thou shalt have treasure in heaven: and come, ____ __ ___ ____ follow me.	-RV
And Jesus looking upon him loved him, and said to him, "You lack one thing; go, sell what you have, and give to the poor, and you will have treasure in heaven; and come, ____ __ ___ _____ ___ follow me."	-RSV
Jesus looked at him and loved him. "One thing you lack," he said. "Go, sell everything you have and give to the poor, and you will have treasure in heaven. Then come, ____ __ ___ _____ follow me."	-NIV

Appendix B. Impact of the Changing Scriptures

Greek (TR: Received Text; WH: a Critical Text)	Mark 10:24
οι δε μαθηται εθαμβουντο επι τοις λογοις αυτου ο δε ιησους παλιν αποκριθεις λεγει αυτοις τεκνα πως δυσκολον εστιν τους πεποιθοτας επι τοις χρημασιν εις την βασιλειαν του θεου εισελθειν	-TR
οι δε μαθηται εθαμβουντο επι τοις λογοις αυτου ο δε ιησους παλιν αποκριθεις λεγει αυτοις τεκνα πως δυσκολον εστιν ___ _____ ___ ____ _____ εις την βασιλειαν του θεου εισελθειν	-WH

English: Based on Received Greek Text	Mark 10:24
And the disciples were astonished at his words. But Jesus answereth again, and saith unto them, Children, how hard is it **for them that trust in riches** to enter into the kingdom of God!	-KJV
And the disciples were astonished at His words. But Jesus answered again and said to them, "Children, how hard it is **for those who trust in riches** to enter the kingdom of God!	-NKJV
And the disciples were astonished at His words. But Jesus answering again said to them, Children, how hard it is **for those who trust in riches** to enter into the kingdom of God!	-MKJV

English: Based on Critical Greek Texts	Mark 10:24
And the disciples were amazed at his words. But Jesus answereth again, and saith unto them, Children, how hard is it **for them that trust in riches** to enter into the kingdom of God!	-RV
And the disciples were amazed at his words. But Jesus said to them again, "Children, how hard it is ___ ____ ____ _____ _____ to enter the kingdom of God!	-RSV
The disciples were amazed at his words. But Jesus said again, "Children, how hard it is ___ ____ ____ _____ __ _____ to enter the kingdom of God!	-NIV

Impact: The Socialist implication of the change is clear. The topic that Jesus was discussing was that trusting in riches is an obstacle to entering the Kingdom of God. The change distorts the entire point that Jesus made in the next verse and suggests that only those who have no riches can enter the Kingdom. Promoters of the Social Gospel insist that Jesus was thinking about the "righteous society on earth" when He said these words.[10]

[10] Rauschenbusch, *Christianity and the Social Crisis*, p. 76.

While Men Slept...

We Live Not By Bread Alone, but by Every Word of God

Greek (TR: Received Text; WH: a Critical Text)	Romans 10:17
αρα η πιστις εξ ακοης η δε ακοη δια ρηματος θεου	-TR
αρα η πιστις εξ ακοης η δε ακοη δια ρηματος χρισ-του	-WH

English: Based on Received Greek Text	Romans 10:17
So then **faith** *cometh* by hearing, and hearing by the **word of God**.	-KJV
So then **faith** *comes* by hearing, and hearing by the **word of God**.	-NKJV
Then **faith** *is* of hearing, and hearing by the **Word of God**.	-MKJV

English: Based on Critical Greek Texts	Romans 10:17
So **belief** cometh of hearing, and hearing by the **word of Christ**.	-RV
So **faith** comes from what is heard, and what is heard comes by the **preaching of Christ**.	-RSV
Consequently, **faith** comes from hearing **the message**, and **the message** is heard through the **word of Christ**.	-NIV

Greek (TR: Received Text; WH: a Critical Text)	Luke 4:4
και απεκριθη ιησους προς αυτον λεγων γεγραπται οτι ουκ επ αρτω μονω ζησεται ο ανθρωπος αλλ επι παντι ρηματι θεου	-TR
και απεκριθη προς αυτον ο ιησους γεγραπται οτι ουκ επ αρτω μονω ζησεται ο ανθρωπος ___ ___	-WH

English: Based on Received Greek Text	Luke 4:4
And Jesus answered him, saying, It is written, That man shall not live by bread alone, **but by every word of God**.	-KJV
But Jesus answered him, saying, "It is written, 'Man shall not live by bread alone, **but by every word of God**.'"	-NKJV
And Jesus answered him, saying, It is written that "man shall not live by bread alone, **but by every word of God**."	-MKJV

Appendix B. Impact of the Changing Scriptures

English: Based on Critical Greek Texts	Luke 4:4
And Jesus answered unto him, It is written, Man shall not live by bread alone ___ __ __ ___ ____ __ ___.	-RV
And Jesus answered him, "It is written, 'Man shall not live by bread alone ___ __ __ ____ ___ __ ___.'"	-RSV
Jesus answered, "It is written, 'Man does not live on bread alone ___ __ __ ___ ___ __ ___.'"	-NIV

Impact: Paul repeated the words of Habakkuk 2:4 in Romans 1:27 (also see Galatians 3:11 and Hebrews 10:38), "The just shall live by faith." In Romans 10:17, we learn that the faith by which we live comes from hearing the Word of God. Jesus said that we inherit everlasting life by believing in Him (see John 3:16). That is, faith is required. Therefore, as Jesus said, every Word of God is essential for our life. Bread is needed for our physical life, but every Word of God, which is omitted in the Critical Text versions, is essential for our spiritual life.. Without His Word, we are without faith, which is required for us to believe in the saving sacrifice of Jesus Christ unto everlasting life!

While Men Slept...

Appendix C. A Note of Warning: Try the Spirits

A letter written by Charles F. Parham on December 1, 1906 concerning a counterfeit spiritual movement he witnessed in Los Angeles, California:

A NOTE OF WARNING

"Throughout the history of all religious reformations and movements which have brought to light new spiritual life and power, the truth always has been veiled by the shadows, mists and clouds of wild-fire, fanaticism, and everything else that the devil through his agents could invent to conceal the real and the good, and to mystify those who were seeking for more light and power. Everything that could be brought to bear has been thrown about it to hide it from the world.

"As it has been in the past, so it will ever be. Only those who are willing to go down beneath the veil, tearing it away that they may view the real in all it's beauty and splendor, and expose the counterfeit that seems so like the real, facing the fanaticisms, in a self-forgetful spirit—only such will be able to bring to the surface the pure truth of God, that the world may view His great wonders which are revealed so mysteriously.

"Never were God's servants surrounded with more deceptive counterfeits of real divine experience than in this day and age; and never was it more imperative that all should stand firm and steadfast for the truth.

"So many different agencies are employed to imitate the real and the 'magician's' work is so well nigh perfect, that it often is indeed hard to distinguish the true and false.

"It is for his reason that I am writing this. And I earnestly urge all to search their own hearts, that they may learn for a certainty that they are in no way deceived or mislead, or in any way coming short of the truth and the light, for which we are looking; and that they may know for a certainty that they are really on the Lord's side and led by no influences save that of the Holy Spirit.

"I have witnessed great dangers in the work here in Los Angeles, and in pointing them out I shall not refer to indi[vi]duals, but to the work itself as a whole, that we all may see the error of our way and get back to God.

"Throughout the summer I was greatly encouraged, and truly rejoiced at the reports of the work that was sweeping the California field. Every breeze across the continent wafted tidings of victories achieved until it seemed as if the whole Pacific Coast would be taken for God. Through this glorious onward march, although absent in body I was present in spirit beholding the wonderful victories and triumphs, as well as some defeats, and waiting patiently for our God to free me from many hindrances and allow me to come here that I might be used of Him in every helpful way.

"After much hard labor in Missouri, Kansas and Texas and the conduction of the great state rally in the city of Houston, and the visiting of many missions throughout Texas, I went north to conduct the encampment for the States of Missouri and Kansas, held in Baxter, Kansas. When this meeting was well under way God told me to go to Zion City, and the work accomplished there is now known far and near.

"For some time I had been in touch with many friends who knew the extremes that had crept into the meeting in California, and also with others who were anxious to know if the work there truly represented the teachings of the Apostolic Faith Movement; meanwhile workers which had been sent there and who were well acquainted with the work wrote me repeatedly to come quickly to the rescue.

"At last, the work in Zion City being thoroughly established, God said to me, "Go to California." So, leaving the work there in the hands of thoroughly competent persons, I came to Los Angeles.

522

Appendix C. A Note of Warning: Try the Spirits

"I feel that it was in God's order for me not to reach here sooner than I did, and I may say here that, although many forms of fanaticism have crept in, I believe every true child of God will come out of this mist and shadow stronger and better equipped against all extremes that are liable to present themselves at any time in meetings of this kind.

"Let me say, in speaking of different phases of fanaticism that have been obtained here, that I do so with all lovingkindness and at the same time with all fairness and firmness. I have no desire to assert my authority (for I have none to assert over the people of God), but to help and strengthen, and forever make plain to all people that extremes, wild-fire, fanaticism, and everything that is beyond the bounds of common sense and reason, do not now and never have had any part or lot in Apostolic faith work and teachings.

"Let me speak plainly with regard to the work as I have found it here. I found hypnotic influences, familiar-spirit influences, spiritualistic influences, mesmeric influences, and all kinds of spells, spasms, falling in trances, etc. All of these things are foreign to and unknown in this movement outside of Los Angeles, except in the places visited by the workers sent out from this city.

"A word about the baptism of the Holy Ghost. The speaking in tongues is never brought about by any of the above influences. In all our work the laying on of hands is practised only occasionally, and then for the space of only a minute or two. No such thing is known among our workers as the suggestion of certain words and sounds, the working of the chin, or the massage of the throat.

"Nonsense! The Holy Ghost needs no help! When the recipient of the Holy Ghost comes into proper relations with God the speaking in tongues comes as naturally as any other gift from Him. There is always the real and the false, and anything outside of the operation of the Holy Ghost is counterfeit.

While Men Slept...

"There are many in Los Angeles who sing, pray and talk wonderfully in other tongues, as the Spirit gives utterance, and there is jabbering here that is not tongues at all. I know that people sometimes fall under the power of God, and that there are times that God thus deals with his creature's that resist Him; but these cases are exceptional and are not general. The falling under the power in Los Angeles has, to a large degree, been produced through a hypnotic, mesmeric, magnetic current.

"The Holy Ghost does nothing that is unnatural or unseemingly, and any strained exertion of body, mind, or voice is not the work of the Holy Spirit, but of some familiar spirit, or other influence brought to bear upon the subject. The Holy Spirit is always strengthening, uplifting, vitalizing, and invigorating; while that of any other spirit is always devitalizing and degenerating, with the tendency to drag down.

"How vastly important it is that we try the spirits; and not yield to every influence brought to bear upon us! Let us guard carefully against every form of fan[a]ticism, and stand firm and true, helping one another and reasoning together.

"Having guarded this Pentecostal blessing from it's earliest infancy, I feel that it is still my duty to stand against anything and everything that will in any way prove a hindrance to others, or to the advancement of the work. The corrections which I seek to make are for the good of all, and the condemnation of none, that we may rise to all the heights of power and strength possible, and go on together in His name for the evang[e]lization of the world. The Holy Ghost never leads us beyond the point of self-control or the control of others, while familiar spirits or fan[a]ticism lead us both beyond self-control and the power to help others."[1]

---

[1] Parham, *The Life of Charles F. Parham*, pp. 166-170.

Bibliography

[American Bible Revision Committee], *Documentary History of the American Committee on Revision: Prepared by Order of the Committee for the Use of the Members* (New York: Printed, Not Published, 1885).

[Anon.] "Basis of Unity and Hearty Co-operation" on the Part of the Faculty with Pres. Mahan, Asa Mahan (1799-1889) Papers, [1764] 1835-1985, Accession No. 223, Processed by Brian A. Williams (Oberlin, Ohio: Oberlin College Archives, April 1992).

[Anon.], *Georg Wilhelm Friedrich Hegel's Leben, beschrieben durch Karl Rosenkranz, Berlin, 1844*, Review Art. IV. In *The Princeton Review*, October 1848.

[Anon.], *Record of the Convention for the Promotion of Scriptural Holiness Held at Brighton, May 29th to June 7th, 1875* (Brighton: W. J. Smith and London: S.W. Partridge and Co., c1896; Reprinted in *"The Higher Christian Life: Sources for the Study of the Holiness, Pentecostal, and Keswick Movements*, Donald W. Dayton, ed., New York and London: Garland Publishing, Inc., 1985).

[Anon], *Account of the Union Meeting for the Promotion of Scriptural Holiness held at Oxford, August 29 to September 7, 1874* (London: S.W. Partridge & Co., c1875; Reprinted in *"The Higher Christian Life: Sources for the Study of the Holiness, Pentecostal, and Keswick Movements*, Donald W. Dayton, ed., New York and London: Garland Publishing, Inc., 1985).

[Mahan, Asa], "Peace Congress at Paris," *The Oberlin Evangelist*, Oct 10, 1849.

[The World Council of Churches], *The New Delhi Report: The Third Assembly of the World Council of Churches, 1961* (New York: Association Press, 1962).

1550 Textus Receptus Text, In *Online Bible*, Version 8.11 (Winterbourne, Ontario, Canada: Timnathserah, Inc., 2000).

1769 Authorized Version, In *Online Bible*, Version 8.11 (Winterbourne, Ontario, Canada: Timnathserah, Inc., 2000).

1881 Westcott Hort Greek Text, In *Online Bible*, Version 8.11 (Winterbourne, Ontario, Canada: Timnathserah, Inc., 2000).

1982 New King James Version, In *Online Bible*, Version 8.11 (Winterbourne, Ontario, Canada: Timnathserah, Inc., 2000).

Adhav, Shamsundar Manohar, *Pandita Ramabai: Confessing the Faith in India Series—No. 13* (Madras, India: The Christian Literature Society, 1979).

Allen, Gay Wilson, *Waldo Emerson: A Biography* (New York: The Viking Press, 1981).

Alpha for Catholics: UK Bishop on Alpha's "Incredible Achievement," Alpha News, USA ed., No. 6, April-July, 2000.

American & Foreign Anti-Slavery Society, The Thirteenth Annual Report of the American & Foreign Anti-Slavery Society, Presented at New York, May 11, 1853 with the Addresses and Resolutions (New York: The American & Foreign Anti-Slavery Society, 1853).

Andersen, Hans Christian, *The Emperor's New Clothes*, Designed and Illustrated by Virginia Lee Burton (Boston: Houghton Mifflin Co., 1949).

Anthon, Charles, *A Manual of Greek Literature from the Earliest Authentic Periods to the Close of the Byzantine Era* (New York: Harper & Brothers, 1853).

Anon., "Memorial Minute: John Alexander Mackay*, 1889-1983*," *Theology Today*, vol.. 40, no. 4, http://theologytoday.ptsem.edu/jan1984/v40-4-editorial2.htm, January 1984.

Anon., "Moriah C. M. Chapel: Evan Roberts-The Man-What was He Like?," 2001, http://www.moriah1904.ukgateway.net/evan.htm.

Anon., "Spiritualism, Chapter 2," *The Catholic World*, vol. 18, no. 105, December, 1873.

Anon., Khasi Hills, 2001, http://www.newdelhi.net/india/DiscoverIndia/Meghalaya/khasi.html.

Anon., Review of *The Works of Plato*, In *The Princeton Review*, vol. 36, no. 2, April, 1864.

Arnold, Duane Wade-Hampton, *The Early Episcopal Career of Athanasius of Alexandria* (Notre Dame, Indiana: Notre Dame University Press, 1991).

Arthur, William, *The Tongue of Fire, or the True Power of Christianity* (New York: Harper & Brothers, Franklin Square, 1880).

Athanasius, St, Bishop of Alexandria, http://ccel.wheaton.edu/a/athanasius/athanasius-EB.html.

Athenagoras, *Writings of Athenagoras*, B. P. Pratten, trans. In *The Anti-Nicene Fathers the Writings of the Fathers Down to A.D. 325, The Ante-Nicene Fathers*, vol. 2, ch. 10, Alexander Roberts and James Donaldson, eds. (Albany, Oregon: Sage Software, 1996, American Reprint of the Edinburgh ed., July, 1975).

Atlhusser, Louis, *For Marx*, Ben Brewster, trans. (New York: Pantheon Books, 1969).

Backhouse, Edward, *Early Church History to the Death of Constantine*, 2nd ed., Charles Tylor, ed. (London: Hamilton, Adams & Co., 1885).

Baring, Anne and Jules Cashford, *The Myth of the Goddess: Evolution of an Image* (London: Penguin Books Ltd., 1993).

Barrows, John Henry, ed., *The World's Parliament of Religions: An Illustrative and Popular Story of the World's First Parliament of Religions, Held in Chicago in Connection with the Columbian Exposition of 1893*, vol. 1. (Chicago: The Lakeside Press, H. H. Donnelley & Sons, 1893).

Barry, Joseph, *Infamous Woman: The Life of George Sand* (Garden City, New York: Anchor Press/Doubleday, 1978).

Barthel, Manfred, *The Jesuits: History & Legend of the Society of Jesus*, Mark Howson, trans. and adapt. (New York: William Morrow and Company, Inc., 1984).

Bartleman, Frank, *Around the World by Faith: With Six Weeks in the Holy Land* 2nd ed. (Los Angeles: Frank Bartleman, undated; Reprinted in *Witness to Pentecost: The Life of Frank Bartleman, with a Preface by Cecil M. Robeck, Jr.* (New York and London: Garland Publishing, Inc., 1985)).

Bartleman, Frank, *From Plow to Pulpit; From Maine to California* (Los Angeles: Frank Bartleman, 1924; Reprinted in *Witness to Pentecost: The Life of Frank Bartleman, with a Preface by Cecil M. Robeck, Jr.* (New York and London: Garland Publishing, Inc., 1985)).

Bartleman, Frank, *How Pentecost Came to Los Angeles: As It Was in the Beginning*, 2nd ed. (Los Angeles: Frank Bartleman, 1925; Reprinted in *Witness to Pentecost: The Life of Frank Bartleman, with a Preface by Cecil M. Robeck, Jr.* (New York and London: Garland Publishing, Inc., 1985)).

Bea, Augustin Cardinal, *Unity in Freedom: Reflections on the Human Family* (New York and Evanston: Harper & Row, Publishers, 1964).

Beam, Kathryn L. and Traianos Gagos, eds., *The Evolution of the English Bible: From Papyri to King James* (Ann Arbor: University of Michigan Press, Ann Arbor, 1997).

Becket, J. C., *A Short History of Ireland* (London: Hutchinson University Library, 1958).

Berman, David, *A History of Atheism in Britain: From Hobbes to Russell* (London, New York, and Sydney: Croom Helm, 1988).

Betts, C. J., *Early Deism in France: From the So-Called "Deistes" of Lyon (1564) to Voltaire's "Lettres Philosophiques" (1734)* (The Hague, Boston, and Lancaster: Martinus Nijhoff Publishers, 1984).

Biographical Note on Henry Edward Manning (1808-1892) Collection, 1826-1891, Manuscript No. 002 (Atlanta, Georgia: Archives & Manuscripts, Pitts Theology Library, Emory University) http://www.pitts.emory.edu/text/mss002.html

Birdsall, J. Neville, *Textual Criticism and New Testament Studies* (Birmingham, England: University of Birmingham, 1984).

Bloch-Hoell, Nils, *The Pentecostal Movement: Its Origin, Development, and Distinctive Character* (Halden, Norway: Universitetsforlaget, 1964).

Blumhofer, Edith Waldvogel, *The Assemblies of God: A Popular History* (Springfield, Missouri: Gospel Publishing House, 1985).

Boyesen, Hjalmar H., *Goethe and Schiller: Their Lives and Works, Including a Commentary on Goethe's "Faust"* (New York: Charles Scribners Sons, 1901).

Bradley, Dan F., "Oberlin Theology—From Mahan to Horton," *The Oberlin Alumni Magazine*, vol. 29, no. 6, March 1, 1933 (Oberlin, Ohio: Oberlin College Archives, 1933).

Brandreth, Henry Renaud Turner, "Approaches of the Churches Towards Each Other in the Nineteenth Century," In *A History of the Ecumenical Movement, 1517-1948*, ch. 6, Ruth Rouse and Stephen Charles Neill, eds. (Philadelphia: The Westminster Press, 1954).

Brenton, Lancelot C. L., (Jeremiah 51:26), *The Septuagint with Apocrypha: Greek and English*, Originally published by Samuel Bagster & Sons, Ltd., London, 1851 (Peabody, Massachusetts: Hendrickson Publishers, 1987).

Broad, C. D., *Religion, Philosophy and Psychical Research* (New York: Harcourt, Brace & Company, Inc., 1953).

Brose, Olive J., *Frederick Denison Maurice: Rebellious Conformist* (Athens, Ohio: Ohio University Press, 1971).

Brown, Frank Burch, *The Evolution of Darwin's Religious Views*, National Association of Baptist Professors of Religion Special Studies Series, No. 10 (Macon, Georgia: Mercer University Press, 1986).

Brown, Jerry Wayne, *The Rise of Biblical Criticism in America, 1800-1870: The New England Scholars* (Middletown, Connecticut: Wesleyan University Press, 1969).

Bruce, F. F., *History of the Bible in English From the Earliest Versions* (New York: Oxford University Press, 1978).

Bryant, M. Darrol and Frank Flinn, *Introduction, Scouting the Frontier*, In *Interreligious Dialogue: Voices from a New Frontier*, M. Darrol Bryant and Frank Flinn, eds., (New York: Paragon House, 1989).

Brzezinski, Zbigniew, *Out of Control: Global Turmoil on the Eve of the Twenty-First Century* (New York: Simon and Schuster Inc., 1995).

Budhananda, Swami, *Worship of God as Mother*, The Vedanta Kesari (Madras-4, India: Sri Ramakrishna Math), vol. 49 (6), October, 1962.

Burgon, John William, *Proof of the Genuineness of God Manifested in the Flesh*, In *Unholy Hands on the Bible*, vol. 1., Jay P. Green, Sr., ed. (Lafayette, Indiana: Sovereign Grace Trust Fund, 1990).

Burgon, John William, *The Last Twelve Verses According to the Gospel of Mark*, In *Unholy Hands on the Bible*, vol. 1., Jay P. Green, ed. (Lafayette, Indiana: Sovereign Grace Trust Fund, 1990.

Burgon, John William, *The Revision Revised: A Critique of the English Revised Version of 1881, with Application to the Modern Translations*, In *Unholy Hands on the Bible*, vol. 1, Jay P. Green, ed. (Lafayette, Indiana: Sovereign Grace Trust Fund, 1990).

Burgon, John William, *The Secret Spanking of Westcott and Hort,* In *Unholy Hands on the Bible*, vol. 1., Jay P. Green, Sr., ed., (Lafayette, Indiana: Sovereign Grace Trust Fund, 1990).

Burgon, John William, *The Traditional Text of the New Testament,* In

Unholy Hands on the Bible, Edward Miller, ed., vol. 1, Jay P. Green, ed. (Lafayette, Indiana: Sovereign Grace Trust Fund, 1990).

Cabot, James Elliot, *A Memoir of Ralph Waldo Emerson* (Boston and New York: Houghton, Mifflin and Company, 1888).

Cairns, Earle E., *Christianity Through the Centuries,* 3rd ed. (Grand Rapids, Michigan: Zondervan Publishing House, 1996).

Campbell, Thomas, *The Jesuits, 1534-1921: A History of the Society of Jesus from Its Foundation to the Present Time*, vol. 2. (New York: The Encyclopedia Press, 1921).

Carson, D. A., *The King James Version Debate: A Plea for Realism* (Grand Rapids, MI: Baker Book House, 1992).

Carwardine, Richard, *Transatlantic Revivalism: Popular Evangelicalism in Britain and America, 1790-1865* (Westport, Connecticut and London: Greenwood Press, 1978).

Cassier, Ernst, *The Philosophy of the Enlightenment*, Fritz C. A. Koelln and James P. Pettegrove, trans. (Princeton, NJ: Princeton University Press, 1979).

Chadwick, John White, *Old and New Unitarian Belief* (Boston: Geo. H. Ellis, 1894).

Chadwick, Owen, *Michael Ramsey: A Life* (Oxford: Clarendon Press, 1990).

Chakraborty, Nirod Baran, "The Holy Mother as a Spiritual Force," In *Bulletin of the Ramakrishna Mission Institute of Culture*, vol. 27, no. 12 (Calcutta: Ramakrishna Mission Institute of Culture, December 1976).

Chakravarti, Uma, *Rewriting History: The Life and Times of Pandita Ramabai* (New Delhi: Kali for Women, 1998).

Chapman, J. Wilbur, *The Life and Work of Dwight L. Moody* (Chicago and Philadelphia: International Publishing Co., 1900).

Chapman, Raymond, *Faith and Revolt: Studies in the Literary Influence of the Oxford Movement* (London: Weidenfeld and Nicolson, 1970).

Cheyney, Edward P., *A Short History of England* (Boston and others: Ginn and Company, 1904).

Clement of Alexandria, "Exhortation to the Heathen," In *The Ante-Nicene Fathers: Translations of The Writings of the Fathers down to A.D. 325*, vol. 2, *Fathers of the Second Century*, Alexander

Roberts and James Donaldson, eds. (Grand Rapids: Wm. B. Eeerdmans Publishing Company, Reprinted 1979).

Coleman, Simon, *The Globalisation of Charismatic Christianity: Spreading the Gospel of Prosperity* (Cambridge: Cambridge University Press, 2000).

Cooper, John M., *Introduction*, In *Plato: Complete Works*, John M. Cooper and D. S. Hutchinson, eds. (Indianapolis, Indiana: Hackett Publishing Company, 1997).

Coppa, Frank J., *Pope Pius IX: Crusader in a Secular Age* (Boston: Twayne Publishers, A Division of G. K. Hall & Co., 1979).

Cornish, Francis Warre, *The English Church in the Nineteenth Century, Part II* (London: Macmillan and Co., 1910).

Cort, John C., *Christian Socialism: An Informal History* (Maryknowll, NY: Orbis Books, 1988).

Council of Nice, In Valesius, *Annotations on the Life and Writings of Eusebius Pamphilus*, S. E. Parker, trans., In *The Ecclesiastical History of Eusebius Pamphilus, Bishop of Caesarea, In Palestine*, Translated from the Original with an Introduction by Christian Frederick Cruse and an Historical View of the Council of Nice by Isaac Boyle (Grand Rapids, Michigan: Baker Book House, 1990).

Courtney, Janet E., *Freethinkers of the Nineteenth Century* (London: Chapman & Hall, Ltd., 1920).

Cox, Harvey, *Fire from Heaven: The Rise of Pentecostal Spirituality and the Reshaping of Religion in the Twenty-First Century* (Reading, Massachusetts: Addison-Wesley Publishing Company, 1995).

Cragg, Gerald R., *Reason and Authority in the Eighteenth Century* (Cambridge: Cambridge University Press, 1964).

Crouter, Richard, In the Introduction to *Friedrich Schleiermacher On Religion: Speeches to Its Cultured Despisers,* Richard Crouter, intro., trans., and notes (Cambridge: Cambridge University Press, 1988).

Crowe, Terrence Robert, *Pentecostal Unity: Recurring Frustration and Enduring Hopes* (Chicago: Loyola University Press, 1993).

Cunningham, Lawrence S., "Mary in Catholic Doctrine and Practice," *Theology Today*, vol. 56, no. 3, October, 1999.

Daniels, William Haven, *D. L. Moody and his work, by Rev. W. H. Daniels* (Hartford: American Publishing Company, 1876).

Davies, Horton, *Worship and Theology in England From Watts and*

Wesley to Maurice, 1690–1850 (Princeton, New Jersey: Princeton University Press, 1961).

Dayton, Donald W., *Theological Roots of Pentecostalism* (Grand Rapids, Michigan: Francis Asbury Press of Zondervan Publishing House, 1987).

De Beer, E. S., ed., *The Correspondence of John Locke*, vol. 4 (Oxford: Clarendon Press, 1979).

de Guibert, Joseph, *The Jesuits: Their Spiritual Doctrine and Practice*, William J. Young, trans. and George E. Ganss, ed. (Chicago: The Institute of Jesuit Sources in cooperation with Loyola University Press, 1964).

de Purucker, G., *Fountain-Source of Occultism*, Grace F. Knoche, ed. (Pasadena, California: Theosophical University Press, 1974).

de Semlyen, Michael, *All Roads Lead to Rome? The Ecumenical Movement* (Bucks, England: Dorchester House Publications, 1993).

de Zirkoff, Boris, "Compiler's Notes," In *H. P. Blavatsky: Collected Writings, 1883*, Boris de Zirkoff, compiler (Los Angeles: Philosophical Research Society, Inc., 1950).

de Zirkoff, Boris, compiler, *H. P. Blavatsky: Collected Writings, 1883* (Los Angeles: Philosophical Research Society, Inc., 1950).

de Zirkoff, Boris, compiler, *H. P. Blavatsky: Collected Writings, 1874-1878*, vol. 1 (Wheaton, IL: The Theosophical Press, 1966).

Dearmer, Percy, *Socialism and Christianity*, Pub. Fabian Society, Fabian Tract No. 133, 1907, page 3. (Referenced by Bernard Mends, "John Trevor - The Labour Church And Socialist Sunday Schools," http://www.qbradley.freeserve.co.uk/labourchurch.html, 1999).

Dedication Letter, In *The Holy Bible, 1611 Edition, King James Version*: *A Word-for-Word Reprint of the First Edition of the Authorized Version Presented in Roman Letters for Easy Reading and Comparison with Subequent Editions* (Nashville: Thomas Nelson Publishers, Undated).

Delling, Gerhard, *Johann Jakob Griesbach: His Life, Work and Times*, Ronald Walls, trans., In *J. J. Griesbach: Synoptic and Text-critical Studies, 1776-1976*, Bernard Orchard and Thomas R. W. Longstaff, eds. (Cambridge: Cambridge University Press, 1978).

Dickens, Charles, *A Tale of Two Cities*, In *Charles Dickens: Four Complete Novels* (Avenel, New Jersey: Gramercy Books/Random House Value Publishing, Inc., 1982).

Distad, N. Merrill, *Guessing at Truth: The Life of Julius Charles Hare* (Shepherdstown: The Patmos Press, 1979).

Documents of the Revolution of 1848 in France, J. H. Robinson, ed., Readings in European History (Boston: Ginn, 1906; Hanover Historical Texts Project February, 1997).

Douay-Rheims Version, *The Holy Bible Translated from the Latin Vulgate: Diligently Compared with the Hebrew, Greek, and Other Editions, in Divers Languages: The Old Testament First Published by the English College, at Douay, A.D. 1609; and the New Testament First Published by the English College at Rheims, A.D. 1582* (New York: Edward Dunigan & Brother, 1850).

Du Plessis, David, as told to Bob Slosser, *A Man Called Mr. Pentecost* (Plainfield, New Jersey: Logos International, 1977).

Durant, Will, *The Reformation: A History of European Civilization from Wyclif to Calvin: 1300-1564* (New York: MJF Books, 1957 and 1985).

Edwards, Francis, *The Jesuits in England: From 1580 to the Present Day* (Tunbridge Wells, Kent: Burns & Oates, 1985), p. 162.

Ehrenstrom, Nils, "Movements for International Friendship and Life and Work, 1925-1948," In *A History of the Ecumenical Movement, 1517-1948*, ch. 12, Rouse and Neill, eds.

Elliott, Charles, *Subjective Theory of Inspiration*, In *The Princeton Review* (New York: July-December, 1881).

Emerson, Ralph Waldo, *The Complete Sermons of Ralph Waldo Emerson*, Ronald A. Bosco, ed. (Columbia and London: Ralph Waldo Emerson Memorial Association, University of Missouri Press, 1991).

Erasmus, Desiderius, *The Life of the Eminent Doctor Jerome of Stridon Composed Mainly from His Own Writings by Desiderius Erasmus of Rotterdam*, In *Collected Works of Erasmus*, James E. Brady and John C. Olin, eds. (Toronto: University of Toronto Press, 1992).

Eusebius of Caesarea, "The Church History of Eusebius," Arthur Cushman McGiffert, trans with Prolegomena and notes, bk. 3, ch.

25, In *A Select Library of Nicene and Post-Nicene Fathers of the Christian Church*, vol. 1, 2nd series, Philip Schaff and Henry Wace, eds. (Grand Rapids, Michigan: Wm. B. Eerdmans Publishing Company, 1979).

Eusebius Pamphilus, "The Life of the Blessed Emperor Constantine," bk. 4, ch. 34, Ernest Cushing Richardson, rev. trans. with Prolegomena and notes, ed., In *A Select Library of Nicene and Post-Nicene Fathers of the Christian Church*, vol. 1, 2nd Series, Philip Schaff and Henry Wace, eds. (Grand Rapids, Michigan: Wm. B. Eerdmans Publishing Company, 1979).

Eusebius, *The Ecclesiastical History*, vol. 2, ed. published with H. J. Lawlor, J. E. L. Oulton, trans. (London: William Heinemann Ltd, 1932).

Farnell, Lewis R., *Greece and Babylon: A Comparative Sketch of Mesopotamian, Anatolian, and Hellenic Religions* (Edinburgh: T. & T. Clark, 1911).

Faupel, D. William, *The Everlasting Gospel: The Significance in the Development of Pentecostal Thought* (Sheffield, England: Sheffield Academic Press, 1996).

Fee, Gordon D., *Modern Text Criticism and the Synoptic Problem*, In *J. J. Griesbach: Synoptic and Text-critical Studies, 1776-1976*

Ferguson, Charles W., *The New Books of Revelations: The Inside Store of America's Astounding Religious Cults* (Garden City, New York: Doubleday, Doran & Company Inc., 1928; printed for Chicago: The Private Editions Company, 1930).

Fiddes, Paul S., "The Theology of the Charismatic Movement," In *Strange Gifts? A Guide to Charismatic Renewal*, David Martin and Peter Mullen, eds. (Oxford: Basil Blackwell Publisher Ltd., 1984).

Fife, Robert Herndon, *The Revolt of Martin Luther* (New York and London: Columbia University Press, 1957).

Figgis, J. B., *Keswick from Within* (London: Marshall Brothers, Ltd., 1914; Reprinted in *"The Higher Christian Life:" Sources for the Study of the Holiness, Pentecostal, and Keswick Movements*, Donald W. Dayton, ed. (New York & London: Garland Publishing, Inc., 1985).

Finegan, Jack, *Encountering New Testament Manuscripts: A Work-*

ing Introduction to Textual Criticism (Grand Rapids, Michigan: William B. Eerdmans Publishing Company, 1974).

Finney, C. G., "Induement of Power," In Asa Mahan, *The Baptism of the Holy Ghost* (London: Elliott Stock, 1876).

Finney, Charles Grandison, *Memoirs of Rev. Charles G. Finney. Written by Himself* (New York: A. S. Barnes & Company, 1876).

Fish, Henry C., *Pulpit Eloquence of the Nineteenth Century: Being Supplementary to the History and Repository of Pulpit Eloquence, Deceased Divines; and Containing Discources of Eminent Living Ministers in Europe and America with Sketches Biographical and Descriptive* (New York: Dodd, Mead & Company, Publishers, 1871).

Fleming, William Kaye, *Mysticism in Christianity* (New York and Chicago: Fleming H. Revell Company, 1913).

Foakes-Jackson, F.J., *Eusebius of Pamphili* (Cambridge: W. Heffer & Sons Ltd., 1933).

Franklin, R. W., *Nineteenth-Century Churches: A History of a New Catholicism in Wurttemberg, England, and France*, In *Modern European History: A Garland Series of Outstanding Dissertations*, William H. McNeill, Gen. Ed. (New York and London: Garland Publishing, Inc., 1987).

Froude, James Anthony, *Thomas Carlyle: A History of His Life in London, 1834-1881*, vol. 1 (New York: Charles Scribner's Sons, 1910).

Fulop-Miller, Rene, *The Power and Secret of the Jesuits*, F. S. Flint and D. F. Tait, trans. (New York: Viking Press, 1930).

Gaines, David P., *The World Council of Churches: A Study of Its Background and History* (Peterborough, New Hampshire, Richard R. Smith, Noone House, 1966).

Gairdner, W. H. T., *Echoes from Edinburgh, 1910: An Account and Interpretation of the World Missionary Conference* (New York: Fleming H. Revell Company, 1910).

Galton, Francis, *Imagining a Utopia - or Laputa, MacMillan's Magazine*, vol. 11 (November, 1864-April, 1865), pp. 157-166, 318-327, referenced in http://www.cimm.jcu.edu.au/hist/stats/galton/macm9.htm.

Garrard, Mary N., *Mrs. Penn Lewis* (London: The Overcomer Book

Room; Reprinted and Web Published by Toni Cauchi, Architech Information Designs, Inc., http://revival-library.org/catalogues/world6/garrard/foreshadowings.ihtml, 2001).

Gary B. McGee, "'Latter Rain' Falling in the East: Early-Twentieth-Century Pentecostalism in India and the Debate over Speaking in Tongues," *Church History*, vol. 68 no. 3, September 1999.

Gauld, Aland, *The Founders of Psychical Research* (London: Routledge & Kegan Paul, 1968).

Geisler, Norman L. and William E. Nix, *A General Introduction to the Bible, Revised and Expanded* (Chicago: Moody Press, 1986).

Gibbons, James Cardinal, *The Faith of Our Fathers: Being a Plain Exposition and Vindication of the Church Founded by Our Lord Jesus Christ* (Rockford, Illinois: Tan Books and Publishers, Inc., 1980 [Originally published: Baltimore: The John Murphy Company, 1876]).

Gibson, William, *Church, State, and Society, 1760-1850* (New York: St. Martin's Press, 1994).

Goff, James R., Jr., *Fields White Unto Harvest: Charles F. Parham and the Missionary Origins of Pentecostalism* (Fayetteville: The University of Arkansas Press, 1988).

Gorky, Maxim, *Letter from Gorky to Stalin*, (lcweb@loc.gov Library of Congress, posted November 13, 1995).

Grady, William, *Final Authority: A Christian's Guide to the King James Bible* (Schererville, Indiana: Grady Publications, Inc., 1997).

Grant, R. M., *Gnosticism and Early Christianity*, 2nd ed. (New York & London: Columbia University Press, 1966).

Grant, Robert M., *Eusebius as Church Historian* (Oxford: Clarendon Press, 1980).

Graves, Charles L., *Life and Letters of Alexander Macmillan* (London: Macmillan and Co., Ltd., 1910).

Gray, Robert, *Cardinal Manning: A Biography* (New York: St. Martin's Press, 1985).

Green, Jay P., Sr., *The Interlinear Bible: Hebrew-Greek-English*, 2nd ed. (Lafayette, Indiana: Sovereign Grace Publishers, 1986).

Green, Miranda, *Celtic Goddesses: Warriors, Virgins and Mothers* (London: British Museum Press, 1995).

Greeven, Heinrich, *The Gospel Synopsis From 1776 to the Present*

Day, Robert Althann, trans., In *J. J. Griesbach: Synoptic and Text-critical Studies, 1776-1976*, Bernard Orchard and Thomas R. W. Longstaff, eds. (Cambridge: Cambridge University Press, 1978).

Griesbach, J. J., *Commentatio qua Marci Evanelium totum e Matthaei et Lucae commentariis decerptum esse monstratur,* Bo Reicke, intro., In *J. J. Griesbach: Synoptic and Text-critical Studies, 1776-1976.*

Gunstone, John, *Pentecostal Anglicans* (London: Hodder and Stoughton, 1982).

Hall, Alfred, *Fifty Points in Favour of Unitarianism* (London: British and Foreign Unitarian Association, 1910).

Hansard Volume (House of Commons Debates), Session 1993-94, vol. 248, 17th October 1994 - 3rd November 1994, http://www.parliament.the-stationery-office.co.uk/pa/cm/cmse9394.htm.

Hanson, J. W., *Universalism: The Prevailing Doctrine Of The Christian Church During Its First Five Hundred Years* (Boston and Chicago: Universalist Publishing House, 1899), pp. 93-94.

Hare, Julius Charles, *To William Wordsworth*, In *[Augustus William and Julius Charles* Hare], *Guesses at Truth by Two Brothers*, new ed. (London: Macmillan and Co., 1876).

Harrison, John F. C., ed. *Introduction to Utopianism and Education*, (New York: Teachers College Press, Teachers College, Columbia University, 1968).

Hasler, August Bernhard, *How the Pope Became Infallible: Pius IX and the Politics of Persuasion* (Garden City, NY: Doubleday & Co., Inc., 1981).

Havel, Vaclav, Quoted in Jane R. Elgass, "Honorary Degree for Vaclav Havel," *Michigan Today*, The University of Michigan, Ann Arbor, vol. 32, no. 3, Fall, 2000.

Hawley, John Stratton, "Prologue: The Goddess of India," In *Devi: Goddesses of India*, John S. Hawley and Donna M. Wulff, eds. (Berkeley and Los Angeles: University of California Press, 1996).

Heine, Ronald, *Reading the Bible with Origen*, In *The Bible in Greek Christian Antiquity*, Paul M. Blowers, ed. and trans., Based on *Bible De Tous Les Temps,* vol. 1, *Le monde grec ancien et la*

Bible, C. Mondesert, ed. (Notre Dame, Indiana: University of Notre Dame Press, 1997).

Helvidius, Post-Nicene Fathers, vol. 6, Philip Schaff and Henry Wace eds. (Grand Rapids, Michigan: Eerdmans Pub. Co., 1892; rep. 1983).

Hennesey, James, *The First Council of the Vatican: The American Experience* (New York: Herder and Herder, 1963).

Hill, Hamilton and John Keep, "Minutes of the Trustee Meeting of Oberlin College, August 28, 1850, John Keep, Chairman, Hamilton Hill, Secretary (Oberlin, Ohio: Oberlin College Archives, 1850).

Hislop, Alexander, *The Two Babylons* (Ontario, California: Chick Publications, no date; first published as a pamphlet in 1853 and greatly expanded in 1858).

Hodge, Charles W., ed., *The Biblical Repertory and Princeton Review for the Year 1861,* vol. 33 (Philadelphia: Peter Walker, 1861).

Hodge, Charles W., *Proposed Revision of the English Bible*, In *The Biblical Repertory and Princeton Review*, Charles Hodge and Lyman H. Atwater, eds. (New York: Charles Scribner & Co., 1871).

Holborn, Hajo, *A History of Modern Germany, 1648-1840* (New York: Alfred A. Knopf, 1964).

Holborn, Hajo, *A History of Modern Germany: The Reformation* (New York: Alfred A. Knopf, 1976).

Hollenweger, Walter J., *Pentecostalism: Origins and Developments Worldwide* (Peabody, Massachusetts: Hendrickson Publishers, Inc., 1997).

Hollenweger, Walter J., *The Pentecostals: The Charismatic Movement in the Churches*, 2nd print. (Minneapolis: Augsburg Publishing House, 1973).

Hollenweger, Walter, "Two Extraordinary Pentecostal Ecumenists," *The Ecumenical Review*, vol. 52, July 2000.

Horne, Alistair, *Harold Macmillan, 1894-1956*, vol. 1 (New York: Viking Penguin Inc., 1988).

Hort, Arthur Fenton, *Life and Letters of Fenton John Anthony Hort*, vol. 1, (London: Macmillan & Co., 1896).

Hort, Arthur Fenton, *Life and Letters of Fenton John Anthony Hort,* vol. 2, (London: Macmillan & Co., 1896).

Hovell, Mark, *The Chartist Movement*, T. F. Tout, ed. (Manchester: Manchester University Press and London: Longmans, Green & Co., 1918).

Hudson, Charles Frederic, *A Critical Greek and English Concordance of the New Testament, Prepared by Charles F. Hudson under the Direction of Horace L. Hastings... Revised and Completed by Ezra Abbott*, 2nd ed., rev. (Philadelphia: J. B. Lippincott & Co., 1871).

Hughes, Thomas, *Memoir of Daniel Macmillan* (London: Macmillan and Co., 1882).

Hullyer, Paul C., "A Short History Of The Cambridge Clergy Training School And Westcott House, 1881-1996," http://www.ely.anglican.org/westcott/history.htm, 1999.

Hurst, John Fletcher, *History of Rationalism Embracing A Survey of the Present State of Protestant Theology* (New York: Eaton Mains, 1901).

Hywel-Davies, Jack, *The Life of Smith Wigglesworth: One Man, One Holy Passion* (Ann Arbor, Michigan: Servant Publications, 1988).

International Bible Society, *The Holy Bible, New International Version* (Grand Rapids, Michigan: The Zondervan Corporation, 1984).

International Missionary Council, *The Jerusalem Meeting of the International Missionary Council, March 24-April 8, 1928* (New York and London: International Missionary Council, 1928).

Irenaeus Against Heresies, bk. 3, ch. 10, Proofs of the Foregoing, Drawn from the Gospels of Mark and Luke, http://www.ccel.org/fathers2/ANF-01/anf01-60.htm#P7297_1937859, Christian Classics Ethereal Library, Calvin College, May 27, 1999.

Jamieson, Robert, A.R. Fausset, and David Brown, *A Commentary, Critical and Explanatory on the Old and New Testaments*, vol. 2 (New York: S.S. Scranton and Company, 1873).

Jefferson, Thomas, *The Writings of Thomas Jefferson*, Saul K. Padover, ed. (Lunenburg, Vermont: The George Macy Companies, Inc, 1967).

Jellicoe, Sidney, *The Septuagint and Modern Study* (London: Oxford at the Clarendon Press, 1968).

John XXIII, Pope, *Meditations for the Council*, In *The Pope Speaks*, vol. 8, no. 1, 1962.

John XXIII, Pope, *The Council and the Separated Brethren*, In *The Pope Speaks*, vol. 8, No. 1, 1962.

Jones, Brynmor Pierce, *An Instrument of Revival: The Complete Life* of *Evan Roberts (1878-1951)* (South Plainfield, New Jersey, 1995).

Josephus, *The Works of Josephus*, bk. 12, chs. 1 and 2, William Whiston, trans. (Peabody, Massachusetts: Hendrickson Publishers, 1985).

Journal of the Society for Psychical Research, vol. 8, p. 260, 1898, In Aland Gauld, *The Founders of Psychical Research* (London: Routledge & Kegan Paul, 1968).

Joyce, G. H., *The Pope*, In *The Catholic Encyclopedia*, Charles G. Herbermann et al., eds., vol. 12 (New York: The Encyclopedia Press, 1913).

Kant, Immanuel, *Foundations of the Metaphysics of Morals and What is Enlightenment?*, 2nd ed., rev., Lewis White Beck, trans. (Upper Saddle River, New Jersey: Prentice-Hall, Inc., 1997).

Kenyon, F. G., *The Text of the Greek Bible* (London: Gerald & Co., Ltd., 1975).

Kenyon, Frederic, *Our Bible and the Ancient Manuscripts* (London: Eyre & Spottiswoode, 1948).

Kerenyi, C., *The Gods of the Greeks* (London: Thames and Hudson, 1951).

Kidd, B. J., *A History of the Church to A.D. 461*, vol. 2, A.D. 313-408 (Oxford: The Clarendon Press, 1922).

Kildahl, John P., *The Psychology of Speaking in Tongues* (New York: Harper & Row, 1972), pp. 50-51, Cited in Quebedeaux, *The New Charismatics*.

Kilpatrick, G. D., *Griesbach and the Development of Text Criticism*, In *J. J. Griesbach: Synoptic and Text-critical Studies, 1776-1976*.

Kingsley, Charles, *Sermons on National Subjects* (London: Macmillan and Co., 1890).

Kirk, Norris Edward, *Lectures on Revivals* (Boston: Congregational Publishing Society, 1875).

Koch, George Byron, "Pumped and Scooped?" *Christianity Today*, vol. 39, no. 10 (11 September 1995).

Kosambi, Meera, "Multiple Contestations: Pandita Ramabai's Educational and Missionary Activities in Late Nineteenth-Century India and Abroad," *Women's History Review*, vol. 7 no. 2, 1998.

LaBerge, Agnes N. O., *What God Hath Wrought: Life and Work of Mrs. Agnes N. O. LaBerge, Nee Miss Agnes N. Ozman* (Chicago:

Herald Publishing Co. Press, Date Unavailable; reprinted New York and London: Garland Publishing, Inc., 1985).

Lamarch, Paul, *The Septuagint: Bible of the Earliest Christians*, In *The Bible in Greek Christian Antiquity*, Paul M. Blowers, ed. and trans., Based on *Bible De Tous Les Temps,* vol. 1, *Le monde grec ancien et la Bible*, C. Mondesert, ed. (Notre Dame, Indiana: University of Notre Dame Press, 1997).

Larsen, Robin et al., eds. *Emanuel Swedenborg: A Continuing Vision* (New York: Swedenborg Foundation, Inc., 1988).

Latourette, Kenneth Scott, *A History of Christianity to A.D. 1500,* vol. 1 (New York: Harper San Francisco, 1975).

Latourette, Kenneth Scott, *A History of Christianity: A.D. 1500-A.D. 1975,* vol. 2 (New York: HarperSanFrancisco, 1975).

Latourette, Kenneth Scott, *A History of the Expansion of Christianity,* vol. 1, *The First Five Centuries* (Grand Rapids, Michigan: Zondervan Publishing House, 1970).

Latourette, Kenneth Scott, *Christianity in a Revolutionary Age, A History of Christianity in the Nineteenth and Twentieth Centuries,* vol. 2, *The Nineteenth Century in Europe-The Protestant and Eastern Churches* (New York: Harper & Brothers, Publishers, 1959).

Lavan, Spencer, *Unitarians and India: A Study in Encounter and Response*, 2nd ed. (Boston: Skinner House, 1984).

Leask, Nigel, "Coleridge and the Idea of a University," *Queens' College Record 1998*, http://www.quns.cam.ac.uk/Queens/Record/1998/Academic/coleridge.html, 1998.

Letter XCV, From Pope Anastasius To Simplicianus, In *A Select Library of Nicene And Post-Nicene Fathers*, series 2 vol. 6 -- *St. Jerome: Letters and Select Works*, Philip Schaff and Henry Wace, eds. (Grand Rapids: Wm. B. Eerdmans Publishing Company, 1954).

Lightfoot, J. B., *Dissertations on the Apostolic Age* (London: Macmillan and Co., 1892).

Lightfoot, Joseph Barber, *On A Fresh Revision of the English New Testament* (London: Macmillan and Co., 1891).

Locke, John, *The Works of John Locke, Four Letters on Toleration* (London: Ward, Lock and Co., Undated).

Lord, W. H., *The Modern English Pulpit*, In *The Presbyterian Quarterly and Princeton Review*, New Series, No. 8, October, 1873.

Ludlow, John, *The Autobiography of a Christian Socialist*, A.D. Murray, Ed. and Intro. (London: Frank Cass and Company Ltd., 1981).

Luibheid, Colm, *Eusebius of Caesarea and the Arian Crisis* (Dublin: Irish Academic Press, 1981).

Lutzow, The Count, *The Life & Times of Master John Hus* (London: J. M. Dent & Co. and New York: E. P. Dutton & Co., 1909).

LXX Septuagint, In *Online Bible*, Millennium ed. (Winterbourne, Ontario, Canada: Timathaserah, January 14, 2002).

Machiavelli, Niccolo, *The Prince, A New Translation with an Introduction by Harvey C. Mansfield, Jr.* (Chicago: The University of Chicago Press, 1985).

Machin, G. I. T., *Politics and the Churches in Great Britain in 1832 to 1868* (Oxford: Clarendon Press, 1977).

Machin, G. I. T., *Politics and the Churches in Great Britain in 1869 to 1921* (Oxford: Clarendon Press, 1987).

Mackay, John A., *Christianity on the Frontier* (New York: The Macmillan Company, 1950).

Mackay, John A., *Ecumenics: The Science of the Church Universal* (Englewood Cliffs, New Jersey: Prentice-Hall Inc., 1964).

Macmillan, Margaret Burnham, *The Methodist Church in Michigan: The Nineteenth Century* (Grand Rapids: The Michigan Area Methodist Historical Society and William B. Eerdmans Publishing Company, 1967).

Macnicol, Nicol, *Builders of Modern India: Pandita Ramabai* (Calcutta: Association Press, 1930).

Madden, Edward H. and James E. Hamilton, *Freedom and Grace: The Life of Asa Mahan* (Metuchen, NJ and London: The Scarecrow Press, Inc., 1982).

Mahan, Asa, "Reminiscences and Reflections," *Divine Life*, vol. 13, May 1890, p. 292. In Oberlin College Archives, Asa Mahan (1799-1889) Papers, [1764] 1835-1985, Accession No. 223, Processed by Brian A. Williams (Oberlin, Ohio: Oberlin College Archives, April 1992).

Mahan, Asa, *Autobiography: Intellectual, Moral, and Spiritual* (London: T. Woolmer, 1882; reprinted New York: AMS Press, 1979).

Mahan, Asa, In Asa Mahan (1799-1889) Papers, [1764] 1835-1985, Accession No. 223, Processed by Brian A. Williams (Oberlin, Ohio: Oberlin College Archives, April 1992).

Mahan, Asa, *Modern Mysteries: Explained and Exposed* (Boston: John P. Jewett and Company; Cleveland: Jewett, Proctor and Worthington; New York: Sheldon, Lamport and Blakeman; London: Trubner and Co., 1855).

Mahan, Asa, *The Baptism of the Holy Ghost* (London: Elliot Stock, 1876).

Mahan, Asa, *The Phenomena of Spiritualism: Scientifically Explained and Exposed* (London: Hodder and Stoughton, 1875).

Mahan, Asa, *The Phenomena of Spiritualism: Scientifically Explained and Exposed* (New York, Chicago, and New Orleans: A. S. Barnes and Co., 1876).

Malkin, Irad, *Religion and Colonization in Ancient Greece* (Leiden, The Netherlands: E. J. Brill, 1987).

Margoliouth, H.M., *Wordsworth and Coleridge 1795-1834* (London: Oxford University Press, 1953).

Martin, David, "The Political Oeconomy of the Holy Ghost," In *Strange Gifts? A Guide to Charismatic Renewal*, David Martin and Peter Mullen, eds. (Oxford: Basil Blackwell Publisher Ltd., 1984).

Marx, Karl and Friedrich Engels, *Manifesto of the Communist Party*, In *Karl Marx and Friedrich Engels On Religion*, Introduced by Reinhold Niebuhr (New York: Schocken Books, 1964).

Marx, Karl and Friedrich Engels, *Manifesto of the Communist Party*, In *Karl Marx and Friedrich Engels On Religion*, Introduced by Marx, Karl, A *Contribution To The Critique Of Hegel's Philosophy Of Right*, Introduction, In *Deutsch-Franzosische Jahrbucher*, February, 1844, Annette Jolin and Joseph O'Malley, trans., Joseph O'Malley, ed. (Cambridge: Cambridge University Press, 1970).

Masterman, Howard, *Chapter 4. The Confusion in International Relations*, In *Christianity and the Crisis*, Percy Dearmer, ed. (London: Victor Gollancz Ltd, 1933).

Maurice, F. D., *The Claims of the Bible and of Science: Correspon-*

dence Between a Layman and the Rev. F. D. Maurice on Some Questions Arising Out of the Controversy Respecting the Pentateuch (London and Cambridge: Macmillan and Co., 1863).

Maurice, Frederick Denison, *The Kingdom of Christ or Hints to a Quaker Respecting the Principles, Constitution and Ordinances of the Catholic Church*, vol. 1, new ed. based on the 1842 2nd ed. of, Alec R. Vidler, ed. (London: SCM Press Ltd, 1958).

Maurice, Frederick Denison, *The Kingdom of Christ*, vol. 2, new ed. based on the 1842 2nd ed. of, Alec R. Vidler, ed. (London: SCM Press Ltd, 1958).

Maurice, Frederick Denison, *Theological Essays*, First Published in 1853, Introduced by Edward F. Carpenter (New York: Harper & Brothers, Publishers, 1957).

Maurice, Frederick, ed., *The Life of Frederick Denison Maurice: Chiefly Told in His Own Letters*, vol. 1 (New York: Charles Scribner's Sons, 1884).

Maurice, Frederick, ed., *The Life of Frederick Denison Maurice: Chiefly Told in His Own Letters*, vol. 2 (New York: Charles Scribner's Sons, 1884).

Maynard, Michael, *A History of the Debate Over 1 John 5, 7-8: A Tracing of the Longevity of the Comma Johanneum With Evaluations of Arguments Against its Authenticity* (Tempe, AZ: Comma Publications, 1995).

McBrien, Richard P., *Lives of the Popes: The Pontiffs from St. Peter to John Paul II* (New York: HarperCollins Publishers, Inc., 1977).

McCarter, P. Kyle, Jr., *Textual Criticism: Recovering the Text of the Hebrew Bible* (Philadelphia: Fortress Press, 1986).

McConnell, Francis J., *The Essentials of Methodism* (New York and Cincinnati: The Methodist Book Concern, 1916).

McDonnell, Kilian, "The Death of Mythologies: The Classical Pentecostal/Roman Catholic Dialogue," *America*, vol. 172, no. 10 (25 March 1995).

McGee, Gary B., "'Latter Rain' Falling in the East: Early-Twentieth-Century Pentecostalism in India and the Debate over Speaking in Tongues," *Church History*, vol. 68 no. 3, September 1999.

McGee, Gary B., "Pentecostal Phenomena and Revivals in India: Implications for Indigenous Church Leadership," *Internationaal*

Bulletin of Missionary Research, vol. 20, no. 3, July 1996.

McGiffert, Arthur Cushman, "Prolegomena. The Life and Writings of Eusebius of Caesarea, The Life of Eusebius," ch. 1, Arthur Cushman McGiffert, trans. with Prolegomena and notes, In *Nicene and Post-Nicene Fathers of the Christian Church*, series 2, vol. 1, Philip Schaff and Henry Wace, eds. (Grand Rapids, Michigan: Reprinted by Wm. B. Eerdmans Publishing Co., 1979).

McLoughlin, William G., "Revivalism," In *The Rise of Adventism: Religion and Society in Mid-Nineteenth-Century America*, Edwin S. Gaustad, ed. (New York, Evanston, San Francisco, and London: Harper & Row, Publishers, 1974).

McNall, Burns Edward, *The Counter Reformation* (Princeton, New Jersey: D. Van Nostrand Company, 1964).

Merivale, Charles, *Autobiography and Letters* (Oxford, 1898), pp. 97-99, Quoted in Distad, *Guessing at Truth: The Life of Julius Charles Hare.*

Mill, John Stuart, *Autobiography*, In *The Harvard Classics*, vol. 25, Charles Elliott, ed. (New York: P. F. Collier & Son Corporation, 1937).

Miller, David, "Modernity in Hindu Monasticism: Swami Vivekananda and the Ramakrishna Movement," *Journal of Asian and African Studies*, vol. 34, February 1999.

Miller, Edward, *Introduction* to John William Burgon, *The Traditional Text of the New Testament,* In *Unholy Hands on the Bible*, Miller, Edward, ed., vol. 1, Jay P. Green, ed. (Lafayette, Indiana: Sovereign Grace Trust Fund, 1990).

Modern King James Version of the Holy Bible (Lafayette, Indiana: Jay P. Green, Sr., Sovereign Grace Publishers, 1999).

Monaghan, Patricia, *The New Book of Goddesses and Heroines* (St. Paul, Minnesota: Llewellyn Publishers, 1998).

Monteiro, Mariana, *The Life of Saint Jerome: The Great Doctor of the Church in Six Books from the Original Spanish of the Reverend Father Fray Jose de Siguenza, 1595* (London: Sands and Co., 1907).

More, Thomas, *Utopia*, with an Introduction by Jenny Mezciems (New York and Toronto: Alfred A. Knopf, 1992).

Morgan, Timothy C., "The Alpha-Brits are Coming: a British Course

for non-Christians Aims to Transform North American Evangelistic Outreach," *Christianity Today*, vol. 42, no. 2 (9 February
1998).

Morley, John, *The Life of William Ewart Gladstone*, 3 vols. In 2, vol.
1, new ed. (New York: The Macmillan Company, 1911).

Morley, *The Life of William Ewart Gladstone*, 3 vols. In 2, vol. 2,
new ed. (New York: The Macmillan Company, 1911).

Muller, F. Max, *Natural Religion: The Gifford Lectures Delivered
before the University of Glasgow in 1888* (London: Longmans,
Green, and Co., 1889).

Muller, F. Max, *Theosophy or Psychological Religion; The Gifford
Lectures Delivered before the University of Glasgow in 1892*
(London, New York, and Bombay: Longmans, Green, and Co.,
1903; First ed. pub. 1893).

Nelson, Shirley, *Fair, Clear, and Terrible: The Story of Shiloh, Maine*
(Latham, New York: British American Publishing, 1989).

Neumann, Erich, *The Great Mother: An Analysis of the Archtype*,
Ralph Manheim, trans. for the Bollingen Foundation, Inc., Series
47 (New York:., Pantheon Books Inc., 1954).

Newsome, David, *The Wilberforces and Henry Manning: The Parting of Friends* (Cambridge, Massachusetts: The Belknap Press of
Harvard University Press, 1966).

Nicolini, Quoted from, *History of the Jesuits*, pp. 387-406, In Thompson, *The Footprints of the Jesuits*.

Nigg, Walter, *The Heretics*, Richard and Clara Winston, trans. and
eds. (New York: Alfred A, Knopf, Inc., 1962).

Nikhilananda, Swami, *Vivekananda: A Biography*, 4th Indian ed.
(Calcutta: Advaita Ashrama, 1982).

Nikhilananda, Swami, *Vivekananda: The Yogas and Other Works*,
revised ed. (New York: Ramakrishna-Vivekananda Center, 1953).

O'Conner, Edward D., "The Immaculate Conception and the Spirituality of the Blessed Virgin," In *The Dogma of the Immaculate
Conception: History and Significance*, Edward Dennis O'Conner,
ed. (Notre Dame, Indiana: University of Notre Dame Press, 1958).

O'Connor, Edward D., *The Pentecostal Movement in the Catholic
Church* (Notre Dame, Indiana: Ave Maria Press, 1971).

On Christian Doctrine, bk. 2, written 397 A.D., J.F. Shaw, trans., In

A Select Library of the Nicene and Post-Nicene Fathers of the Christian Church, vol.. 2, *St. Augustin's City of God and Christian Doctrine*, Philip Schaff, ed., 1886 ed. (Grand Rapids, Michigan: Reprinted by Wm. B. Eerdmans Publishing Co., 1979).

Origen, *Origen's Commentary on the Gospel of John, Book I*, Allan Menzies, trans., In *The Ante-Nicene Fathers,* vol. 10, A. Roberts and J. Donaldson, eds. (Albany, Oregon: The Sage Digital Library Collections, Sage Software, 1996).

Orr, J. Edwin, *The Flaming Tongue: The Impact of Twentieth Century Revivals* (Chicago: Moody Press, 1973).

Orsini, G. N. G., *Coleridge and German Idealism: A Study in the History of Philosophy with Unpublished Materials from Coleridge's Manuscripts* (Carbondale: Southern Illinois University Press, 1969).

Orsini, Mathieu, *Life of the Blessed Virgin, Mother of God; with the History of the Devotion to Her*, J. Sadlier, trans. (New York: D. & J. Sadlier & Co., c1854).

Pache, Rene', *The Inspiration and Authority of Scripture*, Helen I. Needham, trans. (Salem, Wisconsin: Sheffield Publishing Company, Moody Bible Institute of Chicago, 1969).

Packer, J. I., *Beyond the Battle for the Bible* (Westchester, Illinois: Cornerstone Books, 1980).

Paine, Thomas, *Rights of Man* (Lunenburg, Vermont: The George Macy Companies, Inc., 1961).

Paino, Paul E., personal communication with author, November 22, 2000.

Parham, Sarah E., *The Life of Charles F. Parham: Founder of the Apostolic Faith Movement* (Joplin, Missouri: Hunter Print. Co., c1930; reprinted New York and London: Garland Publishing Inc., 1985).

Patterson, M. W., *A History of the Church of England* (London: Longmans, Green and Co., 1909).

Paul VI, Pope, "A New Spirit of Friendship: Address of Pope Paul VI to Christian Observer Delegates Attending the Third Session of the Ecumenical Council," In *The Pope Speaks*, vol. 10, no. 1, 1964.

Paul VI, Pope, "Exploring the Mystery of the Church: Address of

Pope Paul VI at the Close of the Third Session of the Second Vatican Ecumenical Council," In *The Pope Speaks* vol. 10, no. 1, 1964.

Paul VI, Pope, "The Universal Fatherhood of the Pope," In *The Pope Speaks*, vol. 10, no. 1, 1964.

Paul VI, Pope, In *Marialis Cultus: Apostolic Exhortation for the Right Ordering and Development of Devotion to the Blessed Virgin Mary*, February 2, 1974, http://www.ewtn.com/library/PAPALDOC/P6MARIAL.HTM.

Paul VI, Pope, In *Second Vatican Council II Closing Speeches and Messages*, December 8, 1965, http://listserv.american.edu/catholic/church/papal/paul.vi/p6closin.txt.

Paul VI, Pope, *Marian Devotion for the Modern Christian: An Address of Pope Paul VI to Marian Congregations*, In *The Pope Speaks*, vol. 9, 1963.

Paul VI, Pope, *Vatican II: The Decree on Ecumenism*, vol. 10, no. 1, 1964.

Penn-Lewis, Jessie, *The Awakening in Wales: and Some of the Hidden Springs* (Originally Published in England by The Overcomer Literature Trust, Ltd.; Fort Washington, Pennsylvania: Christian Literature Crusade, 1993).

Penn-Lewis, Jessie, with Evan Roberts, *War on the Saints*, unabridged ed. (1st ed. published in 1912; New York: Thomas E. Lowe, Ltd., 10th printing of 9th ed., 1994).

Percival, Henry R., ed. "Historical Introduction, The Third Ecumenical Council: The Council of Ephesus, The Seven Ecumenical Councils of the Undivided Church," Henry R. Percival, ed., In *A Select Library of the Nicene and Post-Nicene Fathers of the Christian Church*, series 2, vol. 14, Philip Schaff and Henry Wace, eds. (Grand Rapids, Michigan: Wm. B. Eerdmans Publishing Company, Reprinted 1979), pp. 192-195.

Pettersen, Alvyn, *Athanasius* (London: Geoffrey Chapman, 1995).

Philip Schaff, "The Reformation in Prussia. Duke Albrecht And Bishop Georg Von Polenz, § 99, Propagation And Persecution Of Protestantism In Germany Till 1530, ch. 6, The Reformation from A.D. 1517 to 1648," vol. 7, In *The History of the Christian Church*, http://www.ccel.org/s/schaff/history/7_ch06.htm.

Bibliography

Phillips, Paul T., *A Kingdom on Earth: Anglo-American Social Christianity, 1880-1940* (University Park, Pennsylvania: The Pennsylvania State University Press, 1996).

Phillips, Thomas, *The Welsh Revival: Its Origin and Development* (Edinburgh and Carlisle, Pennsylvania: The Banner of Truth Trust, 1989; reprinted from the 1860 publication).

Pius IX, Pope, "Letters Apostolic of Our Most Holy Lord Pius IX, by Divine Providence Pope, Concerning the Dogmatic Definition of the Immaculate Conception of the Virgin Mother of God," In *Life of the Blessed Virgin, Mother of God; with the History of the Devotion to Her*, J. Sadlier, trans. (New York: D. & J. Sadlier & Co., 1854).

Plato, *The Republic*, In *Plato: Complete Works*, John M. Cooper and D. S. Hutchinson, eds. (Indianapolis, Indiana: Hackett Publishing Company, 1997).

Pollard. Alfred W., *Records of the English Bible: The Documents Relating to the Translation and Publication of the Bible in English, 1525-1611* (London & New York: H. Frowde, Oxford University Press, 1911).

Pollock, J. C., *The Keswick Story: The Authorized History of the Keswick Convention* (London: Hodder and Stoughton, 1964).

Porter, Wendy J., "The Worship of the Toronto Blessing?" In *The Toronto Blessing—or Is It?*, Stanley E. Porter and Philip J. Richter, eds. (London: Darton, Longman and Todd Ltd., 1995).

Preston, Gene, "The Toronto Wave: Holy Laughter is Contagious," *The Christian Century*, vol. 111 no. 33 (16 November 1994).

Price, Clive, *Spiritual Renewal Around the World: How the British Rediscovered the Bible, Charisma*, August, 1999, pp. 58-100.

Price, Ira Maurice, *The Ancestry of Our English Bible*, 2nd ed. (Philadelphia: The Sunday School Times Company, 1907).

Purcell, Edmund Sheridan, *Life of Cardinal Manning: Archbishop of Westminster*, vol. 1 (New York: Macmillan and Co., 1896).

Purcell, Edmund Sheridan, *Life of Cardinal Manning: Archbishop of Westminster*, vol. 2 (New York: Macmillan and Co., 1896).

Purdy, William, *The Search for Unity: Relations between the Anglican and Roman Catholic Churches from the 1950s to the 1970s* (London: Geoffrey Chapman, 1996).

Putnam, George Haven, *The Censorship of the Church of Rome and Its Influence Upon the Production and Distribution of Literature*, vol. 1 (New York: Benjamin Blom, 1967).

Quebedeaux, Richard, *The New Charismatics: The Origins, Development, and Significance of Neo-Pentecostalism* (Garden City, New York: Doubleday & Company, Inc., 1976).

Ramabai, Pandita, Quoted in *Pandita Ramabai Through Her Own Words: Selected Works*, Meeri Kosambi, ed. (Oxford: Oxford University Press, 2000).

Ramsey, Arthur M., *F. D. Maurice and the Conflicts of Modern Theology: The Maurice Lectures, 1948* (Cambridge: Cambridge University Press, 1951).

Ranaghan, Kevin and Dorothy, *Catholic Pentecostals* (Paramus, New Jersey and New York, New York, 1969).

Raser, Harold E., *Phoebe Palmer: Her Life and Thought*, In *Studies in Women and Religion*, vol. 22 (Lewiston, New York and Queenston, Ontario: The Edwin Mellen Press, 1987).

Rauschenbusch, Walter, *Christianity and the Social Crisis* (New York: The Macmillan Company, 1907, Reprinted in 1912).

Reardon, Bernard M. G., *From Coleridge to Gore: A Century of Religious Thought in Britain* (London: Longman Group Ltd., 1971).

Reed, John Shelton, *Glorious Battle: The Cultural Politics of Victorian Anglo-Catholicism* (Nashville: Vanderbilt University Press, 1996).

Reedy, Gerard, *The Bible and Reason: Anglicans and Scripture in Late Seventeenth-Century England* (Philadelphia: University of Pennsylvania Press, 1985).

Reicke, Bo, *Griesbach's Answer to the Synoptic Question*, Ronald Walls, trans., In *J. J. Griesbach: Synoptic and Text-critical Studies, 1776-1976.*

Religious Controversies of the Nineteenth Century: Selected Documents, A. O. J. Cockshut, ed. (Lincoln: University of Nebraska Press, 1966).

Review of the Works of S. T. Coleridge, In *The Princeton Review*, vol. 20, No. 2, April 1848.

Ridley F. A., *The Jesuits: A Study in Counter-Revolution* (London: Secker and Warburg, 1938).

Rigg, James H., *Modern Anglican Theology with a Prefix of the Memoir of Canon Kingsley,* 3rd ed. rev. (London: Wesleyan Conference Office, 1880).

Robertson, Archibald, "Prolegomena," *Select Writings and Letters of Athanasius, Bishop of Alexandria,* Archibald Robertson, ed., In *A Select Library of the Nicene and Post –Nicene Fathers of the Christian Church,* 2nd series, vol. 4, Philip Schaff and Henry Wace, eds. (Grand Rapids: Wm. B. Eerdmans Publishing Company, reprinted 1978; 1891).

Robertson, Pat, *The New World Order* (Dallas, London, Vancouver, and Melbourne: Word Publishing, 1991).

Robinson David, *The Unitarians and Universalists* (Westport, Connecticut: Greenwood Press, 1985).

Rogers, Arthur Kenyon, *English and American Philosophy Since 1800: A Critical Survey* (New York: The Macmillan Company, 1922).

Rogerson, J. W., *The Bible and Criticism in Victorian Britain: Profiles of F. D. Maurice and William Robertson Smith,* In *Journal for the Study of the Old Testament, Supplement Series 201* (Sheffield, England: Sheffield Academic Press, 1995).

Rolland, Romain, *The Life of Vivekananda and the Universal Gospel,* 6th impression, E. F. Malcolm-Smith, trans. (Calcutta: Advaita Ashrama, 1965).

Roller, Lynn E., *In Search of God the Mother: The Cult of Anatolian Cybele* (Berkeley: University of California Press, 1999).

Rose, Ruth, "Voluntary Movements and the Changing Ecumenical Climate," In *A History of the Ecumenical Movement, 1517-1948,* ch. 7, Ruth Rouse and Stephen Charles Neill, eds. (Philadelphia: The Westminster Press, 1954).

Rosten, Leo, ed. *Religions of America, Ferment and Faith in an Age of Crisis: A New Guide and Almanac,* (New York: Simon and Schuster, 1963.

Royle, Edward, *Victorian Infidels: The Origins of the British Secularist Movement, 1791-1866* (Manchester: Manchester University Press, 1974).

Ryan, Charles James, *H. P. Blavatsky and the Theosophical Movement: A Brief Historical Sketch* (Point Loma, California: Theosophical University Press, 1937).

While Men Slept...

Sandeen, Ernest R., "Millennialism," In *The Rise of Adventism: Religion and Society in Mid-Nineteenth-Century America*, Edwin S. Gaustad, ed. (New York, Evanston, San Francisco, London: Harper & Row, Publishers, 1974).

Sanders, Charles R., Coleridge and the Broad Church Movement: Studies in S. T. Coleridge, Dr. Arnold of Rugby, J. C. Hare, Thomas Carlyle, and F. D. Maurice (New York: Octagon Books, 1972).

Schaff, David S., *The Life of Philip Schaff* (New York: Charles Scribner's Sons, 1897).

Schaff, Philip and Henry Wace, eds., *A Select Library of Nicene and Post-Nicene Fathers of the Christian Church: St. Athanasius: Selected Works and Letters, Prolegomena*, ch. 2, pt. 3, 2nd series, vol. 4 (Grand Rapids, Michigan: Wm. B. Eerdmans Publishing Company, 1971).

Schaff, Philip and Henry Wace, eds., *Post-Nicene Fathers*, vol. 6, (Grand Rapids, MI: Eerdmans Pub. Co., 1892; rep. 1983).

Schaff, Philip, *History of the Apostolic Church with a General Introduction to Church History*, Edward D. Yeomans, trans. (New York: Charles Scribner, 1859).

Schaff, Philip, ed., *St. Augustin's City of God*, Marcus Dods, trans., 1871, In *A Select Library of the Nicene and Post-Nicene Fathers of the Christian Church*, Vol. 2, *St. Augustin's City of God and Christian Doctrine*, (Grand Rapids, Michigan: Wm. B. Eerdmans Publishing Co., 1979; reprint of the 1886 ed.).

Schaff, Philip, *History of the Christian Church Chapter IX: Theological Controversies, and Development of the Ecumenical Orthodoxy* (Oak Harbor, WA: Logos Research Systems, Inc., 1997, according to the 1910 ed. of Charles Scribner's Sons; Dallas, TX: The Electronic Bible Society, 1998), http://www.ccel.org/s/schaff/history/3_ch09.htm#_edn1

Schaff, Philip, *History of the Christian Church*, vol. 2, *Ante-Nicene Christianity, A.D. 100-325* (New York: Charles Scribner's Sons, 1883).

Schaff, Philip, *History of the Christian Church*, vol. 3, *Nicene and Post-Nicene Christianity from Constantine the Great to Gregory the Great, A.D. 311-600*, 5th ed., rev. (Grand Rapids: Wm. B. Eerdmans Publishing Company, 1981; Charles Scribner's Sons, 1910).

Schaff, Philip, *History of the Christian Church*: *Nicene and Post-*

Nicene Christianity from Constantine the Great to Gregory the Great, A.D. 311-600, vol. 3 (New York: Charles Scribner's Sons, 1886).

Schaff, Philip, *Introduction on the Revision of the English Bible*, In J. B. Lightfoot, Richard Chenevix Trench, and C. J. Ellicott, *The Revision of the English Version of the New Testament*, J. B. Lightfoot, Richard Chenevix Trench, and C. J. Ellicott (New York: Harper & Brothers, Publishers, 1873).

Schaff, Philip, *The History of the Christian Church*, vol. 7, *History Of Modern Christianity, The German Reformation*, 2nd ed. (Grand Rapids: Wm. B. Eerdmans Publishing Company, 1980; Revised, Charles Scribner's Sons, 1910).

Schleiermacher, Friedrich, *On Religion: Speeches to Its Cultured Despisers*, Richard Crouter, intro, trans. and notes (Cambridge: Cambridge University Press, 1988).

Scholasticus, Socrates, *The Ecclesiastical History*, bk. 1, ch. 1, A. C. Zenos, rev. and notes, In *A Select Library of Nicene and Post-Nicene Fathers of the Christian Church, vol. 2, Socrates, Sozomenus: Church Histories*, Philip Schaff and Henry Wace, eds. (Grand Rapids, Michigan: Reprinted by Wm. B. Eerdmans Publishing Co., 1979).

Seager, Richard Hughes, ed., *The Dawn of Religious Pluralism: Voices from the World's Parliament of Religions, 1893* (La Salle, Illinois: Open Court Publishing Company, 1993).

Shah, A. B., *The Letters and Correspondence of Pandita Ramabai*, compiled by Sister Geraldine (Bombay: Maharashtra State Board for Literature and Culture, 1977).

Sidgwick, Arthur and Eleanor Mildred Sidgwick, *Henry Sidgwick: A Memoir by A. S. and E. M. S.* (London: Macmillan and Co., Ltd., 1906).

Singer, Charles Gregg, *The Unholy Alliance* (Tyler, Texas: Institute for Christian Economics, 1975).

Smith, G. Vance, *Christianity: What It Is Not, and What It Is,* In *Christianity and Modern Thought* (Boston: American Unitarian Association, 1873).

Smith, Timothy L., *Revivalism and Social Reform In Mid-Nineteenth-Century America* (New York and Nashville: Abingdon Press, 1957).

Smith, William, *A New Classical Dictionary of Greek and Roman Biography, Mythology and Geography, partly based upon the Dictionary of Greek and Roman Biography and Mythology* (New York: Harper & Brothers, 1851).

Snowden, James H., *The Coming of the Lord: Will it be Premillennial?*, 3rd ed., rev. (New York: The Macmillan Company, 1922).

Solly, Henry, *These Eighty Years Or, The Story of an Unfinished Life*, vol. 2 (London: Simpkin, Marshall, & Co., Ltd., 1893).

Sozomen, Salaminius Hermias, *The Ecclesiastical History of Sozomen, Comprising a History of the Church from A.D. 323 to A.D. 425*, bk. 5, chs. 1-3, Nicephorus Callistus, arranger, Chester D. Hartranft, rev., In *A Select Library of Nicene and Post-Nicene Fathers of the Christian Church*, vol. 2, *Socrates, Sozomenus: Church Histories*, Philip Schaff and Henry Wace, eds. (Grand Rapids, Michigan: Wm. B. Eerdmans Publishing Co., reprinter, 1979).

Stanley, A. P., *Judgement on "Essays and Reviews," "Edinburgh Review," July 1864*, In *Religious Controversies of the Nineteenth Century*, Cockshut, ed.

Stanley, Arthur Penrhyn "The Prospects of Liberal Theology," *Addresses and Sermons Delivered During a Visit to the United States and Canada in 1878*, ch. 2 (New York: Macmillan & Co., 1879), pp. 9-10.

Stanley, Arthur Penrhyn, *Lectures on the History of the Eastern Church* (New York: Charles Scribner's Sons, 1900).

Sterling, John, In *Catholic World*, vol. 7, issue 42, Sept. 1868, p. 812.

Stevenson, J., *Studies in Eusebius* (Cambridge: Cambridge University Press, 1929).

Strong, James, "Hebrew and Chaldee Dictionary," In *The Exhaustive Concordance of the Bible: Showing Every Word of the Text of the Common English Version of the Canonical Books and Every Occurrence of Each Word in Regular Order, Together with Dictionaries of the Hebrew and Greek Words of the Original, with References to the English Words* (Peabody, Massachusetts: Hendrickson Publishers, undated; a reprint of the original).

Swedenborg, Emanuel, *On the New Jerusalem and Its Heavenly*

Bibliography

Doctrine, As Revealed from Heaven, to Which are Prefixed Some Observations Concerning the New Heaven & the New Earth, trans. from Latin, 5th ed. (London: Society for Printing and Publishing the Writings of the Hon. Emanuel Swedenborg, 1812; Originally published in 1758).

Swedenborg, Emanuel, *The Apocalypse Revealed, Wherein are Disclosed The Arcana There, Foretold, Which Have Hitherto Remained Concealed,* trans. from Latin (Philadelphia: J. B. Lippincott Company, 1887).

Swedenborg, Emanuel, *The True Christian Religion; Containing the Universal Theology of the New Church, Foretold by the Lord in Daniel, VII. 13, 14, and in the Apocalypse, XXI. 1, 2.,* trans. of the Latin (New York: American Swedenborg Printing and Publishing Society, 1873).

Synan, Vinson, *The Holiness-Pentecostal Tradition: Charismatic Movements in the Twentieth Century,* 2nd ed. (Grand Rapids, Michigan and Cambridge, U.K.: William B. Eerdmans Publishing Company, 1997).

The Bible in its Ancient and English Versions, H. Wheeler Robinson, ed. (London: Oxford at the Clarendon Press, 1940).

The Biblical Repertory and Princeton Review for the Year 1861, vol. 33, Charles Hodge, ed. (Philadelphia: Peter Walker, 1861).

The Holy Bible, Revised Standard Version: Containing the Old and New Testaments, (New York: Thomas Nelson & Sons, 1952; Copyright by National Council of Churches of Christ: New Testament, 1946, Old Testament, 1952).

The Journal of the Rev. John Wesley, A. M., vol. 6, Nehemiah Curnock, ed. (London: Charles H. Kelly, 1779).

The New Testament of Our Lord and Saviour Jesus Christ Translated Out of the Greek: Being the Version Set Forth A.D. 1611 Compared with the Most Ancient Authorities and Revised A.D. 1881 (Oxford: Oxford University Press, 1881).

Thompson, R. W., *The Footprints of the Jesuits* (Cincinnati: Cranston & Curts and New York: Hunt & Eaton, 1894), p. 22.

Thorton, W. H., *Reminiscences of an old West Country Clergyman* (Privately Printed) pp. 71-73, quoted in Graves, *Life and Letters of Alexander Macmillan.*

Thuesen, Peter J., *In Discordance with the Scriptures: American Protestant Battles over Translating the Bible* (New York and Oxford: Oxford University Press, 1999).

Tischendorf, Constantine, *Introduction*, In *The New Testament: the Authorized English Version; with Introduction, and Various Readings from the Three Most Celebrated Manuscripts of the Original Greek*, Tauchnitz ed., vol. 1000 (Leipzing: Bernard Tauchnitz, 1869).

Toews, John E., *Hegelianism: The Path Toward Dialectical Humanism, 1805-1841* (Cambridge: Cambridge University Press, 1980).

Tolstoi, Lyof N., *The Kingdom of God is Within You*, In *The Complete Works of Lyof N. Tolstoi* (New York: E. R. Dumont, 1899).

Torrens, James S., "Admiring Cardinal Suenens (Leo Joseph Cardinal Suenens, 1904-1996) (Obituary)," In *America*, vol. 174 no. 20, June 22, 1996.

Toward the Recovery of Unity: The Thought of Frederick Denison Maurice, John F. Porter and William J. Wolf, eds. (New York: The Seabury Press, 1964).

Trevelyan, George Macaulay, *England Under the Stuarts* (London: Methuen & Co. Ltd. and New York: G.P. Putnam's Sons, 1924).

Turnbull, H. W., ed., *The Correspondence of Isaac Newton, 1688-1694*, vol. 3 (Cambridge: Cambridge University Press for the Royal Society of London, 1961).

Ulrich, Eugene, *The Old Testament Text of Eusebius: The Heritage of Origen*, In *Eusebius, Christianity, and Judaism*, Harold W. Attridge and Gohei Hata, eds. (Detroit: Wayne State University Press, 1992).

Unitarian Universalist Association, *"We Are Unitarian Universalists", pamphlet #3047*, In *Unitarian Universalism in Brief* (Boston: Unitarian Universalist Association, 1995), http://uua.org/uubrief.html.

Valesius, Annotations on the Life and Writings of Eusebius Pamphilus, S. E. Parker, trans., In *The Ecclesiastical History of Eusebius Pamphilus, Bishop of Cesarea, In Palestine*, Christian Frederick Cruse and Isaac Boyle, trans. and eds. (Grand Rapids, Michigan: Baker Book House, 1990).

Vermaseren, Maarten J., *Cybele and Attis: the Myth and the Cult* (London: Thames and Hudson, 1977).

Vidler, Alec R., *The Church in an Age of Revolution: 1789 to the Present Day* (Harmondsworth, Middlesex: Penguin Books Ltd, 1961).

Vineeth, Francis, "Theology of Adisabda and OM," ch. 15, In *Indian Christian Spirituality*, D. S. Amalorpavadass, ed. (Bangalore, India: National Biblical Catechetical and Liturgical Centre, 1982).

Vireswarananda, Swami, *The Complete Works of Swami Vivekananda*, Part IV, 4th ed. (Mayavati, Almora, Himalayas: Advaita Ashrama, 1932).

Vischer, Lukas, *The Ecumenical Movement and the Roman Catholic Church,* In *The Ecumenical Advance: A History of the Ecumenical Movement*, vol. 2: 1948-1968, Harold E. Fey, Editor (Philadelphia: The Westminster Press, 1970).

Vivekananda, Swami, In *The Complete Works of Swami Vivekananda*, vol. 6, Swami Tadrupananda, ed., (Calcutta: Advaita Ashrama, 1978).

Vivekananda, Swami, In *The Complete Works of Swami Vivekananda*, vol. 8, Swami Tadrupananda, ed., (Calcutta: Advaita Ashrama, 1977).

Vivekananda, Swami, quoted in U. Thant, *Swami Vivekananda—The Spiritual Ambassador of India, The Vedanta Kesari* (Madras-4, India: Sri Ramakrishna Math), vol. 50 (4), August 1963.

Von Ranke, Leopold, *The History of the Popes During the Last Four Centuries*, vol. 2 (London: G. Bell and Sons, Ltd., 1913).

Walker et al., *A History of the Christian Church*, 4th ed. (New York: Charles Scribner's Sons, 1985).

Wallace, Lillian Parker, *The Papacy and European Diplomacy: 1869-1878* (Chapel Hill: The University of North Carolina Press, 1948).

Walters, Kerry S., *Rational Infidels: The American Deists* (Durango, Colorado: Longwood Academic, 1992).

Ward, Julian, "Pentecostal Theology and the Charismatic Movement," In *Strange Gifts? A Guide to Charismatic Renewal*, David Martin and Peter Mullen, eds. (Oxford: Basil Blackwell Publisher Ltd., 1984).

Ware, John, *Memoir: Life of Henry Ware, Jr.,* vol. 1 (Boston: American Unitarian Association, 1874).

Weber, Timothy P., *Living in the Shadow of the Second Coming:*

American Premillennialism, 1875-1925 (New York and Oxford: Oxford University Press, 1979).

Webb, James, *The Occult Underground* (LaSalle, Illinois: Open Court Publishing Company, 1974).

Webster's Seventh New Collegiate Dictionary (Springfield, Massachusetts: G. & C. Merriam Company, 1969).

Welch, Claude, *Protestant Thought in the Nineteenth Century*, vol. 1, *1799-1870* (New Haven and London: The Bross Foundation, Yale University Press, 1972).

Wesley, John, *On The Trinity Advertisement, Sermon LV*, In *The Works of John Wesley,* vol. 6, (Albany, Oregon: The Sage Digital Library Collected Works, Sage Software, 1996).

Westcott, Arthur, *Life and Letters of Brooke Foss Westcott*, vol. 1 (London: Macmillan & Co., 1903).

Westcott, Arthur, *Life and Letters of Brooke Foss Westcott,* vol. 2 (London: Macmillan & Co., 1903).

Westcott, Brooke Foss, *A General View of the History of the English Bible* 3rd ed., rev. by William Aldis Wright (London: Macmillan and Co., Ltd., 1905).

Westcott, Brooke Foss, *A General View of the History of the English Bible*, 1st ed. (London and Cambridge: Macmillan and Co., 1868).

Westcott, Brooke Foss, *Social Aspects of Christianity* (London and Cambridge: Macmillan and Co., 1887).

Westcott, Brooke Foss, *The Bible In The Church; A Popular Account of the Collection and Reception of the Holy Scriptures in the Christian Churches* (London & Cambridge: Macmillan and Co., 1866).

Westminster Confession Of Faith (Glasgow: Free Presbyterian Publications, 1990; first published in 1646).

White, James R., *The King James Only Controversy: Can You Trust the Modern Translations?* (Minneapolis, Minnesota: Bethany House Publishers, 1995).

White, William, *Life of Emanuel Swedenborg, Together with A Brief Synopsis of His Writings, Both Philosophical and Theological* (Philadelphia: J. B. Lippincott & Co., 1884).

Wigmore-Beddoes, D.G., *How the Unitarian Movement Paid its Debt to Anglicanism*, In *Transactions of the Unitarian Historical Society*, vol. 13, no. 2, October, 1964.

Wilberforce, Reginald G., *Life of the Right Reverend Samuel Wilberforce, D. D., Lord Bishop of Oxford and Afterwards of Winchester with Selections from His Diaries and Correspondence*, vol. 3 (London: John Murray, 1882).

Wilkinson, Benjamin G., *Our Authorized Bible Vindicated*, In *Which Bible?*, David Otis Fuller, ed. (Grand Rapids, Michigan: Institute for Biblical Textual Studies, 1990).

Williams, C. H., ed., *English Historical Documents: 1485-1558*, (New York: Oxford University Press, 1971).

Williams, Monier, *Religious Thought and Life in India, Part 1: Vedism, Brahmanism, and Hinduism* (London: John Murray, 1883).

Wilson, A. N., *God's Funeral* (London: John Murray, 1999).

Wood, H. G., *Frederick Denison Maurice* (Cambridge: Cambridge University Press, 1950).

Wright, Conrad, *The Beginnings of Unitarianism in America* (Hamden, Connecticut: Reprint by Archon Books of Starr King Press 1955 ed., 1976).

Yoder, Donald Herbert, "Christian Unity in Nineteenth-Century America," *A History of the Ecumenical Movement, 1517-1948*, Ruth Rouse and Stephen Charles Neill, eds. (Philadelphia, Westminster Press, 1954)

Young, B.W., *Religion and Enlightenment in Eighteenth-Century England: Theological Debate from Locke to Burke* (Oxford: Clarendon Press, 1998).

Young, David, *F. D. Maurice and Unitarianism* (Oxford: Clarendon Press; New York: Oxford University Press, 1992).

Zikmund, Barbara Brown, *Asa Mahan and Oberlin Perfectionism*, Doctoral Dissertation (Durham, North Carolina: Department of Religion, Duke University, 1969).

Zimmer, *Die indische Weltmutter*, pp. 179ff, Quoted in Erich Neumann, *The Great Mother*.

While Men Slept...

Index

Index

While Men Slept...

W